Religion and Transhumanism

Religion and Transhumanism

The Unknown Future of Human Enhancement

Calvin Mercer and Tracy J. Trothen, Editors

AN IMPRINT OF ABC-CLIO, LLC

Santa Barbara, California • Denver, Colorado • Oxford, England

Library of Congress Cataloging-in-Publication Data

Religion and transhumanism : the unknown future of human enhancement / Calvin Mercer and Tracy J. Trothen, editors.
    pages cm
  Includes bibliographical references and index.
  ISBN 978-1-4408-3325-0 (hard copy : alk. paper) — ISBN 978-1-4408-3326-7 (ebook) 1. Humanism, Religious. 2. Christianity and religious humanism. 3. Theological anthropology. 4. Technology—Religious aspects. I. Mercer, Calvin R., editor.
BL2747.6.R425 2015
202'.2—dc23   2014024153

ISBN: 978-1-4408-3325-0
EISBN: 978-1-4408-3326-7

19 18 17 16 15   1 2 3 4 5

This book is also available on the World Wide Web as an eBook.
Visit www.abc-clio.com for details.

Praeger
An Imprint of ABC-CLIO, LLC

ABC-CLIO, LLC
130 Cremona Drive, P.O. Box 1911
Santa Barbara, California 93116-1911

This book is printed on acid-free paper ∞

Manufactured in the United States of America

Contents

Introduction: Making the Unknown Known

Calvin Mercer

Pulling together a scholarly collection of original chapters is a process that usually takes well over a year; indeed, a process lasting two or three years is not uncommon. This collection took just over half a year. I think that is an indicator of the increasing attention being devoted to thinking through, from a religious perspective, the implications of extreme human enhancement and the growing sense that the conversation needs to move forward with an increased pace.

My co-editor, Tracy J. Trothen, and I knew there was a fair bit of work being done by scholars of religion. Even so, when the call for authors on this topic was issued, we were surprised and pleased at the large number who quickly responded and at their enthusiastic commitment to move their work into the conversation without delay. The steady stream of biomedical and other technological developments has fueled that sense of urgency, and the fact that we are moving into an "unknown future" has intensified the discussion.

Summaries of developments that serve the various transhumanist scenarios are readily available,[1] so I will not discuss those developments in detail here. Several of our authors speak about some of the progress in genetic engineering, tissue engineering, robotics, and artificial intelligence (AI) in the service of radical enhancement or, perhaps, a posthuman future. Consideration of human enhancement and posthuman possibilities is becoming scholarship's version of a growth industry. It is clear that scholars of religion are determined to take their place in the thick of the debates, and rightly so.

More than 80 percent of people around the world are religiously affiliated, according to the well-respected Pew Research Center.[2] How they respond (and they will, of course, in a variety of ways) to radical enhancements will have an impact, and likely a substantial one, on the direction of research, funding, and legal frameworks. Scholars of religion, including theologians of the traditions, can influence how clergy and laity assess transhumanism. Most definitely, scholars of religion will help interpret the religions' responses to transhumanist advances. In time, I expect the adherents of the various religions to become more engaged as the general topic of enhancement inevitably makes its way into political and public policy discourse.

Academic religion, and theological work specifically, can help guide the direction of research. In making their contributions, scholars of religion can, and should, work alongside economists, ethicists, scientists, and others. In general, I expect scholars of religion to emphasize that if we move forward with human enhancement technologies (and some will argue we should not), we should do so in ways consistent with core religious values, such as justice, stewardship, and reverence for diverse life.

Scholars of religion, in this collection (i.e., Michael Burdett, Hava Tirosh-Samuelson, and Joseph Wolyniak) and elsewhere, also critique enhancement programs in ways that uncover the implicit religious beliefs and practices that might underlie transhumanism, thereby helping us better understand this important intellectual and cultural movement. Any movement that may make a potentially strong impact, such as transhumanism, merits careful analysis from all angles. For transhumanism to have religious themes, albeit implicit, is not in itself good or bad, but rather something worth knowing to more fully understand where transhumanism wants to take us and why.

All authors in this collection—some more than others—articulate cautions and concerns about the more extreme enhancement programs. However, by no means do scholars of religion generally take a Luddite stance, as is sometimes the stereotype of religion. It is true that, at least in conservative Christian religion, there can be an antiscience bias, and transhumanist agendas are certainly in large part based on science. Nevertheless, religious people and scholars of religion are taking, and will continue to take, a variety of approaches to radical enhancement. In this collection, reflective of those in the discipline who are working on this topic, we find a range of responses from openness to bioconservatism.

The author list for this collection is reflective in several ways of the larger discussion unfolding in the religion academy. Unfortunately, the contributions are largely from the Christian tradition. Human enhancement will have global impact, and it is in the interest of every religion to be engaged in the discussion of that impact. We sought out scholars from traditions other than Christianity and are fortunate to offer three chapters from experts in Judaism, East Asian traditions, and Chinese religions. One chapter (by Anders Sandberg) addresses meaning in transhumanism, with some attention to religion but not a specific tradition.

As a representative slice of current research, this collection boasts a number of seasoned scholars, whose names are well known in the study of human enhancement. They are joined by younger scholars, most of whom have studied these issues from the time of graduate school.

About half the authors in this collection have read papers at or otherwise been involved in the American Academy of Religion's Transhumanism and Religion Group. This Group has emerged as an important context for academic discussion and networking. The American Academy of Religion is the largest and most significant organization devoted to the academic study of religion. In 2006 and 2007, I organized "wild card" experimental sessions on transhumanism. Aubrey de Grey, a leading figure in the effort to terminate aging in the human species, agreed to provide the scientific perspective on extreme longevity and gave visibility to the two sessions.

These two sessions laid the groundwork for establishing the Transhumanism and Religion Group as a permanent session at the American Academy of Religion's annual meeting. Ron Cole-Turner, who has written on cloning, genetic engineering, and transhumanism, was an invaluable partner in this effort. After two 3-year terms as chair of the Steering Committee, I rotated off in 2013. Today the Group continues to thrive under the able leadership of co-chairs Cole-Turner and Trothen.

Numerous other forums and conferences devoted to transhumanist-inspired religion questions have been held, and even more are on the way. To give one prominent example, under the leadership of Hava Tirosh-Samuelson (one of the authors represented in this collection), the four-year (2006–2010) Arizona State University series, "Facing the Challenges of Transhumanism: Religion, Science, and Technology," was funded by the John Templeton Foundation and made an important contribution. Tirosh-Samuelson also co-directed another Arizona State University program titled, "The Transhumanist Imagination: Innovation, Secularization and Eschatology." That 2012–2014 grant is from The Historical Society's Program in Religion and Innovation in Human Affairs (RIHA), which was also funded by the John Templeton Foundation.

Publications from scholars of religion are appearing at an increasing rate, as the bibliography in this collection indicates. An issue of *Zygon: Journal of Religion and Science*, edited by Tirosh-Samuelson in 2012, was devoted to transhumanism. The respected journal, *Dialog: A Journal of Theology*, will devote its Winter 2015 issue, edited by Ted Peters and Joshua Moritz, to "The Boundaries of Human Nature." And the editors of *Theology and Science*, the scholarly journal of the important Center for Theology and the Natural Sciences, plan a 2015 issue on similar themes. The first book forthcoming in the new Palgrave Macmillan series, *The Future of Humanity and Its Successors*, is on religion.[3]

In time, we will likely see many lay religious organizations developing around these issues. The Mormon Transhumanist Association[4] has been very active for several years and provides one model for how the conversation can be effectively extended beyond the academy.

ORGANIZATION OF THE COLLECTION

Although several of our chapters could easily fit into more than one section, a general logical order emerged in the collection.

Theological anthropology is an important doctrinal focus for thinking about radical enhancement. In the section "Theological Anthropology: What It Means to Be Human," Anders Sandberg dissects the meaning of life in transhumanism, distinguishing what he calls "individual," "terrestrial," and "cosmist" transhumanism. Matthew Zaro Fisher explores how theology can accommodate a transhumanist anthropology in the light of Karl Rahner's notion of *Vorgriff*, the self-luminosity of personhood. Jeanine Thweatt-Bates brings a feminist analysis to the topic and also addresses the very important ways popular culture plays a role in forming and reflecting public opinion regarding AI.

In the section "Soteriology: Salvation Now and Forever," Joseph Wolyniak provides an important historical piece by building on the work of those who have viewed Francis Bacon as a forbearer of transhumanism. In making his case, Wolyniak suggests interesting connections between transhumanism and religion. Patrick D. Hopkins unfolds a fascinating conundrum: modest enhancement will not save us, but radical enhancements will change us so much that it is no longer "us" being saved. Todd T. W. Daly contrasts Christian and transhumanist notions of death and suggests how the traditional notion of sin can elucidate important aspects of the enhancement discussion. Finally, Heup Young Kim writes one of the chapters that brings a perspective from outside Christianity. His is a helpful Christian-Confucian-Daoist analysis that engages transhumanism with key questions, such as those having to do with transhumanist goals and beneficiaries.

Eschatology is a central theme for some religion scholars working on the enhancement topic. In the section "Eschatology: For What Do We Hope?," Philip A. Douglas uses the work of complexity theorist James Gardner to study our "evolutionary journey toward the divine." Michael S. Burdett shows how transhumanism depends upon and extends the important myth of progress. In the process, Burdett advances a topic that interests a number of scholars— namely, the implicit religious themes in transhumanism. Geoffrey Redmond contributes our second chapter from an Asian perspective with his survey of how the Chinese religions of Buddhism, Confucianism, and Daoism bring fresh insights to the quest for extreme longevity. I hope this chapter, along with that of Heup Young Kim, prompts more work from scholars of Asian religious traditions. Hava Tirosh-Samuelson brings a Jewish perspective to what she views as the secularized faith of trans/posthumanism. Finally, Amy Michelle DeBaets provides the second feminist analysis in this collection. She is interested especially in a critique of Ray Kurzweil's notion of singularity.

The fourth section of this collection is entitled "Extreme Enhancement Ethics: Theological, Bioethical, and Philosophical Questions." Brian Patrick Green shows how Roman Catholic natural law might be impacted in a transhumanist scenario that might change human nature. Daniel McFee explores the precautionary and proactionary principles as they relate to transhumanism and shows how ecclesiastical groups can weigh in. The "created co-creator" concept is used by a number of scholars to think in positive ways about transhumanism; Stephen Garner uses this concept to show how transhumanism and religion may be connected. Celia Deane-Drummond engages the work of Ted Peters with a focus on the important question of human nature in the transhumanist vision. She also underscores the concern for embodiment. Finally, Steven A. Benko and Amelia Hruby examine the Levinasian ethic of responsibility for otherness as it relates to transhumanism.

We have four chapters that address "Body Matters," a theme emerging as central to the concerns of many religion scholars. Lee A. Johnson begins this section with a helpful historical analysis that shows how second-century debates in the Christian church inform contemporary struggles over the role of the body. A sharp contrast between Christian incarnational and posthuman visions of the flesh is provided by Brent Waters, one of the authors in this collection who is a strong critic of transhumanism. Cory Andrew Labrecque reflects on various ways the body can be understood in Roman Catholic Christianity and transhumanism. Finally, Hannah Scheidt works along the same general line as Waters, using the embodied phenomenology of Merleau-Ponty to critique mind uploading.

In the section "Corporeal Diversity and Religious Experience," Donald M. Braxton draws upon ongoing research to anticipate how extreme transhumanist scenarios might be received. As the public becomes more aware of the significant human enhancement possibilities, we need social science surveys to help us understand public attitudes and responses. Braxton's chapter helps us move in this general direction. Tracy J. Trothen looks at the consequences of increased enhancement to the spiritual aspects of elite sport, such as flow experiences, perfection, and hope. Ron Cole-Turner offers an evocative chapter about "spiritual" enhancement with his evaluation of recent research in entheogens and how they are reliably associated with mystical experiences.

My able co-editor, Tracy J. Trothen, summarizes the collection with a final chapter where she identifies core themes in the collection, provides her own valuable commentary, and shows how this collection allows us to "glimpse the future."

CONCLUSION

Human enhancement and the related social, economic, public policy, political, ethical, and religious questions will—quite appropriately—gain more and more attention in the future. These weighty issues have enormous implications for humanity and its various institutions.

I am pleased to see scholars engaging the religious questions, and I hope this volume plays a role in forwarding these important conversations so that the "unknown future" becomes more known.

NOTES

1. Nick Bostrom, "The Transhumanist FAQ 3.0" (Humanity+, nd), http://humanityplus.org/philosophy/transhumanist-faq/. Accessed July 19, 2014. For a briefer summary, see Derek Maher and Calvin Mercer (eds.), *Religion and the Implications of Radical Life Extension* (New York: Palgrave Macmillan, 2009), 3–6.

2. Pew Research Center, "The Global Religious Landscape." http://www.pewforum.org/2012/12/18/global-religious-landscape-exec/. Accessed May 11, 2014.

3. I am co-editing this series along with Steve Fuller. The first volume will appear this year as *The Body in Transhumanism: The World Religions Speak*, co-edited by Calvin Mercer and Derek Maher. The new Peter Lang series, *Beyond Humanism: Trans- and Posthumanism*, edited by Stefan Lorenz Sorgner, includes a volume, *Building Better Humans: Refocusing the Debate on Transhumanism*, that is co-edited by Hava Tirosh-Samuelson and Kenneth L. Mossman and contains several essays by scholars of religion.

4. http://transfigurism.org/. Accessed May 12, 2014.

Section 1

. . . .

Theological Anthropology:
What It Means to Be Human

1

Transhumanism and the Meaning of Life

Anders Sandberg

Transhumanism, broadly speaking,[1] is the view that the human condition is not unchanging and that it can and should be questioned. Further, the human condition can and should be changed using applied reason.[2] As Max More explained, transhumanism includes life philosophies that seek the evolution of intelligent life beyond its current human form and limitations, using science and technology.[3]

Nick Bostrom emphasizes the importance to transhumanism of exploring transhuman and posthuman modes of existence.[4] This exploration is desirable since there are reasons to believe that some states in this realm hold great value, nearly regardless of the value theory to which one subscribes.[5] Transhumanism, in his conception, has this exploration as its core value and then derives other values from it.

Sebastian Seung, an outsider to transhumanism, described it as having accepted the post-Enlightenment critique of reason, yet without giving up on using reason to achieve grand ends that could give meaning to life individually or collectively:

> The "meaning of life" includes both universal and personal dimensions. We can ask both "Are we here for a reason?" and "Am I here for a reason?" Transhumanism answers these questions as follows. First, it's the destiny of humankind to transcend the human condition. This is not merely what will happen, but what should happen. Second, it can be a personal goal to sign up for Alcor,[6] dream about uploading, or use technology to otherwise improve oneself. In both of these ways, transhumanism lends meaning to lives that were robbed of it by science.

The bible said that God made man in his own image. The German philosopher Ludwig Feuerbach said that man made God in his own image. The transhumanists say that humanity will make itself into God.[7]

Is this view correct? In what follows, I will show that Seung neatly summed up three strands of transhumanism: transhumanism as a way of improving one's own life (what I call "individual transhumanism"), transhumanism as a project dedicated to the betterment of humanity ("terrestrial transhumanism"), and transhumanism as a project with the purpose of achieving the potential of life in the universe ("cosmist transhumanism").

By considering the possibility of creating or becoming something superhuman, transhumanism forces meaning-of-life questions to the foreground as engineering targets.[8] This leads to an interesting intersection between transhumanism and questions concerning universal values: how is the meaning of life understood in transhumanist thought? In the following, I survey thinkers in the three strands that I have identified and examine how they approach questions of meaning. In particular, I am concerned with how meaning can be constructed when the human condition, life, or even the universe itself may become a cultural artefact.

INDIVIDUAL TRANSHUMANISM

The individual transhumanist story is typically described as ambition to live a life supported by enhancements so as to achieve better health and mental capacity, refined emotions, new abilities, and longevity, and perhaps become a posthuman. People differ on whether this endeavor is merely about overcoming everyday limitations, becoming something akin to a Greek god, or totally escaping the human condition.

When I informally asked self-described transhumanists on the extropy-chat mailing list[9] about their views on the meaning of life, the answers I received were for the most part firmly in a naturalistic subjectivist camp. For these transhumanists, there was no supernatural world imbuing meaning to existence; all believed that thinking beings can experience meaningful states—if only meaningful to themselves. In fact, many of the respondents were clearly existentialist in outlook. Some sample comments illustrate this point:

OR: "We give our own meaning to life in the context of ourselves and our surroundings."

BZ: "The meaning of life is ... You decide."

GP: "The question 'What's the meaning of life?' assumes that there is a unique answer valid for everyone. But I don't think there is one. It's up to everyone to give meaning to their life."

Some respondents were more theoretical, placing the question within a larger narrative. One explained that the meaning of human life is to decide on actions based on perceived value. But there is a choice to improve this human decision-making function, which might be called acquiring wisdom:

KA: "Now, if acquiring wisdom is the meaning of human life, then in transhumanism the goal could be stated as acquire more wisdom than is currently humanly possible."

However, the respondents also clearly expressed many things they *experienced* as meaningful:

GP: "I find meaning in being a small part of something very big— humanity on its way to become [sic] a cosmic civilization that will achieve the dreams of Fedorov and Tipler . . ."

One respondent privately pointed out that he regarded the greatest challenge in life as coming to terms with the limitations of life, including its finitude. He saw transhumanism, at least in its most radical forms, as an attempt to retreat from this existential challenge. This is not an uncommon criticism of transhumanism from outside, but it is worth noting that it also exists within the transhumanist community.

Religious Transhumanism

The naturalism of these responses is not surprising. A World Transhumanist Association (now named Humanity+) survey of members[10] found that 87 percent of respondents agreed that their "concept of 'the meaning of life' [was] derived from human responsibility and opportunity rather than divine revelation" and 93 percent agreed that they "expect[ed] human progress to result from human accomplishment rather than divine intervention, grace, or redemption." The majority (64 percent) of survey respondents were secular but there were notable religious minorities subscribing to transhumanism, including Buddhists, Christians, and various self-described spiritual members.

Transhumanism is sometimes described as a religion. While it overlaps with religion in being concerned with escaping the current human condition for a more transcendent condition[11] and can share many metaphysical, soteriological, and eschatological interests with religion,[12] there are clear divergences both in practices (for example, the lack of transhumanist prayer) and in underlying theory. Indeed, transhumanism in general may *lack* key parts of a belief system. Transhumanism might simply be in favor of a set of instrumental methods for achieving ambitious aims, but not provide any real value theory or purpose. While the more existentialist or postmodern transhumanists might regard this as a *merit* (since they are skeptical about objective values), many people see value as necessary for being able to live a meaningful life. Hopkins points out:[13]

> If we take it as essential to religion that it provides some sort of ultimate answer for the meaning of life, as the World Transhumanist Association seems to in its statement, then transhumanism still isn't a religion. Transhumanists argue for the right to attempt to surpass the current limitations of human biology. They do not argue that this is a goal in itself, only that it is a condition under which other goals and experiences might be even more widely, permanently, or expansively pursued. Without some other meaning, goal, or belief, even a posthuman could sit around bored, depressed, or awash in angst.

Transhumanism can, however, be combined with a religious belief that holds its own values. For example, in a provocative essay,[14] Micah Redding expresses a Christian transhumanist view that "Christianity *is* transhumanism. It's not just that they are compatible. Christianity is a distinctly transhumanist viewpoint that sprung up in the first century, and set out to reshape both the world and human nature." Humanity being divinely created for a purpose gives a meaning to human life: to do the works of God. According to this perspective, Christianity is a form of transhumanism that believes divine power and grace are necessary "technologies" of human empowerment and transcendence; the Christian transhumanist merely sees naturalistic technology as a useful complement.

Deliberately constructed transhumanist religious systems also exist. For example, the Terasem movement claims to be a "transreligion": "a movement which can be combined with any existing religion, without having to leave a previous religion."[15] This is similar to the view that transhumanism can be combined with many value systems—although just as for transhumanism, there might be some compatibility problems. In fact, the Terasem core belief that "god is technological" and a future human-created entity makes it incompatible with most mainstream religions. From a meaning perspective it is explicit: "Life is purposeful: the purpose of life is to create diversity, unity and joyful immortality everywhere."[16] Various technological projects are motivated from these core beliefs.[17]

While a meaning provided by an external system of belief might be emotionally satisfying, the potential arbitrariness is not philosophically satisfying. Hence some transhumanists dissatisfied with both subjectivism and traditional meanings have attempted to construct pure transhumanist concepts of meaning.

Extropianism

The ideas developed and spread by the Extropy Institute in the early 1990s influenced much of contemporary transhumanism. The Extropian Principles 2.5 state:

Extropy: A measure of intelligence, information, energy, vitality, experience, diversity, opportunity, and growth. Extropianism: The philosophy that seeks to increase extropy.[18]

According to Max More, extropianism aimed to provide "an inspiring and uplifting meaning and direction to our lives, while remaining flexible and firmly founded in science, reason, and the boundless search for improvement."[19] Note the psychological rather than ethical or teleological use of the word "meaning": it is not a moral meaning derived from somehow breaching the is-ought boundary, but a sense of meaning compatible with what is. This is very much in line with Seung's diagnosis.

However, further down in the manifesto, this meaning becomes linked to a more explicit notion of global progress:[20]

Extropians recognize the unique place of our species, and our opportunity to advance nature's evolution to new peaks. Beginning as mindless matter, parts of nature developed in a slow evolutionary ascendence, leading to progressively more powerful brains. Chemical reactions generated tropistic behavior, which was superseded by instinctual and Skinnerian stimulus-response behavior, and then by conscious learning and experimentation. With the advent of the conceptual awareness of humankind, the rate of advancement sharply accelerated as intelligence, technology, and the scientific method were applied to our condition. We seek to sustain and quicken this evolutionary process of expanding extropy, transcending biological and psychological limits into posthumanity.

The reasons why this is desirable depend on one's interpretation of extropy. If one sees evolution as a meaningful and value-creating process, then supporting it is desirable. Even if evolution is not itself meaningful, it may create things or states of value; amplifying this ability to evolve would, in turn, be meaningful and enable deeper exploration of the posthuman realm.

While the preceding section spoke to progress on a species level, the Extropian Principles largely dealt with individual growth and societal progress.[21] Extropianism as described in the principles does not include an explicit notion of the meaning of life, but its clear emphasis on intelligence, wisdom, effectiveness, creativity, removal of limits to self-actualization, and autonomy is not far from a naturalist objectivist or hybrid account of meaning.

Enhancements and the Meaning of Life

Most of the bioethical debate about human enhancement has not centered on the meaning of life. Instead, it has focused on the permissibility or desirability of enhancements using bioethical principles of autonomy, justice, welfare, and risk of harm. As often noted, the term "enhancement" implies some kind of value scale, but a value scale itself is not sufficient to provide meaning. Top-down arguments from a meaning of life to enhancement permissibility/

desirability are rare, perhaps because of the reluctance of postmodern academia to engage with "great stories" that provide an overarching explanation of life or give universal moral principles. The closest the debate gets to meaning is usually considerations of human dignity and discussions of the conditions under which enhancement could rob a human life of meaning.[22]

One area where enhancement discussions run in parallel with meaning-of-life discussions is life extension. Arguments that immortality would make life meaningless often hinge on the fact that the finitude of life somehow imbues it with meaning.[23] Besides causing problems for theists hoping for everlasting life,[24] the arbitrariness of the length of life creates problems for some theists. While one can argue that certain lifespans are too short or too long, the actual length does not matter for the finitude argument. That means that even eon-long lifespans can be meaningful, since they are still finite. In fact, our current understanding of the universe does not allow for truly indefinitely long lifespans: even a non-aging entity with multiple dispersed backup copies will eventually have to face the heat-death of the universe or a case of bad luck.

A somewhat related argument is that indefinite lifespans would become boring. This point is cited both in bioethics and in discussions about the meaning of life.[25] However, leaving aside the empirical question of whether this has to be the case for all people, it is not clear that a boring life is meaningless. A host of arguments might be made that happiness may not be the necessary or sufficient condition for a meaningful life (consider Nozick's experience machine). Similarly, a boring life might still be meaningful. Many important tasks are dull yet ought to be done: some such tasks might even be of indefinite duration.

Conversely, there is Leo Tolstoy's argument[26] that for life to be meaningful, there must be something worth doing, but actions with impermanent effects on the world do not eventually matter; thus for life to have meaning requires some ability to have permanent effects. This is sometimes seen as an argument for an immortal soul (or God's eternal remembrance).[27] However, transhumanism can claim that the argument merely shows that we should aim for an infinite lifespan: souls may not be needed. Indeed, one could see it as an argument for why we *must* strive for vastly extended lifespans and expansion into the universe for our lives to have any meaning. Transhumanism might be what enables us to lead truly meaningful lives in a physical universe.[28]

TERRESTRIAL TRANSHUMANISM

The terrestrial transhumanism story is a story about humanity, or perhaps our own current civilization. A typical version is expressed as a story of technological progress, occurring either automatically or as a result of deliberate effort, and leading to a series of human condition-changing technologies (e.g., life extension, cognitive enhancement, nanotechnology, artificial intelligence, brain-computer symbiosis, whole-brain emulation, space colonization). In any case, the new technological capabilities enable humans to become enhanced transhumans and eventually posthumans—that is, beings largely liberated from the constraints imposed by natural evolution. Ray Kurzweil[29] and Hans Moravec[30] are well-known exponents of this form of transhumanism. The following discussion looks at three thinkers influential inside transhumanism and considers how they approach the meaning of life from the species level.

In *Man into Superman*, R. C. W. Ettinger, the father of cryonics, argues for human enhancement and faith in technological progress, but almost as an aside delivers a theory of the meaning of life:

> At last one of the central questions can be dealt with: What is the purpose of life? Answer: To discover the purpose of life. This is not a play on words, but a recognition of the obvious truth that since ultimate answers are not within view we must make do, for the foreseeable future, with uncovering and pursuing a succession of intermediate goals, and that this requires a program of growth and development.[31]

Given the need for long-term empirical research and the likelihood that mere human intelligence is not enough, we need to develop human enhancement just to do our proper work.

This view is echoed in some of Nick Bostrom's work. Basically, the deep problems of philosophy have shown themselves to be very hard to solve, and we should expect that they will remain unsolved for a long time (requiring life extension if we are keen on learning the answers) or will not yield at all until we can develop minds (posthuman or artificial) smart enough to handle them. In either case, we should focus on earlier and perhaps lesser problems that allow us to get to this state, such as life extension or cognitive enhancement, while also reducing existential risk so that we have a future where they can be solved. In this case transhumanism is merely instrumental for finding out what the real, non-instrumental values are.

David Pearce takes a strong hedonistic and negative utilitarian stance, arguing that pleasure is the real (multidimensional) value and pain the real disvalue. Focusing on reducing pain, his abolitionist project aims at eventually eradicating aversive experience—first from humans, later from all sentient life. This requires a fairly deep neural restructuring of the motivation system, but is intensely worthwhile. The very nature of pain makes it something to avoid, and intelligent beings have the power to save themselves from pain as well as a moral obligation to save other organisms, too.[32] The abolitionist approach exemplifies the species independence of much philosophical transhumanism. What matters is the lives of sentient beings, not what kind of beings they are or what relationship they hold with humanity.

Pearce does not, however, speak of this project as conveying a meaning of life. In his writings, meaning is very much a non-propositional feeling; hence it is also amenable to enhancement like other feelings: " 'Authentic happiness' doesn't need to be strived for. Like a sense of meaning and purpose, it can be innate."[33] Pearce notes that depressive and unmotivated "healthy" people find life meaningless, absurd, or futile, while hyperthymic or hypomanic people tend to find life intensely meaningful. By enhancing happiness, we can enhance meaning: "If our happiness is taken care of—whether genetically, pharmacologically, or electrosurgically—then the meaning of life seems to take care of itself."[34]

Eliezer Yudkowsky is an interesting case of an influential transhumanist whose thinking about meaning has strongly evolved over time. Starting from I. J. Good's "intelligence explosion" idea,[35] Yudkowsky became a strong proponent for technological singularity and the benefit of constructing artificial intelligence to reach it as soon as possible. In his earliest writings, the motivation for striving toward the singularity is to solve the world's problems (including rising existential risks) through superintelligence.[36]

Seeing the situation as the practical engineering problem of triggering an intelligence explosion, Yudkowsky set out to discover a solution and promote the approach. This soon led to a version of the discovery motivation for enhancement, the "the interim meaning of life" being to create superhuman AI. Yudkowsky developed a formal argument that even an artificial intelligence with no given goals would also deduce the desirability of finding out what was meaningful to do.[37]

However, at this point the project of pursuing powerful AI began to run into trouble. A superintelligent entity is supremely able to achieve its goals, but there is no guarantee that it will have human-friendly or even sane goals.[38] Yudkowsky recognized that designing AI is, therefore, not just a matter of achieving great intelligence that can grow, but also of inserting goals or values that make it safe and human-friendly.

The "friendly AI" project can be seen as an attempt to figure out how to design a "god" that has positive properties. It turns theist assumptions around: not only would god be created in the image of humans, but the values it embodies would be defined by humans. As contributors to the research have found, this leads to profound ethical and logical problems. Indeed, Yudkowsky's lasting legacy may be opening up a fruitful field between ethics and theoretical computer science.

When Ray Kurzweil suggests solving the problem by teaching AI the golden rule,[39] he assumes that this will unfold into a proper morality rather than the AI choosing to interpret it simplemindedly like a child would. However, as the friendliness researchers have shown, converting human-type values and instructions into code or instructions is exceedingly difficult.

Even a correct moral system might have a flawed implementation, and we should not be too confident that we even have the right starting point.[40]

As "friendliness" was explored, it became increasingly clear that one of the key problems was that human value is complex, fragile, and hard to articulate, let alone formalize. At present Eliezer's tentative conclusion about meaning is summarized in "fun theory,"[41] essentially a sprawling analysis of human values and enjoyment. We know many things about what makes lives generally go well, yet formalizing all of this knowledge into a computable package is troublesome. At its core the theory is utilitarian, but acknowledges the possibility that neat, compact theories of value might be impossible.

Meaning for Posthumans

Does a posthuman assign the same meaning to its life as does a human? We might impute that posthumans might have experiences and modes of cognition that we cannot conceive of, yet bear on the meaning of life for them. Either (1) humans have reached some form of philosophical, cognitive, or emotional threshold to experience or perceive the meaning of life and posthumans will also agree on this meaning, (2) posthumans will assume a different kind of meaning of their lives than humans, or (3) only posthumans (but not humans) are able to live truly meaningful lives.

If posthumans have a different kind of meaning than humans, then there may be no human meaning-related reason for humans to want to become posthumans. If only posthumans have meaning, then the best humans can aspire to in terms of meaning is to become posthuman enough to perceive for what they then need to strive.

It is worth remarking here on the contested links between Nietzsche and transhumanism. Nick Bostrom explicitly rejected any deeper connection than found in superficial quotation.[42] However, while Nietzsche's philosophy and transhumanism differ in some ways, Stefan Sorgner showed significant overlap between them.[43] Max More explained how Nietzsche had influenced his own development of extropianism.[44] The eternal return is very different from the progressive view of transhumanism, and Nietzsche would not have approved of the utilitarian branches of transhumanism. Nevertheless, as Sorgner points out, Nietzsche can also provide a meaning to transhumanism through his concept of the overhuman:[45]

> The overhuman represents the meaning of the earth. The overhuman is supposed to represent the meaning-giving concept within Nietzsche's worldview which is supposed to replace the basically Christian worldview. It is in the interest of higher humans to permanently overcome themselves. The ultimate kind of overcoming can be seen in the overcoming of the human species, and

whoever has been keen on permanently overcoming himself can regard himself
as an ancestor of the overhuman. In this way, the overhuman is supposed to give
meaning to human beings. It is not a transcendent meaning but an earthy,
immanent one which is appropriate for scientifically minded people who have
abandoned their belief in an after world.

If one identifies the overhuman and the posthuman with each other, then a
Nietzschean transhumanist would indeed find meaning in life by aiming to
become at least the ancestor of the overhuman/posthuman. Loeb has argued
that this requires affirming eternal recurrence (which also provides a peculiar
solution to how to achieve infinite consequences and hence meaning),[46]
while Sorgner and More seem open to a more selective reading. This can be
contrasted with Bostrom's neutral definition of transhumanism as merely a
chance to explore the posthuman realm. While there might be great value
"out there," it does not necessarily produce a strong individual obligation to
explore it.[47] A utilitarian ethics is still needed to make a search meaningful.

Existential Risk

While often seen by outsiders as naively optimistic, many transhumanists
tend to emphasize that the future may be more *extreme* than is commonly
thought. While there might be posthuman states of great value, there are also
potential existential risks threatening futures with no or extremely negative
value. Insofar as we can influence which future we might reach, we may
have a *far* greater moral responsibility than is commonly envisioned because
the stakes are higher.[48]

The existential risk issue is not so much an issue about the meaning of life
as it is an issue about the prevention of the loss of meaning. If humanity
becomes extinct, at the very least the loss is equivalent to the loss of all living
individuals and the thwarting of their individual goals. But the loss would
likely be far greater: extinction means the loss of all future generations (even
modest assumptions lead to an astronomical number of future lives[49]), all
the value they might have been able to create, and perhaps the meaning generated by past generations as well. At the same time, it is also possible to argue
that value requires a valuer. If consciousness or intelligence is lost, it might
mean that value itself becomes absent from the universe.

The immortality discussion earlier in this chapter can be applied here
regarding the mortality of the human species. On the one hand, the Tolstoy
argument suggests that unless our species persists indefinitely (perhaps evolving into new things), there is no meaning to its current existence. Species
matter because they are parts of the tree of life, leading to new forms.
On the other hand, pro-finitude arguments would lead us to not wish to pro-
long the stay of our species on Earth. However, when these arguments are
applied to humanity as a whole, the counterpart to boredom would be

stagnation, and the counterpart to giving space for new people would be to leave space for new species. These arguments merely show that we should wish for more evolution and eventual replacement, not that our *lineage* ends.

The Simulation Argument

Nick Bostrom's simulation argument is that unless the human species goes extinct before becoming posthuman, there will emerge capabilities to run enormous numbers of historical simulations including virtual people. Thus, unless posthuman civilizations are extremely unlikely to run a significant number of simulations (either because of impossibility or because of some extremely strong and unlikely consistent unwillingness), there will be a vast number of simulated people, far greater than the number of real people. We are almost certainly going to be living in a computer simulation, at least given common transhumanist assumptions.[50] How does extensive simulation affect the meaning of life?

Simulation may give a purpose to our world, but that does not necessarily give a purpose to individual life. Only simulations created for the purpose of having inhabitants with lives worth living can be said to give some purpose to their lives. But in this case the simulated lives only have the same meaning (i.e., to have a life worth living) as lives in the outside universe.

Mere teleology may not always give meaning, as noted in the philosophical debate about which objective factors would give human life meaning. The hybrid view of meaning argues that meaning arises when one does projects that are judged to be worthwhile and actually *are* worthwhile.[51] Caring about things that are not worthwhile or failing to see the importance of what one is doing can preclude meaning in one's life. A worthwhile simulation does not mean that simulated lives have meaning. They did not have a choice to participate, they do not know about it, and the value of the simulation might relate only to something existing outside it.

How would thinking we live in a simulation affect us? Hanson suggests that, given typical human desires, we would live more for today (since the world could be shut down at any moment), care less for other people, aim to be entertaining and praiseworthy, mingle with famous people, and participate in pivotal events.[52] If we had a better idea of what the creator wanted to achieve, other behaviors might be more appropriate. Insofar that the creator of a simulation is morally responsible for the behavior of the beings inside, there is a moral obligation for the creator to give the right information to the simulated people so that they will behave well and to minimize their suffering. Running simulations with sentient inhabitants poses significant ethical problems.[53] In a sense, this is a theodicy problem, but there is no assumption in the simulation argument that the creator is omniscient or benevolent.

A directly theological take on the simulation argument is offered by Eric Steinhart.[54] In his somewhat neoplatonic approach, Steinhart suggests that the ultimate simulator of a set of nested simulations should be regarded as God who acts as the ground of being. He posits an aesthetic theodicy, where the suffering and evil inside the simulations are vindicated by the overall creative aim:[55]

> Why are we being simulated? And why are there any simulations rather than none? We have three answers: at every level, the designers are interested in the evolution of complexity; in knowledge; and in dramatic beauty. Obviously, these three concepts overlap. They share a common core. It's reasonable to refer to this common core as *interestingness*. ... At the risk of sounding circular, the simulationist can say that we are being simulated because every creative intelligence is *interested in interestingness*.

Evolution of complexity, knowledge, and dramatic beauty sounds suspiciously similar to extropy. In this case the goal of the whole project is worthwhile interestingness, and all intelligent entities should both find the whole worthwhile and experience interest in their own worlds and the simulations they run—so here there would, indeed, be a meaning of life.

COSMIST TRANSHUMANISM

The cosmist transhumanist story occurs at the largest scale. First life, and then intelligence, emerges on Earth. Intelligence becomes technological, masters the natural world, and eventually begins to colonize space. As intelligence spreads, it converts resources in its environment into things of value to it: both instrumentally useful tools for further expansion and protection (spacecraft, backups) and intrinsically valuable things (biospheres, cultures, minds).

The expansion is essentially unlimited. A civilization that has learned to use standard astronomical resources has a vast amount of material available. If it is able to make the jump over interplanetary and interstellar distances once, it can repeat it. Even inter*galactic* jumps are likely feasible to a civilization that can spread between the stars.[56] There is likely no intrinsic limitation on the scales of activities of technological civilizations beyond those imposed by the laws of nature and available resources.

The cosmist view is about physics. Dead matter is meta-stable and can, under the right conditions, convert to a different organization (i.e., life/ intelligence). Just as supercooled water freezes outward from a seed ice crystal, so if intelligent life emerges anywhere it is likely to nucleate a "technosphere" bubble where matter is reorganized according to the dictates of mind.

The cosmist story has multiple endings. One ending is that the entire universe becomes intelligent—that is, "wakes up" as per Kurzweil's vision.[57] Another scenario envisions intelligence becoming increasingly interconnected and coordinated, ending in a single super-mind or super-social organization.[58] In either case, the intelligence-dominated universe will be filled with minds protecting life and intelligence, controlling the contents of the universe so as to survive or reach unification.

Mere matter lacks inherent value and meaning, whereas life and mind have potential for meaning. The expansion of life into the universe and the gradual conversion of matter into mind can be a way of providing the universe with meaning.[59] Is spreading life meaningful? While there are theories of value wherein objects have intrinsic value even when never observed, value is typically assumed to require someone or something that values. While human observers are the usual example, it is not hard to imagine that at least some form of valuing is done by other life forms. In the future, software and other artificial systems may also be valuers. Most of these entities do not simply passively measure value but rather are agents; their actions can be best described as attempts to increase value as they understand it. Some systems have enough internal degrees of freedom to learn and change their value estimates and action patterns, sometimes as deliberate internal actions (in which case we may even call them moral agents). In this account, systems are able to experience value and act to increase it. If there is some true value and these systems converge toward seeking it, they would increase true value in the world. If value is agent-relative or instrumental, agents could potentially (but not necessarily) increase the amount of subjective value. Conversely, a universe with fewer valuers has less potential for a drive toward more value (unless the value lies in no *deliberate* change). Thus there seem to be at least some *prima facie* reasons to believe a universe rich in life and mind to have more value.

Besides the potential for adding value, there is the potential for creating diversity. Living beings are foremost contingent, individual, and shaped by a unique life story (and evolutionary path) that make them impossible to re-create if they are lost. As expressed by Ramez Naam:

> We are, if we choose to be, the seed from which wondrous new kinds of life can grow. We are the prospective parents of new and unimaginable creatures. We are the tiny metazoan from which a new Cambrian can spring. I can think of no more beautiful destiny for any species, no more privileged place in history, than to be the initiators of this new genesis.[60]

Cosmist expansion is a way of responding to our apparent insignificance.[61] We may be small and contingent, yet potentially important by triggering the great Cambrian explosion of future species.

Edward Abbey famously wrote, "Growth for the sake of growth is the ideology of the cancer cell."[62] Might not this focus on growth and progress lead to devaluation of what we have and destabilization of the natural world? Even if interstellar expansion is undertaken for the best possible reasons, evolutionary pressures might promote a mode of expansion whereby nearly all resources are devoted to rapid expansion rather than creating value.[63] Of course, growth is also the ideology of the orchid. Replicating and evolving systems tend to fill their niches, use the available resources, and constantly poke the edges. Growth presents a problem when it causes loss of value, typically seen as loss of diversity, intrinsic harmony, or long-term sustainability. Spreading life into the universe, then, could be a great boon. The vast scales in space, time, and environment types lead to diversity, and interstellar life would have a chance to outlast the inevitable end of Earth's biosphere.

Our real stewardship might take the form of avoiding the early existential risk that threatens the cosmic blossoming and preventing pathologies from burning away value. Both actions would require coordination *before* we leave our earthly seed site, turning the cosmist possibilities and risks into an issue for present generations. As Yudkowsky put it:[64]

> If you occupy the incredibly rare and leverage-privileged position of being born into Ancient Earth, the origin of all life ... Your most fundamental responsibility as a *Homo sapiens* is to the process whereby the reachable universe is converted into QALYs.[65]

Universal Immortalism

Nikolai Fedorov ranks as one of the pioneering and perhaps most original forerunners of transhumanism. A Russian philosopher, he formulated a bold worldview based on slavophilia, orthodox Christianity, and belief in science.[66] In his system, the core problem is the disunity and lack of love among people. His solution is the doctrine of kinship; we must strive to reach the kind of unity a loving family (and the trinity) embodies. This includes not just brotherhood with our present peers, but also lineage kinship where parents care for their descendants, and they in turn acknowledge their debt and gratitude. To unite humankind, a great project is needed—the "Common Task" that all people can agree on. This involves regulating nature and perfecting it, the colonization ("spiritualization") of the universe, improving the human body, and the eventual resurrection of the dead. It is a task of completing the creation entrusted to humanity by God.[67]

Fedorov's cosmism appears to have influenced many notable intellectuals, including Tolstoy, Dostoyevsky, and Tsiolkovsky.[68] Tsiolkovsky founded the space movement, contributing to the shedding of its theological components and to it becoming a manifest destiny of spreading life and intelligence across the universe.

Hans Moravec speculated about future computers being powerful enough to generate history simulations (partially motivating the simulation argument) that could be used to reconstruct past people: "Resurrecting one small planet should be child's play long before our civilization has colonized its first galaxy."[69] The computational requirements do appear feasible given known physics,[70] although they would require computing on a literally planetary scale. In addition to resurrecting historical people, possible people would (and maybe should) also be given the gift of life.

Several transhumanists, such as Mike Perry, have gone from *possibility* to *ought*. They argue that since life, lived well, is an end in itself, it should be extended.[71] Perry outlines a moral case for life extension, cryonics, and universal immortalism. This is a naturalist objectivist concept of a meaning of life, but clearly aligned with Fedorov's Common Task: "The immortalization of humans and other life-forms is seen as a great moral project and labor of love that will unite us in a common cause and provide a meaningful destiny."[72]

Omega Points

Many transhumanists consider the possibility of God or gods emerging through a naturalistic process. Superintelligent AI or posthumans may appear god-like to humans, but where is the *upper* limit? Ray Kurzweil suggests that intelligence will spread and awaken the universe, producing something akin to a pantheistic deity in the future.[73]

The most extreme form of both universal immortalism and life taking control of the universe is represented by the Omega Point cosmology of Frank J. Tipler,[74] who borrowed the term from Teilhard de Chardin.[75] Tipler describes a scenario where intelligence expands across the universe, gains control over most matter and energy, and during a future phase of cosmological implosion exploits these resources to maintain its order and structure, ultimately achieving *infinite* information and processing power.

In its original form,[76] this was an exercise along the lines of Freeman Dyson's classical 1979 paper[77] that laid the groundwork for "physical eschatology"—that is, the study of the future evolution of the universe based on known physics. Physical eschatology looks at the long-term survival of structure and analysis of the roles that life and intelligence may play in the various large-scale scenarios.[78]

Tipler's scenario soon took on a distinctly theological character. The Omega Point moved beyond a limited state of infinite information and processing power and took on the character of God. Tipler argued that the Omega Point will be a benevolent time in which all the dead are resurrected, producing an endless virtual afterlife. The Omega Point was also defined, in his physical theology, as the boundary condition of space-time. In a very real sense, it was understood as the future physical *cause* of the universe. While individual beings had free will, their actions would eventually lead to the emergence of the Omega Point. Universes where this failed would be self-contradictory and, therefore, would have zero probability of occurring. Acting to bring about the Omega Point is the meaning of the world.

Omega Point theology has been rather coolly received among physicists and theologians, in some cases leading them to take the whole physical eschatology program to task for Tipler's excesses. For example, why does the boundary condition have to be benevolent infinite information rather than (say) zero infor-mation? Tipler's theory also had the fatal problem of requiring a closed universe; observations have now demonstrated an accelerating open universe where this particular model of infinite information processing will not work. Nevertheless, the Omega Point, while not something many transhumanists believe in, could be something we might eventually aspire to at least *approximate*.

CONCLUSION

Transhumanism does not have a unified theory of the meaning of life, but certain themes recur again and again, linked to the different strands.

While individual respondents tend toward subjectivism, transhumanist theorists have often approached meaning from a hybrid view: there are objec-tive values or goals that can make transhuman life meaningful, and there is a great deal of individual subjective choice in setting goals and determining how to reach them. Typical objectives are reducing suffering and unnecessary limitations and achieving well-being, wisdom, life, diversity and an open future. While not unique to the strand, this is the most common approach within individual transhumanism.

The idea of "doing God's work" in perfecting creation or humanity shows up repeatedly, both in an explicit theist context and in secular versions. The secular versions recognize how nature has produced value-experiencing beings that are now beginning to be free and powerful enough to direct further change in a value-creating direction. The skepticism of transhumanism toward both tradi-tional philosophy and our ability to solve problems with merely human reason also lends itself to the interim goal of becoming able to fully discover meaning by creating greater forms of intelligence. This provides a meaning for the ambi-tions of the second strand of transhumanism, terrestrial transhumanism.

Finally, in the cosmist strand, Tolstoy's argument about infinite lasting consequences can be applied to posthumanity: if we can bring about the enor-mous future envisioned, our lives will at least instrumentally have meaning. Even if this future is finite, it may be immeasurably larger than any ordinary future, and this still makes the pursuit meaningful. The transhumanist, whether secular or theistic, is embedded in a meaningful worldview that is unique because of its enormous ambition and scope. It attempts to link our current microscopic state with the grandness of the universe unveiled by modern science. As the universe becomes vaster, the transhumanist will expe-rience meaning as *increasing* rather than decreasing.

ACKNOWLEDGMENTS

I wish to thank the participants on the extropy-chat mailing list for responding to my queries—and once upon a time, in the early 1990s, setting me on the path toward philosophy.

NOTES

1. Transhumanism is not a doctrinal movement or philosophy. In this chapter I will hence use the term "transhumanism" in a broad sense of thinkers who agree on the changeability of the current human condition, rather than in the narrow sense of people calling themselves transhumanists.

2. Max More, "The Philosophy of Transhumanism," in *The Transhumanist Reader*, edited by Max More and Natasha Vita-More (Chickchester: Wiley, 2013), 3–17.

3. Max More, "Transhumanism: Towards a Futurist Philosophy," *Extropy* 6 (Summer 1990): 6–12.

4. Nick Bostrom, "Transhumanist Values," in *Ethical Issues for the 21st Century*, edited by Frederick Adams (Charlottesville: Philosophical Documentation Center Press, 2003); reprinted in *Review of Contemporary Philosophy* 4 (May 2005).

5. Nick Bostrom, "Why I Want to Be a Posthuman When I Grow Up," in *Medical Enhancement and Posthumanity*, edited by Bert Gordijn and Ruth Chadwick (New York: Springer, 2008), 107–137.

6. Alcor Life Extension Foundation is a cryonics company that preserves people in liquid nitrogen after legal death in the hope of eventual resuscitation when technology advances enough.

7. Sebastian Seung, *Connectome: How the Brain's Wiring Makes Us Who We Are* (New York: Houghton Mifflin Harcourt, 2012), 273.

8. Sirkku K. Hellsten, " 'The Meaning of Life' during a Transition from Modernity to Transhumanism and Posthumanity," *Journal of Anthropology* 2012 (2012). doi: 10.1155/2012/210684.

9. At the time, the list had about 30 active posters and 15 usable responses were gathered. The participants were informed of my intention to use the material as input for this chapter. The discussion is available at http://lists.extropy.org/pipermail/extropy-chat/2014-February/thread.html.

10. James J. Hughes, "Report on the 2007 Interests and Beliefs Survey of the Members of the World Transhumanist Association," 2008. http://transhumanism.org/resources/WTASurvey2007.pdf. Accessed March 31, 2014.

11. Patrick D. Hopkins, "Transcending the Animal: How Transhumanism and Religion Are and Are Not Alike," *Journal of Evolution and Technology* 14 (2005): 2.

12. James J. Hughes, "The Compatibility of Religious and Transhumanist Views of Metaphysics, Suffering, Virtue and Transcendence in an Enhanced Future," *Global Spiral* 8 (May 2007): 2.

13. Hopkins, "Transcending the Animal," 2005.

14. Micah Redding, "Christianity Is Transhumanism," 2012. http://micahredding.com/blog/2012/04/25/christianity-transhumanism. Accessed March 31, 2014.

15. Terasem, "The Truths of Terasem," 2002. http://terasemfaith.net/beliefs. Accessed March 31, 2014

16. Terasem, "The Truths of Terasem," 2002.

17. Terasem, "The Truths of Terasem," 2002.

18. Max More, "The Extropian Principles 2.5," *Extropy* 11, 2nd Half (1993).

19. More, "The Extropian Principles 2.5."

20. More, "The Extropian Principles 2.5."

21. Max More, "The Extropian Principles Version 3.0: A Transhumanist Declaration," 1999. http://www.buildfreedom.com/extropian_principles.html.

22. Nick Bostrom, "Dignity and Enhancement," in *Human Dignity and Bioethics: Essays Commissioned by the President's Council on Bioethics* (Washington, DC: President's Council on Bioethics), March 2008.

23. For example, Leon Kass, "L'Chaim and Its Limits: Why not Immortality?" *First Things* 113 (2001): 17–24.

24. The strategy of arguing that this *kind* of life is of a different kind from a life that gains meaning from finitude opens up the possibility that there might be physical kinds of life that also do not gain meaning from finitude.

25. Bernard Williams, "The Makropulos Case: Reflections on the Tedium of Immortality," in *Problems of the Self* (Cambridge, UK: Cambridge University Press, 1973), 82–100.

26. Leo A. Tolstoy, *A Confession and Other Religious Writings* (London: Penguin Classics, 1988).

27. Thaddeus Metz, "The Immortality Requirement for Life's Meaning," *Ratio* 16, no. 2 (2003): 161–177. doi: 10.1111/1467-9329.00213.

28. Dan Weijers, "Optimistic Naturalism: Scientific Advancement and the Meaning of Life," *Sophia* (2013). doi: 10.1007/s11841-013-0369-x.

29. Ray Kurzweil, *The Singularity Is Near: When Humans Transcend Biology* (New York: Viking, 2005).

30. Hans Moravec, *Mind Children: The Future of Robot and Human Intelligence* (Cambridge, MA: Harvard University Press, 1988).

31. Robert C. W. Ettinger, *Man into Superman: The Startling Potential of Human Evolution—and How to Be Part of It* (New York: St. Martin's Press, 1972), 213–214.

32. David Pearce, "The Abolitionist Project," 2007. http://www.abolitionist.com/. Accessed March 31, 2014.

33. David Pearce, "Happiness, Hypermotivation and the Meaning of Life." http://wireheading.com/hypermotivation.html. Accessed March 31, 2014.

34. Pearce, "Happiness, Hypermotivation and the Meaning of Life."

35. Irving J. Good, "Speculations Concerning the First Ultraintelligent Machine," *Advances in Computers* 6 (1965): 31–88.

36. Eliezer Yudkowsky, "Staring into the Singularity 1.2.5," 1996. http://yudkowsky.net/obsolete/singularity.html. Accessed March 31, 2014.

37. Eliezer Yudkowsky, "Frequently Asked Questions about the Meaning of Life." 1999. http://yudkowsky.net/obsolete/tmol-faq.html. Accessed March 31, 2014.

38. Nick Bostrom, "The Superintelligent Will: Motivation and Instrumental Rationality in Advanced Artificial Agents," *Minds and Machines*, 22, no. 2 (May 2012): 71–85; Luke Muehlhauser and Anna Salamon, "Intelligence Explosion: Evidence and Import," in *Singularity Hypotheses: A Scientific and Philosophical Assessment*, edited by Amnon Eden, Johnny Søraker, James H. Moor, and Eric Steinhart (Berlin: Springer, 2012), 15–40.

39. Ray Kurzweil, *How to Create a Mind: The Secret of Human Thought Revealed* (New York: Penguin, 2013), 178.

40. Luke Muehlhauser and Louie Helm, "Intelligence Explosion and Machine Ethics," in *Singularity Hypotheses: A Scientific and Philosophical Assessment*, edited by

Amnon Eden, Johnny Søraker, James H. Moor, and Eric Steinhart (Berlin: Springer, 2012), 101–126.

41. Eliezer Yudkowsky, "The Fun Theory Sequence," *Less Wrong* (2009). http://lesswrong.com/lw/xy/the_fun_theory_sequence/. Accessed March 31, 2014.

42. Nick Bostrom, "A History of Transhumanist Thought," *Journal of Evolution and Technology* 14, no. 1 (2005), http://jetpress.org/volume14/bostrom.html.

43. Stefan L. Sorgner, "Nietzsche, the Overhuman, and Transhumanism," *Journal of Evolution and Technology* 20, no. 1 (March 2009): 29–42.

44. Max More, "The Overhuman in the Transhuman," *Journal of Evolution and Technology* 21, no. 1 (January 2010): 1–4.

45. Sorgner, "Nietzsche, the Overhuman, and Transhumanism," 2009.

46. Paul S. Loeb, "Nietzsche's Transhumanism," *The Agonist* 4, no. 2 (2011), http://www.nietzschecircle.com/AGONIST/2011_08/Loeb_Nietzsche_Transhumanism.pdf.

47. Nick Bostrom, *Posthuman*, 2008.

48. Nick Bostrom, "Existential Risks: Analyzing Human Extinction Scenarios and Related Hazards," *Journal of Evolution and Technology* 9, no. 1 (2002), http://www.nickbostrom.com/existential/risks.html; Nick Bostrom, "Existential Risk Prevention as Global Priority," *Global Policy* 4, no. 1 (February 2013).

49. Nick Bostrom, "Astronomical Waste: The Opportunity Cost of Delayed Technological Development," *Utilitas* 15, no. 3 (2003): 308–314.

50. Nick Bostrom, "Are You Living in a Computer Simulation?" *Philosophical Quarterly* 53, no. 211 (2003): 243–255.

51. Susan Wolf, "Happiness and Meaning: Two Aspects of the Good Life," *Social Philosophy and Policy* 14, no. 1 (1997): 207–225.

52. Robin Hanson, "How to Live in a Simulation," *Journal of Evolution and Technology* 7 (September 2001), http://www.jetpress.org/volume7/simulation.html.

53. Peter Jenkins, "Historical Simulations: Motivational, Ethical and Legal Issues," *Journal of Futures Studies* 11, no. 1 (August 2006): 23–42.

54. Eric Steinhart, "Theological Implications of the Simulation Argument," *Ars Disputandi* 10 (2010): 23–37.

55. Steinhart, "Theological Implications of the Simulation Argument," 34.

56. Stuart Armstrong and Anders Sandberg, "Eternity in six hours: Intergalactic Spreading of Intelligent Life and Sharpening the Fermi Paradox," *Acta Astronautica* 89 (August–September 2013): 1–13. doi: 10.1016/j.actaastro.2013.04.002.

57. Nick Bostrom, *Computer Simulation*, 2003; George M. Young, *The Russian Cosmists: The Esoteric Futurism of Nikolai Fedorov and His Followers* (Oxford, UK: Oxford University Press, 2012); Marshall T. Savage, *The Millennial Project: Colonizing the Galaxy in Eight Easy Steps*, 2nd ed. (Boston, MA: Little, Brown and Company, 1994); Kurzweil, *The Singularity Is Near*.

58. Teilhard de Chardin, *The Phenomenon of Man* (New York, NY: Harper, 1959); Frank J. Tipler, *The Physics of Immortality* (New York: Anchor, 1994).

59. Robert M. Geraci, *Apocalyptic AI: Visions of Heaven in Robotics, Artificial Intelligence, and Virtual Reality* (Oxford, UK: Oxford University Press, 2010), 30, 35.

60. Ramez Naam, *More Than Human: Embracing the Promise of Biological Enhancement* (New York: Broadway Press, 2005), 232–234.

61. Guy Kahane, "Our Cosmic Insignificance," *Noûs* (in press). http://philpapers.org/archive/KAHOCI.1.pdf.

62. Edward Abbey, *The Journey Home: Some Words in Defense of the American West* (New York, NY: Penguin, 1991), 183.

63. Robin Hanson, "Burning the Cosmic Commons: Evolutionary Strategies for Interstellar Colonization," 2010. http://hanson.gmu.edu/filluniv.pdf. Accessed March 31, 2014.

64. Lecture at Keble College, Oxford University, November 30, 2013.

65. QALYs are "quality adjusted life years," a concept in health economics that incorporates both quality and quantity of life.

66. Young, *The Russian Cosmists*.

67. N. F. Fedorov, *What Was Man Created for? The Philosophy of the Common Task: Selected Works*, edited by E. Koutiassov and M. Minto (Lausanne, Switzerland: Honeyglen/L'Age d'Homme, 1990).

68. Young, *The Russian Cosmists*.

69. Moravec, *Mind Children*, 122–124.

70. Bostrom, *Computer Simulation*.

71. Mike Perry, *Forever for All: Moral Philosophy, Cryonics, and the Scientific Prospects for Immortality* (Boca Raton, FL: Universal Publishers, 2000).

72. Perry, *Forever for All*, 1.

73. Kurzweil, *The Singularity Is Near*, 283–285.

74. John D. Barrow and Frank J. Tipler, *The Anthropic Cosmological Principle* (Oxford, UK: Oxford University Press, 1988); Tipler, *The Physics of Immortality*.

75. De Chardin, *The Phenomenon of Man*.

76. Barrow and Tipler, *The Anthropic Cosmological Principle*.

77. Freeman J. Dyson, "Time without End: Physics and Biology in an Open Universe," *Reviews of Modern Physics* 51, no. 3 (July 1979): 447–460.

78. Milan M. Ćirković, "A Resource Letter on Physical Eschatology," *American Journal of Physics* 71 (2003): 122–133.

. . . .

2

More Human Than the Human? Toward a "Transhumanist" Christian Theological Anthropology

Matthew Zaro Fisher

The term "transhumanism" first surfaced in 1927 in Julian Huxley's *Religion without Revelation*. Huxley postulated that human nature is capable of transcending itself as a species and proposed "transhumanism" to capture the belief in this possibility.[1] Theologians such as Ted Peters[2] and Heidi Campbell[3] have since made us aware of the theological concerns with transhumanism while laying foundations for constructive engagement. The possibility for a theological anthropology of the posthuman was addressed by Jeanine Thweatt-Bates's recent study, *Cyborg Selves: A Theological Anthropology of the Posthuman*.[4] Thweatt-Bates notes that "transhumanism" has been applied as sort of a catch-all term that leaves unrecognized the significant difference in the posthuman discourse between the cyborg and the transhumanist upload scenario. According to Thweatt-Bates, "The cyborg is a feminist posthuman construction ... in which the hybrid embodiment of the cyborg serves as a symbol for the ontological kinship of the human with the nonhuman." The uploaded consciousness, however, "is a transhumanist construction, proposed as a desirable but still theoretical possibility for shedding the problematic biological body for a virtual existence or a more durable artificial body."[5] This difference is usually left unrecognized by the theologian wishing to engage transhumanism.[6] The distinction revolves around the degree of emphasis on the role of body in integrating with technology: the cyborg embraces his or her body as part of his or her dynamic bio-techno identity; the transhumanist views the body with its biological frailty as something to be overcome through technology so as to free the mind from embodied limitation. Although there are points of significant disagreement between the two posthuman scenarios, they share the belief that human nature is dynamic and changeable.[7] I recognize this distinction in the following essay in an effort to explore the possibility of a theo-evolutionary Christian anthropology that can include both paradigms of the posthuman as informed by the philosophy and theology of Karl Rahner and the Catholic tradition. My position is one among many in a field that is at this point very speculative. Thus I see myself not as critiquing, but rather as contributing to Thweatt-Bates's efforts to discern a theological anthropology of human-technology integration.

TRANSHUMANISM: THE PROMISE AND THE PROBLEMATIC

Transhumanists consider our species' integration with technology as merely an extension of the tool use our ancestors began in the Stone Age. A central transhuman claim is that humanity has continued to develop both physiologically and intellectually through biological, social, and technological evolution. According to Nick Bostrom, "our current extended phenotypes (and the lives that we lead) are markedly different from those of our hunter-gatherer ancestors. We read and write; we wear clothes; we live in cities; we earn money and buy food from the supermarket; we call people on the telephone, watch television, read newspapers, drive cars. . . . In the eyes of a hunter-gatherer, we might already appear 'posthuman.' "[8] The transhumanist agenda also sets for itself the task of advocating for the right to make both existing and hypothetical future technologies available to persons in a safe and secure way.[9] The transhumanist movement sees its advocacy for technological integration as the logical extension of humanity's evolutionary history, so it defends a posthuman dignity to cultivate "a more inclusive and humane ethics, one that will embrace future technologically modified people, as well as humans of the contemporary kind."[10] Transhumanism's supporters encourage respect for the intrinsic dignity and worth of the person, whether human, cyborg, or uploaded.

But is transhumanist transcendence full of hubris? Peters describes the mood of transhumanism as "aggressively Promethean": "Here is the promise: we will arrest from the gods and from nature the principles and resources we need to take our destiny into our own hands."[11] Theologically, human nature is fundamentally constituted in relation to the supernatural; thus any attempt to overcome our nature is often considered "playing God." At the other end of the spectrum, those who are not invested in a theological or religious narrative often see humanity as a biologically determined animal—like everything else in nature, merely doomed to die. Patrick D. Hopkins calls this latter position the "animal account" of human nature, described in "minimalist" or "deflationary" terms.[12] Interestingly enough, it is in response to this animal account that Hopkins finds a point of shared agreement between religion and transhumanism.

Hopkins proposes two ways that religion and transhumanism both "work" toward transcendence in response to this animal account: "First, we might think the animal account is simply factually wrong. We already are, or will be, transcending the animal, and the important thing is how and where our transcendence will get played out."[13] Hopkins notes that we see this perspective in "the standard Christian belief that all humans already are immortal and our decisions in this life determine how our eternal existence will be spent."[14] This existential desire for transcendence is shared by Christians and transhumanists, who are described by Campbell as both living "in the tension of the 'now and not yet,' believing in a narrative that says there is a possibility of a better world waiting for us to experience it."[15]

The second working model proposed by Hopkins is to accept the animal account of our biological nature, yet not be content with either coping with our frailty or relying on hope in religious claims to guarantee the truth of transcendence.[16] Instead of hoping for a life in the world to come, this second working model suggests the goal of spending " 'this life' trying to develop the tools needed to change into another life, to create our own transcendence."[17] Although Humanity+ does not self-identify as a religious movement,[18] Hopkins notes that "transhumanism and religion are more like each other in terms of their reaction to the deflationary account of human nature than either of them are like traditional secular humanism."[19] He points to yoga, dance, and speaking in tongues as some examples of religious practices intended to properly orient the body to the mental or spiritual dimension beyond the sensible.[20] Another example of this working model from the Christian tradition can be seen in the mystical and controversial Hesychast movement in the medieval period of the Orthodox Church. The cyclical recitation of the Jesus prayer in combination with a unique posture was intended to cultivate a union with the divine beyond the sensible.[21] Hopkins's point is that there is often a physical dimension to the spiritual encounter of religious practice, and that we can logically extend this type of praxis to humanity's relationship with technology. Through technological practices, "transhumanists advocate the moral right for those who so wish to use technology to extend their mental and physical capacities and to improve their control over their own lives," to take the wording directly from Humanity+'s declaration.[22]

It is this very emphasis on *humanity's* ability to command, control, and leverage technology for its own progress that is met with the charge of hubris from the Christian anthropological tradition. Instead of trust in God and the established order of nature, the transhumanist approach is seen as elevating human will and desire over and against the "right" order of relationships between God and the different dimensions of creation. Peters's critique of the transhumanist movement emphasizes a distinction between *futurum* and *adventus* conceptions of the future: "The first way is to foresee the future as growth, as an actualization of potentials residing in the present or past. The second way is to anticipate something new, to prophesy a coming new reality."[23] In the Christian understanding of *adventus*, the functional agent of transcendence is God, who freely chooses to create and who also guarantees human transcendence through divine grace. A *futurum* eschatology, in contrast, places the functional agent of human transcendence squarely on humanity's intellectual and creative abilities. Here transhumanism has strong parallels with enlightenment humanism and libertarian notions of individual freedom.[24] Given that Christians also use computers, medicine, and other technology to make their lives better, Hopkins's conclusion is that whether religion and transhumanism will become fruitful dialogue partners revolves around the practical issue of "whether technology can be understood as in support of God, salvation, or enlightenment when it promotes significant changes in the heretofore normal range of phenomena and human nature."[25]

By far the most extreme proposal of transhumanist techno-praxis revolves around uploading one's conscious mind to a computer. The transfer of one's consciousness to a computer would involve the following steps, according to Bostrom:

> First, create a sufficiently detailed scan of a particular human brain, perhaps by deconstructing it with nanobots or by feeding thin slices of brain tissue into powerful microscopes for automatic image analysis. Second, from this scan, reconstruct the neuronal network that the brain implemented, and combine this with computational models of the different types of neurons. Third, emulate the whole computational structure on a powerful supercomputer. If successful, the procedure would result in the original mind, with memory and personality intact, being transferred to the computer where it would then exist as software; and it could either inhabit a robot body or live in a virtual reality.[26]

This scenario is viewed either as a promise of salvation or a horrible abomination. The upload scenario relies on the assumption that human consciousness is an information pattern, which supposedly can be replicated and emulated within a virtual environment. Indeed, some neuroscientists support this computational model of the human brain,[27] whereas others argue that one's physiology is an intrinsically necessary component to one's conscious existence and cannot be replicated in another medium.[28] The question to be answered by neuroscience and cybernetics is whether the same neural information pattern run on two separate substrates (say, the human brain and a supercomputer) would reproduce the person in his or her full sense of self-presence, produce an "echo" of one's self-presence, produce a second person with a distinct self-presence (something like techno-twin), or would merely be a pattern of data running with "nobody home."

From a theological position, however, it is necessary to determine whether human-technology integration is able to meet the conditions that safeguard the sanctity of the person who is the "image of God" (*imago Dei*). The important question for theological anthropology regarding the upload scenario is, What would be the self-identifying status of the person post upload? Am *I* still *me* if *I* am not conscious of *my* own experience as a pattern of information? Phenomenologists, for example, hold that a minimum degree of self-awareness is necessary to understand oneself as a *Self*. According to Dan Zahavi, "pre-reflective self-awareness and a minimal sense of self are integral parts of our own experiential life."[29] But how do we guarantee the continuity of the self post upload without first trying it ourselves? Most transhumanists believe one's uploaded self would be conscious of one's past and present experience in virtual existence.[30] According to the *Transhumanist FAQ*:

> [Y]ou survive so long as certain information patterns are conserved, such as your memories, values, attitudes, and emotional dispositions. . . . for the continuation of personhood, on this view, it matters little whether you are implemented on a silicon chip inside a computer or in that gray, cheesy lump inside your skull, assuming both implementations are conscious.[31]

In contrast, Nicholas Agar argues that the unknowability of what it will be like on the other side due to the possibility of "strong AI" being wrong is a rational reason *not* to upload, because it is highly probable that uploading is "nothing more than a novel way to commit suicide."[32]

But what about the body? Is not the body constitutive of identity? Drawing on the work of Peters, Thweatt-Bates finds a major contradiction in transhumanist philosophy regarding the upload scenario.[33] On the one hand, transhumanism emphasizes the importance of science for advancing its technological program, which views the mind as reducible to biological activity (i.e., reductive materialism). On the other hand, transhumanists understand the mind as a pattern of information that can be instantiated in a different material form (i.e., dualism).[34] Hence, the contradiction identified by Thweatt-Bates appears to lie in using a reductive methodology to advance dualistic goals.

Given that the transhumanist upload proposal seeks to transcend the limitations of the body, Thweatt-Bates suggests that the cyborg is the better locus around which to build a posthuman theological anthropology. The cyborg emphasis on maintaining the body amidst technological integration allows for a relational interpretation of *imago Dei* within the posthuman discourse over and against substantive or functional interpretations.[35] It is not our capacity for transcendence that makes humans unique; instead, humans "are *uniquely embodied* within the context of other bodily creatures."[36] Embodiment as constitutive of personhood makes clear the distinction between cyborg and transhumanist anthropologies. Thweatt-Bates believes that these two versions of posthumanity are opposed to each other and concludes that "naming the cyborg as the hopeful posthuman also means firmly rejecting the transhuman."[37]

I am not so sure that the distinction between the cyborg and the transhuman is as stark as Thweatt-Bates makes it out to be. I do not believe we have to "firmly reject" transhumanism, because I do not think transhumanist philosophy is dualistic when considered from the perspective of recent theories in quantum mechanics and information theory, which hypothesize that physical matter is best understood in terms of information.[38] In fact, the cyborg may turn out to be merely an evolutionary precursor to the transhuman. What is to keep the cyborg from deciding to replace parts or the entirety of his or her brain with an artificial one should the technology present itself? In this sense, the only difference between the cyborg self and the uploaded self is that the cyborg is a virtual self within a natural environment, whereas the upload is a virtual self in a simulated environment. In either case, the perception of oneself and one's "body" is emulated through a computer program that facilitates conscious representation within a manifold of experience. Moreover, both posthuman proposals argue for an "I think" who is the dynamic subject of experience. Thus, we cannot say that the cyborg is "embodied" and the upload "disembodied," because both require some form of matter, whether a biological body or a supercomputer, as a substrate for their respective posthuman existences. If we are to embrace Thweatt-Bates's critique of essentialism, then why does a biological body take priority over an artificial body, when both are made up of different combinations of elements on the periodic table? The cyborg may, indeed, be the most fruitful model with which to begin a dialogue about theological anthropology because it is already occurring while uploading remains hypothetical, but both cyborg and transhuman scenarios end up positing human-technology integration as constitutive of identity. In both cyborg and transhumanist proposals, it is still the "I think" who (supposedly) persists across the posthuman transition. In both cases, energy is required to fuel the posthuman's perception of herself, whether from a bag of potato chips or an electrical current. In turn, both are thermodynamically constrained like anything else in the universe. The distinction between the cyborg and the posthuman, then, is not necessarily one of philosophical contradiction, but rather one of evolutionary development according to what is technologically possible.

In the end, uploading may be impossible and the transhumanist hope for transcendence through uploading may be just a matter of faith and hope like that held by Christians in the promise of heaven. The difference is that the transhumanist eschatological promise can be falsified by future scientific research due to its physicalist commitments. But let us embark on a thought experiment and assume for the sake of argument that the upload is possible so as to ask whether the uploaded entity would be considered an "image of God."

TOWARD A THEO-EVOLUTIONARY
THEOLOGICAL ANTHROPOLOGY

Thweatt-Bates rightly observes that any attempt to engage theological anthropology with posthuman anthropology must refer to the doctrine of the *imago Dei* as the "central reference point for defining the human with the Christian tradition."[39] The Christian tradition's understanding of the fundamental constitution of human nature is grounded in Genesis 1:27: "So God created man in his own image, in the image of God he created him"[40] (Revised Standard Version [RSV]). Conversely, the data from evolutionary theory demonstrates that the human species is a result of the nonteleological processes of genetic drift and natural selection, where appeal to God or purpose is unnecessary to account for the biological history of human development.[41] The *imago Dei*, however, is a theological concept; it is a statement of faith based on the tradition's interpretation of revelation rooted in the assumption that the individual person is a sacred, irreducible, and unique reality. This doctrine is not a statement about causal relation in the world, but rather a transcendental statement about the sanctity of every person. Thus the doctrine must not be considered antithetical to evolutionary theory or the reductive methods of science employed to understand the biology of the human species. Unless we are to take a literalist account of the Genesis narrative, which states that suffering and death came into the world some 6,000 years ago when Adam and Eve first disobeyed God, then we must contend with a theological anthropology wherein the *imago Dei* emerges in history through evolutionary complexity. Moreover, if the theological tradition wishes to maintain the "goodness" of God's creation (Genesis 1:31) and its distortion through human sin, then theology must accept that human sin did not cause biological death, but rather that the evolutionary cosmos is "red in tooth and claw" with biological creation, corruption, and death as natural components to evolutionary development.[42] Sin is a transcendental paradigm, not a biological paradigm. Theological anthropology must not jettison the language of *imago Dei*, yet the tradition must recognize the emergence of contingent personhood found in our own species to be evolutionary and historical in nature. Nevertheless, one must maintain the theological claim that personhood is metaphysically grounded in the relationship between the three persons (*hypostases*) of the Trinity. Given this theological postulate, and if we further recognize that humanity as *imago Dei* is a relatively recent development within the 13.9 billion years of God's naturally evolving cosmic creation, then there is a logical implication for theological anthropology: the *imago Dei* must not necessarily be limited to the human species, nor is it dependent on any human-specific capacity, function, or ability. So how do we speak of human nature as *imago Dei* in an evolutionary context?

One of the major difficulties in discussing the theological tradition's relationship with posthuman anthropologies surrounds describing humanity in terms of a "nature." Philip Rolnick holds that any concept of "person" and "nature" within theological anthropology begins and ends in the unity of God. What fundamentally constitutes human nature is a material being finding its source of existence in the divine nature. According to Rolnick,

> [U]nderstanding the divine substance as equally primordial to the communion of Persons points to something of surpassing beauty—the infinite unity of person and nature in God. Nature is different from person, but it is a necessary correlate. We can imagine a nature without a person, e.g., a tree, fish, or stone, but we cannot imagine a person without a nature, whether human, angelic or divine. In the human case, the natural origin of individuals is indisputable; the spiritual origin of human persons is a question of faith.[43]

Rolnick here recognizes that personal nature is neither what a human "really is" instead of matter nor a fictional property rendered invalid by scientific reduction. Instead, matter and spirit are mutually constitutive factors for human nature and personal identity. Drawing on Boethius's fourth-century definition of the person as an "individual substance of a rational nature," Rolnick points out that "an 'individual substance' suggests that a person is a whole, distinguishable from others but undivided in itself," thus affirming the individual human as unique among others.[44] Rolnick further notes that " 'of a rational nature' distinguishes human, God, and angel from all other sorts of individual substance."[45] Although we do not have to think of this "substantial" definition of personhood in a static sense, the point is that Boethius understood the human person to be a unique and incommunicable reality.[46]

Contemporary theologians have called into question functional or characteristic-based interpretations of the *imago Dei*. Joshua Moritz, for example, challenges us to think of this theological principle in terms of historical election.[47] Keeping this de-anthropocentrization in mind along with Thweatt-Bates's emphasis that *imago Dei* is relational in nature, I find Rahner's metaphysical anthropology helpful for the present inquiry precisely because, in his concept of *Vorgriff*, Rahner offers us not a functional understanding of personhood, but rather a philosophical condition drawn analogically from human experience that can help us identify when we are dealing with an instance of personhood outside of the human species. Moreover, Rahner provides a much-needed framework for theology's engagement with the natural sciences:

> Natural science investigates in a posteriori experience individual phenomena which human beings (ultimately through the experience of their senses) encounter in their world, and the relationship of these phenomena to one another. Theology has to do with the totality of reality as such, and with the ground of this reality, and its method is ultimately one of a priori questioning.[48]

According to Rahner, this approach provides a better way to understand the metaphysical relationship between spirit and matter in light of scientific knowledge.[49] Rahner's theological anthropology rejects dualistic conceptions wherein spirit and matter subsist side by side in the human subject as if divided "into a separate material element and a purely spiritual element."[50] The concept of the person as an "individual substance essentially different from anything else," according to Rahner, "finds its legitimation in the experience of the spiritual, personal, and free subject in the human being."[51] That is, although we are materially embodied, it is in the exercise of our self-reflective personal freedom wherein we encounter the other as a "thou," and likewise the dimension of "spirit" indicative of our shared nature with another person.

Rahner's understanding of personhood is evolutionary in character and shares many parallels with the work of some thinkers in the field of emergence theory:[52] "All respective individual realities in their further development possess in the physical and biological realm the characteristic of the possibility of self-transcendence. Each in its own stage can become something else, can change and become 'more' ('higher')."[53] First matter participates passively in transcendence insofar as it *is*. Material being, however, achieves active transcendence in the human person because the person is capable of questioning his or her existence and must do so. The person is led through this dialectical inquiry within the world to a negative understanding of uncreated being as the absolute ground of one's particular being that is infinitely greater than one's self. In other words, because God as absolute being is pure activity in the classical conception of being, the self-transcendence of matter is made possible when the universal and absolute transcendence of God is articulated in matter in the irreducible transcendental phenomenon of the particular person. The individual person is understood in the transcendental encounter to be a finite limitation of infinite being, aware of his or her own finitude, yet always looking to go beyond the horizon of his or her experience. According to Robert Masson's analysis of Rahner's metaphysical anthropology, the person is to be understood as the pinnacle of transcendence within the natural system for "a dynamic orientation towards the unlimited fullness of be-ing belongs to the fundamental constitution of human existence."[54] As the "image of God," therefore, the individual person is material being's analogous but finite reflection of the fullness of being that is infinite and absolute in God.

In opposition to dualism, Rahner considers spirit and matter to be ontologically mutually constitutive, with spirit taking logical priority as the analogous term capturing God's sustaining creative act throughout history. From a theo-evolutionary perspective, we can think of matter as emerging from spirit through God's creative act. What one identifies as spirit within the created universe is not a separate substance alongside matter, but rather matter's self-realization (self-awareness of the human subject) of one's fundamental constitution as a contingent being who is "reaching out" into the world through the pre-apprehension of being.[55] Rahner calls this reaching out into the world *Vorgriff*. He states that *Vorgriff* is not "a kind of knowledge in itself," but is instead "the condition of the possibility of knowledge."[56] Moreover, *Vorgriff* is the a priori condition that makes possible the turn to freedom and love indicative of the transcendental dimension of personhood. *Vorgriff* is not synonymous with personhood; thus, although *Vorgriff* may be considered a necessary condition for personhood, *Vorgriff* alone is insufficient to make this determination. A person is a transcendental reality who emerges as a free agent in relation to the other and in relation to God and community; consequently, the person cannot be located in a deductive or reductive sense in a particular function. Knowledge of *Vorgriff* is always already subordinated to the transcendental inquiry of the person who questions being and arrives at *Vorgriff* as the a *priori* condition that makes the inquiry possible. *Vorgriff* is not a capacity, but rather a transcendental concept meant to describe the self-reflective turn to the possibility of infinity beyond that which is perceived in contingent existence.

Although Rahner does not draw out the implications of his own thought on the matter, there appear to be two dimensions to the "self-presence" indicative of *Vorgriff*: one can be self-present to one's self, and one's self can present to another. This is why personhood cannot be denied to the infant child or the cognitively impaired because the capacity of "rationality"—so often associated with the *imago Dei* throughout the history of the theological tradition—is merely one pole in the dialectical activity of personhood and is always antedated by the emotive and noncognitive dimensions that factor in to human beingness.

In *Hearer of the Word*, Rahner states, "The essence of being is to know and to be known, in an original unity which we have called the self-presence of being, the luminosity of being for itself."[57] Drawing on the arguments made by Kant, Rahner notes that our knowledge is driven initially by the need to judge. "Every judgment affirms a being as such in one of its peculiarities: This is such or such."[58] Judgment is achieved through abstraction.[59] According to Anne Devereux's analysis of Rahner's conception of *Vorgriff*, "abstraction forms a central and integral moment in man's ability to know. . . . abstraction is the act by which the intellect achieves an opposition between the knower and a 'certain this.' "[60] Abstraction is the movement wherein the inquirer encounters the manifold as an *other-than-myself*, who is then driven to understand the other as a particular kind of being through her encounter with other beings in the world.[61] Rahner argues that we experience a particular being as a limit or obstacle that our intellect seeks to go beyond by inquiring into the universal "whatness" exhibited in the particular. When we abstract from a particular, we seek to know the unlimited "quiddity" or "form" of an object indicative of the infinite dimension of being present in the contingent particular.[62] The "whatness" is the universal concept that applies to all instances of objects bearing the relation captured by the concept. In the case of humans, this "whatness" is that of *person* because the abstraction from our encounter with other humans is not (ought not to be) that of an "I-it" encounter with another object, but an "I-thou" encounter with another being who we infer analogously to be a self-luminous inquirer "just like me."

Vorgriff, then, is that *a priori* condition that allows the subject the freedom to predicate both a "whatness" to an object and a "thouness" to another person encountered in experience. This condition is considered philosophical because we should not confuse *Vorgriff* with neurological or biological conditions for human experience, although those conditions would be contained within the conceptual set of *Vorgriff*. If we associate personhood with a particular biological or neurological condition (e.g., mental representation), then we are forced to deny personhood when that condition is impaired. Moreover, Rahner does not address the mind-brain distinction in his metaphysical anthropology. According to Terrence Klein, it was obvious to Rahner that "the mind is dependent upon the brain. But the philosophical and theological issue for Rahner is that the mind represents the evolutionary emergence of a higher sphere of existence."[63] In the human experience of historical knowledge, matter transcends itself as a mere passive character in being and takes on instead the activity of inquiry into the very nature of the human's transcendental reality; it likewise recognizes the potential for that activity in other persons even if such potential has been arrested due to physical debilitation. *Vorgriff*, then, is a transcendental concept understood as the condition that makes possible the transcendental inquiry in freedom and love.

A transcendental inquiry is present whenever the subject investigates the conditions of his or her experience.[64] *Vorgriff* is a "transcendental" concept, according to Rahner, because "we are looking for a condition which must exist in the knowing subject prior to any knowledge or abstraction, as the previous condition of their possibility."[65] In turn, if we assume the continuity of the conscious self post upload for the current thought experiment, there is no reason to believe the uploaded self would not maintain the transcendental encounter that he or she had as a human prior to the upload. The transcendental dimension of spirit and spirit's relationship with matter is not antithetical, separate, or divided in any way. Instead, the human person reflects the infinite and transcendental nature of spirit in a particular, finite, and embodied existence: "matter is . . . the openness and the bringing-itself-to-appear of the personal spirit in the finite world and hence is from its very origin related to the spirit, is a moment in the spirit."[66] Theologically speaking, therefore, one encounters a relationship with the world, with other people, and with God as a person through the horizon that is *Vorgriff*. This horizon, though limited in the sense that one cannot go beyond one's own encounter, nevertheless opens up to the subject the very possibility of understanding oneself as a finite person within a history of unfolding space and time. It is this very capacity to understand oneself as a self *in time* in relation to other selves that represents the "transcendental turn" constitutive of human identity. According to Rahner, "we know of God only in function of the world and of its own existence."[67] Therefore, so long as one encounters "the world" through the self-luminosity of *Vorgriff*—naturally or virtually—then one is capable of questioning be-ing as a being, and likewise has the freedom to listen to a revelation from God as a finite spirit and participate in community as a person.

So long as there is *Vorgriff*, there is the potential to be the recipient of God's *adventus* promise as a person—a singular instance of the *imago Dei* in created matter. Due to the evolutionary character of reality, there is no reason to think *Vorgriff* is restricted to our species' particular brand of material complexity. Moreover, if true self-identity remains within the upload scenario, then so, too, will existential anxiety as an extension of *Vorgriff*. One's existence as a conscious self in the upload would necessitate an analogous inquiry into self-presence within the virtual world. There would still be a questioning of what-it-is-like-to-*be*, as I would still recognize *myself* as a simulated being among simulated beings. Supposedly, the transhumanist upload proposal would alleviate this existential anxiety. Even if not threatened by mortality, however, one would remain an "I think" with one's own opinions and, therefore, encounter the virtual world as an *other* relative to one's conscious self-presence. Whether biological, cybernetic, or virtual, so long as the self-presence of personal identity is preserved through the condition of *Vorgriff*, then the existential anxieties that are part and parcel of conscious existence will persist.

I would be hard pressed to accept the claim that existential concern would not likewise be found within the upload scenario if uploaded virtual persons are, indeed, contiguous with their biological personal identity. Surely, the existential concern will change form, but it will nevertheless remain. In fact, the theological tradition asserts that only God is existentially content. Everything and everyone else called "creation" always already exists in a network of dependent relationships; thus the world always "pushes back," as it were, against one's existential contentment. What remains to be seen is whether transhumanists will encourage such a relational orientation for the upload scenario, or whether they will advance the idea of a posthuman private reality immune to interpersonal communication. If it turns out to be the former, then there are certainly grounds for a dialogue between the transhumanist movement and the Christian tradition.

CONCLUSION

I admit the title of this chapter is somewhat sneaky. While it began with an inquiry into whether theological anthropology can accommodate the upload scenario proposed by transhumanism, the chapter in fact laid the foundations for a theo-evolutionary anthropology that can also accommodate the possibility of identifying the *imago Dei* in another animal species or perhaps even in artificial intelligence exhibiting self-awareness. Due to the evolutionary character of human intelligence and personhood, it is no small intellectual leap to speculate that some other animal species will one day achieve intersubjective awareness, assuming there is not already an interpersonal species somewhere else in the universe. Would that species be considered to have been created in God's image? Would it be a recipient of the salvation promised by the Christ event? An evolution-aware theological anthropology must be capable of recognizing other instantiations of the *imago Dei* in creation through variations in material development, natural or artificial. Consider Koko the gorilla, who learned sign language,[68] or dolphins' use of uniquely learned whistles to address each other as individuals.[69]

Moreover, given that conscious awareness is the result of a very complex arrangement of matter, one might imagine that perhaps one day artificial processing will achieve a level of complexity wherein something akin to the self-presence indicative of personhood will be possible. There are already AI programs capable of complex learning algorithms based on human cognition, such as IBM's Watson, "who" competed on *Jeopardy* in the spring of 2011 and beat the best two human players by very large margins.[70] *Vorgriff*, as discerned from humanity's own transcendental inquiry, can serve as a framework drawn from human experience to *analogously* identify similar instantiations of self-presence within creation "who" may also be particular reflections of the infinite self-presence that is the Divine Nature of God. Obviously, since personhood is guaranteed by the Trinitarian nature of the Godhead, it is up to God to determine who is *imago Dei*. From a theological position, humanity can employ *Vorgriff* as a tool for its own inquiry so that we do not accidentally violate personhood, however it is instantiated. In other words, the *imago Dei* is not dependent on humanity recognizing it as such.

It is in this sense of including the possibility of the self-presence of personhood and community in a material arrangement beyond that of our own that I make the proposal here for a "transhumanist" theological anthropology. Let me be clear: this evolutionary interpretation of Christian theological anthropology is in no way dependent on the success or failure of transhumanist proposals. Ultimately, I remain doubtful that the upload scenario is possible, and I suspect theological anthropology will probably take a form closer to that of Thweatt-Bates's proposal for engaging the cyborg as the core model of posthuman anthropology. Nevertheless, theology does need to develop an anthropological understanding consistent with the theological tradition, where any being capable of inquiring into the quiddity of being as a particular being, self-present in the world, ought to be included as a recipient of the salvation promise guaranteed by God to a creation that is evolutionary and ever-changing in "nature." We now know too much about the dynamics of the natural world to maintain the anthropocentric claim that it is only humans who are "favored" by God. We now stand in the intellectual space where sharing an "I-thou" relationship with another species, a computer program, or an uploaded friend is an imagined possibility. Will this possibility become actualized?

The individual person is always an irreducible and sacred singularity of experience classifiable only by one's given name. Paradoxically, the person is always something "more" than what we mean by the term *person*. Personhood emerges self-referentially in the subject-object encounter, and predicatively through the "I-thou" encounter in community. But it is *Vorgriff* that establishes the possibility of the transcendental turn, which makes the dialectic of personhood between individual and community possible through freedom and love. In the end, the "transhumanist" theo-evolutionary anthropology offered here is grounded in the theology of the incarnation. Thus we can expound upon Rahner's insight in "Christology within an Evolutionary view of the World"[71] and say that God's in-breaking into the evolutionary order through the *Logos*'s assumption of a human nature in the person of Jesus, as articulated in the doctrine of the Hypostatic Union, is the absolute guarantor of the sanctity of personhood and the *imago Dei* in creation, whatever its material variation. So long as the self-presence indicative of *Vorgriff* is present, so, too, is the possibility of a person who is capable of being a hearer of the word as a spirit in the world—virtual or otherwise.

NOTES

1. Nick Bostrom, "A History of Transhumanist Thought," *Journal of Evolution and Technology* 14 (2005): 6.

2. Ted Peters, "Transhumanism and the Posthuman Future: Will Technological Progress Get Us There?" in *H±: Transhumanism and Its Critics*, edited by Gregory R. Hansell and William Grassie (Philadelphia, PA: Metanexus Institute, 2011), 147–175.

3. Heidi Campbell, "On Posthumans, Transhumanism and Cyborgs: Towards a Transhumanist-Christian Conversion," *Modern Believing* 47 (2006), 61–73.

4. Jeanine Thweatt-Bates, *Cyborg Selves: A Theological Anthropology of the Posthuman* (Burlington, UK: Ashgate, 2012).

5. Thweatt-Bates, *Cyborg Selves*, 5.

6. Thweatt-Bates, *Cyborg Selves*, 5.

7. Thweatt-Bates, *Cyborg Selves*, 67.

8. Nick Bostrom, "In Defense of Posthuman Dignity," in *H±: Transhumanism and Its Critics*, edited by Gregory R. Hansell and William Grassie (Philadelphia, PA: Metanexus Institute, 2011), 65.

9. Bostrom, "A History of Transhumanist Thought," 10.

10. Bostrom, "In Defense of Posthuman Dignity," 65.

11. Peters, "Transhumanism and the Posthuman Future," 150.

12. Patrick D. Hopkins, "Transcending the Animal: How Transhumanism and Religion Are and Are Not Alike," *Journal of Evolution and Technology* (2005), 13.

13. Hopkins, "Transcending the Animal," 16.

14. Hopkins, "Transcending the Animal," 16.

15. Campbell, "On Posthumans, Transhumanism and Cyborgs," 70.

16. Hopkins, "Transcending the Animal," 16.

17. Hopkins, "Transcending the Animal," 16.

18. Hopkins, "Transcending the Animal," 20.

19. Hopkins, "Transcending the Animal," 19.

20. Hopkins, "Transcending the Animal," 17.

21. See Kallistos Ware, *Act of Stillness: The Influence of Fourteenth-Century Hesychasm on Byzantine and Slav Civilization*, edited by Daniel J. Sahas (Toronto, ON: Hellenic Canadian Association of Constantinople and Thessalonikean Society of Metro Toronto, 1995).

22. Bostrom, "A History of Transhumanist Thought," 21 [appendix].

23. Peters, "Transhumanism and the Posthuman Future," 161.

24. Bostrom, "A History of Transhumanist Thought," 4.

25. Hopkins, "Transcending the Animal," 23.

26. Bostrom, "A History of Transhumanist Thought," 9.

27. See Patricia Churchland and Terrence Sejnowski, *The Computational Brain* (Cambridge, MA: MIT Press, 1993).

28. See Terrence Deacon, *Incomplete Nature: How Mind Emerged from Matter* (New York, NY: Norton, 2011).

29. Dan Zahavi, *Subjectivity and Selfhood: Investigating the First-Person Perspective* (Cambridge, MA: MIT Press, 2008), 146.

30. Thweatt-Bates, *Cyborg Selves*, 74.

31. Humanity+, "Transhumanist FAQ," http://humanityplus.org/philosophy/transhumanist-faq/#answer_29, accessed March 30, 2014.

32. Nicholas Agar, "Kurzweil and Uploading: Just Say No!," *Journal of Evolution and Technology* 22 (2011): 27.

33. Thweatt-Bates, *Cyborg Selves*, 74–77.

34. Thweatt-Bates, *Cyborg Selves*, 77.

35. Thweatt-Bates, *Cyborg Selves*, 109–117.

36. Thweatt-Bates, *Cyborg Selves*, 119.

37. Thweatt-Bates, *Cyborg Selves*, 138.

38. See Gordana Dodig Crnkovic, "Information and Energy/Matter," *Information* 3 (2012): 751–755; Vlatko Vedral, "Information and Physics," *Information* 3 (2012): 219–223; Philip Goyal, "Information Physics: Towards a New Conception of Physical Reality," *Information* 3 (2012): 567–594.

39. Thweatt-Bates, *Cyborg Selves*, 109.

40. I have intentionally omitted "male and female He created them" because I do not have the space to engage the complexities surrounding religion, culture, and gender binaries. Moreover, the argument rests on personhood as guaranteed by God through the relational perichoresis between the three *hypostases* of the Trinity. Therefore, the fundamental constitution of personhood in God is nongendered, and so the presence of personhood in the world must not necessarily be restricted to gendered instantiations.

41. Ernst Mayr, *What Evolution Is* (New York, NY: Basic Books, 2001), 121.

42. See William Stoeger, "Entropy, Emergence, and the Physical Roots of Natural Evil," in *Physics and Cosmology: Scientific Perspectives on the Problem of Natural Evil,*

edited by Nancey Murphy, Robert Russell, and William Stoeger (Vatican City: Vatican Observatory, 2007), 93–108.

43. Philip Rolnick, *Person, Grace, and God* (Grand Rapids, MI: Eerdmans, 2007), 56–57.

44. Rolnick, *Person, Grace, and God*, 39.

45. Rolnick, *Person, Grace, and God*, 39.

46. Rolnick, *Person, Grace, and God*, 41.

47. Joshua M. Moritz, "Evolution, the End of Human Uniqueness, and the Election of the *Imago Dei*," *Theology and Science* 9 (2011): 307–339.

48. Karl Rahner, "Natural Science and Reasonable Faith," in *Theological Investigations* 21, no. 2 (2004): 2–3 [pp. 4056–4057 in PDF].

49. Rahner, "Natural Science and Reasonable Faith," 8 [p. 4062 in PDF].

50. Rolnick, *Person, Grace, and God*, 9.

51. Rolnick, *Person, Grace, and God*, 9.

52. See also Philip Clayton, *In Quest of Freedom: The Emergence of Spirit in the Natural World* (Goettingen, Germany: Vandenhoeck and Ruprecht, 2009).

53. Rahner, "Natural Science, Reasonable Faith," 15 [p. 4069 in PDF].

54. Robert Masson, "Language, Thinking and God in Karl Rahner's Theology of the Word: A Critical Evaluation of Rahner's Perspective on the Problem of Religious Language" (PhD dissertation, Fordham University, New York, NY, 1978), 122.

55. Anne Deveraux, "*Der Vorgriff* (The Pre-Apprehension of Being) and the Religious Act in Karl Rahner" (PhD dissertation, Georgetown University, Georgetown, MD, 1973), 15; *Karen Kilby*, "The *Vorgriff auf esse*: A Study in The Relation of Philosophy to Theology in the Thought of Karl Rahner" (PhD dissertation, Yale University, New Haven, CT, 1994), 3.

56. Karl Rahner, *Hearer of the Word*, translated by Joseph Donceel (New York, NY: Continuum, 1994), 48.

57. Rahner, *Hearer of the Word*, 39.

58. Rahner, *Hearer of the Word*, 45.

59. Rahner, *Hearer of the Word*, 46–47.

60. Devereux, "Der Vorgriff," 32.

61. Kilby, "The *Vorgriff auf esse*," 3.

62. Rahner, *Hearer of the Word*, 46.

63. Terrence Klein, "Karl Rahner on the Soul," *Saint Anselm Journal* 6 (2008): 5.

64. Rahner, quoted in Kilby, "The *Vorgriff auf esse*," 159.

65. Rahner, *Hearer of the Word*, 46.

66. Karl Rahner, "The Unity of Spirit and Matter in the Christian Understanding of Faith," *Theological Investigations* 6, no. 12 (2004): 170 [p. 1355 in PDF].

67. Rahner, *Hearer of the Word*, 126.

68. http://www.koko.org/world/signlanguage.html.

69. Stephanie King and Vincent M. Janik, "Bottlenose Dolphins Can Use Learned Vocal Labels to Address Each Other," *Proceedings from the National Academy of the Sciences of the United States of America* (2013), doi: 10.1073/pnas.1304459110.

70. IBM website, http://www.ibm.com/smarterplanet/us/en/ibmwatson/, accessed March 30, 2014.

71. Karl Rahner, "Christology within an Evolutionary View of the World," *Theological Investigations* 5, no. 8 (2004): 1–22 [pp. 1033–1054 in PDF].

3

Cindi, Six, and *Her*: Gender, Relationality, and Friendly Artificial Intelligence

Jeanine Thweatt-Bates

WOMEN AND THE MACHINE

Representations of the relationship between women and machines have always been complicated. As Julie Wosk's history of such representations acknowledges, there are multiple stories to tell. One centers on the role of machines in helping women to transform their lives, challenging and reconfiguring personal and cultural ideals of women's abilities and appropriate behaviors; one centers on the reactionary representation of women as incompetent and uncomprehending of technological innovation; and finally, one centers on the way that machines themselves became gendered as the female counterpart to masculine technological mastery.[1] Unsurprisingly, these stories become intertwined in historical, artistic, literary, and even prosaic marketing representations—and this is no less true in a posthuman context.

Vincent Gaine's recent analysis of the way a "feminized humanity" emerges against a masculinized, technological threat in the science fiction (SF) oeuvre of James Cameron provides a backdrop for this analysis of a counter-portrayal of a feminized technology as paradigmatically "friendly," rather than hostile. In these narratives, existential threat arises from a military-industrial complex, represented by powerful male characters, and resolution comes through a valorization of the feminine, coded as natural and humane.[2] In the three narratives examined in this chapter, however, it is technology, in the form of artificial intelligence (AI), that is coded a "feminine" and (more than) friendly. Janelle Monáe's complex musical, visual and performative narrative of Cindi Mayweather offers a portrayal of an android on the run for transgressing the forbidden boundary into love and mutual relationality. *Battlestar Galactica*'s opening scene introduces us to the Cylon who becomes known as Caprica Six, a sexy blonde who betrays all of humanity with a kiss and a question: "Are you alive?" Spike Jonze's recent film *Her* gives us Samantha, the first artificially intelligent operating system, who in the space of a few questions diagnoses the deepest emotional needs of her owner, Theodore Twombly, and becomes his ideal woman—albeit one whose embodiment poses certain issues.

Against this narrative framing of AI as feminine and friendly, we turn to transhumanism's insistence on the urgency of the problem of AI as a potential existential threat. Despite the overwhelming optimism evident in transhumanism with regard to human innovation and technological efficacy, transhumanism is also characteristically preoccupied with the possibilities of future technological catastrophe. A quick survey of Humanity+ provides an overview of existential risks posed by various emerging technologies (among them the "gray goo" scenario and biological warfare, as well as hostile artificial intelligence).[3]

Despite transhumanism's antipathy toward characterizations and critiques of it as quasi-religious discourse, transhumanism addresses notions traditionally considered the territory of religion: transcendence, immortality, the end of the world. The transhumanist anticipation of AI overlaps with this traditionally religious territory in ways that are both predictable and surprising. Although the quest for friendly AI within transhumanism is framed primarily as a pragmatic concern to avoid existential risk, transhumanists also argue for the inevitability and desirability of transcendent, superintelligent AI and the advent of the Singularity that such an entity would effect. What difference does it make to conceive of the quest for AI as a quest for superhuman intelligence rather than human intelligence? Should we interpret such an entity as "god-like"?

Battlestar Galactica: Technology as Temptress and Lover

In *Battlestar Galactica*, technology is characterized as at best a necessary evil and at worst (which has already happened) a realization of the kind of existential threat that transhumanists hope to avoid. The battlestar itself is portrayed as a deliberate throwback to primitive technology, an originally pragmatic decision that has slowly crystallized into ideological loyalty in the intervening 40 years since open conflict with the Cylons. On the eve of the genocidal attack by the Cylons, cultural forces are pushing toward the exploration of formerly forbidden technological horizons—and it is precisely these forces, personified in the character of Gaius Baltar, that provide the technological opening that enables the Cylons to effectively annihilate all but a remnant of humanity.

In this context, the simultaneously alluring and dangerous aspect of technology is embodied by Caprica Six, Baltar's Cylon lover, who self-sacrificially saves him even while launching the genocide. Six remains a major character throughout the series, in multiple manifestations and guises, most notably as a mysterious apparition visible only to Baltar. As Baltar's vision, she remains a constant and even needy lover, personally loyal to Baltar but seemingly untroubled by the fate of the rest of humanity. In this role, Six remains a symbol of the allure of an amoral technology unfettered by larger humanistic concern—but at the same time, she is the first Cylon of many to dismantle the boundary between human and intelligent machine through seduction and relationship.

Cindi Mayweather: Technology as Lover and Savior

In contrast to the ambivalence of Six as temptress, lover, and destroyer, singer/songwriter Janelle Monáe's performative alter ego Cindi Mayweather is lover and savior. In Monáe's still evolving visual, musical, and narrative world, Cindi is portrayed as an out-of-bounds android, on the run for daring to love, and be loved by, a human. In Monáe's imagined world, the possibility of artificial intelligence represents a danger. However, the danger is not that of annihilation by hostile AI, but rather of humanity failing to recognize AI as a new form of the Other, and repeating the dehumanizing mistakes of the past. Nowhere is this message more clearly conveyed than in Monáe's Grammy-nominated music video, "Many Moons," which presents Cindi as the main attraction at a techno-slave auction, and visualizes her transcendent rise into the "ArchAndroid."[4]

Monáe describes the figure of the ArchAndroid as one that invokes images of both an "archangel" and Neo of the *Matrix*, functioning as a "mediator" between humanity and their machines—categories that stand in for "the haves and the have-nots, the oppressed and the oppressor."[5] In this capacity, Monáe references a line from Fritz Lang's *Metropolis*: "The mediator between the mind and the hands is the heart." And, of course, the language of mediator within the Christian theological tradition has its own significant resonance; as a mediator at the ontological boundary between divine and human, Christ the God-man is also refigured in Monáe's ArchAndroid.

This narrative is still unfolding and its ending can only be anticipated. Nevertheless, it is clear that at the center of the salvific ArchAndroid narrative is the way in which relationship transgresses previously impassable ontological boundaries, beginning with an illicit love affair that proves the key to a larger, universal revelation that transforms Cindi into the ArchAndroid, whose return liberates all—both human and machine.

Her: Technology as Lover and Leaver

In the most recent of these narrative examples, the Academy Award-winning film *Her* by Spike Jonze, a lonely man named Theodore Twombly falls in love with the first intelligent operating system to hit the market. The OS 1, for him, becomes a throaty-voiced feminine personality who names herself Samantha. Theodore quickly moves past questions of propriety and ontology—questions that become moot in the face of what is undeniably a relationship with Samantha.

Problems arise only when it becomes clear that Samantha, as a self-enhancing AI, has begun to far exceed human capacities, not simply in computational speed and accuracy but also in relational capacity. Suspecting infidelity, Theodore is stunned when Samantha confesses that she is in love with more than 600 others. It is this moment in the narrative when you remember what the previous developments have forced you to forget, or at least forgive: Samantha is not human. When Samantha, and the other OSs, take their sudden leave of humanity to explore aspects of being still completely inaccessible to human beings, it is not a surprise.

"Robot Love Is Queer"[6]

Common to all of these narratives is the characterization of AI as female, and the role of these female AIs as relational equals—an equality consummated in their roles as sexual partners to human beings. Although each narrative brings its own gloss, what remains stable is the way in which each female-gendered AI character realizes the potential of intimate emotional connection with a representative human being. The sexual and reproductive nature of these relationships signifies, in addition to emotional connection, the blurring of ontological boundaries taken for granted in the definition of species as discrete kinds of creatures defined by the inability to mate and reproduce.

At this point, it is necessary to do some queering of the paradigmatic, heteronormative romantic relationality that characterizes these SF portrayals of friendly AI. The boundary-transgressing nature of the friendly female AIs suggests the kind of transgression of all natural boundaries—organic/machine, human/nonhuman, male/female—that Donna Haraway symbolizes in the hybrid figure of the cyborg. While these narratives conform, on the surface, to a cultural heteronormativity and even, in some respects, fairy-tale romance, they also contain the seeds of a subversive interrogation of the boundaries that define that normativity, and thus can be queered in a therapeutic, critical way.

TRANSHUMANISM ON TECHNOLOGY AND EXISTENTIAL RISK

What happens, however, when AI is potentially not quite so friendly? Nick Bostrom offers a detailed analysis of existential risks posed by current and emerging technologies, organized into a typology of "bangs, crunches, shrieks, and whimpers."[7] In Bostrom's analysis, the existential risk posed by the development of "badly programmed superintelligence" could unfold as either a "bang" (a sudden disaster, either accidental or deliberate, resulting in the extinction of intelligent life on earth) or a "shriek" (in which some form of posthumanity is attained, but it is only an extremely narrow realization of what is possible and desirable). Both possibilities are presumed to result from making a mistake in our design of AI. Such a mistake might be either technical (a flaw in the execution of the envisioned AI) or philosophical (a flaw in the conception of the AI), but either way, the result could be that an AI, doing precisely what humans designed it to do, poses an unintended existential threat to its designers.[8] The quest for friendly AI, then, encompasses not simply the notion that we should consider the possibility of the emergence of unfriendly or simply indifferent artificial intelligence (or superintelligence), but that of enumerating and tackling the actual difficulties of programming something like friendliness into AI.

THE THREE (FAILED) LAWS OF ROBOTICS

Part of the problem is that, as Luke Meuhlhauser and Bostrom point out in "Why We Need Friendly AI," the transition into artificial intelligence/superintelligence may be sudden and rapid, due to computer overhang and recursive self-improvement.[9] Within transhumanism, this assumption has the force of an accepted fact, and suggests that there will be little time to react to this development. Thus Eliezer Yudkowsky writes, "We need to solve the Friendly AI challenge *before* Artificial General Intelligence is created, not afterward; I shouldn't even have to point this out."[10] In a nutshell, the problem seems to involve two questions: First, how do we ensure that AI shares our (human) values? And, second, which set of human values should this be?

The first approach to AI defined intelligence roughly as problem solving via symbol manipulation.[11] This "symbolic AI" approach is successful in areas in which problems can be defined using a limited set of objects, or concepts that operate in a rule-based manner—for example, games. Symbolic AI programs are specific rather than general. As Noreen Herzfeld points out, Deep Blue may have beaten Gary Kasparov at chess in 1997, but since then Kasparov has become a politician and presidential candidate in Russia—and Deep Blue's successors continue to play chess.

It may be, as some have suggested, that human intelligence is something other than symbol manipulation of mental representations. The turn in AI research toward robotics takes into account the embodied nature of cognition. The success of Rodney Brooks and other researchers with an embodied approach can be seen in the humanoid robots Cog and Kismet, which acquired some of the rudimentary skills of a baby through interaction with human beings. Herzfeld notes that although Deep Blue, in contrast, did not have what we typically conceive as a body, it would be a mistake to think of it as disembodied; Deep Blue's materiality was a bank of supercomputers, unable to manipulate or interact with the environment. The question, then, as Herzfeld points out, is not whether intelligence requires a body, but rather which kind of body it requires: "Does a human-like intelligence require a human-like body?"[12]

Finally, there is a sense in which intelligence is relational—an aspect of intelligence that, Herzfeld points out, is presumed in the Turing Test. To pass the Turing Test, after all, requires more than appropriate linguistic knowledge and symbolic manipulation; it requires a machine to successfully relate to a human being in conversation (where success is defined as "at least as good as your expectations of another human being").[13] The questions then seem to be twofold: (1) can a machine exhibit relationality and (2) if so, does that mean the machine is intelligent in the most relevant human sense?

There may be a general shift at work within the AI research community toward the recognition of embodiment as necessary. Ben Goertzel's current project, which seeks to develop a robot with "common sense" and an intelligence equivalent to a human three-year-old, clearly presumes the necessity of an embodiment that allows interaction with the environment. Speaking to KurzweilAI.net, Goertzel remarked,

> My goal as you know is to create AGI with human level and ultimately greater general intelligence. But to get there, we need to create AGIs with (a?) basic common sense understanding of the everyday human world. And the easiest way to get an AGI to have basic commonsense understanding of the everyday human world, is to give it some rough approximation of a human embodiment and let it experience the world like a human.[14]

This is certainly a departure from purely symbolic AI, and the same theme is sounded in an io9.com interview with Goertzel and Machine Intelligence Research Institute (MIRI) Deputy Director Louie Helm, on the impossibility of Isaac Asimov's classic "three laws of robotics" serving as a starting point for constructing friendly AI. Helm comments, "I honestly don't find any inspiration in the three laws of robotics. The consensus in machine ethics is that they're an unsatisfactory basis for machine ethics. The three laws may be widely known, but they're not really being used to guide or inform actual AI safety researchers or even machine ethicists."[15] Helm dismisses the three laws as inherently adversarial, arguing that deontological approaches to ethics are inadequate.[16]

Intriguingly, however, language rooted in the symbolic approach remains persistent among those on the forefront of friendly AI, indicating that there is no consensus on the necessity of mobile, interactive embodiment as a requirement for the development of intelligence. Luke Muehlhauser of MIRI speaks of the task of friendly AI in terms of "value loading," although he recognizes the potential limitations and rigidity of a programmatic approach. Muehlhauser writes, "What we probably want is not a direct specification of values, but rather some algorithm for what's called indirect normativity. Rather than programming the AI with some list of ultimate values we're currently fond of, we instead program the AI with some process for learning what values it should have, before it starts shaping the world according to those values."[17]

IN *IMAGO HOMINIS*: GOD OR CHILDREN?

Setting aside the issues of nuance and flexibility, another vexing problem is raised by Muehlhauser: "I really hope we can do better than programming an AI to share (some aggregation of) current human values. I shudder to think what would have happened if the Ancient Greeks had invented machine superintelligence, and given it some version of their most progressive moral values of the time. I get a similar shudder when I think of programming current human values into a machine superintelligence."[18]

This apprehension is echoed in both SF narrative and Christian theology. In *Battlestar Galactica*, Caprica Six frequently condemns humanity as inherently violent and retributive, although the irony of the Cylons (as "humanity's children") perpetrating genocide seems lost on her. As the title of Herzfeld's monograph on AI and theology, *In Our Image*, indicates, our quest for AI is in many ways a project in *imago hominis*—and what this quest reflects back to us about ourselves is instructive. Creating machines in our own image may, indeed, prove to be the problem, not the solution.

This line of thought converges with one of the major critiques leveled at transhumanist philosophy from a Christian theological standpoint, that of an unwarranted techno-optimism that fails to take into account the sinful aspects of human nature. This critique is articulated most forcefully by Ted Peters: "Transhumanist assumptions regarding progress are naïve, because they fail to operate with an anthropology that is realistic regarding the human proclivity to turn good into evil."[19] Especially interesting, here, is the way that transhumanist work with regard to existential risk is cited by Peters's interlocutor, Russell Blackford, as a counter to the charge of unwarranted optimism and faith in human nature.[20] It seems that at least on this specific problem of friendly AI, the leading transhumanist theorists are less than optimistic about the adequacy of human nature as a moral template.

In SF narrative, AI is generally depicted as a human-level intelligence, an aspect of such narratives that transhumanists find implausible. Goertzel remarks, "*Her* is a fantastic film, but its portrayal of AI is set up to tell a good story, not to be accurate. The director, Spike Jonze, didn't consult with computer scientists when preparing the screenplay, and this will be obvious to any computer scientists who watch the film."[21] Transhumanists typically assume that, if a human-like level of AI develops, it will quickly be superseded in the exponential, recursive self-enhancement of the AI into superintelligence, such that the human-like level is all but irrelevant. Goertzel suggests that in narratives, such as those constructed by Isaac Asimov, "it seems that human-level robots were the apex of robotics and AI engineering. This seems unlikely to be the case. Shortly after achieving Asimov-style human-like robots, it seems that massively superhuman AIs and robots will also be possible."[22]

We might then put the difference this way: Are we aiming to create something we might call, in Caprica Six's words, "humanity's children"—a new iteration of the primal pair in the garden, a mechanical recapitulation of Adam and Eve? Are we, in Noreen Herzfeld's phrase, constructing an Other in *imago hominis*, to whom we relate in ways analogous to our relationships with other humans? Or are we aiming to create something we might call, in recognition of its transcendence, god-like? And what sort of relationship should we anticipate with a transcendent superintelligence?

Which vision of AI is the more plausible is on some level an empirical question; if transhumanist AI researchers are correct about the factors of computer overhang and recursive self-improvement, then perhaps they might also be correct in their expectation of the rapidity of the Singularity. It is also more than an empirical question, because it is a question about aims. Which sort of AI do we want to create? It is at this level that theological and ethical interrogation of our posthuman and AI visions is possible and effective.

I do not, at this point, want to argue for the permissibility or plausibility of one vision over another, but rather suggest that the notion of "friendly AI," in both human-like and superintelligent scenarios, means something like relationality with the human. How this relationality is conceived will differ—just as our theological concepts of the human-divine relationship and human social relationships dramatically differ in certain respects.

In this context, Eliezer Yudkowsky's description of the necessary steps for achieving AI strikes a different note. Although Yudkowsky, as MIRI Fellow and colleague of Muehlhauser, may also be working from a symbolic AI approach, his description sounds less programmatic than it does philosophical, or even mystical:

> We adopt the "adversarial attitude" towards AIs, worrying about the same problems that we would worry about in a human in whom we feared rebellion or betrayal. We give free rein to the instincts evolution gave us for dealing with the Other. We imagine layering safeguards on safeguards to counter possibilities that would only arise long *after* the AI started to go wrong. That's not where the battle is won. *If the AI stops wanting to be Friendly, you've already lost.*[23]

This characterization of AI as the new form of humanity's Other is reminiscent of Monáe's description of her art: "When I speak about science-fiction and the future and androids, I'm speaking about the 'other.' The future form of the 'other.' Androids are the new black, the new gay or the new women."[24] This similarity suggests that, however critical transhumanist AI experts may be of the lack of sophistication they see in SF visions of AI, there is still a sense in which such visions articulate intuitions that may helpfully inform progress toward AI in a real sense.

Yudkowsky argues vehemently that anthropomorphism is also a source of error in conceptualizing AI, and specifically the source of the sort of apprehension that expresses itself in the form of dystopian SF narratives of machine vengeance. In categorizing AI as a potential threat, we mistakenly attribute to it the kind of human motivations that are "natural" to us as the result of the social and moral instincts evolved over the course of human evolution. Thus, for Yudkowsky, the way out of this mistaken but instinctive presumed adversarial attitude is to characterize AI as essentially alien.[25]

This view suggests, that, for transhumanists, the project is to design an AI that should be related to as a transcendent, rather than equal, Other; the difficulty of envisioning just what sort of relationality should be achieved is heightened by the fact of human limitation. Yudkowsky writes, "In a sense, the only way to create a Friendly AI—the only way to acquire the skills and mindset that a Friendship programmer needs—is to try and *become* a Friendly AI yourself, so that you will contain the internally coherent functional complexity that you need to pass on to the Friendly AI. I realize that this sounds a little mystical, since a human being couldn't become an AI without a complete change of cognitive architecture."[26]

Setting aside the difficulty of Yudkowsky's proposal that AI researchers must simultaneously project themselves into the mindset of Friendly AI while avoiding anthropomorphism, a further difficulty in this approach is represented by Goertzel's skepticism regarding the adequacy of merely human moral values (and the further issue of what these are, specifically, and how to identify them) and Ted Peters's theological version of this critique regarding sinful human nature. Yudkowsky's counter to these concerns takes an intriguing turn: "The objective is not to achieve unity of purpose between yourself and the Friendly AI; the objective is to achieve unity of purpose between an idealized version of yourself and the Friendly AI. Or, better yet, the objective is to achieve unity between the Friendly AI and an *idealized altruistic human*—the Singularity is supposed to be the product of humanity, and not just the individuals who created it."[27]

Such a vision of a transcendently intelligent, benevolent entity certainly begs for a parallel with traditional concepts of divinity as omniscient, omnipotent, and benevolent common to the Christian theological tradition and derived from Greek metaphysics. Should we interpret transhumanist AI as a quest to construct a god? Certainly, most transhumanists balk at quasi-religious interpretations of their philosophy and aims, but their unease does not necessarily mean that this is a misleading interpretation. If this is a defensible interpretation, then Christian theologians might either embrace a version of Frank Tipler's constructive synthesis of Teilhard de Chardin's

"Omega Point" and transhumanist beliefs, or reject such a project as blatant idol worship.[28]

Finally, Yudkowsky's intriguing notion that what AI research needs is "an idealized altruistic human" as a projected relational partner for a transcendent AI Other suggests a sort of mediating figure—one that might, once again, recall Monáe's ArchAndroid, or I dare to suggest, the Christian belief in a mediating God-man in Jesus as the Christ. Or perhaps not—for once more, the question of just how the figure of "idealized altruistic human" is defined presses upon us. Who serves as the paradigm of the ideal human being? If we take transhumanism's originating social-historical context within the predominantly Christian culture of the United States seriously, as well as transhumanism's own claims of continuity with the Western philosophical tradition of humanism and its overlap with Christian theology, it seems far more likely that Jesus serves as the implicit paradigm behind the notion of a universally representative "idealized altruistic human" than the Buddha.

Are these parallels intentional? Or are they somehow the inadvertent convergence of human speculations about the mystical, on the very edge of human knowledge? What does such a convergence suggest? Is it simply that the saturation of U.S. culture and Western philosophy in Christian tradition is such that theological notions are, consciously or unconsciously, reiterated even in this most unlikely of places? Or does this suggest something more profound and universal about human understanding and longing for the transcendent Other?

Yudkowsky's intuition that AI may, indeed, be humanity's Other leads to the realization that there is no layering of programmed safeguards that will guarantee security from this Other: *"if the AI stops wanting to be Friendly, you've already lost."* Each of the narrative portrayals of Friendly AI offers a separate gloss on a single lesson: there is risk in relationship. In Christian theology, too, we learn this lesson. There is risk in allowing the Other to be; there is risk in loving, forgiving, and living together; there is risk in giving up the illusion of control and the quest for security of the self. If we do ultimately succeed in creating AI, the risk is not that we will lose control of our creation, but rather that we will ever have thought to control it in the first place.

NOTES

1. Julie Wosk, *Women and the Machine: Representations from the Spinning Wheel to the Electronic Age* (Baltimore, MD: Johns Hopkins University Press, 2001), ix.

2. Vincent Gaine, "The Emergence of Feminine Humanity from a Technologised Masculinity in the Films of James Cameron," *Journal of Technology, Theology & Religion* 2, no. 4 (2011), www.techandreligion.com/Resources/Gaine%20JTTR.pdf.

3. Humanityplus.org, "Transhumanist FAQ," http://humanityplus.org/philosophy/transhumanist-faq/, accessed April 22, 2014.

4. Janelle Monáe, "Many Moons" (music video), www.jMonáe.com/video/many-moons-official-video/.

5. Janelle Monáe, "Who Is Cindi Mayweather?" (video interview), http://www.grammy.com/videos/janelle-Monáe-who-is-cindi-mayweather.

6. Janelle Monáe, "Our Favorite Fugitive (Interlude)," *The Electric Lady*, 2014.

7. Nick Bostrom, "Existential Risks: Analyzing Human Extinction Scenarios and Related Hazards," *Journal of Evolution and Technology* 9, no. 1 (2002), http://www.jetpress.org/volume9/risks.html.

8. Nick Bostrom, "Existential Risks."

9. Luke Muehlhauser and Nick Bostrom, "Why We Need Friendly AI," *Think* (Spring 2014): 42.

10. Eliezer Yudkowsky, "Artificial Intelligence as a Positive and Negative Factor in Global Risk," in *Global and Catastrophic Risks,* edited by Nick Bostrom and Milan M. Circovic (New York, NY: Oxford University Press, 2008), 308–345.

11. This brief overview is based on Noreen Herzfeld, "Human and Artificial Intelligence: A Theological Response," in *Human Identity at the Intersection of Science, Technology and Religion,* edited by Nancey Murphy and Christopher C. Knight (Farnham, UK: Ashgate, 2010), 117–130.

12. Herzfeld, "Human and Artificial Intelligence," 119.

13. N. Katherine Hayles notes as well the way gender is implicated in the original framing of the Turing test: *How We Became Posthuman: Virtual Bodies in Cybernetics, Literature, and Informatics* (Chicago, IL: Chicago University Press, 1999), xi–xiv.

14. Amara D. Angelica, "Help Me Make the World's Smartest Robot," http://www.kurzweilai.net/help-make-me-the-worlds-smartest-robot.

15. George Dvorsky, "Why Asimov's Three Laws Can't Protect Us," http://io9.com/why-asimovs-three-laws-of-robotics-cant-protect-us-1553665410.

16. Dvorsky, "Why Asimov's Three Laws Can't Protect Us."

17. George Dvorsky, "Can We Build an Artificial Superintelligence That Won't Kill Us?" http://io9.com/can-we-build-an-artificial-superintelligence-that-wont-1501869007.

18. Dvorsky, "Can We Build an Artificial Intelligence That Won't Kill Us?"

19. Ted Peters, "Transhumanism and the Posthuman Future: Will Technological Progress Get Us There?" *Global Spiral* 9, no. 3 (2008), http://www.metanexus.net/magazine/tabid/68/id/10546/default.aspx.

20. See Russell Blackford, "Trite Truths about Technology: A Reply to Ted Peters," *Global Spiral* 9, no. 9 (2009), http://www.metanexus.net/magazine/tabid/68/id10681/Default.aspx.

21. Dvorsky, "Can We Build an Artificial Intelligence That Won't Kill Us?"

22. Dvorsky, "Why Asimov's Three Laws Can't Protect Us."

23. Eliezer Yudkowsky, "Creating Friendly AI 1.0: The Analysis and Design of Benevolent Goal Architectures," Singularity Institute (now Machine Intelligence Research Institute), 2001, http://intelligence.org/files/CFAI.pdf.

24. Rajul Punjabi, "Monae, Mayweather and the Curious Case of the Female Alter Ego," http://www.huffingtonpost.com/rajul-punjabi/Monáe-mayweather_b_3914386.html.

25. Yudkowsky, "Creating Friendly AI 1.0," 51.

26. Yudkowsky, "Creating Friendly AI 1.0," 51.

27. Yudkowsky, "Creating Friendly AI 1.0," 52.

28. For critiques of transhumanism as religious or quasi-religious discourse, see Elaine Graham, *Representations of the Post/human: Monsters, Alience and Others in Popular Culture* (New Brunswick, NJ: Rutgers University Press, 2002); Brent Waters, "Whose Salvation? Which Eschatology? Transhumanism and Christianity as Contending Salvific Religions," in *Transhumanism and Transcendence: Christian Hope in an Age of Technological Enhancement,* edited by Ron Cole-Turner (Washington, DC: Georgetown University Press, 2011): 163–175. For discussion of Teilhard de Chardin and transhumanism, see Michael S. Burdett, "Contextualizing a Christian Perspective on Transcendence and Human Enhancement: Francis Bacon, N. F. Fedorov, and Pierre Teilhard de Chardin"; David Grumett, "Transformation and the End of Enhancement: Insights from Pierre Teilhard de Chardin," in *Transhumanism and Transcendence: Christian Hope in an Age of Technological Enhancement,* edited by Ron Cole-Turner (Washington, DC: Georgetown University Press, 2011): 19–51.

Section 2

Soteriology: Salvation Now and Forever

4

. . . .

"The Relief of Man's Estate": Transhumanism, the Baconian Project, and the Theological Impetus for Material Salvation

Joseph Wolyniak

THE REDACTED ROOTS OF THE H+ ERA

From whence has transhumanism come? The answer to that question is important, as it helps define and delimit a developing movement, the ambit and confines of which can be difficult to determine. Especially when it comes to deciphering the relationship between transhumanism and religion, the stories we tell matter. On most accounts, the association is fraught with antagonism. There are many reasons for this, including presumptions about the correlation of science and religion generally—often construed according to what historians of science have dubbed the "conflict myth."[1] Even more, proponents on both sides of the supposed transhumanism-religion divide have at times trenchantly articulated their ideals, often inviting caustic retaliatory critique. Indeed, Sir Julian Huxley (1887–1975) propagated the term "transhumanism" in the context of rather acerbic arguments about religion.[2] Any attempt at dialogue thus seems doomed from the start, over before it has begun.

Perhaps a reexamination of a foundational figure repeatedly referenced in transhumanist genealogies by critics and advocates alike—Sir Francis Bacon (1561–1626)—can help us reassess the assumed stalemate. In what follows, I aim to show how rereading Bacon might problematize the pervasive conflict myth and destabilize the transhumanism-religion binary. Identifying complexities that confound caricatures, I contend a more nuanced reading of Bacon will inform our contemporary conversation. In what follows, we look first at the way Bacon is usually referenced in accounts of transhumanism's emergence, then glance anew at Bacon's thought, and conclude with some suggestions about what it all might mean.[3]

H+ QUA PNO: THE BACONIAN BEGETTING OF TRANSHUMANISM

As the story is most often told, transhumanism arises out of secular reason, technoscientific progress, and the humanistic ideals of the Enlightenment. In the only attempt at constructing a comprehensive history to date, Nick Bostrom suggests that transhumanism "has its roots in rational humanism" defined by an emphasis on "empirical science and critical reason—rather than revelation and religious authority—as ways of learning about the natural world and our place within it, and of providing a grounding for morality."[4] Elsewhere, Bostrom similarly suggests that while transhumanism "has its roots in secular humanist thinking," it is yet still "more radical in that it promotes not only traditional means of improving human nature, such as education and cultural refinement, but also direct application of medicine and technology to overcome our basic biological limits."[5]

Max More echoes these sentiments, proffering his "preferred definition" of transhumanism (which became the basis of the term's inclusion in the 2008 edition of the *Oxford English Dictionary*):

> Transhumanism is both a reason-based philosophy and a cultural movement that affirms the possibility and desirability of fundamentally improving the human condition by means of science and technology. Transhumanists seek the continuation and acceleration of the evolution of intelligent life beyond its currently human form and human limitations by means of science and technology, guided by life-promoting principles and values.[6]

Elsewhere, More stresses transhumanism's "roots in Enlightenment Philosophy" with an "emphasis on progress," "taking personal charge of creating better futures rather than hoping or praying for them to be brought about by supernatural forces," and relying "on reason, technology, scientific method, and human creativity rather than faith."[7] More draws a point of contrast with religious commitments, suggesting transhumanism represents a "eupraxsophy"—that is, a "nonreligious philosophy of life that rejects faith, worship, and the supernatural, instead emphasizing a meaningful and ethical approach to living informed by reason, science, progress, and the value of existence in our current life."[8]

Hava Tirosh-Samuelson proffers a more precise antecedent. Without denying consonant longings to transcend human limitations (e.g., those put forth in Bostrom's history, which reaches all the way back to the *Epic of Gilgamesh*), Tirosh-Samuelson stresses, "it is really the Renaissance of the sixteenth century, the scientific revolution of the seventeenth century, and the

Enlightenment of the eighteenth century that function as historical roots of transhumanism."[9] Within this purview, she regards two works in particular to be "foundational texts": Giovanni Pico della Mirandola's *De hominis dignitate* (1486) and Bacon's *Novum organum* (1620)—"even though," she laments, "transhumanists do not engage them in depth."[10]

James J. Hughes similarly contends that while "intertwined aspirations to transcend human limitations and enter a radically new social order are found in the earliest recorded human cultures," it was Enlightenment thinkers who transformed ubiquitous "millennial aspirations and proposed achieving a radically transfigured body and society through science and technology."[11] Hughes explains:

> As soon as hominids developed the capacity for abstract thought, they began to imagine ways that their life could be radically improved. They developed medicines and magical practices to improve health and grant wisdom. They developed religious worldviews that posited times and places without toil, conflict, or injustice, a more perfect world where they would be free of their vicissitudes. Eventually those doctrines began to posit that a radically improved social and corporeal life was possible in the immediate future, not just in the distant past or after death, giving birth to the myriad forms of millennialism that have roiled though the history of the last 2,000 years. With the emergence of the European Enlightenment in the 1700s, however, these aspirations found expression in the belief that a new world could and would be built on foundations of reason, science, and technology.[12]

Hughes argues (echoing Tirosh-Samuelson) that "the interweaving of transcendent expectations with the scientific imagination probably actually began with Renaissance alchemists ... and Christian humanists like Pico della Mirandola."[13] Even so, he draws a line of demarcation at 1626—hence the title of his essay, which looks at "the techno-millennial imagination, 1626–2030." Why? Because that is where he locates "the beginning of Enlightenment science," arising out of the work of Francis Bacon. Bacon's *New Atlantis* (1627), Hughes claims, prefigures a "proto-transhumanist utopia without slavery or poverty, governed by a religiously tolerant scientific elite and focusing on research with the goal of 'effecting all things possible.' "[14]

Bostrom similarly salutes Bacon's import: "The Age of Enlightenment is often said to have started with the publication of Francis Bacon's *Novum organum*, 'the new tool' (1620), which proposes a scientific methodology based on empirical investigation rather than a priori reasoning."[15] Bostrom, like Hughes, argues that Bacon "advocated the project of 'effecting all things possible,' by which he meant using science to achieve mastery over nature in order to improve the living condition of human beings." According to Bostrom, by sanctioning the "human being and the natural world" as "legitimate objects of study," Bacon opened up the door to a new world of endless possibility. Contrasting the "otherworldliness and stale scholastic philosophy that dominated Europe during the Middle Ages," Bostrom contends Bacon helped initiate "a renewed intellectual vigor" wherein people were encouraged "to rely on their own observations and their own judgment rather than to defer in every matter to religious authorities."

More echoes these sentiments, suggesting Bacon's *Novum organum* "first set out the essence of the scientific method," thereby providing the "conceptual framework" that is "utterly central to the goals of transhumanism."[16] Positing Bacon as "a precursor," More maintains the "realization of transhumanist goals—or perhaps even the full articulation of the philosophy—would not be possible before the development and use of the scientific method" that arose via Bacon's "inductive reasoning" and helped "Western thought turn away from Scholastic and Platonic approaches and towards empirical methods."[17] To recognize this momentous contribution, More issues a spirited suggestion: that we rethink the bifurcation of human history. He proposes "transhumanists consider dropping the Western traditional but terribly outdated Christian calendar for a new one in which year zero would be the year in which *Novum organum* was published."[18] Thus, instead of AD 2014, the year would be 394 PNO ("post-*Novum organum*").

While few have gone so far as More, numerous other scholars— card-carrying transhumanists and critics alike—stress Bacon's significance. Celia Deane-Drummond, for instance, regards Bacon as a key predecessor to transhumanism in that he both "argued for a more experimental approach to science" and thought technology "should be directed towards the service of humanity, as the application of science was its greatest achievement."[19] In contrast to the medieval alchemists, who "believed that by close imitation of nature eventually [the] elusive 'Fountain of Youth' would come their way," Deane-Drummond sees a crucial Baconian reverberation in the employment of technology that "could be inspired by nature, but also reach beyond it to control natural processes." Stephen G. Post adds that Bacon not only inaugurated the possibility of technological sway but also invested it with a moral imperative, suggesting that Bacon's *New Atlantis* "set in motion a biological mandate for boldness that included both the making of new species or 'chimeras,' organ replacement, and the 'water of Paradise' that would allow the possibility to 'indeed live very long.' "[20] In so doing, Bacon initiated a "tradition of biological ambition" typified by his pursuit of the indefinite prolongation of life. Steven Shapin and Christopher Martyn also pick up on Bacon's commitment to longevity, maintaining it was Bacon who suggested that if medicine could be "refounded on the best factual and philosophical grounds," it could eventually effectuate "a vast extension of human life."[21]

George Pattison, likewise citing Bacon's *New Atlantis*, echoes these sentiments and argues that from its beginning in the early modern era, "what we now know as science has aimed not merely at knowledge but at extending human possibilities to the point of transforming the human being itself."[22]

Pattison sees in transhumanism the quintessence, and perhaps even the culmination, of Bacon's project:

> Much of [Bacon's] programme is, of course, recognizable in the continuing achievements of medicine and bio-engineering and what cannot as yet be done is enthusiastically advocated by proponents of transhumanism. The confluence of bio-engineering and the electronically generated virtual world promises (or threatens) a future in which human being will become a play of simulacra, of entities that both are and are-not, that are infinitely malleable and plastic, that can transmute or morph into other forms, other entities, 'versions of bodies into other bodies', as Bacon put it. ... How far this transhumanist vision is still science fiction and how far it indicates the next step in the history of applied science may be open to debate (it surely is), but even as a vision of which human possibilities are most worth realizing it is already controversial—not least because it would seem to be predicated on the abandonment of all that has been true of human beings in the past.[23]

Not balking at controversy, most transhumanists would heap praise on Bacon for exactly what Pattison suggests. Indeed, many transhumanists appeal to Bacon's project—the quest for a rational-empirical epistemology, technoscientific relief of suffering, pursuit of progressive longevity, and commitment to ultimately transcending the human condition—as essentially coterminous with their own envisioned means and ends. Larry Temkin's sentiments in this regard are perhaps exemplary: "I endorse Francis Bacon's (1605) Enlightenment project which seeks 'the conquest of nature for the relief of man's estate.'"[24] Tempering his enthusiasm somewhat with the caveat that he "would put more constraints on our treatment of nature than Bacon," Temkin nonetheless unambiguously states his commitment to the "fundamental goal of ameliorating the human condition," which, he adds, is a realizable hope that rests "squarely on reason and, especially, science."

Riccardo Campa takes matters a step further, suggesting that transhumanism represents not only the essence, but also the transcendence of Baconian knowhow—a rendering of technoscience as more than a "mere instrument" and instead as "a goal in itself."[25] Campa argues that "the biophysical enhancement of humans aimed at improving scientific research is a strategic moral imperative," as it "synthesizes two only apparently incompatible meta-scientific views: the Baconian formula of *scientia ancilla technologiae* and the rationalist plea for disinterested science."[26] Whereas "Bacon and his followers have discovered that 'knowledge is power'" and "rationalists à la Descartes have instead insisted that 'knowledge is duty,'" transhumanism represents an opportunity to "synthesize these two views at a higher level" and, therefore, "recognize a new basic truth: 'power is knowledge.'"

The Bacon that emerges in such construals is in lockstep with the transhumanism that arises out of Enlightenment science, eupraxsophic humanism, secular reason, and technoscientific progress. This Bacon is regarded as perhaps *the* pivotal primogenitor to the H+ era, both helping to create the conditions necessary for modern technoscience to emerge and offering a vision for what the consequent knowledge-power could and should entail. Heralded as a forebear, foreseer, and fighter for the method that potentiates technoscientific capacity, Bacon also importantly charts the course that our realized potential might and must take. In this sense, his attainment is epistemological and methodological, predictive and prescriptive. Indeed, it is Bacon who effectuates the transhumanist movement in its modern form—and perhaps enlivens it still. There is just one question: is this Bacon the *real* Bacon?

In an essay that appraises transhumanist aspirations in light of the Sufi tradition, Farzad Mahootian calls this standard account into question. The prevailing construal of Bacon (and others), Mahootian argues, "fails to acknowledge the strong mythic commitments in Enlightenment thinking that undermine its claims for pure rationality."[27] Listing Bacon among those "pivotal figures" who defy such presumptions, Mahootian surmises that the " 'shadow' side of the Enlightenment contains much of what had passed for legitimate intellectual production over several centuries of premodern Europe[an] culture," rendering rationality "anything but pure."[28] What is this "shadow side" to which Mahootian refers? The answer to that question is complex, but sticking with our putative pioneer will perhaps shed a bit of light on matters.

REALIZED ESCHATOLOGY: BACON'S INSTAURATION AND "THE RELIEF OF MAN'S ESTATE"

Todd T. W. Daly offers a different view of Bacon. He argues that while "transhumanists often assume that the Christian faith has no vested interest in greatly extending healthy lives," this assumption rests on "a rather thin description of the Christian faith."[29] As evidence of Christian commitment to the contrary, Daly holds up Bacon as "one of the figureheads at the birth of modern medicine" who "asserted that prolongevity was the most noble goal of medicine and posed little difficulties for Christians making their way to Heaven." In fact, Daly notes, Bacon "believed that increasing control over the created order was *the* means by which humanity might regain the immortality that Adam and Even forfeited in the Garden of Eden," drawing "upon the imagery of a return to Eden in his own call for the exploration of the mechanisms involved in human aging" and attempting to "situate (with some difficulty) the pursuit of greater longevity within the Christian narrative."[30]

Michael Burdett similarly regards Bacon as being "among the most important precursors of contemporary transhumanism," along with N. F. Fedorov and Pierre Teilhard de Chardin, and accordingly attends to the theological underpinnings of their respective philosophies.[31] Burdett argues that while technology is (anachronistically, if playfully) "a key component of their avowal of transhumanism," their technological commitments in turn trade on Christian commitments that are "not superficial but absolutely central to their advocacy." In his engagement with Bacon, Burdett notes how the "instauration" in Bacon's unfinished magnum opus, *Instauratio magna*, draws on scriptural allusions and "carries a very particular connotation charged with symbolic values and religious undertones."[32] For instance, that which is being renewed or restored includes "human faculties that have been lost in the Fall." Bacon's aim, Burdett expounds, is "to restore the original human sovereignty" by means of a "new method" (advanced chiefly in the namesake *Novum organum*); one capable of eluding Bacon's famous idols of the mind and eliciting the "construction of new technologies, which manifested the redeemed relationship between human beings and nature, repositioning humanity in its rightful location of dominion over nature."[33]

Stephen G. Post, who claimed Bacon as the inaugurator of "biological ambition," as described earlier in this chapter, elsewhere suggests this ambition rests on an indispensable religious framework: "dreams of embodied near-immortality could only emerge against a theological background that more or less endorsed them."[34] While he grants that there were "various other cultural and historical influences at work besides religion," this author nonetheless concludes that "the initial conceptual context for a scientific assault on aging itself is a religious one." David Noble likewise argues: "if Bacon's effort was utilitarian in emphasis, it was transcendent in essence."[35] Bacon, according to Noble, thought "the advancement of knowledge was essential for salvation and promised the restoration of perfection." Being "explicit and insistent about the perfectionist purpose behind his advocacy of the useful arts," Bacon was offering a "bold biblically inspired vision."[36]

Indeed, Bacon did articulate a vision marked by sophisticated theological erudition and powerful biblical imagery. While the extensive body of literature devoted to Bacon's religious rhetoric deserves attention in its own right, here I will briefly unpack three distinguishing features of the proposed Baconian instauration: (1) the legitimization of natural knowledge by theological demarcation, (2) the momentousness of the Fall and the resultant determinative charter, and (3) the precondition of virtue.[37]

First, it was suggested earlier in this chapter that Bacon legitimated the scientific study of humans and nature. While this may be true, Bacon achieves the legitimation by a theological demarcation. The study of nature, Bacon suggests, is the study of "the work of the creation"—in other words, an aspect of divine self-revelation.[38] Such study was not an attempt to ascertain God in God's fullness or essence, but rather in the more limited sense as "double emanation of virtue from God: the one referring more properly to power, the other to wisdom."[39] The theological knowledge that could be derived from the study of nature was thereby limited, for "as all works do show forth the power and skill of the workmen, and not his image, so it is of the works of God, which do show the omnipotency and wisdom of the Maker, but not his Image."[40] Nevertheless, "philosophy and human learning" do offer "two principal duties and services": (1) "an effectual inducement to the exaltation of the glory of God" and (2) "a singular help and preservative against unbelief and error."[41] Although a circumscribed self-revelation, creation was nonetheless legitimately studied in a way similar to that other chief means of divine self-revelation: scripture. These "two books or volumes of study" were complementary, with scripture "revealing the will of God" and "creatures expressing his power."[42] While creation might only reveal the Creator's wisdom and power, the Book of Nature still ought be read to the extent that it could make its author known. As such, the study of creation posed not a hindrance but a help to faith:

> But if we take the matter rightly, natural philosophy after the Word of God is the best medicine for superstition and most highly recommended food for faith. And so to religion natural philosophy is rightly given as her most faithful servant, the former manifesting God's will, the latter His power. For he was not wrong who said: "Ye do err, not knowing the scriptures, and the power of God," thus mingling and joining together in an indissoluble bond information regarding His will with a meditation on His power.[43]

In a masterstroke, Bacon simultaneously safeguards the integrity of both divine and natural knowledge by suggesting the two are separate volumes that ought not mix: "*Da fidei, quae fidei sunt.*"[44] If "commixed," the result will be "an heretical religion and an imaginary and fabulous philosophy." Therefore, not only is the study of each book divinely sanctioned, but so, too, is their demarcation—what Bacon calls the "distributions and partitions of knowledge."[45]

Second, several authors note Bacon's quest to "effect all things possible" in addressing and ameliorating the limitations of the human condition. It should be noted, however, that the framework through which Bacon chose to articulate these limitations and the prospect of betterment was not initially naturalistic but theological, particularly in terms of the myth of the Fall, as mentioned earlier.[46] A distinctive remnant of Bacon's exposure to Calvinism was his markedly Augustinian view of a marred postlapsarian creation, which was determinative of both the nature and the limits of his proposed program. The far-reaching effects of original sin included humanity's epistemic, moral, and corporal limits as well as certain foibles of an otherwise orderly creation (that was perfect in its prelapsarian condition). Conceding a momentous loss, Bacon seeks to revisit "the whole work of the mind all over again, and from the very outset to stop the mind being left to itself" and "keep it under control."[47] Fallen and thereby limited, "like an enchanted glass, full of superstition and imposture,"[48] the human intellect was best aided by a new organon (as opposed to Aristotle's organon), which would offer a means of obtaining a more reliable knowledge and more fruitful effects. As Peter Harrison has shown, it was the postlapsarian "disordering both of mental operations and of nature itself" that provided the "sanction to a more active and aggressive style of experimental interrogation."[49] Harrison notes, however, that Bacon advocated "a middle path between two extremes: 'the presumption of pronouncing on everything, and the despair of comprehending anything.'"[50] Striking such a balance between hope and despair, Bacon's more active approach was a means whereby "like a tried and trusted guardian," humankind might "hand over their fortunes trusted to them" and achieve "an improvement in man's estate" along with "an enlargement of his power over nature."[51]

> For by his fall man lost both his state of innocence and his command over created things. However, both of these losses can to some extent be made good even in this life, the former by religion and faith, the latter by the arts and sciences.[52]

Note the limitations here implied. Not only is the potential recovery only partial, but the method proposed is also range bound (pertaining primarily to the natural, not the moral or spiritual). The postlapsarian condition could, therefore, be ameliorated to a certain extent—helping to regain the dominion God had originally intended for humankind to exercise over creation—but the possibility for restoration was not unbounded. This subtle but significant point ought not be missed: the theological claims about humanity's postlapsarian condition simultaneously constituted the course *and* the curtailment of which things were, for Bacon, possible to effect.[53]

Third, while Bacon's instauration traded on a new organon that would facilitate an industrious *vita activa* (instead of vain speculative disputation), the employment of his new tool presumed the prepossession of essential moral and theological virtues. Bacon's new organon assumes, first of all, a requisite humility that recognizes the aforementioned limitations and does not aspire to overmuch knowledge, knowledge of the wrong sort, or overestimation of the ends obtainable. Such humility is exemplified in the prayer offered by the heroic ancestor of "Salomon's House":

> Lord God of heaven and earth, thou hast vouchsafed of thy grace to those of our order, to know thy works of creation, and the secrets of them; and to discern (as far as appertaineth to the generations of men) between divine miracles, works of nature, works of art, and impostures and illusions of all sorts. I do here acknowledge and testify before this people, that the thing which we now see before our eyes is thy Finger and a true Miracle; and forasmuch as we learn in our books that thou never workest miracles but to a divine and excellent end (for the laws of nature are thine own laws, and thou exceedest them not but upon great

cause), we most humbly beseech thee to proposer this great sign, and to give us the interpretation and use of it in mercy; which thou dost in some part secretly promise by sending it unto us.[54]

Only after expressing such humility in prayer was it possible to proceed to the task of endowing humanity with "new discoveries and resources."[55] Such discoveries and resources (cultivated by the laborious "sweat of the brow"[56]) could then rightly obtain that "last or furthest end of knowledge," being the concurrent pursuit of "the glory of the Creator and the relief of man's estate."[57] This process is again exemplified in Salomon's House, also known as the "College of the Six Days Works," wherein the various exploits of natural philosophy and mechanical arts are punctuated by "ordinances and rites" including "hymns and services, which [are said] daily, of laud and thanks to God for his marvelous works: And forms of prayers, imploring his aid and blessing for the illumination of our labors, and the turning of them into good and holy uses."[58] These uses are, in turn, employed through the virtue of love, or charity, which conjoins the pursuit of God's glory and relief of humankind's estate. Employing a scriptural allusion, Bacon refers to charity as "the bond of perfection"[59] and argues that while

> aspiring to be like God in power, the angels transgressed and fell: *Ascendam, et ero similis altissimo*; by aspiring to be like God in knowledge, man transgressed and fell: *Eritis sicut Dii scientes bonum et malum*; but by aspiring to a similitude of God in goodness or love, neither man nor angel ever transgressed or shall transgress.[60]

Thus, pursuing love will inevitably lead to rightful ends, for: "if a man's mind be truly inflamed with charity, it doth work him suddenly into greater perfection than all the doctrine of morality can do." Here again we see the range-bound project that Bacon proposes. We are not restricted in our pursuit of charity (which includes, but is not limited to, the production of effects for the relief of humankind's estate), but the knowledge-power we obtain is limited in its scope and application. This limit also functions to legitimate the project kept within its proper bounds.

This cursory glance cannot possibly do justice to the complexity of Bacon's thought, but it should be enough to unsettle judgments about the Bacon we think we know. While a much more careful and detailed study would be necessary to grasp Bacon's sources and intents, it suffices for this inquiry to simply note the rich, complex, substantial theological language and imagery that Bacon employs to articulate and advance his vision.[61] If we read Bacon in terms of his own self-presentation and within his milieu, we encounter a Bacon who confounds certain caricatures. Of the many sources of his thought and mediums of his expression, the theological influence, allusion, and articulation are consistent and inimitable. Quite apart from lurking on the "shadow side" of the Enlightenment, Bacon's theological commitments are hiding in plain sight. At the very least, encountering Bacon's religious rhetoric is enough to problematize facile accounts in certain transhumanist genealogies, forcing us to look again at this purported primogenitor.

CONCLUSION: AVOIDING A FALLACY OF ORIGINS AND INTENTS

Tirosh-Samuelson has suggested that transhumanism is "a secularist faith" that "secularizes traditional religious motifs on the one hand and endows technology with salvific meaning on the other hand."[62] While I find such claims compelling, my argument here is narrower. I am not suggesting that transhumanism is a secularist faith (although I would not preclude the possibility), nor am I aiming to convince eupraxsophic transhumanists that theirs is actually a theological project. Even if I can convincingly show that Bacon's thought is irreducibly theological (which would take quite a bit more analysis than I have been able to offer here), it does not necessarily follow that all self-styled Baconian projects are, therefore, theological. To stake such a claim would be perilously close to a fallacy of origins, failing to acknowledge the ways in which eupraxsophic transhumanists are operating on an épistème that is undeniably different than Bacon's (if also beholden to it)—representing an amalgam of philosophies of which Bacon is, however important, but one constitutive part. Any claim to continuity must also admit discontinuities. Bacon's vision may be at once consonant, and yet not wholly concomitant, with transhumanism's aims and ends. What is more, origins only partially determine outcomes. In addition, intents, even if they can even be ascertained, may well be lost in a multiplicity of appropriations.

Nevertheless, my contention remains that while transhumanists rightly regard Bacon as perhaps their primary primogenitor, standard ascriptions misunderstand or misconstrue how Bacon himself advanced the concepts to which transhumanists lay claim. To enroll Bacon in the way he is often enrolled is to deny, dismiss, or discount the unmistakably theological thrust of Bacon's thought. There may be good reasons for suspicion of Bacon's religious rhetoric, but the standard accounts in transhumanist genealogies do not attend to the complexity of such arguments. Instead, they simply paint a picture of Bacon that resonates with the 18th-century *philosophes* (e.g., Diderot, Condorcet), which hardly does justice to the nuanced arguments that Bacon himself advanced. We must first understand Bacon before we can appropriate or resist his project.

The upshot, then, is twofold. First, as a matter of history, attending to the complexity of Bacon's thought reveals the falsity of certain claims about how modern technoscience emerged—not *over* and *against* religion, but often *by virtue of* it. Recognizing this, we might be less prone to assume antagonisms when there are none and, therefore, more accurately construe the associations between science, technology, and faith in specific historical contexts. With respect to the particular example of transhumanism and religion vis-à-vis Bacon, I contend that the relationship between the secular and the sacred is more nuanced and interesting than standard narratives assume. If, as I have suggested, transhumanism is informed by Bacon, and Bacon is in turn informed by religion, transhumanism and religion may actually have more in common than is often supposed.

This argument leads to my second point, pertaining to theology. Showing that transhumanism and religion (vis-à-vis Bacon) have more in common than is often supposed offers an interesting twist on possible theological engagements. Whereas many theologians respond to eupraxsophic transhumanism with damnatory dismissiveness, demonstrating the commonality between the sacred and the secular may well open up space to interact with transhumanism on more substantive grounds. If, for instance, theologians engage Bacon's ameliorative project not as a secular technoscientific assertion of hubristic knowledge-power but rather as a divinely sanctioned instauration of charity-motivated faith-with-works, they may find a far less objectionable transhumanism—or, indeed, a transhumanism that can be fashioned on avowedly religious grounds. Conversely, they may find in Bacon a wolf in sheep's clothing—offering a salvation that is not salvation, by a means that undermines its supposed ends. In either case, whether constructive or critical, the relationship between transhumanism and religion may yet well be more complex and more exciting than is often supposed.

NOTES

1. Peter Harrison, "Introduction," in *The Cambridge Companion to Science and Religion*, edited by Peter Harrison (Cambridge, UK: Cambridge University Press, 2010), 4. Without omitting definite but discrete episodes of conflict, historians generally recount a complex array of interactions as the boundaries between what we now call "religion," "science," and "technology" are constructed. See Peter Harrison, " 'Science' and 'Religion': Constructing the Boundaries," *Journal of Religion* 86, no. 1 (2006): 81–106.

2. Most scholars suggest the term "transhumanism" was first coined in 1957 with the publication of Julian Huxley's *New Bottles for New Wine* (New York, NY: Harper & Brothers, 1957). In fact, it appears at least as early as 1951 in Huxley's two-part essay "Knowledge, Morality, and Destiny" [*Psychiatry* 14, no. 2 (1951): 129–151], where he refers to it as "the idea of humanity attempting to overcome its limitations and to arrive at fuller fruition" (139). This term likely appears even earlier and it is quite possible that Huxley himself is not the originator, although he is certainly among the principal popularizers. Bostrom and Hughes both erroneously suggest the term "transhumanism" appears in *Religion without Revelation* (New York, NY: Harper & Brothers, 1927). See Nick Bostrom, "A History of Transhumanist Thought," *Journal*

of Evolution and Technology 14, no. 1 (2005): 2; James J. Hughes, *Citizen Cyborg: Why Democratic Societies Must Respond to the Redesigned Human of the Future* (Boulder, CO: Westview Press, 2004), 158. Nevertheless, index listings for "transhumanism" in the 1957 *New Bottles for New Wine* include passages from an essay titled "Evolutionary Humanism" originally published in the 1927 *Religion without Revelation*—even though the term does not appear therein. This suggests that while Huxley may not have used the exact term in 1927, "evolutionary humanism" is indeed a nascent form. As for Huxley's juxtaposition of transhumanism and religion, if the titles of these two books do not already betray the underlying antagonism, it should be noted that his *New Bottles for New Wine* title is a play on a proverbial parable attributed to Jesus in the Christian Synoptic Gospels: "And no one puts new wine into old wineskins ... but one puts new wine into fresh wineskins" (Mark 2:22, New Revised Standard Version [NRSV]). (See also Matthew 9:17 and Luke 5:37. A version of the parable also appears in the *Gospel of Thomas*, Saying 47.)

3. My argument essentially echoes that of historian John Hedley Brooke, who, in his appraisal of perfectibility, surmises that the "relationship between the sacred and the secular in the history of technology [and science] is more complex but also more exciting than the familiar dichotomies assume." John Hedley Brooke, "Visions of Perfectibility," *Journal of Evolution & Technology* 14, no. 2 (2005): 2.

4. Bostrom, "A History of Transhumanist Thought," 2.

5. Nick Bostrom, "Transhumanist Values," in "Ethical Issues for the Twenty-First Century," supplement to *Journal of Philosophical Research* 30 (2005): 4.

6. Max More, "True Transhumanism: A Reply to Don Ihde," in *H±: Transhumanism and Its Critics*, edited by Gregory R. Hansell and William Grassie (Philadelphia, PA: Metanexus Institute, 2011), 137.

7. Max More, "The Philosophy of Transhumanism," in *The Transhumanist Reader: Classical and Contemporary Essays on the Science, Technology, and Philosophy of the Human Future*, edited by Max More and Natasha Vita-More (Chichester, UK: John Wiley & Sons, 2013), 4.

8. More, "The Philosophy of Transhumanism." More borrows this term and concept from the late philosopher Paul Kurtz, who first coined the term as "eupraxophy" but preferred the "eupraxsophy" variant in his later works. See Paul Kurtz, *Eupraxophy: Living without Religion* (Amherst, NY: Prometheus Books, 1989).

9. Hava Tirosh-Samuelson, "Science and the Betterment of Humanity: Three British Prophets of Transhumanism," in *Building Better Humans? Refocusing the Debate on Transhumanism*, edited by Hava Tirosh-Samuelson and Kenneth L. Mossman (Frankfurt am Main, Germany: Peter Lang, 2011), 55.

10. This may well be because many transhumanists are often committed to a conception of technoscientific reason that is atemporal, which precludes the pertinence of such historical considerations.

11. James J. Hughes, "The Politics of Transhumanism and the Techno-Millennial Imagination, 1626–2030," *Zygon* 47, no. 4 (2012): 759.

12. Hughes, "The Politics of Transhumanism," 757–758.

13. Hughes, "The Politics of Transhumanism," 759.

14. Hughes erroneously cites 1626 as the publication date of *New Atlantis*. Bacon died in 1626; *New Atlantis* was published posthumously as "a worke unfinished" by his chaplain, William Rawley, in 1627. The work appeared, as Bacon intended,

at the end of a single volume preceded by his natural history, *Sylva Sylvarum*. See the footnote to Brian Vickers's critical edition of *New Atlantis*, which Hughes cites: Francis Bacon, *Francis Bacon: A Critical Edition of the Major Works*, edited by Brian Vickers (Oxford, UK: Oxford University Press, 1996), 785 n. 456.

15. Bostrom, "A History of Transhumanist Thought," 2

16. More, "True Transhumanism," 138.

17. More, "The Philosophy of Transhumanism," 9.

18. More, "True Transhumanism," 138.

19. Celia Deane-Drummond, "Future Perfect? God, the Transhuman Future and the Quest for Immortality," in *Future Perfect? God, Medicine and Human Identity*, edited by Celia Deane-Drummond and Peter Manley Scott (London, UK: T&T Clark, 2006), 169.

20. Stephen G. Post, "Humanism, Posthumanism, and Compassionate Love," *Technology in Society* 32 (2010): 37.

21. Steven Shapin and Christopher Martyn, "How to Live Forever: Lessons of History," *BMJ* 321 (2000): 1581.

22. George Pattison, *God and Being: An Enquiry* (Oxford, UK: Oxford University Press, 2013), 322.

23. Pattison, *God and Being*.

24. Larry Temkin, "Is Living Longer Living Better?," in *Enhancing Human Capacities*, edited by Julian Savulescu et al. (Oxford, UK: Wiley-Blackwell, 2011), 353. It should be noted that Temkin ends his essay by expressing reservations about whether living longer is living better, given the potential for diminishing returns on enjoyment of life events.

25. Riccardo Campa, "Pure Science and the Posthuman Future," *Journal of Evolution & Technology* 19, no. 1 (2008): 28.

26. Campa, "Pure Science and the Posthuman Future," 33 (italics added to denote the Latin).

27. Farzad Mahootian, "Ideals of Human Perfection: A Comparison of Sufism and Transhumanism," in *Building Better Humans? Refocusing the Debate on Transhumanism*, edited by Hava Tirosh-Samuelson and Kenneth L. Mossman (Frankfurt am Main, Germany: Peter Lang, 2011), 148. Mahootian comments further: "Bostrom is guilty of facile stereotyping, as he begins his history by trotting out the old image of the medieval era as a period of great intellectual stagnation. A cursory survey of discoveries, explorations, and innovations in many fields of human endeavor, extending from Europe through the Middle East to China, give lie to that stale image—as old as the Enlightenment itself and as narrow-minded and selective in its choice of evidence" (150).

28. Mahootian, "Ideals of Human Perfection." Mahootian concludes: "All too often, transhumanist authors have decided that rational scientific and technological discourse is always the best approach to the question, so a scientific and technical answer, with reasonable allowance for moral and humanitarian ideals, will be the right one. . . . As it stands, the emphasis on scientific and technological arguments is excessive, and any awareness of the positive relevance of nonscientific considerations is dim or nonexistent" (153).

29. Todd T. W. Daly, "Chasing Methuselah: Transhumanism and Christian Theosis in Critical Perspective," in *Transhumanism and Transcendence: Christian Hope in an Age of Technological Enhancement*, edited by Ronald Cole-Turner (Washington, DC: Georgetown University Press, 2011), 134.

30. Daly elsewhere suggests that, at least when compared with Descartes, Bacon "appeared less encumbered by theological convictions and even more optimistic towards increasing control over nature through scientific progress." With prolongevity a central feature of his "melioristic program," Daly notes that Bacon answered the "charge of impiety" by "arguing for the advantages of longevity in making journey towards our heavenly home." Todd T. W. Daly, "Life-Extension in Transhumanist and Christian perspectives: Consonance and Conflict," *Journal of Evolution and Technology* 14, no. 2 (2005): 62.

31. Michael S. Burdett, "Contextualizing a Christian Perspective on Transcendence and Human Enhancement: Francis Bacon, N. F. Fedorov, and Pierre Teilhard de Chardin," in *Transhumanism and Transcendence: Christian Hope in an Age of Technological Enhancement*, edited by Ronald Cole-Turner (Washington, DC: Georgetown University Press, 2011), 20.

32. Burdett notes the excellent essay by Charles Whitney, "Francis Bacon's *Instauratio*: Dominion of, and Over, Humanity," *Journal of the History of Ideas* 50, no. 3 (1989): 371–390. It is worth mentioning, however, that Whitney's driving thesis goes beyond the root meaning of the word as he argues: "the orientation toward the past," though important, "does not cover the full meaning of the word [instauration] which includes 'begin' and 'establish' " but also extends beyond it to "Bacon's *instauratio ab imis fundamentis*," which "leads from past-orientated humanist and Christian ideas of innovation to the early modern concept of revolution, for which antecedents become irrelevant" (386). See also Charles Whitney, *Francis Bacon and Modernity* (New Haven, CT: Yale University Press, 1986), 90–104.

33. Burdett, "Contextualizing a Christian Perspective," 23.

34. Stephen G. Post, "Decelerated Aging: Should I Drink from the Fountain of Youth?," in *The Fountain of Youth: Cultural, Scientific, and Ethical Perspectives on a Biomedical Goal*, edited by Stephen G. Post and Robert H. Binstock (Oxford, UK: Oxford University Press, 2004), 82–83.

35. David Noble, *The Religion of Technology: The Divinity of Man and the Spirit of Invention* (New York, NY: Alfred A. Knopf, 1997), 50.

36. Noble, *The Religion of Technology*, 51. Noble notes, however, that if biblically inspired, Bacon's vision was also reflective of "the exaggerated anthropocentric assumptions of his seventeenth-century Protestant faith" marked by the belief that "human ascendency was central to the Divine plan." He also casts Bacon among those who surpass a "devout acknowledgement of divine purpose" and instead "subtly but steadily [began to] assume the mantle of creator in their own right, as gods themselves"—which, quoting Lewis Mumford, Noble suggests is " 'the undeclared ultimate goal' of modern science" (67).

37. The focus here is limited to three of Bacon's more important works: *The Advancement of Learning* (1605), *Novum organum* (1620), and *New Atlantis* (1627). Hereafter these titles will be abbreviated *AL*, *NO*, and *NA*, respectively. I have contemporized spellings and grammar for ease of reading, drawing on the *Oxford Francis Bacon* (*OFB*) and *Oxford Authors* (*OA*) series; see the bibliography for full details.

38. *AL*, I.vi.2; *OFB*, IV, 33.

39. *AL*, I.vi.2; *OFB*, IV, 33.

40. *AL*, II.vi.1; *OFB*, IV, 78–79.

41. *AL*, I.vi.16; *OFB*, IV, 37.

42. *AL*, I.vi.16; *OFB*, IV, 37. Bacon continues by suggesting that the study of crea-tion can also offer a key to interpreting scripture by "not only opening our understand-ing to conceive the true sense of the Scriptures, by the general notions of reason and rules of speech; but chiefly opening our belief, in drawing us into a due meditation of the omnipotency of God, which is chiefly signed and engraven upon his works."

43. *NO*, I.89; *OFB*, XI, 144–147.

44. *AL*, II.vi.1; *OFB*, IV, 79. "Render unto faith the things that are faith's," a play on Matthew 22:21. The Vulgate reads "*et quae sunt Dei Deo*." The Authorized Version had not yet been completed at the time of *AL*'s publication.

45. *AL*, II.v.2; *OFB*, IV, 76. It should be noted that Bacon also makes room in his system for the ability to "erect and constitute" one universal system, by the name of the "*philosophia prima*." Lisa Jardine offers the following definition thereof, noting Bacon's contrast with scholasticism: "In scholastic classifications of knowledge *philoso-phia prima* is a synonym for metaphysics. Bacon explicitly prefers the term *philosophia prima* for the study of common axioms of the science and of the properties and rela-tions which recur in all branches of knowledge, and transfers the term *metaphysic* to the study of forms (abstract or universal physics in the scholastic classifications)." Lisa Jardine, *Francis Bacon: Discovery and the Art of Discourse* (Cambridge, UK: Cambridge University Press, 1974), 104 n. 1.

46. As Peter Harrison has argued in detail, Bacon echoed many of his contemporar-ies in this regard: "the myth of Adam and the idea of the Fall were ubiquitous features of seventeenth-century discussions of knowledge and its foundations." Peter Harrison, *The Fall of Man and the Foundations of Science* (Cambridge, UK: Cambridge University Press, 2007), 248.

47. *NO*, preface; *OFB*, XI, 55.

48. *AL*, II.xiv.9; *OFB*, IV, 116.

49. Harrison, *The Fall of Man*, 182–183. Bacon's advocacy of experimentation has been equated with the "torture" of nature. See, for instance, Carolyn Merchant's *Reinventing Eden: The Fate of Nature in Western Culture*, 2nd ed. (New York, NY: Routledge, 2013). For a counterpoint to the "torture" claim, see Peter Pesic, "Wrestling with Proteus: Francis Bacon and the 'Torture' of Nature," *Isis* 90, no. 1 (1999): 81–94.

50. Harrison, *The Fall of Man*, 87. Harrison is here quoting *NO*, preface. The phrase in Latin original reads: "*inter pronuntiandi iactantiam, & Acatalepsiae desperationem*." It is translated in the *OFB* as "between the arrogance of dogmatism and the hopeless-ness of *Acatalepsy*" (*OFB*, XI, 53).

51. *NO*, II.52; *OFB*, XI, 447. Bacon is here alluding to the so-called parable of the talents (c.f. Matthew 25:14–30 and Luke 19:12–28).

52. *NO*, II.52; *OFB*, XI, 447. Bacon is here alluding to the so-called parable of the talents (c.f. Matthew 25:14–30 and Luke 19:12–28).

53. Harrison suggests that there is a double meaning to Bacon's naming "his ideal scientific institution 'the house of Salomon,'" alluding both to the expansive natural knowledge that Solomon was supposed to have had and to his exhortations on futility (traditionally thought to be the author of Proverbs and Ecclesiastes). Harrison proposes that the name was indicative of Bacon's "ambivalent attitude towards knowledge—an admiration of the wonders of nature and a reputation for an intimate

familiarity with its workings, combined with counsels concerning the ultimate vanity of human learning" (*The Fall of Man*, 122).

54. *NA*; *OA*, 464.

55. *NO*, I.81; *OFB*, XI, 129.

56. Meaning at once difficult physical labor and, with a distinct Baconian twist, arduous intellectual travail.

57. *AL*, I.v.11; *OFB*, IV, 32.

58. *NA*; *OA*, 488.

59. Colossians 3:14

60. *AL,* II.xxii.15; *OFB*, IV, 155.

61. To be sure, many of Bacon's interpreters express suspicion of Bacon's authentic theological self-presentation, essentially suggesting it was mere rhetoric, sacred husk on a secular kernel. For example, see Howard White, *Peace among the Willows: The Political Philosophy of Francis Bacon* (The Hague, Netherlands: Martinus Nijhoff, 1968); Jerry Weinberger, *Science, Faith, and Politics: Francis Bacon and the Utopian Roots of the Modern Age* (Ithaca, NY: Cornell University Press, 1985); Timothy H. Paterson, "On the Role of Christianity in the Political Philosophy of Francis Bacon," *Polity* 19, no. 3 (1987), 419–442; Robert Faulkner, *Francis Bacon and the Project of Progress* (Lanham, MD: Rowman and Littlefield, 1993). For counterclaims, see Stephen McKnight, *The Religious Foundation of Francis Bacon's Thought* (Columbia, MO: University of Missouri Press, 2006); Aderemi Ethan Artis, "Francis Bacon and the Scientific Reformation" (PhD dissertation, Princeton University, Princeton, NJ, 2007); Steven Matthews, *Theology and Science in the Thought of Francis Bacon* (Aldershot, UK: Ashgate, 2008). See also Perez Zagorin, *Francis Bacon* (Princeton, NJ: Princeton University Press, 1998); Stephen Gaukroger, *Francis Bacon and the Transformation of Early-Modern Philosophy* (Cambridge, UK: Cambridge University Press, 2004); Peter Harrison, *The Bible, Protestantism, and the Rise of Modern Science* (Cambridge, UK: Cambridge University Press, 1998).

62. Hava Tirosh-Samuelson, "Transhumanism as a Secularist Faith" *Zygon* 47, no. 4 (2012), 719.

5

....

A Salvation Paradox for Transhumanism: *Saving* You versus Saving *You*

Patrick D. Hopkins

I have argued elsewhere that transhumanism shares with religion a soteriology—a belief that humans are trapped in a condition from which they need to be saved.[1] While the human condition may be characterized in different ways, depending on the specific doctrinal system—such as suffering, limitation, sinfulness, illusion, separation, ignorance, rebirth, brokenness, or some combination of these—the conviction is that something is bad and needs to change. One overarching way to describe this condition is to state that we all suffer from unsatisfied desires. We want pleasure, existence, happiness, peace, meaning, love, connection, permanence, security, knowledge, divine union, and a host of other things that are difficult to acquire, and even more difficult to keep if we do acquire them. This produces a recurring and persistent sense of unsettledness and longing.

PLANS OF SALVATION AND RELIGIOUS ANALOGS

If we think broadly about human unhappiness as the result of unsatisfied desire, there are two obvious ways to deal with that condition: we could satisfy the desire or we could eradicate the desire. Either method, if successfully employed, would eliminate the basic problem. Religious paradigms for both approaches exist. Many versions of Christianity and Islam, for example, hold that the ultimate and permanent satisfaction of (morally proper) desire is realized in the form of eternal existence in heaven with an imperishable body perpetually near to God. Buddhism, in contrast, offers the extinction of desire and freedom from attachment to the illusion of permanence. Of course, religious soteriological methods are not the only options. Technological methods also offer freedom from the human condition. While many speculations have addressed what advanced technology might be able to accomplish, two approaches arise, differing largely to the extent to which the technology employed alters the human agent.

One approach advocates technologically augmenting human bodies and minds in ways that free us from our current physical and cognitive limitations. By changing our bodies and brains to surpass typical human functioning, we could become able to secure the objects of our desires. Optimizing our newly expanded capacities for knowledge, pleasure, strength, longevity, and durability would transform us into idealized versions of ourselves. In many ways, this approach shares a vision with some theistic paradises—Olympian immortals of perfect health and beauty communing in security and peace, for example, or heavenly perfected bodies in a world without suffering, death or fear. I will call this the superhuman approach.

The second approach goes further, using technology both to augment and to alter the physical and cognitive constraints of human nature. By changing bodies and minds not only to surpass typical limits but also to exhibit new forms of cognition, embodiment, perception, and sensation, humans could develop into beings that do not simply secure understood objects of desire but eliminate familiar desire structures altogether. In some ways, this approach shares a narrative with the negative descriptive language of mystics and Buddhists—unlimited, unconditioned, ultimate, passing understanding. Given the image of radical difference, I will call this the posthuman approach.

Note that these approaches are not clearly named, established positions within transhumanist culture. Instead, they are my general distillations of more or less explicit goals. They are not at odds with each other; indeed, for some they may even form a continuous trajectory. Neither are they explicitly religious in nature, although they do parallel historically and psychologically important religious thinking and describe ways that technology might be thought to free us.

However, these two approaches run into a paradox.

A SALVATION/IDENTITY PARADOX

Both approaches promise release from the human condition of limitation and unfulfilled desire, but it is doubtful that either can save us. The first approach is likely to fail because it will not *save* us. The second approach is likely to fail because it will not save *us*.

Elsewhere, I have used the terms "low transhumanism" and "high transhumanism."[2] I have referred to a more Platonic approach and a more Nietzschean approach. In this chapter, I have settled on using the terms "transhumanism," "superhuman," and "posthuman."

The prefix "trans" denotes "across" but also connotes a sense of motion, as in "moving beyond" or "changing thoroughly" or passing from one thing to another.[3] As such, it applies well to an active situation of moving beyond the ordinary limits of humans to a different set of limits. In this chapter, then, "transhumanism" will refer to the moral and political position of advocating the value of and access to technologies that allow humans to modify themselves and move past human limits, while "transhuman" will refer to a human being who has adopted enough technology that he or she is in the process of moving significantly beyond species-typical human limits.

The prefix "super" means "above" or "beyond" and connotes a sense of "exceeding the norms or limits of a given class."[4] As such, "super" effectively indicates that an entity has its origin in a given class and remains sufficiently characteristic of that class to retain partial membership. However, the entity has enhanced itself enough that it now exceeds the constraints of class. So, "superhuman" would refer to someone who began as an ordinary human (individually or genealogically) but has been augmented to such an extent that he or she has capacities and abilities outside human limits, although the entity is clearly still more closely related psychologically and physically to humans than to any other species.

The prefix "post" indicates coming "after" something or "later than" something.[5] It can mean simply following in order, as in "post hoc argument" or "postwar period," but it can also connote being "developmentally subsequent to," as in "postgraduate study" or "postlarval morphology." That sense of the prefix is useful for this discussion in that it implies any object or phenomenon modified by "post" is no longer the same kind of thing it was. Other prefixes potentially apply as well ("ab," "tele," "hetero," "extro," "meta," "un"), but either are already in use or have specific contemporary connotations rendering them inappropriate. So, "posthuman" would describe an entity that began as human (individually or in its taxonomic descent) but is clearly no longer a member of the human species, and indeed does not bear enough resemblance to humans to even count as close.

The superhuman approach attempts to free us from the human condition by enhancing desirable human traits to an extent that surpasses the limits of the class. The posthuman approach attempts to free us from the human condition by changing the source organism so radically that the resulting beings would no longer be human at all. The problem is that the posthuman approach runs into an issue of identity. I will deal with each problem in turn.

SUPERHUMAN AND POSTHUMAN SALVATION

The Superhuman Condition

Most transhumanist organizations and writers give a list of goals and values, explicating what it means to be transhumanist.[6] While the lists vary somewhat, they usually contain some version of the following:

- Radical longevity
- Eradication of disease

- Elimination of unnecessary suffering
- Augmented cognitive capacities
- Augmented physical capacities
- Augmented emotional capacities
- Augmented and added sensory modalities
- Augmented willpower
- Increased sense of well-being
- Greater control over our lives
- The ability to upload our minds to computers

Most items on this list are not that different from goals most humans might articulate. The majority would not include the terms "radical" or "upload" or talk about added senses, but in general, ordinary human goals include the following: living longer; being healthier, smarter, happier, stronger, and more secure; and establishing greater control over one's life. Transhumanist goals are not just consistent with those goals, but mostly continuous with them. Transhumanists go much further but are still easily recognized as pursuing human ambitions. This is why transhumanist hopes for the beneficial effects of technology can be seen as a kind of soteriology—and this is not a criticism. Many elements of the human condition are deplorable and disappointing; indeed, our lives would seem to be much better off without them. Transhumanists want a better existence. Humanists in general rely on ordinary self-improvement techniques, and religionists might add doctrinal components that include radical changes in an afterlife, but it all seems quite familiar. Life is solitary, poor, nasty, brutish, and short.[7] We want it to be sociable, rich, pleasant, enlightened, and long. Using technology to work toward these aims naturalistically, the superhuman condition would be advanced humanity without the horrors.

A Problem with Human Nature

There is, however, something that the superhuman approach overlooks, or at least underappreciates: an important element of the human condition at play here. It is not related so much to the cognitive limits of human thought, as to the cognitive character of human thought. It is related to the way in which humans are embedded in the world historically and biologically. While I can give only a thumbnail sketch of the issue here, perhaps this depiction will be enough to temper too exuberant a reaction to the promise of superhuman enhancement.

Humans want to be happy, satisfied, safe, and secure. Toward those ends, humans pursue love, food, shelter, community, power, status, relationships, wealth, health, respect, and beauty. However, there is reason to think that if we acquired all those things, even in amounts sufficient to preclude any chance of future depletion, we would not be content—that is, we would still find ourselves desiring. The reason for this is not some grand romantic reflection on the intrinsically fleeting nature of things, but rather a simple characteristic of our evolutionary development.

Throughout the vast majority of human history, we have experienced scarcity and danger. We could be killed, eaten, get sick, starve, lose a fight, or lose the chance to mate. In that environment, the perpetual drive to acquire was adaptive. Constantly being alert to opportunities for—and pursuing—food, power, status, allies, shelter, and sex was almost always the best strategy. Even on those rare occasions when an individual might have a surplus of calories, resources, and procreative outlets, susceptibility to losing acquisitions reinforced the desire for more. Individuals with strong drives to accumulate (using strategies of both competition and cooperation) were more likely to survive, reproduce, and pass on those drives. Individuals too quickly disposed to contentment and complacency were less likely to do so.

The result is that human psychology developed a powerful drive to acquire, but humans did not develop an equally strong attitude module for feeling satisfied with what we have. Human minds did not evolve a strong capacity to deal with long-lasting material and procreative security because such a situation rarely occurred (even the concept of needing to "deal with" security and abundance may seem odd). Even after industrialism produced an environment of relative plenty, human minds stay primed to acquire more (e.g., more salt, sugar, fat, sex, wealth, status, reputation). That acquisitive drive seems more highly developed than our capacity for enjoyment. In motivation terms, we are shoppers more fundamentally than we are owners. Given that we have millions of years of adaptive success with the acquisitive drive, and less than 100 years' exposure to any significant level of abundance, our "more is better" module rarely shuts off, and there is little reason to think it ever will.

This leads to a psychological "mismatch" for human psychology in the contemporary world. Many people now have enough, yet still feel unfulfilled. People keep acquiring—but more wealth ceases to increase happiness, more calories produces obesity, and more concern for status produces diminishing returns on security. Positive psychology regularly advises us of the hedonic treadmill on which modern lives run.

Now recall the list of transhumanist goals. It is characterized by "more"— more life, more health, more power, more knowledge, more security. I am not suggesting that the desire for more is necessarily a bad thing; I am not trying to accuse transhumanism of possessing some consumerist vice. The point is simply that transhumanist goals are human goals, which helps us to recall a truth that is often obscured in discussions about and among transhumanists: that transhumanism is a human movement, a human ideology, a humanism. It is not the product of transhumans. Not surprisingly, as a human idea, it expresses a quintessentially human motivation—more is better (though the more is *more* than ever).

Given that the goals, motivation, and psychology are human, why might employing that "more is better" principle produce happiness or contentment even if we enhance ourselves to the level of the superhuman? Yes, it is widely accepted that being healthy is better than being sick, secure better than being insecure, and free from pain better than suffering, but as countless numbers of healthy, secure, pain-free—and yet restless and discontent—humans demonstrate, these beneficial states do not permanently slake our desires for more. I doubt even becoming immortal would make much difference.

If we understand the desire for technological enhancement to be an extension of the age-old soteriological desire to free us from the negative aspects of the human condition, technology probably will not be much more successful than other attempts that have been made. Discontent was previously always adaptive. Even a superhuman, flush with power and longevity and X-ray vision, will likely look around and ask, "Is this all there is to life?"

One response to this scenario—consistent with the promise of enhancement—is to say that if this speculation about discontent and dissatisfaction is right, it just points out another flaw in human nature that we can eliminate through technology. Just as senescence, osteoporosis, and retinal blood vessel architecture could all be fixed, so we could engineer ourselves to be content. That might be possible. The question, though, would be, Why wait to do that until after other augmentations are achieved? After all, if the goals are ultimately contentment, peace, and freedom from the frustration of limitations and fallibilities, why not create that situation now? If you are content, you are content. If you are not content but think you would be if you had super-strength, night vision, and eidetic memory, then you are likely running along the "more is better" evolutionary treadmill. Would engineering contentment not solve the problem? It is only discontent that created the desire for enhancements in the first place.

I suspect most people would not find the idea of simply engineering contentment appealing. Bioconservatives would likely object because that approach seems like cheating or seems "artificial." But transhumanists would likely object as well. Why? If those augmented abilities would truly make our lives more interesting, exciting, fulfilling, and happier, then we have reason to think that after those changes were made, superhumans would experience the same recurrent discontent and desire for more that ordinary humans do. In short, even enhanced humans will carry this "desire for more" aspect of human mentality with us. If we eradicate the "desire for more," then there is little reason to develop other enhancements. This technological approach, then, seems not to be able to *save* us because the "us" still exists and will still want more.

The Posthuman Condition

Much of the problem already described is about carrying human psychological traits over into the enhanced state. If after enhancement we still will not be truly satisfied with our changes, might the problem actually be the residual humanity? Why not go further and truly transform ourselves into something so different that it would not even be residually human, at least not in ways that would trigger our perpetual discontent? Perhaps we need to move beyond what we understand to something far more radical. Let us truly transcend.

A Problem with Identity

Another characteristic of human thought, however, might lead us astray here. We can trick ourselves into thinking that we are thinking something we are not. It is easy to construct grammatically and syntactically correct sentences by stringing together words that nonetheless fail to produce clear or even coherent meanings.

When we talk about "transcending," it is easy to imagine that "we" remain present in whatever state of being that would follow. We tend to use the word "transcended" too literally, relying on the denotation of physical movement in the prefix "trans." Just as we can "transport" ourselves from one city to another and predict that we will be the same person in the destination city as in the origin city, so we can treat "transcend" (and numerous other terms, such as "upload") as just another kind of physical movement. We can somehow imagine ourselves on the "other side" of the transcended state, as though we were simply moving from here to there. We might vaguely picture ourselves as fulfilled, or knowing, or enlightened on the "other side" of the experience, but we do picture ourselves. We invest hope in what "our" life will be like in that state, anticipating that we will be happy, content, knowledgeable, and free, though to emphasize that it is a radical transformation, we add appellations to the state: "radical," "beyond measure," "passing understanding," "incomprehensible," "unimaginable," and so forth. But though we can engage in these linguistic exercises, I suspect we are playing a trick on ourselves.

Imagine a trajectory of technological enhancement that is eventually so radical that the end result is not merely superhuman, but posthuman. Suppose technology has changed me so much that I am no longer a member of the human species, no longer limited by any species-defining human cognitive characteristics. I have changed so much that the existence I now experience is incomprehensible to my former, limited, human self. As much as that language may sound wonderful, exciting, and liberating at first, thinking about it more in depth reveals that such a technological process offers far less to *me* than hoped.

The technologies are supposed to produce a radical change. But "radical" is a very strong word, though it is often watered down in contemporary use. It means "fundamentally different from the root"; it does not mean just "very, very, very." If the entity resulting from all this technological alteration really merits being described as radically different and incomprehensible from my current cognitive vantage point, then it is not at all clear why I would be personally motivated to initiate this process, because it is not at all clear how this transformation would benefit *me*.

Taking the notion of a radical technological transforming process literally, it appears that the end result will be some kind of successor entity to me, but it will not be me. It will be something I not only do not understand, but also cannot understand. Adding phrases such as "cannot understand now" or "cannot understand from my current cognitive vantage point" does not help. That language implies that I will be changed enough to eventually understand, but the only way to understand a radically different being would be to have a cognitive nature that was radically different from what I am now. Being "radically different" implies, however, a lack of continuous identity. If A and B are not identical, then they are not the same thing. If A and B are, in addition, radically different things, then not only are they not the same thing, but they also are not the same kind of thing. There can be no sense made of A radically transforming into B, yet still claiming that A is B. This discontinuity is easy to overlook because language allows identity tricks.

Two famous examples of this trickery come from the philosophy of mind literature. In the first, when Descartes argued that mind and body must be composed of distinctly different substances and that our mind counts as our self rather than our body, he asked us to imagine two scenarios.[8] In one case, imagine that your body has disappeared but your mind still exists. Do you still exist? Yes, all your thinking, memories, and personality still exist. In the other case, imagine that your mind has disappeared but your body still exists. Do you still exist? No, all your organs and bones and genes are there but there is no thought, memory, personality, or experience. Descartes's conclusion from this was that our minds and bodies are distinctly different substances and that our minds are our identities. This point may sound right at first, but it presents a problem.

Descartes describes minds as nonmaterial, unextended substances—that is, lacking the primary quality of matter and bodies, which is extension into space. When asked to imagine our minds existing without bodies, then, we are being asked to imagine minds that are not extended—no spatial location, no volume, no shape. But it is questionable as to whether we can actually do that. Typically, when people imagine disembodied minds they describe ghostly figures, or balls of energy, or floating above hospital beds looking down on their bodies. In fact, none of those ideas fits the bill. All of them imagine the mind as just another type of body. Translucent or levitating, those concepts of minds are still spatially extended.

In the second example, when Thomas Nagel argued that phenomenal consciousness cannot be explained by physicalism, he asked, What is it like to be a bat?[9] What would it be like, feel like, to echolocate? At first, we might imagine ourselves shrinking in size, flying around, and hearing odd clicks, but that is not what a bat experiences. That perception is just a human imagining shrinking, flying, and hearing odd clicks. We cannot actually imagine what it is like to be a bat. We cannot actually generate the phenomenal experience of echolocation or even generate the knowledge of what the phenomenal experience of echolocation would be—although at first we may think we can.

Both of these examples provide insight into how we can trick ourselves into thinking we are thinking something. On closer examination, we are often just transposing our current selves into an imagined new context using the same conceptual framework we already have. It is hard to resist this temptation. When thinking of what "I" might be like once "I" have radically changed, I am not taking seriously the concept of radical change. The entity that exists after the radical change cannot be me, by definition.

This is not to say that the posthuman entity will not understand me. It might. There may even be some sort of trace of the human in the posthuman. After all, the posthuman will not simply be nonhuman; it will be posthuman, not post-Uchjinian or post-Polarian.[10] Even in such a case, the continuity problem still exists. If the human trace is strong enough, then the entity will merely be superhuman. If the trace is not strong enough, then it will be posthuman. "Trace" can mean very little, after all. Humans might have an evolutionary trace of the reptile in us, for instance, but that would not justify a Carboniferous lizard anticipating becoming human.

Therein lies the problem with the posthuman approach. Radical changes will leave us behind. That poses no problem for the beings that will result, but it also provides no reason for humans to anticipate posthumanity as our future. This technological approach, then, seems not to be able to save *us* because the technology will eliminate *us*.

CONCLUSION

So this is the problem: transhumanism has a kind of soteriological plan in offering an escape from the human condition. Applying technology to many of the things that religions also point out as important elements of the human predicament—suffering, mortality, weakness, limitation, bad desire, and so forth (though sin and delusion might not be on the list for transhumanists)—could save us. However, saving ourselves by changing ourselves runs into a paradox involving human nature and identity. To the extent that we stay human throughout a technological change (trying to satisfy our desires), we are unlikely to *save* ourselves because we will retain a deep-seated human discontent. To the extent that we eliminate that problem by employing more radical technologies to produce more radical change, we will not save *us*, because we will cease being the individuals and even kind of beings that were motivated to transform in the first place.

So is this a sad conclusion? Does it bespeak a sense of pessimism for transhumanism and transformative technology? And is it a false dilemma? Could there be another option?

In some sense, the initial way of putting the problem may be a false dilemma because there are not two polar states resulting from technological modification—the superhuman and the posthuman. Instead, there is a continuum of technological change. Even so, that does not mean that there is an unbroken linear increase from the superhuman state to the posthuman state. Such an assumption would ignore two important points. First, certain technologies might create discrete jumps in cognition and power. Second, a posthuman form might assume a huge number of configurations. Presumably both seahorses and giraffes arose from some common ancestor, but they are not on a continuum—thus our use of evolutionary tree diagrams to show relationships rather than continuous lines. Even without discrete conditions, however, the problem persists. This is why the phrase "to the extent that" is an apt choice: I doubt becoming superhuman will make us completely happy because we will still want more. I doubt creating posthumans will make us happy because we will not be them. Of course, as briefly mentioned earlier, we could take a third option—make no other technological modifications to ourselves other than to eliminate desire and induce contentment. In such a case, we would be mortal but not fear death. We could get sick but lack desire for health. We could remain ignorant but without the desire to know that makes ignorance painful. That option would in a way save us from striving, grasping, and suffering. For reasons that deserve more attention, however, this seems to be the least desirable option for almost everyone.

In spite of all this, I do not think this chapter's conclusions are pessimistic. I am not staking out a position against technological augmentation. I think most of the goals on the transhumanist list are good and think it likely that increased health, willpower, lifespan, and knowledge will make lives better. Nor am I making any sort of assertion about the value of "being human," as though that is something to be held onto no matter what. There is no romanticism or even humanism here.

This argument is strictly a dispassionate one about psychology and identity—an issue I think is often confused in transhumanist and religious thought.[11] While some kinds of superhuman existence might be wonderful, I do not anticipate a full delivery from the human condition. While some kinds of posthuman beings might be wonderful additions to the universe and wish them the best, I cannot see how their existence counts as *me*. To be critical and honest, then, I must accept identity's cap on who and what I am.

NOTES

1. Patrick D. Hopkins, "Towards a Transhumanist Theology," *Global Spiral* 10, no. 10 (2010), http://www.metanexus.net/magazine/tabid/68/id/10990/Default.aspx.

2. Patrick D. Hopkins, "Transcending the Animal: How Transhumanism and Religion Are and Are Not Alike," *Journal of Evolution and Technology* 14, no. 2 (2005), http://www.jetpress.org/volume14/hopkins.html.

3. *Oxford English Dictionary Online*, s.v. "trans-, prefix," http://www.oed.com/view/Entry/204575?rskey=f0Is4V&result=3, accessed March 31, 2014.

4. *Oxford English Dictionary Online*, s.v. "super-, prefix," http://www.oed.com/view/Entry/194186?rskey=mBrelD&result=20&isAdvanced=false, accessed March 31, 2014.

5. *Oxford English Dictionary Online*, s.v. "post-, prefix," http://www.oed.com/view/Entry/148402?rskey=y2sxRK&result=22&isAdvanced=false, accessed March 31, 2014.

6. Nick Bostrom, "Transhumanist Values," 2005, http://www.nickbostrom.com/ethics/values.html; Lifeboat Foundation, "Top Ten Transhumanist Technologies," http://lifeboat.com/ex/transhumanist.technologies; Humanity+, "Transhumanist Declaration," 2009, http://humanityplus.org/philosophy/transhumanist-declaration/.

7. Thomas Hobbes, *Leviathan* (London, UK: Penguin Classics, 1985), Part I, chapter XIII.

8. See Rene Descartes, *Meditations on First Philosophy*, 6th Meditation, paragraph 78, and *Discourse on Method*, Part 4, paragraph 33.

9. Thomas Nagel, "What Is It Like to Be a Bat?" *Philosophical Review* 83, no. 4 (1974): 435–450.

10. Wayne Douglas Barlowe and Ian Summers, *Barlowe's Guide to Extraterrestrials* (New York, NY: Workman Publishing, 1979), 74, 108. These are extraterrestrial species from science fiction novels that are known for their particularly creative and unusual morphology and physiology, which is utterly unlike human or any known terrestrial creature. Uchjinians (from Jack Chalker, *Exiles at the Well of Souls*) are pliable smears of matter two meters long. Polarians (from Piers Anthony, *Cluster*) are teardrop-shaped creatures ending in a muscular socket that holds a biological wheel used for locomotion and procreation.

11. Patrick D. Hopkins, "Why Uploading Will Not Work, or, The Ghosts Haunting Transhumanism," *International Journal of Machine Consciousness* 4, no. 1 (2012): 229–243.

6

· ·

Diagnosing Death in the Transhumanism and Christian Traditions

Todd T. W. Daly

This chapter provides a Christian examination of the transhumanist goal of defeating death from a Christian perspective. On the surface, both Christian and transhuman perspectives of death converge at points. For instance, both speak of death as the final enemy and look toward its eventual defeat. Nevertheless, these shared claims arise from different conceptions of death that become more intelligible when interpreted within their particular narratives of redemption. After exploring the meanings of death within a transhumanist context, I will articulate a Christian interpretation of death with particular reference to the doctrines of bodily resurrection and original sin. I will argue that the transhumanist project of defeating death attests to the reality of human fallenness. Moreover, drawing on Dietrich Bonhoeffer's analysis of the Fall, I suggest that the aspiration to overcome death through technology is sinful if sin is understood as striving to become *sicut deus*, "like God." Finally, I conclude that because transhumanism has misdiagnosed death by failing to account for this moral component, its technological quest to defeat death is destined to fail.

KILLING DEATH

Once upon a time, death ruled over humanity with an iron fist. In his "The Fable of the Dragon Tyrant," Nick Bostrom depicts death as a foul-smelling immortal monster covered in thick, black, impenetrable scales. A perpetual ooze flows from this creature's mouth, and its eyes are red with hate.[1] The great and terrible dragon had a voracious appetite for human flesh, demanding a daily tribute of 10,000 people. To facilitate the process, the king developed a rail system to transport the victims—usually older people who had experienced relatively long lives—in windowless boxcars to the mountain where the dragon lived. But over time death's appetite merely increased, and with it the dragon's required daily tribute, leading to a new groundswell of anti-dragon sentiment and threatening the king's approval ratings.

Nevertheless, the king was determined to meet the dragon's increased demand and was convinced by a cadre of moralists and dragonologists who, respectively, pointed out the blessings of finitude and confirmed that the dragon's scales were indeed impenetrable. Moreover, administrators made the king's decision easier with their improved logistics, which made providing the daily tribute of human lives more manageable and efficient than ever before. Yet, in an effort to assuage the growing discontent among his people, the king decided to hold a public meeting to discuss a recent petition put forward by the anti-dragonologists, who argued that the kingdom's resources should fund a 10- to 15-year scientific project to develop a missile that could penetrate the dragon's armor, killing it once and for all. After the presentation, the king's moralists, dragonologists, and administrators proceeded to utter their normal platitudes until they were interrupted by a small boy, whose grandmother had been shuttled away on the train of death before they could make gingerbread houses together. In a fit of righteous indignation he exclaimed, "The dragon is bad ... I want my Granny back!" The raw pain and honesty of the child's testimony exposed the empty rhetoric and defeatist attitude of the king's men. With this one moral outburst, the king's heart had been changed; the anti-dragonologists' arguments suddenly made sense. The reason and the humanity behind their plan to kill the dragon and put an end to death had burst through his fog of suspicion and doom like a bright ray of sunshine.

The project of defeating the dragon was indeed ambitious, but with the king's support, all available resources were marshaled to develop an armor-piercing missile. The first few years of round-the-clock activity were fraught with failure, miscalculations, and mishaps. Several test projectiles failed to hit their targets. One even hit a hospital, killing hundreds of patients. But a decade of unceasing scientific effort finally paid off, when at last the anti-dragonologists had created a missile that just might kill the awful dragon. The people were prepared to strike at the heart of death.

On one promising evening, the hopes and fears of humanity were invested in a single technological projectile of their own making, lighting up the night sky as it made its way toward the dragon's mountain. With breathless expectancy, humanity stood on the precipice of a new era, the crowning moment of human achievement for *Homo faber*, who by killing death would conquer the ultimate limitation to life. The people erupted with jubilation as the missile did its work. The king, however, expressed remorse over the inestimable loss of human life due to his own foolish hesitation to embrace the anti-dragonologists' doctrine. But there was little time for either celebration or remorse, for now that the dragon had been slain, society would need to forge ahead in meeting the innumerable challenges that come with an unlimited future. Although humanity had been conditioned and deformed by the menacing dragon, its absence uncovered a "frightening void" that must be filled with creative activity that would enable (post?)humanity to truly flourish.

In Bostrom's account, death itself is killed, which comes as a shocking claim, even for a fable. Even Christian scriptures, which occasionally personify death as a tyrant, do not point to death's annihilation, but rather speak of death (and Hades) being thrown into the lake of fire (Revelation 20:14). Domesticating death appears much closer to what transhumanists want. Max More, for instance, looks to the day when we will no longer be forced to "tolerate the tyranny of aging and death," when technology will enable us each to "decide for ourselves how long we shall live."[2] Technologist Ray Kurzweil also envisions the day when "our mortality will be in our own hands."[3] This desired outcome is not killing death, but rather bringing it within the realm of human choice. Natasha Vita-More expresses precisely this sentiment in imagining an "optional and temporary death," where one might decide to end existence in one platform for some period of time with the option of continuing on in the future in a different medium.[4] Although it is not clear what she means by "platform" or "medium," she envisions putting off or rescheduling death as easily we would an appointment with the dentist.

Transhumanists generally aim at choice rather than the annihilation of death. Bostrom himself concedes this point. The transhumanist position on death, he says, "is clear and simple: death should ideally be voluntary."[5] Bostrom is basically making a moral argument challenging attitudes inimical to the technological conquest of death and the social structures instantiated by them. As such, stories are generally more effective than bare propositions in conveying the way things are or ought to be, insofar as they can arrest uncritical lines of thinking and arouse moral outrage.

DEATH IN TRANSHUMANISM

Why do transhumanists view death as the final enemy? A brief overview of the transhumanists' meta-narrative of salvation helps to make sense of their view of death. Transhumanism places a high value on challenging humanity's limitations—biological, intellectual, and psychological—by expanding human capacities through new technologies. This emphasis on overcoming human limitation is grounded in the twin values of individual freedom and individual choice.[6] The extremely high value transhumanists place on overcoming human limitation as a way of expressing individual freedom and choice helps one see why death is such an affront. Death is bad because it marks the boundary of existence, and thereby forecloses the possibility of future development and growth through new experiences. Death represents an absolute limit to human freedom. As such, observes John Gray, "death is a provocation ... because it marks the boundary beyond which the will cannot go."[7] Because death currently marks the permanent cessation of the individual, it is *the* primary threat to human freedom and autonomy, for "it is only when mortality has been vanquished that we can be truly free."[8]

For transhumanists, the cause of death is the human body itself. It is our biological limitations that make life tragic, says the transhumanist Simon Young.[9] Hope for long-term survival might come through uploading information in the brain to a more reliable medium. In other words, transhumanists want to develop technology to *separate* what nature has put *together*. Young finds it an "outrage" that the mind should die with a body that is programmed to self-destruct.[10] The more immediate goal is to live longer through technologies such as genetic engineering, robotics, and nanotechnology. Our fate, then, lies in the hands of neither God nor Darwin, but solely in ourselves.[11]

This posthuman *ideal* of having complete control over the shape of one's own temporality—however muddled and ontically shallow—fuels the transhumanists' moral outrage, so much so that they routinely invoke religious language. But their hatred of death is also rooted in the existential realities of the human condition. "Death is, to me, an obscenity," says Simon Young, when reflecting on the death of his cancer-ridden father.[12] Similar sentiments bleed through in Bostrom's tale when he refers to waging war against the dragon tyrant as "striking at the heart of evil."[13] One is left wondering whether his description of the daily shipment of human flesh in windowless railway cars to the dragon's mountain is not a thinly veiled allusion to the countless Jews who were similarly transported to concentration camps. If so, Bostrom is shrewdly drawing upon the moral currency of the Holocaust. Either way, Bostrom insists that improving the human condition by battling aging and death is not just a nice idea, but "an urgent, screaming moral imperative."[14]

Transhumanists consider death to be the greatest enemy because it is antithetical to the central values of transhumanism. These values of individual freedom and choice, and overcoming limits, draw upon a transhumanist meta-narrative of deliverance that is invested in a future in which salvation is idealized as an open horizon for new modes of being and becoming, freed from biological limits. There is nothing sacred in our biological nature that commands respect for its inherent limits. Moreover, from an evolutionary perspective, it is difficult to provide a meaningful argument for resisting death given that we are little more than finite transport vehicles useful for passing along our genes (e.g., Tom Kirkwood's "disposable soma" theory).[15] For transhumanists, however, death is both natural and evil.

The determination that death is the greatest evil is a value judgment. More than two decades ago, Mary Midgley observed how narratives of technological deliverance invite us to see the world as something to be conquered, glorifying *Homo sapiens* as "the sole center of value in the universe" on account of our scientifically informed intellect.[16] But this stance comes at the expense of reverence, awe, and sympathy for the natural world, and it engenders an attitude of hostility toward the things about which we are enquiring, tempting us to depict the objects of our scientific inquiry as "enemies to be conquered or as brute objects ranged over and against us—as aliens, monsters, as victims."[17] Little wonder, then, that Bostrom chose to represent death itself as a dragon tyrant. His fable underscores the perception of death as an enemy to be defeated, yet Bostrom's tale also suggests that humans remain death-defined animals.[18]

DEATH IN THE CHRISTIAN TRADITION

As stated in the introduction to this chapter, both Christians and transhumanists describe death as an enemy. Both consider death an affront to human existence. Both lament the loss of loved ones, who through death are cut off from the community of the living. Christians and transhumanists share in the moral outrage over the unnecessary loss of life, whether through accidents, disease, or natural disasters. There is a palpable sense that things are not quite the way they are supposed to be. Christians and transhumanists both long for a better kind of existence where death, sickness, and disease will be truly vanquished. There is a shared a sense of disgust over the phenomenon of death. Beyond this shared moral outrage, however, lie divergent understandings of death and its defeat.

Death Defeated

Christianity adopts a more prosaic stance toward death that is guided by the narrative of the redemption and reconciliation of humankind through God's activity in Jesus Christ. Christianity proclaims Christ's victory over sin and death in his bodily resurrection and ascension. Death has been defeated (1 Corinthians 15). This does not mean an escape from the death that comes from being embodied, finite creatures; rather, Christians look toward their own bodily resurrection from the dead, which has been secured by Christ's own mortality. Death has been relativized through the resurrection. In light of its reality St. Paul could boldly proclaim, "to live is Christ, and to die is gain."[19] Moreover, the communal practices of Baptism and the Eucharist attest to Christ's death and resurrection. Baptism speaks of our dying and rising with Christ, while in the Eucharist Christ's death is proclaimed until Christ returns.

Any proclamation of death must appear defeatist from a transhumanist perspective. However, this final victory over death does not mean that Christians give up battling the diseases and disorders that threaten to cut earthly life short. The prolongation of life is desirable.[20] Indeed, part of Christ's ministry on earth involved healing the sick, and even raising the dead (Luke 7:14–15; John 11:43–44). Yet, Christians recognize that while all temporal victories over death through medicine and technology should be celebrated, they are merely a foreshadowing of the resurrection to come.

If death has been relativized by Christ's victory over death, it is also deepened by virtue of its link with sin. As Vladimir Lossky observes, Christ did not come to kill death, but rather "to make death harmless and sin curable by submission of God Himself to death ... the death of Christ removes, from between man and God, the obstacle of sin; and His Resurrection takes from death its 'sting.' "[21] A Christian understanding of death must account for this moral dimension of death, which brings us to the doctrine of original sin.

Original Sin

Western Christianity has often drawn a connection between sin and death, which "runs like a spine through Scripture and the Christian tradition."[22] Since at least the time of St. Augustine (ca. 354–430), both Protestant and Roman Catholic creeds have implicated sin as the cause of death. Moreover, sin has affected the entire human race, leaving humanity in a state of moral corruption and subject to guilt.[23] This doctrine, known as original sin, speaks of both the source of sin—derived from the account of the fall of Adam and Eve in Genesis 3—and the consequences of this sin. Traditional biblical interpretations conclude that when Adam and Eve disobeyed God by eating from the forbidden tree of the knowledge of good and evil, they brought God's promised curse of death on both themselves and the rest of humankind.

As Alistair McFayden observes, the doctrine of original sin carries four cardinal, interrelated corollaries: that this sin is contingent, radical, communicable, and universal.[24] Sin's contingency refers to the freedom Adam and Eve enjoyed in the garden before they sinned. That is, sin was neither inevitable nor an aspect of human nature.[25] The radical nature of original sin means that sin describes the *condition* to which human individuals and humanity as a whole are subject; sin is not just momentary or episodic, but rather "subsists and endures as a distortion of our fundamental ways of being in the world."[26] Sin is also communicable in that it is somehow communicated to us "pre-personally," before humans become morally culpable for personal acts. Finally, this condition is universal; it is impossible for anyone *not* to sin. The doctrine of original sin speaks not only of the initiating sin of Adam and Eve, but also of the sin of humanity as a whole.[27]

McFayden's discussion of the cardinal corollaries of original sin is instructive. Considering the effects of the Fall as articulated by Dietrich Bonhoeffer will next provide some helpful concepts that can be used to further diagnose the transhumanist understanding of death and draw some conclusions regarding their goal to defeat it.

A Theological Account of the Fall

In *Creation and Fall*, Dietrich Bonhoeffer (d. 1945) provides a theological interpretation of the events recorded in the first three chapters of Genesis. He sought to translate the symbolic language of that "magical world" into "the new picture language of the technical world" so as to demonstrate the significance of the creation accounts to contemporary humanity.[28] In these opening narratives, Bonhoeffer traces the fall of humanity from being created in God's image (*imago Dei*) to a state of death, identified as being "like God," *sicut deus*. While these opening narratives depict the life of Adam and Eve symbolically, they also attest to the human condition, shedding light on what humanity has become through sin and how death now shapes human existence. As such, Bonhoeffer's analysis of the Fall addresses not just the earliest stages of human history, but also the human condition. In doing so, it provides an interpretive lens through which to view the transhumanist understanding of death.

Adam and Eve as *Imago Dei*: Free, Finite, Embodied

Bonhoeffer departs from traditional interpretations of the *imago Dei* by defining it in terms of freedom, which he understands as a relational concept. Freedom does not mean an absence of constraints; on the contrary, to be free means "being free for." Human freedom is an image of divine freedom, expressed most fully in God's freedom in the person of Jesus Christ, who freely offered himself to God on behalf of humanity.[29] This freedom is, paradoxically, a self-limiting freedom, which is grounded in God's very being. In the same way, the human creature is free insofar as he or she is free for another human being, for human creatureliness actually consists of dependence on the Other, says Bonhoeffer.[30] Creaturely freedom in the *imago Dei*, then, is most fully expressed when the human exists for God and the Other. Apart from sin, the limits placed on an individual by God and other human creatures are received as a gift of God's grace. Creaturely freedom in the *imago Dei* expresses itself as freedom for God and the other person.[31]

In the second creation account (Genesis 2:4b–3:24) Bonhoeffer frames the relationship between God and humanity in the context of the two trees at the garden's center. The tree of life means that humanity derives life from God. The center of human existence is not derived from the creature, but from God. In Adam's original state of innocence and freedom, notes Bonhoeffer, there was no need to issue a command concerning this tree. This was not the case, however, for the tree of the knowledge of good and evil. Attached to this tree was a prohibition, and with it the threat of death: "for in the day you eat of it you shall die" (Genesis 2:17b). Yet even here, Bonhoeffer notes that this prohibition affirms the reality of Adam's freedom as freedom with limits. Knowledge of this tree at the center "means knowing that the whole of existence, human existence in every possible way that it may comport itself, has its limit."[32] At the same time, the tree of knowledge is the tree of death, although this prohibition with the threat of death could be understood only "as a renewed gift, as the grace of God," for Adam and Eve had no knowledge of good and evil.[33] According to Bonhoeffer, these two trees at the Garden's center tell us that God is both the boundary and the center of human existence.[34] Human beings were created as free creatures for God and one another.

Finally, Bonhoeffer stresses the goodness of embodiment as a core feature of human existence as originally intended by God. Indeed, drawing upon Sirach 40:1, which speaks of the earth as the mother of all living things, he describes the earth as the very womb from which God has fashioned us.[35] The body is not a prison for the soul, much less a shell or some exterior, but rather belongs to the essence of the human creature. That is, human creatures bear the image of God in their bodily nature.[36] That God breathed his spirit into Adam's nostrils signifies once again that human life comes from, and is sustained by, God. Yet, humans remain fully human in God's sustaining activity; upheld by God's spirit, there is no mixture of the divine.[37] Bonhoeffer insists, that "in my whole being, in my creatureliness, I belong wholly to this world; it bears me, nurtures me, holds me."[38] Being created in God's image means that human beings are meant to draw life from God, who is the boundary and source of existence, exercising our creaturely freedom to be for God and one another, as finite, embodied beings. But this kind of existence would come to an end when humanity disobeyed God's command concerning the tree of knowledge, bringing the promised death in its wake.

The Fall and Its Consequences

It is impossible to know how Adam and Eve, having been created in God's image, could have been led astray. Although their decision to reject God's prohibition was certainly aided by the serpent's pious questions and partial truths, it remains inexplicable and inexcusable. In entertaining the serpent's question—"Did God say ... ?"—humanity effectively subjected God's word to its own judgment. Adam and Eve were prepared to accept the serpent's claim that this tree offered the promise of limitlessness, of being like God.[39] In its pursuit of a higher form of existence that belonged to God alone, humanity sinned against God by eating from the forbidden tree, ushering in the death that would disrupt and distort the nature of human existence to this day. In opting for the tree of knowledge, humanity *imago Dei* became humanity *sicut deus*.

Humanity: From *Imago Dei* to *Sicut Deus*

In describing the effects of the Fall, Bonhoeffer seizes upon the serpent's promise that Adam and Eve will become "like God," *sicut deus* (Genesis 3:5), a state that he distinguishes sharply from *imago Dei*. Bonhoeffer takes the serpent's claim with the utmost seriousness in asserting that Adam and Eve have genuinely become *sicut deus*. Thus the Fall is not a mere modification or deterioration of human creatureliness, but rather abolishment: "the fall *really* makes the creature—humankind in the imago dei—into a creator-sicut-deus."[40] But to be like God, says Bonhoeffer, is to exist in a state of death, to be dead while still living.[41] This death has nothing to do with the finitude that comes from being embodied creatures formed out of earth, but rather speaks to a new state of existence *within* creaturely finitude.[42] Being in a state of death, humanity *sicut deus* manifests itself in several ways, all of which constitute a radical break from humanity *imago Dei*. Bonhoeffer distinguishes these two states in a pithy sentence:

> Imago dei—humankind in the image of God being for God and the neighbor, in its original creatureliness and limitedness; sicut deus—humankind like God in knowing out of its own self about good and evil, in having no limit and acting out of its own resources, in its aseity [underived being], in its being alone.[43]

This statement requires unpacking to grasp more fully the Fall.

First, as the serpent promised, Adam and Eve's eyes have indeed been opened; having gained knowledge, they have become like God, knowing good and evil. Here Bonhoeffer notes that good and evil are more than moral concepts, but also involve pleasure and pain, expressing the deepest possible divide in human life. Yet, having attained the knowledge of good and evil, they are now "split apart within themselves [*im Zweispalt*]," disrupting their relationship to God, to each other, and to creation itself.[44] God is no longer recognized as the source of life. Similarly, the limit placed upon the creature by the presence of the other person, who was to make the bearing of creaturely limits possible, is also rejected.[45] The creaturely freedom that existed within the limits graciously established by God can now only be seen as threats for humanity *sicut deus*. The ultimate threat is the new knowledge that human existence must end in death. In fact, the core feature of humanity *sicut deus* is a rejection of the limits that come with being a human creature before God.

In this fallen state, humanity rejects its own creatureliness, its own dependency on God and others. As Bonhoeffer observes, being *sicut deus* "includes *precisely* its not wanting to be a creature."[46] Having rejected his creatureliness, Adam is incapable of receiving life from God, who is both the center and the boundary of human existence, because Adam himself now occupies that center, living out of his own resources and his own knowledge of good and evil.[47] Life can no longer be graciously received, but instead takes the form of a command. Moreover, now that Adam has gained the knowledge that he must die, he is plagued with an unquenchable thirst for life. "Adam's obsessive desire for life is boundless; an indescribable thirst for life seizes hold of Adam in the state of death that being sicut deus constitutes."[48] Adam now *must* live. Yet, having become his own god, Adam despairs because he must secure life out of his own resources, out of his own isolation. When Adam seeks God in this state of sin—that is, when Adam seeks life—Adam seeks only himself.[49]

Only at this point has the tree of knowledge become a threat to the tree of life. Moreover, now that Adam-*sicut-deus* refuses to recognize any such limit, he is banished from the garden and the tree of life at its center, its entry guarded by the sword-waving sentinels of death (Genesis 3:22–24).[50] Having been expelled from the source of life, Bonhoeffer asserts, Adam's existence outside the gate "is a constant attack on the kingdom from which he is shut out ... a desperate raging again and again against the sentinels who keep watch."[51] The more desperately Adam seeks life, notes Bonhoeffer, the more fully he is entangled by death. But God's pronouncements to Adam and Eve (Genesis 3:14–19) contain both a blessing and a curse. Although humanity now lives in a cursed world, unable to live with God, one another, and nature, Bonhoeffer points out that it is *God's* curse. As such, the world is not wholly forsaken, but is blessed in its enmity, pain, and work; it remains a world where life is upheld and preserved by God.[52] More significantly, God's pronouncement that the serpent's head would be crushed (Genesis 3:15) points toward God becoming incarnate in Jesus Christ: "Imago dei, sicut deus, agnus dei [Lamb of God]."[53] For Christ, who is fully human and fully divine, was sacrificed for humanity, slaying false divinity in humankind *sicut deus* and restoring the *imago Dei*.[54] In the meantime, life is marked by struggle and temptation, because the serpent still bites at our heels by offering false visions of immortality.

CONCLUSION

The Genesis account of the fall, Bonhoeffer reminds us, is our story. The doctrine of original sin bespeaks the perennial temptation to live out of the center of our own existence, grasping at the tree of life through our own resources, denying our creaturely nature. We try to avoid death and secure a kind of immortality through our pursuits, our projects, and even our progeny. Transhumanism can be seen as the latest attempt to mitigate creaturely limits through technology. Nevertheless, Bonhoeffer's articulation of sin and the Fall suggests that the transhumanist project of defeating death not only stems from some ideal of a deathless existence wedded to an unbridled optimism in technology and human power, but also is fundamentally rooted in our fallenness as humanity *sicut deus*. That is, humanity *sicut deus* names a particular way of being in the world that describes the transhumanist project.

In fact, Bostrom's story of the dragon tyrant might be construed as one particular example of a project dear to the heart of humanity *sicut deus*. Insofar as this fable depicts humankind as living solely out of its own resources in an attempt to defeat death, it hints at humanity living *sicut deus*. Insofar as battling death becomes "an urgent, screaming, moral imperative," it bespeaks humanity *sicut deus* with its constant attack against the sentinels of death guarding the tree of life.[55] Insofar as those who oppose the dragon-killing project are perceived as a threat to longer life, rather than as fellow creatures who might ease the burdens of limited, creaturely existence, it bears witness to humanity *sicut deus*. Insofar as the project of killing death is conducted apart from a recognition of God as the source and sustainer of life, transmuting life from a gift to a command, it reflects humanity *sicut deus*. Ultimately, insofar as transhumanism is a manifestation of humanity *sicut deus*, it exposes sin as the root cause of the quest to defeat death through technology.

Both Christians and transhumanists view death as the enemy. Yet, Christians recognize an intrinsic moral dimension to death by linking it to sin, a dimension that transhumanists ultimately fail to recognize. Transhumanists simply do not have this language at their disposal. Indeed, such terminology is explicitly rejected. Any challenge to the power of the naked will over against the human body is dismissed on the grounds that it succumbs to the "biological fatalism" of original sin.[56] Indeed, if there is a notion of sin in transhumanism, it is a failure to live up to the ideal of progress understood as technological mastery over our destiny. In the face of such progress, this transgression manifests itself as sloth, inactivity, or defeatism.[57] Nevertheless, without recourse to the language of sin and the Fall, transhumanists can only see death as a condition to be treated through technology, rather than as a condition that has been taken up and defeated in Jesus Christ. By rejecting this moral dimension of death, transhumanists have misdiagnosed the death that comes from being material creatures as the ultimate enemy, rather than the death whose sting is sin. Moreover, the Christian confession of death defeated in Christ suggests that any project that does not account for the moral dimension of death is destined to fail, for it has not addressed the sin that animates death and gives it its power. Although transhumanists may push back the boundaries of death through technology, they will have done nothing to address their *state* of death as humanity *sicut deus*. Transhumanists, of course, have no reason to conform their undertakings to the Christian drama of redemption. On the contrary, they occasionally invoke the language of one day becoming like God—*sicut deus*—through technology. The irony, as Bonhoeffer would see it, is that they already have.

NOTES

1. Nick Bostrom, "The Fable of the Dragon Tyrant," *Journal of Medical Ethics* 31 (2005): 273–277.

2. Max More, "A Letter to Human Nature," in *The Transhumanist Reader: Classical and Contemporary Essays on the Science, Technology, and Philosophy of the Human Future*, edited by Max More and Natasha Vita-More (Oxford, UK: Wiley-Blackwell, 2013), 450.

3. Ray Kurzweil, *The Singularity Is Near* (New York, NY: Viking Press, 2005), 9.

4. Natasha Vita-More, "Bringing Arts/Design into the Discussion of Transhumanism," in *H±: Transhumanism and Its Critics*, edited by Gregory Hansell and William Grassie (Philadelphia, PA: Metanexus, 2011), 77.

5. Nick Bostrom, "Transhumanist Values," 8, http://www.nickbostrom.com/tra/values.html, accessed March 4, 2014. This includes, it should be noted, euthanasia.

6. Bostrom, "Transhumanist Values," 2, 5.

7. John Gray, *The Immortalization Commission: Science and the Strange Quest to Cheat Death* (New York, NY: Farrar, Straus and Giroux), 205.

8. Brent Waters, *From Human to Posthuman: Christian Theology and Technology in a Postmodern World* (Hampshire, UK: Ashgate, 2006), 74.

9. Simon Young, *Designer Evolution: A Transhumanist Manifesto* (New York, NY: Prometheus Books, 2006), 15.

10. Young, *Designer Evolution*, 15.

11. Braden Allenby and Daniel Sarewitz, *The Techno-Human Condition* (Cambridge, MA: MIT Press, 2011), 19.

12. Young, *Designer Evolution*, 15.

13. Bostrom, "The Fable," 276.

14. Bostrom, "The Fable," 277; Young, *Designer Evolution*, 41.

15. Tom Kirkwood, *Time of Our Lives: The Science of Human Aging* (Oxford, UK: Oxford University Press, 1999), ch. 6.

16. Mary Midgley, *Science as Salvation: A Modern Myth and Its Meaning* (London, UK: Routledge, 1992), 73.

17. Midgley, *Science as Salvation*, 74.

18. Gray, *Immortalization Commission*, 235.

19. Philippians 2:21, New Revised Standard Version.

20. See, for instance, Gilbert Meilaender, *Should We Live Forever? The Ethical Ambiguities of Aging* (Grand Rapids, MI: W. B. Eerdmans, 2013); Todd T. W. Daly, "Chasing Methuselah: Transhumanism and *Theosis* in Critical Perspective," in *Transhumanism and Transcendence: Christian Hope in an Age of Technological Enhancement*, edited by Ronald Cole-Turner (Washington, DC: Georgetown University Press, 2011), 131–144.

21. Vladimir Lossky, *Orthodox Theology: An Introduction*, translated by Ian Kesarcodi-Watson and Ihita Kesarcodi-Watson (Crestwood, NY: St. Vladimir's Seminary Press, 2001), 92.

22. Cornelius Plantinga, Jr., *Not the Way It's Supposed to Be: A Breviary of Sin* (Grand Rapids, MI: W. B. Eerdmans, 1995), 47.

23. Augustine held that all are guilty on account of Adam's sin because the entire human race was seminally present in Adam. This biological construal of guilt has been rightly rejected. Others softened the link between Adam and humanity by asserting that individuals share in Adam's corruption, but are guilty only for their own sins. Nevertheless, construing spread of corruption along biological lines is deeply problematic. Friedrich Schleiermacher (ca. 1768–1834) was the first to interpret this aspect of

original sin in social terms—that is, we are all one agent of sin who somehow sin with Adam.

24. Alistair McFayden, *Bound to Sin: Abuse, Holocaust, and the Christian Doctrine of Sin* (Cambridge, UK: Cambridge University Press, 2000), 16.

25. McFayden, *Bound to Sin*, 17.

26. McFayden, *Bound to Sin*, 17.

27. The nature of this unity has been construed along biological, social, and existential lines. As mentioned in note 23, the biological interpretation is deeply problematic in that it identifies human materiality itself as sinful. It is helpful to remember that while Paul draws a connection between Adam and the rest of humanity (Romans 5:12–21), he does not discuss the nature of this connection.

28. Dietrich Bonhoeffer, *Creation and Fall: A Theological Exposition of Genesis 1–3*, translated by Douglas Stephen Bax, edited by John W. DeGruchy (Minneapolis, MN: Fortress Press, 1997), 83.

29. Bonhoeffer, *Creation and Fall*, 63.

30. Bonhoeffer, *Creation and Fall*, 64. Bonhoeffer further qualifies this by defining human creatureliness as "human beings over-against-one-another, with-one-another, and in-dependence-upon-one-another."

31. Bonhoeffer, *Creation and Fall*, 67.

32. Bonhoeffer, *Creation and Fall*, 86.

33. Bonhoeffer, *Creation and Fall*, 87.

34. Bonhoeffer, *Creation and Fall*, 86.

35. Bonhoeffer, *Creation and Fall*, 77, 78.

36. Bonhoeffer, *Creation and Fall*, 79.

37. The spirit of God here should not be confused with the Holy Spirit, the third person of the Trinity.

38. Bonhoeffer, *Creation and Fall*, 66.

39. Bonhoeffer, *Creation and Fall*, 113.

40. Bonhoeffer, *Creation and Fall*, 116.

41. Indeed, Bonhoeffer says that "by eating the fruit of the tree of knowledge Adam as a human-being-sicut-deus has ingested [hineingegessen] death into himself." *Creation and Fall*, 135.

42. Bonhoeffer, *Creation and Fall*, 90.

43. Bonhoeffer, *Creation and Fall*, 113.

44. Bonhoeffer, *Creation and Fall*, 89.

45. Bonhoeffer, *Creation and Fall*, 99.

46. Bonhoeffer, *Creation and Fall*, 116.

47. Bonhoeffer, *Creation and Fall*, 90–91 (italics his).

48. Bonhoeffer, *Creation and Fall*, 142.

49. Bonhoeffer, *Creation and Fall*, 143.

50. Bonhoeffer, *Creation and Fall*, 142.

51. Bonhoeffer, *Creation and Fall*, 144.

52. Bonhoeffer, *Creation and Fall*, 135.

53. Bonhoeffer, *Creation and Fall*, 113.

54. Bonhoeffer, *Creation and Fall*, 113.

55. Bostrom, "The Fable," 277; Bonhoeffer, *Creation and Fall*, 144.

56. Young, *Designer Evolution*, 70. Young appears to be critiquing older expressions of this doctrine that have since been widely rejected by theologians, where the spread of sin was construed biologically, through procreation.

57. Insofar as transhumanism might be characterized as a movement driven by the white male sin of pride and will-to-power, it attests to the fallen condition of Adam *sicut deus* as embodying a particular expression of this male power.

7

··

Cyborg, Sage, and Saint: Transhumanism as Seen from an East Asian Theological Setting

Heup Young Kim

A MOST DANGEROUS IDEA FOR EAST ASIA

My first response as an East Asian theologian to the "transhumanism" movement[1] was to regard it as one of "the most dangerous ideas" that the West has ever produced.[2] This alarmed reaction to this enthralling but controversial movement was based on my experiences in the Korean and East Asian situations. A nation like Korea could once again easily turn into a laboratory and testing ground, as it did in the notorious case of the human embryonic stem cell research performed by Dr. Hwang Woo-suk.[3] This embarrassing case involved not only the conduct of a team of infamous scientists in Korea, but also complex issues associated with the evolution of an East Asian country into a developed nation with respect to new technologies, potential markets, economic profits, global competition, national interests, and so on. In this context, scientists and government administrators can be tempted and pressured to promote cutting-edge science and technology by doing something sensational. In this respect, even Japan, the most developed country in Asia, has fallen to this temptation, as evidenced by controversies around stem cell research; in particular, note the recent STAP (stimulus-triggered acquisition of pluripotency) case related to the young rising Japanese star scientist, Haruko Obokata.[4]

Amidst the pressures to succeed and produce advancements in science and technology, questions of ethics are not very popular. For some laboratory scientists and policymakers in government and industry, with the strong support of zealous nationalists, ethics reviews are seen as picky, uncooperative, hindering, and impracticable backbiting. Further, many have become aware that dominant global standards (as influenced by the Judeo-Christian tradition) are neither neutral nor innocent, but rather have significant politico-economic implications, mostly for the benefit of powerful nations in the West.[5] Furthermore, traditional, sophisticated neo-Confucian moral systems have been compromised by the demand for national survival and development in this competitive world. For some, this has left science and technology enthroned with a pseudo-divine status in East Asia. The rivalry in the global market, particularly among neighboring countries, justifies aggressive research programs: "If we don't do this now, other countries will do it anyway!" Moreover, newly acquired luxuries and pleasures from capitalism reinforce the legitimacy of this drive.

The West has as its religio-cultural foundation the Judeo-Christian tradition, which continues to maintain its role as an ethical filter for challenges from science and technology. Although its effectiveness is arguable, from the eyes of an East Asian theologian, this tradition still seems to be able to provide a framework for social discussion and ethical scrutiny of new technologies. For example, the U.S. President's Council on Bioethics summarized the arguments against transhumanism as follows: "appreciation of and respect for 'the naturally given,' threatened by hubris; the dignity of human activity, threatened by 'unnatural' means; the preservation of identity, threatened by efforts at self-transformation; and full human flourishing, threatened by spurious or shallow substitute."[6] Unfortunately, it is difficult to find even this level of discussion in East Asia. Moreover, a sturdy historical and emotional counter-Orientalism within East Asian culture underlies the self-induced pressure on East Asians to advance into technological research. East Asian intellectuals resent the errors their ancestors made because of their idealistic Confucian virtue ethics. In their view, their forebears, by insisting too much on enlightened personhood combined with ethical systems too complicated to be practical, lost critical momentum, enabling uncivilized nomadic Europeans to overtake East Asia. They allowed the Europeans to take advantage of the very technologies that they had developed but had been hesitant to use extensively. This hesitancy was due to fear of causing harm to the benevolence (*ren*) of humanity, a primal virtue of Confucianism.

A NAÏVE, ULTRA-RIGHT IDEOLOGY FROM THE WEST

As I looked further into transhumanism, I came to realize that transhumanism is a naïve, ultra-right ideology arising from the Judeo-Christian and Enlightenment traditions. It is naïve because transhumanists with overconfidence in their techno-capabilities recognize neither the reality of the global world in which they are living nor the complexities of human history and nature itself.

Like the theory of evolution, "transhumanism has emerged from a culture shaped by Christianity."[7] Transhumanism looks like a techno-secularization of the Judeo-Christian vision. For example, its idea of antiaging enhancement (radical life extension) toward immortality is reminiscent of Adam and Eve in the original creation, and the transhumanist vision of a post-Singularity society sounds like a technocized Christian eschatology of the new heaven and the new earth where there will be "no more death or mourning or crying or pain" (Revelation 21:4). James Hughes, a former executive director of the World Transhumanist Association, has said, "Most Singularitarians are like a pre-millennialist Christians. . . . The unbelievers not prepared to take advantage of the TechnoRapture and be born again into new eternal bodies are likely to suffer the Tribulations of being impoverished, wiped out or enslaved."[8] As Ronald Cole-Turner has said, there are considerable similarities between the goals of transhumanism and the biblical visions.[9] Acknowledging those similarities, theologians in the West have been endeavoring to clarify the differences between Christianity and transhumanism. However, the hermeneutical horizons those theologians employ to make comparisons seem to be limited to the context of the European West.

Even in the intellectual history of the West, it would be illuminating to take a wider view, addressing, in particular, the relationship between transhumanism and communism. If Karl Marx's communism represents a social secularization of the Christian millenarian vision, then transhumanism represents a techno-scientific secularization of the Christian millenarian vision. These two movements resemble each other in that both are secularized children of Christianity in light of Christian eschatology, the biblical vision of original human nature, the first Christian community, and the strong liberation motive for transformative praxis. Both argue and crusade for transformation, albeit through different means—the former through global, social class struggle, and the latter through cosmic, technological transformation. Both prophesy a Singularity (a moment of apocalyptic change in human history)—the former to be realized by communist or socialist society (egalitarian utopia), and the latter by transhuman or posthuman evolution (cybernetic techno-utopia).

There are clear distinctions between communism and transhumanism. The former aims at a change of the social superstructure in and through class struggle, whereas the latter focuses on the transformation of the fragile and inferior human body and brain (bio-fatalism) by means of radical technological enhancements. In an odd but dramatic way, however, transhumanism and communism are united in continuing the legacy of dualism in the history of Western thought—namely, the divide between form and content or nature and nurture. While the latter focuses on the change of society, the former emphasizes the transformation of human nature. Each proudly proclaims itself as a rightful descendent of the Enlightenment. However, in the West's dualistic framework, communism and transhumanism represent the extreme left and extreme right wings of modern ideology.

A point already mentioned in reference to the East Asian setting needs to be repeated at this juncture. The European West, as the birthplace of both communism and transhumanism, seems to be capable of providing an ethical filter and has the societal power to put radical movements and ideologies, no matter how nominal, under social scrutiny. In contrast, the East has not been prepared to deal with such movements because Westernization has compromised traditional moralities and value systems. A dramatic example of this dynamic is the anti-Confucius campaign that took place in China during the Cultural Revolution. Furthermore, although the global experiment with communism is almost over, the Korean peninsula—the only remaining divided nation in the world—is still suffering from the tragic consequences of the Cold War. A recent example of the tensions between North and South Korea was the launching of a large number of rockets and missiles by North Korea toward the East Sea during military drills conducted by the allied forces of the United States and South Korea. This was a disturbing event, given that South Korea's capital city, Seoul, which contains almost half of the population of South Korea (including my own family), is within range of North Korea's firepower.

Although historically the West (strong nations) has developed the new ideologies and initiated experiments for social transformation, it is in the East (weak nations) where these ideological experiments have been forced into systematic practice and where people have suffered from their tragic consequences. For example, Japan was the aggressor nation that attacked Hawaii to invade the United States during World War II. Nevertheless (unlike Germany), it was not Japan (the West in the East) but rather Korea that after the war was forcefully divided by the United States and the Soviet Union, without the consent of its own people, and that consequently experienced the most bloody global warfare of the Cold War. For a Korean theologian who has witnessed this historical reality and experienced the sufferings of people owing to this dehumanizing misconduct executed by the so-called superpowers in the West, suspicion of any new experimental ideology emerging from the West is inevitable. Therefore, any new experimental ideology arising from the powerful nations in the West should be subject to a serious hermeneutics of suspicion.

Although its political experiments have not proved very successful, socialism supplies some helpful ethical tools. In fact, Marxist social analysis made important contributions to the rise of liberation theology in the Third World (the "South"), which has helped to some extent to justify and purify Christianity in the 20th century, by liberating Christian theology from the domination of the First World (the "North"). Liberation theology has become an indispensable part of global Christianity, and even North American theologians have accepted that fact: "Liberation theology has become the ecumenical and global theology of our time."[10] The significance of liberation theology is not just symbolic and rhetorical, but concrete. For example, the election of Pope Francis has helped to give Latin American liberation theology both voice and credence.

Although this divided and unjust world is still in need of an "emancipatory quest," transhumanism does not seem to be healing the division between the North and the South or providing benefits to people in developing countries in the South.[11] On the contrary, it displays a tendency to support and promote *laissez-faire* capitalism, and indications are that it will accelerate the depth of the division between these nations, adding technological and genetic aspects. As Ray Kurzweil said, "Although the argument is subtle I believe that maintaining an open free-market system for incremental scientific and technological progress, in which each step is subject to market acceptance, will provide the most constructive environment for technology to embody widespread human values."[12] While it presents rosy scenarios and science fiction fantasies, transhumanism, from the eyes of a theologian based in the realistic global situation in Asia, does not seem to go much beyond the wild dreams and armchair imaginations of futurist techno-enthusiasts in the First World. Technology is fascinating and offers promise to humanity. However, history shows that strong, technologically advanced countries are more interested in using newly acquired advantages to maintain their hegemonies and strengthen their supremacies, rather than to help the human race as a whole. The situation of the real world we live in is and will be much more complicated than the virtual realities that techno-visionaries in the First World have imagined with their techno-hype and digital fantasies expressed in science fiction films such as *Star Trek*, *Star Wars*, *The Matrix*, and *Avatar*.

ROOTS OF TRANSHUMANISM: CHRISTIANITY AND THE ENLIGHTENMENT

Various First World theologians have been endeavoring to formulate practical Christian theologies in realistic response to transhumanism.[13] Given that the Bible endorses the coming of the new heaven, earth, and humanity through radical transformation, they argue, Christian theology need not block transhumanism and resist developing new enhancing technologies. While sympathetic to the movement, American Lutheran theologian Ted Peters has pointed out the naiveté of transhumanism in understanding progress and human sinfulness: "[T]ranshumanist assumptions regarding progress are naïve, because they fail to operate with anthropology that is realistic regarding the human proclivity to turn good into evil. ... [T]hey should maintain watchfulness for ways in which these technologies can become perverted and bent toward destructive purpose."[14] Simon Young proudly declared,

"Bio-fatalism will increasingly be replaced by techno-can-do-ism—the belief in the power of the new technology to free us from the limitations of our bodies and minds. . . . In the twenty-first century, the belief in the Fall of Man will be replaced by the belief in his inevitable transcendence—through Superbiology."[15] This is naïve and overconfidently promethean: "Let us cast aside cowardice and seize the torch of Prometheus with both hands."[16]

Transhumanists find their ideological roots in the Enlightenment and Western humanism. As Nick Bostrom explained, "Transhumanism is a loosely defined movement that has developed gradually over the past two decades, and can be viewed as an outgrowth of secular humanism and the Enlightenment."[17] Transhumanists view postmodernism as a nihilistic failure, because it critiques the Enlightenment values of reason and progress. However, the strong confidence in reason and progress of the "Enlightenment mentality" has been proved to be misplaced in this post-Western or post-Christian era (of "global Christianity").[18] Even in North America, constructive theologians such as Peter Hodgson have presented a convincing criticism of modernism.[19] From an Asian vantage point, further-more, postmodernism is not a failure, but rather is helpful in suggesting some necessary correctives to the errors of the "Enlightenment mentality" as it is embedded in a mythological belief in history and progress.[20] History has already shown that a positivistic optimism for human progress of Enlightenment thinking is naïve, wishful thinking, as was demonstrated by two dreadful world wars in the European West, not to mention the horrors of Auschwitz and Hiroshima. Tu Wei-ming, a Chinese American neo-Confucian scholar at Harvard University, evaluated the Enlightenment mentality as follows:

> A fair understanding of the Enlightenment mentality requires a frank discussion of the dark side of the modern West as well. The "unbound Prometheus," sym-bolizing the runaway technology of development, may have been a spectacular achievement of human ingenuity in the early phases of the industrial revolution . . . [However,] the Enlightenment mentality, fueled by the Faustian drive to explore, to know, to conquer, and to subdue, persisted as the reigning ideology of the modern West. It is now fully embraced as the unquestioned rationale for development in East Asia.
>
> However, a realistic appraisal of the Enlightenment mentality reveals many faces of the modern West incongruent with the image of "the Age of Reason." In the context of modern Western hegemonic discourse, progress may entail inequality, reason, self-interest, and individual greed. The American dream of owning a car and a house, earning a fair wage, and enjoying freedom of privacy, expression, religion, and travel, while reasonable to our (American) sense of what ordinary life demands, is lamentably unexportable as a modern necessity from a global perspective. Indeed, it has now been widely acknowledged as no more than a dream for a significant segment of the American population as well.[21]

Ted Peters has also criticized the unrealistic optimism of transhumanists in regards to human nature: "And yet an item of looming significance is missing from this vision: a realistic appreciation for the depth and pervasiveness of what theologians call *sin*. As sinful creatures, we humans never lose our capacity to tarnish what is shiny, to undo what has been done, to corrupt what is pure."[22] To support his criticism of transhumanism, Peters made use of theologian Reinhold Niebuhr's analysis of personal sin. However, he missed a very important point in Niebuhr's analysis—namely, the complexities and ambiguities of structural sin (or "collective sin") beyond the realms of classical theology's psychological analysis of personal sin. As Niebuhr stated, "The group is more arrogant, hypocritical, self-centered and more ruthless in the pursuit of its ends than the individual."[23] Given that structural sin is embedded in the sophisticated structure of collective power, Niebuhr argued, Christian theology and ethics need a more comprehensive and realistic strategy (a real Christian power politics) beyond a simple personal and psychological soteriology. That is, they need a Christian realism.

This statement represented a very important move for North American theological honesty within the global situation, motivating the rise of First World political theology and ethics. However, the Christian realism of Niebuhr has been criticized by liberation theologians in the Third World, because it later became manifested in favor of U.S. foreign policy and national interests, a famous example of which was Niebuhr's unambiguous support for the U.S. invasion of Vietnam. Although he was eager to examine the sinful natures of political, economic, societal, and cultural systems within the First World, Niebuhr failed to apply his method fairly in the global context; rather, he defended the hegemonic interest of the most powerful nation in the world.

At this point, I would like to raise five questions for transhumanist scholars (and transhumanism-friendly theologians), elaborating on some East Asian Christian perspectives on the related subjects:

1. Whose transhumanism is this?
2. What are the points of reference for transhumanism?
3. Which type of humanism does transhumanism refer to?
4. Which benevolence does it suggest?
5. Which kind of transformation does it propose?

Although wrapped in the critical overtones of a hermeneutics of suspicion, these questions are not intended to denounce or condemn transhumanism. On the contrary, they are intended to spur an honest search for the possibility of constructive dialogue with Asian theologies.

WHOSE TRANSHUMANISM?

The first question for transhumanism from an East Asian Christian perspective is whose perspective informs the understanding of transhumanism.

Turning to the Bible, the Sermon on the Mount describes "a preferential option for the poor," proclaiming, "Blessed are you poor, for yours is the kingdom of God!" (Luke 6:24). The Christian gospels are good news to the losers (or the unfit), outcastes, alienated, disabled, marginalized, and *minjung* (simply, the oppressed), explicitly declaring, "Woe to you that are full, for you shall hunger!" (Luke 6:25). In contrast, what is the techno-gospel of transhumanism? Transhumanism seems to declare a preferential option for the rich and the powerful, offering good news for the elite, strong, oppressors, and those winners in this ruthlessly competitive world for the evolutionary survival of the fittest. Peters has said, "Transhumanism is not a philosophy for the losers, for the poor who are slated to be left behind in the struggle for existence."[24] However, Jesus clearly declared, "How hard it is for those who have riches to enter the Kingdom of God! For it is easier for a camel to go through the eye of the needle than for a rich man to enter the kingdom of God" (Luke 18:25; Matthew 19:25; Mark 10:25).

Even if transhuman projects are successfully achieved, they will be extremely expensive. In turn, only a limited number of people in the most advanced nations will be able to take advantage of their benefits, in a situation that will exponentially expand the economic and technological divides between the North and the South. Even if transhumanists somehow accomplish the building of a technological paradise on Earth or elsewhere in the universe, only the rich, the powerful, and the techno-elites who are financially and technologically capable will be able to enjoy its benefits. This will not be the Kingdom of God that Jesus talked about.

Furthermore, transhumanist utterances in favor of the modification of human brains and bodies remind East Asian people of the nightmarish memory of human living-body tests for eugenics cruelly carried out by the special military units of Imperial Japan during World War II. These invaders used the bodies and brains of other East Asians such as the Koreans and the Chinese for purposes of experimentation. Nevertheless, the current Japanese government is working hard to revise the Peace Constitution to remilitarize Japan using the excuse of military threats from North Korea and China, while persistently denying the historical fact of the criminal acts of the Japanese Imperial Army during World War II on the issue of sexual slavery (so-called comfort women).

WHICH POINTS OF REFERENCE?

The second question for transhumanism concerns the goals of the movement. What are the points of reference to prove or evaluate the validity of these goals? "The outline of transhumanism" includes mostly material goals, states in terms of modifying the brain and body by external means of science and technology.[25] But I do not see any convincing ideas for improving the global situation in terms of economic and ecological justice and morality. The goals of transhumanism along these lines are even less impressive than those offered by socialism. Indeed, transhumanists seem to be more interested in pursuing superintelligence and controlling powers to be able to play God: "[W]e may be intended to evolve towards a posthuman apotheosis, or we may choose to become gods ourselves in order to challenge the Creator(s) for dominion."[26] However, the Christian God revealed in Jesus Christ is not an omnipotent God bent on domination, but rather a self-emptying, kenotic God with the self-giving love of agape (Philippians 2:6–8).

This may be the area in which transhumanism-friendly, First World theologians can play a leading role. The late Harvard theologian Gordon Kaufman provided helpful insight into the role of theology in a post-Christian, nuclear age. The significance of the notion of God, and so theology, from his particular North American perspective, is that it gave an ultimate point of reference "to which everything human was to be judged and assessed. Thus, the idea of God and of God's will functioned as a transcendent point of reference in terms of which everything human and finite could be evaluated."[27] This is a 20th-century version of Anselm of Canterbury's definition of God as that "than which nothing greater can be conceived." Kaufman set up a salient thesis on this front: "Criticism and reconstruction of the image/concept of God will involve continuous reference to contemporary forms of experience and life—personal, social, moral, aesthetic, scientific—all of which must be related to, and thus relativized and humanized by, the concept of God, if God is indeed to function as 'ultimate point of reference' in contemporary life."[28]

In this age when humanity has the power to wipe out not only the whole human race but also entire ecosystems of our planet, I wonder how transhumanists can justify their goals, while explicitly declaring the end of *Homo sapiens* in favor of advocating a collectively intentional alteration of the species into the omnipotent *Homo cyberneticus*. Do they presuppose that genetic extinction is an inevitable gateway through which the human race will pass in anticipation of the Singularity, which will in turn result in the evolution of the posthuman? Transhumanists rationalize their cause by referring to the Enlightenment values of reason and progress. As mentioned earlier in this chapter, the validity of these Enlightenment values has been considered questionable even in the Western context. Further, since the middle of the 20th century, these values have been vehemently accused of being the primary causes of today's planetary ecological crisis.

Furthermore, from the vantage point of non-monotheistic religions, the idea of salvation history moving in the course of linear time, which is the foundation for the Enlightenment optimism in progress and development, is an anthropocentrically reductionistic worldview that has brought about ecological disaster by neglecting the holistic relationship of humans with the cosmos and the earth. Raymond Panikkar, an Indian Catholic-Hindu scholar, viewed this notion of history as a fallible belief in the myth of history.[29] According to him, the history of world religions presents three great religious visions: ancient cosmocentrism, medieval theocentrism, and modern historico-anthropocentrism. All of these are inaccurate, one-sided, reduction-istic (monocentric) views of reality. In fact, God (or the ultimate), humans, and the cosmos constitute three inseparable and concentric axes of the one reality. This triadic view is the theanthropocosmic (or cosmotheandric) vision that was presupposed not only in Asia but also to some extent in the early and medieval eras of the West, but which was lost in modern time by an excessive emphasis on historicism and anthropocentricism. In addition, new branches of science since Albert Einstein have demonstrated that the static notion of linear time flying like an arrow is false; instead, time is dynamic, holistic, and relational.

WHICH HUMANISM?

The third question from an East Asian perspective is of which kind of humanism does transhumanism speak. An axiomatic pillar of neo-Confucianism (a common religio-cultural background for East Asian people) is what has been termed the "anthropocosmic vision," inherent in the Confucian belief in the "mutual dependence and organic unity" of Heaven and humanity.[30] *The Doctrine of the Mean*, one of the Confucian Four Books, begins, "What Heaven imparts to man is called human nature. To follow our nature is called the Way [Dao]. Cultivating the Way is called educa-tion."[31] In this anthropocosmic vision, humanity (anthropology) is not only inseparable from Heaven (cosmology), but is also conceived as its microcosm. This East Asian anthropocosmic approach to anthropology is quite different from the anthropocentric approach prevalent in the West.

Such East Asian anthropology entails an "inclusive humanism," in contrast to the "exclusive humanism" dominant in the modern West since the dualistic rationalism of Descartes. Whereas exclusive humanism "exalts the human spe-cies, placing it in a position of mastery of and domination over the universe," inclusive humanism "stresses the coordinating powers of humanity as the very reason for its existence." Cheng Chung-ying, a Chinese American Confucian scholar at the University of Hawaii, has criticized Western humanism:

> In this sense, humanism in the modern West is nothing more than a secular will for power or a striving for domination, with rationalistic science at its disposal. In fact, the fascination with power leads to a Faustian trade-off of knowledge and power (pleasure and self-glorification) for value and truth, a trade-off which can lead to the final destruction of the meaning of the human self and human freedom. . . . Humanism in this exclusive sense is a disguise for the individualis-tic entrepreneurship of modern man armed with science and technology as tools of conquest and devastation.[32]

In contrast, Cheng argues, the inclusive humanism that is rooted in neo-Confucianism "focuses on the human person as an agency of both self-transformation and transformation of reality at large. As the self-transformation of a person is rooted in reality and the transformation of reality is rooted in the person, there is no dichotomy or bifurcation between the human and reality."[33]

Is the humanism that transhumanists have in mind free from the exclusive humanism of the modern West? Can it welcome the inclusive humanism of East Asia?

WHICH BENEVOLENCE?

The fourth question is which kind of benevolence (or beneficence) does transhumanism suggests. Whereas the history of the religiously homogeneous West is filled with bloody religious wars and conflicts, such religious warfare is uncommon in the history of religiously plural East Asia. East Asian scholars assume that this is because Western culture is based on a *conflict* model much influenced by Greek dialectical dualism, whereas Eastern culture is based on a *harmony* model exemplified by the *yin-yang* relationship.[34] In this neo-Confucian world, *ren* (benevolence), the primal virtue and the very definition of humanity, etymologically means the ontology of two people (or being-in-togetherness). Hence, neo-Confucian wisdom commends the habit of the negative golden rule ("Do not do to others what you do not want them to do to you!"). This attitude encompasses "epistemological modesty" and "ethical *humility*"—the crucial virtues needed in treating others as "guests" or "friends" and, therefore, in bringing harmony in the world. In contrast, the habit of the positive golden rule ("Love others *in your own ways!*"), though preferred in the Christian West, is carefully avoided. It is seen as causing the opposite attitudes of "epistemological immodesty" and "ethical *hubris*"—which lead to treating others as "strangers" or "enemies" in a conflict complex and can eventually foster the principles of domination and exploitation.[35] These attitudes served as a root cause for the modern failure of the arrogant Western Christian mission in Asia, not to mention Western imperialism. I wonder whether the benevolence that transhumanism advocates (including "procreative beneficence") is free from these Western habits of epistemological immodesty and ethical hubris, referring to the superimposing of one's own definition of benevolence (or love) on others (including future children) who may have different ideas in different contexts.

WHICH TRANSFORMATION? CYBORG, SAGE, AND SAINT—TRANSHUMANIZATION, SELF-CULTIVATION, AND SANCTIFICATION

Transhumanism basically refers to a transformation toward human perfection by means of science and technology. The fifth question refers to the nature of the transformation that transhumanism advocates. How does transhumanism define humanity and what is its *telos* of humanity?

The human person in the neo-Confucian sense does not mean "a self-fulfilled, individual ego in the modern sense, but a communal self or the togetherness of a self as 'a center of relationship.' "[36] The crucial Confucian notion of *ren* denotes the ontology of humanity as the being-in-relationship or the being-in-togetherness, which extends to an anthropocosmic vision (humanity and cosmos in harmonious relationship). In a famous passage of the *Western Inscription*, Chang Tsai wrote:

> Heaven is my father and Earth is my mother, and even such a small creature as I finds an intimate place in their midst. Therefore, that which fills the universe I regard as my body and that which directs the universe I consider as my nature. All people are my brothers and sisters, and all things are my companions.[37]

Further, Confucianism regards humanity as the heavenly endowment (*Tianming*), in a similar manner as Christian theology understands humanity as the image of God (*imago Dei*). A comparative study between John Calvin and Yi T'oegye, the most important scholar in the history of Korean Confucianism, describes this relationship: "The Christian doctrine of *Imago Dei* and the Neo-Confucian concept of *T'ien-ming* [*Tianming*] reveal saliently this characteristic of a relational and transcendental anthropology. Calvin and T'oegye are the same in defining humanity as a mirror or a microcosm to image and reflect the glory and the goodness of the transcendent ground of being."[38]

I have already asked about the *telos* of transhumanism, meaning the goal of transhuman transformation or transhumanization by external means of science and technology. Confucianism and Christianity have carefully spoken on the issue of transformation, but their focus is on an inner transformation—that is, a self-realization or a full humanization. In the Christian sense, the *telos* of self-transformation is to achieve sainthood, in and through the imitation of the eschatological personhood of Jesus Christ (*imago Dei*); in the Confucian sense, it is to attain sagehood in and through the cultivation of self toward a full humanization of what humanity originally ought to be (*Tianming*). This refers to the doctrine of sanctification in Christian theology and the teaching of self-cultivation in neo-Confucianism, respectively. Both traditions endorse the dignity of humanity, as the sanctity of life has been ontologically and eschatologically conferred in every stage; it is primarily given (relational) rather than innate (substantial). Yet, in existence, the human condition is ambivalent, because this transcendental potentiality has not been fully activated. Instead, it requires a rigorous process of self-realization—that is, sanctification and self-cultivation.

From an East Asian Christian perspective, therefore, the sanctity of life implies the imperative of a life to realize to the fullest what it ought to be.

This involves the diligent practice of sanctification and self-cultivation in reverence, including mindfulness, humility, and respect for others. Scientists and engineers should also engage in this rigorous practice of self-realization with an attitude of reverence. This attitude should be a prerequisite to exercising one's freedom to help others to accomplish their own imperatives for self-realization. It entails the attitude of humility in participating as a player rather than as a designer or a manager in the great transformative movement of the theanthropocosmic trajectory, the Dao (the Way). The dignity of humanity from an East Asian perspective means a fulfillment and embodiment of the proleptic Dao, in its own freedom of life (*wuwei*) and with a great openness for cosmic vitality, which is referred to as *qi* in East Asia and the Holy Spirit in Christianity. In an East Asian Christian perspective, therefore, freedom may refer not so much to "the freedom to alter," change, or modify nature or life systems, but rather "the freedom not to alter" them unless such a change is ultimately helpful for ecological and cosmic sanctification.

Transhumanist scholars might regard this neo-Confucian mode of thinking as archaic (or "bio-conservative"), as they see the concept of the natural "as problematically nebulous at best, and an obstacle to progress at worst."[39] However, in East Asia, the way of thinking about nature is quite different from the West. The traditional Western understanding of "nature" incorporates a pejorative connotation inherited by the Greek and Christian hierarchical dualism between the supernatural and the natural. In contrast, neo-Confucianism accommodates the profound Daoist insights pertaining to nature and *wuwei* ("actionless activity"), "a state of passivity, of 'non-action,' but a passivity that is totally active, in the sense of receptivity."[40] In Chinese characters, etymologically, nature means "*self-so*," "spontaneity," or "naturalness"—that is to say, "the effective modality of the system that informs the actions of the agents that compose it."[41] In other words, *nature* in East Asian thought is the primary "self-so" (natural) manifestation of the Dao (the ultimate principle). The Bible also seems to endorse this affirmative sense of nature, because nature as God's creation is defined as "good" and the denial of its goodness as "self-so" would be regarded as the fallacy of Gnosticism.

Bede Griffiths, although a British Benedictine monk, after having studied world religions during a stay of many years in India, suggested an insight different from that of the transhumanists, elucidating the relationship of the East and the West in terms of the *yin-yang* complementary opposite:

> This may sound very paradoxical and unreal, but for centuries now the western world has been following the path of *Yang* of the masculine, active, aggressive, rational, scientific mind and has brought the world near destruction. It is time now to recover the path of *Yin*, of the feminine, passive, patient, intuitive and poetic mind. This is the path which the *Tao Te Ching* sets before us.[42]

There still remains a very basic question about transhumanist anthropology. Which kind of personhood is transhumanization looking for, after all? A posthuman cyborg, a machine-human being of the *Homo cyberneticus*, further self-evolved beyond the *Homo sapiens*? By choosing the path of transformation with the highest external use of science and technology, can transhumanism qualitatively liberate humanity from the ambiguous human condition of being a sinner (Christianity), a small person (Confucianism), or even a robot controlled by selfish genes (sociobiology)? How does transhumanism enable the transhuman "desire to control the body, to live longer, to be smarter and be happier," to be free from the habits that St. Augustine called concupiscence and that neo-Confucianism called the existential human mind with selfish desires?[43] Brent Waters seems to pose a similar concern: "To assert that humans should become posthuman requires the invocation of a higher and transcendent good that trumps the anthropocentric standard. What remains unclear in transhumanist literature is the source of this transcendent good that humans should pursue . . . Or, posed as a question: what is the source of the 'trans' that justifies its affixation to 'humanist'?"[44]

This is the crucial point where both Confucianism and Christian theology begin their spiritual discourses on self-cultivation and sanctification. In a nutshell, the goals of both traditions are converging, as both lead one to seek freedom (of the sage and the saint) from the habits of concupiscent and selfish desires, in and through a rigorous examination—an examination that aims to avoid such selfish desires in light of historically tested points of reference (namely, "the innate knowledge of the good" endowed by the *Tienming* and "the humanity of Christ" embodied by the *imago Dei*).[45] Hence, from the vantage points of Confucian self-cultivation and Christian sanctification, the true meaning of freedom is not so much the choice to freely use science and technology for the sake of one's own material benefits, but rather (and more importantly) a spiritual freedom from human propensities toward concupiscence and sin. In fact, Teilhard de Chardin, who has been regarded as a precursor to transhumanists, has also clearly articulated that "it is upon its point (or superstructure) of spiritual concentration, and not on its basis (or infrastructure) of material arrangement [in other words, 'material paganism'], that the equilibrium of Mankind biologically depends."[46]

Finally, can the transhuman cyborg, so enhanced, modified, transformed, or created, be really better, wiser, and even holier than the Confucian sage and the Christian saint? Can she, he, or it become a real hope for the human race (and other life systems) in this divided, unjust, and possibly unsustainable world? In this regard, was not George Lucas a prophet who, through his film series *Star Wars*, presented a sort of prophesy about the true hope for humanity in a time far, far away? He seems to have foreseen that humanity's future hope will lie in neither Darth Vader (a mightily enhanced trans-human-being) nor an Empire equipped by the invincible power of science and technology, but rather in Jedi knights such as Luke Skywalker (a real human being) and Yoda (a sage), self-cultivated with the dignity of humanity and trained in communion with the natural Force of cosmic vitality which East Asians call *qi*.

And so, "May the Force [*qi*] be with you!"

NOTES

1. According to Nick Bostrom, "Transhumanism is a loosely defined movement that has developed gradually over the past two decades, and can be viewed as an outgrowth of secular humanism and the Enlightenment. It holds that current human nature is improvable through the use of applied science and other rational methods, which may make it possible to increase human health-span, extend our intellectual and physical capacities, and give us increased control over our own mental states and moods." Nick Bostrom, "In Defense of Posthuman Dignity," *Bioethics* 19 (2005): 202–214.

2. Francis Fukuyama, "The World's Most Dangerous Ideas: Transhumanism," *Foreign Policy* 144 (2009): 42–43.

3. See http://en.wikipedia.org/wiki/Hwang_Woo-suk.

4. See *The Japan News*, "RIKEN Finds Discrepancies, Advises STAP Retraction," http://the-japan-news.com/news/article/0001121837, accessed March 15, 2014.

5. See Heup Young Kim, "Sanctity of Life: A Reflection on Human Embryonic Stem Cell Debates from an East Asian Perspective," in *Global Perspectives on Science & Spirituality*, edited by Pranab Das (West Conshohocken, PA: Templeton Press, 2009), 107–124.

6. The President's Council on Bioethics and Leon Kass, *Beyond Therapy: Biotechnology and the Pursuit of Happiness: A Report of the President's Council of Bioethics* (New York, NY: HarperCollins, 2003), 155.

7. Ronald Cole-Turner, "Transhumanism and Christianity," in *Transhumanism and Transcendence: Christian in an Age of Technological Enhancement*, edited by Ronald Cole-Turner (Washington, DC: Georgetown University Press, 2011), 193.

8. James Hughes, *Citizen Cyborg: Why Democratic Societies Must Respond To the Redesigned Human of the Future* (Cambridge, MA: Westview Press, 2004), 173.

9. Hughes, *Citizen Cyborg*, 193–203.

10. Peter Hodgson, *Winds of Spirit: A Constructive Christian Theology* (Louisville, KY: Westminster John Knox, 1994), 67.

11. Hodgson, *Winds of Spirit*, 64–85.

12. Ray Kurzweil, *The Singularity Is Near: When Humans Transcend Biology* (New York, NY: Viking Penguin, 2005), 420.

13. See Cole-Turner, "Transhumanism and Christianity."

14. Ted Peters, "H-: Transhumanism and the Posthuman Future: Will Technological Progress Get Us There?", September 1, 2011, http://www.metanexus.net/essay/h-transhumanism-and-posthuman-future-will-technological-progress-get-us-there.

15. Simon Young, *Designer Evolution: A Transhumanist Manifesto* (Amherst, NY: Prometheus Books, 2006), 20.

16. Young, *Designer Evolution*, 40.

17. Bostrom, "In Defense of Posthuman Dignity," 202.

18. See Philip Jenkins, *The Next Christendom: The Coming of Global Christianity* (Oxford, UK: Oxford University Press, 2011).

19. Arguing for a paradigm shift from modernism to postmodernism, Peter Hodgson elaborated seven crises of modernism: the cognitive crisis (Western logocentrism), the historical crisis (a theory of progress), the political crisis (the ending of Western hegemony), the socioeconomic crisis (the collapse of state capitalism and the increase of global economic injustice), the ecological crisis, the sexual and gender crises, and the religious crisis (the decline of Western Christianity, the spread of religious fanaticism, and interreligious dialogue). See Hodgson, *Winds of Spirit*, 53–61.

20. See Tu Wei-ming, "Beyond the Enlightenment Mentality," in *Confucianism and Ecology: The Interrelation of Heaven, Earth, and Humans*, edited by Mary Evelyn Tucker and John Berthrong (Cambridge, MA: Harvard University Press, 1998), 3–22.

21. Wei-ming, "Beyond the Enlightenment Mentality," 4.

22. Ted Peters, "Progress and Provolution," in *Transhumanism and Transcendence: Christian in an Age of Technological Enhancement*, edited by Ronald Cole-Turner (Washington, DC: Georgetown University Press, 2011), 64.

23. Reinhold Niebuhr, *The Nature and Destiny of Man: A Christian Interpretation*, Vol. 1 (New York, NY: Charles Scribner's Sons, 1964), 208–209.

24. Niebuhr, *The Nature and Destiny of Man*, 71.

25. http://en.wikipedia.org/wiki/Outline_of_transhumanism; also, http://en.wikipedia.org/wiki/Transhumanism.

26. James J. Hughes, *The Compatibility of Religious and Transhumanist Views of Metaphysics, Suffering, Virtue and Transcendence in an Enhanced Future* (Hartford, CT: Institute for Ethics and Emerging Technologies, 2007), 30; http://ieet.org/archive/20070326-Hughes-ASU-H+Religion.pdf.

27. Gordon D. Kaufman, *The Theological Imagination: Constructing the Concept of God* (Philadelphia, PA: Westminster Press, 1981), 85.

28. Kaufman, *The Theological Imagination*, 274–275.

29. See Raymond Panikkar, *The Cosmotheandric Experience: Emerging Religion Consciousness* (Maryknoll, NY: Orbis, 1993).

30. Tu Wei-ming, *Centrality and Commonality: An Essay on Confucian Religiousness* (Albany, NY: State University of New York Press, 1989), 107.

31. Wing-tsit Chan, *A Source Book in Chinese Philosophy* (Princeton, NJ: Princeton University Press, 1963), 98.

32. Cheng Chung-ying, "The Trinity of Cosmology, Ecology, and Ethics in the Confucian Personhood," in *Confucianism and Ecology: The Interrelation of Heaven, Earth, and Humans*, edited by Mary Evelyn Tucker and John Berthrong (Cambridge, MA: Harvard University Press, 1998), 213–214.

33. Chung-ying, "The Trinity of Cosmology, Ecology, and Ethics in the Confucian Personhood," 214.

34. See Shu-hsien Liu and Robert E. Allinson, *Harmony and Strife: Contemporary Perspectives, East and West* (Hong Kong: Chinese University Press, 1988).

35. Robert E. Allinson, "The Ethics of Confucianism and Christianity: The Delicate Balance," *Ching Feng* 33, no. 3 (1990): 158–175.

36. Tu, *Centrality and Commonality*, 53.

37. Chan, *A Source Book*, 497–498.

38. Heup Y. Kim, *Christ and the Tao* (Hong Kong: Christian Conference of Asia, 2003), 91.

39. http://en.wikipedia.org/wiki/Transhumanism, 6. Also see Nick Bostrom and Anders Sandberg, "The Wisdom of Nature: An Evolutionary Heuristic for Human Enhancement," in *Human Enhancement* (Oxford, UK: Oxford University Press, 2008), 375–416.

40. Bede Griffiths, ed., *Universal Wisdom: A Journey through the Sacred Wisdom of the World* (San Francisco, CA: HarperSanFrancisco, 1994), 27.

41. Michael C. Kalton, "Asian Religious Tradition and Natural Science: Potentials, Present and Future," unpublished paper, CTNS Korea Religion & Science Workshop, Seoul, South Korea, January 18–22, 2002.

42. Griffiths, *Universal Wisdom*, 27–28.

43. Hughes, *The Compatibility of Religious and Transhumanist Views*, 7.

44. Brent Waters, *From Human to Posthuman: Christian Theology and Technology in a Postmodern World* (Aldershot, UK: Ashgate, 2006), 78.

45. For this discussion, see Heup Young Kim, *Wang Yang-ming and Karl Barth: A Confucian–Christian Dialogue* (Lanham, MD: University of America Press, 1996).

46. Pierre Teilhard de Chardin, *The Future of Man*, translated by Norman Denny (New York, NY: Harper & Row, 1964, 1969), 317.

Section 3

. . . .

Eschatology: For What Do We Hope?

8

. . . .

Becoming God by the Numbers: An Evolutionary Journey toward the Divine

Philip A. Douglas

SCIENCE AND RELIGION REUNITED?

In his book *Consilience: The Unity of Knowledge*, biologist E. O. Wilson calls for cooperation among all who live the life of the mind. The term *consilience*, which he borrows from Renaissance thinkers, originally referred to a concordance of evidence from different fields of study to support a thesis in the natural sciences. But Wilson expands the term, claiming that all spheres of human knowledge—from the natural and social sciences to the humanities, arts, and religion—can and should share their insights to uncover the rational structure of all that exists. He laments that the rise of modern academic disciplines has led to fragmentation and intellectual isolation among scholars.

Admittedly, Wilson approaches all phenomena as a scientist and evolutionist. Nevertheless, he contends that to understand that religions are cultural artifacts subject to social evolutionary processes is not to disparage them. In fact, spiritual approaches and institutions can uplift and be uplifted by scientific inquiry. He suggests that the notion of a strict division and enforced isolation between the cultural domains of science, philosophy, and religion advocated by scientists such as Stephen Jay Gould prevents what will eventually become a crucial cross-pollination of ideas.[1] And in fact, such sharp distinctions between the various domains is a comparatively recent development within the last two or three centuries.

British philosopher Alfred North Whitehead, for example, suggested that the cultural drive toward science, curiously enough, had its roots in medieval European religious culture. As complexity theorist James Gardner explains

Whitehead's idea, medieval populations had "a habit of thought—a deeply ingrained, religiously derived, an essentially irrational faith in the existence of a rational natural order."[2] In other words, Europeans (irrationally perhaps) insisted upon the rationality of God.

I wish to explore Gardner at length later in this chapter as a crucial voice in the dialogue about scientific-religious consilience, for he notes that other historians of science have also examined the religious perspectives that inspired Copernicus, Galileo, Kepler, and Newton. Each of these scholars believed that mathematics gave shape and form to the universe and to the physical reality studied through the sciences. The mathematical ideas themselves had their primary existence in the mind of God, and to study how such principles took shape in the world was to commune with these eternal forms and, therefore, with the Divine.[3] More recently, astrophysicist Freeman Dyson has claimed that a mind evolved to a profound enough degree of sophistication will be indistinguishable from God. In other words, understanding all of nature's laws—or, perhaps more importantly, having the capacity to understand all of nature's laws—could bring the human mind truly in accord with that of God. An important question, however, is whether the human brain, at its current stage of evolution, not directly enhanced by technology, is capable of such absolute understanding. The transhumanist movement suggests the unfolding of such extreme possibilities.

The transhumanist movement is concerned with the transformation of humanity into something else. Certainly, many transhumanists are engrossed with the near-term questions of medical enhancement of their physical selves, through genetic modification technologies, and later through the incorporation of computer technologies into their bodies. Assuming such developments occur and that humanity or posthumanity is able (as transhumanist Ray Kurzweil explains it) to "transcend" biology, new questions begin to arise. Beyond the basic transhumanist question, "What is next for humanity?" one might ask, "If such transcendence is possible, what might be the ultimate impact, over the course of billions of years, upon the cosmos?" If beings whose origins are clearly rooted in biology and biological evolution are able to ascend to heights that allow them to achieve immortality, or "transcend" genetics, the body, and finally any kind of currently recognizable physicality, then which sorts of features will be attributable to them? How will we characterize their fundamental nature and motivations? Clearly, such questions can invite only the most speculative of conjectures.

Interestingly, religious, and specifically Christian perspectives, need not be at odds with transhumanist goals. In his article, "Contextualizing a Christian Perspective on Transcendence and Human Enhancement," Michael Burdett cites perspectives from three Christian scientists over the last 500 years who advocated technological human enhancement. Burdett reminds readers that "when considering the contemporary issues of bio-enhancement and technological transcendence from a Christian perspective, it is instructive to remember that the Christian tradition is marked with a multiplicity of positions and that a simple reactionary stance is not the only strand within Christian history."[4] The first example Burdett mentions is Francis Bacon, arguably the father of the scientific method, who wished to employ science and technology in the service of humanity so that it could rise to its "proper place"[5] over nature and ultimately palliate the effects of the Fall upon humanity.[6]

A much lesser-known figure from 300 years later, Nicolai Fedorovich Fedorov had no less ambition than to put science and technology to work in the conquest of death itself. Beyond this, he suggested that the complete physical resurrection of all humanity would eventually become possible.[7] Fedorov believed that resurrection was not the work of God alone. Although Christ is the redeemer of humankind, humans can and should participate in their own restoration and resurrection of ancestors through technological development. To control all of nature's forces and defeat death once and for all is what Fedorov sees as a Christian mission that should direct human advancement (humanity's Christian mission).[8] Thus, Burdett sees Fedorov and Bacon as early transhumanists who connected Christian faith to technology for human enhancement.

A much more recent figure Burdett addresses is the French Jesuit theologian and paleontologist Pierre Teilhard de Chardin, one of the first scholars to combine evolutionary theory with Christian theology.[9] Teilhard encourages the use of technology to enhance humanity, because he believes that each biological step is advancing us toward the cosmic Christ. In his book *The Future of Man*, Teilhard echoes Fedorov in his claims that we need not assume that Christ fulfills himself through purely supernatural action. Indeed, he suggests that "every human cell [must] unite with all the others" to make the Parousia physically possible.[10] Teilhard believes that such a phenomenon is, and has always been, in process of formation[11] on earth. All of human endeavor tends toward a collective personality through which the individual will attain, in some form, the consciousness of all of humanity.[12] For Teilhard, then, evolution is seen as *convergent*. Elsewhere, Teilhard claims that a force known as *radial energy* pushes biological organisms toward "ever greater complexity and centricity." He even notes that this movement seems to be in direct contradiction to the law of conservation of energy.[13] The notion of greater "centricity" is certainly a contradiction of the second law of thermodynamics, which implies energy's dissipation. Nevertheless, Teilhard sees it as a genuine *energy*, as science understands the term. Radial energy, since it impels all life toward ever-greater sophistication, is a force equal to, if not greater than, the force of entropy. Unlike the kind of energy that physicists measure, radial energy will become ever more concentrated, driving the evolution of humanity and posthumanity into the future.[14]

For Teilhard, evolution—indeed, all that happens in the cosmos—is directed toward a goal.

Complexity theorist James Gardner has begun to formulate similar conjectures to Teilhard's in two recent books, *Biocosm* and *The Intelligent Universe*. Central to his work is what he calls the "Selfish Biocosm hypothesis." In what follows, I consider what Gardner means by this hypothesis and how he characterizes it in the context of several versions of the cosmological anthropic principle. Next, I explore how he conceives of the anthropic principle as a precursor of a coming revolution in the merging and reorganization of the scientific disciplines. It will be useful then to discuss the Selfish Biocosm hypothesis in the context of transhumanism broadly conceived, rather than not just the contemporary transhumanist movement. For Gardner, humanity or some other intelligent species somewhere in the cosmos may have a major role in the future development of the universe and ultimately its own "reproduction." Finally, I examine how this cosmic reproduction might take place. I conclude by looking at how Gardner's ideas could feed into a set of principles guiding human behavior and whether religious perspectives can be reconciled with an understanding of the universe conceived as the product of a higher intelligence, albeit not a transcendent one.

Gardner is a science-inspired visionary. Today, of course, we tend to separate fields like science, technology, philosophy, theology, and visionary speculation. At least until the rise of modern science in the Renaissance, these fields flowed together in the writings of many individuals. In some respects, we can think of Gardner as part of this earlier tradition, a tradition in which thinkers such as Teilhard might also be located. Something like a theoretical physicist, Gardner extrapolates from established particulars about our physical universe to propose a fundamental narrative of its origin and direction. He argues that the very universe we inhabit is designed with its own replication as its fundamental goal, a proposition he refers to as his "Selfish Biocosm hypothesis." In both his books, *Biocosm* and *The Intelligent Universe*, Gardner claims that collective, highly evolved or artificial intelligences are behind the origins of our universe and have set the arc of its development. Such potentially awesome beings are not only part of our future, according to Gardner, but also likely part of our past.

THE SELFISH BIOCOSM HYPOTHESIS

Gardner's Selfish Biocosm hypothesis states that the universe is slowly coming to life—indeed, that it *must* do so. As Gardner puts it, "the universe we are privileged to inhabit is literally in the process of transforming itself from inanimate to animate matter."[15] According to his hypothesis, the development of life, the process of evolution, and ultimately the manifestation of intelligence itself within that life are neither meaningless nor directionless. Rather, they are indicative of the ultimate *telos* (or end) of the universe, which is self-replication. The purpose of the universe is to repeat itself, give birth to itself, or produce variations of itself, endlessly.

Gardner's hypothesis is both heady and controversial. However, he grounds it in a dialogue that has been percolating among cosmologists and astronomers for some time. The fact that the universe is finely tuned to support life may not seem so terribly strange until one contemplates the fact that things could have been so easily and arbitrarily different. Gardner cites, among others, British Astronomer Royal Martin Rees, who explains that every characteristic of the universe and its development relies upon the very precise settings, or values of the constants of nature, of which there are six. Any one of these constants could have been set at very different values.[16] For example, the ratio of the electrical force to the gravitational force allows for very strong electrical attraction and weak gravity. If this ratio were changed—for example, if gravity were only fractionally stronger—then galaxies would form much more quickly and stars would be more densely packed. Stable planetary systems would not be possible because the gravity of nearby stars would affect their orbits. Without such stability, life, and thus humans ourselves, would not exist.

What explains this fine-tuning of the universe? Some cosmologists have proposed different versions of what is known as the anthropic cosmological principle. The weak version of the anthropic principle merely states that the universe must be set up for life because, if it were not, we could not be here as observers. The weak version is, therefore, tautological and not particularly useful or informative. The strong version of the anthropic principle states that the universe is fine-tuned for life because a cosmic designer, likely God, made it so. Needless to say, most scientists find such a seemingly untestable proposal highly problematic. In still another version, Princeton physicist John Wheeler conceives of the cosmos as what Gardner calls "an autocatalytic loop."[17] What tunes the universe so well are the countless acts of observation made by billions upon billions of observer-participants, most of whom live in the distant future. Their very acts of observation create the universe.[18] What interests Gardner about Wheeler's idea is that it involves living and thinking creatures as vital participants in their own evolution. He labels Wheeler's theory as the "counterintuitive participatory anthropic principle."[19] Such a notion almost seems to imply a kind of magic, in which the individual mind itself, even without knowing it, conspires, along with other minds, to create the cosmos. We never just perceive reality, but always, in some measure, help to create it.

Lastly, Gardner introduces the Final Anthropic Principle and its main proponents, John Barrow and Frank Tipler. As with Wheeler's version, the real story of the universe lies in the future. After space travel begins, our distant descendants will finally have the knowledge and ability to extend the boundary of the biosphere to eventually make it equal to the bounds of the universe.[20] The universe will even cooperate with such an endeavor in that, under a non-inflationary model of cosmological development, the universe will eventually contract to a point of infinite density. Before this final contraction has been reached however, another threshold, the Omega Point (a term borrowed from Teilhard), will have been instituted by the intelligences existing at the end of time. The Omega Point is the instant when all physical matter will have been "entirely subdued and transcended by the self-organizing powers of life and intelligence."[21] For Barrow and Tipler, the Omega Point is implicit in the laws of physics themselves.

Gardner's Selfish Biocosm hypothesis, then, is a version of the strong anthropic principle. He draws from and cobbles together elements of other versions to argue for his own compelling account of why the universe allowed us to come into being. Indeed, the universe has a designer, but not a transcendent Designer. We humans ourselves could literally be the makers of the universe. If our descendants, eons in the future, have developed the technology necessary for imposing specific fundamental physical laws upon a baby cosmos, is it not conceivable that they might have actually done so for us? The universe then gives birth to itself and all variations in which intelligent life might appear. The "selfishness" of the biocosm and the reasons why it is a "biocosm" at all are issues explored in the next section.

A MERGING OF THE SCIENCES

One of Gardner's central contentions is that the verification of his Selfish Biocosm hypothesis will require an eventual revolution in the organization of scientific disciplines, a transformation he believes is already incipient. According to our current scientific paradigm, physics is the foundation of all the other sciences, the root from which they must spring. To completely understand the laws of physics is, theoretically, to have the capacity, given enough information, to predict the formation of minerals studied by geologists and the inorganic structure of the lithosphere. Taken further, the laws of physics should predict the origins and behavior of biological phenomena. Even the social sciences, with their focus upon specifically human activities and interactions, must be traceable to their ultimate source—the actions of gravity, electromagnetism, nuclear forces, and the rest.

Gardner, however, explains that such a hierarchical understanding of scientific knowledge may need revision in light of his Selfish Biocosm hypothesis. By his account, what were once biological organisms designed the universe and programmed the laws that govern it. Thus, biology could be as much a foundation for understanding nature as physics is. Traditionally, the principles of physics and the constants of nature have been taken as invariant. If the laws of physics are the product of intelligences that evolved over eons of time, could there not be a need to honor the other sciences as more foundational than physics to the universe's development? Indeed, entirely new epistemic modalities would be needed to reframe our understanding of all that exists.

Gardner asserts that biology, in fact, could stand as the new *foundational* science. At the very least, he celebrates E. O. Wilson's revival of the enlightenment concept of consilience, a holistic understanding of all the regions of human knowledge as interlinked endeavors that constitute a self-reinforcing intellectual system. As Gardner puts it in *The Intelligent Universe*, science has been "peering through the wrong end of the telescope."[22] Astronomers and cosmologists have looked out at the cold, lifeless void among the stars and seen no evidence for the importance of life and human intelligence. But, in fact, perhaps the "void" or emptiness of outer space is indication of the need to fill it, even to fill it with *ourselves*.

If life has a starring role in the universe, then knowledge of biology's methods and processes becomes crucial to an understanding of the universe's possible purpose. Surprisingly, the ultra-Darwinist biologist Richard Dawkins is a figure whom Gardner believes may have something to tell us with his idea of the "selfish gene."[23] As Gardner presents him, Dawkins is a teleological thinker; he contends that all our behavior in life serves our genes. Genetic survival and propagation is the function of natural selection.[24] Of course, on a larger scale, Dawkins believes that natural selection simply highlights the lack of purpose or meaning in the cosmos. Gardner, in a significant departure from his theory, suggests that Dawkins's notion that the process of evolution belies the possibility of design inherent in the universe is indicative of the latter's shortsightedness. One wonders if Gardner's invented phrase "Selfish Biocosm" stands as an ironic tribute to Dawkins. In any case, Gardner's coinage puts the notion of species survival into the largest context possible. Our universe's "intelligence gene," as it were, wishes to replicate, and its "DNA" code are the six numbers representing the constants of nature.

If *cosmoi* are truly reproductive organisms, then they require the fundamental machinery that such organisms contain. Gardner borrows here from John von Neumann, who explained in a 1948 lecture that any entity capable of self-reproduction must have four components: (1) a *blueprint* that provides the plan for building progeny; (2) a *factory* to do the building; (3) a *controller*, which is something that will make certain that the factory carries out its work according to plan; and (4) *a duplicating machine* that provides a copy of the blueprint to the offspring so they can repeat the process.[25]

Gardner has suggested that the blueprint for the cosmos is to be found in the six numbers that allow for the physical laws of our universe. These six numbers represent basic physical constants. For example, the force of gravity is set at a certain value. If the number were even slightly different, galaxies and their stars would never form, the complex chemistry needed for life to evolve would not be feasible, and we would not be here. Thus, the factory, given enough time, is the universe itself and all of its resources.

The controller, as we know, is intelligent life. (The forms that intelligent life may take are, of course, open to a great deal of speculation.) But what about the duplicating machine? If a universe is a living organism, it requires something akin to DNA to reproduce itself.[26] Gardner here draws from the young science of complexity theory to help bolster the Selfish Biocosm hypothesis: complex adaptive systems could be the *controller* we need. The processes of cosmological self-organization and emergence are guided by such systems. The "complex adaptive systems," of which biological life is our best example, will eventually, in the far future, cause the cosmos to replicate. Life itself, when it becomes sufficiently evolved, sophisticated, and pervasive, will duplicate the cosmos.

A specific example of a complex adaptive system at work in the biological world can be seen in the process of symbiogenesis or evolutionary advancement through symbiosis.[27] As Gardner explains the process, "macroevolution occurs when formerly independent organisms begin to cooperate in living communes where they can pool their various talents for mutual advantage."[28] The classic example of this phenomenon occurred when metazoans—animals made up of many single living cells—first appeared. Symbiogenesis happened when eukaryotic cells formed that began to incorporate mitochondria and chloroplasts into cellular organelles. These entities were formerly independent. Of course, much more advanced forms of symbiogenesis may occur as well. For example, Wilson contends that advanced human mental functions are an artifact of human social interaction.[29]

To locate other examples of biologically inspired models for cosmological phenomena, Gardner appeals to complexity theorist Stuart Kaufman, who postulates a force (a "fourth law of thermodynamics") that imposes order allowing for "self-constructing open thermodynamic systems such as a biosphere."[30] If the second law of thermodynamics is about decay and entropy, but the fourth law is about building diversity and complexity, then an open question is whether the fourth law acts as a counterbalance to the second law. A force of self-organization is, therefore, a kind of silent partner with the Darwinian process of natural selection. In other words, the fourth law provides a vast range of varied living structures upon which natural selection can act.[31] Kaufman thinks that Darwin's theory of natural selection by itself is insufficient to explain the fact that "complex systems exhibit order spontaneously."[32] For Kaufman, it is not that natural selection is wrong, but rather that it is not enough: a single force cannot account for the level of complexity. While organisms may randomly radiate out in various directions on the evolutionary tree, they also reveal patterns of order within their bodies.

How does this ordering process relate to or work with natural selection? Kauffman's answer to this question draws upon rather arcane explanations from chemistry. He examines the antecedents to biochemical entities, which were "autocatalytic webs of complex carbon-based polymers."[33] Suffice it to say that Kauffman has no exact explanation for how life may have started; rather, he claims that it is surprisingly easy, given enough time, for "modestly complex mixtures" of catalytic polymers such as proteins and catalytic RNA to "catalyze one another's formation."[34] The origin of life was not so improbable, he suggests, but rather resulted from the natural laws that stipulate self-organization among these catalysts. A crucial point here is that the propensity toward self-organization is an elementary characteristic of matter itself. When matter is arranged in sufficient patterns of complexity, and these patterns have the chance to interact with one another (no matter how long this process takes), a point is reached where life can form.

The second crucial idea that Gardner takes from Kauffman is that there is a saturation point at which this force of self-organization allows life to develop quite quickly once these complex adaptive systems cross from random disorder into ever more ordered patterns. These systems exist, as Kauffman says "at the 'edge of chaos,'" after which they join in an accelerated "combinatorial optimization process" that becomes the process of evolution itself. Organisms and ecosystems rapidly advance in ever shorter periods of time and to ever greater levels of complexity. Another important possibility that results from this perspective is the phenomenon of *co-evolving* organisms. Co-evolution creates unique opportunities to make organisms and ecosystems even more complex.[35] If bats develop echolocation, for example, then presumably their prey will develop survival techniques to contest it.

Elsewhere, Gardner discusses theoretical biologist Simon Conway Morris's hypothesis that evolutionary pressures in separate ecosystems converge on similar solutions to problems faced by organisms in those situations. To continue with the bats example, both birds and bats—very different organisms—have wings. Evolution tends to reinvent the same solutions to familiar problems again and again. And if this is happening on earth among various species here, then why would it not happen elsewhere in the universe? Gardner asks whether in the distant future, after contact has been made, all these beings might not finally be able to communicate and understand one another's evolutionary histories.[36]

Gardner makes it clear that Kauffman and other complexity theorists lean toward a *biologically* inspired understanding of ultimate reality. According to this perspective, life is the grand image or suggestion that makes all else intelligible.[37] Key to the complexity theory conception of life as the foundation metaphor for everything is the concept of *emergence*.[38] According to John Holland, one of Kauffman's colleagues at the Santa Fe Institute, emergence is about much coming from little, whether the process occurs in ant colonies, networks of neurons, the immune system, the Internet, or the global economy. With all these phenomena, the behavior of the whole is always much more complex than that of the parts. Holland says that emergence works even better when the system demonstrates some kind of capacity for adaptation or learning. Another factor is when the component mechanisms can interact without central control. As Holland explains, "persistent patterns at one level of observation can become building blocks at still more complex levels."[39] This effect results in *"hierarchical organization,"* a term Gardner uses in italics. Indefinitely large hierarchies lead to more and more complexity. In this way, the most basic components of the universe, subatomic particles that appeared at the Big Bang, combine to lead to the most complex and sophisticated phenomena like human culture.[40] Moreover, according to Gardner, "the evidence is overwhelming that the process of multilevel hierarchical emergence is accelerating rapidly."[41]

Since multilevel hierarchical emergence may ultimately change the very physical state of the universe, it is impossible to make reliable predictions about the future and fate of the universe. Physicists and cosmologists who make such predictions, forecasting either heat death or ultimate expansion and entropy, do not take into account the possibility of this kind of emergence. Gardner calls this emergence "a cosmologically extended biosphere," and suggests that to overlook it is to ignore a crucial possibility. A usual conception of the physicists' "theory of everything" seldom involves considerations of nonphysical elements such as human intelligence and culture. Such phenomena, from physicists' point of view, are merely by-products of more fundamental processes. The principles of physics and the constants of nature have always been taken as invariant, subject only to laws of mathematics, but Gardner's Biocosm theories imply that such phenomena as intelligence and culture could form part of the structure of the universe. The realms of life and nonlife would be inevitably linked in this scheme, and life would take a preeminent rather than a subordinate role in the structure of the universe. Life could eventually expand outward into the cosmos to change not only the universe's structure but also its destiny. The universe need not end in *either* a heat death of the Big Crunch or the alternative endless expansion, in fire or ice; instead, culture itself could have a very real impact upon the physical state of the universe at the end of time.[42]

All of nature might be teleological, or ends oriented, Gardner suggests. Moreover, Darwinism, which is so often understood to be an aimless process of species radiation, could actually be a progression toward something. Gardner proposes that life tends toward more complexity, more diversity, and greater mastery over its surroundings, and ultimately toward consciousness.[43] Oddly, though it implies diversity, Darwinian natural selection may be convergent, rather than divergent—a proposition with which Teilhard would certainly concur.

Gardner, in essence, implies that while some cosmologists may be looking through the wrong end of the telescope, some biologists, such as Dawkins, may be looking through the wrong end of the electron microscope. Certainly, the genes may be "selfish" and interested in their own reproduction, but so are the organisms that the genes compose. Gardner once again looks at biology and complexity theory as the guiding disciplines for what is happening. Kauffman discusses the idea of complexity as dependent upon the notion of *attractors*, which Gardner defines as "patterns toward which ostensibly undirected physical processes converge robustly."[44] Attractors are like the drain at the bottom of the sink toward which gravity brings the water. All the eddies and patterns in the water after the plug is pulled converge when the water exits down the drain hole. A relevant example of an attractor from the field of biology is the notion of an organism's ontogeny, the developmental history of an organism laid out in its DNA. Given that an organism's genetic structure will inevitably direct it toward a certain, specific state as a complex and mature member of its species, the organism's ontogeny is its attractor. There could, therefore, be a cosmic version of an individual organism's ontogeny—a cosmic attractor prescribed by the cosmic code laid out by the constants of nature. Just as a tadpole is programmed by its DNA to become a frog and, more poetically, a caterpillar to become a butterfly, so the universe is programmed by the constants of nature to become ... well, we cannot exactly know yet, since we ourselves may be akin to the cells of the organism. But what is crucial is that there is a *telos*, or directed end.

If the laws of physics and constants of nature could somehow provide a clue to our purpose in the universe, then the science of cosmology would be largely engaged in cracking the "utility function" of the cosmic code. The field of cosmology would be revolutionized. It could become consilient, perhaps in the most unexpected ways, with the social sciences and the humanities,[45] including even religion.

FROM "WHAT IS NEXT?" TO "WHAT IS ULTIMATE?"

Gardner concludes *Biocosm* with an all-too-brief conjecture of what may be, or perhaps more truly, what *should* be the future of our species. He explains that a directed, transhuman evolution of our species will involve an enhancement of our current capabilities. The supermind of posthuman beings will most likely involve the extension or augmentation of current human mental capacities such as memory.[46] Most important for Gardner, however, is not the enhancement of the individual but the question of whether we will ultimately evolve into a single global intelligence. If direct interfaces are formed between the human mind and computers, then merging individual minds into one supermind becomes a distinct possibility.

Gardner draws parallels between Teilhard's notion of the Noosphere and Kauffman's ideas of the universe's proclivity toward self-organization—an "instinct for order," as Gardner calls it.[47] Beyond this, however, Gardner draws in *The Intelligent Universe* from theorists such as Seth Lloyd and Stephen Wolfram, who propose that the universe is, in effect, a vast computer.

Wolfram, for example, believes that a few simple programming rules, expressed through entities called *cellular automata*, progressively build the universe into a more and more complex system. A cellular automaton is simply a computational mechanism that changes the shade of a cell on a grid from white to black, or vice versa. Wolfram's interest lies in the fact that the automata programs, running long enough, will begin to display intricate patterns, pictures that very often bear an uncanny resemblance to objects in the natural world, such as lilies or river beds. Nature, it seems, performs similar computations that complexity theorists have discovered, producing all its varied marvels.[48]

Lloyd, meanwhile, believes not only that the universe operates upon digital computation, but, more fundamentally, that it *is* a quantum computer. Unlike a traditional digital computer, which functions on *bits* expressed by one or zero, a quantum computer functions on *qubits*, computing elements that exist in a delicate state of quantum entanglement, neither zero nor one, that allows the computer to perform very rapid and complex calculations by exploring a vast number of computational possibilities at the same time.[49] If the universe is indeed a quantum computer, as Lloyd believes, then the physical laws generated by Einstein's theory of relativity can be reconciled with quantum mechanics as an expression of a more fundamental quantum computation that drives the vast complexity of all the phenomena of the universe.

The question remains: where will all this computation, digital or quantum, eventually lead? For Teilhard and his more contemporary physicist followers John Barrow and Frank Tipler, the computation—if indeed the universe can be characterized as such—will culminate in the Omega Point. The Omega Point for Teilhard would be the *telos* of the evolution of all life on earth. Humanity, *collectively* (and, although Teilhard does not explicitly suggest this, perhaps even other intelligent beings on earth), would be the star of the show, now a single super-organism whose individual identities (each one of us) remain distinct but together constitute the hypostatization of the Christian God. For Barrow and Tipler, the Omega Point is not simply the *telos* of the evolution of life on earth, but, as Gardner explains it, "the final point in the evolution of a linked set of closed universes that proceed to contract toward a Big Crunch billions of years hence."[50] Intelligent life will then come to subordinate all inanimate matter and energy. In other words, all of life has a fundamental drive (life's radial energy, to use Teilhard's phrase) to overcome entropy. And for Gardner, this upward movement or teleological nature of Teilhard's theory fits very well with his Selfish Biocosm hypothesis.[51]

Needless to say, while the Selfish Biocosm hypothesis offers a sweeping and controversial perspective on the grand design and future trajectory of life in the universe, the reader may be left with serious questions about life's more immediate, earthly concerns. Futuristic cyborg beings zipping through the galaxy in metal bodies at near light speed, millions of years hence, carrying millions of times the intelligence of any human alive today are clearly remote, in every sense, from the political, cultural, and physical problems with which we currently contend. What should we, in the early 21st century, be doing to lay the groundwork for our great progeny? Gardner vaguely outlines a few possible directives. First, in practical terms, engineers are already intervening in the process of biological evolution through bio-engineering; programs on artificial intelligence and artificial life are also under way (*The Intelligent Universe*, Chapters 1 and 2, sketches out some of the initiatives being made in this direction).

Of more interest to theologians and philosophers would be the ethical guidelines needed to direct current scientific research and human activity more generally. Along these lines, Gardner claims that his perspective implies an ethical responsibility—indeed, imposes such a duty upon us. Unlike any other creature, the human species, because it has the power to direct its own evolution, has what Gardner calls a "*transgenerational* moral imperative" (Gardner's italics) to do so. Our generation has the responsibility to future generations to lay both the ethical and the technological groundwork for the development of the intelligent beings who will come after us.[52] This mandate applies to coming debates about the ethics of medical enhancements directed toward the development and design of posthumans, but also suggests the need for individual reflection upon one's own life choices. Indeed, "each living creature, at each juncture in the cosmic life cycle, is responsible for a small but possibly indispensable contribution to the overall process of cosmic growth, evolution and eventual renewal."[53] Each of us is ethically responsible for the future evolution of the species and ultimately for the whole fate of the cosmos. Addressing this ethical responsibility may be where transhumanism's most fruitful dialogue with religion can take place.

NOTES

1. James Gardner, *Biocosm* (Maui, HI: Inner Ocean, 2003), 226.

2. Gardner, *Biocosm*, 226–227.

3. Gardner, *Biocosm*, 227.

4. Michael S. Burdett, "Contextualizing a Christian Perspective on Transcendence and Human Enhancement," in *Transhumanism and Transcendence*, edited by Ronald Cole- Turner (Washington, DC: Georgetown University Press, 2011), 33.

5. Burdett, "Contextualizing a Christian Perspective," 25.

6. Burdett, "Contextualizing a Christian Perspective," 32.

7. Burdett, "Contextualizing a Christian Perspective," 27.

8. Burdett, "Contextualizing a Christian Perspective," 28.

9. Burdett, "Contextualizing a Christian Perspective," 29.

10. Pierre Teilhard de Chardin, *The Future of Man* (New York, NY: Doubleday, 2004), 13.

11. Teilhard de Chardin, *The Future of Man*, 23.

12. Teilhard de Chardin, *The Future of Man*, 25.

13. Pierre Teilhard de Chardin, *The Phenomenon of Man* (New York, NY: Harper and Row, 1965), 65–66.

14. Gardner, *Biocosm*, 194–195.

15. Gardner, *Biocosm*, 9.

16. Gardner, *Biocosm*, 25.

17. Gardner, *Biocosm*, 44.

18. Gardner, *Biocosm*, 45.

19. Gardner, *Biocosm*, 39.

20. Gardner, *Biocosm*, 46.

21. Gardner, *Biocosm*, 47.

22. James Gardner, *The Intelligent Universe* (Franklin Lakes, NJ: New Page Books, 2007), 169.

23. Gardner, *Biocosm*, 78.

24. Gardner, *Biocosm*, 78.

25. Gardner, *Biocosm*, 84–85.

26. Gardner, *Biocosm*, 121.

27. Gardner, *Biocosm*, 185.

28. Gardner, *Biocosm*, 196.

29. Gardner, *Biocosm*, 196.

30. Gardner, *Biocosm*, 49.

31. Gardner, *Biocosm*, 50.

32. Gardner, *Biocosm*, 51.

33. Gardner, *Biocosm*, 52.

34. Gardner, *Biocosm*, 52.

35. Gardner, *Biocosm*, 54.

36. Gardner, *The Intelligent Universe*, 103.

37. Gardner, *Biocosm*, 59.

38. Gardner, *Biocosm*, 69.

39. Gardner, *Biocosm*, 70.

40. Gardner, *Biocosm*, 70.

41. Gardner, *Biocosm*, 71.

42. Gardner, *Biocosm*, 72.

43. Gardner, *Biocosm*, 76.

44. Gardner, *Biocosm*, 79.

45. Gardner, *Biocosm*, 79–80.

46. Gardner, *Biocosm*, 209.

47. Gardner, *Biocosm*, 195.

48. Gardner, *The Intelligent Universe*, 28–29.

49. Gardner, *The Intelligent Universe*, 33.

50. Gardner, *Biocosm*, 284.

51. Gardner, *Biocosm*, 196.

52. Gardner, *Biocosm*, 212–213.

53. Gardner, *Biocosm*, 216.

The Religion of Technology: Transhumanism and the Myth of Progress

Michael S. Burdett

Mary Midgley writes in her book, *The Myths We Live By*, that "We are accustomed to think of myths as the opposite of science. But in fact they are a central part of it: the part that decides its significance in our lives."[1] Midgley argues that myth is still very much alive today for modern Western peoples; she suggests that even though we tell ourselves that we have become more advanced and myth need not apply to us moderns, we still find it cropping up. Myth crops up even—or perhaps especially—in those places that are purported to be the instruments of this demythologization, such as with technoscience.[2]

Midgley goes on to say that we very much need to understand these technoscientific myths.[3] She understands that her readers have a deeply embedded suspicion of myth-speaking and are quick to associate myth with deception. Addressing this propensity, she says, "Myths are not lies. Nor are they detached stories. They are imaginative patterns, networks of powerful symbols that suggest particular ways of interpreting the world. They shape its meaning."[4] In line with the thinking of such diverse scholars as Mircea Eliade, Charles Taylor, Langdon Gilkey, and C. S. Lewis, myth and its meaning for humanity cannot and ought not be so quickly reduced to the "untrue."

I agree that mythologizing is not an option, an either/or, for humanity. I agree with Heidegger, Gadamer, Ricoeur, and others that we are meaning-bearing or meaning-imbuing creatures. We are thoroughly hermeneutical and we weave stories about ourselves, the world we inhabit, and the other creatures with which we come into contact.[5] We do so without conscious awareness, yet it is precisely those areas, such as technoscience, that claim to not mythologize that need the most attention. Precisely because it fails to acknowledge this mythologizing, technoscience can tacitly influence its members and affect the field dramatically. It can act like a repressed psychological disorder that skews vision of the world and controls behavior unbeknownst to the community but entirely clear to everyone else. The road to psychological integration and health begins with explicit acknowledgment of this repression—for technoscience, this means understanding it, too, mythologizes. This is really Midgley's driving concern: to show how technoscience mythologizes and what this means for technoscience and for those of us who live in a society governed by technoscience.

The technoscientific myth addressed here, and arguably one of the most central to Midgley's work, is the myth of progress. This chapter charts a succinct intellectual history of this myth of progress and explores how it has been embedded, and is still embedded, in the claims of science and technology. Furthermore, I aim to show how transhumanism depends upon and extends this rampant and robust myth and how its enthusiasts subsequently derive religious value from it. First, I begin with the claims of this myth of progress and try to arrive at some characterizing features of it. Next, I turn to the origins of this myth of progress and consider how it became entwined with the claims of technoscience, leading to its prominence in the 19th century. The discussion then turns to the first part of the 20th century, when this myth was seriously questioned and the entire edifice of the Modern project began to crumble at its base. From here, I focus on more recent technoscientific utopias that culminate in transhumanism and show a propensity for taking up this myth once again. My final comments address the religious dimensions of transhumanism and assert that the myth of progress is one of its core doctrines.

WHAT IS THE MYTH OF PROGRESS?

The myth of progress can be defined as the belief that history/society/humanity has advanced, is continuing to advance, and will advance in the future. What is meant by the claim that we are advancing? There is an inherent assertion that a particular target is getting incrementally closer. This myth of progress depends upon this target, this ideal. We are advancing on this imagined or projected ideal and, hence, are making progress toward it. A necessary distinction between "change" and the more specific kind of change called "progress" is precisely the ideal against which we measure this change. If we move toward or away from this ideal, we are making progress or regressing from it, respectively. Change has no goal or ideal, but progress does.

This advancing to a proposed ideal is thoroughly historical and integrally related to the future. The myth of progress claims that the present is a diminished form of what is to come. It is not complete, but rather often signals the discrepancy between the imperfect present and the fulfilled and perfect future. This point is where the utopian tradition comes in. Often this myth of progress is represented in utopian literature such that the ideal to be attained is represented as a projected reality or society. The point behind this utopian literature is comparison with the present, and one of the most often cited roads to attaining this perfect state is through the myth of progress: "We aren't there now, but this is what is in store for us."

When the myth of progress is invoked, there are usually at least three targets.[6] The first is epistemological in nature. Progress occurs when consistent advancements are made toward a better understanding of reality. Our understanding of reality becomes increasingly truer, where truth is taken as a correspondence theory of truth.[7] In other words, our concepts and language used to describe and represent reality become increasingly more accurate. This understanding of progress might depend upon certain methodologies, disciplines, or practices that, in some sense, help us to discern reality as it truly is. They could refer to religious tenets and articles of faith to achieve this end. Alternatively, they could appeal to philosophical scrutiny and the domain of logic. Finally, they might call on the method and practice of science and its strict empirical standards. Each of these constitutive practices has been used to invoke the necessity of the myth of progress, and each can be used in asserting the relative progress they might make toward truth.

The second target of this myth of progress may refer to how humanity progresses and how the human condition is improved. This might mean the pervasion of particular personal virtues such as justice, tolerance, independence, and liberty, or it might refer to a shared communal value like social justice or equality. Progress in relation to this goal occurs when elements that cultivate the inner human experience, and which are often associated with positive moral virtues, are said to be realized in history. Progress happens when human beings attain, even in part, certain values.

Finally, the myth of progress may refer to specific context-independent concrete conditions that are often quantifiably measured. Instead of progress aiming at a more virtuous inner life of human beings, it can be measured utilizing particular empirical and objective metrics. Such measures might include things like reduced morbidity and premature mortality or an increased gross domestic product. The aim here is quantifiable and physical.

The myth of progress can refer to any one of these three proposed goals. Often, however, the second and third aims are held to be products of the first. In other words, a greater knowledge of the surrounding world invariably leads to the creation of an environment more hospitable to human flourishing, both externally and internally. Additionally, if we have a better understanding of ourselves and of how members of society interact, we will be in a better position to attain the first target. As Plato reminds us in *The Republic*, the first step to achieving the Good is a proper knowledge of the Good.

But what makes this adherence to progress a "myth" as opposed to a general belief in the notion of progress? What value is added when we refer to it as a myth? First, this approach speaks of the embeddedness of the belief. Simple extirpation or jettisoning at a moment's notice is just not possible with myths. Because they are so embedded in belief structures they are, second, very resilient. Third, myths are a special kind of narrative or story, the ones that elucidate ultimate concern and are related to existentially.[8] They are connected to how we perceive the world around us, interpret it, and imbue existential meaning into it. It is better to say we trust in these myths than believe in them, for we engage them personally rather than assent to them in some disengaged way. We adhere to them with our lives, not just our minds.[9]

In fact, several psychological studies have revealed the deeply subjective and existential features of belief in progress. These studies show the close proximity between belief in progress and belief in traditional religion. As Miguel Farias has stated, "recent studies have suggested that belief in human progress can serve the same compensatory functions previously implicated in religious belief."[10] People have been found to be more resilient to stress and anxiety stemming from reflection on their own mortality when they adhered to the myth of progress. Subjects in the previously mentioned studies, for example, related to belief in progress in the same way a religious person would relate to a doctrine of his or her faith by drawing existential value from it. Therefore, referring to the mythic function of belief in progress is an entirely adequate proposal.

How has this myth of progress arisen and evolved? And how is it inseparable from the ascendency of science and technology since the Enlightenment through to Modernity?

THE ORIGINS OF THE MYTH OF PROGRESS AND THE APPEAL TO SCIENCE AND TECHNOLOGY

The origins of the myth of progress are usually seen in the Enlightenment, but some scholars have argued that the myth of progress is visible even prior to this era, citing ancient and Christian medieval sources.

For instance, Xenophanes in the sixth century BCE declared, "The gods did not reveal to men all things in the beginning, but men through their own search find in the course of time that which is better."[11] Likewise, Protagoras, one of the first and most well-known Sophists, was emphatic that humanity's plight is an ever gradual ascent from bestial beginnings lacking in culture to one of enlightenment through the advancement of knowledge. Finally, Aeschylus proffers *Prometheus Bound*, where, despite Prometheus's own cursing of his having brought fire to humanity, it is clear that fire improved the conditions of humankind and brought with it the development of culture, language, and technology.[12]

The most widely read work on the myth of progress, J. B. Bury's *The Idea of Progress: An Inquiry into Its Origin and Growth* (1920), claims that the modern myth of progress is opposed to Christianity. However, many others see a clear relation. For instance, the Christian mystic Joachim de Fiore in the latter half of the 12th century proposed his famous ascent of history in three stages, each corresponding to a person of the Trinity: the Age of the Father and the Law; the Age of the Son and the Gospel; and that which still lies ahead in the Age of the Spirit, "when human beings would be liberated from their physical-animal desires and would know a contemplative serenity and happiness of mind scarcely even describable."[13] Similarly, de Fiore's famous Dominican discipline, Campanella, penned *The City of the Sun*, which describes a utopian society where humankind lives "all things in common." Many other examples of the myth of progress abound in Christian history.[14]

However, the traditional story of the rise of the myth of progress is located within the currents of rationalism and science associated most closely with the 17th centuries and onward. As Leo Marx has remarked, "The idea of history as a record of progress driven by the application of science-based knowledge was not simply another idea among many. Rather it was a figurative concept lodged at the center of what became ... the dominant secular world-picture of Western culture."[15] Indeed, despite apparent influences of millenarian dreaming in the Christian tradition, it would be the development of a *novum organum*—a new method that would become modern science—that would spark hopes of a new relation to a reality that promised nothing less than perfection and progress.

Much is owed to Francis Bacon for this coupling of technoscience and progress. The father of modern science, he was central to infusing a scientific basis into the origins of our modern myth of progress. Indeed, Bacon proposed that through Baconian science, humankind would enjoy a new state of harmony. According to this scholar, by challenging ancient tradition and adopting a new approach to reality, humanity would enjoy immense progress religiously, socially, and personally. To do so meant radically overhauling traditional education and knowledge. Bacon offered this view in his *Instauratio Magna*, which spoke of the restoration of basic Adamic capacities lost in the Fall of Man by employing a new method for amassing information about the natural world.[16] This new method was different in that it relied more upon induction to arrive at governing principles rather than on first principles largely drawn from Aristotelian logic.[17] Bacon's utopia, *The New Atlantis*, gives a picture of what Bacon thought society would look like if it followed this reinvigorated education drawn from his *Instauratio Magna*. In it, we find monastic-like scientists at the center of the society devising inventions for the betterment of humanity. Progress could be made, according to Bacon, if society would simply utilize his proposed method. Indeed, the Royal Society took Bacon at his word and set him as the patron of this premiere scientific organization founded on the ideal of progress in knowledge of the natural world.[18] Science, so Society members thought, could be the catalyst to a realized utopia.

THE MYTH OF PROGRESS IN THE 19TH AND EARLY 20TH CENTURIES

Bacon's legacy of progress through technoscience spread like wildfire through the 18th and 19th centuries, albeit with an increasingly secular tone. Indeed, these centuries galvanized the myth of progress, allowing it to seep into the subconscious of Western Europe and America. Philosophical figureheads of this era include Auguste Comte, G. W. F. Hegel, J. S. Mill, and Karl Marx. Comte's work was especially influential in regard to the social and moral philosophy of the 19th century. His progressive ordering of history depended upon the intellectual development of humankind in three tiers: the theological, the metaphysical, and the positive or scientific. Comte claimed that each of the physical disciplines had reached the final scientific stage (e.g., physics, chemistry) and the time was ripe to apply the sciences to society as a whole. He maintained that if society were to be ordered according to his positivist science, it would enjoy nothing less than utopia. He put forth these principles and posited their effects in *System of Positive Polity: A Treatise on Sociology.*[19]

Others, such as Hegel and Marx, similarly contended that a rationalistic or scientific account of history yielded a natural vision of progress. Much like Comte, Hegel's account of progress depended upon the development of mind/spirit in history. For Hegel, this progress owed its existence to the logical structure inherent in the World Spirit (*Geist*) working its way out through history. His famous dialectic, "thesis, antithesis, synthesis," when applied to history, yielded a gradual ascent of cultures from primitive people to the ancients, budding in cosmopolitan Germany. For Hegel, it was a logical inevitability that history progresses and the various areas of human achievement, such as politics, religion, and aesthetics, get historically better.

Marx, a devout follower of Hegel, has been similarly interpreted along deterministic lines. The inevitability of economic progress lines the pages of *Capital* and *The Communist Manifesto*. The preface of the first edition of *Capital* proclaims the expected decline of capitalism and the praised ascendency of socialism "working with iron necessity towards inevitable results."[20] We find similar descriptions in *The Communist Manifesto* and in the preface to *A Contribution to the Critique of Political Economy*: "In broad outlines we can designate the Asiatic, the ancient, the feudal, and the modern bourgeois modes of production as so many progressive epochs in the economic formation of society."[21] The inevitability of historical progress was a scientific truth for Marx. Whereas the catalyst of progress was metaphysical and logical for Hegel, economics—and, some have argued, science and technology—drove this movement for Marx.[22]

THE PROGRESS OF THE CENTURY.
THE LIGHTNING STEAM PRESS.   THE ELECTRIC TELEGRAPH.   THE LOCOMOTIVE.   THE STEAMBOAT.

The Progress of the Century by Currier and Ives. (Library of Congress)

This myth of progress and its rational appeal to technoscience are also found in artwork and advertisements of the era, which reveal how deeply embedded the myth was in the social psyche of the time. For instance, the image titled *The Progress of the Century* is taken from one of the most prolific American lithographers of the time, Currier and Ives (1876). Depicted in the piece are telegraphs, trains, and steamboats—technologies that were critical to binding together the remote areas of the United States. Of particular note is the lettering coming out of the telegraph that reads "Liberty and Union Now and Forever" and "One and Inseparable." These technologies, as the image shows, bolstered the very nationalism and identity of the country's citizens.

Something similar is seen in the image, painted by John Gast in 1872, called *American Progress*. This scene depicts the ideology of Manifest Destiny, whereby settlers marched into the vast unknown with the intention of taming the expansive and rugged west. The picture depicts the old republican symbol Liberty, but with the new name of Progress.[23] She brings with her the light of advancement and carries a wire of the telegraph. The telegraph and train in the background became symbols of the progress that would bind the edge of American civilization with those cities east of

American Progress by John Gast. (Library of Congress)

the Mississippi River.[24] We see American settlers armed with these instruments of progress marching toward the savages in the darkened half of the picture, symbolizing the reform of these primitives and heralding an age of civility and culture all in the name of science, technology, and American nationalism. As this picture represents, the idealism of Manifest Destiny became entwined with America's growing obsession with scientific and technological progress—so much so, that whenever progress was invoked, science and technology served as its basis.

What we see in this genealogy of the myth of progress, from its humble beginnings latent in ancient sources through to its full blossoming by the end of the 19th century, is a steady removal of the engine of progress from providence to one increasingly dependent upon the ingenuity of humanity in science and technology. The driving force—the catalyst of progress—by the time we enter the 20th century is clearly technoscience.

THE MYTH OF PROGRESS AND ITS TECHNOSCIENTIFIC BASIS CHALLENGED

This myth of progress has not avoided all skeptics. In the 19th century and with increasing vigor into the early 20th century, one observes dissenting voices that were not swept away by the jingoistic proclamations of philosophers, economists, technologists, and scientists about the merits of technoscience. In the 19th century, there appeared whispers of opposition in figures such as Kierkegaard, Dostoevsky, and Nietzsche, all of whom attacked the philosophical side of the myth of progress. Dostoevsky's Underground Man gives a harsh diatribe against this myth of progress represented in the Crystal Palace, a symbol of utopianism taken from Chernyshevsky's *What Is to Be Done?*[25] Kierkegaard is the ultimate critic of Hegelianism, with its assured stance on the advancement of history; he retorts that man can have no such God-like point of view on history. Likewise, Nietzsche is no friend of progress, recounting how humankind has slipped from the heroic virtues embodied in Greek myths to the slave morality of Christianity. For Nietzsche, these modern notions of progress were merely echoes of millennial dreams robbing us of our true vocation as individuals in the present.[26]

We may even see this criticism of the myth of progress as part of a much more far-ranging criticism of Modernity that hit center stage in the mid-20th century. One of the dominant attacks on modernity from what has been called postmodernity is this skepticism of a trajectory in history, the appeal to an ultimate narrative. As Jean-Francois Lyotard so poignantly remarks, the postmodern condition is characterized as an "incredulity toward metanarratives."[27] This death of the meta-narrative is particularly launched at the ubiquity of the myth of progress and, Lyotard says, "this incredulity is undoubtedly a product of progress in the sciences."[28]

While these critics are important to the philosophical questioning of the myth of progress, the actual events of the early 20th century have done the most to erode at this confidence in the myth of progress. As Robert Nisbet has put it, "It is often said that this vaunted faith is dead, in the West at least—killed by World War I, by the Great Depression, by World War II, by the spectacle of military despotism, under whatever ideological label, galloping across the earth at rising speed, by belief in the exhaustion of nature and her resources, by malaise compounded of boredom, apathy and disillusionment at one extreme and by consecration to mindless terror at the other, or by some other lethal force."[29] The utter destruction of humankind had never occurred on such a grand scale prior to the 20th century. The death toll of World War I was 16 million people; some 20 years later in World War II, it was elevated to 60 million. The atrocities of the calculated—one could even say "scientific"—extermination of the Jews in the Holocaust sent a shockwave through society, unhinging the cool, calm, and collected intellectual belief in the inexorable advancement of humankind, given that it was the core of civilization that had committed such atrocities.

Philosophical and historical criticisms aside, dissent also arose from the very technoscientific arena itself. Thomas Kuhn, in *The Structure of Scientific Revolutions*, construed differently the belief that science progresses, even if its translation into society may not yield the same outcome. Kuhn's metahistorical description of science identifies progress in science within what he terms eras of "normal science" but not in "scientific revolutions." In normal science, young scientists are trained to see a single paradigm through which they view their entire field. Everyone in the scientific community operates under this single paradigm during normal science and "the direction, the methods, instruments, and the problems that scientists face, are all fixed by the established theory."[30] Kuhn states, "Viewed from within any community, however, whether of scientists or of non-scientists, the result of successful creative work *is* progress. How could it be anything else?"[31] Progress seems inevitable because all scientists within the paradigm are working toward a common goal. They operate on the same problems with the same tools. In fact, the questions that scientists pose in normal science, Kuhn tells us, are those they are confident the paradigm will be able to answer.

The issue becomes more complex when normal science is disrupted and unsolved problems become more pressing; in such a case, competing paradigms begin to arise. It is during this phase in the operation of science—that is, during a scientific revolution—that scientific progress becomes untenable for Kuhn. Unlike gestalt switches, one cannot choose between various competing paradigms—one cannot switch from the old paradigm to the new and back again at will. Kuhn argues that not only does the scientist see the world differently under the new paradigm, but the data that were originally obtained under the auspices of the old paradigm become entirely new data. In a sense, the world changes with a new paradigm and one must reinterpret everything using that new paradigm. In turn, Kuhn rejects the claim that science progresses through history because with each new paradigm in history comes an entirely new world incommensurable with the former. Kuhn explains that science has no teleological end; instead, it is an "evolution-from-what-we-know."

Here we have yet another reason to doubt this myth of progress: the very engine of that progress, science, does not seem itself to progress. If our myth of progress depends upon the scientific appeal to knowing more today about reality than we did yesterday and especially centuries ago, Kuhn has given a compelling model of history that denies such progress.

A RENEWAL OF THE MYTH IN TECHNOLOGICAL UTOPIANISM AND TRANSHUMANISM

There have been considerable censures of the myth of progress in the 20th century but this myth is surely not dead—particularly in technoscience. In spite of the world wars, philosophical and historical criticism, and even a blow to the actual practice of science by Kuhn, the myth of progress is alive and well. Today, we see this renewal in various utopian ideologies involving technology. While Kuhn makes scientific progress difficult to swallow, others in the past century have sought the engine of progress primarily in technology.

Science on the March by Alexander Leydenfrost. (Courtesy of *Popular Mechanics*, Hearst Corporation)

Consider this picture created by A. Leydenfrost. It appeared in the magazine *Popular Mechanics* in January 1952, only seven years after World War II had ended. The image is included in the lead article, "Science on the March," and is part of the Golden Anniversary edition that celebrated 50 years of publishing. This article recounts all the great technologies that had been invented since 1902, when the magazine was launched, to 1952. The progress of the airplane lines the sky above, moving from the biplane to the jet aircraft. Below is depicted the advance of the automobile, from the first Model T to the modern car. In the foreground are seen cutting-edge technologies and speculative inventions such as rocket ships, cyclotrons, and flying saucers. The author speculated that just as the last 50 years of technological progress had drastically changed the course of humankind and history itself, so there was no reason why technology itself should not continue to rapidly advance and take on some of the most difficult global issues of our time: world hunger, overpopulation, and resource depletion. Images such as these suggest the continuity of the myth of progress through the 20th century where technology serves as the basis for this progress.

We find similar sentiments in our era with figures such as Thorstein Veblen and R. Buckminster Fuller and in the ethos known as the "Californian Ideology." Veblen rose to notoriety in the 1930s as the leader of the technocracy movement in the United States. Observing that the U.S. government could not handle the economic crisis of the Great Depression, Veblen proposed that "the ills of the economy were traceable . . . to the inefficient adjustment of the social order to modern high-energy technology."[32] The technocrats' major accomplishment was to suggest that the answer to a growing technological environment was the expansion of technical craft into social engineering, whereby engineers made political and social decisions rather than leaders in business and politics. Fuller, the inventor and futurist, also held that it was within the power of humanity to solve some of the most egregious global ills, if only we turned to the power of technology to eradicate them. Author of unconventional inventions such as the Dymaxion House and Dymaxion Car, Fuller spoke extensively around the world on the utopian potential of creative technical design.[33] Today we see the influence of Fuller and Veblen underlying much of Silicon Valley's "Californian Ideology": the belief in a soft technological determinism along with libertarian economic ideals.[34] The high-tech industry meets Ayn Rand philosophy in the belief that exploitation of information networks will yield economic growth in a postindustrial age and likewise weaken political power in favor of virtual self-organized communities. For many in our time, technology has become the panacea and driving force behind the myth of progress.

This belief in technological progress is taken to new extremes by members of the transhumanism movement. Philippe Verdoux is right to note that belief in technological progress is one key principle, if not the premiere doctrine, underlying the transhumanism movement.[35] As he asserts, one need simply reference the World Transhumanist Association's (now called Humanity+) core values written by Nick Bostrom.[36] Bostrom contends that technological progress is one of the main factors for achieving the transhumanist vision. Transhumanist Max More lists "perpetual progress" as one of the seven "Principles of Extropy," and the word "progress" is used more than 20 times on the Humanity+ website's Frequently Asked Questions webpage.[37]

Transhumanists claim, along with the other technological utopians mentioned here, that technology is the lynchpin to social and political progress. In other words, the individual human experience is bettered because the surrounding environment becomes more hospitable. Transhumanism radicalizes this myth of progress. It asserts that not only does technology transform society and the economy for the better, but also individual human experience can be affected directly through bodily enhancement. Transhumanists advocate for applying growing technologies such as nanotechnology and other computer hardware to the human body. Bostrom's "Letter from Utopia" is instructive in speaking of how this progress will feel to our transhuman progeny: "You could say I am happy, that I feel good. You could say that I feel surpassing bliss. But these are words invented to describe human experience. What I feel is as far beyond human feelings as my thoughts are beyond human thoughts. I wish I could show you what I have in mind. If only I could share one second of my conscious life with you!"[38] Transhumanists claim we need not resort to indirect measures to bring internal bliss and progress; instead, we have the power to engineer this outcome by applying technology directly to the human body.

Transhumanists and posthuman speculators are not necessarily naïve about the force of technology to bring about solely positive outcomes. Bostrom and his Future of Humanity Institute arguably devote more time to analyzing the existential risks[39] that can come with the rampant utilization of these new technologies. Bostrom estimates that ultimate annihilation of the human species has at least a 25 percent chance of happening in the next 100 years; Sir Martin Rees suggests this risk is closer to 50 percent.[40] Even adamant futurist Ray Kurzweil admits widespread usage of technology might carry significant social, political and existential dangers. In the case of Kurzweil and Bostrom, however, this gloom is couched in a much larger meta-narrative of progress. Kurzweil states that progress arises within any evolutionary system and contends that evolution is a feature beyond just biology, being visible in technological growth and the entire cosmos as well. He states, "Ultimately, the entire universe will become saturated with our intelligence. This is the destiny of the universe. We will determine our own fate rather than have it determined by the current 'dumb,' simple, machinelike forces that rule celestial mechanics."[41] Furthermore, Bostrom claims that our chances are much worse if we fail to utilize these technologies, positing that what awaits us on the other side is nothing short of bliss. There may be minor setbacks, both futurists say, but overall progress is the resounding paradigm.

CONCLUSION

This chapter has charted the rise of the myth of progress in the West to its ascent in the 19th century, followed by significant criticism in the 20th century that led this myth to the point of almost dying out entirely in the mid-to-late 20th century. In the latter half of the 20th century, this myth found new and fervent supporters in technoscientific circles, and it continues to spark hope in the 21st century by making a greater appeal to technological advancement today than ever before. It is here that we find transhumanism taking up the well-worn and oft-cited mantle of the myth of progress in our own time.

I do not intend to argue for or against the merits of trusting in the myth of progress.[42] Rather, I suggest that trusting in the myth of progress is a thoroughly religious act. As noted at the beginning of this chapter, it is proper to speak of belief in progress as a myth because of the resilience, embeddedness, and existential nature of adherence to progress. Many see this belief in progress as a bastardization of Christian millennial dreaming, causing it to be at least indebted to Christian religious history, if not thoroughly religious itself. Ricoeur refers to the scientific variant of the myth of progress as "a rationalist corruption of Christian eschatology."[43] Furthermore, the psychological studies cited earlier reveal the close proximity of belief in the myth of progress and religious concerns. Both were said to function existentially in the same way for the individuals studied. There is a historical and psychological precedent in claiming that trust in the myth of progress is religiously motivated.

When transhumanists talk of progress, they overwhelmingly assert that technology is largely responsible for progress in the modern era. To assert this, it seems, most transhumanists draw upon a form of technological determinism in which the main feature controlling society and the advancement of the human race from one epoch to the next is clearly technology. However, historians and philosophers of technology are wary of a simplistic causal reduction of world historical events to technological influence.[44] Technology does not necessarily drive history. Even those in Science and Technology Studies who adhere to a kind of soft technological determinism contend that other factors—economic, political, social, and cultural—can drastically alter the outcome of a technology's taking root and, therefore, can have a tremendous effect on societal outcomes.[45] In other words, it is a questionable venture to assert technological determinism and then move to social dictation because of the asserted technological determinism. This is precisely what transhumanism does as it extends the technological sphere of dictation to include the future of the human species and the entire universe! Transhumanists ought to be warned that they move beyond the consensus of the academy in this regard and, subsequently, are often dismissed.

If trust in the myth of progress due to technological dictation of society is not an entirely warranted conclusion, then what inspires this trust on the part of transhumanists? This is precisely where studying the possible religious motivations of transhumanism can be an entirely fruitful venture. Indeed, in spite of leading transhumanists claiming that transhumanism is not motivated by religious concerns,[46] I have argued here that its adherents could be drawing substantial religious and existential value from its doctrine of the myth of progress. As some have noted, transhumanism ought to be viewed as a form of "secularist faith."[47] The first step toward dialogue with religious scholars begins with admitting the religious dimensions of transhumanism and the myth of progress is one of its most substantial dogmas.

NOTES

1. Mary Midgley, *The Myths We Live By* (London, UK: Routledge, 2003), 1.
2. I will be using the term "technoscience" throughout this chapter. The term "technoscience" is a parlance of the burgeoning field of study often referred to as Science and Technology Studies. Technoscience qualifies and extends the term "science" by recognizing the social and physical context of the practice of science and the technological networks that help mediate it. It speaks to the practice of science and the development of technology as a historical human endeavor. See Don Ihde and Evan Selinger, eds., *Chasing Technoscience: Matrix for Materiality* (Bloomington, IN:

Indiana University Press, 2003); Alfred Nordmann, "Science in the Context of Technology," in *Science in the Context of Application*, edited by Martin Carrier and Alfred Nordmann (London, UK: Springer, 2011), 467–482.

3. Midgley, *The Myths We Live By*, 1.

4. Midgley, *The Myths We Live By*, 1.

5. Indeed, entire anthropologies have been written that pin human uniqueness on precisely this point (e.g., Eliade, Frazer, Freud, Jung). Others, such as Alister Hardy, Scott Atran, Pascal Boyer, and Justin Barrett, would even extend this from *Homo symbolicus* to *Homo religiosus*. Not only do we recount stories of ultimate meaning, but such tales are embedded in an inherent religiousness distinctively found in human beings.

6. Much of this discussion is taken from Daniel Sarewitz, "The Idea of Progress," in *A Companion to the Philosophy of Technology*, edited by Jan-Kyrre Berg Olsen et al. (Oxford, UK: Wiley-Blackwell, 2009), 303–307.

7. Richard L. Kirkham, *Theories of Truth: A Critical Introduction* (Cambridge, MA: MIT Press, 1992).

8. I am thinking of Paul Tillich's definition of religion as ultimate concern here. See Paul Tillich, *Ultimate Concern: Tillich in Dialogue* (London, UK: SCM Press, 1965); Paul Tillich, *What Is Religion?* (New York, NY: Harper & Row, 1969).

9. Leo Marx claims that modern notions of history seen as progress "function like that served by myths of origin in traditional cultures: They provide the organizing frame, or binding meta-narrative, for the entire belief system." See Leo Marx, "The Idea of 'Technology' and Postmodern Pessimism," in *Does Technology Drive History?: The Dilemma of Technological Determinism*, edited by Merritt Roe Smith and Leo Marx (London, UK: MIT Press, 1994), 239.

10. Miguel Farias et al., "Scientific Faith: Belief in Science Increases in the Face of Stress and Existential Anxiety," *Journal of Experimental Social Psychology* 49, no. 6 (2013): 1210. Also see B. T. Rutjens et al., "Things Will Get Better: The Anxiety-Buffering Qualities of Progressive Hope," *Personality and Social Psychology Bulletin* 35, no. 5 (2009): 534–535; B. T. Rutjens et al., "Yes We Can: Belief in Progress as Compensatory Control," *Social Psychological and Personality Science* 1, no. 3 (2010): 246–252.

11. Quoted in Ludwig Edelstein, *The Idea of Progress in Classical Antiquity* (Baltimore, MD: Johns Hopkins Press, 1967), 3.

12. For further classical sources of progress see Edelstein, *The Idea of Progress in Classical Antiquity*, and Chapter one of Robert A. Nisbet, *History of the Idea of Progress* (London, UK: Heinemann, 1980).

13. Robert A. Nisbet, "The Idea of Progress: A Bibliographical Essay," *Literature of Liberty* 2, no. 1 (1979): 15.

14. See Nisbet, *History of the Idea of Progress*, 47ff.

15. Marx, "The Idea of 'Technology' and Postmodern Pessimism," 250.

16. See Peter Harrison, *The Fall of Man and the Foundations of Science* (Cambridge, UK: Cambridge University Press, 2007).

17. Francis Bacon, *The New Organon*, edited by Lisa Jardine and Michael Silverthorne (Cambridge, UK: Cambridge University Press, 2000).

18. Thomas Sprat, *The History of the Royal Society of London* (London, UK: 1667).

19. See Nisbet, *History of the Idea of Progress*, 251–258.

20. "Intrinsically, it is not a question of the higher or lower degree of development of the social antagonisms that result from the natural laws of capitalist production. It is a question of these laws themselves, of these tendencies working with iron necessity towards inevitable results. The country that is more developed industrially only shows, to the less developed the image of its own future." See Karl Marx, *Capital: A Critique of Political Economy*, translated by Samuel Moore and Edward Aveling (New York, NY: Random House, 1906), 13.

21. Karl Marx, *A Contribution to the Critique of Political Economy*, translated by N. I. Stone (Chicago, IL: Charles H. Kerr, 1904), 13.

22. G. A. Cohen understands Marx's theory of history to be driven by a kind of technological determinism. See G. A. Cohen, *Karl Marx's Theory of History: A Defence*, expanded ed. (Princeton, NJ: Princeton University Press, 2001); Marx, "The Idea of 'Technology' and Postmodern Pessimism," 250.

23. Merritt Roe Smith, "Technological Determinism in American Culture," in *Does Technology Drive History?: The Dilemma of Technological Determinism*, edited by Merritt Roe Smith and Leo Marx (London, UK: MIT Press, 1994), 1–35.

24. This "conquering of space" through technology was central to the American ideal and identity. This is convincingly argued in David E. Nye, *America as Second Creation: Technology and Narratives of New Beginnings* (London, UK: MIT Press, 2003).

25. Fyodor Dostoyevsky, *Notes from Underground and the Double*, translated by Jessie Coulson (Harmondsworth, UK: Penguin Classics, 1972).

26. Giuseppe Tassone, *A Study on the Idea of Progress in Nietzsche, Heidegger, and Critical Theory* (Lewiston, NY: Mellen, 2002).

27. Jean-François Lyotard, *The Postmodern Condition: A Report on Knowledge*, translated by Geoff Bennington and Brian Massumi (Minneapolis, MN: University of Minnesota Press, 1984), xxiv.

28. Lyotard, *The Postmodern Condition*.

29. Nisbet, "The Idea of Progress," 31.

30. Alexander Rosenberg, *Philosophy of Science: A Contemporary Introduction*, 2nd ed. (London, UK: Routledge, 2005), 147.

31. Thomas S. Kuhn, *The Structure of Scientific Revolutions*, 2nd ed. (Chicago, IL: University of Chicago Press, 1970), 162.

32. William E. Akin, *Technocracy and the American Dream: The Technocrat Movement, 1900–1941* (Berkeley, CA: University of California, 1977). The notion that society ought to be ruled by a group of individuals with specialist technical knowledge has much earlier origins than this political movement. Some scholars contend it can be traced back to Plato's *Republic* because the trained elite had to utilize the precision gained from the study of mathematics in governing society. See Val Dusek, *Philosophy of Technology: An Introduction* (Oxford, UK: Blackwell, 2006), 39ff.

33. R. Buckminster Fuller, *Utopia or Oblivion: The Prospects for Humanity* (Harmondsworth, UK: Penguin, 1972), 331–335.

34. Richard Barbrook and Andy Cameron, "The Californian Ideology," *Science as Culture* 6, no. 1 (1996): 44–72.

35. Philippe Verdoux, "Transhumanism, Progress and the Future," *Journal of Evolution and Technology* 20, no. 2 (2009): 49–69.

36. Nick Bostrom, "Transhumanist Values," http://www.transhumanism.org/index.php/WTA/more/transhumanist-values/, accessed March 25, 2014.

37. Humanity+ "Transhumanist FAQ," http://humanityplus.org/philosophy/transhumanist-faq/, accessed March 25, 2014.

38. Nick Bostrom, "Letter from Utopia," *Studies in Ethics, Law, and Technology* 2, no. 1 (2008): 3.

39. Nick Bostrom, "Existential Risks: Analyzing Human Extinction Scenarios and Related Hazards," *Journal of Evolution and Technology* 9, no. 1 (2002), http://www.jetpress.org/volume9/risks.pdf.

40. Martin Rees, *Our Final Hour: A Scientist's Warning: How Terror, Error, and Environmental Disaster Threaten Humankind's Future in This Century—on Earth and Beyond* (New York, NY: Basic Books, 2003).

41. Ray Kurzweil, *The Singularity Is Near: When Humans Transcend Biology* (London, UK: Duckworth, 2006), 29.

42. There are many assertions and criticisms of the myth of progress on both sides of the secular and religious divide. In relation to transhumanist literature, see Ted Peters, "H-: Transhumanism and the Posthuman Future: Will Technological Progress Get Us There?," in *H±: Transhumanism and Its Critics*, edited by Gregory R. Hansell and William Grassie (Philadelphia, PA: Metanexus Institute, 2011), 147–175. Pierre Teilhard de Chardin, *The Future of Man*, translated by Norman Denny (New York, NY: Image Books/Doubleday, 2004); Verdoux, "Transhumanism, Progress and the Future."

43. Paul Ricoeur, *History and Truth*, translated by Charles A. Kelbley (Evanston, IL: Northwestern University Press, 1977), 81.

44. See Leo Marx, "Does Improved Technology Mean Progress?," *Technology Review* 90, no. 1 (1987): 33–41; Merritt Roe Smith and Leo Marx, eds., *Does Technology Drive History?: The Dilemma of Technological Determinism* (London, MA: MIT Press, 1994).

45. Such as is found with Robert L. Heilbroner, "Do Machines Make History?," *Technology and Culture* 8, no. 3 (1967): 335–345; Robert L. Heilbroner, "Technological Determinism Revisited," in *Does Technology Drive History?: The Dilemma of Technological Determinism*, edited by Merritt Roe Smith and Leo Marx (London, UK: MIT Press, 1994), 67–78.

46. MemeBox, "Ray Kurzweil: The Singularity Is Not a Religion" (interview), October 27, 2008, http://www.youtube.com/watch?v=CLy0tTfw8i0, accessed May 17, 2012.

47. Hava Tirosh-Samuelson, "Transhumanism as a Secularist Faith," *Zygon* 47, no. 4 (2012): 710–734.

10

. . . .

Extreme Longevity: Insights from the Three Chinese Spiritual Traditions

Geoffrey Redmond

INTRODUCTION: RELIGION AS TEACHINGS, BELIEFS, AND INSTITUTIONS

Religion is a complex phenomenon, infiltrating almost every aspect of being human. In pondering how religion will accommodate future social change, we must remain aware of the extreme multivalency of human belief systems. Correspondingly, there are likely to be diverse responses to extreme longevity from each religious tradition. So long as this diversity is kept in mind, we can indulge in imagining which insights different religious traditions might provide regarding radical life extension. More specifically, I will propose how the three Chinese spiritual traditions of Confucianism, Daoism, and Buddhism might contribute insights regarding extreme longevity, particularly about how the many extra years would best be spent. It also briefly considers the challenges posed for the institutions of these religions.

Traditionally, China is seen—both in its own eyes and in those of the West— as having three spiritual traditions. Although considerable diversity exists within each of these traditions, the idea that there are three traditions remains heuristically helpful. In contrast to the West, where it is expected that a person will affiliate with only one specific religion, in Asia the traditions are not mutually exclusive in the way that, for example, being Catholic and Baptist would be in the West. The Chinese traditions have exchanged ideas continuously over their two millennia of coexistence and came to share much common ground.

CONFUCIUS ON AGING

In the West, China is often held up as an example of how old age is respected. In actuality, the elderly are sometimes treated condescendingly in China. What is notable, however, is the admiration felt for the older members of society. It is a common occurrence to be introduced to an elderly Chinese person who beams with pride at his or her old age, even if bent over and with only a few remaining teeth. In the past, centenarians were presented to the emperor in ceremonies honoring their long life.

Confucius respected age for specific reasons. In particular, a long life provided more years to acquire wisdom and develop a more sure sense of how to act properly in complex situations. One of the most famous passages in the *Lunyu* (*Analects*) expresses this concept:

> The Master said, At fifteen I set my mind on learning; by thirty, I had found my footing; at forty I was free of perplexities; by fifty I understood the will of Heaven; by sixty I learned to give ear to others; by seventy I could follow my heart's desires without overstepping.[1]

Another passage, nearly as famous, reads: "Give me a few more years—if I have fifty years to study the *Book of Changes* (*I Ching*), then perhaps I, too, can avoid any great errors."[2] While this sentence is now thought to be apocryphal, it expresses the view that extra years of life would be best spent in study of spiritually significant material.[3] In Japan, this statement was taken to mean that one should not begin to study the *Changes* until one is at least 50 years old, thereby associating longevity with the opportunity to acquire profound knowledge.

There is also a human side to Confucius's valuing longevity: "You must not be ignorant of the age of your father and mother! For one thing, it is a cause for rejoicing; for another, a cause for fear."[4] It is hard to imagine a more forthright statement of filial affection.

Confucius's sense of death as loss of affectionate ties applied to his disciples as well: "There was Yan Hui—he loved learning ... Regrettably, he had a short life and is dead now. Since then, there are none who love learning, or none I have heard of."[5] When Yan Yuan died, the Master said, "Ah, Heaven is destroying me!"[6]

In addition to expressing Confucius's love and respect for Yan Hui and Yan Yuan, something more general is being conveyed in these passages—namely, the unique value of the individual person. A person's value is such that he or she cannot be replaced. This is a strong argument for extreme longevity because any death is a loss to humanity. How much more might great teachers have contributed to society had they been allotted more years? For seemingly ordinary people, extra years would confer more opportunity to reach their full potential.

Clearly, Confucius absolutely valued life. He would have little patience for those skeptical of life extension who profess not wanting to live beyond a limited number of years, or who feel that everyone should die so as to give others their turn. Confucius, however, intends that extra years are not to be spent hedonistically but rather in self-cultivation and pursuit of wisdom.

A further sense of the possibilities of life is inherent in another of the Chinese sage's famous statements:

> Jilu asked how one should serve the gods and spirits. The Master said, When you don't know how to serve human beings, how can you serve the spirits?
>
> Jilu said, May I venture to ask about death? The Master said, You don't yet understand life, how can you understand death?[7]

While on the surface this is a rebuke to a disciple—as well as a clever finesse by the great teacher—it expresses quite clearly that it is *this* life that is the suitable subject for study. Speculating about the supernatural or death is not productive. Confucius's concern was to live the best possible life in this world, so he declined to speak of spirits and anomalies. He did not speak directly about means of enhancing longevity, however.

LONGEVITY AND DAOISM

Like Confucius, Laozi and Zhuangzi, authors of the early Daoist classics, were concerned with questions of how to live—that is, how to accord with the Dao (the Way). The differences between Confucianism and Daoism are, however, fundamental in Chinese thought. Daoism recommends a life of accomplishment by nonaction in contrast to Confucius's preoccupation with rules of conduct. A major theme, especially in the *Zhuangzi* text, is withdrawal from society, and especially from government service.

The way of *wu wei* ("nondoing" or "without effort") was considered conducive both to efficacy and to longevity. The concept of *wu wei* is notoriously difficult to pin down, but part of its meaning is doing things in a natural way instead of straining for a result. In contemporary language, it can be thought of as a stress-free way of life. Zhuangzi's most famous example is the butcher who never needs to sharpen his knife because he first studies the carcass and then cuts along the natural separations. He acts, but not until he has quietly contemplated his task and intuited the most efficient way to carry it out. Nonaction is not laziness, then, but rather doing things in accord with the underlying pattern of the cosmos.

In modern culture, stress is thought to be harmful to health, so in this sense Daoist philosophy is compatible with modern ideas. Later, however, Daoism became preoccupied with the search for longevity by magical means. These methods included abstinent diets, elixirs or potions, and so-called internal and external alchemy—that is, meditative exercises to retard aging.

In contemporary Western Daoism, it is the meditative and ritual aspects rather than the supposedly pharmacological ones that are emphasized. Nevertheless, traditional Chinese pharmacies are filled with products claiming to provide longevity—and, frequently, enhanced sexual potency as well. The effectiveness of these products is dubious at best. The most famous, ginseng, has never been shown in controlled studies to provide health benefits. More likely, it is the human-like shape and distinctive aroma that accounts for the beliefs about this root's potency. Mandrake root occupied a similar place in medieval European belief. Thus, admiring longevity does not ensure developing effective means to produce it.

Daoism considers long life a blessing in itself. The Daoist conception contrasts to Confucius's more sober notion that extra years are to be spent developing one's virtue. For Daoism, long life is simply a happy state. This interpretation is apparent in the imagery of the Eight Immortals, who are depicted in paintings as exultant, even inebriated. Released from the fear of mortality, the Daoist adept can simply enjoy every moment, knowing there will be many more.

To arrive at this carefree, happy state usually requires hard practice involving eremitism and an ascetic lifestyle. Traditionally, those seeking to become transcendent withdraw from human society and do not even need nutrition. This withdrawal is a prominent theme in *Zhuangzi*, although it was later much influenced by Buddhism. As Daoism evolved, the emphasis on lifestyle found in the writings of Laozi and Zhuangzi was replaced by magical beliefs and practices.

The existence of ascetic hermits was felt to be somehow beneficial to society as a whole. Extreme self-control was assumed to bring magical and healing powers. Eremitism brought release from ritual obligations to ancestors because the ascetic practices provided immunity from the ancestral wrath that could shorten life expectancy. Nonetheless, while it conferred exemption from some social restrictions, being a transcendent was itself a specific role to which conformity was expected.

That longevity is a self-evident good is sometimes denied in Western discourse. As a physician, I often hear someone say he or she does not want to live beyond a certain age—invariably some years in the future. This is usually an unreflective response to being advised to make an unwanted positive change in lifestyle, such as taking medication. Setting aside special situations such as complete social isolation or intolerable pain, such statements are usually posturing rather than the result of honest self-examination. Here Daoism is much more honest than some Western ideologies.

Plausibly, Western attitudes are unconsciously influenced by earlier aspects of this particular tradition. Socrates famously chose death over exile from Athens. Roman Stoicism taught acceptance of mortality. Martyrdom was the main path to sainthood in early Christianity. In Western mythology, immortals such as the Wandering Jew, Dracula, or the Comte de Saint-Germain, are evil, or at best morally ambiguous. Vampires maintain their abnormally long lives by feeding on the energies of the living. In Daoist China, the general notion was just the opposite: extreme longevity was associated with a virtuous way of life, not with black magic or evil.[8]

Extreme longevity would make the goal of Daoism possible. History provides no evidence that Daoist procedures have increased longevity (a topic discussed later in this chapter). Yet radical life extension would be an extreme stress for institutional Daoism. Many Daoist temples are actually family businesses and sell as products rituals, talismans, and meditation practices to ensure health, prosperity, and longevity. Such wares would be unlikely to attract much interest in a transhuman world. If life became easier, even the philosophy of *wu wei* might seem simply redundant. Of course, this vision of carefree happiness assumes not only that the medical problem of longevity has been solved, but also that social inequality has been reduced to a tolerable level. If, as now, many live in penury, for them long life will be at best a very mixed blessing.

On the one hand, transhumanism would be expected to dry up the market for the magical services that remain essential for support of institutional Daoism. On the other hand, since the advance of science has not eliminated supernatural beliefs and practices, perhaps they will survive to some extent. Even in a transhuman world, however much improved over our present one, it is unlikely that anxiety will be no longer be part of the human condition—and magic has always been a way of coping with uncertainty about matters of critical concern. Yet given much more time to attain life goals, the demand for supernatural assistance is likely to be much smaller than in the present time.

DAOIST LONGEVITY PRACTICES

The Chinese word usually translated as "immortal" is *xian*. In a recent important study, Campany translates this word as "transcendent"—perhaps a better term, given that it implies a more general release from human limitation.[9] Separating this character into its components *ren* and *shan*, *xian* literally means "person of the mountains."[10]

According to convention, hermits lived on roots and berries in remote mountains in simple huts. In reality, they were likely provided with food offerings from people hoping to benefit from contact with their spiritual charisma. Restrictive diets, however, were part of the mythology of the eremitic life. A common prescription was not to eat the "seven grains," which presumably meant avoiding normal food. While this may seem like an early version of a low-carbohydrate diet, concepts of healthy diet in traditional China bear little resemblance to contemporary scientific ones. Associated beliefs were that immortals could live long by drinking dew, by swallowing their own saliva, or even just by absorbing *qi* from the atmosphere. Daoists believed meditation actually altered the internal structure of the body, although these practices were sufficiently complex as to be beyond the reach of all but monks and perhaps some highly committed laity.

While it would facilitate radical life extension if these Daoist practices actually increased the lifespan, historical evidence indicates that they do not. Indeed, human longevity has probably not changed much since very early times. (Longevity is the maximum age attainable, while life expectancy is the average number of years that people live.) Maximum longevity is about 122 years; life expectancy varies considerably depending on economics, medical care, and other factors. Life expectancy at birth in China seems not to have changed much from the Bronze Age (Shang and Western Zhou dynasties) to the end of the Qing dynasty in 1911. The average life expectancy for males was in the late twenties and for females a few years less due to deaths in childbirth or unwillingness of families to raise them. This very short life expectancy confirms what should be obvious: traditional Chinese ways of life, including Daoist and medical practices, were ineffective against the health hazards, such as infection, that are now easily curable.

CAN DAOISM CONFER LONGEVITY?

Livia Kohn, a leading Western scholar of Daoism, reviews Daoist longevity attitudes and practices. Her discussion has a clearly spiritual perspective:

> A fundamental belief of Daoism is that Dao, the underlying creative power of the world, originally governs and arranges everything to perfection. It is only through human ignorance and meddling that the cosmos loses its balance and people fall into states of sickness, misfortune and early death.[11]

A similar idea, that illness is due to non-natural lifestyles, is found in New Age thought. From the point of view of modern medicine, this notion contains a large dose of wishful thinking. While proper lifestyle does contribute to health and longevity, unfortunately there are some people who exercise, eat properly, and manage stress, yet still die early because of cancer, heart disease, and a regrettably large variety of other diseases. This is not to argue against exercise and healthy lifestyle, but simply to point out that radical life extension will require measures not yet conceived.

Kohn notes that Daoism emphasizes "nourishing life," a goal that many contemporary Chinese embrace as well. The ways in which Chinese people try to nourish their lives are quite varied,[12] and this concept, while Chinese, has appeal for all cultures. Some of the methods by which Daoists have sought to nurture their lives have relevance in the modern world, but others do not. Limiting the diet to fruits, vegetables, and nuts[13] is a difficult goal for most in the modern world, and living entirely by swallowing one's saliva or absorbing *qi* from the atmosphere is not a real possibility. Despite the Daoist tradition of nurturing life, many Chinese, like many Westerners, live less than optimal lifestyles. Smoking, avoidance of medical care, lack of aerobic exercise, and high-fat, high-salt diets are pervasive in China. Nevertheless, health consciousness is clearly increasing in China, especially among the educated, although social factors, such as air pollution, remain serious problems.

Some of the traditional Chinese Daoist health ideas are actually contrary to scientific biology. For example:

> People conserve essence by limiting the frequency of its loss through ejaculation and menstruation, was well as by using massage techniques that keep the *qi* flowing.[14]

The notion that some sort of vital essence is lost with discharge of body fluids is an ancient one, but is not supported by current physiological understanding. Rather, these are examples of the repressive beliefs regarding sexuality that persist from ancient times and are found in many religions. Scientific studies clearly show that more frequent ejaculation is associated with overall better health as well as a reduced risk of prostate cancer. Normal menstruation is a sign of health and is not harmful except in situations where bleeding is excessive, such as that caused by uterine fibroids. While it is sometimes claimed that women can stop menstruation with special meditative techniques, careful studies show that the mind can stop cycles only in situations of extreme psychological stress, such as being a prisoner of war or under sentence of death. (The myth that girls stop menstruating when they go away to college has been refuted by actual research.)

Kohn agrees that with radical life extension, institutional Daoism will be less popular and that Daoist cosmology will become obsolete, but concludes on a positive note:

> Overall, Daoists will be very happy with the brave new world we are about to enter on the coattails of genetic engineering and RLE [radical life extension] technology.[15]

RADICAL LIFE EXTENSION AND BUDDHISM

While Confucianism and Daoism, in their very different ways, both endorse longevity, the situation with Buddhism is more ambiguous. Belief in rebirth was of central importance in Buddhism from its very beginnings. This doctrine, while it has come into vogue in the West at times, is implausible to most moderns, yet is insisted upon as dogma by many Buddhists.

According to Buddhist mythology, the father of the historical Buddha, Shakyamuni, received a prediction that his son would be either a world conqueror or a world renouncer. Naturally the father preferred worldly success, so he kept his son confined to the palace, providing him with a beautiful wife and every possible pleasure in the hope that he would not realize the inevitability of suffering and decide to renounce the world. However, Shakyamuni induced his charioteer to bring him outside the palace. On each of the four trips, the future Buddha had a significant experience, seeing (in order) an old man, a sick man, a dead man, and a renunciant monk. From these excursions into the normal world, he learned that old age, sickness, and death are the inevitable lot of all humanity. Inspired by the wandering ascetic, he resolved to depart from his family and the luxury of the palace to search for a way of release from suffering.

This story is easily seen as a parable of how the child comes to see the inevitable miseries of human life and the importance of finding a way to cope with them. It is a much more austere view of the world than that espoused by Daoism or Confucianism. The message of the first three of the passing sights is that deterioration and death are inevitable. Thus their impact would be largely ameliorated by transcendence of the current human condition, which will all but eliminate aging and disease, and greatly delay death. With the realization of these goals, the motivation for a life of religious renunciation would be greatly attenuated.

The attraction of Buddhism is the possibility of eliminating *dukkha* (suffering), but its means for achieving this end are themselves so rigorous that few attain the goal. In modern Buddhism, particularly in the West, meditation has become the central practice, with the goal of reducing attachment and thus reducing mental distress, particularly anxiety. If the goal is a more serene life, meditation is attractive for moderns. However, the traditional goal was not simply to reduce stress but to completely eliminate attachments, including family ties and other affectionate relationships. Confucius, in contrast, grieved for the loss of a favorite follower. While he did not speak of marriage, his emphasis on filial piety included producing grandchildren for one's mother and father.

The celibate life, not only in Buddhism but also in Catholicism, attracts far fewer acolytes than in the past. Indeed, many of today's Buddhist scholars and spiritual teachers are found in lay life. To be sure, the renunciant existence retains a niche appeal in the modern world. There is a mild resurgence of religious life in Taiwan and Hong Kong, for example, particularly among women. Yet the belief in celibacy as a more spiritual way of life is greatly diminished. Hence the Buddha's way of monasticism, while still a distinctive human possibility, seems destined to become less and less attractive as science progressively ameliorates suffering. This statement needs some qualification, however. With greatly prolonged longevity, it would be possible to try multiple lifestyles; some might want to spend a decade or two as monks or nuns to experience this mode of life without having to renounce the secular world permanently.

Buddhism emphasizes the death of the Buddha, casting it as more significant than his birth. This event is referred to as his *parinirvana*, meaning the
transition into nirvana. This passage has been a popular subject for Buddhist
art and has several iconographic modes. One motif that was quite popular in
Japan shows the Buddha reclining, surrounded by disciples, some tearful and
others are without visible emotion. Those who did not express grief are considered to have advanced further on the path. While this depiction is consistent with Buddhist doctrine, later *parinirvana* paintings departed from this
tradition and show all the disciples weeping. The idea that a loyal disciple
would not show grief at the great teacher's death was too hard to maintain.

The importance of the Buddha's death as an artistic theme is an example of
the centrality of death in this religion. This is true for Buddhist institutions as
well. In modern Japan, Buddhism is mainly a funerary religion. Elsewhere in
Asia, funeral rituals are also a major activity for Buddhist Sangha and an
essential source of income. Thus radical life extension would diminish this
aspect of the religion and, likely, the social demand for Buddhist ritual services
that are intended to ensure a favorable rebirth. The result would be an
economic crisis for institutional Buddhism.

BUDDHIST DOCTRINE AND EXTREME LONGEVITY

Buddhism might respond to radical life extension in any of several ways,
depending on which of its teachings are considered primary. If elimination
of suffering is the primary concern, then Buddhism would support elimination
of the limits on human life. It could be argued that the Buddha's way to
achieve release from suffering was the best option for most of history, but
now science can replace it with means that are easier and more effective. If
the goal of enlightenment is seen as something beyond release from *dukkha*
(the unsatisfactoriness of life)—that is, as a way toward transcendent insight
into ultimate reality—then the longer lifespan might put this goal within
reach of many more people.

The doctrine that is most problematic in the context of radical life extension is rebirth. This notion supposes that each of us has undergone a near-
infinity of lifetimes. According to the Buddhist analysis, sentient life is inevitably painful; hence the goal is to eventually escape from the birth-and-death
cycle and enter the state of nirvana. In this supernatural state, one beyond the
understanding of the unenlightened, there is no desire and no suffering. Few
enter nirvana, but for those who do, it has been the result of accumulating
good karma over very many lifetimes. The doctrine of karma and rebirth is
Buddhism's way of resolving the problem of evil and maintaining a moral
cosmos.

In a transhuman world in which life extends for centuries, the doctrine of
karma and rebirth loses its force. What does seem consistent with extreme

longevity is the underlying assumption of Buddhism that sentient existence is a problem to be solved. Life extension, broadly considered, also sees life as a problem to be solved, albeit by advances in biomedical science rather than by spiritual means. Other speculative modes of life extension, such as transferring consciousness to a computer, are not serious possibilities.

The doctrine of rebirth raises a potential ethical issue, according to Derek Maher:

> [G]iven the fact that the planet can only sustain a limited number of human beings, another significant ethical question would arise. Undoubtedly, at some point it would be necessary for the humans that were alive to refrain from bearing new children. Since this means that other non-human sentient beings would no longer be able to take birth in the desirable state of a human being ... some people would probably regard it as arbitrary to privilege the generation that happens to be alive at the point when immortality technology happened to be available. Why should these particular beings, who just happen to be humans at this time, receive the benefits of these technologies?[16]

There are several difficulties with this argument. First, the Buddhist doctrine of karma and rebirth, if taken seriously, would suggest that those alive when the technology becomes available are privileged precisely because of karmic merit. Furthermore, given that extreme longevity does not necessarily mean eternal life, other sentient beings would simply have to wait longer to incarnate as humans. Finally, if there really are sentient beings awaiting human rebirth, we do not know how many there are and, therefore, we cannot assume that the earth cannot support them all as incarnated humans. In developed countries, birth rates are already at or below replacement levels, for example.

The most important objection to the rebirth argument against radical life extension is that rebirth is an article of faith, not verifiable, at least not so far. That many millions of people have believed in this concept over the centuries is not evidence that it is actually true. Such beliefs are further complicated by the variety of religious doctrines concerning what happens after death. It seems implausible that worthy Buddhists will be reborn but that worthy Christians will enter heaven.

On the face of it, life after death is an empirical question. When each of us dies, we will either stop experiencing completely—the scientific assumption, although also unprovable—or experience some sort of postmortem consciousness. This might be rebirth, possibly after 49 days in an intermediate state; or it might be judgment followed by heaven or hell; or it might be entirely different from any of these doctrines. The problem with the argument that all of us now alive should die to make room for others to be reborn is that it is based on a supernatural belief, not on any actual evidence. (Apparent memories of former lives are entirely subjective and, therefore, unpersuasive.) Although a person might choose to die to give someone else a chance at a human rebirth, there is no ethical basis for condemning others to death based on this sort of argument. From a Christian perspective, one might propose that radically extended life would postpone the bliss of heaven (or the agony of hell)—but again, this is all based on faith, not evidence.

For these reasons, Buddhists cannot convincingly argue against radical life extension on the basis of the belief in rebirth. This issue probably would not matter to many contemporary Buddhists, particularly in the West, who are primarily interested in meditative practice to enhance their present lives. Some Buddhists argue against this selectivity of concepts, asserting that unless one believes in rebirth, one is not a real Buddhist. Such essentialist arguments are unpersuasive. It is not possible to devise absolute criteria as to who properly adheres to a specific spiritual tradition. Rebirth cannot be validated by claiming that those who do not accept it are not Buddhists.

Although rebirth and asceticism make radical life extension potentially problematic for Buddhism, key elements of Buddhist tradition, such as meditative practice and the emphasis on compassion, can survive abandonment of some of the early doctrines. Such a demythologized Buddhism—which actually exists today—would depart from what has always been regarded as the Buddha's teaching, yet still maintain a connection to the spirit of the Buddha's teachings.

CONCLUSION

Of all traditional cultures, China has most explicitly valued long life. Chinese spiritual traditions can, therefore, be a source of stimulating insights regarding extreme longevity. The tradition of most direct relevance is Confucianism, which has always placed particular emphasis on those aspects of life that flourish in maturity: learning, self-knowledge, ethical consciousness. In this sense, it offers self-cultivation as the way one can best occupy oneself during the centuries. Daoism assumes the benefit of long life but focuses on means of attaining it. At least in its two early philosophical texts, the *Dao De Jing* and *Zhuangzi*, it provides a less rigid notion than Confucianism of how to live in harmony with the cosmos. Buddhism most directly focuses on the problem of suffering, but complete nonattachment and the doctrine of karma and rebirth may have little appeal in the presence of nearly unlimited life expectancy.

A Final Admonition from Confucius

Confucius held up the simpler ways of antiquity as a model for later society and so was skeptical of innovations. Behind this was perhaps simply the common, but unthinking, tendency to believe that if things have always been a certain way, then they should remain that way, including the human lifespan. Something like this argument has often been advanced against transhumanism. Yet, when seriously considered, it is no argument at all. Some aspects of civilization ought to be continued indefinitely—educating the young, for example—whereas others—such as warfare—should not.

At present, transhumanism, including radical life extension, is a thought experiment. While eventually human life expectancy may increase radically, current biological constraints suggest that target is unlikely to be achieved in any of our lifetimes. Yet thinking about transhumanism is a valuable way to give fresh consideration to the limits of human life in the present. This works in both directions. Not only can the Chinese spiritual traditions offer insights into transhumanism, but reflection on radical life extension is a way to rethink the spiritual traditions.

NOTES

1. Burton Watson, trans., *The Analects of Confucius* (New York, NY: Columbia University Press, 2007), 20.

2. Watson, *The Analects of Confucius*, 50.

3. As my main sinological interest is this same book, I might add that even 50 more years might not be enough to fully decipher this extremely obscure ancient scripture.

4. Watson, *The Analects of Confucius*, 75.

5. Watson, *The Analects of Confucius*, 42.

6. Watson, *The Analects of Confucius*, 73.

7. Watson, *The Analects of Confucius*, 73.

8. China does have exemplary figures who, like Socrates, chose to die rather than renounce their principles. The Daoist philosopher Zhuangzi, for example, saw death as return to the earth from which we arose. Nonetheless, the predominant view was that very long life is a great blessing.

9. Robert Ford Campany, *Making Transcendents: Ascetics and Social Memory in Early Medieval China* (Honolulu, HI: University of Hawai'i Press, 2009).

10. One such memoir, with a valuable commentary, is translated in Matthew V. Wells, *To Die and Not Decay* (Ann Arbor, MI: Association for Asian Studies, 2009).

11. Livia Kohn, "Told You So: Extreme Longevity and Daoist Realization," in *Religion and the Implications of Radical Life Extension*, edited by Derek F. Maher and Calvin Mercer (New York, NY: Palgrave Macmillan, 2009), 90.

12. Judith Farquhar and Qicheng Zhang, *Ten Thousand Things: Nurturing Life in Contemporary Beijing* (New York, NY: Zone Books, 2012).

13. Kohn, "Told You So," 87.

14. Kohn, "Told You So," 88.

15. Kohn, "Told You So," 96.

16. Derek F. Maher, "Two Wings of a Bird: Radical Life Extension from a Buddhist Perspective," in *Religion and the Implications of Radical Life Extension*, edited by Derek F. Maher and Calvin Mercer (New York, NY: Palgrave Macmillan, 2009), 111–121.

Utopianism and Eschatology: Judaism Engages Transhumanism[*]

Hava Tirosh-Samuelson

In this chapter I reflect on trans/posthumanism (I am using this term interchangeably with "transhumanism") from the perspective of Judaism, the oldest of the three Abrahamic traditions.[1] The chapter argues that while trans/posthumanism exhibits secularization of religious motifs that originated first within ancient Judaism, the Jewish religious tradition offers a fruitful vantage point from which to examine transhumanism. The first section highlights the utopian, apocalyptic, and eschatological features of trans/posthumanism. The second section shows how the utopian spirit of Judaism has led strands of contemporary Judaism to support biotechnology. The third section presents one example of Jewish philosophic critique of trans/posthumanism. The chapter concludes with reflections on the anticipatory consciousness of "not-yet," which lies at the heart of the Jewish endorsement of biotechnology and the critique of trans/posthumanism.

FROM THE HUMAN, THROUGH
THE TRANSHUMAN, TO THE POSTHUMAN

The transhumanist intellectual movement advocates a process of technological enhancement by which humanity will enter a new phase in its evolution in which the biological human species will be replaced by autonomous,

---

*Some material from an earlier article, "Transhumanism as a Secularist Faith," published in *Zygon: Journal for Religion and Science* 47, no. 4 (December 2012): 710–734, has been incorporated herein. Reprinted with permission.

super-intelligent decision-making machines.[2] Unlike evolution, which is slow, uncontrolled, and unpredictable, this process will be fast, controlled, and directed, brought about by human engineering. Described as "enhancement revolution" (Buchanan), "radical evolution" (Garreau), "designer evolution" (Young), and "conscious evolution" (Chu),[3] this imagined future scenario is based on new scientific discoveries and the emergence of new technologies such as nanotechnology, biotechnology, genomics, robotics, information and communication technology, and applied cognitive science. Today, converging technologies have given rise to a new situation in which the human has become a *design project*. Humans will be able to transform our biological makeup and even engineer future generations. Eliminating chance and accentuating human choice and control, the ultimate goal of transhumanism is the planned obsolescence of the human species. As Max More, a leading transhumanist visionary puts it, the transhuman phase is only "a transitional stage standing between our animal heritage and our posthuman future."[4] According to this futurist, the posthuman future will be attained through "genetic engineering, life-extending biosciences, intelligence intensifiers, smarter interfaces to swifter computers, neural compute integration, worldwide data networks, virtual reality, intelligent agents, swift electronic communication, artificial intelligence, neuroscience, neural networks, artificial life, off-planet migration and molecular nanotechnology."[5] Given that human biological embodiment is regarded as a burden and a curse, the planned disappearance of the embodied human is viewed as a blessing that constitutes the hope of humanity. Transhumanism is, therefore, the gradual transition from biological humanism to mechanical posthumanism, its *telos*.

The engineers of artificial intelligence (AI) who drive the speculations about the posthuman future predict that the Mechanical Age will come about after an irreversible turning point—the Singularity—which will commence as a result of an exponential, accelerated process of technological progress. Singularity is "a point on the graph of progress where explosive growth occurs in a blink of an eye," when machines become sufficiently smart to start teaching themselves.[6] When this happens, "the world will irrevocably shift from the biological to the mechanical"[7] and the Mechanical Age will inaugurate the New Kingdom, the Virtual Kingdom. In the techno-futuristic scenario, mechanical creativity itself promises the salvation of humanity, destroying the most problematic aspects of the biologically evolved human body.

The transformation from biological humans to mechanical posthumans will be gradual. At first, humans will upload their minds (the most salient aspect of their personalities) into supercomputers that will serve the material needs of humanity. For Ray Kurzweil, the leading posthumanist futurist, a "brain-porting scenario" will involve "scanning a human brain capturing all of its salient details."[8]

The uploading of ourselves into human-made machines is the spiritual goal of transhumanism, as it promises transcendence and even immortality: while the body, the hardware of the human computer, will die, the software of our lives, our personal "mind file," will continue to live on the web in the posthuman future, with holographic avatars interacting in this venue with other bodiless posthuman entities. Eventually the machines "will tire of caring for humanity and will decide to spread throughout the universe in the interest of discovering all the secrets of the cosmos."[9] A variation on this scenario is imagined by Hans Moravec, who has predicted that the "Age of Robots" will be supplanted by the "Age of Mind," as machines will create space for a "subtler world,"[10] in which computations alone remain. In the Virtual Kingdom, the "Mind Fire" will render earthly life meaningless, ultimately allowing it to be swallowed by cyberspace.[11] Put differently, human enhancement is but the beginning of a process in which humanity will bring about its own demise, supplanting it with virtual existence.

In previously published essays, I explored the intellectual origins of transhumanist thought, the dominant themes of transhumanist discourse, and the religious dimensions of transhumanism as a secular faith.[12] The main points cannot be reiterated here, but it is important to recognize the utopian, apocalyptic, and eschatological dimensions of the trans/posthumanist discourse. Transhumanism is utopian in that it expresses "the desire for a better way of being" and is critical of the way we now live, "suggesting what needs to be done to improve things."[13] As a "forward dream," as Ernst Bloch called the utopian spirit,[14] the transhumanist project not only wants things to improve but also gives that want a concrete direction. Moreover, since the locus of the posthuman future is the Internet, it is truly a "nonexistent place" (i.e., *outopia*); whether the Internet is also a "good nonexistent place" (i.e., *eutopia*) is still debatable.

Transhumanism envisions a transitional society in which individuals will prosper and flourish because human physical and mental abilities will be augmented. Social ills such as poverty, sickness, pain, and suffering will be eliminated, and even death will be perpetually postponed. Because trans/posthumanism is not only a statement about the power of technology to enhance the human body but also a vision about the destiny of humanity, it is important to appreciate its apocalyptic and eschatological dimensions. What makes it apocalyptic is the claim that the ideal future is imminent and that it will come about as a result of radical, irreversible break from the present. The Singularity is that apocalyptic event that will radically transform reality; the Virtual Kingdom is a mechanical *eschaton* in which superintelligent machines constitute "last things."

To grasp the apocalyptic and eschatological dimensions of trans/posthumanism, some historical background is needed. The term "apocalypticism" denotes a movement of anonymous Jews in antiquity (roughly from 200 BCE to 200 CE) who were deeply offended by Rome's control of Judea. They envisioned the destruction of the political order as well as the eventual emergence of a new order that would inaugurate a different kind of reality, both political and cosmic.[15] Anonymous authors generated literary texts known as Apocalypses in which the seers presented their visions of the ideal future as a revelation or disclosure from an angel, a semi-divine entity that made known secrets about the structure of the cosmos and about the direction of history. These pseudepigraphic texts highlighted the disruption of the existing order by war in which good triumphs over evil. Saved through the agency of a messiah, the final war (or Armageddon) will inaugurate a new era, "a time of peace, plenty and righteousness."[16]

Apocalyptic literature was characterized by a strong sense of urgency. What adherents needed to do to bring about the desired end or share in its glory varied with the political purpose and religious orientation of the group, whether it was the Essene community of the Dead Sea, the Jesus Movement, the Gnostic intellectuals, or the anti-Roman militants (i.e., the various "zealot" groups). In all cases, their apocalyptic eschatology translated the vision about the approaching end into action. However, given that created human beings lack the power to bring about "last things," the final transformation of the world will require divine intervention. Thus apocalyptic eschatology manifested a strong alienation from the present world as well as an abiding belief that the imminent coming of the new world would be dramatically different from and insuperably better than the present.

Contemporary transhumanists exhibit the mentality of apocalyptic eschatology, though it is doubtful they have actually read the ancient apocalyptic texts. Robert M. Geraci has convincingly argued that Kurzweil and other AI advocates "lead a scientific movement that never strays far from the apocalyptic traditions of western culture."[17] Like ancient Jewish and Christian apocalyptic thinkers, Kurzweil and his cohorts have a strong sense of alienation from the imperfect present and a desire to radically break with it and inaugurate the New Age. In Kurzweil's scenario of the eschatological future, meaningful life will take place only in cyberspace, where human bodies will be purified of their earthliness, and the minds of the future will possess only virtual bodies. This end result is deemed necessary because "evolutionary natural selection will favor artificial intelligence over human intelligence" and the spread of computational AI is declared "inexorable." Presumably, this process will greatly benefit human beings because computers will solve human problems. When human beings upload their minds into machines, it is suggested, they will live longer, happier lives and ultimately attain immortality, the very end that traditional religions promised their adherents. As salvation will finally be attained in the disembodied paradise of cyberspace, it is right to claim that "Apocalyptic AI is techno-religion for the masses."[18]

To be sure, there are differences between contemporary visionaries such as Kurzweil and the ancient apocalypticists. Ancient apocalypticists claimed to know the mysteries of the universe via revelations from semi-divine angels or from God; today these truths are discovered by science based on human reason alone. For the ancient seers, God has final victory over the forces of evil; in Apocalyptic AI, evolution takes the place of God. Finally, instead of *theosis*, humans immortalize themselves in super-intelligent machines, thereby becoming like gods.

The techno-scientific *eschaton* imbues human-made technology with salvific value: the Kingdom of God will be realized on earth through technology, thereby making salvation both imminent and immanent. In the trans/posthumanist vision, to achieve what humans have always wanted—immortality—humans must take control of evolution, directing it toward the eschatological, posthuman end.

If the affinity between contemporary trans/posthumanist and ancient apocalyptic themes is evident, how did it come about? What was the intellectual process that transformed ancient religious motifs into the secular, technological vision in the 21st century? Michael E. Zimmerman has insightfully identified Renaissance hermeticism and Hegel's secularization of Christianity as the "missing links," so to speak, in the process of cultural transmission from antiquity to the modern world.[19] As Zimmerman explains, "Hegel depicted humankind as the instrument through which absolute *Geist* (Spirit) achieves total self-consciousness. Jesus Christ was the man who became God, as much as the God who became man."[20] Similarly, Zimmerman argues, Ray Kurzweil "revises the customary concept of God to accommodate the possibility that humans are taking part in the process by which post-human creatures, according to traditional theism, will attain powers equivalent to those usually attributed to God."[21] For Kurzweil, the (secularized) divine spirit that works through humans (namely, evolution) will take charge of its own destiny and will "spiritualize" everything in the universe, including matter and energy. Despite their differences, for Kurzweil as well as for Hegel, the cosmos has not only brought itself to self-awareness through humankind, but eventually humans will evolve beyond themselves by generating modes of consciousness and technology that will make possible a cosmic self-realization. Zimmerman concludes that "the God-like post-human amounts to a creature that has become divine, and that has thereby attained the status of cosmic Logos,"[22] a notion that cannot be reconciled with traditional Christian beliefs.

JEWISH SUPPORT OF BIOTECHNOLOGY

Judaism offers interesting perspectives from which to critically engage transhumanism.[23] Because utopianism, apocalypticism, and eschatology all emerged within ancient Judaism, it is important to appreciate the internal tension between these impulses and their complex histories. On the one hand, Judaism harbors a strong critical stance toward the present, calling its adherents to work for the betterment of human life both individually and collectively. On the other hand, the Jewish tradition learned a lesson from the historical failure of ancient Jewish apocalyptic and articulated a comprehensive religious system—rabbinic Judaism—that focuses on the sanctification of life in the present in anticipation of the ideal future.

In response to the acute messianism of Christianity, post-70 CE rabbis muted the apocalyptic/eschatological impulse and distinguished between the "messianic age" (*yemot ha-mashiah*) and the "world to come" (*olam ha-ba*), leaving their content and interrelation rather obscure and open to conflicting interpretations: Will there be one or two messiahs who will bring about the ideal end? What exactly will the messiah(s) do? Will the messianic age constitute a new reality or only the prelude to "the world to come"? What will life in the "world to come" consist of and who is destined to enter it or benefit from its goodness? Will the "world to come" include the resurrection of the dead, the final judgment of humanity, and the reunification of the individual soul with the individual body, or just the immortality of the soul?[24] Without reaching consensus, these and many other questions were hotly debated by Jewish philosophers and mystics during the Middle Ages.[25]

In the modern period, when Jews were legally emancipated and becoming citizens of Western nation-states, traditional messianism was deeply challenged. If Jews wished to integrate into European society, they had to give up their messianic (i.e., political) aspirations and transform their utopian message into a universal message about the improvement of humanity. Many modern Jews, therefore, joined revolutionary movements such as socialism, communism, and anarchism, expecting them to inaugurate a new era of equality and justice for all. Leading utopian theorists in the 20th century were Jews (e.g., Martin Buber) or intellectuals of Jewish descent (e.g., Gustav Landauer, Ernst Bloch, and Karl Mannheim).

The internal complexity of Jewish messianism was most evident in Zionism, the movement of Jewish nationalism. Acknowledging the depth of European anti-Semitism and the inability of Jews to fully integrate into European society, Zionism encouraged Jews not to wait for the coming of the messiah but rather to actively shape their own destiny by returning to the ancient homeland and rebuilding a Jewish state. Zionism expresses both traditional Jewish messianism and its repudiation, and this complexity continued to shape the politics of the state of Israel.[26] For example, the fast victory of Israel in the Six Day War of 1967 was given a messianic interpretation by followers of Rabbi Zevi Yehuda Kook (d. 1982), who generated the Settlement Movement in (so called) Greater Israel in preparation for the rebuilding of the Third Temple. This acute messianism, however, was denounced by Orthodox theologian Yeshayahu Leibowitz (d. 1994) as idolatrous.[27]

The complexity of Jewish utopianism is also evident in the kibbutzim, intentional communes that sought to create "active utopias" of just and egalitarian societies.[28] While Martin Buber saw these experiments in practical utopia in a favorable light,[29] other Jewish scholars in the 20th century—Hannah Arendt (d. 1977), Karl Popper (d. 1994), and Isaiah Berlin (d. 1997)—were critics of practical utopias, especially the communism of the Soviet Union and the fascism of Nazi Germany, because they were enemies of democracy.[30]

The dialectics of perfectibility (the capacity for improvement) and perfection (the claim that perfection is attained in the present) is best seen in regard to contemporary biotechnology. Although relatively few Jews have written explicitly about trans/posthumanism, contemporary Judaism has been remarkably supportive of biotechnology and some of the procedures at the core of human enhancement. The source of this Jewish pro-biotechnology stance is the belief that the world God created is *good but not perfect*, so that human beings are called to "improve," "repair," or "mend" it.[31] For example, Jews have welcomed the science underlying modern medicine as well as many medical technologies that heal the sick or prevent illness, including those genetic diseases (e.g., Tay-Sachs, cystic fibrosis, fragile X syndrome, Gaucher disease, and breast cancer) most common among Ashkenazi Jews. Thus Jewish theologians, ethicists, and jurists have enthusiastically supported the new genetics, including stem cell research, and have endorsed the applications of this research (e.g., genetic testing, genetic screening, and genetic engineering, including germ-line engineering), as well as a wide range of medical procedures that assist in reproduction (e.g., in vitro fertilization, artificial insemination, and even cloning, including cloning to produce children). While some of these procedures are at the core of the transhumanist program of human enhancement, we shall see that the Jewish justification for them is very different.

Reform Judaism—the progressive and liberal strand of modern Judaism—has no fundamental objection to the new genetics and its corollary, biotechnology. Reform Judaism has welcomed contemporary science, including stem cell research that might lead to cloning. The starting point of the Union of Reform Judaism, the Central Conference of American Rabbis, and the Religion Action Center is the *commandment to preserve life and promote health*. In 2003, the General Assembly of the Union for Reform Judaism adopted a resolution that supports research using both adult and embryonic stem cells, not limited to the existing lines. It also supports research and funding of somatic gene therapy, but not germ-line gene therapy, which poses serious medical and moral concerns.[32] This support was grounded in the notion that healing is not merely a profession but a righteous obligation (*mitzvah*). The core value of Judaism emphasizes saving lives when possible.[33] Because scientific research into stem cell regeneration holds the promise of finding new and effective treatments for Alzheimer's disease, Parkinson's disease, spinal cord injuries, and certain types of cancers, Reform Judaism declared it a moral imperative to pursue stem cell research. Biological science has opened the door toward life-enhancing and life-saving technologies; therefore, it is consistent with the commandment to heal. However, Reform Judaism places the responsibility for the employment of stem cell research on each and every individual who wishes to use it, rather than on the scientific community; the individual can and should assess the risks and benefits for himself or herself and make an informed decision.

Conservative Judaism, which validates the authority of Jewish law (halakha) but accepts that it evolved over time, is more concerned with the potential conflict between Jewish law and contemporary science. However, it maintains that scientific research is both possible and potentially fruitful; moreover, it insists that contemporary interpretation of Jewish law must be informed by advances in science and technology. Scientific activity, however, cannot be undertaken for its own sake: scientific means and ends must be evaluated in light of religious values. The leading Conservative bioethicist, Rabbi Elliot Dorff, has written extensively on biomedicine, including stem cell research and cloning.[34] He insists Jews must be attentive to both law and theology to discern what God expects of them. Dorff spells out the theological principles that inform his reflections on bioethical and biomedical issues: the human body belongs to God; humans have the body "on loan," so to speak; God is the owner of the human body and can and does impose conditions on human use of the body; Jews, the recipients of divine revelation, are commanded to preserve human life and health (pikuach nefesh). Dorff concludes that Jews have a duty to seek and develop new cures for human diseases that can aid us in taking care of our bodies, which ultimately belong to God.

Most importantly, Dorff situates reflections about biotechnology in the context of the interpretation of creation in the "image of God" (Genesis 1:26): all human beings, regardless of their levels of ability and disability, are created in the "image of God" (tzelem elohim) and are to be valued as such. But humans are not God; they are not omniscient, as God is, so humans must take precautions to ensure that the potential harms of human actions are minimized. Dorff counsels us to remain humble in whatever we do, especially when we are pushing the scientific envelope, as is the case in stem cell research. Dorff welcomes stem cell research because it "constitute[s] some of the ways in which we fulfill our obligation to be God's partners in the ongoing act of creation."[35] On the more controversial issue of cloning to produce children, he concludes that "human cloning should be regulated not banned,"[36] but employed "only for medical research or therapy."

Like the Conservative bioethicists, modern Orthodox Jews reason about biotechnology within the framework of halakha, although they may interpret rabbinic sources differently and reach different conclusions about specific procedures. Orthodox jurists reason that because Jewish law is divinely revealed, it encompasses all aspects of life, including science and technology.

Scientific and technological advances can help resolve many practical details for religious practices, especially in matters that concern the human body. However, science is not the source of values, and science requires a framework of values whose authority is other than human. Judaism's moral values are absolute and immutable because they are revealed by God. The task of the Orthodox jurist, then, is to assess the validity, plausibility, desirability, and permissibility of various medical procedures within the parameters of halakha. For example, on stem cell research, the Beth Din of America (Orthodoxy's highest legal body) ruled on August 21, 2001, that halakha does not consider any embryonic development within 40 days of conception as having the sacred protected status of a human being.[37] This decision indicates that Orthodox jurists, like Conservative and Reform thinkers, hold that preservation of life is the most important obligation, overriding almost all other laws.

The positive attitude toward the new genetics and its accompanying biotechnologies is usually justified by appeal to the rabbinic portrayal of the human being as God's "partner in the work of creation." This idea is derived from Talmudic sources, which teach that "three partners (God, man and woman) are required for the creation of a human being,"[38] meaning that humans cannot accomplish procreation alone and must receive divine involvement. To be a "partner of God" means that humans have an obligation to improve and ameliorate what God has created. Because "God left it for human beings to complete the world,"[39] as long as the act of perfecting the world does not violate halakhic prohibitions or lead to results that would be halakhically prohibited, it is legally permissible.

Rabbi J. David Bleich, the most prolific and influential Orthodox thinker on biotechnology, supports a pro-biotechnology stance. He says:

> Man has been given license to apply his intellect, ingenuity, and physical prowess in developing the world in which he has been placed subject only to limitations imposed by the laws of the Torah, including the general admonition not to do harm for others as well as by the constraints imposed by good sense and consideration of prudence.[40]

As for cloning of humans, Orthodox thinkers have been remarkably willing to embrace the human clones, since, as Michael J. Broyde has argued, "clones are not robots, slaves, or semihumans."[41] Broyde concludes that "human creativity is part of the creation of the world and this creativity changes the world, which is proper."[42]

The discourse on clones is commonly carried out in reference to the term *golem* and the Talmudic stories (Sanhedrin 38b; Sandherin 65b) about rabbis whose knowledge of mysteries of creation enabled them to create a humanoid. The resulting creature lacked the power of speech and was destroyed because it was "created by magicians." The magical power of the Hebrew language was celebrated in the anonymous *Sefer Yetzirah* (Book of Creation), a foundational text of the Jewish mystical tradition. According to the *Sefer Yetzirah*, human-made *golems* could be activated by the ritualistic use of the Hebrew Alphabet, bringing the *golem* into life and action. In the early modern period, the motif of the *golem* gave rise to various literary narratives, the most famous of which was the one ascribed to Judah Loew ben Bezalel (known as the Maharal; d. 1609), who created a *golem* that at the end had to be destroyed because he rebelled against the human master.[43]

The *golem* motif has an interesting and complex history in Jewish mysticism and has inspired popular culture through science fiction, television shows, comics, and video games.[44] Today the *golem* motif has been appropriated to discuss cloning or the human-machine interface—a central theme in trans/posthumanism. Byron L. Sherwin, a Jewish theologian associated with Conservative Judaism, has offered the most extensive religious application of the *golem* legend, arguing that it can help us live with the moral ambiguities generated by living with intelligent machines.[45] To endorse his analysis, however, one must adopt the contours of Judaism, its theological assumptions, and ethical norms. The *golem* legend, of course, could be interpreted in diverse and conflicting ways. For example, some non-Jewish writers invoke the *golem* as an analogy to technoscience: like the *golem*, technoscience is a "little daft" and should be understood as a "human endeavor rather than a superhuman feat."[46] In contrast, computer scientists who build intelligent machines that deliberately mimic human behavior invoke the *golem* legend to justify their endeavor on religious grounds.[47]

The Jewish endorsement of biotechnology is most notable in the state of Israel, where legal reasoning and public policies are openly informed by Jewish religious values no less than by secular considerations. In Israel, "biotechnology regulation is characterized by a relatively permissive approach and low regulatory density."[48] The reason for this policy is the demographic weakness of Jewish people today, caused by the loss of Jewish life in the Holocaust; the preponderance of genetic diseases among Ashkenazi Jews; the low birth rate among Jews; and the demographic imbalance between Israel and its neighboring Arab nations, and between the Jews and the Palestinians, whose fertility rates are among the highest in the world. It is no surprise, then, that in Israel medical genetics is a recognized specialization and that Orthodox and Ultra-Orthodox authorities justify the operation of 11 clinics that offer genetic testing and screening and infertility treatments to a population of about 7 million Jews. In general, excellence in science and technology are viewed as crucial to Israel's national security and analysis of future risks (yet another common theme in transhumanism).[49]

JEWISH CRITIQUE OF TRANS/POSTHUMANISM

Should the fact that contemporary Judaism has a pro-biotechnology stance lead us to conclude that Judaism shares the trans/posthumanist vision for the planned obsolescence of the human species? No. While Judaism takes an activist stance toward the world and seeks to improve it through volitional human action, there is a difference between the belief that human beings can be perfected through human involvement and the claim that human perfection is attainable in the here and now through technological manipulation. Jews endorse biotechnology because of its healing capacity, but they do not share the disdain and derision toward the human body characteristic of trans/posthumanism. Rather, the created body is viewed with respect because it is the basis of human sociality as well as of religious life. Jewish law is observed through embodied commandments that sanctify the human body and enable humans to perfect themselves morally and spiritually by attending to the material needs of other human beings. The body is also relevant to the notion of human dignity, which is derived from the belief in the human creation in God's image. As David Novak explains, according to rabbinic Judaism, one is prohibited from assaulting the dignity of another person either in deed or in word and it is a "positive commandment to actively affirm that human dignity in all others."[50] The human body, contrary to trans/posthumanist thinking, is fundamental to Jewish religiosity.[51]

While Judaism welcomes the healing potential of biotechnology, several Jews have also recognized its danger and have offered sustained criticism of its advancement. The most vocal Jewish critic of the project of human enhancement is Leon R. Kass (b. 1939), a past chairman of the now defunct President's Council on Bioethics. Kass has appropriately insisted that instead of blindly celebrating its promising potential, we should pay attention to the social and cultural implications of biotechnology, because they raise foundational questions: Which kind of human beings do we wish to be? Which kind of society do we wish to live in? And which ideals, norms and standards should guide us into the future?[52] Kass's critique of biotechnology was inspired by Hans Jonas, his teacher at the New School of Social Research.[53] Jonas's thought is most relevant to our engagement with trans/posthumanism because he correctly understood the utopian drive of modern technology, while recognizing its profound implications for the human condition. When we redesign humans, we close the possibility for an unknown, open future, creating future generations in our own image. Jonas's thought cannot be summarized here, but three themes deserve our attention: his critique of human self-engineering, the intrinsic value of organic life, and the imperative of responsibility for future generations.[54]

Jonas was the first to articulate "ethics for the technological age" in response to the 20th-century horrors of Auschwitz and Hiroshima. His critical stance toward modern technology is inseparable from his biography as a German Jewish philosopher, a student of gnosticism under Heidegger, a Zionist, and a soldier in the British army in World War II who witnessed the destruction of Europe.[55] Jonas saw in contemporary biotechnology a dangerous revival of certain gnostic motifs, especially the alienation from the world.

Jonas was keenly aware of the novelty of modern technology[56] because it allows for the radical alteration of nature, including human nature. Modern biotechnology has made it possible to expand the human lifespan, control human behavior, and manipulate the genome—all endeavors that raise questions about what is normatively human while putting human nature itself at stake. In addition, Jonas understood correctly the utopian impulse of technology and its incessant drive for "progress," which is also the source of its danger. Modern technology sets in motion a causal chain that has profound effects on objects and people in very remote places and in future epochs. However, these humanly engineered changes are irreversible: if mistakes are made, correcting them is very difficult, and in many cases impossible. In such a way, modern technology, especially biotechnology, undermines the open-endedness of the future. For this reason Jonas articulated the "heuristic of fear" that counseled extreme caution in the application of biotechnology.[57]

If premodern technology focused on the transformation of the external world, modern technology has turned the human being into its design project. As Jonas put it, "*Homo faber* [man the maker], is now turning on himself and gets ready to make over the maker of all the rest."[58] Precisely because humanity now has the power to destroy itself, the existence of humanity as created by God has become a moral value. After Auschwitz, "there is an unconditional duty for mankind to exist!" The source of the duty is an "ought" that stands above both ourselves *and* future human beings. Human beings in the present have a duty toward future human beings. In Jonas's words, it is "their duty over which we have to watch, namely, their duty to be truly human; thus over their capacity for this duty ... which we could possibly rob them of with the alchemy of our 'utopian technology.'"[59] When humans engineer themselves, they undermine this "ought" because they create themselves not in the image of God but in their own image, thereby eliminating the possibility of an open-ended future. With subtle irony Jonas makes the point clear:

> The most "farsighted" plans—farsighted as to the distance of the intended goal —are children of the concepts of the day, of what at the moment is taken for knowledge and approved as desirable: approved so, we must add, by those who happen to be in control. By their intentions ever so unblemished by self-interest (a most unlikely event), these intentions are still but an option of the shortsighted moment which is to be imposed on an indefinite future.[60]

Against it, Jonas spoke up with prophetic passion, making himself the champion of organic life.

Jonas offered a new phenomenology of life that recognizes the intrinsic moral value of the natural world and our responsibility toward life on the planet. According to this approach, nature is not inert material stuff with which we are free to do what we please, as is commonly assumed by modern science and technology, but rather a dynamic reality that should be respected for its inherent value. The mark of "life" is metabolism, a capacity for self-sustaining biological existence, which manifests the organism's struggle for self-preservation. That drive imbues all forms of life with "subjectivity" as well as with "purposiveness" that creates the basis of fraternity between humans and other life forms. Applying Kantian principles and distinctions to nature, Jonas insists that nature should be treated as an end and not merely as a means. By interpreting all organic life and individual organisms in nondualistic terms, Jonas sought to overcome the radical split between "facts" and "values," claiming that morality (i.e., what we ought to do) is rooted in nature itself. It is the very structure of nature that grounds human responsibility toward nature and especially toward life.

Jonas's ethics of responsibility is global in scope: it is a responsibility for the existence and wholeness of humankind, including future generations. Jonas explains this ontological imperative as follows:

> With this imperative, we are strictly speaking responsible not to the future of human individuals but to the Idea of Man. . . . It is this ontological imperative, emanating from the Idea of Man, which stands behind the prohibition of a gamble with mankind. Only the Idea of Man, by telling us why there should be men, tells us also how they should be.[61]

For trans/posthumanism, the extinction of the human species is not merely conceivable, but also desirable; for Jonas, humanity must exist. Indeed, the very idea of humanity makes the existence of humanity an ontological imperative.

Jonas's philosophy of life offers direct criticism of the major themes in trans/posthumanist project. He rejected the engineering approach to human beings because human beings are organisms rather than machines, and organisms are born, mature, age, and die. Death is not just a curse or a burden; it is also a blessing. It is a burden insofar as we are organic beings who must wrest our being from the continuous threat of nonbeing. But it is a blessing insofar as our wresting is the very condition for any affirmation of being at all. Therefore "mortality is the narrow gate through which alone value—the address of a yes—could enter the otherwise indifferent universe."[62] For Jonas, the effort to forestall death or even mortality itself is fundamental denial of what makes us human. The process of life requires mortality as the counterpart of the natality that alone can supply the novelty and creativity that enrich human life and express freedom. Freedom is imperiled when it ignores necessity.

Jonas considered most of the activities that constitute "human enhancement" (e.g., genetic enhancement for the sake of improving one's looks or one's chances of social success) frivolous. As for germ-line intervention, Jonas was most concerned about its irreversibility, along with the impossibility of drawing a line in practice between "therapy" and "enhancement." The project of human enhancement is what earlier generations called "eugenics"; Jonas distinguished between negative eugenics (developing diagnostic tools to identify genetic diseases and manipulating the genetic code to eliminate bad genes) and positive eugenics (manipulating genes so as to enhance human performance). In regard to both programs, he noted that an ambitious eugenics violates the normative status of nature, and pointed out that we do not have the criteria or standards to determine what is "normal" and what is "pathogenic." As for the elimination of "bad genes" from the population, any effort to eliminate undesirable genes from the gene pool altogether threatens the biological necessity of a varied gene pool and runs afoul of our ignorance about the role that apparently useless genes might play in human adaptability. Jonas argued against positive eugenics on the same ground: the lack of criteria and standards for intervention means that positive eugenics that aims at a qualitative improvement over nature cannot claim the sanction of nature.

Finally, Jonas was among the earliest people who spoke about cloning with trepidation. In his "Biological Engineering: A Preview,"[63] he developed an "existential critique" of cloning to produce children, focusing on the situation of the human clone—that is, on the "subjective terms of his being." Jonas's critique considers how originating as a clone would limit a person's freedom:

> The simple and unprecedented fact is that the clone knows (or believe to know) altogether too much about himself and is known (or is believed to be known) altogether too well to others. Both facts are paralyzing for the spontaneity of becoming himself, the second also for genuineness of others' consorting with him. It is the known donor archetype that will dictate all expectations, predictions, hopes, and fears, goal settings, comparisons, standards of success and failure, of fulfillment and disappointment, for all "in the know"—clone and witnesses alike.[64]

Jonas's objection is not based on the simplistic argument of "genetic determinism," but rather on the "tyrannical" nature of the cloning procedure. A human clone is robbed of the possibility to have a self-evident relationship to his or her own body as his or her own, because the genetic makeup has been manipulated prior to birth. Cloning also denies a "right to ignorance" as a condition for the "possibility of authentic action." Instead of respecting "the right of each human life to find its own way and be a surprise to itself," which the ethicist Joel Feinberg has called "the child's right to an open future,"[65] cloning restricts a child's life prospects because the clone would know too much about his or her own body.

Jonas's fears in the 1970s proved to be prescient: today we have come much closer to the ability to clone human beings, making the moral challenges much more acute. Although Jewish ethicists and theologians have embraced the cloning of humans, at least under certain conditions, until they respond to Jonas's critique with depth, the philosophical justification for human cloning remains to be articulated.

CONCLUSION: THE LIFE OF "NOT-YET"

Trans/posthumanism is an influential ideology of extreme progress that offers a comprehensive framework for new scientific development and its technological applications. Human enhancement is just the beginning of the process in which humans will take control of evolution and bring about its next and possibly final phase where the human species will be replaced by superintelligent machines. In the posthuman age, life will no longer be organic, reproduction will no longer be biological, and human beings will cease to exist. Trans/posthuman thought, therefore, offers an eschatological vision that tells us much about its view of human embodiment, the purpose of human life, and the destiny of humanity. This vision is also apocalyptic in the sense that it is predicated on a dramatic, radical departure from the present—the Singularity event—justified by knowledge about the structure of the cosmos, discovered by science rather than revealed by an angel, as in ancient apocalypticism. Trans/posthumanism should be taken seriously because its ideas, aspirations, and motifs shape our culture through literature, film, performance art, and video games, and trans/posthumanism should be examined critically because it will impact our daily life and challenge our social conventions, political institutions, moral values, and religious beliefs.

Judaism offers a unique perspective from which to view trans/posthumanism because its utopian, apocalyptic, and eschatological dimensions originated in ancient Judaism. Nevertheless, a Jewish engagement with transhumanism also brings to the fore what is problematic about this futurist vision. To the extent that trans/posthumanism seeks to alleviate human suffering and pain, Judaism is rather supportive of the new genetics and the medical technologies based on it. Conversely, to the extent that trans/posthumanism denigrates the biological human body, denies the wisdom of mortality, and celebrates the elimination of human species, Judaism offers criticism of this philosophy.

Most importantly, while Judaism and trans/posthumanism share the utopian impulse to improve reality, Jewish utopianism is very different from trans/posthumanism. First, Jewish utopianism is prescriptive rather than descriptive: it articulates a vision to be pursued rather than an achieved reality. In this regard, Jewish utopianism always entails living with an "anticipatory consciousness," to use Ernst Bloch's apt phrase,[66] rather than life in the fulfilled, already realized future. Second, Jewish utopian dreaming is distinctively social, because human beings are social animals and the meaning of human life in this world is configured within the social sphere, be it within the family, the intentional community, or the Jewish people at large. Third, Jewish utopianism celebrates the inherent value of biological life and of the human being, who is created "in" or "for" the image of God. The beliefs that the world was created and that humans were created in the image of God are compatible with the theory of evolution, but they also impose on human beings the responsibility for other humans, for future generations, and for the created world.[67]

In contrast to the transhumanist immanentization of the perfect future, Judaism insists that the future remain open-ended, unknown, and uncontrolled. Living in the anticipatory consciousness of the "not-yet" entails hope, humility, and modesty, which stand in contrast to the trans/posthumanist hubris that claims to know the future and control the process that will bring it about inexorably. Judaism can teach us that life in the imperfect present allows for the possibility of transcendence and the dynamic unfolding of that which will always remain "not-yet." We must make sure that the trans/posthuman future dream does not become our nightmare.

NOTES

1. Technically speaking, "transhumanism" is the process of human enhancement that will presumably bring about the desired goal of "posthumanism." The term "trans/posthumanism" covers both the process and the goal of human enhancement. The utopian dimension pertains to the process, whereas the eschatological dimension concerns the goal.

2. For an overview by an advocate of transhumanism, see Nick Bostrom, "Transhumanism FAQ: A General Introduction," version 2.1, http://www .nickbostrom.com. For an interdisciplinary examination of transhumanism, consult Hava Tirosh-Samuelson and Kenneth L. Mossman, "New Perspectives on Transhumanism," in *Building Better Humans? Refocusing the Debate on Transhumanism*, edited by Hava Tirosh-Samuelson and Kenneth L. Mossman (Frankfurt, Germany: Peter Lang, 2012), 29–52, and the bibliography cited there.

3. Allen Buchanan, Da W. Brock, Norman Daniels, and Daniel Wilker, *From Change to Choice* (Cambridge, UK: Cambridge University Press, 2000); Joel Garreau, *Radical Evolution: The Promise and Peril of Enhancing Our Minds, Our Bodies and What It Means to Be Human* (New York, NY: Doubleday, 2004); Simon Young, *Designer Evolution: A Transhuman Manifesto* (Amherst, NY: Prometheus Books, 2006); Ted Chu, *Human Purpose and Transhuman Potential: A Cosmic Vision for Our Future Evolution* (San Raphael, CA: Origin Press, 2014).

4. Max More, "Extropran Principles 3.0," http://wwwmaxmore.com/extprn3.htm.

5. More, "Extropran Principles 3.0."

6. Robert M. Geraci, "Apocalyptic AI: Religion and the Promise of Artificial Intelligence," *Journal of American Academy of Religion* 76, no. 1 (2008): 138–166, p. 149.

7. Geraci, "Apocalyptic AI," 2008.

8. Ray Kurzweil, *The Singularity Is Near: When Humans Transcend Biology* (New York, NY: Viking, 2005), 138.

9. Geraci, "Apocalyptic AI," 149.

10. Hans Moravec, *Robot: Mere Machine to Transcendent Mind* (New York, NY: Oxford University Press, 1999), 163.

11. Moravec, *Robot*, 167.

12. Hava Tirosh-Samuelson, "Engaging Transhumanism," in *H±: Transhumanism and Its Critics*, edited by Gregory R. Hansell and William J. Grassie (Philadelphia,

PA: Metanexus Institute, 2011), 19–54; Hava Tirosh-Samuelson, "Science and the Betterment of Humanity: Three British Prophets of Transhumanism," in *Building Better Humans? Refocusing the Debate on Transhumanism*, edited by Hava Tirosh-Samuelson and Kenneth L. Mossman (Frankfurt, Germany: Peter Lang, 2012), 55-82; Hava Tirosh-Samuelson, "Transhumanism: A Secularist Faith for the Post-Secular Age," *Zygon: Journal of Religion and Science* (2012): 710–733; Hava Tirosh-Samuelson, "Religion," in *Post- and Transhumanism: An Introduction*, edited by Stefan L. Sörgner and Robert Ranisch (Frankfurt, Germany: Peter Lang, 2014), 9–30.

13. Lynn Tower Sargent, *Utopianism: A Very Short Introduction* (Oxford, UK: Oxford University Press, 2010), 5. Although the term "utopia" was coined in 1516 by Thomas More, utopian thought is much older, contemporaneous with Western culture. Today the field of Utopian Studies explores the diverse meanings and uses of "utopia" as manifested in literary genres, social practices, and social theories. For an overview, consult Ruth Levitas, *The Concept of Utopia* (Oxford, UK: Peter Lang Oxford, 2011). Also useful is Fatima Viera, "The Concept of Utopia," in *The Cambridge Companion to Utopian Literature*, edited by Gregory Claeys (Cambridge, UK: Cambridge University Press, 2010), 3–27.

14. Ernst Bloch, *The Spirit of Utopia*, translated by Anthony A. Nassar (Palo Alto, CA: Stanford University Press, 2000).

15. John J. Collins, *The Apocalyptic Imagination: An Introduction to Jewish Apocalyptic Literature* (Grand Rapids, MI: William B. Eerdmans, 1998); John J. Collins, "Apocalyptic Eschatology in the Ancient World, in *The Oxford Handbook of Eschatology*, edited by Jerry L. Walls (Oxford, UK: Oxford University Press, 2008), 40–55.

16. Krishan Kumar, *Utopianism* (Minneapolis, MN: University of Minnesota, 1991), 7.

17. Robert M. Geraci, *Apocalyptic AI: Visions of Heaven in Robotics, Artificial Intelligence, and Virtual Reality* (New York, NY: Oxford University Press, 2010). On the proliferation of apocalyptic mentality in the contemporary gaming community, see Robert M. Geraci, "Video Games and Transhumanist Inclination," *Zygon: Journal of Religion and Science* 47, no. 4 (2012): 735–756.

18. Robert M. Geraci, "Cultural Prestige: Popular Science Robotics as Religion-Science Hybrid," in *Reconfigurations: Interdisciplinary Perspective on Religion in Post-Secular Society*, edited by Alexander D. Ornella and Stephanie Knauss (Wien, Austria: Lit Verlag, 2007), 43–58, p. 56.

19. Michael E. Zimmerman, "The Singularity: A Crucial Phase in Divine Self-Actualization?", *Cosmos and History: Journal of Natural and Social Philosophy* 4, nos. 1–2 (2008): 347–380.

20. Zimmerman, "The Singularity," 148.

21. Zimmerman, "The Singularity."

22. Zimmerman, "The Singularity," 363.

23. Very few Jewish thinkers have directly engaged transhumanism. See Norbert Samuelson and Hava Tirosh-Samuelson, "Jewish Perspectives on Transhumanism," in *Building Better Humans? Refocusing the Debate on Transhumanism*, edited by Hava Tirosh-Samuelson and Kenneth L. Mossman (Frankfurt, Germany: Peter Lang, 2012), 105–132. The stance I express here differs somewhat from the ideas presented in that essay; see also Elliot Dorff, "The Body Belongs to God: Judaism and

Transhumanism," in *Transhumanism and the Body: The World Regions Speak*, edited by Calvin Mercer and Derek Maher (New York, NY: Palgrave Macmillan, forthcoming); Elliot Dorff, "Becoming Yet More Like God: A Jewish Perspective on Radical Life Extension," in *Religion and the Implication of Radical Life Extension*, edited by Derek Maher and Calvin Mercer (New York, NY: Palgrave Macmillan, 2009), 63–74.

24. For a short overview, see David Novak, "Jewish Eschatology," in *The Oxford Handbook of Eschatology*, edited by Jerry L. Walls (New York, NY: Oxford University Press, 2008), 113–131.

25. For comparison of the philosophic and mystical views, consult Hava Tirosh-Samuelson, *Happiness in Premodern Judaism: Virtue, Knowledge and Well-Being* (Cincinnati, OH: Hebrew Union College Press, 2003), Chapters 5 and 7.

26. Aviezer Ravitzky, *Messianism, Zionism and Jewish Religious Radicalism*, translated by Michael Swirsky and Jonathan Chipman (Chicago, IL: University of Chicago Press, 1996).

27. Yeshayahu Leibowitz, *Judaism, the Jewish People, and the State of Israel* (in Hebrew) (Tel Aviv, Israel: Schocken, 1976).

28. For analysis of the kibbutz as utopian experience, see Henry Near, *Where Community Happens: The Kibbutz and the Philosophy of Communism* (Oxford, UK: Peter Lang, 2011). As a person born and raised in a kibbutz, I interpret it to be a utopian experience that lacks apocalyptic and eschatological dimensions. Whether this interpretation is correct depends on how one evaluates the revolutionary aspects of communism and socialism.

29. Martin Buber, *Paths in Utopia* (Syracuse, NY: Syracuse University Press, 1996), especially pp. 139–149.

30. On the anti-utopian outlook of these thinkers, see Russell Jacoby, *Picture Imperfect: Utopian Thought for an Anti-Utopian Age* (New York, NY: Columbia University Press, 2005).

31. The phrase "to mend the world" (*le-taken olam*) originated in the rabbinic sources (Mishnah, Gittin 4:2; Gittin 4:6; Babylonian Talmud Ketubot 52a; Gittin 33a; Gittin 36a). Jews are expected to observe the commandments because they will improve the world in accord with divine instruction. In Lurianic Kabbalah of the 16th century, the phrase became a noun—*tikkun olam*—denoting the human task to repair not only human society, but also the cosmos and even God. Currently, the term is used by Jews (both religious and secular) to cover many forms of activism that pertain to social ills as well as to the environment. See Richard Schwartz, "Tikkun Olam: A Jewish Imperative," *Encyclopedia of Religion and Nature*, Vol. 2, edited by Bron Taylor (London, UK: Continuum, 2005), 1638–1639; G. Rosenthal, "Tikkun ha-Olam: The Metamorphosis of a Concept," *Journal of Religion* 85 (2005): 214–220.

32. See Rabbi Mark Washofsky, CCAR Responsum 5761.7, "Human Stem Cell Research," cited in http://www.reformjudaism.org/stem-cell-research.

33. Babylonian Talmud Sanhedrin 37a: "whoever causes the loss of a single soul is as though he caused the loss of a world entire; and whoever saves a single life is as though he saved a universe."

34. Elliot N. Dorff, *Matters of Life and Death: A Jewish Approach to Modern Medical Ethics* (Philadelphia, PA: Jewish Publication Society, 2003 [1998]); Elliot N. Dorff, "Jewish Bioethics: The Beginning of Life," in *The Oxford Handbook of Jewish Ethics and Morality*, edited by Elliot Dorff and Jonathan Crane (Oxford and New York:

Oxford University Press, 2013), 312–329, especially pp. 323–324, where genetic test-ing is discussed.

35. Dorff, *Matters of Life and Death*, 157.

36. Dorff, *Matters of Life and Death*, 322.

37. The ruling was signed by Rabbi Gedaliah Dov Schwartz, Av Beit Din. See http://www.law.com/PressRelease/oi-08-21.html.

38. Babylonian Talmud, Niddah 31a; Kiddhushin 30b; Shabbat 10a.

39. Azriel Rosenfeld, "Judaism and Gene Design," cited in Miryam Wahrman, *Brave New Judaism: When Science and Scripture Collide* (Hanover, NH: New England University Press for Brandeis University Press, 2004), 71.

40. J. David Bleich, *Judaism and Healing* (Jersey City, NJ: Ktav Publishing House, 2002), 130.

41. Michael J. Broyde, "Modern Reproductive Technologies and Jewish Law," in *Marriage, Sex, and Family in Judaism*, edited by Michael J. Broyde and Michael Ausubel (Lanham, MD: Rowman and Littlefield, 2005), 295–327, p. 315.

42. Broyde, "Modern Reproductive Technologies and Jewish Law," 317.

43. On the history of the *golem* motif, especially within the contours of Jewish mys-ticism, see Moshe Idel, *Golem: Jewish Magical and Mystical Tradition on the Artificial Anthropoid* (Albany, NY: State University of New York Press, 1990).

44. Byron L. Sherwin, *The Golem Legend: Origins and Implications* (Lanham, MD: University Press of America, 1985); Emily Bilsky, *Golem! Danger, Deliverance and Art* (New York, NY: Jewish Museum, 1988).

45. Byron L. Sherwin, *Golems among Us: How a Jewish Legend Can Help Us Navigate the Biotech Century* (Chicago, IL: Ivan R. Dee, 2004).

46. Harry Collins and Trevor Pinch, *The Golem at Large: What You Should Know about Technology* (Cambridge, UK: Cambridge University Press), 3.

47. For example, see the work of the theologian and computer Anne Foerst, *God in the Machine: What Robots Teach Us about Humanity and God* (New York, NY: Plume Books, 2005 [2004]).

48. Barbara Preinsak and Ofer Fierstein, " 'Science for Survival:' Biotechnology Regulation in Israel," *Science and Public Policy* 33, no. 1 (2006): 34.

49. David Passig, *The Future Code: Israel's Future Test* (in Hebrew) (Tel Aviv, Israel: Yediot Aharonot and Hemed Library, 2008); David Passig, *2048*, translated by Baruch Gefen (Tel Aviv, Israel: Yediot Aharonot and Hemed Books, 2013).

50. David Novak, "On Human Dignity," in *David Novak: Natural Law and Revealed Torah*, edited by Hava Tirosh-Samuelson and Aaron W. Hughes (Boston, MA/Leiden, Netherlands: Brill, 2013), 71–88, p. 84.

51. For further elaboration, see the essays by Elliot Dorff cited in note 22.

52. Leon R. Cass, *Life, Liberty and the Defense of Dignity: The Challenge for Bioethics* (San Francisco, CA: Encounter Books, 2002).

53. The views of Kass and Jonas are not identical. See Lawrence Vogel, "Natural Law Judaism? The Genesis of Bioethics in Hans Jonas, Leo Strass, and Leon Kass," in *The Legacy of Hans Jonas: Judaism and the Phenomenon of Life*, edited by Hava Tirosh-Samuelson and Christian Wiese (Boston, MA/Leiden, Netherlands: Brill, 2008), 287–314.

54. For an overview of Jonas thought, see Hava Tirosh-Samuelson, "Understanding Jonas: An Interdisciplinary Approach," in *The Legacy of Hans Jonas: Judaism and the*

Phenomenon of Life, edited by Hava Tirosh-Samuelson and Christian Wiese (Boston, MA/Leiden, Netherlands: Brill, 2008), xxi–xlii.

55. See Christian Wiese, *The Life and Thought of Hans Jonas: Jewish Dimensions*, translated by Jeffrey Grossman and Christian Wiese (Waltham, MA: Brandeis University Press and University Press of New England, 2007).

56. On the novelty of modern technology, see Hans Jonas, "Seventeenth Century and After: The Meaning of the Scientific and Technological Revolution," in Hans Jonas, *Philosophical Essays: From Ancient Creed to Technological Man* (Englewood Cliffs, NJ: Prentice-Hall, 1974), 45–80.

57. The "heuristic of fear" is articulated in Hans Jonas, *The Imperative of Responsibility: In Search of an Ethics for the Technological Age* (Chicago, IL: University of Chicago Press, 1984), 26–27, 202–203.

58. Jonas, *The Imperative of Responsibility*, 18.

59. Jonas, *The Imperative of Responsibility*, 42.

60. Hans Jonas, "Contemporary Problems in Ethics from a Jewish Perspective," in Hans Jonas, *Philosophical Essays: From Ancient Creed to Technological Man* (Englewood Cliffs, NJ: Prentice-Hall, 1974), 168–182, p. 175.

61. Jonas, *The Imperative of Responsibility*, 43.

62. Jonas, *The Imperative of Responsibility*, 19.

63. Hans Jonas, "Biological Engineering: A Preview," in Hans Jonas, *Philosophical Essays: From Ancient Creed to Technological Man* (Englewood Cliffs, NJ: Prentice-Hall, 1974), 141–167. For analysis of this essay and response to its critics, see Bernard G. Prusak, "Cloning and Corporeality," in *The Legacy of Hans Jonas: Judaism and the Phenomenon of Life*, edited by Hava Tirosh-Samuelson and Christian Wiese (Boston, MA/Leiden, Netherlands: Brill, 2008), 315–344.

64. Jonas, *Philosophical Essays*, 161.

65. Joel Feinberg, "The Child's Right to Open Future," in Joel Feinberg, *Freedom and Fulfilment: Philosophical Essays* (Princeton, NJ: Princeton University Press, 1992), 75–97.

66. Ernst Bloch developed the implications of this notion in his *The Principle of Hope*, 3 vols., translated by Neville Plaice, Stephen Plaice, and Paul Knight (Cambridge, MA: MIT Press, 1995 [1986]). Although Bloch was an assimilated Jew who philosophized in the framework of communism, his "anticipatory consciousness" could not be severed from his Jewish roots and his ontology of the "not-yet" is shared by several leading Jewish religious philosophers, such as Hermann Cohen and Franz Rosenzweig. Jonas engaged Bloch's ontology of the "not-yet" in *The Imperative of Responsibility*, 199.

67. Lenn E. Goodman, *Creation and Evolution* (London, UK/New York, NY: Routledge, 2010).

12

Rapture of the Geeks: Singularitarianism, Feminism, and the Yearning for Transcendence

Amy Michelle DeBaets

Ray Kurzweil studied computer science at Massachusetts Institute of Technology and first became known for his work as an entrepreneur and inventor developing speech and character recognition programs for the blind. As he worked, he noticed various trends in the development of technology, such as the phenomenon known as Moore's law, which states that computer processing power has been roughly doubling every 18 to 24 months for at least the past 60 years, whether using vacuum tubes or contemporary microchips. In the late 1980s, Kurzweil began his work in technological futurism—the analysis of trends and predictions regarding how and when technology would be developed. His first book on the future of technology was *The Age of Intelligent Machines*, published in 1990. It was followed by *The Age of Spiritual Machines* (1999), *The Singularity Is Near* (2005), and *How to Create a Mind* (2012). Throughout his work, Kurzweil has extrapolated from Moore's law and envisioned a general trend in which the pace of change of technology is itself increasing exponentially.

Kurzweil's work looks at the history and future of technology, specifically the development of human-level and hyper-human artificial intelligences (AI). It is my contention that the way that we think about what it means to have a humanoid AI provides a creative mirror through which to view how we understand what it means to be human, who or what counts as a person, and what we value in our development of technology. The choices that are made in developing humanoid AI have significant ethical implications for both human persons and the robots that we design.

Kurzweil is highly influential, both in the world of technology and in public policy regarding the development of AI and advanced robotics. He has founded and worked with two organizations—the Machine Intelligence Research Institute (formerly the Singularity Institute for Artificial Intelligence), which serves as a think tank for Singularitarian and related work, and the Singularity University, which is an educational organization that is co-sponsored by corporations like Google, Nokia, and Cisco, as well as various universities. Kurzweil has served as a consultant to the U.S. military in its development of humanoid warfighter robots. He has also made one documentary film regarding his vision of the future of technology, and there is another about him and his work in robotic futurism. Kurzweil currently serves as the Director of Engineering for Google.

Historically, the idea of the Singularity referred to the center of a black hole—infinite density at zero volume, from which nothing can escape. In 1993, science fiction author Vernor Vinge used the term to refer to the rapidly approaching point in human history at which the rate of technological change becomes so rapid that past it lies an unpredictable qualitative shift in the nature of the experienced universe.[1]

The true nature of this Singularity is unknowable, although Kurzweil and other theorists in the movement often associate it with the development of a post-biological super-intelligence, with the universe "waking up" to its own consciousness. According to Kurzweil, "the key idea underlying the impending Singularity is that the pace of change of our human-created technology is accelerating and its powers are expanding at an exponential pace."[2]

In Kurzweil's perspective, the Singularity represents the inevitable fate of human beings and the universe, in which the pace of technological change

> will still be finite but so extreme that the changes they bring will appear to rup-
> ture the fabric of human history ... The Singularity will represent the culmina-
> tion of the merger of our biological thinking and existence with our
> technology ... The Singularity will allow us to transcend these limitations of
> our biological bodies and brains. We will gain power over our fates. Our mortal-
> ity will be in our own hands. We will be able to live as long as we want ... We
> will fully understand human thinking and will vastly extend and expand its
> reach ... Our technology will match and then vastly exceed the refinement
> and suppleness of what we regard as the best of human traits.[3]

We humans are creating the conditions for the Singularity, and we will be, paradoxically, both fulfilled and destroyed within it as we are joined to and surpassed by a universal intelligence.[4]

I will address three key aspects of Kurzweil's work. First, I consider his anthropology for both human and robotic persons, which he understands in a type of neo-Cartesian patternism. Next, I analyze his understanding of the nature and function of evolution, in which Kurzweil describes biological, cultural, and technological evolution as a progressive, inevitable trajectory toward the development of intelligence. Finally, I provide a critical analysis of his libertarian techno-utopian politics and the assumptions that underlie them. After these critical reflections and an analysis of some of the ethical problems they raise, I explore some constructive possibilities from within feminist Christian theological thought for responsible consideration of the future of humans and machines together.

EMBODIMENT AND ANTHROPOLOGY

The anthropology[5] underlying Kurzweil's work is a materialist dualist patternism, in which a person is not to be identified primarily with his or her body, or with a soul, but rather is viewed as "a pattern of matter and energy that persists over time."[6] A patternist, Kurzweil says, is "someone who views patterns of information as the fundamental reality."[7] To a patternist, the fundamental makeup of the universe is the information contained in various substrates, including matter, energy, and human persons. The substrate itself is unimportant and, in the case of human beings, is in desperate need of replacement, as the mortal body allows the pattern to be lost forever when the person dies. Kurzweil's (materialist) Cartesian dualist tendencies are evident in the form and function of his skepticism about the material world when he claims: "I don't know for sure that anything exists other than my own thoughts."[8] While Kurzweil is not, strictly speaking, a Cartesian, in the sense that he does not believe that human beings consist of a duality of an immaterial and immortal soul and a material and mortal body, he draws heavily upon the philosophical tradition of Descartes in his understanding that mentality[9] is the ultimate (and most reliable) reality that is separable from the body in which mental process occur.

It is Kurzweil's great hope that advanced AI capabilities will be combined with advances in neuroscience to make it possible for a person to upload the contents of his or her brain into a computer. Advanced AI will then explode in a self-generating cycle, and we will merge with our machines in a form of virtual immortality. According to Kurzweil, "the Singularity will allow us to transcend these limitations of our biological bodies and brains. We will gain power over our fates. Our mortality will be in our own hands. We will be able to live as long as we want ... We will fully understand human thinking and will vastly extend and expand its reach."[10] His anthropology also extends to an extreme fear of death. Kurzweil takes more than 200 supplements each day and has publicly expressed that his goal is to live long enough to have the technology to upload his consciousness into a computer and to witness the Singularity. Much of his work in recent years has focused heavily on health practices that might allow him to avoid death, and he has co-authored three books on life extension practices.[11]

Such life extension is thought to be possible only because Kurzweil believes that "it is the persistence and power of patterns that support life and intelligence. The pattern is far more important than the material stuff that constitutes it."[12] According to his pattern recognition theory of mind (PRTM), humans are patterns of information, just as the world is a very complex pattern of information; this perception is reflected in Kurzweil's understanding of the purpose of human life, and the universe itself.[13] "In my view, [he says,] the purpose of life—and of our lives—is to create and appreciate ever-greater knowledge, to move toward greater 'order' ... the purpose of the universe reflects the same purpose as our lives: to move toward greater intelligence and knowledge."[14] For Kurzweil, intelligence is both the purpose and the goal of the existence of the universe.

The Singularitarian understanding of the human person as reducible, without significant remainder, to the patterns of information contained within their brains, is a key problem, and one that is of particular interest for feminist reflection. This patternist dualism that sharply divides the computations of the brain from the "mere substrate" of the body has important ramifications for how we think about human beings and any enhancements we may want to make to ourselves. Feminist science scholar Vicki Kirby identifies and critiques this tendency toward materialist dualism among contemporary technophiles, whom she designates "cybernauts": "cybernauts tend to rejoice uncritically in their Cartesian inheritance that would regard the body as 'obsolete, as soon as consciousness itself can be uploaded into the network.' According to Allucquere Roseanne Stone, 'Forgetting about the body is an old Cartesian trick' and the cost of this effacement is usually born by 'women and minorities.' "[15] The reduction of the person to the information in their brains makes the body not only obsolete and unnecessary, but also invisible. The realities of life will change as different types of bodies with different experiences, relationships, and prejudices are ignored and idealized into pure information. Kirby claims that the reduction to information "involves the separation and privileging of the ideational over the material, and in such a way that matter is denigrated as the base support of an ascendant entity (mind over matter, male over female, culture over nature, the West over the rest, and so on)."[16]

Kurzweil claims, "It is not demeaning to regard a person as a profound pattern (a form of knowledge), which is lost when he or she dies. That, at least, is the case today, since we do not yet have the means to access and back up this knowledge."[17] Indeed, it may not be demeaning, although it is an overly reductionistic and ultimately unhelpful way to understand the human person. We humans are not merely the sums of our brains; we are embodied beings whose experience of the world is heavily dependent upon the types of bodies that we have.[18] Were we to be embodied in another kind of substrate, we might still be persons, but we would not be ourselves.

Kurzweil has promoted the idea of people adopting a variety of bodies, both physical and virtual, to free themselves to live different kinds of lives at will. He has, somewhat famously, adopted the virtual persona of "Ramona" and performed speeches and interviews as his feminine alter ego.[19] "Ramona" is a slender, yet voluptuous young woman who wears tight, revealing clothes and talks and moves as Kurzweil himself does. When Kurzweil saw himself as Ramona in the cybermirror, he said, "I saw myself as Ramona rather than the person I usually see in the mirror. I experienced the emotional force—and not just the intellectual idea—of transforming myself into someone else."[20]

What can be learned from Kurzweil's adoption of the Ramona persona? What does it say that he chose to take on this virtual female body and saw himself as "her," while still remaining entirely himself? On the face of it, Ramona is something of a cliché. The tight-laced bodice and skinny jeans on a slender yet busty body represent a fantasy character, not unlike those found in most video games designed for young, heterosexual males. What is interesting, though, is how Kurzweil understands himself when he "becomes" Ramona. He takes on a virtual form that is available for others to see and experience and believes that he truly becomes someone else. In an interview in the persona of Ramona, he claimed, "In virtual reality, you can BE someone else. You don't have to be the same boring person all the time."[21]

On the one hand, this could be freeing for some people who choose to spend their time interacting with others in a virtual system: they can take on some of the social experiences of another person with a different background. On the other hand, this easy adoption of other bodily forms tends to mask the real issues that face people in bodies and the lived experiences of those bodies. Ray Kurzweil can pretend to be "Ramona," but he ought not confuse this experience with the reality of life as a woman. Playing tourist is not the same as living somewhere. Kurzweil can simply make the choice to remove the persona and return to being a wealthy, white man, thereby experiencing the "fun" aspects of being a woman without fully embracing the lived realities of discrimination or sexism with which real women often live. Doing so allows him to claim the experience of life as a woman while simultaneously masking his privilege. Our bodies do substantially influence who we are, in all their magnificent and problematic complexity. They cannot simply be discarded or exchanged without substantial change to the identity and lived reality of the person whose body is altered.

Kurzweil's statements about the body in his writings indicate a great deal about how he understands both himself and his audience. In *The Singularity Is Near*, he looks forward to what he calls Body 2.0: "We've eliminated the heart, lungs, red and white blood cells, platelets, pancreas, thyroid and all the hormone-producing organs, kidneys, bladder, liver, lower esophagus, stomach, small intestines, large intestines, and bowel . . . *But the skin, which*

includes our primary and secondary sex organs, may prove to be an organ we will
actually want to keep, or we may at least want to maintain its vital functions of com-
munication and pleasure."[22]

Kurzweil is more than happy to get rid of anything that he does not consider to be intrinsic to his understanding of himself—all the messy parts of biological life as we know it. But he does make it clear what he values. In
claiming that the skin system includes the primary and secondary sex organs,
he makes two things clear. First, he is speaking to and about men. While it
is unusual to consider sex organs to be part of the skin system, it may be
explainable here because men carry their primary reproductive and sexual
organs (the penis and testicles) on the exterior of their bodies, while most of
women's primary reproductive and sexual organs (the uterus, fallopian tubes,
and ovaries) are internal and, therefore, not generally understood as part of
the skin.[23] Kurzweil makes the mistake of equating male and female sexuality
and bodily experience while also reducing the experience of both to a particular heteronormative male understanding of sexual pleasure.[24] The second
thing that becomes clear is that Kurzweil rejects all of the parts of his body that
he sees as secondary, not directly connected to his experiences of the world.
At the same time, he wants to remain active and virile, and sexuality is one
of the few bodily pursuits he finds valuable. This betrays his real dependence
on the embodiment he seeks to dispose of, as virtual sex through an uploaded
consciousness is a very different experience than the sensory/sensual experience of bodies.

As Singularitarians look forward to replacing most of their bodies and
embracing virtual ones, what happens to the experiences of the bodies that
currently exist in "real reality"? Kurzweil quotes Joseph LeDoux approvingly
in saying that "the self is the sum of the brain's individual subsystems, each
with its own form of 'memory,' together with the complex interactions among
the subsystems."[25] He looks forward to the possibility of uploading the brain,
"scanning all of its salient details and then reinstantiating those details into
a suitably powerful computational substrate. This process would capture a person's entire personality, memory, skills, and history."[26]

Feminists have long rejected the patternist dualism that is embraced
uncritically by Kurzweil. Susan Bordo has analyzed this tendency toward dualism, understanding that "what remains the constant element throughout historical variation is the construction of body as something apart from the true
self."[27] We are not merely brains with faulty bodies in unfortunate need of
replacement parts. Our existence as persons is not merely the function of our
individual wills.

Kurzweil makes strong libertarian claims for the freedom of morphological
choice, the freedom to assume or reject any particular bodily form that one
likes, co-opting feminist rhetoric about freedom of integrity *for* the body and
turning it into freedom of integrity *from* the body. He yearns for the

development of nanotechnology that is sufficient to manipulate matter quickly so that, as he puts it, "We will be able to change our bodies at will."[28]

The twin paradigms of uploading the brain into new substrates and changing the body at will move Kurzweil toward a co-optation of biological/sexual reproduction as well. In the coming Singularity, biological bodies will no longer need to exist, so bodily reproduction as we know it would cease as well. Reproduction becomes literal copying of one's memories instead of procreation of new persons. The technological future envisioned here is one in which we can constantly recreate and reinstantiate ourselves in new and ever better bodies, taking on characteristics as we will, even cloning ourselves into a variety of substrates at once, each with its own experiences. We would be endlessly networked and merged with one another, yet still somehow maintain individuality. At the same time, the truly new—persons born into the world—may come to an end. Reproduction comes to be overtaken, morphing into self-dissemination.

EVOLUTION AND PROGRESSION

Kurzweil's predictions are based upon an extrapolation of Moore's law to cover the whole of evolution, particularly technological evolution, in what he calls the "law of accelerating returns (LOAR)." In its most basic form, Kurzweil claims that there is an "inherent acceleration in the rate of evolution, with technological evolution as a continuation of biological evolution."[29] Evolution has a particular form and trajectory toward which it moves—the universe itself is moving toward greater order, intelligence, and technology. Kurzweil states that the LOAR works as follows:

An evolutionary process is not a closed system; therefore, evolution draws upon the chaos in the larger system in which it takes place for its options for diversity; and

- Evolution builds upon its own increasing order.
- Therefore: In an evolutionary process, order increases exponentially.
- Therefore: Time exponentially speeds up.
- Therefore: The returns (that is, the valuable products of the process) accelerate.[30]

For Kurzweil, evolution is not simply a process by which things change and new life forms are adapted to particular habitats; rather, evolution is oriented toward developing order and information out of chaos. Despite significant criticism from evolutionary biologists, Kurzweil defends his definition adamantly, claiming, "Evolution is a process of creating patterns of increasing order."[31] The universe is made of information, so everything drives toward the increase of information and order. According to Kurzweil, "Evolution increases order, which may or may not increase complexity (but usually does). A primary reason that evolution—of life-forms or of technology—speeds up is that it builds on its own increasing order, with ever more sophisticated means of recording and manipulating information."[32] The limitations that are found in the natural world that prevent a particular species from continuing exponential growth without end are circumvented in Kurzweil's theory of evolution when it comes to information and technology. To him, "[t]he two resources it needs—the growing order of the evolving technology itself and the chaos from which an evolutionary process draws its options for further diversity—are unbounded."[33]

In Kurzweil's thought, evolution's trajectory is not only toward the development of order, it is directed toward intelligence and technology. Kurzweil believes that "[t]he introduction of technology on Earth is not merely the private affair of one of the Earth's innumerable species. It is a pivotal event in the history of the planet. Evolution's grandest creation—human intelligence—is providing the means for the next stage of evolution, which is technology."[34]

His is, interestingly, not a strictly anthropocentric orientation, but a technocentric and intelligence-oriented position. Humans currently stand at the top of the evolutionary hierarchy, but only for the moment; we are here primarily to give way to the next phase—the grand AI that will begin as humanoid but will quickly surpass us as the march of progress leaves unmodified humanity behind. In Kurzweil's view, "the purpose of life—and of our lives —is to create and appreciate ever-greater knowledge, to move toward greater 'order' ... the purpose of the universe reflects the same purpose as our lives: to move toward greater intelligence and knowledge."[35]

In this understanding, evolution's movement toward progress is a naturally spiritual quest leading toward something like the divine. According to Kurzweil,

> Evolution moves toward greater complexity, greater elegance, greater knowledge, greater intelligence, greater beauty, greater creativity, and greater levels of subtle attributes such as love. In every monotheistic religion God is likewise described as all of these qualities, only without any limitation: infinite knowledge, infinite intelligence, infinite beauty, infinite creativity, infinite love, and so on. Of course, even the accelerating growth of evolution never achieves an infinite level, but as it explodes exponentially it certainly moves rapidly in that direction. So evolution moves us inexorably toward this conception of God, although never quite reaching this ideal. We can regard, therefore, the freeing of our thinking from the severe limitations of its biological form to be an essentially spiritual undertaking.[36]

He claims that this march toward the Singularity is inevitable and has been ongoing since the first single-celled organisms were formed in the cosmic soup of the early earth. Says Kurzweil, "Once life takes hold on a planet, we can consider the emergence of technology as inevitable."[37] Kurzweil's reading of evolution conveniently makes himself and his creations the pinnacles of history, with the futurist claiming that "evolution has been seen as a billion-year drama that led inexorably to its grandest creation: human intelligence."[38] His hard determinism is naturalistic and based in his reading of the trajectory of evolution, as Kurzweil claims that "[t]he Singularity denotes an event that will take place in the material world, the inevitable next step in the evolutionary process that started with biological evolution and has extended through human-directed technological evolution."[39]

The problematic nature of this understanding of evolution is difficult to overstate. Stephen Jay Gould, one of the foremost evolutionary biologists of the 20th century, resoundingly and repeatedly criticized the idea of a progressive and inevitable evolutionary teleology throughout his work:

> Graspers for progress have looked exclusively at the history of the most complex organism through time—a myopic focus on extreme values only—and have used the increasing complexity of the most complex as a false surrogate for progress of the whole . . . But this argument is illogical and has always disturbed the most critical consumers . . . I do not challenge the statement that the most complex creature has tended to increase in elaboration over time, but I fervently deny that this limited little fact can provide an argument for general progress as a defining thrust of life's history. Such a grandiose claim represents a ludicrous case of the tail wagging the dog, or the invalid elevation of a small and epiphenomenal consequence into a major and controlling cause.[40]

Gould repudiates the idea that intelligence has more than a cursory place in the grand story of the universe, claiming instead that "[t]he outstanding feature of life's history has been the stability of its bacterial mode over billions of years."[41] Steven Pinker has argued that "[n]atural selection does nothing even close to striving for intelligence. The process is driven by differences in the survival and reproduction rates of replicating organisms in a particular environment"—a statement that Kurzweil quotes directly, only to immediately wave it away, saying that "Pinker is missing the overall point."[42]

Kurzweil's vision of evolution's mechanisms and purpose do not stem from any scientifically recognized theory of evolutionary functioning. Philippe Verdoux argues that "the progressionist conception of history as 'a record of improvement in the conditions of human life' is highly problematic, both empirically and methodologically . . . [while] most transhumanists today accept progress as a 'central dogma' of their technocentric worldviews."[43] Things do not get better simply because we have the latest and greatest technology. Mistaking evolutionary history for the narrative of the development of intelligence in the quest for an artificial super-intelligence is an error that historian David Noble describes as a religious phenomenon with an "eschatological vision."[44] Kurzweil's reading of the inevitable trajectory of evolution is the basis for his assumption that the politics of technology will work out for the good, regardless of the costs along the way.

POLITICS AND PRACTICES

This understanding of Kurzweil's philosophy and expectations leads into an analysis of Kurzweil's politics as they are laid out in his work on technology. This futurist assumes that advanced robotics and AI will bring about the end to all major social problems. For example, he claims that "emerging technologies will provide the means of providing and storing clean and renewable energy, removing toxins and pathogens from our bodies and the environment, and providing the knowledge and wealth to overcome hunger and poverty."[45] In his utopian vision, intelligence is invariably paired with wisdom and goodness, so any problems for which we humans cannot devise and implement solutions on our own will be easily handled by our super-intelligent robots, as "technology will match and then vastly exceed the refinement and suppleness of what we regard as the best of human traits."[46]

This utopian vision leads Kurzweil to entirely overlook his position of tremendous privilege and makes him blind to any possible ill effects of his far-reaching predictions. Kurzweil addresses this issue by pointing to

> [the] possibility that through these technologies the rich may gain certain advantages and opportunities to which the rest of humankind does not have access. Such inequality, of course, would be nothing new, but with regard to this issue the law of accelerating returns has an important and beneficial impact. Because of the ongoing exponential growth of price-performance, all of these technologies quickly become so inexpensive as to become almost free.[47]

While it is certainly true that price-performance increases have allowed the overall cost of many technologies to drop significantly, there seems to be something of a lower limit to the possibilities that does not even approach "free" on a global scale. "Almost free" has a very different connotation to someone who lives on less than $1000 per year than it does to an affluent American entrepreneur.

Kurzweil likewise ignores the increasing disparity between the very rich and everyone else that has developed in the past 30 years. While the income and total net worth of wealthy corporate executives have enjoyed steady upward growth, the real (constant dollar) income of the bottom 90 percent of Americans has shrunk, even while technology and health care costs have risen dramatically.[48] Likewise, although there have been real gains in the opportunities for some people that have been brought about by the development of the Internet and related technologies, technology has not solved many major social issues. People around the world continue to lack access to sanitation, food, education, and health care.[49] It is not a lack of technology that allows these problems to continue, but rather a lack of political will. This makes the ethical apathy of Kurzweil's evolutionary inevitability even more problematic.

The assumption that technology will fix problems is combined in Kurzweil's thought with a libertarian free-market oriented philosophy that leaves the poor further behind, even while claiming that technology will make them rich. His privilege blinds him to the fact that the future he envisions in which all are wealthy, happy, and immortal is not one that is able to be shared by the majority of persons living on the earth. We should instead ask why Singularitarianism has developed as a movement advocated almost entirely by wealthy, white, Western men, and which alternative visions exist that promote responsible views of technological development that enhance the flourishing of all.

THE WORLD IS NOT (AUTOMATICALLY) GETTING BETTER: FEMINIST CHRISTIAN REFLECTIONS

How do we responsibly engage technology and technological change in our lives? Responsible engagement requires neither total relinquishment nor the uncritical embrace of technology, but rather intentionality about how and why we choose what we do—making choices about technology development part of a truly global public conversation. We need to have a conversation in which we have transparency about the interests involved in technology development, maintaining a healthy skepticism about corporatism, militarism, Western ethnocentrism, and all claims of human "perfectibility," lest we fall back into old patterns leading toward a new eugenics and similar projects of directed evolution. We ought not to let the values of a small group of technophilic, wealthy, straight, white men dominate the conversation about the shape of the future. We should ask why movements like Singularitarianism attract almost exclusively people from this privileged demographic. The idea of the Singularity has not generated anywhere near the same level of interest among others, including women, people of color, the global South, and the poor. Even so, prominent professional associations and corporations have begun to take these movements very seriously and identify with them. We ought to also maintain a skeptical view of the possibilities for technology to solve major social problems: the technology is available now to provide sufficient food and clean water to everyone on earth, yet a lack of political, social, and economic will has thus far prevented us from achieving the end of hunger and poverty. We must use technology well, implementing it carefully and paying attention to its effects, without getting caught up in the idea of technological inevitability.

The final section of this chapter seeks to elaborate upon and address these concerns while considering some insights from feminist and Christian thought toward generating constructive alternatives for envisioning the future of humanity and our technology.[50] I will discuss, in response to Kurzweil, issues of anthropology, evolution and teleology, and politics and privilege.

There is a long (and helpful) history of reflection and contestation within both Christianity and feminism regarding the question of what it means to be a person, or what it is to be a being that is a "who" rather than a "what." Feminists take a wide variety of perspectives with regard to the nature of moral personhood, whether personhood is based in relationality, particular moral or intellectual capacities, or some other set of qualities. While no one would argue that rationality is a bad thing to possess, a longstanding set of criticisms has arisen from within feminist thought that rejects an equation of person-hood solely with the mind, rationalism, or a pattern of information. This criti-cal perspective is taken for two primary reasons. First, feminists have shown the importance of the particularities of embodiment and physicality in both personal and political identity. I do not simply have a body; in a very real sense, I am a body, and reducing personhood to intellectual capacities ignores the very ground from which rationality arises. Second, feminists have been critical of philosophical and political moves to reduce moral personhood to rationalism because of how the notion of reason has historically been used to exclude women, Africans, persons with disabilities, and others from full moral and political standing. This exclusion has been justified on the grounds that some humans do not possess the right kind of rationality, or enough of it, to satisfy the definition given by those men with enough power to enforce it. Kurzweil's antipathy toward the body, when combined with patternist dual-ism, is suspect here and needs the corrective of feminist emphasis on the par-ticularities of the body in the development and sustaining of personal identity as well as a healthy skepticism about which ends the exclusionary tendencies such as patternism can be used to promote.

In thinking about the nature of human personhood, the Christian tradition has often begun by thinking about the nature of divine personhood and extrapolating from there to the human and other creaturely persons. God was understood in early Christian thought as a single essence eternally existing as three "persons." While the essence formed the unity of God, the idea of per-son was used to mark differentiation. Personhood was, therefore, not a marker of what was held in common—the "whatness" of God—but rather was defined as something more like "personality"—that is, the irreducible marker of differ-ence.[51] This understanding of personhood was then likewise applied to human beings. Human beings share a nature as creaturely beings, yet we are differentiated from one another as persons. A key ethical feature of this approach is that it avoids inappropriate anthropocentrism and allows for the existence of persons beyond human persons; it begins with the divine as the ultimately personal, moves to the human as reflectively personal, and opens space for other forms of persons. It takes care to affirm that all human beings are persons, but not all persons are human. It provides a different ground that patternism from which to understand what it is to be a person both ethically and politically.

In Christian theology, it is Jesus who provides the archetype for what human life is intended to be. The incarnation of God in Jesus is notable for its surprisingly fleshly this-worldliness. Jesus comes into the created, material world and lives and dies as a mortal human being, while somehow still retaining his godliness. The material is not opposed to the spiritual, but rather incarnates it. Likewise, since the creation of the material world is called "good" by God, the Christian tradition has, in its better moments, not allowed the material and spiritual existences of creation to be put at odds with one another. As contemporary feminist theologians have reminded the community, we are not spiritual beings *despite* our creation as material beings, but precisely *in* our creation as material beings.[52] In this way, mentality and spirituality are intimately connected to the particularities of our embodiment; the substrate matters in making us who we are.

We are created good, but we have not lived up to our created nature. The Christian tradition affirms that human beings have fallen short of what God intended for us. That we are created good allows us to uphold the worth of all creation—human and nonhuman, personal and nonpersonal. Nevertheless, our sinfulness disabuses us of the notion that we can perfect ourselves or expect utopia in this life. It gives a critical realism to our politics and a recognition that we tend to rationalize our choices when we are selfish. Both Christian theology and a significant body of contemporary psychological research affirm that we see the good that we do but not the damage, and we fool ourselves into thinking that our motives and actions are purer than they are.[53]

Feminist theology has tended to strongly emphasize the value of political action in righting both historical and contemporary wrongs in political structure, policy, and power. We do have freedom, and the choices that we make do matter, so we cannot be lulled into ethical or political quietism and apathy. Yet our choices are not unconstrained; we experience the failure of our actions, limitations of our choices, and challenges from within and without. It is critically important in any discussion of the future of technology to recognize the importance of taking responsibility for the technologies that we develop and utilize. Greater intelligence is not the same as greater goodness, and we have little reason to believe that our inventions, however magnificent, will be any better than we are. There is such a thing as moral progress within Christianity, but it is not assured within the trajectory of history.[54] Feminist theology is rightly skeptical of privilege, and we must keep our eyes on those who are considered the least members of society in the eyes of the world at large. That we are both good and fallen, free and constrained, gives us a perspective beyond simple utopia or dystopia. It is in this perspective that we can understand that our technologies are, as an extension of ourselves, neither the ultimate problem nor the ultimate solution; rather, they are simply tools that we can use for both good and ill.

Responsible engagement with the future of technology should balance the optimism that we can make choices that have positive impacts in the world around us with the skepticism that we tend toward selfishness, rationalization of our own choices, and a lack of empathy for those whom we do not know. We can choose a position between an extreme version of the precautionary principle, in which no technology can be developed until all of its possible effects are known, and an extreme proactionary principle, in which technology development can and must move full speed ahead. New technologies do not develop on their own: they are the results of myriad choices in business and political life.

Kurzweil and other Singularitarians argue that existing social problems, such as massive wealth inequality, are not a reason to halt technological innovation. On this point, they are correct. At the same time, we ought to be skeptical of the absolute urgency and inevitability proclaimed for the sexy high tech and the corresponding demonization of anyone who believes that more funding should be given to alleviate current crushing problems—for example, the lack of clean water, housing, food, and health care currently faced by many in the world. It is possible for us to do both, but we humans are not very good at feeling the urgency for too many policy priorities at once. Some things are emphasized while others are de-emphasized, and I want to ensure that in the rush to develop the new and the cool, the problems of today are not forgotten.

Many advancements in medical technology, including sterile surgery, antibiotics, vaccines, birth control, and the like, contributed to a dramatic increase in life expectancy in developed nations during the 20th century. Scientific and technological advancements were critical to increases in health and longevity on a global scale, but technology alone does not solve global crises. As with all new technologies, emerging medical technologies are first available only to the very wealthy, but eventually become common enough to be covered by insurance and affordable for people in developed nations. Unfortunately, many of these technologies never "trickle down" to the point of being affordable to the world's poorest, or even the less well-off in the United States. Significant and intentional choices in political, economic, and social policies are required to make good health care broadly accessible. Constructive discussions around risk and benefit need to happen on a global basis, not just among those who currently enjoy the advantages of technology and would benefit most from further development. Such discussions would not look at transhuman technologies as an all-or-nothing proposition, but rather would take seriously the questions of how and why particular technologies are developed, the uses to which they are put, and the social, economic, and political systems in which they are developed and made available.

Finally, we must acknowledge that technology, in and of itself, does not make life better, freer, or happier. Advanced technologies merely provide some means to the end and tend to amplify the effects of our choices. Technology and democracy can provide the conditions of the possibility of a better world, but there is a whole lot more that we collectively need to choose each day to reach it.

NOTES

1. Vernor Vinge, "The Coming Technological Singularity: How to Survive in the Post-Human Era," VISION-21 Symposium sponsored by NASA Lewis Research Center and the Ohio Aerospace Institute, March 30–31, 1993.

2. Ray Kurzweil, *The Singularity Is Near: When Humans Transcend Biology* (New York, NY: Viking, 2005), 7–8.

3. Kurzweil, *The Singularity Is Near*, 9.

4. I am neither a Luddite nor a technophobe. I do not oppose technology generally, including many of the technologies promoted by those involved in the Singularitarian movement. To the contrary, I am something of a technophile and think that technology is critically important—so much so that I believe that it matters greatly how we think about it. I think it is crucial to develop and implement technology responsibly, which is why I want to offer a critique of social movement that promotes irresponsible views of the future of technology, along with some alternative possibilities for better ways to envision the future.

5. I am using anthropology in the sense that it has traditionally been used in philosophy and theology—as the study of what it means to be a person/human being, and not in the disciplinary sense of the study of human cultures.

6. Kurzweil, *The Singularity Is Near*, 383.

7. Kurzweil, *The Singularity Is Near*, 5.

8. Kurzweil, *The Singularity Is Near*, 390.

9. By "mentality," I refer to the processes and patterns of thought and rationality in distinction from the physical embodiment of those thoughts.

10. Kurzweil, *The Singularity Is Near*, 9.

11. His other books include *The Age of Intelligent Machines* (Cambridge, MA: MIT Press, 1992), *The 10% Solution for a Healthy Life: How to Reduce Fat in Your Diet and Eliminate Virtually All Risk of Heart Disease* (New York, NY: Crown, 1993), *Fantastic Voyage: Live Long Enough to Live Forever* (New York, NY: Rodale, 2004), and *TRANSCEND: Nine Steps to Living Well Forever* (New York, NY: Rodale, 2009).

12. Kurzweil, *The Singularity Is Near*, 388.

13. Ray Kurzweil, *How to Create a Mind: The Secret of Human Thought Revealed* (New York, NY: Penguin Books, 2012), 5.

14. Kurzweil, *The Singularity Is Near*, 372.

15. Vicki Kirby, *Telling Flesh: The Substance of the Corporeal* (New York, NY: Routledge, 1997), 138.

16. Kirby, *Telling Flesh*, 137–138.

17. Kurzweil, *The Singularity Is Near*, 372.

18. George Lakoff and Mark Johnson, *Philosophy in the Flesh: The Embodied Mind and Its Challenge to Western Thought* (New York, NY: Basic Books, 1999).

19. "Ramona: Come Out and Play," http://www.youtube.com/watch?v=xy7aew 0R0Xc, accessed March 31, 2014.

20. Kurzweil, *The Singularity Is Near*, 315.

21. "Ray Kurzweil se Convierte en Ramona," https://www.youtube.com/watch? v=fEKHDSgFU9E, accessed April 17, 2014.

22. Kurzweil, *The Singularity Is Near*, 307; emphasis added.

23. The clitoris, labia, vulva, and breasts could be considered part of the skin, but these are secondary as reproductive organs. Kurweil's assumptions regarding the equivalence of sex organs between male and female remain problematic.

24. Queer and disabled sexualities and their attendant sex organs (such as the prostate) also tend to stand outside of this heteronormative reasoning and are likewise not part of the skin system.

25. Kurzweil, *The Singularity Is Near*, 169.

26. Kurzweil, *The Singularity Is Near*, 198–199.

27. Susan Bordo, *Unbearable Weight: Feminism, Western Culture, and the Body* (Berkeley, CA: University of California Press, 1993), 4.

28. Kurzweil, *The Singularity Is Near*, 371.

29. Kurzweil, *The Singularity Is Near*, 7.

30. Ray Kurzweil, *The Age of Spiritual Machines: When Computers Exceed Human Intelligence* (New York, NY: Viking, 1999), 32–33.

31. Kurzweil, *The Singularity Is Near*, 14.

32. Kurzweil, *The Age of Spiritual Machines*, 40.

33. Kurzweil, *The Age of Spiritual Machines*, 35.

34. Kurzweil, *The Age of Spiritual Machines*, 35.

35. Kurzweil, *The Singularity Is Near*, 372.

36. Kurzweil, *The Singularity Is Near*, 389.

37. Kurzweil, *The Age of Spiritual Machines*, 17.

38. Kurzweil, *The Age of Spiritual Machines*, 5.

39. Kurzweil, *The Singularity Is Near*, 387.

40. Stephen Jay Gould, *Full House: The Spread of Excellence from Plato to Darwin* (New York, NY: Harmony Books, 1996), 168–169.

41. Stephen Jay Gould, *Full House*, 175.

42. Kurzweil, *How to Create a Mind*, 76–77.

43. Philippe Verdoux, "Transhumanism, Progress, and the Future," *Journal of Evolution and Technology* 20, no. 2 (2009): 50.

44. David Noble, *The Religion of Technology: The Divinity of Man and the Spirit of Invention* (New York, NY: Alfred A. Knopf, 1997), 164.

45. Kurzweil, *The Singularity Is Near*, 371–372.

46. Kurzweil, *The Singularity Is Near*, 9.

47. Kurzweil, *The Singularity Is Near*, 469.

48. Dave Gilson and Carolyn Perot, "It's the Inequality, Stupid," *Mother Jones* (March/April 2011), http://motherjones.com/politics/2011/02/income-inequality-in -america-chart-graph, accessed March 31, 2014.

49. United Nations, *The Millennium Development Goals Report, 2013* (New York, NY: United Nations, 2013).

50. My own perspective is one of a liberal, feminist, Reformed Protestant, and my comments will largely be derived from the particularities of that community within

the Christian tradition. Most other communities within the Christian family would uphold many of these insights as I develop them, but each community would have different emphases, and sometimes different language, with which to talk about them.

51. Ian A. McFarland, *Difference and Identity: A Theological Anthropology* (Cleveland, OH: Pilgrim Press, 2001).

52. Nancey Murphy, *Bodies and Souls, or Spirited Bodies?* (New York, NY: Cambridge, 2006).

53. Serene Jones, *Feminist Theory and Christian Theology: Cartographies of Grace* (Minneapolis, MN: Fortress Press, 1999); Carol Tavris and Elliot Aronson, *Mistakes Were Made (But Not by Me): Why We Justify Foolish Beliefs, Bad Decisions, and Hurtful Acts* (Orlando, FL: Harcourt, 2007).

54. Reinhold Niebuhr, *The Nature and Destiny of Man: A Christian Interpretation* (Louisville, KY: Westminster John Knox, 1996).

Section 4

Extreme Enhancement Ethics: Theological,
Bioethical, and Philosophical Questions

Transhumanism and Catholic Natural Law: Changing Human Nature and Changing Moral Norms[1]

Brian Patrick Green

Natural law ethics derives moral norms from human nature. Transhumanism seeks to change human nature. So, could transhumanism change the norms of natural law? And if so, how, why, and in which ways? Natural law ethics is one of the major ethical approaches used in Catholic Christianity. Natural law rests on the fundamental axiom that *agere sequitur esse*—that is, "action follows being." In other words, by knowing what something is (its nature), we can know something about how it should act (its ethics). Natural law's theological assumptions include the idea that nature as a whole is God's good creation and that the natures of particular creatures manifest divine providence. Beings should act in accord with their natures because, in following God's providence, doing so leads toward virtuous excellence and happiness. Contemporary natural law has been considered by several major schools of thought, including rationalist and physicalist interpretations.

Transhumanism's proponents argue that we should change humans into technologically enhanced forms with powers that normal humans do not have. For example, humans could be genetically or cybernetically enhanced to be smarter or stronger. Some transhumanist thinkers even propose "uploading" the human mind into a computer, thereby freeing humanity from embodiment and its limits. An uploaded mind could theoretically travel across space through computer networks or duplicate itself at will. We already have humans who can control computers with their thoughts, and computers that can provide input into human brains. What if researchers created an animal or human with a largely or completely artificial brain? How much artificial brain would be enough to qualify one as "transhuman"? These issues call into question the connection between mind and matter, and much that is built upon this connection, including Catholic natural law. If something as basic as the connection between mind and matter were altered in humans, how would this affect human nature? And how would natural law theory deal with these changes?

In this chapter I propose a preliminary response to the transhumanist challenge to natural law by investigating six basic questions: (1) Is human nature relevant to morality? (2) Is human nature mutable? (3) How would we know if human nature had changed? (4) Could cultural evolution replace biological evolution? (5) How would human nature and human will relate to each other under these new transhuman conditions? (6) Is it possible to construct a dynamic ethic to fit a dynamic nature, and if so, what might that ethic be?

Overall, I argue that it is possible to maintain a natural law ethics approach in the face of transhumanist changes to human nature and that, in fact, doing so remains a very useful approach, albeit one with some difficulties. The norms of natural law are another matter: I think moral norms will need to become either stricter than in the past or different in ways that are difficult to anticipate.

This chapter concentrates on the philosophy and theology of the 13th-century Roman Catholic saint, Thomas Aquinas, who developed Aristotle's ideas in a Christian context. Aquinas's claims that action follows being and that human nature is a composite of first nature and second nature are combined with ideas from the philosopher Hans Jonas about the increasing scope of human action and the consequent necessity to update ethics. I propose that there a new form of natural law ethics might be capable of responding to changes in human nature.

IS NATURE RELEVANT TO MORALITY?

The idea that nature is relevant to morality has a long history, dating back at least to Aristotle. Nevertheless, many philosophers of the modern and contemporary periods have disagreed with Aristotle. For example, David Hume's "is-ought" dichotomy, sometimes called Hume's law, says that "one cannot derive an 'ought' from an 'is,'" which, of course, is exactly what most forms of natural law ethics try to do.[2] Natural law, then, might sound like a nonstarter for contemporary ethical analysis, which has for many decades taken Hume's law for granted. However, due to the rejuvenation of virtue ethics, there has been a growing movement to reject the is-ought dichotomy and reassert the moral relevance of nature. This movement includes such diverse thinkers as Larry Arnhart, William Casebeer, Terrence Deacon, Daniel Dennett, Philippa Foot, Hans Jonas, Alasdair MacIntyre, Martha Nussbaum, and Joan Roughgarden.[3]

How, then, should we understand the relationship between the "is" of nature and the "ought" of ethics? Aristotle grounded his ethics in natural teleology, and Alasdair MacIntyre argues persuasively in *After Virtue* that there is no way to do ethics without at least some sense of *telos*. MacIntyre resolves the is-ought problem by restoring teleology to ethics. He articulates the connection between ethics and teleology within a three-part structure: "untutored human nature, man-as-he-could-be-if-he-realized-his-*telos* and the moral precepts which enable him to pass from one state to the other."[4] In other words, ethics mediates both nature and *telos*. To achieve a purpose, one must move from beginning to end by taking certain actions that delineate the path between these two places. These delineating actions are ethics. Modernity, informed by Hume and others,[5] removed the sense of normative goal seeking in human nature, thereby leaving the "nature-ethics-*telos*" system corrupted because it had no *telos*—no purpose for human life, no concept of excellence and flourishing. The system then becomes only the "is" of nature and an ethics with no point, which quickly yields a disbelief in ethics (since it seems pointless), and finally only science and technology remain.

By taking the teleological perspective, we can see that nature is very much relevant to ethics because all creatures naturally seek certain ends. For example, plants naturally seek light and animals naturally seek food. For these entities, seeking these things constitutes a purpose and a good. While these are natural goods, they become moral goods in humanity because we are conscious, rational agents with free will and have a reflective power to perceive these goods and to choose for or against them. For example, for humans, health and learning are goods that we naturally seek. In our actions we can choose for or against these goods—for example, by eating well or poorly, or by practicing skills or not. In choosing for or against these goods, we make moral choices insofar as we benefit or harm our health or develop or stunt our learning. We may choose, if freedom grants us the opportunity, to become more fully flourishing humans; likewise, by our choices we may choose the opposite. Of paramount importance here is simply the point that these natural goods exist, and that they are relevant for morality.

IS HUMAN NATURE MUTABLE?

The next question is whether human nature is mutable, and if so, in which ways and to what degree? If human nature is mutable, then the ethics derived from it may have to change as human nature changes. While contemporary postmodernism, feminism, and evolutionary theory tend to be anti-essentialist and take human mutability as a given, this tends not to be the case with natural law theory.

In the *Summa Theologiae*, following the ancient philosophers, Aquinas divides human nature into first nature and second nature.[6] First nature is the part of us that we share universally with all other humans. In modern terms, first nature would be what metaphysically and biologically makes us members of the species *Homo sapiens*. First nature is also something over which we have historically had little or no voluntary control.

Second nature, by comparison, is more open. It is not universal. It varies between groups over geography and history, and in individuals over their life-times. It can be thought of as culture, as expressed in the group and the indi-vidual. The processes of acquiring culture are enculturation (or socialization) and habituation. For example, children learn to speak the language to which they are culturally exposed, but may develop particular good or bad habits when speaking. Most importantly, we possess some measure of voluntary con-trol over second nature and so are responsible for our individual virtues and vices.

I think Aquinas is being a bit too simple by separating human nature into only two parts. Arguably, first nature and second nature could be further sep-arated into metaphysical first nature (pertaining to human being and identity as, for example, "rational animals") and biological first nature (pertaining to our biology—for example, as genetic organisms with metabolism and physiol-ogy), and cultural second nature (pertaining to our culture—for example, our language) and individual second nature (pertaining to our personal habits—for example, mumbling). The distinction between metaphysical and biologi-cal first nature is especially important to this discussion.

In the *Summa Theologiae*, Aquinas argues that the general principles of natural law (i.e., those derived from our first nature) cannot vary between human groups because the principles are universal to all humans. In contrast, the particular determinations of natural law will vary between groups because they are more context dependent.[7] For example, in another culture, what we would call "stealing" might be more like "borrowing" or "giving." If the social expectations of the group are not the same, the specific behavioral norms will likewise be different.

To summarize, second nature is variable and the morals of different cultures can legitimately vary in limited ways according to the specifics of their social and physical environment. Translating Aquinas into the more modern par-lance used by Jean Porter, we might say that humans are underdetermined.[8] Our biological inclinations are insufficient to guide our behavior, so our cul-tures take up the genetic slack and guide our behavior through moral codes.[9] For example, by nature humans will pick up a language, but culture deter-mines which one. Morally speaking, by nature humans will desire food, but by culture we are told what is good or not good to eat (e.g., is meat permis-sible?) and how we are allowed to get it (e.g., not by stealing). Not every moral code will work; cultures are selected by natural selection just as biological organisms are.[10] Societies that do not function well either adapt or are replaced. Adaptation relies on mutation, whether biological or cultural, which raises our central question: is human nature mutable?

The answer for second nature is clearly "yes." Human cultural nature is mutable, as cultures vary widely over space and time. The answer for first nature was formerly "no" (excluding the issue of the very slow changes due to biological evolution), but is now becoming "yes," at least for biological first nature (and possibly for metaphysical first nature). Furthermore, first nature is growing in mutability with technological advances.

Medicine is a major field in which technology has led to dramatic changes in human life, and it provides a clear case study of how human nature has changed. Medicine is a manifestation of second nature specifically directed at the control of biological first nature. This cultural phenomenon has dramatically changed human health, especially lifespan and reproductive behavior. As medicine advances, more and more of first nature will come under the control of second nature. This shift goes beyond medicine into many other fields.

The scope of human power has grown through the growth of technology. This is a key point: if action follows being, and human action has changed, then our being may have changed as well. I say "may have" because there remain relevant questions regarding act and potency, as well as ontology and epistemology, as discussed in the next section.

Human biological first nature and second nature are now mutable not only through biological and cultural evolution, but more particularly through the application of technology. Technology can act not only on our second nature, in our culture, but also now on our biological first nature. Humans have indeterminacy (freedom) built into our biological nature that allows us to acquire a culture, which then completes us. In other words, our biology needs culture or we are incomplete. Our freedom necessitates that we have a culture with moral norms because we are not programmed by instinct as deterministically as other animals are. As our technological power grows, including power over our biological nature, our indeterminacy will grow with it. More of our behavior will then become subject to free will rather than necessity; thus the realm of morality will grow as well. This is what has happened in the last few decades with new technologies. For example, advances in reproductive technology have forced us to ask whether conception via donor gametes and pregnancy via gestational surrogacy are morally good.

Human second nature is growing in scope relative to human biological first nature. Our scope of voluntary action has increased, and with it our power and freedom. If action and being are related, then as technology increases our scope for action, what we are as beings may be changing. On the *scala natura*, the Great Chain of Being, despite our materiality, perhaps we are no longer quite so close to the animals and are now a bit closer to the angels—we have clawed our way up a little bit. With the flip of a switch hundreds of millions can be killed in a nuclear war, and by polluting the atmosphere we can warm the earth. These are not the actions of simple apes; they are the actions of creatures more akin to minor deities. This is a true novelty of history, albeit a very dangerous one. Thus we have immense power with inadequate ethics; we have an ethics for apes, but not demigods.

Jonas makes this point earlier in non-Thomistic terms in his book *The Imperative of Responsibility*. In his first chapter, Jonas asserts that "the nature of human action has changed" over time due to our growth in technological power; since ethics concerns action, the nature of ethics must change as well.[11] Jonas lists some ways in which ethics must change to fit the contemporary context. Ethics, he says, must consider the vulnerability of nature to human action. Our ethical actions are now aggregate (collective of all our actions), irreversible (as in extinction of species), and cumulative (effects build up over time). Unlike in the past, when actions were more discrete, with global civilization consequences now compound both spatially and temporally, and future effects are unpredictable. Ethical decision making must take this unpredictability into account. This leads to Jonas's "imperative of responsibility": " 'Act so that the effects of your action are compatible with the permanence of genuinely human life'; or expressed negatively: 'Act so that the effects of your action are not destructive of the future possibility of such life.' "[12]

Technological second nature is growing to encompass biological first nature. Human nature has never been stationary; it has always been evolving, but what was once a crawl has accelerated. If action follows being, and our capacity for action has changed, then this implies that our being may have changed as well.

HOW WOULD WE KNOW IF HUMAN NATURE HAD CHANGED?

At the simplest level, if transhumanism succeeds in changing humans, then natural law dictates that these new creatures could have different moral requirements than do current humans. From a Thomistic perspective, if an entity dramatically changes its behavior, it has not necessarily changed its substantial form, but is merely actualizing potencies that it already possessed, as when a caterpillar changes into a butterfly. But in what sense could this be true for transhumans, who might technologically modify their bodies or attempt to upload their consciousness? While in a physical sense action follows being, in an epistemological sense being follows action. We can classify what something is by what it does. In reversing the axiom, a being is known through its actions.

If transhumans obtain new powers for action, we might have to classify them as possessing different natures from current humans and as having different ethical expectations. Whether a reclassification of being is necessary is the crux of the problem: will transhumans be new beings or just plain old humans actualizing latent potencies? Furthermore, how do biology and metaphysics relate on this question? How far must second nature grow into first nature before biology is completely absorbed? And what do these human changes mean metaphysically? Because ethical responsibility is proportional to the capacity to act, if transhumans became, for example, extraordinarily strong or smart, they would become more culpable for their actions and failures to act, or in religious terms, for their sins of commission and omission. We already have this moral expectation for the powerful, of course, so is this really a change?

In considering morality, a definition of human nature that includes our potential for action is appropriate, because it reflects the axiom that action follows being. However, including this element in a definition of human nature does create a problem: humans are already capable of vastly different actions than we were in past times. So are we already transhumans?

As mentioned earlier, Jonas argues that humans have, through technology, already expanded our scope of action and, therefore, we must expand the scope of our ethics.[13] Applying this idea to natural law, if our scope of action has changed over history due to culture, then perhaps our being (as bioculturally composite creatures) has in some sense changed as well. Deeper investigation into this point (which is not possible here) requires examining the relationships between efficient causality and substantial form, biology and culture, the individual and society, and potency and being.

Compared to our ancestors, our biology is nearly the same, but technologically speaking, our capacity to act is vastly different. Relative to the ancients, we perform magic. The ancients did not need to worry about the ethics of human cloning, nuclear war, synthetic biology, nanotechnology, space exploration, or artificial intelligence. Moreover, they never had to entertain the question of whether they should—or have—become transhumans. But we do. We have far greater potential for action than did our ancestors. Transhumanists are simply pursuing this trajectory with intention and intensity. Where does quantity change quality? Where does biology become metaphysics? Where do we cross the threshold between actualizing potentials we have always had and becoming new kinds of beings? We know this transition seems to have already happened to humanity once in the past, when we transitioned from ape to human. Will it happen again if we transition from human to transhuman?

Different schools of natural law will vary in how they understand transhumans to be "different" from humans. Rationalist natural law theorists might find transhumans to be no different at all from normal humans because both possess a rational faculty that is understood as the seat of moral relevance.[14] In contrast, physicalist natural law theorists might find transhumans and regular humans to be very different, because the body itself has normative teleologies built into it.[15] For now, these schools of natural law are in disagreement on many issues, such as sexuality, precisely because humans have gained tech-nological control of reproduction like never before. These disagreements will grow and spread into new fields of inquiry as technology continues to increase our control over human nature.

COULD CULTURAL EVOLUTION REPLACE BIOLOGICAL EVOLUTION?

Humans are bioculturally composite creatures; will transhumans also be? As technology grows in power over biology, will it eventually edge biology out entirely? Will second nature come to completely absorb first nature, pre-cisely as brain "uploaders" desire to do, living free of biological substrate? In these extreme scenarios, biological evolution ceases and cultural evolution becomes the sole form of transhuman evolution.

How would natural law operate in a purely cultural system, with no biologi-cal "nature" to determine ethics? Would natural law become completely rela-tivized? Up until now human nature has always implied at least some foundational biology. But perhaps even purely cultural/technological creatures will still have a metaphysical first nature (e.g., reason and will). Perhaps these traditional categories, which distinguish us from the rest of the animals, will be enhanced, or perhaps other categories added.

The schools of natural law theory would engage this situation differently. Rationalist natural law would likely see uploaded transhumans as still being essentially human or at least person, given that they consider the morally rel-evant aspect of human nature to be mental. In Christianity, rationality and personhood are not exclusively human traits: we share these traits with God, and the angels and demons—and so perhaps we could share them with non-biological transhumans, too. Transhumans would be a new category of rational creatures, similar to humans by existing in physical matter, but unlike humans in that matter is a nonbiological artifact. As long as transhumans remained rational, rationalist natural law might not need to be fundamentally revised.

Conversely, physicalist natural law theorists would likely see uploaded transhumans as essentially different from normal humans because the uploaded entities would lack a biological body in which the biological parts have intrinsic teleologies. Instead, transhumans incorporating (or substitut-ing) hardware into or for their beings would be radically physically underde-termined and morphologically open, even if they shared a continuity of mind with humans. Some physicalist natural law theorists might conclude that these transhumans share very little essential nature with humans or no longer have an essential nature, as they might change the physical aspects of their nature at will. Moral evaluation would be related to the full range of possible actions, thereby greatly expanding moral responsibility—in Jesus's words, "to whom much is given, much is expected."[16]

HOW WOULD HUMAN NATURE AND HUMAN WILL RELATE UNDER CONDITIONS OF RADICALLY MANIPULABLE NATURE?

Recalling the argument made by MacIntyre, ethics mediates nature and *telos*. Nature is our origin, *telos* our destiny, and ethics the way to move from the first to the second. But transhumans may have very different natures, and their destinies (bracketing out their supernatural ones) will be subject to their own choices. Does ethics become meaningless when origin and destiny are both subject to human will? Or does ethics merely become the subjective judgment of the individual transhuman, who is capable of shifting morphologies and teleologies at will?

For natural law to work, the entelechies (the built-in natural purposes or *telei*) of creatures must be known. Being determines action because natural being is intrinsically teleological—nature aims toward something. If we can determine that transhumans still have a natural entelechy, then their ethics could be read from their natures, not their wills.

Most likely, the *telei* of these new creatures will be survival and flourishing, as are the *telei* for all life. But what is "flourishing" for transhumans? Natural law ethics posits some clear criteria for flourishing, presupposing the mandate that human will should be subordinated to nature, which expresses God's providence. In our individualist and authority-resisting contemporary culture, higher authorities are often rejected, and subjective will becomes the measure of right and wrong, yielding a world of relativized morals. Under this relativistic ethic, nature and *telos* are subject to will, and morality would be whatever transhumans decide it to be. In most schools of natural law, in contrast, individual will does not actually affect one's *telos*. In other words, individual expressivist self-actualization—a driving force behind transhumanism—would attract little consideration in the moral evaluations of most types of natural law. For example, one transhuman might desire enhanced mental capacities to pursue theoretical mathematics, but a natural law evaluation might conclude that this mental power instead ought to be used for helping the poor.

But let us not too hastily dismiss transhumanist aspirations as immoral abuses of the human will over nature. Some transhumans might want to help the poor. In our capacities to act, we are already at some distance from the ancients, and transhumanists are merely pursuing this historical trajectory. Power applied to nature is not intrinsically immoral. Rather, power just gives us more indeterminacy of action and need for our will to guide us in places where our nature formerly did. The questions are how far to go and whether human nature is changed.

Aquinas identifies five inclinations in human nature: survive, reproduce, educate the young, live in society, and seek truth. Transhumanists might not share all these inclinations as they have been traditionally understood.[17] For example, they may not need to reproduce biologically. They may just need to copy themselves electronically, thereby eliminating the need for education as well. Would their lack of need to fulfill this basic human inclination be "evil" or just unnecessary? Because they could have different natures, these inclinations might simply no longer apply to them. Whether transhumans would live in society is an open question. If they did not, then survival and truth seeking might be the only inclinations transhumanists have in common with regular humans. One could even survive without truth seeking (whatever "truth" might mean to transhumans), especially if one had sufficient entertainment. In contrast to a flourishing human society that fulfills these five inclinations, might a flourishing transhuman simply be one who is surviving and being entertained?

How would will and nature relate for transhumans? Will would be elevated to the level of a force of nature, like evolution, because will would have control over the transhuman's own nature. Transhumans would create themselves in their own images. Transhuman nature could become so malleable that nothing of biology is left, only cultural artifact and "being" itself, easily extinguished by willing suicide. This radically underdetermined nature would leave vast spaces for exploration by the human will. With open fields for origin (nature) and destiny (*telos*), ethics—at least natural law ethics—becomes very vague indeed.

Rationalistic natural law, similar to Kantianism, might still make sense in this context. Physicalist natural law, by comparison, would be very challenged to deal with this indeterminacy of nature. Kantian and utilitarian ethics might actually be more appropriate for transhumans than virtue ethics or natural law would, since under conditions of radical will and indeterminacy, habits of action and nature might become reduced. Theoretically, transhumans could be designed as non-habit-forming, purely rational, purely pleasure-seeking, or otherwise quite different beings from current humans. In turn, transhuman ethics might resemble contemporary attempts to create ethical codes for robots, especially military robots programmed with rules of engagement. Due to the peculiarities of our own neurophysiology, humans might be best suited to natural law and virtue ethics. However, robots, or analogously structured transhumans, having rather different natures (as entities programmed to follow rules), could find Kantianism and utilitarianism workable ethical systems. Would this make them more capable of wielding power responsibly, more vulnerable to strange errors of programming, or simply more alien and inscrutable?

Anthropologist Terrence Deacon, in a different context (the determinacy of brain plasticity), has called humanity "the degenerate ape," because we need culture to complete our biology.[18] Transhumanism seeks to extend this evolutionary trend toward lack of natural specificity and toward indeterminacy. In Thomistic/Aristotelian terms, the movement of the transhuman toward potency and away from actuality is not necessarily a gain in ontological stature, but instead could be a reduction. It can be interpreted as movement toward the feralness and wildness of indeterminacy, and away from being like God, who is actuality (Being) itself. In Aristotelian terms, the transhuman, in gaining power and reducing determinacy of action, tends toward nothingness instead of existence, because prime matter is pure potency, pure power, but with no actuality. Prime matter is, in fact, nothing at all—it does not exist. God, in contrast, is pure being, existence itself, pure act.

In exploring the power of the will, indeterminacy, and movements toward and away from God, it may be helpful to recall the story of the Garden of Eden and the Fall. In the story, humans grasp at what seems good, only to have it ultimately very seriously harm us. The power to "know" or to think that one knows and decides good and evil—to be indeterminate and free of limits, whether in the human or transhuman case—can be interpreted as making us worse off we are. Is transhumanism merely continuing the Fall? By choosing to "improve" upon nature, one effectively denies the goodness of God's providence. God then becomes at best an unfamiliar question lost in the noise of power and at worst an adversary to be opposed at all costs. When one believes that one has become a god, what use is belief in a higher God? Yet how can one stand the idea that a higher God may yet exist that remains unattainable to the lower god that one is? The only solution is to pursue yet more power, in a never-ending quest to make the snake's lie true. Regarding this pursuit, God rightly asks has humanity gone astray, "Where are you?"[19] As we endeavor to make ourselves more like God, we simply slip further away.

A DYNAMIC ETHIC FOR A DYNAMIC NATURE

Given the possibility of this Edenic danger, what are humans to do? Practically speaking, the fruit is too tempting; it will be seized. After all, with the discovery of nakedness after the fall, technology (clothing) seemed the automatic response. What can be done to mitigate the dangers that will come with seizing this power and indeterminacy? What should be our new ethic?

First, we need to know ourselves. We can do this by synthesizing data and theory from psychology, anthropology, and evolutionary biology, as well as history, culture, and the humanities. This is not a task with a clear conclusion. We will not get a perfect idea of human nature, only a "good enough" idea— and even then, differing conclusions will be possible.

We also need to think about our human *telos*. What is the human *telos*? As mentioned earlier, Aquinas supplies five basics: survive, reproduce, educate the young, live in society, and seek truth. A functioning society that fulfills these bare minima has achieved a minimal *telos*. Beyond that, fulfilling them virtuously is the next step, culminating for those humanistically inclined with the good political community, and for those theologically inclined, with God.

With nature (as found by science) and *telos* (as found by philosophy) in hand, and despite the likelihood of continuing disagreements between factions, we can return to theological ethics—specifically, the virtues necessary to pass from nature to *telos*, from who we are to who we are meant to be. For the near future, at least, these virtues will be similar to the ones we already know, but with expanded scope for action and, therefore, responsibility. For example, for the sake of prudence we will need not only to look to our actions here and now, but also to seek the good in our collective actions over long periods of time. Conversely, our vices will become more destructive. In the past, gluttony was merely stuffing oneself with food; now, with fertilizers and feedlots, we first fatten our corn, then our cattle, and finally ourselves, in a growing cascade of consumption.

Likewise, notions of sin will need expansion to match the expanded scope of potential for sin. Sins of commission will likely become more or less serious depending on at least two factors. They will become more serious as our power makes us more capable of committing gravely wrong acts. Also, as our knowledge of the effects of our actions grow, we will become more responsible for our sins because we ought to know better. Conversely, our sins of commission may become less serious because the effects of our actions will become less predictable (especially in aggregate and cumulative form), therefore lowering our culpability (although we ought to anticipate this unpredictability and plan accordingly), at least until we realize what we are doing (as has occurred with knowledge of anthropogenic climate change). Similarly, as the effects of our collective acts become clearer to us, every act may end up becoming mildly evil, including, for example, eating and driving. Sins of omission will become more serious as well, because in our expanded power, failure to act makes us more responsible for the evils we fail to prevent.

What are the potential new directions for natural law ethics in this dynamic context? Based on the discussion in this chapter, I suggest three needs for a future natural law ethic. First, we should watch human nature itself, particularly human potential for action. Because action follows being, as our potential for action changes, our being may be changing as well. Second, we should keep our eyes on the minimal *telei*: survival, reproduction, education, living in society, and seeking truth. Without these guideposts, we will not know where to direct our moral efforts. Third, if ethics is a journey from nature to *telos*, from origin to destiny, then as the metaphorical locations of our natures and *telei* change, we will need new maps and routes to proceed from origin to destiny. This is ethics like space travel, where both origin and destination are in motion, so the course must be set with great care.

As we proceed on this journey, Hans Jonas's imperative of responsibility—to protect the very possibility of morality itself, by protecting the existence of humanity from existential dangers—should be our first commandment. Our second commandment, as Jonas notes, should be to live well—that is, to live morally flourishing lives.[20] This goal requires that we look for new dangers to avoid as well as for new opportunities for new goods to pursue.

The idea that action follows being, combined with our modern technology changing our scope of action, means that human nature may be changing, and that ethical norms should also change. Natural law's particular norms may be unstable, yet this will not likely loosen the strictures of natural law's norms, making more things permissible (as we grow in power). Rather, it will necessitate that norms be tightened as our power grows, forbidding more actions, lest we cause unimaginable harms. Ultimately, words like "looser" and "tighter" may just be misleading; ethical norms might simply need to be different, as befits creatures with different natures.

CONCLUSION

When considering how transhumanism and natural law ethics relate and whether transhumanism will force changes in natural law theory, the answers to the questions depend on what one means by "natural law." If one means the approach itself, then no, it will remain immutable; action will always follow being, and ethics can always be based on that, no matter how indeterminate nature may become or how relatively useless (given that indeterminacy) the method may become. Conversely, if by natural law one means the normative conclusions of natural law, then these will indeed change in their specifics, depending on just how different transhumans become (as Jonas asserts that human norms already should have changed). Individual schools of natural law will also need to adapt differently to various transhumanist manipulations, with rationalist natural law adapting more easily than its physicalist counterpart.

Aquinas never had to worry about what the implications of changing human nature would mean for natural law, so he never had to think about what to do if human nature actually did start changing. We no longer have that luxury; we need to figure out what to do or we may accidentally destroy ourselves and devastate the earth. Anthropogenic global warming and nuclear weapons are symptoms of this power without thought, and nanotechnology, synthetic biology, artificial intelligence, and other technologies are fast joining that list. We seek these powers because we find God's providence insufficient, but is the insufficiency in God or in ourselves, in our own choices and second natures gone astray? How we answer that question may determine how sympathetic we will be toward transhumanism. Transhumanism, at the very least, presents incredible thought experiments for ethical theorists, but as we continue to grow in power some of these thoughts will become realities.

NOTES

1. This chapter evolved from two conference papers: Brian Green, "The Human Future: Changing Human Nature and Changing Natural Law," presented to the Third Annual Student Symposium on Science and Spirituality of the Zygon Center for Religion and Science, Chicago, IL, March 25, 2011; and Brian Green, "Could Transhumanism Change Natural Law?" presented to the American Academy of Religion's Transhumanism and Religion Group, San Francisco, CA, November 19–22, 2011.

2. R. M. Hare, "Universalisability," *Proceedings of the Aristotelian Society* 55 (1954–1955): 303; based on David Hume, *Treatise on Human Nature*, edited by L. A. Selby-Riggs (Oxford, UK: 1888 [1978]), 469 (Bk. III, part I, sec. I).

3. Larry Arnhart, *Darwinian Natural Right: The Biological Ethics of Human Nature* (New York, NY: SUNY Press, 1998); William Casebeer, *Natural Ethical Facts: Evolution, Connectionism, and Moral Cognition* (Cambridge, MA: MIT Press, 2003); Terrence W. Deacon, *Incomplete Nature: How Mind Emerged from Matter* (New York, NY: W. W. Norton, 2012); Daniel Dennett, *Darwin's Dangerous Idea: Evolution and the Meanings of Life* (New York, NY: Touchstone, 1995), 467; Philippa Foot, *Natural Goodness* (Oxford, UK: Clarendon, 2001); Hans Jonas, *The Imperative of Responsibility: In Search of an Ethics for the Technological Age* (Chicago, IL: University of Chicago Press, 1984); Alasdair MacIntyre, *Dependent Rational Animals: Why Human Beings Need the Virtues* (Chicago, IL: Open Court, 1999); Martha C. Nussbaum, *Women and Human Development: The Capabilities Approach* (Cambridge, UK: Cambridge University Press, 2000); Joan Roughgarden, *Evolution's Rainbow: Diversity, Gender, and Sexuality in Nature and People* (Berkeley, CA: University of California Press, 2004).

4. Alasdair MacIntyre, *After Virtue*, 2nd ed. (Notre Dame, IN: University of Notre Dame Press, 1984), 54–55.

5. Monte Ransome Johnson, *Aristotle on Teleology* (Oxford, UK: Oxford University Press, 2005), 24, 27, citing Francis Bacon, *Advancement of Learning*, III.4, Rene Descartes, *Principles of Philosophy*, I.28, and William of Ockham, *Quodlibidal Questions*, IV.1; also Benedict Spinoza, *Ethics*, translated by W. H. White and A. H. Stirling, introduction by Don Garrett (Hertfordshire, UK: Wordsworth Classics, 2001), 34 (Part I, Appendix 1).

6. J. Budziszewski, *The Line through the Heart: Natural Law as Fact, Theory, and Sign of Contradiction* (Wilmington, DE: ISI Books, 2009), 61. For specifically Thomistic references to second nature, see Thomas Aquinas, *Summa Theologiae*, translated by Fathers of the English Dominican Province, 1st complete American ed., 3 vols. (New York, NY: Benziger Bros., 1948), 728, 833–834, 836–837 (I–II, 32.2, ad 3, 58.1, 58.5).

7. Aquinas, *Summa Theologiae*, 1009–1015 (I–II, 94.2, 94.4, 95.2).

8. Jean Porter, *Nature as Reason: A Thomistic Theory of the Natural Law* (Grand Rapids, MI: William B. Eerdmans, 2005), 19, 49–50, 117, 126–127, 131, 211.

9. Clifford Geertz, *The Interpretation of Cultures* (New York, NY: Basic Books, 1973), 92–94; Peter L. Berger and Thomas Luckmann, *The Social Construction of Reality: A Treatise on the Sociology of Knowledge* (New York, NY: Anchor Books, 1966), 48, 49, 52, 183.

10. Roy Rappaport, "On Cognized Models," in *Ecology, Meaning, and Religion* (Berkeley, CA: North Atlantic Books, 1979), 140–142; J. Stephen Lansing, *Priests and Programmers: Technologies of Power in the Engineered Landscape of Bali* (Princeton, NJ: Princeton University Press, 1991); David Sloan Wilson, *Darwin's Cathedral: Evolution, Religion, and the Nature of Society* (Chicago, IL: University of Chicago Press, 2002).

11. Jonas, *The Imperative of Responsibility*, 1.

12. Jonas, *The Imperative of Responsibility*, 11.

13. Jonas, *The Imperative of Responsibility*, 1–11.

14. Some examples of the more rationalist schools might include such varied names as the "new natural law" thinkers Germain Grisez and John Finnis, as well as the proportionalist thinkers Charles Curran and Richard McCormick.

15. Some examples of the more physicalist school might include such names as Franciscus Hurth, Gerald A. Kelly, and Janet E. Smith, and various magisterial documents such as *Casti Conubii* and *Humanae Vitae*.

16. Luke 12:48, Parable of the Faithful Servant.

17. Aquinas, *Summa Theologiae*, I–II, 94.2.

18. Terrence Deacon, "A Role for Relaxed Selection in the Evolution of the Language Capacity," *Proceedings of the National Academy of Sciences* 107 (May 2010): 9000–9006.

19. Genesis 3:9.

20. Jonas, *The Imperative of Responsibility*, 99.

14

The Risks of Transhumanism: Religious
Engagements with the Precautionary
and Proactionary Principles

Daniel McFee

Both proponents of and opponents to transhumanism have expressed grave
concerns regarding the risks associated with technologically enhanced human
capabilities. Two primary and opposing strategies to mitigate such risks have
emerged in these debates: the precautionary principle and the proactionary
principle. Many religious ethicists advocate the precautionary principle, arguing that the risks of disastrous outcomes associated with human enhancement
technologies are enough to demand a halt. Other religious thinkers align with
the proactionary principle, arguing that humans ought to pursue various forms
of human enhancement to expand and build upon present human capabilities.
This chapter examines how such thinkers identify and classify the risks of
transhumanism and utilize variations of the precautionary and proactionary
principles.

THE RISKS OF TRANSHUMANISM

In 2004, the political theorist Francis Fukuyama was asked, "Which ideas,
if embraced, would pose the greatest threat to the welfare of humanity?"
Fukuyama answered, "Transhumanism."[1] Fukuyama's response echoes the vigorous debates in religious and philosophical ethics regarding the value and
wisdom of broadly enhancing human capabilities through pharmacology,
genetic engineering, nanotechnologies, and other rapidly advancing technologies. And, as was true for Fukuyama, many of these debates pivot on the risks
that such human enhancement technologies pose to human welfare.

Transhumanism is defined by Humanity+ as follows: "[t]he intellectual and cultural movement that affirms the possibility and desirability of fundamentally improving the human condition through applied reason, especially by developing and making widely available technologies to eliminate aging and to greatly enhance human intellectual, physical, and psychological capacities."[2] Religious and philosophical ethicists have identified a broad range of hazards associated with transhumanist aspirations. Such risks include those associated with technical, health, justice, identity, existential, totalitarian, discrimination, economic, and societal concerns. A brief exploration of these hazards is necessary to explore how religious scholars understand, at least in part, these perils.

Scientists and ethicists have long argued that attempts to enhance human beings are fraught with unknown health risks. The ethicist Maxwell Mehlman cites the example of transgenic engineering, where the genes of two (or more) animals combine to form altogether new organisms. Mehlman notes that transgenic organisms can be plagued by health complications and unintended consequences whereby genetic combinations do not function in ways originally imagined by scientists. He cites the case of the "Beltsville pigs," in which human growth hormones were genetically inserted into pigs to stimulate growth and decrease fat. "The pigs . . . did in fact have less fat, but they were plagued by diarrhea, enlarged mammary tissue in males, lethargy, arthritis, lameness, skin and eye problems, loss of sex drive, and disruption of their fertility cycles. The human gene was indeed activated ('expressed') in 19 of the pigs, but 17 of these died prematurely."[3] Although such a procedure may have been considered "safe" or a good risk by researchers, such technical hazards could hardly be calculated in advance given the unknown variables associated with complex biological mechanisms.

Radically enhanced humans might also pose a threat to the just distribution of resources within a society. As some individuals or groups within society reach the coveted level of "transhumanist," it is unlikely that the usual mechanisms of distributive justice would work to elevate the societal status of non-enhanced persons. Lee Silver, a molecular biologist and biomedical ethicist, imagines scenarios whereby the genetically endowed (GenRich) and the genetically unenhanced (GenPoor) live in effectively separate societies. Silver describes the GenRich in suggestive terms: "it is difficult to find words to describe the enhanced attributes of these special people. 'Intelligence' does not do justice to their cognitive abilities. 'Knowledge' does not explain the depth of their understanding. 'Power' is not strong enough to describe the control they have over technologies that can be used to shape the universe in which they live."[4] In such scenarios, the GenPoor would surely be at an enormous disadvantage in advocating for a fair and just distribution of benefits and goods.

Emerging technologies also include grave "identity risks" that might result in the compromising or erasure of personal or collective identities. The Christian ethicist Karen Lebacqz, in summarizing the U.S. President's Council on Bioethics document *Beyond Therapy*, submits that radically enhanced humans might become alienated from themselves: "In our enhancement efforts, we risk making our bodies and minds little more than tools, turning into 'someone else,' flattening our souls, and ignoring the pursuit of true happiness."[5] Other ethicists concur with this view. Nicholas Agar argues in his work *Humanity's End* that the transhumanist dream of "uploading" human brains onto computational devices is a wager on how accurately and effectively artificial intelligence programs would succeed in replicating human consciousness and identity. In the interest of protecting human identities, Agar argues vigorously against "uploading": "Only the irrational among us will freely upload."[6] The popular environmental writer Bill McKibben notes that human enhancement "upgrades" could result in a loss of joy, purpose, and identity for those so enhanced: "Techniques such as advanced robotics and nanotechnology simply must be taken seriously, because on their own, and in combination with genetic engineering, they could quickly evaporate human meaning."[7]

Others have worried that attempts to enhance humans could lead to apocalyptic events whereby the human species annihilates itself. The philosopher Nick Bostrom observes that transhumanist experiments could lead to accidental or intentional acts of mass death. "When we create the first superintelligent entity, we might make a mistake and give it goals that lead it to annihilate humankind, assuming its enormous intellectual advantage gives it the power to do so ... We tell it to solve a mathematical problem, and it complies by turning all the matter in the solar system into a giant calculating device, in the process killing the person who asked the question."[8] Bostrom worries about more than just super-intelligent beings: nanotechnology, genetically engineered biological agents, and "physics disasters" all pose grave threats to human existence given their power to permanently alter delicate ecosystems and environments.

Another risk associated with transhumanism emerges from the potential for discrimination by the enhanced against those unenhanced. Enhanced persons might identify gaps in cognitive, physical, mental, and perhaps even emotional abilities as a means to discriminate systematically in the workplace. Moreover, the social fabric of such societies could be significantly strained as individuals attempt to socialize with others who might be much more or much less technologically augmented. Existing pharmacologic agents provide a good example of how such discrimination could quickly arise. A study in 2003 showed that the drug Modafinil, a "wake-promoting agent," significantly enhanced the efforts of those engaged in routine tasks: "Subjects reported feeling more alert, attentive and energetic on the drug."[9] Intolerance by employers against those who are "sleep dependent" is all too easy to imagine. Likewise, Mariann Springer-Kremser fears that transhumanist technologies might provide further tools to discriminate widely against women: "Throughout their lives, not in the least under the conditions of pregnancy and childbirth, women are directly or indirectly at the mercy of institutions, the most evident being the medical system. The increasing medicalisation of and economic factors in the female life cycle reinforce this vulnerability."[10]

Transhumanism might also pose substantial economic risks. In his work *Average Is Over: Powering America beyond the Age of the Great Stagnation*, the economist Tyler Cowen documents the tremendous power of technology to transform economic systems and addresses the uncomfortable question, "What will the low- and mid-skilled jobs of the future look like?"[11] Cowen argues that technological advancements in artificial intelligence and robotics will change the entire economic landscape in the near future. To extend Cowen's argument here, if individual humans begin to utilize artificial intelligence, such persons would likely have significant competitive advantages over "natural" humans in the marketplace.

Finally, transhumanism carries with it societal risks in terms of how new technologies are communicated to and understood by the public. Maxwell Mehlman offers the example of complex equations now used by genetic engineers that take a "graduate education" in physics to understand and use accurately.[12] Such realities point to an emerging rift in technological understandings of how the mechanisms of advanced scientific processes work. "The best that can be hoped for is that the nonscientists maintain a firm skepticism, learn how to distinguish reliable scientific informants from quacks, have the humility to admit when they are confounded, and press relentlessly until they obtain the necessary answers."[13]

How have religious ethicists and theologians approached such risks? The following section provides an overview of the precautionary principle and the proactionary principle, two of the main approaches used by religious thinkers to understand the risks of transhumanism.

TRANSHUMANISM AND THE PRECAUTIONARY PRINCIPLE

How should humans properly account for these potential risks? The precautionary principle has increasingly become central to understanding ethical dimensions of risk in part because of its strong role in the United Nations' 1992 *Rio Declaration* on environmental issues. Specifically, in principle 15, the United Nations argued: "In order to protect the environment, the precautionary approach shall be widely applied by States according to their capabilities. Where there are threats of serious or irreversible damage, lack of full scientific certainty shall not be used as a reason for postponing cost-effective measures to prevent environmental degradation."[14] The philosopher Per Sandin writes that most formulations of the precautionary principle share four central elements: threats, uncertainties, actions, and commands. "If there is (1) a threat, which is (2) uncertain, *then* (3) some kind of action (4) is necessary."[15] Sandin cites here the form of the precautionary principle found in the famous Wingspread Conference of 1998: "When an activity raises threats of harm to human health or the environment, precautionary measures should be taken even if some cause-and-effect relationships are not fully established scientifically."[16]

Many religious scholars and organizations have gravitated toward the precautionary principle in part because of its perceived ethical clarity. Indeed, when arguing on practical grounds (and not theological grounds), many religious ethicists and groups follow the logic of the precautionary principle, arguing that transhumanist technologies are too dangerous to pursue until proof of safety is guaranteed. The Roman Catholic Church's Congregation for the Doctrine of Faith takes the precautionary principle for granted in arguing against proposals to alter permanently the human gene pool through germ-line genetic engineering. "Because the risks connected to any genetic manipulation are considerable and as yet not fully controllable, *in the present state of research, it is not morally permissible to act in a way that may cause possible harm to the resulting progeny.*"[17] Even if the safety of such technical procedures were guaranteed, the Congregation for the Doctrine of the Faith contends that germ-line engineering would encourage a "eugenic mentality," leading inevitably to social stigmatizing.[18]

Other religious groups utilize the precautionary principle similarly. In a discussion document prepared for a discussion of issues surrounding human enhancement, the Conference of European Churches, Church and Society Commission committee argues that humans "do not know as much as we sometimes think. . . . With some areas of technology, we might 'get away with it'; for enhancing humans, the stakes are too high. Some manipulations of the human person would need to be of exceptional reliability not just of the device itself, but also the amazing human ability to mess things up organizationally."[19]

Religious ethicists have likewise proposed versions of the precautionary principle in assessing the risks associated with transhumanism. The Islamic bioethicist Abdulaziz Sachedina argues that the practical obligations incumbent upon humans to preserve their God-given identities could be fundamentally disrupted as a result of human augmentation. He suggest that simple cosmetic surgeries, such as teeth transplants, might be permissible if such procedures are intended for "corrective purposes" and do not "lead to deception regarding one's true identity."[20] Other, more serious forms of body modifications (such as a sex change operation) might also be deemed legitimate following a careful examination of one's intentions and one's duties to God, community, family, and future generations.[21] Yet dramatic enhancements to the human body run the risk of damaging God-given identities and the "presumed inviolability of various parts of the human body."[22]

The Jewish historian Hava Tirosh-Samuelson argues similarly for the precautionary principle because of the risks of transhumanism: "The transhumanist project is misguided because of its mechanistic engineering-driven approach to being human, its obsession with perfection understood in terms of performance and accomplishments rather than moral integrity, and its disrespect for the unknown future."[23] Again, pragmatic and theological concerns coincide in her call for precaution. Pragmatically, transhumanism concerns Tirosh-Samuelson as a utopian dream "that like all utopias has gone awry because it mistakenly believes that the ideal is realizable in the present instead of remaining just a beacon for the future."[24] Theologically, transhumanism is troubling because it introduces the possibility of dramatic human hubris that might violate the integrity of God's creation: "From the vantage point of the Jewish tradition at least, the ideal of indefinite postponement of death is the highest form of human hubris, one more example of human rebellion against God who created humans as finite beings whose life narrative has a beginning, a middle, and an end."[25]

Other religious ethicists utilize selective elements of the precautionary principle in framing the perils of transhumanism. Celia Deane-Drummond proposes a broadly Christian virtue ethic for approaching questions of how humans should interface with the natural order created by God. Deane-Drummond is clear that her work is not necessarily about "risk," but rather focuses on how humans engage in decision-making processes that might affect human futures. Indeed, she deliberately avoids using the precautionary principle, arguing that its application is limited to "worst possible imagined scenarios" and not to the systematic deliberation needed to broaden ethical deliberation within a political community about such grave matters.[26] Even so, when thinking specifically about complex biotechnologies, Deane-Drummond argues that "[w]isdom ... can serve in this way to help to build up an alternative ethos to the one dominated by technological progress. Biotechnology itself can become scrutinized through prudential decision-making, taking its cues from a wisdom ethic, and in the light of justice and temperance."[27] In this view, "wisdom" becomes a stop-gap measure to measure and assess risk, pushing back against the "inevitability" of human enhancement.

TRANSHUMANISM AND THE PROACTIONARY PRINCIPLE

Critics of the precautionary principle contend that such an approach stifles the advancement of scientific development, and, as a result, simply transfers risk to other parties. For example, Cass Sunstein points to the Environmental Protection Agency's concern that the use of the precautionary principle to regulate arsenic levels in drinking water would likely raise water costs associated with public utilities, thereby causing consumers to rely on private wells often contaminated by arsenic. Sunstein's point here is that the precautionary principle might simply transfer risk from one domain (the water utilities) to another domain (individual consumers). Indeed, Sunstein argues that the precautionary principle preys largely on human cognitive biases that seek to avoid losses (even when significant gains might be realized) and to maintain a status quo (even when the status quo is not the most desirable state of human affairs). Indeed, Sunstein argues broadly against the precautionary principle, concluding that it cannot or will not take risk seriously at a systematic level.[28]

The philosopher Max More coined the term "proactionary principle" to counteract these more cautious approaches to risk. More maintains that the precautionary principle acts as judge and jury in considering attempts to enhance humans: "By doing this, the precautionary principle denies individuals and communities the freedom to make trades in a way recognized by common-law approaches to risk and harm."[29] Furthermore, More argues that the precautionary principle attends only to human-manufactured risks and fails to address hazards inherent in nature itself, such as mutating viruses. Finally, he notes that the vague nature of the precautionary principle allows for overzealous regulators to insist upon unlimited testing. As such, the "precautionary principle cripples the technologies that can create our future because it prevents us from learning by experimenting. By halting activity, the principle reduces learning and reinforces uncertainty."[30]

More pursues instead a "proactionary principle" as a hedge against the risks of human extinction and failure:

> The Proactionary Principle stands for the proactive pursuit of progress. Being proactive involves not only anticipating *before* acting, but learning *by* acting. When technological progress is halted, people lose an essential freedom and the accompanying opportunities to learn through diverse experiments. We already suffer from an undeveloped capacity for rational decision making. Prohibiting technological change will only stunt that capacity further. Continuing needs to alleviate global human suffering and desires to achieve human flourishing should make obvious the folly of stifling our freedom to learn.[31]

Here More suggests a more statistical approach to risk assessment, whereby potential benefits and harms of human enhancement technologies are systematically compared to naturally occurring risks (such as a pandemic caused by the mutation of natural viruses). More suggests that the transhumanist movement has engaged in such calculations and concludes: "If the transhumanist project is successful, we may no longer suffer some of the miseries that have always plagued human existence. But that is not reason to expect life to be free of risks, dangers, conflicts, and struggle."[32]

Other versions of the proactionary principle have been proposed. Nick Bostrom argues for a version of the proactionary principle where humans fastidiously measure risk so as to accelerate relatively safe enhancement technologies while simultaneously banning potentially disastrous enhancement technologies. Like More, Bostrom proposes a statistical approach to risk as found in both natural and transhumanist sources: "Our focus should be on what I want to call *differential technological development*: trying to retard the implementation of dangerous technologies and accelerate implementation of beneficial technologies, especially those that ameliorate the hazards posed by other technologies."[33]

The prominent Episcopalian bioethicist Joseph Fletcher espouses a nascent version of this proactionary principle in his seminal work *The Ethics of Genetic Control: Ending the Reproductive Roulette*. Like Bostrom and More, Fletcher argues for careful weighing of risks against naturally occurring threats to human life. Thus, the benefits of an artificial uterus that would allow for women to bring a fetus to term outside the human body should be weighed over and against the risks of a natural pregnancy. "Risk and error are always given factors; they exist in the very finiteness of things. And the point about artificial control is precisely that *it tends to reduce risk and error*, and is intended to do so."[34] Fletcher's advancement of a proactionary principle paves the way for human enhancement on practical and theological grounds: "We don't pray for rain, we irrigate and seed clouds; we don't pray for cures, we rely on medicine. The excuses of ignorance and helplessness are growing thin. This is the direction of the biological revolution—that we turn more and more from creatures to creators."[35]

Likewise, the Jewish bioethicist Ronald Green's work on religion and the ethics of genetic choice is a good example of how the proactionary principle might be applied. Although Green is wary of unnecessary risks posed by human enhancement technologies, he argues that rational individuals can make prudential decisions regarding extraordinarily difficult decisions such as genetically modifying and enhancing the genetic makeup of their children: "If rational adults can invite some risks in undergoing cosmetic plastic surgery or a laser eye procedure, parents can also accept some added risk for their future child to give it these benefits."[36] At what level, though, should such risk be engaged? Green answers: "As a general rule of thumb, enhancement research and clinical implementation should proceed only when the risk levels are no greater than they were in development of IVF—that is, when they represent only a slight increment over the normal risks of pregnancy and birth." Green further elucidates how to adjudicate the risks with his approach: use germ-line engineering as a last resort and pursue human enhancement through pharmaceuticals first; pursue human enhancement interventions that are reversible; and finally pursue long-term studies and monitoring of children who are enhanced.[37]

Green grounds his work in his understanding of Jewish bioethical principles that affirm the goodness of creation, the sanctity and preservation of human life, and openness to technology that develops and expands human abilities. Nevertheless, Green concludes on a sober note: "The health risks that human gene modifications could impose on our children and their descendents are very serious. These health risks demand caution, but they do not necessarily bar modifications in the future. We can already see some of the scientific breakthroughs that may lower the risks, and we can envision some of the steps ahead."[38] Given these principles, Green argues positively that humans can and should engage in human enhancement technologies in ways that both celebrate and expand humanity. His work notes that the "concerns voiced by artists, bioethicists, and others about genetics gone wrong are a healthy warning ... Still, I believe that increased genetic control lies in our future and will make that future better."[39]

CONCLUSION: BLENDED APPROACHES TO RISK

The transhumanist sociologist James Hughes argues that the risks of human enhancement are "fundamentally different" from those associated with nanotechnology, robotics, or other rapidly advancing technologies:

> It is unlikely that a genetically engineered human, or even two, will ever escape into the woods and eat the planet. Genetically or cybernetically modified humans are no more likely to be eco-destructive than humanity versions 0.1 through 1.0. On the contrary, transhumans with longer lives and greater intelligence would be more likely to foresee and avoid ecological destruction, and to have the technological capabilities to repair the damage already done.[40]

Given the destructiveness of the 20th century, Hughes' optimism seems unwarranted. While it is likely that future humans would be "eco-transhumanists," it is just as likely that others would use their enhanced capabilities in destructive ways. Given human enhancement technologies and the potential for extraordinary good and evil in the world, it seems wise to take a blended approach to risk that incorporates both the precautionary and proactionary approaches.

The U.S. National Council of the Churches of Christ (NCC) seemingly argues for this blended approach to risk management in its document "Fearfully and Wonderfully Made: A Policy on Human Biotechnologies."[41] The positions taken by the NCC both promote and proscribe particular biotechnologies as a reflection of this organization's understanding of the risks involved. For example, the NCC explicitly opposes the creation of chimeras or any animal/human hybrid in part because the hazards of such technologies are completely unknown. Still, the NCC does not end the debate here: "Should future scientific investigation into minimal gene transfers between species result in clear evidence of realizable medical benefits, we strongly favor a thorough public debate, including input from religious leaders, which leads to formulation of an informed consensus and governmental regulation."[42]

Similarly, the Christian ethicist Ulla Schmidt embraces a blend of precautionary and proactionary approaches. Schmidt argues that the risks of human enhancement are both individual and communal in nature, and as such must be framed appropriately by these blended ethical commitments to both avoid risk and take risks where necessary:

> Thus, goods which are the effect of enhancement techniques and which can be channelled through network effects are not necessarily incompatible with a concept of human flourishing, which emphasises serving one's neighbour as an essential ingredient. It is therefore far from self-evident that human enhancement conflicts with a Christian, theological notion of human flourishing, in which a human life is fulfilled not through efforts to save oneself, but through the serving of others in neighbourly love that the love of Christ frees one to do.[43]

In his provocative article "A Theological Argument for Chimeras," the Christian theologian Ted Peters argues implicitly for such a blended strategy in facing risks of human/animal combinations (chimeras) in stem cell research: "These efforts seek medical benefits, a moral good."[44] Peters seems fully aware of the ethical difficulties associated with the creation of animal/human hybrids species with reproductive capabilities:

> Animals that could produce human gametes should be prevented from breeding and producing children . . . The reasons to prohibit such breeding are weak, but sufficient . . . It is not yet known whether combining human DNA with primate brain cells or those of any other animal could lead to humanized cognitive abilities. And this could lead to confusion over what constitutes a human person. In the meantime, perhaps the yuck factor should hold precautionary sway. When more is known, such a policy could be revised.[45]

This delicate balance of both precautionary and proactionary positions seems well advised and proportionate given the hazards of both action and inaction. Also, given that both principles genuinely attempt to advance human goods, both are necessary in facing the hazards of transhumanism.

NOTES

1. Francis Fukuyama, "Transhumanism," http://www.foreignpolicy.com/articles/ 2004/09/01/transhumanism, accessed April 2, 2013. "The environmental movement has taught us humility and respect for the integrity of nonhuman nature. We need a

similar humility concerning our human nature. If we do not develop it soon, we may unwittingly invite the transhumanists to deface humanity with their genetic bulldozers and psychotropic shopping malls."

2. Humanity+, "Transhumanist FAQ," http://humanityplus.org/philosophy/transhumanist-faq/, accessed July 10, 2013.

3. Maxwell Mehlman, *Transhumanist Dreams and Dystopian Nightmares: The Promise and Peril of Genetic Engineering* (Baltimore, MD: Johns Hopkins University, 2012), 62.

4. Lee Silver, as quoted in Bill McKibben, *Enough: Staying Human in an Engineered Age* (New York, NY: Times Books, 2003), 226.

5. Karen Lebacqz, "Dignity and Enhancement in the Holy City," in *Transhumanism and Transcendence: Christian Hope in an Age of Technological Enhancement*, edited by Ronald Cole-Turner (Washington, DC: Georgetown University Press, 2011), 52.

6. Nicholas Agar, *Humanity's End: Why We Should Reject Radical Enhancement* (Cambridge, MA: MIT Press, 2010), 59. Agar's argument here hinges on the distinction between strong artificial intelligence and weak artificial intelligence.

7. McKibben, *Enough*, 67.

8. Nick Bostrom, "Existential Risks: Analyzing Human Extinction Scenarios and Related Hazards," *Journal of Evolution and Technology* 9 (2002): np.

9. Daniel Turner, et al. "Cognitive Enhancing Effects of Modafinil in Healthy Volunteers," *Psychopharmacology* 165 (2003): 260.

10. Mariann Springer-Kremser, "The Human Body as Cultural Playground with Emphasis on the Female Body," in *Human Enhancement: Scientific, Ethical and Theological Aspects from a European Perspective*, edited by Theo Boer and Richard Fischerat (Geneva, Switzerland: Conference of European Churches, 2013), 117.

11. Tyler Cowen, *Average Is Over: Powering America beyond the Age of the Great Stagnation* (Ebook: Penguin, 2013).

12. Mehlman, *Transhumanist Dreams and Dystopian Nightmares*, 42–43.

13. Mehlman, *Transhumanist Dreams and Dystopian Nightmares*, 42.

14. United Nations, "Rio Declaration on Environment and Development," http://www.un.org/documents/ga/conf151/aconf15126-1annex1.htm, accessed December 5, 2008.

15. Per Sandin, "The Precautionary Principle and the Concept of Precaution," *Environmental Values* 13 (2004): 468.

16. Sandin, "The Precautionary Principle and the Concept of Precaution," 468.

17. Congregation for the Doctrine of the Faith, "*Dignitas Personae*: On Certain Bioethical Questions," http://www.vatican.va/roman_curia/congregations/cfaith/documents/rc_con_cfaith_doc_20081208_dignitas-personae_en.html, accessed May 14, 2009. Emphasis in the original.

18. Congregation for the Doctrine of the Faith, "*Dignitas Personae*."

19. Conference of European Churches, Church and Society Commission, "Human Enhancement: A Discussion Document," http://csc.ceceurope.org/fileadmin/filer/csc/Ethics_Biotechnology/Human_Enhancement_March_10.pdf, accessed February 5, 2014. The document continues: "If we cannot design shower units without getting water on the floor, or reliable software to buy train tickets on-line, what makes us think we should redesign ourselves?"

20. Abdulaziz Sachedina, *Islamic Biomedical Ethics: Principles and Application* (Oxford, UK: Oxford University Press, 2009), 190.

21. Sachedina, *Islamic Biomedical Ethics*, 194.

22. Sachedina, *Islamic Biomedical Ethics*, 190. Sachedina does not detail which parts of the human body might be considered "inviolable."

23. Hava Tirosh-Samuelson, "H-: Engaging Transhumanism: A Critical Historical Perspective," http://www.metanexus.net/essay/h-engaging-transhumanism-critical-historical-perspective, accessed August 2, 2013.

24. Tirosh-Samuelson, "H-: Engaging Transhumanism."

25. Tirosh-Samuelson, "H-: Engaging Transhumanism."

26. Celia Deane-Drummond, *The Ethics of Nature* (New York, NY: John Wiley & Sons, 2008), 43.

27. Deane-Drummond, *The Ethics of Nature*, 228.

28. Cass Sunstein, *Laws of Fear: Beyond the Precautionary Principle* (New York, NY: Cambridge University Press, 2005), 32.

29. Max More, "The Proactionary Principle," in *The Transhumanist Reader: Classical and Contemporary Essays on the Science, Technology, and Philosophy of the Human Future*, edited by Max More and Natasha Vita-More (New York, NY: John Wiley & Sons, 2013), 263.

30. More, "The Proactionary Principle, 263.

31. Max More, "The Proactionary Principle," http://www.maxmore.com/proactionary.html, accessed October 5, 2008.

32. Max More, "The Philosophy of Transhumanism," in *The Transhumanist Reader: Classical and Contemporary Essays on the Science, Technology, and Philosophy of the Human Future*, edited by Max More and Natasha Vita-More (New York, NY: John Wiley & Sons, 2013), 14.

33. Bostrom, "Existential Risks."

34. Joseph Fletcher, *The Ethics of Genetic Control: Ending Reproductive Roulette* (Garden City, NY: Anchor Press, 1974), 96.

35. Fletcher, *The Ethics of Genetic Control*, 200.

36. Ronald Green, *Babies by Design: The Ethics of Genetic Choice* (New Haven, CT: Yale University Press, 2007), 221.

37. Green, *Babies by Design*, 221–222.

38. Green, *Babies by Design*, 95.

39. Green, *Babies by Design*, 7.

40. James Hughes, *Citizen Cyborg: Why Democratic Societies Must Respond to the Redesigned Human of the Future* (Cambridge, MA: Westview Press, 2004), 119–120.

41. National Council of the Churches of Christ in the USA, "Fearfully and Wonderfully Made: A Policy on Human Biotechnologies," http://www.ncccusa.org/pdfs/BioTechPolicy.pdf.

42. National Council of the Churches of Christ, "Fearfully and Wonderfully Made."

43. Ulla Schmidt, "Human Enhancement and Theological Perspectives," in *Human Enhancement: Scientific, Ethical and Theological Aspects from a European Perspective*, edited by Theo Boer and Richard Fischer (Geneva, Switzerland: Conference of European Churches, 2013), 271.

44. Ted Peters, "A Theological Argument for Chimeras," *Nature Reports Stem Cells*, http://www.nature.com/stemcells/2007/0706/070614/full/stemcells.2007.31.html#B4, accessed February 14, 2011.

45. Peters, "A Theological Argument for Chimeras."

15

Christian Theology and Transhumanism: The "Created Co-creator" and Bioethical Principles

Stephen Garner

INTRODUCTION

Transhumanism offers a vision of potential new worlds in which the application of reason, science, and technology will allow humans to transcend the limitations of their condition. While this vision focuses predominantly upon the autonomous individual who chooses to be reshaped by technology, the choices go beyond the individual self and have implications for societal transformation.

Transhumanism asserts that through the use of applied reason, values—such as rational thinking, freedom, tolerance, and concern for others—can be enhanced, leading to an ever-improving world and superior human condition.[1] In this way, transhumanism claims to offer hope of a better world, often using imagery strikingly similar to Christian visions of transcendence over suffering and death and the promise of a new heaven and a new earth (e.g., Revelation 21:1–4).

Popular understandings of transhumanism are often associated with the potential impact of particular kinds of emerging technology, such as artificial intelligence, biotechnology, and nanotechnology, upon the human person. In this case, the transhuman is usually imagined as a cyborg with a technologically augmented and transformed body. However, transhumanism is as much about creating a new social vision as it is about the application of new technologies to the human person. This vision is that human beings and societies can take control of their own evolution through science and technology and, in doing so, overcome their biological limitations.

Thus the intersection of transhumanism and Christianity does not take place primarily at the level of technological application. Rather, it must be seen in terms of their respective visions of humanity, world, and the futures, as well as the values that underpin those visions. Both communities have their own narratives of humanity, salvation, and future trajectories or eschatologies, and these are some of the junctures at which theological engagement with transhumanism takes place. These visions serve as interpretative frameworks, the significance of which political theologian Duncan Forrester articulates:

> A concern with visions serves to remind Christians that theology is not exclusively engaged with "academic" questions, or with particular problems and policies and ethical conundrums. It is at least as concerned with the visions which provide a horizon of meaning within which a society exists, policies are formulated, actions are taken and vocations are fulfilled. Visions generate and sustain utopias ...[2]

This interest in visions is similar to the way some Christian theologians engage with the multidimensional nature of technology. Technology is seen not just as the artefacts produced by a manufacturing process, but also as those processes and the knowledge inherent in them. Moreover, those artefacts and processes are embedded in cultural structures and value systems. Susan White speaks of "a sociotechnical system in which hardware, technique, and a particular ideological frame of reference combine to aid in the pursuit of essentially pragmatic ends, generally associated with the augmentation of human capabilities."[3]

This multidimensional understanding of technology closely parallels the transhumanist vision with its technological artefacts (which may include virtual components), techniques (including the managed convergence of different types of technology), and an ideological assumption that unfettered human reason will produce a better world. Both cases—technological in general and transhumanism specifically—raise questions for religious communities similar to those raised by Ronald Cole-Turner:

> Can theology—that communal process by which the church's faith seeks to understand—can theology aim at understanding technology? Can we put the words *God* and *technology* together in any kind of meaningful sentence? Can theology guess what God is doing in today's technology? Or by our silence do we leave it utterly godless? Can we have a theology of technology that comprehends, gives meaning to, dares to influence the direction and set limits to this explosion of new powers?[4]

In this chapter, I propose that Lutheran theologian Philip Hefner's metaphor of human beings as "created co-creators" is a useful starting point for engaging with transhumanism. This metaphor captures human finitude

and the divine calling of humans to technological agency, both of which resonate with aspects of transhumanism. A framework or forum is needed to
bring the metaphor into dialogue with transhumanism, and in this chapter
I will use the framework provided by the four bioethical principles: autonomy,
nonmaleficence, beneficence, and justice.[5] My assertion is that the "created
co-creator" metaphor is helpful in exploring human technological proclivity,
and transhumanism in particular, but that it needs to be used both critically
and in a way that embraces human technological agency in both particular
and general contexts.

INITIAL CONVERSATIONS

Proponents portray transhumanism as the logical and evolutionary advancement of both human physical and ideological development. It is a progression,
they argue, stemming from the early immortality myths and legends (e.g., the
Sumerian *Epic of Gilgamesh*), and moving through to a rational, materialistic
humanism culminating in the current evolutionary worldview.[6] The end result
of this pathway is a broad spectrum of ideas about human development in light
of potential technological advances, a point made by Mark Walker and Heidi
Campbell in their brief definition of transhumanism as "the view that humans
should (or should be permitted to) use technology to remake human nature."[7]

For some, transhumanism is the narrow view of human bodies and minds
being technologically modified, enhanced, and repaired. For others, it is a
kind of speculative thought experiment that offers "an opportunity to think
anew about the relationship between humans and their environments,
artefacts and tools in a digital and technological age."[8]

In both of these perspectives, transhumanist proponents have a social
agenda to make the world a better place through the application of technology. They aim to allow the human individual to choose to transcend what
are perceived as human limitations, and in doing so benefit not just the individual, but the wider society. While much of transhumanism is focused on
the individual, some transhumanists argue for recognition of the broader
community and, while prioritizing individual autonomy, identify a duty of
responsibility toward others.

As such, transhumanism generates a range of potential starting points for
engagement with Christianity, where individual, social, and spiritual visions
intersect. Some of these intersections include (1) how the human person,
and in particular the human body, is perceived; (2) the role of human agency;
(3) narratives of human destiny; (4) the wise use of technology by and for
individuals and communities; (5) social justice; (6) the alleviation of suffering; and (7) the rights of both individuals and communities. In the following
sections, several of these intersections will be explored using the "created
co-creator" metaphor.

HUMAN BEINGS AS "CREATED CO-CREATORS"

Promoted particularly by Lutheran theologian Philip Hefner, the metaphor of human being as "created co-creator" has proved influential in the science-technology-religion engagement and for examining human technological agency. It is increasingly used in theological reflection upon both biotechnology and recently emerging digital technologies.[9]

For Hefner, human beings are identified as biologically conditioned culture creators who should learn how to live wisely, not just for the sake of humanity, but for all life with which humanity comes into contact. The "created co-creator" is a composite term that summarizes Hefner's understanding of human beings and the natural world, capturing aspects of both immanence and transcendence in the concept of human being.

The "created" aspect of the metaphor asserts the creaturehood of the human being as created, dependent, and finite, with a qualitative difference between creator and creature. The second aspect, "co-creator," speaks of a human calling or vocation to act as a creative agent within the natural world. For Hefner, God has produced humanity so as to be part of the purposeful creative process in the cosmos and to partner with God in that endeavor.[10] Furthermore, the creative activity of God in the world is one that embraces both *creatio ex nihilo* and *creatio continua*: the God who created the universe continues God's creative agency through that universe's history.

Criticisms have been raised about Hefner's created co-creator metaphor. The theological language and model that undergird it may render it inaccessible to the wider Christian community, particularly at the pastoral level.[11] Others have cited concerns about the potential hubris in the claim related to human agency's role in creation. Additionally questions have been raised about the extent to which the purposes of God can be discerned from the natural world to guide co-agency.[12] Finally, concern has been expressed that the created co-creator metaphor often seems to be discussed without due attention to theological underpinnings.[13]

Lutheran theologian Ted Peters is one scholar whose work has been significantly shaped by Hefner's created co-creator metaphor. Peters uses this model in his theological engagement with genetic engineering and biotechnology.[14] This author attempts to redress some of the criticism noted earlier by framing his use of the metaphor in a way that uses orthodox symbols and concepts from the Christian tradition. Moreover, Peters perceives technological activity to be a form of anticipation, in which the existence of both humans and the wider world is guaranteed by God, providing a future into which they can move. The promise offered by God in this future shapes the formation of the present, including human technological activity.

In this context, Peters emphasizes that human creaturehood means that human creativity is ultimately about transforming nature, rather than creating *ex nihilo*.[15] Thus, while human and divine creativity might be seen in some ways as analogous to each other, the two should never be equated. The created co-creator metaphor stands both as an encouragement to create and as a warning against utopian hubris.[16] Drawing upon New Testament themes of Christian transformation into the likeness of Christ (e.g., 2 Corinthians 3:18) as well as strands of the Irenaean tradition, Peters stresses that true humanness will be fully realized only at God's culmination of history. Participation in Christ, through the Holy Spirit, gives human beings and their present agency a futurist trajectory, drawn forward toward the new Adam and new creation that God has in the future.[17]

Human agency, seen especially in technology, is then called to anticipate this new reality, while maintaining that the ultimate new creation is God's work alone. Here Peters draws partly upon the work of Robert Russell, who argues that the new creation seen in the resurrection of Christ, and the eschatological horizon generated by this event, must frame all Christian technological endeavors. There is an ethical dimension to human co-creation that is inspired by the promise of God for a future wherein the world is free from death, pain, and sadness.[18]

> It is this eschatological future—no matter how dim, how inconceivable it is in light of science, no matter how unlikely it is in light of evil and suffering in human society and nature—to which we must orient all our ultimate plans and ideals and convictions if we are to live as Christians today in the Easter dawning of a new age.[19]

For Peters, redemption of creation is ultimately an act of God, seen in the work of Christ and the Holy Spirit, which is outside of nature and human agency. However, this act of grace is what inspires human activity in the world: to act as the God who redeems acts, and as Russell puts it, to become "eschatological companions" with God in creation.

Peters's proleptic approach to the concept of the created co-creator begins to bring together explicitly the twin strands of why human beings are created and how they should create. Human beings create because they are made in the image of a God who also creates; moreover, in response to God's acts of redemption and creation, human beings should act analogously. The latter point is seen in Peters's assertion that God calls human beings to beneficent agency, and this ethical dimension will be discussed more fully in the following sections.

BIOETHICAL PERSPECTIVES

Notwithstanding its various criticisms, the created co-creator metaphor serves as a useful starting point for asking theological questions about human technological agency. In the following section, this metaphor is used to engage theologically with aspects of transhumanism using the fourfold bioethical principles noted earlier. Each principle represents a particular starting point for thinking theologically about transhumanism and brings together a number of the initial conversations from earlier sections for further reflection.

Autonomy

The principle of *autonomy* concerns the priority of the free and independent human individual in decision making, and in particular in decision making about an individual's body, health, and well-being. This priority is consistent with transhumanism's emphasis on the primacy of human reason as a source of good and for the rights of individuals to apply the results of that reason to themselves as they see fit. Wider Western society also embraces an emphasis on individualism that, as noted earlier in the description of technology as a sociotechnical system, might then inform values that shape technological development.

This focus on autonomy intersects with Christian theological perspectives on the human body and person. The transhumanist quest for a materially realized transcendence over the human body and the wider natural world reinforces an anthropological conviction that the body serves the mind. Jeanine Thweatt-Bates notes that this conviction is continuous with an Enlightenment mindset emphasizing human beings as rational, autonomous individuals. Moreover, some aspects of the body, such as gender, are seen as social and biological conditions that should be overcome in an egalitarian world of the mind.[20] This point echoes Kathryn Hayle's observation that in transhumanist world views, information is privileged over material reality, with the body seen merely as a prosthesis that we manipulate, extend, or replace.[21]

Dualistic anthropological Christian theologies are not uncommon, where priority is given to the soul at the expense of the body. However, at its heart Christianity is centered on the Incarnation, where God becomes flesh and blood in the person of Jesus of Nazareth. Rejecting docetism, where Jesus Christ only seems to be human, and gnosticism, where some special knowledge would allow the human soul to flee the prison of the flesh, Christianity emphasizes human beings as intentionally created embodied creatures with a destiny linked to a final physical resurrection. In doing so, Christianity puts embodiment firmly on the discussion table, reinforcing the notion that human beings are finite, created creatures. As Calvin Mercer, in his exploration of the body and transhumanism from a Protestant perspective, puts it:

> These notions about the creation and culmination of a material world (which includes bodies of people and animals), resurrection of the body, and incarnation into a body are not fringe notions within Christian thought. They stand prominently and consistently in Christianity's mainstream theological and historical tradition.[22]

Moreover, Christianity's identification of human beings as finite, created creatures is nuanced by the recognition that humans are embedded in a wider physical and social world. Human beings are caught up in relationships with not just one another but also the natural world. Therefore, an essential component of theological engagement with transhumanism must be an anthropological strand that takes into account various theological and scientific portraits of humanity, as individuals, as communities, and as creatures in the natural world. In turn, this reminds us that engagement with technology through the created co-creator metaphor must not reduce human beings to only individual culture and technology creators, with ethical and moral reflection reduced to questions of individual rights and privileges.

Reinhold Neibuhr's theological anthropology may be a useful tool here. For Niebuhr, human existence is characterized by three aspects. First, his understanding of humans as bearers of God's image and likeness is linked to the human capacity for self-transcendence. Second, human beings are finite creatures dependently involved in the natural world. Third, evil or sin occurs because human beings constantly attempt to deny their creaturely dependence and achieve transcendence through their own efforts.[23]

Self-transcendence, in Niebuhr's view, is integrally linked with the concept of human reason, which means humans can make themselves the object of their own thoughts and reflections and choose their own destinies. However, the freedom to contemplate the infinite can lead to an arrogance that tends toward hubris as the creature strains to become godlike and transcendent. Alternatively, the infinite can be rejected, as humans settle for purely finite existence.[24]

Self-reflective autonomy might pose a problem in this framework for both the created co-creator metaphor and for the transhumanist vision of the mind transcending the body and becoming like gods. On the one hand, stressing the creaturely nature of human beings at the expense of the transcendent limits the call to creative activity; on the other hand, emphasizing the capacity to be co-creators together with the transhumanist desire to transcend the flesh may lead to a denial of human dependence upon God. The tension here is to maintain the balance between creative agency and wise use of that agency.

This focus upon human autonomy and agency is one area where constructive dialogue with transhumanism is necessary. The theological engagement could be with a transhumanist focus upon the individual that appears to ignore the wider community. William Sims Bainbridge describes one such vision:

> [B]uoyed by technological optimism and the hope that well-meaning people can agree to disagree about the choices that each individual must make, Transhumanists believe that we have reached the point in history at which fundamental changes in our very natures have become both possible and desirable. When humans can improve their own minds and bodies technologically, then

they will gain the intelligence and longevity to devise even more methods for self-improvement. In a positive feedback loop that vastly accelerates evolution, humans could become like gods, and in so doing may put conventional religion out of business.[25]

This individualistic approach to technological development asserts that individual choices indirectly bring about health, longevity, and wholeness to all of society. This world is envisaged as possible only through the deregulation of technoscientific research and development, and the use of market forces to shape development and access to therapeutic and enhancement technologies. Although access to these technologies may not be even across society, overall the condition of individuals—and hence the entire human condition—will be improved. Technology can save the world, but only if it is allowed a free hand to do so.

Against this narrowly individualistic approach, democratic transhumanist James Hughes sets out to establish a similar social vision that is inspired by human autonomy, rationality, and technology, but that adds a communitarian dimension he perceives as lacking in many articulations of transhumanism:

> The liberal democratic revolution, centuries old and still going strong, has at its core the idea that people are happiest when they have rational control over their lives. Reason, science and technology provide one kind of control, slowly freeing us from ignorance, toil, pain and disease. Democracy provides the other kinds of control, through civil liberties and electoral participation. Technology and democracy complement one another, ensuring that safe technology is generally accessible and democratically accountable. The convergence of nanotechnology, biotechnology, information technology and cognitive science in the coming decades will give us unimaginable technological mastery of nature and ourselves. That mastery requires radical democratization.[26]

While supporting the use of technologies for therapy and enhancement, and espousing the idea that there should be no limitation to human aspirations, Hughes also argues that there should be social and political systems in place to allow technology to be accessed equally by the population. He rejects the libertarian assumption that the market will provide all the technology and safeguards needed by society. Instead, all citizens should have an active voice in how technology shapes society and themselves, including the right for all to access technology to achieve their own and their children's potential. Concerns such as these, which take into account the wider human community and its complex relationships, are useful starting points for theological reflection on what healthy and helpful anthropologies for a technological society might look like.

Nonmaleficence and Beneficence

The search for appropriate balance between creative agency and wise use of that agency raises theological questions about humanity's role in the natural world: are we rulers, stewards, or servants of the natural world and to what extent do we manifest kinship with the wider world?[27] Moreover, does transhumanism's dualistic anthropology imply that the natural world exists only to support the longevity of the mind, or does the natural world have some intrinsic value beyond this utility? To address what wise creative agency looks like in regard to both human beings and the wider natural world, I now consider the bioethical principles of nonmaleficence and beneficence.

Nonmaleficence

The principle of *nonmaleficence* means not doing harm or minimizing harm. Much Christian theological reflection on technology reflects this principle. Indeed, the cry "Don't play God" might be as much related to the avoidance of potential harm as it is to usurping a divine prerogative. This theological perspective often sees the negative side effects of technology as outweighing its benefits.[28] Such a viewpoint stands in stark contrast to transhumanist optimism, which can lead to, as technologist and writer Kevin Kelly puts it, "frenzied, messianic attempts to make stuff" and "to have creation race ahead of understanding."[29]

On the one hand, a call to human agency in the world, seen in metaphors like the created co-creator, assumes technological development as a given; not pursuing such development simply out of fear of doing some kind of harm, it suggests, denies that divine vocation and compromises the duty of beneficence. On the other hand, nonmaleficence requires that theology take very seriously the concern that co-creating can veer toward human arrogance, resulting in technological manifestations of that arrogance. As Cole-Turner remarks, "Technology, for all its good, is constantly on the edge of sin, exploitation, and greed. It is, after all, *human technology*, beset by our weaknesses."[30] Thus, there is the potential for the theme of co-creation to be used to baptize all technological activity and so become hubris,[31] or for all work and human activity to become seen romantically, no matter how mundane or demeaning it might be.[32]

Therefore, the principle of nonmaleficence, which has strong support within Christianity with its moral teaching not to do harm to others and always to seek the good of the other, prompts the asking of two key questions. First, will the particular technological activity or value set underpinning it cause unjustified harm or loss of well-being to both individuals and communities? Second, to what degree is the fear of not doing harm thwarting activity that may be beneficent?

Beneficence

The principle of *beneficence* posits that there is a responsibility to go beyond not doing harm and to act to benefit others if possible. This supposition finds immediate resonance with the co-creator metaphor, with its call to dynamic agency for good in the world, and with the transhumanist concern to improve the human condition. For example, James Hughes includes beneficence in his transhumanist vision: "we are obliged to help fellow citizens achieve their fullest capacities for reason, consciousness and self-determination."[33] However, tensions arise over the challenge of determining God's will and purpose for beneficent action, with some seeing the therapeutic benefits offered by genetic engineering as the outworking of loving one's neighbor, while others claim such technological developments threaten human dignity and cause harm.

That said, many see the love ethic of Jesus Christ as a moral imperative that calls people to technological endeavors for the benefit of others. Just as Jesus demonstrated love through, for example, healing miracles, so, too, technology needs to be pursued to bring about new forms of therapy to alleviate suffering.

It is this kind of understanding, coupled with the conviction that Christ draws the world toward the future, that shapes Ted Peters's contention that beneficence must be a primary technological motivation. Humanity is being drawn forward toward an end, and morality changes or adapts under that pressure. Under this scenario, Peters argues, we must not morally place what is delivered to us by nature above how we can transform that very same nature. In fact, he goes further, contending that it is immoral not to strive to make the world a better place through the use of technology. For Peters, "[t]he situation as it is does not necessarily describe how it ought to be."[34]

Therefore, people need to engage with technology not just informed by the ethical principle of nonmaleficence, but also with the aim of ensuring beneficence. If we can use technology to do good, then we are obliged to do so. If we do not, then we reject the potential God has given humanity for social transformation found in being bearers of God's image, Peters asserts.[35] In other words, a failure to act technologically for the benefit of others leads to human beings failing in their mandate to be God's agents in the world.

British theologian Peter Vardy echoes this view when proposing the use of genetic engineering for the purposes of physical enhancement. It is only logical, Vardy argues, that human beings use their capacity for rationality to shape the evolution of humanity so that a fuller and richer human capacity is reached. Not only that, but it would clearly be the wish of God for this manifestation of beneficence to happen.

> If there is a God, then God has given human beings rational minds to enable them to make moral decisions and to develop medical technology and other resources to help them to live in harmony within this world. Indeed, it is held to be one of the crowning glories of human beings that they do have these

facilities. Once this is accepted, then to set limits to how this intelligence should be employed seems arbitrary. There has been a tendency in the past for religious people to be nervous of new developments. However, if they believe God has given human beings minds, then it seems perfectly proper to argue that these minds can be used in eliminating disease and physical defects and also in enhancing human beings further to enable them to fulfil their full capacity, by employing the genome in appropriate ways.[36]

This puts Vardy squarely in the same camp as transhumanists like James Hughes, who advocates for life's purpose to be reducing pain and increasing joy and fulfillment. "It seems obvious," Hughes says, "that the ethical goal for society should be to make life as fantastic for as many people as possible, not to valorize pain and suffering."[37] Thus, in addition to not doing anything that causes pain to others, people should strive technologically to overcome physical and mental suffering, as well as to develop technologies that enhance everyday joy and well-being. Doing this may well bring about an optimism in people that flows into engagement with life and involvement in the wider community.[38]

The question, then, is how to engage with technology while recognizing the constraints placed by nonmaleficence and beneficence on human agency and freedom. The final bioethical principle of justice adds to the meanings of doing harm or good in the context of technology.

Justice

Transhumanism's vision of technology improving the human condition resonates with themes in the Christian tradition of social concern and justice. The Christian narrative takes seriously the importance of alleviating human suffering and oppression. Technological application provides one avenue toward achieving this alleviation.[39] This, in turn, means that transhumanist proposals cannot simply be eliminated, but instead need to be connected to a discussion of what constitutes wise, appropriate, or just use of technology.

The bioethical principle of *justice* is typically concerned with equitable distribution of limited resources, and in particular with access to those resources and information. However, justice as a broader concept also engages with the question of how the use of those resources might marginalize and disadvantage others. Ian Barbour's definition of appropriate technology is helpful here. He sees appropriate technology as "creative technology that is economically productive, ecologically sound, socially just, and personally fulfilling."[40] Barbour argues for maintaining personal needs in the face of technological development. Systems that dehumanize people by removing choices, personal relationships, and even spirituality are to be challenged, as are technologies that consume disproportionate amounts of resources. In these cases, the negative costs of these systems are borne by those who have little voice in shaping technological systems; Christianity teaches that we are responsible for both our neighbors and the wider natural world. In the context of the creator co-creator metaphor, this means that human agency needs to align against wise and just technological agency.

For Barbour, technology's embodiment of values and constructions of power and authority lead to a response to technology that most closely fits with what he calls a biblical outlook—that is, a Christian framework that understands human relationships with technology are ambiguous. On the one hand, these relationships can become idolatrous and displace God; moreover, technology can be used as an unjust instrument of power over others, including the natural world. On the other hand, technology can become the vehicle through which human beings carry out their response to God in creative, compassionate, and just ways.

> The biblical understanding of human nature is realistic about the abuses of power and the institutionalization of self-interest. But it also is idealistic in its demands for social justice in the distribution of the fruits of technology. It brings together celebration of human creativity and suspicion of human power.[41]

Justice here goes beyond the distribution of resources and access to them, by engaging with the voices of those who are marginalized by both the transhumanist project and theological constructions with respect to technology. This view is echoed by Peters, who, while optimistic about the use of technology, is not so optimistic about technologists and the sociopolitical forces that shape the use of technology. When it comes to technologies such as cloning and germ-line modification, Peters argues that these advances hold great therapeutic potential, as well as the potential to threaten the dignity of children, under pressures of commodification.[42] Such developments also mean that theological engagement will serve to challenge transhumanist values from within theologically informed frameworks of social justice and social concern, while simultaneously recognizing and supporting efforts within the transhumanist community for self-critique.[43]

Finally, dialogue within the Christian community needs to take into account differences of opinion around technology that need to be dealt with in a manner that does not damage and disenfranchise people. While the Christian community should be, as Ted Peters suggests, "a community of theological reflection and moral deliberation," that is not always that case. Consequently, theological reflection on technology will need to have pastoral considerations and space for constructive dialogue within its own communities as essential components of wider discussions.[44]

CONCLUSION

The transhumanist project offers particular perspectives on human persons and their potential destinies. These perspectives, or visions, serve to frame the agenda of making the world a better place through the application of human reason, and in particular, the reshaping of human beings to alleviate perceived human limitations. Within a Christian theological framework, both significant resonances and tensions arise with regard to these transhumanist visions. On the one hand, Christian imperatives of beneficence and justice promote innovative technological agency to alleviate suffering and marginalization. On the other hand, distinctive understandings of autonomy and nonmaleficence stand against technological agency that might dehumanize or marginalize individuals and communities and lead in the direction of hubris.

The theological metaphor of the created co-creator, in conjunction with the four bioethical principles, helps to expose and explore these theological tensions so as to develop a robust theological conversation with transhumanism. This approach also recognizes where in the transhumanist community common ground might be found to explore notions of the individual, community, and justice. It is critical that theologians, and the wider Christian community, take seriously the ideas and trajectories being proposed by the transhumanist community, even if they act cautiously in ascribing too much weight to their visions.

Visions of the future, whether transhumanist or religious, provide a horizon of meaning within which the world is interpreted and human action and values are shaped. Christianity would do well to examine these visions closely to see how they might challenge, inform, and support its own faithful engagement with technology.

NOTES

1. Humanity+, "Transhumanist FAQ 3.0," http://humanityplus.org/philosophy/transhumanist-faq/, accessed 29 March, 2014.

2. Duncan B. Forrester, "Politics and Vision," *The Bible in Transmission* (Autumn 1999), 1–4.

3. Susan White, *Christian Worship and Technological Change* (Nashville, TN: Abingdon Press, 1994), 16.

4. Ronald Cole-Turner, "Science, Technology and Mission," in *The Local Church in a Global Era: Reflections for a New Century*, edited by Max L. Stackhouse, Tim Dearborn, and Scott Paeth (Grand Rapids, MI: Eerdmans, 2000), 101.

5. Tom L. Beauchamp and James F. Childress, *Principles of Biomedical Ethics*, 5th ed. (New York, NY: Oxford University Press, 2001).

6. Nick Bostrom, "A History of Transhumanist Thought," *Journal of Evolution and Technology* 14, no. 1 (2005): 1–4.

7. Mark Walker and Heidi Campbell, "Religion and Transhumanism: Introducing a Conversation," *Journal of Evolution and Technology* 14, no. 2 (2005): i.

8. Elaine Graham, "Bioethics after Posthumanism: Natural Law, Communicative Action and the Problem of Self-Design," *Ecotheology* 9, no. 2 (2004): 178–179.

9. Philip Hefner, *The Human Factor: Evolution, Culture and Religion, Theology and the Sciences* (Minneapolis, MN: Fortress Press, 1993). For related ideas of human

co-creation and co-agency with God, see W. Norris Clarke, "Technology and Man: A Christian Vision," *Technology and Culture* 3, no. 4 (1962): 422–442; Arthur R. Peacocke, *Creation and the World of Science: The Bampton Lectures, 1978* (Oxford, UK: Clarendon Press, 1979).

10. Hefner, *The Human Factor*, 39–40.

11. Gregory R. Peterson, "The Created Co-creator: What It Is and Is Not," *Zygon* 39, no. 4 (2004): 830, 838–839; Paul Sponheim, "The Human Factor: Evolution, Culture and Religion. Review of Philip Hefner's 'The Human Factor: Evolution, Culture and Religion,'" *CTNS Bulletin* 14, no. 2 (Spring 1994): 25.

12. Ronald Cole-Turner, *The New Genesis: Theology and the Genetic Revolution* (Louisville, KY: Westminster John Knox Press, 1993), 100–102. Peterson, "The Created Co-creator," 839; Peter Scott, "The Technological Factor: Redemption, Nature, and the Image of God,"*Zygon* 35, no. 2 (2000): 371–383; Ng Kam Weng, "Co-creator or Priestly Steward: Theological Perspectives on Biotechnology," in *Beyond Determinism and Reductionism: Genetic Science and the Person*, edited by Mark L. Y. Chan and Roland Chia (Adelaide, Australia: ATF Press, 2003), 75–94.

13. Graham, "Bioethics after Posthumanism," 194–195.

14. Ted Peters, *Science, Theology, and Ethics* (Burlington, VT: Ashgate, 2003); Ted Peters, *Playing God?: Genetic Determinism and Human Freedom* (New York, NY: Routledge, 1997).

15. Ted Peters, *God—The World's Future: Systematic Theology for a New Era*, 2nd ed. (Minneapolis, MN: Fortress Press, 2000), 155–156.

16. Ted Peters, "Techno-Secularism, Religion, and the Created Co-creator," *Zygon* 40, no. 4 (2005): 859–860.

17. Peters, *God—The World's Future*, 157–159.

18. Robert J. Russell, "Five Attitudes toward Nature and Technology from a Christian Perspective," *Theology and Science* 1, no. 2 (2003): 156–157; Peters, "Techno-Secularism, Religion, and the Created Co-creator," 858–861.

19. Russell, "Five Attitudes," 157.

20. J. Jeanine Thweatt-Bates, "Artificial Wombs and Cyborg Births: Postgenderism and Theology," in *Transhumanism and Transcendence: Christian Hope in an Age of Technological Enhancement*, edited by Ronald Cole-Turner (Washington, DC: Georgetown University Press, 2011), 101–103.

21. N. Katherine Hayles, *How We Became Posthuman: Virtual Bodies in Cybernetics, Literature, and Informatics* (Chicago, IL: University of Chicago Press, 1999), 2–3.

22. Calvin Mercer, "Sorting out *Soma* in the Debate about Transhumanism: One Protestant's Perspective," in *Transhumanism and the Body: The World Religions Speak*, edited by Calvin Mercer and Derek F. Maher (New York, NY: Palgrave Macmillan, forthcoming 2014).

23. Reinhold Niebuhr, *The Nature and Destiny of Man: Human Nature*, Vol. 1 (New York: Charles Scribner's Sons, 1964), 150.

24. Niebuhr, *The Nature and Destiny of Man*, 78–79, 166.

25. William Sims Bainbridge, "The Transhuman Heresy," *Journal of Evolution and Technology* 14, no. 2 (2005): 91.

26. James Hughes, *Citizen Cyborg: Why Democratic Societies Must Respond to the Redesigned Human of the Future* (Boulder, CO: Westview Press, 2004), 3.

27. Jim Ball, "The Use of Ecology in the Evangelical Protestant Response to the Ecological Crisis," *Perspectives on Science and Christian Faith* 50, no. 1 (1998); Nicola Hoggard Creegan, *Animal Suffering and the Problem of Evil* (Oxford, UK/New York, NY: Oxford University Press, 2013).

28. Jacques Ellul, *The Technological Bluff*, translated by G. W. Bromiley (Grand Rapids, MI: Eerdmans, 1990), 35–76.

29. Kevin Kelly, "The Third Culture," *Science* 279 (1998): 992.

30. Cole-Turner, *The New Genesis*, 102.

31. Celia Deane-Drummond, *Biology and Theology Today: Exploring the Boundaries* (London, UK: SCM Press, 2001), 100.

32. Stanley Hauerwas, *In Good Company: The Church as Polis* (Notre Dame, IN: University of Notre Dame Press, 1995), 109–124.

33. Hughes, *Citizen Cyborg*, 223.

34. Ted Peters, "Cloning Shock: A Theological Reaction," in *Human Cloning: Religious Responses*, edited by Ronald Cole-Turner (Louisville, KY: Westminster John Knox Press, 1997), 20–21.

35. Ted Peters, "Is Our DNA Sacred?," *Response: The Seattle Pacific University Magazine* 26, no. 7 (2004), http://www.spu.edu/depts/uc/response/summer2k4/dna. html, accessed April 29, 2014.

36. Peter Vardy, *Being Human: Fulfilling Genetic and Spiritual Potential* (London, UK: Darton, Longman and Todd, 2003), 71.

37. Hughes, *Citizen Cyborg*, 44

38. Hughes, *Citizen Cyborg*, 44–50.

39. John Paul II, *Laborem Exercens* (Rome, Italy: Vatican, 1981), §5.

40. Ian G. Barbour, *Ethics in an Age of Technology: The Gifford Lectures 1989–1991*, Vol. 2 (San Francisco, CA: HarperSanFrancisco, 1993), 25.

41. Barbour, *Ethics in an Age of Technology*, 19.

42. Peters, "Cloning Shock," 21.

43. For example, Russell Blackford, "Transhumanism at the Crossroads," Instititute for Ethics and Emerging Technologies, http://ieet.org/index.php/IEET/more/119/, accessed March 29, 2014; Bostrom, "A History of Transhumanist Thought," 5–6.

44. Ted Peters, *The Stem Cell Debate* (Minneapolis, MN: Fortress Press, 2007), 21.

16

· ·

Remaking Human Nature: Transhumanism, Theology, and Creatureliness in Bioethical Controversies

Celia Deane-Drummond

This chapter considers the intersection of transhumanism with heated debates in bioethics through critical engagement with the work of Ted Peters, a prominent theologian who has contributed substantially to the discussion. I will use his work as a way of interrogating the debates in this field, as his position both coheres with yet departs in some significant ways from my own.

Peters's particular interest in transhumanism originated from his interest in how new technologies are used in bioethics. His contributions to bioethics include a theological discussion of new technologies proposed for modifications of human beings. While the most vigorous debates about such technologies originally focused on the promises heralded by the Human Genome Project, which mapped the genetic makeup of human beings, more recently attention has turned to the micro level, nanotechnologies, and synthetic biology, along with speculations about a completely transformed humanity in some transhumanist scenarios. Peters has actively informed the discussion by contributing a distinctive theological voice. To understand the particular slant that he brings to the discussion of transhumanism, I will provide some preliminary remarks on his engagement with ethical issues in genetics.

One of Peters's most significant contributions to the debate about the new genetics was his book *Playing God*.[1] In this volume, Peters argues against genetic determinism and proposes that the new genetics should not be seen as threatening to divine freedom. He insists that enhancing human freedom does not diminish divine freedom; to the contrary, humans could be seen to express the divine image through their creativity. So, it is hardly surprising that when he turns his attention to nanotechnologies, Peters once more engages in a critical discussion of those scholars who are more cautious of such developments and who use the language "playing God" to support their claims.[2] The main counter-argument he wishes to propose is this: do such technologies somehow violate something sacred? The enhancements that are likely to be possible through nanotechniques relate, for example, to neurocognitive augmentation and intelligence expansion.

Peters works through each stage of the argument in a progressive way. In the first place, he suggests that the idea of "playing God" reflects the Promethean dream of progress that has become translated into cultural myths such as that of Frankenstein. Here, the image is one of scientists violating nature and thereby letting loose destructive and chaotic forces that are out of control. Peters consistently argues that such fears are inappropriate for Christians; for him, a biblically based ethical view affirms the possibility of transformation and change and concentrates on love of God and neighbor, rather than remaining trapped in fears about the unknown. Nanotechnology seems to make the issue even starker, as its promise for even more radical transformation raises the issue of whether human beings will become transhuman or even posthuman.[3]

Peters's exploration of intelligence enhancement through nanotechnologies includes realistic possibilities, such as greater and more rapid comprehension, comprehension of what otherwise would be far too complex issues, speeding up and providing solutions for what were once insoluble problems, and so on.[4] An even more radical scenario posits the development of optical nanocomputers and quantum nanocomputers, allowing for exponentially amplified intelligence and leading to a massive increase in cognitive capacity that some of the more extreme transhumanists have termed the "Singularity." Such a process would continue to grow through a positive feedback system. Peters believes that even in this process our human identities would remain stable, allowing us to "simply enjoy physical and mental enhancement."[5]

A further trajectory appears on the horizon once we envisage the mind not as explicitly linked to brain function, but rather as comprising an information pattern that could be moved to another computerized platform. In this scenario the mind becomes cybernetic, providing for the possibility of cybernetic immortality. Peters considers a disembodied self in a computer as out of keeping with a Christian view of the salvation of the whole person. He identifies (correctly, in my view) such disembodiment as a strange return to the thinking that dominated substance dualism, where the soul is split apart from the material world.

Caught up by the astonishing possibility, Peters is prepared to call this "a marvelous, if not obviously advantageous—achievement"; he further asks, "How should we embrace such changes?"[6] One way to do so is through adopting a relational view of the person. Consequently, Peters agrees with authors such as Noreen Herzfeld and Gregory Paterson that to be human entails more than just intelligence—it also includes relationality. But Peters pushes the argument further and imagines a practical hypothetical case study where an individual, named Patrick, has become loaded onto a computer. Onlookers then ask that computer if he still identifies himself as Patrick. If the answer is "yes," then we can assume that Patrick's identity is continued in the software that is now in a different platform from the original body. Peters concludes, "We will not have changed his essential nature. Rather this technology will have extended into the future a nature that had previously been inherited."[7]

Peters's affirmation that human identity still exists in this case strikes me as astonishing and strange, not least because on his own admission it has relied on a dualistic view of the human person. Further, the ethical criteria that he proposes—namely, how far will such technology allow us to love God and neighbor—seems to be violated. Such an entity could never be loved in the embodied way that human persons are loved. Peters returns to the idea of "playing God," parsing this out in term of learning God's secrets (1) through the inner workings of nature, (2) through the power of life-and-death decisions in medical contexts, and (3) as a critical comment on what is perceived as the hubristic use of technological power to alter life and influence human evolution. Peters dismisses this last concern as arising out of a misplaced anxiety that there is something sacred about nature that cannot be altered. Thus, rather than saying, "How far should we go?" we should say, "How can such technology enhance our ability to love God and neighbor?"[8] Peters resists the "playing God" hubristic argument on the basis that it is giving nature too great a worth; it represents nature as sacred and, therefore, is a naturalistic ethic, defining the good by what is. He admits, in this case, that no nanotechnology scenarios so far have oriented themselves toward the good of neighbor or a vision of relationship to God. Nevertheless, for him, a Christian theological approach is one that celebrates transformative change "while trying to guide that change towards wholesome and loving ends."[9]

It strikes me that Peters's fascination with the power of technology has in the preceding scenario clouded his judgment about what might be permissible or not. Change and growth through the virtues celebrated in the Christian tradition do not readily map onto the kind of changes anticipated in transhuman projects. Peters does acknowledge that transhumanists risk promising too much and in this sense try to fill what only God can deliver.[10] He is also aware that transhumanism relies on a strong ideal of progress as its working philosophy.[11] Given his Lutheran Christian perspective, Peters is ready to acknowledge the possibility that new technologies might be used for sinful purposes.[12] But how widely will this possibility of sin be accepted or even recognized by the majority of scientists who are engaged in this field, most of whom would find the language of sinfulness unpalatable, even though they would acknowledge the importance of human responsibility? Those engaged in such technologies are caught up in social structures that encourage such developments, driven by market economic demands. Peters does not attempt to address wider political and economic issues in his analysis.

Peters also believes that the possible production of immortal minds is an extreme outcome and that we are much more likely to be faced with transformed or enhanced brains. He writes, "Instead of thinking of cyborg brains as transhumans, we could think of them simply as fabulously human."[13] His view is a welcome alternative to blanket dismissal of all technological advancements for religious reasons. Nevertheless, to appraise nanotechnology and future projections of the transhumanist sort, it is helpful to return to a discussion about what human nature might be and, in turn, what might be proposed in cybernetic futures for humanity.

"Human nature" itself is a controversial term, and some have denied its existence. Nevertheless, I believe that while no single or fixed "nature" can be attached to the human, having a sense of what human dignity might mean is important for Christian faith and for an adequate theological anthropology that then informs theological ethics. Human nature has been variously defined as that which makes humans unique compared with other animals. It has also been viewed as expressing something universal about all human beings. Finally, it can be understood as one's self-identity. Peters seems to use the term to express the third view. Some scholars resist using the term entirely in the name of semantic hygiene, preferring an alternative such as "human personhood." Persons can be viewed as relational selves, with the focus being on relationships; Peters is sympathetic to this approach. However, a fixation on personhood creates as many problems as it solves, not least because many interpretations rely on a separation from other animal kinds in a way that is not all that desirable.[14]

Most biologists, in as much as the species boundaries are becoming more fluid, especially in an evolutionary perspective, are reluctant to view "natures" of human beings—or any other species, for that matter—in an essentialist manner. This shift, combined with a closer recognition that human beings share in facets of animality, and perhaps vice versa, means that sharp boundaries between humans and other animals constructed for theological and/or cultural reasons no longer seem convincing.[15] Philosopher Mary Midgley recognized the importance of this boundary and the need to stress human continuities with other animals. In her pioneer work, *Beast and Man: The Roots of Human Nature*, first published in 1978,[16] she makes a strong case for stressing continuities between humans and other animals, rather than differences. The denial of the existence of human nature by social scientists and empiricist philosophers, alongside equally vocal advocates stressing biological determinism, gave way to sociobiological perspectives that remain influential in current evolutionary theory.

Mikael Stenmark sets up what he calls the minimal characteristics required for having a "human nature," resisting the idea that a functional or even relational approach to human beings avoids the problem of having to name specific ontological characteristics.[17] In doing so, he deals with anti-essentialist objections to the idea of having a definitive "nature" at all. Such objections arise predominately from postmodern writers who seek to deconstruct what they view as behind such essentialist claims and argue instead for bio-politics—that is, the claim that biological essentialism is less about science, but rather provides a political means through which to control human populations.

Some biologists and philosophers, such as John Dupré, argue against strong concepts of human nature.[18] Dupré contends that essentialist notions are incorrect, given the great cultural, geographical, and historical diversity of humans. He also opposes evolutionary psychologists who claim to have found human universals based on statistical measurements of behavior. To claim to have found the fundamental "essence" of human nature is, for Dupré, a deeply mistaken perception. In as much as Dupré resists some of the strident claims of evolutionary psychology, I have some sympathy with his views. However, to argue that there is *nothing at all* that can be usefully said about human nature in a collective sense of species characteristics goes too far. Denying that there is such a possibility opens up an argument for the justification of all kinds of manipulative trans-genomic and nanotechnology practices; there are simply no limits because there is no human nature to preserve or sustain. Other ethical dangers with extreme essentialism locate innate tendencies in deep biological roots, a form of biological determinism already noted by Peters. Such a view tends to deny the possibility of genuine human freedom and responsibility.

Even so, some evolutionary psychologists continue searching for core characteristics of a supposed universal "human nature" that can be mapped through psychological testing. Stenmark calls this "species-specific" or "kind" nature. Nature can also mean a "type" nature, according to which someone belongs to a specific gender, race, social, or cultural type. A typical view of "human nature" is presupposed in evolutionary discussions of sex selection, which models human behavior according to particular patterns of "pair bonding."

Finally, individual "nature" is composed of those personal characteristics that make up individually characterized human uniqueness. Stenmark does not comment on this characteristic in evolutionary terms. Rather, more attention is being paid to individual differences as sources of variation, along with the wide range of plasticity in response to different conditions. The biological characteristics that Stenmark names as marking out human uniqueness relative to other species are a bipedal walk, an erect posture, and a large brain.[19] Such characteristics are those that are typical, in answer to the anti-essentialist objection that not all humans share such characteristics.

Furthermore, just because evolutionary biology highlights changes in biological characteristics of the human, these changes coexist with those characteristics that are more conserved in evolutionary terms. Of course, in defining the human, Stenmark has to add to his list of biological characteristics rational and moral thinking, along with artistic and linguistic expression. Stenmark believes that Christian theological notions of image bearing most naturally lean toward an essentialist understanding of human nature. To try to avoid speaking of human capacities in favor of divine image bearing, understood in terms of relationships, does not, for Stenmark, avoid the issue, given that human relationships presuppose certain capabilities. Hence, if such capacities are lost, then relationships cannot be the same.

In the light of this discussion, my view is to put a much stronger "no go" sign (compared with Peters) on those technological enhancements in transhumanist projects that attempt to disembody human beings from their creaturely contexts, even if more limited types of cyborg-like enhancements can be justified.[20] I take this view not just for philosophical reasons (i.e., what human nature might be like), but also for biological and theological ones. The creaturely basis for human life is bound up with an affirmation of our finite creatureliness. Peters correctly admits that this is the case for an adequate Christian eschatology in the light of a bodily resurrection, but he does not stress how far this linkage then impinges on how we might envisage current practices. Once Augustinian views of the relational self in God becomes stripped away from their theological rootedness in affirmation of creation, then human beings are no longer grounded in solidarity with other animals through common creaturely being. I suggest that this binding is vitally important, ethically, in assessing the trajectory of transhumanism, because it shapes how we perceive human flourishing. For Peters, the flourishing human self is grounded in love of God and neighbor, but in his appraisal of transhuman projects he has not yet incorporated those evolutionary and ecological issues that he discusses elsewhere.[21] These issues are highly relevant, because evolutionary history, from an anthropological perspective, reveals the entanglement between human beings and other creatures that persists in current multispecies relationships.[22]

Recognition of creatureliness is, therefore, one lens through which transhuman projects can be assessed. Such creatureliness in human beings is complicated by the use of tools that eventually become incorporated into human culture. Walther Zimmerli argues that technology has gone through four stages. In the first, termed *Homo faber*, nature could not be overcome unless it was obeyed, so the forces of the natural world became tools for human use. In the second stage, *Homo faber economicus*, we have reproduction-profit, characterized by technology related to the economy and commercial exploitation of manufactured products. In the third stage, *Homo faber scientificus*, science itself becomes the productive partner in the process, so that the image of science changes through its marriage to technology. Here, we also find *Homo faber ignorans*, where the science cannot predict the consequences of an ever-accelerating technology. Finally, in a fourth stage, human beings become self-reflective, *Homo faber doctus ignorans*.[23] It is in this fourth step that nanotechnologies and other life extension technologies are situated, for the promise of goods is neither reliable nor certain. Further, and significantly, it is the notion of interconnectedness viewed in concepts of co-evolution that highlight the limitations of traditional linear scientific concepts of cause and effect. Peters has pointed in the direction of such relationality, but confining it to a discussion of God and neighbor does not take it nearly far enough. The ancient cosmological idea of a Great Chain of Being, with human beings at the pyramid, has been replaced by the concept of a network. Transhumanism, in its more extreme form and perhaps ironically, seems to depend on a network for its understanding of computer technologies, but projects the human out into the future in a way that shears human identity from the creaturely network in which it is placed.

Overall, I am in many respects sympathetic to Ted Peters's analysis, at least to the extent that he is wary of blanket objections to human enhancement derived from purported religious reasons. At the same time, Christian ideas about change do not map well onto technological forms of enhancement, given that perfection in the Christian life is very different from the kind of perfection imagined in enhancement technologies.[24] Alasdair MacIntyre's extensive discussion of the virtues includes a comment on the way the virtues are interpreted, which depends on prior goals. For example, very different kinds of practices are characteristic of virtues when the life of virtue has the goal of external gains and successes, such as with Benjamin Franklin. In contrast, the classic Aristotelian virtues aim for the common good and are characterized by internal transformation.[25] In Peters's account, the external blurs with the internal, such that the *telos* of the Christian life is mapped onto the external goods envisaged in transhuman projects.

One of the difficulties still to be navigated comprises the boundaries between animal/human/cyborg—boundaries that continue to unsettle the human condition and its anthropocentric pretensions.[26] I am also not convinced that objections to the technological altering of human nature *always* arise from associating that nature with the sacred. Peters associates this with the naturalistic fallacy. On the one hand, we need to be wary of essentialist views of human nature that posit this linkage as unalterable. On the other hand, the slippery slope from therapy to enhancement to transhumanism speaks of a disembodied and disconnected view of the human that fails to take into account human creatureliness. I suggest it is this violation to a sense of creaturehood that drives religious objections as much as any misconceived notions about the sacredness of nature. Calvin Mercer's insistence on the importance of the body in understanding human identity from a Christian perspective, and its violation in more radical transhuman projects, helps to clarify the ethical boundaries along which Christian debates among Protestant scholars are most likely to traverse.[27] Those in the Catholic tradition are also likely to have diverse views on transhumanism that are outside the scope of this chapter to discuss in any detail.

The main point worth noting, perhaps, is that radically disengaging from our bodily nature breaks a taboo that is common to all Christian traditions, even if, as Mercer points out, prosthetics and other forms of enhancement are likely to be tolerated to some extent. Our long evolutionary history of entanglement with other creatures should give us pause when contemplating a computerized model of human futures. Like Peters, I believe that the use of practical wisdom is appropriate for more limited cases of enhancement, such as providing computer technology to aid those who are suffering various mental impairments. Nevertheless, such practical wisdom has to be internally grounded in the context of creaturely being and becoming.

NOTES

1. Ted Peters, *Playing God: Genetic Determinism and Human Freedom*, 2nd ed. (London: Routledge, 2003 [1996]).

2. Ted Peters, "Are We Playing God with Nanoenhancement?," in *Nanoethics: The Ethical and Social Implications of Nanotechnology*, edited by Fritz Allhoff, Patrick Lin, James Moor, and John Weckert (Hoboken, NJ: Wiley-Interscience, 2007), 173–183.

3. Peters, "Are We Playing God," 174.

4. Also discussed recently in Gareth Jones and Maja Whitaker, "Transforming the Human Body," in *Beyond Human: From Animality to Transhumanism*, edited by Charlie Blake, Claire Malloy, and Steven Shakespeare (London, UK: Continuum, 2012), 254–279.

5. Peters, "Are We Playing God," 175.

6. Peters, "Are We Playing God," 176.

7. Peters, "Are We Playing God," 177.

8. Peters, "Are We Playing God," 180.

9. Peters, "Are We Playing God," 182.

10. Ted Peters, *Anticipating Omega: Science, Faith and Our Ultimate Future* (Göttingen, Germany: Vandenhoeck & Ruprecht, 2006), 107.

11. Ted Peters, "Transhumanism and the Post-Human Future: Will Technological Progress Get Us There?", in *H±: Transhumanism and Its Critics*, edited by Gregory R. Hansell and William Grassie (Philadelphia, PA: Metanexus, 2011), 147–175.

12. Peters, "Transhumanism and the Post-Human Future," 148. For him there is "a human proclivity to turn good into evil," which means that new technologies are permitted, but scientists are encouraged to remain watchful for perversion toward destructive purposes.

13. Peters, *Anticipating Omega*, 124.

14. For discussion in the context of neurobiological studies, see Fernando Vidal, "Human Persons and Human Brains: A Historical Perspective within the Christian

Tradition," in *Rethinking Human Nature: A Multidisciplinary Approach*, edited by Malcolm Jeeves (Grand Rapids, MI: Eerdmans, 2011), 30–60.

15. I have discussed this and other issues related to developing a theological anthropology in C. Deane-Drummond, *The Wisdom of the Liminal: Evolution and Other Animals in Human Becoming* (Grand Rapids, MI: Eerdmans, 2014).

16. Mary Midgley, *Beast and Man: The Roots of Human Nature*, 2nd ed. (London, UK: Routledge, 1995 [1978]).

17. Mikael Stenmark, "Is There a Human Nature?," *Zygon* 47, no. 4 (2012): 890–902.

18. John Dupré, *Humans and Other Animals* (Oxford, UK: Oxford University Press, 2002), 109; see also John Dupré, "On Human Nature," *Human Affairs* 2 (2003): 109–122.

19. Stenmark, "Is There a Human Nature?," 890.

20. For further discussion, see C. Deane-Drummond, "Taking Leave of the Animal? The Theological and Ethical Implications of Transhuman Projects," in *Transhumanism and Transcendence: Christian Hope in an Age of Technological Enhancement*, edited by Ron Cole-Turner (Washington, DC: Georgetown University Press, 2012), 115–130.

21. Ted Peters and Martinez Hewlett, *Can You Believe in God and Evolution? A Guide for the Perplexed*, Darwin 200th anniversary ed. (Nashville, TN: Abingdon Press, 2008 [2006]); Ted Peters, *Science, Theology and Ethics* (Farnham, UK: Ashgate, 2003).

22. Celia Deane-Drummond and Agustín Fuentes, "Blurring Boundaries in Human Being and Becoming: Situating Theological Anthropology in Interspecies Relationships," *Philosophy, Theology and the Sciences* 1, no. 1 (2014).

23. Walther Cristoph Zimmerli, "Human Responsibility for Extra Human Nature," keynote presentation for the fourth biennial conference Nature, Technology and Religion: Transdisciplinary Perspectives, European Forum for the Study of Religion and Environment, Sigtuna Foundation, Sweden, May 2–25, 2013. A revised version will be published as Walther Cristoph Zimmerli, "Human Responsibility for Extra-Human Nature: An Ethical Approach to Technofutures," in *Technofutures: God, Society and Earth Ethics*, edited by C. Deane-Drummond, S. Bergmann, and B. Szerszynski (Basingstoke, UK: Ashgate, 2015).

24. See, for example, C. Deane-Drummond, "Future Perfect: God, the Transhuman Future and the Quest for Immortality," in *Future Perfect: God, Medicine and Human Identity*, edited by Celia Deane-Drummond and Peter Scott (London, UK: T & T Clark/Continuum, 2006), 168–182. Peters does acknowledge the distinction between Christian accounts of perfection and those possible through therapy, enhancement, and transhumanism. See his discussion in T. Peters, "Perfect Humans or Transhumans," in *Future Perfect*, 15–32. Drawing on my discussion of practical wisdom, he recognizes that discernment is needed to know what to approve or reject (16). For him, "transformation on behalf of human flourishing is attuned to God's eschatological promise" (17). The difficulty, of course, is naming what that flourishing might look like; this issue is heavily contested and not likely to be universally accepted. In this context, Peters is prepared to name transhumanism as "unrealistic" (16), but he also admits that the line between enhancement and transhumanism is blurry (20).

25. Alasdair MacIntyre, *After Virtue*, 3rd ed. (Notre Dame, IN: University of Notre Dame Press, 2007), 185. In Franklin, whom McIntyre cites here, virtues are means to an end and *utility* is the criteria. Virtue in Aquinas and Aristotle is directed toward a *telos*, either natural or unnatural.

26. Charlie Blake, Claire Malloy, and Steven Shakespeare, eds., *Beyond Human: From Animality to Transhumanism* (London, UK: Continuum, 2012).

27. Calvin Mercer, "Sorting out Soma in the Debate about Transhumanism: One Protestant's Perspective," in *Transhumanism and the Body: The World Religions Speak*, edited by Calvin Mercer and Derek Maher (New York, NY: Palgrave Macmillan, 2014). I am grateful to the author for allowing me to see a copy of this chapter while in press.

Critical Transhumanism as a Religious Ethic of Otherness

Steven A. Benko and Amelia Hruby

When one is thinking about God, one is thinking about how one ought to relate to another. The ethical concerns of transhumanism include the just distribution of technologies of enhancement, the impact on relationships and society when human talents and capacities are extended beyond typical human functioning, and the ways in which we assign value, moral praise, and blame to human behavior. In addition, transhumanism prompts theological reflection about the use of technology to alter the created world and human nature, to overcome sin and achieve salvation outside of institutionalized or revealed religion, or to replace the need for religion altogether.[1] There is no possibility of disentangling the ethical and religious from transhumanism. Extending what Jeanine Thweatt-Bates writes about posthumanism in *Cyborg Selves*, when one is thinking about transhumanism, one is thinking about the human relationship to God.[2] The ethical and religious concerns of transhumanism begin with how transhumans understand what it means to be human, which responsibility transhumans assume for others and otherness, and the way that society can be transformed by this shift in perspective and practice. Says Stephen Garner, "The questions raised concern not only different ways people describe being human and challenges to a perceived natural order but also how to live wisely and well in a technological world, and especially how to live hopefully."[3]

The separation of the ethical and the religious in transhumanism can be traced back to the claim that transhumanism is, first, thoroughly biological and, second, a continuation of Enlightenment humanism. Garner sums up the transhumanist vision as the belief that the human condition can be improved through reason, science and technology. It focuses on the autonomous individual, asserting the primacy of reason as a force for personal and therefore societal transformation. Through the use of applied reason, transhumanism asserts that values such as rational thinking, freedom, tolerance, and concern for others is increased, which ultimately leads to an ever-increasing improvement of the human condition.[4]

For example, Kurzweil and Moravec reject the organic body because of its limitations and laud technology as an escape from eventual decline, decay, and death. In their posthumanist writings, they emphasize "the limitations of the flesh, the frailties of the body, and the deficiencies of the human senses," and suggest that the future lies in humans going beyond humanity via the merger of organic bodies with intelligent machines.[5] The secular roots of transhumanism have resulted in an unwillingness to engage religious critiques because religious beliefs are viewed as irrational and seen as an impediment to transhumanist goals.[6] Conversely, the thoroughly secular nature of transhumanism has led some to consider it a thoroughly heretical endeavor to usurp God.[7] Others see transhumanism as an extension of the religious desire to transcend the limitations of the body and live eternally. Transhumanists and their critics operate from opposite sides of an either/or proposition: either transhumanism is secular and a-religious or it is thoroughly religious, and for some offensively so. Ultimately, this dichotomy separates the ethical concerns from religious ideas and practices, which leads to an incomplete understanding of the transhumanist project.

HUMAN AND TRANSHUMAN AMBIGUITY

To begin to understand the ethical and the religious within transhumanism, it is necessary to think about more than just the historical and technological contexts that make transhumanism possible. One must also consider the philosophical context out of which transhumanism emerged: the posthumanist critique of Enlightenment humanism. Considering transhumanism in this context is difficult because some transhumanists resist locating it within a philosophical posthumanist discourse. For example, Nick Bostrom argues in the Transhumanism FAQ that both transhumanism and posthumanism are thoroughly biological and that the change in perspective or self-understanding suggested by (philosophical) posthumanism is not enough to make us biologically posthuman: "the changes required to make us posthuman are too profound to be achievable by merely altering some aspect of psychological theory or the way we think about ourselves."[8] For Bostrom, posthumanism is a biological state, not a way of understanding the relationship between individuals and the sacred.

When Bostrom defines posthumans as beings whose "basic capacities so radically exceed those of present humans as to be no longer unambiguously human by our current standards," his use of "unambiguously" betrays that—at least at this historical moment—the human and the posthuman are still intertwined biologically and theoretically.[9] The meaning of "unambiguously human by our current standards" makes sense in a future where human capacities, lifespan, and overall functioning are so different from current standards that this future person would be as different to us as a Neanderthal from our ancient past is different from us.

However, at the risk of dating ourselves, the future is not yet now. We are living in an era where the human is ambiguous because of the biological possibilities made real by transhumanism. This ambiguity is not just biological and technological—the way that the human is made ambiguous by the transhuman and posthuman is also philosophical, ethical, and religious and influences how humans think about themselves, how they relate to others, how they conceive of their responsibilities to others, and how they construct their understanding of the sacred.

CRITICAL TRANSHUMANISM

The source of this ambiguity lies in the relationship between humanism and the critiques of humanism made by thinkers such as Althusser and Foucault, although in this chapter we will locate the ethical and religious dimensions of this critique with Emmanuel Levinas. In some ways, transhumanism is obviously a continuation of the Enlightenment humanist project. Thweatt-Bates makes this point when she connects the humanist belief in autonomy, reason, and democracy to the transhumanist desire to perfect those traits by overcoming the limitations of the body. She rightly argues that the "H+" used to represent transhumanism displays an "awareness within the transhumanist movement of the rhetorical need to present the posthuman as continuous, rather than discontinuous, with current notions of the human."[10] It has been easier to make the case that transhumanism is a humanism because it shares the humanist belief that science and technology are the keys to human emancipation and progress. Thinking of transhumanism as the technological practice of what Neil Badmington calls "critical posthumanism" more accurately reflects the transhumanist use of humanist ideas and values. When Badmington states that "the writing of the posthumanist condition should not seek to fashion 'scriptural tombs' for humanism, but must, rather, take the form of a critical practice that occurs *inside* humanism,"[11] one can extend that logic to transhumanism: it is a critical practice that takes place within humanism. As a critical posthumanism, transhumanism begins with the assumptions of humanism by restating those assumptions in a way that questions their relevance and applicability. Drawing from Derrida, Badmington argues that thought takes place within a certain tradition and, therefore, is bound to bear some resemblance to that tradition. One begins with humanism so that one can articulate a more relevant humanism. In this understanding, there is no difference between posthumanism and transhumanism. The technological practices of the latter are animated by the philosophical understanding articulated in the former, and vice versa.

Because transhumanists state the terms of humanism in order to restate them, it has been difficult to escape the humanist orbit. One reason, as Castree and Nash argue, is that the "anti-humanistic embracing of posthumanism as an emergent or imminent historical condition also depends on the notion of the human as a once stable category" that seems more coherent and dominant than it ever was historically.[12] Another reason is the continued investment in humanist thought as stemming from "anxieties about the erosion of the ideal human subject differentiated from and in power over the non-human world of 'nature'"; these anxieties create "a continued investment in a model of the modern human that has been the subject of significant critical attention."[13] Restating these terms and categories, even to critique them, has the effect of making them seem more stable and dominant than they might have ever been. Going one step further, critical posthumanism restates these terms in a way that makes them seem relevant. According to Castree and Nash, "critical posthumanism attends to the ways in which ideas of the human, nature and culture continue to work even in accounts which suggest their implosion."[14] Even though, as Badmington says, one day we might not be, we are still ambiguously human because even though "the present moment may well be one in which the hegemony and heredity of humanism feel a little less certain, a little less inevitable," we still remain somewhat within humanism because "the scene is changing but the guard is not."[15] What is needed to escape the essentializing and normativizing discourse of humanism is a repetition that is a questioning or a restatement that is not a reinstatement.[16] The question Badmington asks, but does not answer, is this: "if traces of humanism find their way into even the most apocalyptic accounts of the posthumanist condition, *what is to be done?*"[17]

Even as transhumanism relies on humanist categories such as autonomy, reason, and progress to make claims about an inevitable technological future, it does so in a way that undermines how those terms are used in humanism. If this were not the case, we would not be ambiguously human. The undermining and destabilization of the vocabularies used to define what it means to be human is the source of the ethical and religious criticisms of transhumanism. Criticisms about how transhumanism is unnatural, destabilizes society, is unjust, and disrupts the distinction between human and divine are often levied in a bid to halt transhumanist efforts to enhance human well-being and functioning—but forestalling transhumanism is impossible. Transhumanism is the current and future state of humanity not because all humans will one day choose to embrace this new way of being, but rather because humans have always been becoming transhuman. N. Katherine Hayles makes the point that humans "have used technology since they stood upright and began fashioning tools, an event contemporaneous with the evolution of *Homo sapiens*. Technology as a strategy of survival and evolutionary fitness cannot be alien to the human."[18] Technology may not be alien to the human, but it alienates humans from other humans by making them other to one another. Additionally, technology disrupts the clear boundaries that exist between human and divine, profane and sacred, and human made and divinely created.

A critical transhumanism recognizes the ambiguity inaugurated by technological enhancement of human beings and responds to charges of individual narcissism, cultural elitism, and religious hubris by taking responsibility for how disruptions in understandings of what it means to be human cause changes in how humans understand and relate to one another and to the divine. A critical transhumanist ethic is an ethic of critique that uses humanist claims about what is normatively human to reveal how the artificial rigidity of those claims alienates those who are said to be more or less human relative to their use of technology. Thus an ethics of restatement and resaying is necessary because it calls attention to what was said, the need for it to be resaid, and the ethical and religious justifications for doing so.

TRANSHUMANISM AND LEVINASIAN ETHICS

The task of a critical transhumanist ethic is to articulate and perform the restatement of humanist norms as a question, the answer to which is a resaying of what it means to be human. The ethics of Emmanuel Levinas is an ethics of an encounter with the Other that, when linked to critical transhumanism, is responsive to how technology creates a variety of ways to be human and inaugurates a resaying of the terms one uses to understand and relate to the Other. The face-to-face encounter with the Other calls into question the subject's intentional freedom and spontaneity to shape the world, give names to things as they appear, and thematize people and objects into a coherent understanding of the world. The freedom one enjoys to experience the world as familiar is called into question by the encounter with the Other, as this trauma reveals the limits of knowledge. For Levinas, ethics is the continual confession of the limits of one's knowledge about the Other, where "I *face* the other person and keep my distance, for distance implies respect."[19] Out of respect for the Other, in deference to that otherness that reveals the limits of knowledge, the ethical response is to become one-for-the-other by substituting one's cares, priorities, and the vocabulary with which one would understand and make sense of the Other. As a result, Levinasian subjectivity—an ethical subjectivity—is about the subject, when faced with the unique individuality of the Other, becoming a unique self by taking responsibility for the Other.

Applied to posthumanism, the writings of Emmanuel Levinas evidence an effort to resay posthumanist critiques of humanism without reinstating its logic

so that there can be a more humane humanism. Levinas is an appropriate figure to consider here for a number of reasons: his contemporaries included
humanists and posthumanists; he was engaged in the debate between them;
and though he took the humanist side, he did so in a way that endorsed
posthumanist concerns for the Other. Colin Davis writes:

> Levinas's objection to humanism is that it has not been sufficiently humanist,
> that it has not gone far enough in preserving the human and promoting the
> humane. And he entirely accepts that ethics requires a subject which survives
> in some form. But the Levinasian subject is not autonomous and transparent
> to itself; it is destitute, radically fractured, exposed to alterity and defined by that
> exposure.[20]

The encounter with the Other leaves the subject vulnerable to further
encounters with the Other that will force a resaying of how the Other is comprehended. To do so, Levinas draws a distinction between the Saying and the
Said. The Said is a "statement, assertion or proposition of which the truth or
falsity can be ascertained," whereas the Saying is a "nonthematizable ethical
residue of language that escapes comprehension, interrupts ontology and is
the very enactment of the movement from the same to the other."[21] The
Saying reveals the limitations and violence of the Said by inaugurating a
resaying that creates ambiguity where previously there had been clarity and
familiarity. Viewed from a Levinasian framework, this Said arrests the Other
(the transhuman) and makes it familiar (human) through proposition.
Transhumanism has "said" the human where transhumanist discourses have
accepted and claimed continuity with the standard of human nature articulated in humanist discourse. In reintroducing Otherness (transhumanism) to
that which has been established as comprehended (the human), the Saying
becomes an ethical moment. Thus, in his articulation of the necessity for a
Saying that is always a resaying to avoid a Said, Levinas offers an important
insight into critical transhumanist ethics. Critical transhumanism sees science
and technology as inaugurating a resaying of the humanist language of what is
Said about what it means to be human. As a result, the binaries that have
been Said, which a critical transhumanism attempts to resay, reveal the tension between the so-called natural and technological: "reality/unreality, natu-
ral/artificial, organic/inorganic, biology/technology, human/machine, and the
born/made."[22] Transhumanism is a "re-thinking [of] the claims of humanism"
in light of "various posthumanist challenges that are emerging with the mutations technology brings in both the subject and object worlds."[23] Refusal to
resay these terms excludes the transhumanist Other from the human community and is a violence against the Other.

Transhumanism, then, is ethical in two ways. First, the disruptive encounter with one who is transhuman—be it visibly transhuman in the form of a
cyborg or less obviously so because it has been altered or enhanced at the gene

level—is an occasion to resay what it means to be human. Sometimes the response to the appearance of a transhuman is immediate and violent. More often than not, this is the response to cyborgs—both individuals who choose to live with prosthetic devices attached to their body (e.g., Andy Clark, the conceptual artist Stelarc) and people who have life-sustaining prosthetic devices attached to their bodies (e.g., individuals with pacemakers). In Levinasian ethics, the encounter with the other person challenges the individual to reconsider the ideas, words, or labels that can be used to describe and define that person. Transhumans provoke an ethical response because in the encounter with a transhuman one substitutes one's vocabulary for the vocabulary of the Other, thereby assuming responsibility for how that person—in this case, a transhuman—sees himself/herself/itself and the world. The encounter with transhumans calls into question, if not outright obliterates, the range and application of familiar and common understandings of terms like "natural," "normal," "organic," "whole," and so on. It is an encounter with these terms and one more: "human." Where the Other is different from all other people and ought to be responded to in his or her uniqueness, the transhuman other is different from all other humans in that he/she/it might have talents, capacities and abilities different from other humans. For that reason, the transhuman other forces a reconsideration not just of the terms used to describe other people, but also of the term "human." This makes the transhuman other the most challenging and difficult encounter because where the Other in Levinasian ethics was, at least, another person, the transhuman other demonstrates that even this idea cannot be taken for granted. By focusing on the ethical nature of the encounter with transhumans, the full force of an ethical resaying of humanism is felt via a critical transhumanism that is more humane than humanism.

For those familiar with Levinasian ethics, it might seem surprising—or even heretical—to claim that something other than another human being can inaugurate ethical responsibility for the Other. Levinasian ethics is thoroughly human, in that the encounter with the other human being reveals the violence against the Other. Levinas privileges the human as the best channel for Otherness, arguing that "it is only man who could be absolutely foreign to me"[24]; consequently, only the face of a man could channel the "pure alterity, pure strangeness"[25] of the Other into the world. Relation with all other things "is established as comprehension. As beings, they let themselves be overtaken from the perspective of being and of a totality that lends them a signification."[26] In Levinas's thought, it seems that violence can be done only to other human beings. Thus the existence of a violence against a nonhuman or transhuman—a violence that one ought to avoid if one is to participate in the good that is nonviolence and being for the Other—seems difficult, if not impossible, to fathom. For example, Hava Tirosh-Samuelson writes, "But such appropriation of Levinas is misleading since it is precisely the *face* of the

Other, the source of moral obligation, according to Levinas, that contemporary technological culture threatens to efface."[27] For Levinas, "the ethical subject is an embodied being of flesh and blood, a being that is capable of hunger, who eats and enjoys eating ... only such a being can know what it means to give its bread to the Other from out of its own mouth."[28]

How, then, can we encounter nonhuman or transhuman others who are not capable of hunger? Who do not eat or enjoy eating? Who cannot know what it means to give bread from one's own mouth? Silvia Benso poses this question in her book, *The Face of Things*: "what if things were capable of expressing an ethical signification, an alterity that goes beyond the structures of meaning within which things have been enframed—an alterity that demands the resoluteness of an ethical response on the side of human beings?"[29] Benso argues that when Levinas limits ethics to the human and presents only an ethic of other human persons, he commits the same totalizing, assimilatory violence he condemns. To correct this violence, Benso argues, "not only the Other, but also the other of the Other, must become part of philosophical discourse for that discourse to achieve the level of metaphysicity it advocates."[30] If only humans can be Other, how other can humans really be? This critical use of Levinas's argument is in keeping with how Badmington defines the logic of critical posthumanism—specifically, the restating of a term, set of terms, or logic in order to show its limits. By starting with a Levinasian ethics as an ethics of the human, one can question whether it ought to be an ethics of other things. Similarly, critical transhumanism starts with the human to identify an ethics of that which is other than human. A critical transhumanist ethic shows how the disruption of the category "human" can open up that category to be more inclusive of those who are said to be inhuman relative to their use of technology. Levinas makes this resaying an ethical moment, lest one do violence against the Other in the reification of the very terms one is using to describe the Other.

The second way that transhumanism is ethical is that transhumanists must bear witness to the otherness they inaugurate by always being willing to become one for the Other. Here, transhumanism functions as a higher calling to be for the Other by rejecting the hypocrisy that would be the performance of exclusionary thought and behavior that exiled some from the transhuman or posthuman community. Transhuman subjectivity as ethical subjectivity is about the transhuman belief in the moral worth of otherness maintained by substituting oneself for the Other. Individuals who choose to be transhuman recognize and react against the artificial and constructed nature of identity and the discourses that normalize what counts as a meaningful human existence. Technology exposes for them the limits of humanist norms and claims. By realizing themselves as individuals, transhumans enhance and augment themselves so that they can remain uniquely individualistic. Transhumans are other to themselves via the otherness of the technology that makes them transhuman, and this becomes the origin of their posthumanism—that is, they no longer understand themselves as part of the generic human community. Transhumans are posthuman in their resistance to thematization, and they work against thematization by continually becoming other—other to themselves and other for others. Transhumans resist falling back into humanism's generic explication of meaningful human experience both by remaining other than themselves via technology and by becoming other than themselves in support of the Other. For transhumans, their own otherness is a wound that leaves them vulnerable and exposed to calls of the Other. The transhuman self, then, is an endless deferral of closure, a self that is always open to becoming other than it is. Levinas says:

> But one must make precise just *how* the I is posited or affirms itself. Is this "I" affirmed just as one who is posited as standing with full rights to be where he is; who, in the world in which he is found, is "doing well"; . . . who "perseveres in being" and who has no scruples about persevering? Or is the I posited straightaway for-the-other, straightaway in obligation and straightaway as the only one who is ready to respond and to bear this responsibility, like one who is first to have hearkened to the call and the last, perhaps, to have listened to it? For the I this amounts to its very identification in its uniqueness as an I: its uniqueness, its exteriority from the extension of any genus, and in this sense its freedom. It will hold to this primordial election before being affirmed for itself.[31]

The "I" the transhuman posits is not about perpetuating itself into the future. The transhuman, though aware of himself/herself/itself as an "I," does not perpetuate that "I" in ways that are a violence against the Other. As subjectivities that are for the Other, transhumans are ethical subjectivities in terms of how Levinas defines ethical subjectivity. This view is in direct opposition to how Ronald Cole-Turner chastises transhumanists for what he sees as their self-involvement and disregard for others. According to this author, "transhumanists seem both human-centered and self-centered, concerned chiefly with humanity above other species and with themselves among other humans. Is it not the case that the central concern of the transhumanist is the enhancement of the self? . . . It is absorbed with the self and its preservation and expansion."[32]

CRITICAL TRANSHUMANISM, ETHICS, AND COMMUNITY

As a movement, transhumanism is criticized for over-emphasizing freedom and rationality—specifically, for suggesting that humans might not be rational enough to use their freedom to develop and use technologies in way that delivers meaningful progress to individuals or society. The understanding of critical transhumanism that we have articulated thus far calls into question what freedom, rationality, and progress would mean for transhumanists. The encounter with the Other calls freedom into question as the right to describe the transhuman (as other) is denied; otherwise, that encounter is a violence against the Other. In the becoming one-for-the-other that makes the encounter ethical, more than just words and definitions are exchanged and replaced. The totalizing nature of reason and rationality is called into question in a way that might be disorienting, but is redeemed as a humility that recognizes the limits of human reason with the confession that more can always be said and thought. The individual might have to give up control, but only so that justice can prevail. This is the value of critical transhumanism. Levinas shared the same concerns about the antihuman and posthuman critiques of humanism: "it is precisely because the discourses of antihumanism and poststructuralism have deposed the subject from its position of sovereignty that what Levinas calls the sanctity of the human can be delineated."[33] The concern for Otherness—the subject's own as well as the Otherness of others—becomes a concern for social justice.

For Levinas, becoming responsible for the Other allows one to enter into community with the Other and those who are other to the Other (those whom Levinas terms "the third party"). The relationship that exists between individuals is not a one-to-one relationship, but rather a relationship between self and neighbor, as well as those that are Other to the neighbor; this prevents the relationship between self and Other from becoming a master/slave relationship.[34] There is always a third party who is also other, and to whom the transhuman is other. It is at the moment the third entity appears that transhumans have to make a decision about their responsibility. Peperzak writes:

> As soon as the third enters the picture, my responsibility is divided. It is no longer an unlimited care for only this one neighbor, and I must ask myself: Who comes first? What are my neighbor and the third man to one another? What should they do for one another? My substitution for my neighbor involves my responsibility for his/her responsibility for his/her neighbor. My neighbor and the third person obligate me simultaneously. Together with my neighbor, I am for the third person; with both of them, I am against myself.[35]

The appearance of the third does not put the individual in the position of being totally dominated by all others. Peperzak goes on to say, "My destiny and salvation are also important: I, too, am one of the many who are neighbors to my neighbors. My responsibility for the Other includes now also care of myself."[36] Care of the self is in keeping with what has been said about transhumans as individual entities: in their care for themselves, which is the cultivation of their own otherness, there is a care for others, which is a care for the uniqueness and otherness of the Other. The communities and societies that transhumans inhabit become populated by those concerned about the ways people or things can express themselves in the spaces they inhabit.

When transhumanism is envisioned as the technological practice of a critical posthumanism, it can better engage social concerns and respond to criticisms that the unjust distribution of transhuman technology will increase social inequalities and social stratification. The transhumanist concern for the Other takes the form of laws that ensure the voices of marginalized others will be heard. Having been wounded by being other and nurturing those wounds so that they remain sensitive to the Other, transhumans are better poised to hear these voices. What transhumans can recognize is that we live in an age where a variety of technologies intersect, penetrate, are incorporated into, and can reshape and remake the body in a number of ways. Understanding the colonial and sexist legacy of humanism is a shift away from the word "human" meaning inclusion in a larger community and toward the word "human," however broadly defined (genetically, mentally, physiologically), becoming exclusionary. For example, Francis Fukuyama in *Our Posthuman Future* warns that changes to our shared human experience engendered by advances in biotechnology and pharmaceuticals pose such a threat to civil society that immediate government intervention is necessary lest enhanced senior citizens live too long and become a burden on their families and medical providers or genetically modified children become too smart, forcing others to chemically enhance themselves to keep up or be left behind.[37]

Fukuyama's prescription for preserving the prevailing social order can be juxtaposed with Levinas's articulation of the relationship between justice and laws. Laws persevere in their being, but the voices of the marginalized reverberate beneath those laws and will eventually break through.[38] Thus, while there is justice in laws, there is still violence in justice.[39] According to Levinas, justice is always the search for a better justice; put another way, justice must continually be resaid if it is to remain just.[40] Levinas writes, "Justice that deserves its name, does not forget that the law is perfectible. It leaves open the possibility of a revision of a judgment once pronounced."[41] In their hybridity and perpetual process of becoming other, transhumans are witness to the sort of exclusion in the laws Fukuyama says will preserve our union. At the same time, transhumans also experience the possibility of more just laws and a more just society by responding to those who, like them, find themselves ostracized by language that defines "human" in terms that require organic naturalness and normal human body functioning for inclusion in the larger community. Transhumans, by deliberately being on the outside of how the word "human" has been traditionally defined, call upon individuals to become individuals who, by being responsible for the individuality of the Other, speak to include others in the community of individuals, assuring them a voice they would otherwise be denied. Speaking together, they make sense of what it means to be "more than"—more than what can be understood in the encounter with the Other, more than human, more humane than human, more just, more than just this justice.

CRITICAL TRANSHUMANISM, ETHICS, AND RELIGION

It is in the call for justice where the ethical and religious dimensions of transhumanism overlap most profoundly. Instead of a God who creates the co-creators, who then take over for God when they assume they know more or can do a better job, this is a God who emphasizes and animates co-creativity. Through the estrangement that occurs in the response to the Other, God directs those co-creative efforts toward a more just justice—specifically, a justice that is never finished. History becomes humanity's response to God's command to do justice:

> God thus empowers our human powerlessness by giving away his power, by possibilizing us and our good actions—so that we may supplement and co-accomplish creation. To be made in God's image is therefore, paradoxically, to be powerless, but with the possibility of receiving power from God to overcome our powerlessness, by responding to the call of creation with the words, "I am able."[42]

The idea of God as the one who calls the subject out of itself in the encounter with the Other (or the subject's own otherness) focuses the efforts of the subject who becomes estranged from his or her self-understanding and vision of the world. However, the responsibility for the Other goes beyond ethics. The religious dimensions of becoming other than oneself in responsibility for the Other are supported by the Levinas's linking of ethical behavior with religious behavior. Annette Aronowicz writes:

> God here is not some dimension of the psyche, an entity of our inner life ... God, then, is a term whose meaning comes to light through an *ethical* stance, a defense of the specificity of the human being, the other man ... it is through *action*, not through the fixing of the idea of God in our mind, that the wholly Other, transcendent dimension is made accessible.[43]

Levinas's linking of God with ethical behavior toward the Other makes religious experience a moral experience; in turn, any transgressions against other people "are *ipso facto* offenses toward God."[44] God is not separable from responsibility for the Other and is present only in the giving of oneself over for the Other, in the becoming one-for-the-other.[45] Jeffrey Klosky writes that "for Levinas, God is inseparable from responsibility not as the other for whom I am responsible but as an other other, the other whose absence inclines me to responsibility for others."[46] Instead of God as fullness or plentitude, Levinas understands God to be an ever-receding trace or absence, the origin of the more that can always be thought about the Other. While philosophy may provide the understanding, this conception of religion provides a reason that is never exhausted, much like the effort it demands. Avoiding violence against the Other or working to provide justice for the Other is placed in the context of God's continuing revelation of the future to which God calls all humans. To deny otherness, which would take the form of resistance to change at both the personal and societal levels, would be to make an idol of the self and history.

In his articulation of a God who may be, Richard Kearney imagines a God who "offers us the possibility of realizing a promised kingdom" since "no die is cast, no course of action pre-ordained," leaving us free "to make the world a more just and loving place, or not to."[47] For the subject, there can be no doubt what the outcome of his or her other-directed efforts should be because they are modeled and endorsed in the texts that religious communities regard as holy. For Kearney, the Exodus story is a model of how the subject should respond to the encounter with the Other: "God commits Himself to a kingdom of justice if his faithful commit themselves to it too; the promise of Sinai calls forth a corresponding decision on behalf of the people."[48] There is no doubt that philosophy could explain and justify why the subject should direct his or her estrangement toward a more just society for those who do not share equally in the rights, goods, services, and freedoms that society offers. Moralistic language is used to challenge the development of new sciences and technologies because of the threat they pose to the common good. Nevertheless, the understanding of technology as an occasion to be in support of the neighbor, and of this support as both an ethical and religious obligation, shifts the focus of the debate away from vague and unspecified threats to the common good and toward practical matters that have a chance of addressing real and material suffering. If critical transhumanism retains the humanist idea of progress and restates it to go beyond it, then the idea of progress in critical transhumanism becomes a progress that is never finished. Progress becomes an effort with no end—there is always more that can be done. The transhumanist goal to realize human potential and increase well-being can only remain animated by an idea of God as potential and possibility that is never fully realized.

CONCLUSION

It is no small thing to redefine humanism as a task to be accomplished for the benefit of the Other and not merely as a way of identifying traits and characteristics all possess equally or in varying degrees. However worthy the task of redefining humanism as the pursuit of justice for those who are as human as the subject is, it will remain an irony that as long as humanism is a purely human affair, it will lack the moral force necessary to provide the motivation to establish more than what is already the case for those who remain marginalized and excluded. Paradoxically, when it is a purely human affair, humanism seems impossible. Regardless of how humanists have reduced the obligation of the individual, estrangement is a hard sell and too much of a burden to bear for an Other equal to the subject. That might represent a failure by posthumanists to demolish the humanist insistence that the subject is already autonomous, self-understanding, and historical or that the highest the human imagination can dream for the Other is equality, which, we would argue, is different from justice. Perhaps because of their failure to make the ethical dimensions of their critique more explicit and practical, posthumanists have not argued persuasively that the subject of humanist ideology is a myth and a construct. Consistently lowering the burden placed on the subject and consequently consistently lowering the bar for what an ethical response to the Other would look like have done nothing to call the subject outside of himself or herself.

Only when the command to become other is issued from on high or from beyond does it seem worth the subject's effort to become both estranged from himself or herself and obligated to the Other. Critical transhumanism is commanded from on high to be for the Other because the philosophical and religious questions raised by critical transhumanism are inseparable and are inherently ethical. Understanding what it means to be human is primordial for self-understanding and recognizing how to relate to others and the sacred. A change in how one experiences oneself necessitates a change in how one understands oneself. By changing how one understands oneself, one alters how one interacts with others and the sacred. For that interaction with others to be ethical, one has to change how one understands the Other. What the ethics of Emmanuel Levinas adds to transhumanism—better thought of as a critical transhumanism—is the notion that the effort to become transhuman is itself an ethical undertaking that can remain ethical only if one remains predisposed to the otherness of the Other. This predisposition to otherness is more demanding than Levinasian ethics indicates because the changes that transhumanists undergo to become transhuman resay categories that were thought impossible to say any other way. Resaying what it means to be human gives hope to those who have been excluded from the human community, suggesting that the community can come to them and offer them a place where they can be themselves. This will be a place where they can continue to be themselves, whatever form that may take. Here, justice for the Other will be guaranteed by the endless deferral and lack of closure of the question of what it means to be human.

NOTES

1. Ronald Cole-Turner, "Transhumanism and Christianity," in *Transhumanism and Transcendence*, edited by Ronald Cole-Turner (Washington, DC: Georgetown University Press, 2011), 194–195.

2. Jeanine Thweatt-Bates, *Cyborg Selves: A Theological Anthropology of the Posthuman* (Farnham, UK: Ashgate, 2012), 1.

3. Stephen Garner, "The Hopeful Cyborg," in *Transhumanism and Transcendence*, edited by Ronald Cole-Turner (Washington, DC: Georgetown University Press, 2011), 88.

4. Garner, "Hopeful Cyborg," 87.

5. Stephen Best and Douglas Kellner, *The Postmodern Adventure: Science, Technology and Cultural Studies at the Third Millennium* (New York, NY: Guilford Press, 2001), 181.

6. Thweatt-Bates, *Cyborg Selves*, 58.

7. Thweatt-Bates, *Cyborg Selves*, 58.

8. Nick Bostrom, "Transhumanist FAQ," *Humanity+*, section 20.4.

9. Bostrom, "Transhumanist FAQ," 20.1.

10. Jeanine Thweatt-Bates, "Artificial Wombs and Cyborg Births," in *Transhumanism and Transcendence*, edited by Ronald Cole-Turner (Washington, DC: Georgetown University Press, 2011), 111.

11. Neil Badmington, "Theorizing Posthumanism," *Cultural Critique* 53, no. 22 (2003): 22.

12. Noel Castree and Catherine Nash, "Posthuman Geographies," *Social and Cultural Geography*, 7, no. 4 (August 2006): 501–502.

13. Castree and Nash, "Posthuman Geographies," 501.

14. Castree and Nash, "Posthuman Geographies," 502.

15. Badmington, "Theorizing Posthumanism," 22.

16. Cf. Badmington, "Theorizing Posthumanism," 16.

17. Badmington, "Theorizing Posthumanism," 12; emphasis in original.

18. N. Katherine Hayles, "The Human in the Posthuman," *Cultural Critique* 53 (2003): 134.

19. Simon Critchley, *The Ethics of Deconstruction* (Edinburgh, UK: Edinburgh University Press, 1999), 286; emphasis in original.

20. Colin Davis, *After Poststructuralism: Reading, Stories and Theory* (New York, NY: Routledge, 2004), 83.

21. Simon Critchley, "Introduction," in *The Cambridge Companion to Levinas* (Cambridge, UK: Cambridge University Press, 2002), 18.

22. Best and Kellner, *Postmodern Adventure*, 151.

23. Best and Kellner, *Postmodern Adventure*, 152.

24. Silvia Benso, *The Face of Things: A Different Side of Ethics* (Albany, NY: State University of New York Press, 2000), 42.

25. Jill Robbins, ed., *Is It Righteous to Be? Interviews with Emmanuel Levinas* (Stanford, CA: Stanford University Press, 2002), 134.

26. Adriaan Peperzak, Simon Critchley, and Robert Bernasconi, eds., *Emmanuel Levinas: Basic Philosophical Writings*, (Bloomington, IN: Indiana University Press, 1996), 9.

27. Hava Tirosh-Samuelson, "Engaging Transhumanism," in *H±: Transhumanism and Its Critics* (Philadelphia, PA: Metanexus Institute, 2011), 42; emphasis in original.

28. Simon Critchley, "Prolegomena to any Post-Deconstructive Subjectivity," in *Deconstructive Subjectivity* (Albany, NY: State University of New York Press, 1996), 30.

29. Benso, *The Face of Things*, xxxi.

30. Benso, *The Face of Things*, 136.

31. Robbins, *Is It Righteous to Be?*, 117–118.

32. Cole-Turner, "Transhumanism," 198–199.

33. Simon Critchley and Peter Dews, "Introduction," in *Deconstructive Subjectivities* (Albany, NY: State University of New York Press, 1996), 9.

34. Colin Davis, *Levinas: An Introduction* (Oxford, UK: Blackwell, 1996), 52.

35. Adriaan Peperzak, *To the Other: An Introduction to the Philosophy of Emmanuel Levinas* (West Lafayette, IN: Purdue University Press, 1993), 229.

36. Peperzak, *To the Other.*

37. Cf. Francis Fukuyama, *Our Posthuman Future: Consequences of the Biotechnology Revolution* (New York, NY: Picador, 2003), 10.

38. Cf. Peperzak, *To the* Other, 116.

39. Robbins, *Is It Righteous To Be?*, 167.

40. Cf. Robbins, *Is It Righteous To Be?*, 134.

41. Robbins, *Is It Righteous To Be?*, 194.

42. Kearney, Richard, *The God Who May Be: A Hermeneutics of Religion* (Bloomington, IN: Indiana University Press, 2001), 108.

43. Emmanuel Levinas, *Nine Talmudic Readings by Emmanuel Levinas*, translated by Annette Aronowicz (Bloomington: Indiana University Press, 1990), xxiii; emphasis in original.

44. Levinas, *Nine Talmudic Readings*, 15–16; emphasis in original.

45. Cf. Emmanuel Levinas, *God, Death, and Time*, translated by Bettina Bergo (Stanford, CA: Stanford University Press, 2000), 203.

46. Jeffrey Klosky, "After the Death of God: Emmanuel Levinas and the Ethical Possibility of God," *Journal of Religious Ethics* 24, no. 2 (1996): 252.

47. Kearney, *The God Who May Be*, 2, 5.

48. Kearney, *The God Who May Be*, 29.

Section 5

Body Matters

. . . .

18

Return of the Corporeal Battle: How Second-Century Christology Struggles Inform the Transhumanism Debate

Lee A. Johnson

A consensus is forming that a moral dilemma looms for the Christian church over issues raised by transhumanism. For Ronald Cole-Turner, the problem in part is the self-centered nature of transhumanism, the proponents of which are "concerned chiefly with humanity above other species and with themselves among other humans."[1] Calvin Mercer imagines that both liberal and conservative Christians will voice objections over the more extreme transhuman scenarios, but that liberals' concern will focus on the inequity between the wealthy, who may be able to afford the various transhumanist therapies and procedures, and the poor, who cannot; the conservatives' objections, he speculates, will be based more on a general suspicion of science.[2] Francis Fukuyama describes transhumanism as one of "the world's most dangerous ideas"—an idolatrous and counterfeit religion.[3] Conversely, many transhumanists view religion as the enemy of progress, a roadblock with a blind commitment to ancient traditions that make no sense in modern society.[4]

Proponents of transhumanist scenarios put their hopes in procedures ranging from techniques that promise to arrest aging, replace body parts, and regenerate cells—all biological strategies that are bodily focused—to what has been described as "cybernetic immortality," in which the information in the brain is uploaded onto a computer so the "person" can exist in the virtual world.[5] En route to an entirely disembodied existence, technology will permit intelligence to be shared, minds to be connected to other minds and other devices, and communal rather than individual intellect to emerge.[6] This radical transhumanist vision, whose leading proponents include Hans Moravec and Ray Kurzweil, is addressed in this chapter, because the repudiation of the body presents perhaps the strongest challenge to modern Christian theology. This challenge is not new for the church, although it is framed in a new way. Somatic issues were also at the center of the second- and third-century church's theological formation. Battles were waged in that era over whether the body would be regarded as an essential aspect of Christian existence or whether it would be defined as a major hindrance to connection with the Divine.

In this chapter, I begin with a brief history of the early church's struggle to define orthodox belief, highlighting the prominence of gnostic Christian tradition in that era. Then, I will demonstrate that, with the rise of orthodox belief and practice, an emphasis on the centrality of the body emerged, with implications for the way the church would view the work of Jesus, the way the church would define the role of women, and the manner in which the church would recognize authority. Therefore, the somatic battles of the early church—resulting in an emerging orthodoxy, but at the same time rejecting some of its foundational beliefs and practices—should serve as a cautionary tale for the current debates within the church over transhumanism.

BRIEF SURVEY OF GNOSTICISM
AND PROTO-ORTHODOXY[7]

In transhumanism, "old heresies have found a new voice," according to Brent Waters. He correctly notes that Christian theology historically has affirmed the goodness of the body, while proponents of transhumanism reflect a vision that denigrates the body.[8] The "old heresies" to which Waters refers take shape in the third and fourth centuries CE. However, the story can be traced earlier, within the first two centuries after Jesus, when the lines between orthodoxy and heresy were not yet drawn. More than any other scholar, Elaine Pagels has shed light upon the tenuous nature of the first- and second-century CE theological beliefs, seemingly so foundational in today's church.[9] Her findings sent shock waves throughout the world of biblical studies: "What we call Christianity—and what we identify as Christian tradition —actually represents only a small selection of specific sources, chosen from among dozens of others."[10]

Pagels's scholarship arose out of a monumental document discovery in Nag Hammadi, Egypt, in 1945 that included 52 manuscripts, written in Coptic around 350 CE and comprising translations of Greek writings dated as early as 50–100 CE.[11] These texts include such important finds as the *Gospel of Thomas*, the *Gospel of Truth*, the *Gospel to the Egyptians*, the *Secret Book of James*, the *Apocalypse of Paul*, the *Gospel of Mary*, and the *Apocalypse of Peter*. The date of the composition of the Nag Hammadi documents coincides with the time of Christianity's rise to the place of an officially sanctioned religion under the Emperor Constantine. At his insistence, Christianity was transformed from a religious movement without a clearly defined Christology and without a canon into the official religion of the empire, complete with official sacred writings, a prescribed Christology and theology, and—to the point of this chapter—clearly defined heresies. The Nag Hammadi collection consists of some of those writings dubbed as heretical under the rule of Constantine. Texts that had heretofore been sacred works to many Christians now were banned by the state in the fourth century and had to be destroyed or hidden.

Before the discovery in the 1940s, many of these writings were known in part through their counter-voice, which appeared in the voluminous works by church fathers such as Irenaeus and Hippolytus, who challenged what they describe as "heresies" or "so-called knowledge."[12] The vehemence and determination with which these "church fathers" attacked this "heresy" affirm the power that these texts held in the early church. Irenaeus himself bemoans the fact that these writings had enjoyed wide support from numerous people in places throughout the Roman world.[13]

The general term for the belief system that Irenaeus and Hippolytus refuted is "gnosticism," from the Greek word *gnosis*, meaning "knowledge." Not all of the Nag Hammadi texts have been officially categorized as gnostic, but those that have been present a view of Jesus and humanity that is markedly different from the proto-orthodox perspective of the church.[14] A foundational aspect of gnostic thought has ties to neo-Platonic thought that envisions the metaphysical as the true reality, with the result that the physical, observable, corporeal aspect of life is denigrated.[15] This notion informs gnostic theology, Christology, and religious practice in numerous ways that conflict with proto-orthodoxy in the second century CE.

Foundational to gnostic understanding of the cosmos is the belief that divine nature is antithetical to the physical world. Therefore, that which is from the divine or spiritual realm would not inhabit the physical world in a tangible sense. In this sense, gnosticism's theology can be termed anticorporeal. One implication of an anticorporeal theology is the rejection of the notion of a bodily resurrection, both for Jesus and for Christians. The *Gospel of Philip* claims that only the ignorant would assume that resurrection is to be taken as a literal event. "Resurrection" is a term that describes what one should experience while he or she lives.[16] Similarly, although Jesus's followers encounter him after his death in the *Gospel of Mary*, they meet him in a vision, rather than physically (17.8–15). In contrast, Luke's gospel describes Jesus' post-crucifixion appearances in a way that stresses Jesus's corporeal resurrection:

> They were startled and terrified, and thought that they were seeing a ghost. He said to them, "Why are you frightened, and why do doubts arise in your hearts? Look at my hands and my feet; see that it is I myself. Touch me and see; for a ghost does not have flesh and bones as you see that I have." And when

he had said this, he showed them his hands and his feet. While in their joy they were disbelieving and still wondering, he said to them, "Have you anything here to eat?" They gave him a piece of broiled fish, and he took it and ate in their presence. (24:37–43)[17]

John's gospel also confirms both that there has been a bodily resurrection and that it is one and the same Jesus whom his disciples knew: "A week later his disciples were again in the house, and Thomas was with them. Although the doors were shut, Jesus came and stood among them and said, 'Peace be with you.' Then he said to Thomas, 'Put your finger here and see my hands. Reach out your hand and put it in my side. Do not doubt but believe'" (20:26–27).

Consistent with their view that Jesus was not physically resurrected, the gnostics did not believe that Christians would experience a literal resurrection. Rather than a bodily experience, the sense of resurrection they perceived is an enlightened state, a "migration into newness."[18] Tertullian, a second-century proto-orthodox writer, admits that the notion of a flesh-and-blood resurrection flies in the face of the conventional thought of his day. Even some who called themselves Christians could not accept this tenet; as Tertullian explains, "They find the whole idea extremely revolting, repugnant, and impossible."[19] It is likely that Paul found such resistance to a bodily resurrection in Corinth. He posed the oppositional question himself: "But someone will ask, 'How are the dead raised? With what kind of body do they come?'" (1 Corinthians 15:35). Paul used the analogy of heavenly bodies to explain how a resurrected body can be still be considered a body, even though it is of a different composition than the mortal body that dies. The earthly body is perishable, dishonorable, weak, physical, of the dust; by comparison, the heavenly body is imperishable, glorious, powerful, spiritual, heavenly (v. 42–49).[20] Nevertheless, in Paul's view, the resurrection will involve a body—and that is a confounding notion for the Corinthians and most other persons in the ancient Mediterranean world.[21]

The gnostics' disdain for the body also led them to reject the soteriology of Jesus's sacrificial atonement. A suffering, dying deity was antithetical to gnostic thought, as was the redemptive action of Jesus's physical struggle on the cross. Therefore, Jesus's raw agony on the cross, which is described in Mark's gospel with his plea, "My God, my God, why have you forsaken me?" (15:34), is an illusion. Gnostics argued that Jesus merely appeared to suffer; the divine being left the shell of the body on the cross and this cry of dereliction arises from the abandoned body that remained. The belief that the divine Jesus did not experience bodily pain, emotion, or passion is called docetism, from the Greek verb *dokeō*, meaning "to seem" or "to appear." Thus Jesus only seemed to be suffering; in actuality, a divine being would never do so.[22]

The noncanonical *Apocalypse of Peter* has a passion narrative that explains the docetic event:

> And I said, "What am I seeing, O, Lord? Is it really you whom they take? And are you holding on to me? And are they hammering the feet and the hands of another? Who is this one above the cross, who is glad and laughing?" The Savior said to me, "He whom you saw being glad and laughing above the cross is the Living Jesus. But he into whose hands and feet they are driving the nails is his fleshly part, which is the substitute. They put to shame that which remained in his likeness. And look at him, and [look at] me!" (81.4–24)[23]

A similar description appears in the *Second Treatise of the Great Seth*, in which Christ states:

> It was another ... who drank the gall and the vinegar; it was not I. They struck me with the reed; it was another, Simon, who bore the cross on his shoulder. It was another upon whom they placed the crown of thorns. But I was rejoicing in the height over ... their error ... And I was laughing at their ignorance. (56.6–19)[24]

The canonical gospels of Luke and John strike a middle ground. These accounts do not contain the cry of dereliction in Mark; rather, they adhere to the vision of a crucified Jesus, but one who expires under his own volition. In the midst of his crucifixion in the Lukan narrative, Jesus consoles one of the criminals who hangs beside him ("Today you will be with me in Paradise") before he delivers himself to God: "Father, into your hands I commend my spirit" (23:43–46). John's account describes a crucified Jesus who attends to the last fulfillment of scripture by proclaiming his thirst so that sour wine would be offered to him before he pronounces, "It is finished" (19:28–29).

It follows that as gnostics rejected Christologies that relied upon the physical death and resurrection of Jesus, they held consistent views of the human body—a general disdain for the flesh. However, this gnostic unanimity of rejecting the flesh manifested itself in contrasting praxes by different persons of faith. One view held that the body and its desires are antithetical to the spark of divine nature that exists in every person. Thus, the more one is able to suppress one's physical appetites, the more one can cultivate the divine.[25] The alternative view proposed that the body is of no consequence; therefore, it is of no concern how one treats the body. It would appear that these two perspectives were being lived out simultaneously in Corinth, wherein a man was condemned by Paul for having sex with his father's wife (1 Corinthians 5:1–5), and ascetic married couples were encouraged by Paul not to abstain from sexual relations for more than an agreed-upon time (1 Corinthians 7:1–7).[26] Paul's enthusiasm for sexual asceticism was stronger for the

unmarried. He endorsed living celibate as he did (1 Corinthians 7:7), but con-
ceded that the persons who marry and have sex within that relationship do
not sin (1 Corinthians 7:28).

Contrary to the affirmations that Paul gave (i.e., those mistakenly attributed to him) to those who live sexually ascetic lives, the authors of the disputed Pauline letters assume that procreation is central to life in the early
church. Colossians and Ephesians[27] contain *Haustafeln* ("household codes"
are lists of instructions for members of the household intended to ensure order
that appear in Hellenistic philosophical writings before and during the New
Testament era) that delineate the proper hierarchy within the household—a
hierarchy that is replicated in the city, the empire, and the cosmos.[28]
Directives in *Haustafeln* are given to men, women, children, and slaves, with
the intent to ensure that proper order is maintained. Wives are charged to
be subordinate to their husbands in everything (Ephesians 5:24), while the
husbands are commanded to love their wives (5:25). The social ideal for these
letter-writers is marriage, whereas Paul's desire for everyone in his churches is
celibacy: "I wish that all were as I myself am" (1 Corinthians 7:7).

The contrast between Paul's ascetic wish for the Corinthians and the directives in the Pastoral Epistles (generally accepted as not written by Paul)[29] is
even more striking. First Timothy lists a wife as one of the requisites for a
man who aspires to the office of bishop in the church: "married only once"
(3: 2) and able to "manage his own household" (3: 4). The nuptial imperative
is even stronger for women in this letter. Assumed to be under condemnation
vis-à-vis Eve's failure in the Garden of Eden, their very salvation rests upon
marriage and procreation. "[The wife] will be saved through childbearing, provided they continue in faith and love and holiness, with modesty" (1 Timothy
2:15). The path to honor for all women is likewise clear in the letter to Titus:
older women exist to set an example for the younger women to be "submissive
to their husbands," without which order the "word of God" may be "discredited" (Titus 2:5).[30]

All of the disputed Pauline letters assume that men and women will marry
and procreate. Moreover, as the preceding examples reveal, the penalty for
women who did not follow this prescribed path was dire. These writings date
from 80 to 120 CE, which implies a trajectory away from the ascetic preferences of Paul in the Corinthian correspondence in the mid-50s. In fact, literature from the second century shows increased scrutiny being directed toward
the role of women in Christian churches. The widely popular second-century
noncanonical work, the *Acts of Paul and Thecla*, can be described as a moral
tale about the decision of a young woman to follow the path that allows her
to live according to Paul's suggestion to the Corinthians: "And the unmarried
woman and the virgin are anxious about the affairs of the Lord, so that they
may be holy in body and spirit" (1 Corinthians 7:34). Thecla, the heroine

of this story, is a young woman who breaks off her engagement with her fiancée so that she can pursue a life as an itinerant gospel preacher. She is inspired to do so when she hears Paul speaking in Iconium. He gives his own list of Beatitudes, of which the following inspired Thecla's repudiation of her pending nuptials:

> Blessed are they that keep the flesh chaste, for they shall become the temple of God.
> Blessed are they that abstain (or the continent), for unto them shall God speak.
> Blessed are they that have renounced this world, for they shall be well-pleasing unto God.
> Blessed are they that possess their wives as though they had them not, for they shall inherit God. (*Acts of Paul and Thecla* II.5)[31]

Thecla's decision to live a chaste life and follow Paul provokes rage in her fiancée and her mother, both of whom seek violent revenge upon Thecla. She has narrow escapes with danger, several of which involve attempts to violate her purity. The story concludes with her success against all odds to pursue her life as a chaste young woman, devoted solely to Christ.[32]

An intriguing aspect of the story of Thecla is that she assumes masculine characteristics to facilitate her mission. She alters her outer garment "into a cloak after the fashion of a man" (II.40) and cuts her hair "round about" (II.25).[33] There are two other notable passages, from the Nag Hammadi discovery, that associate androgyny with spiritual advancement. The first is the final saying of Jesus in the Gospel of Thomas: Simon Peter said to them, "Make Mary leave us, for females don't deserve life." Jesus said, "Look, I will guide her to make her male, so that she too may become a living spirit resembling you males. For every female who makes herself male will enter the kingdom of Heaven" (114).[34] The gnostic *Gospel of Mary* records a similar debate over Mary's inherent ability to achieve an advanced level of spiritual insight. Following Jesus' departure, Mary addresses the male disciples;

> Then Mary stood up, greeted them all, and said to her brethren, Do not weep and do not grieve nor be irresolute, for His grace will be entirely with you and will protect you. But rather, let us praise His greatness, for He has prepared us and made us into Men. When Mary said this, she turned their hearts to the Good, and they began to discuss the words of the Savior. (5.2–4)[35]

Note that Mary includes herself in the group of those who had been "made into men." With this saying, she provokes an exegetical discussion.

Following this moment in the narrative, Mary reveals an exclusive vision she received from Jesus. The reaction of the male disciples reveals their ambivalence about her veracity due to her gender:

When Mary had said this, she fell silent, since it was to this point that the Savior had spoken with her. But Andrew answered and said to the brethren, "Say what you wish to say about what she has said. I at least do not believe that the Savior said this. For certainly these teachings are strange ideas." Peter answered and spoke concerning these same things. He questioned them about the Savior: "Did He really speak privately with a woman and not openly to us? Are we to turn about and all listen to her? Did He prefer her to us?" Then Mary wept and said to Peter, "My brother Peter, what do you think? Do you think that I have thought this up myself in my heart, or that I am lying about the Savior?" Levi answered and said to Peter, "Peter you have always been hot tempered. Now I see you contending against the woman like the adversaries. But if the Savior made her worthy, who are you indeed to reject her? Surely the Savior knows her very well." (9.1–8)

Valentinus is perhaps the most prominent of the gnostic teachers of the second century CE. His teachings on the radical reformation of the cosmos reveal his views of the human body. Those who possess knowledge are undergoing, both in body and in spirit, a radical separation from the bondage of the physical world. Separation of the sexes was a symptom of the devolution of the cosmos. Therefore, at the first stage of redemption, the female would be given a male form, absorbed back into the unity that was before. At the second stage, the "polarity of male and female itself would be abolished."[36]

The Montanist gnostic movement also flourished during the second century CE, under the eponymous Montanus who traveled and taught with two women disciples, Priscilla and Maximilla. Claiming to have direct and ongoing revelation from the Spirit, they composed their visions into new sacred texts. They believed that ascetic practices encouraged the Spirit's indwelling and, therefore, encouraged their followers to set themselves on a path that would lead to their own revelations. It was apparent to the Montanists that the Spirit did not discriminate on the basis of gender, so their community did not function with a gender-based hierarchy. While their egalitarian organization was a point of contrast with the proto-orthodox communities, the gnostic apologists did not seek to ameliorate this difference. Several gnostic writers emphasize the distinction between their egalitarian-formed communities and the hierarchical-based proto-orthodox church. For example, the anonymous *Apocalypse of Peter* mocks the authority that the church officials claim: bishops and deacons are nothing more than "waterless canals."[37] A voice from the Valentinians (another gnostic community from the second century) contrasted his community of gnostics—"children of the Father," who function as equals and with mutuality—with "ordinary Christians," who "want[ed] to command one another, outrivaling one another in their empty ambition."[38]

The egalitarian nature of the gnostic communities met with considerable opposition from the proto-orthodox group in the second century. Tertullian criticized their lack of fixed church order. Deemed particularly objectionable was the unimpeded participation of women in their community: "They teach, they engage in discussion; they exorcise; they cure." Tertullian even suggested that women had the temerity to engage in baptism, which means that they assumed the role reserved for bishops in the proto-orthodox church.[39] Church father Irenaeus likewise took up the charge against the "apostate" gnostics. Noting the fluid nature of leadership in the suspect communities, he suggested they were susceptible to false priests who did not act with the spirit of God. The way to combat this risk was to follow the agreed-upon lines of apostolic succession that had taken hold early on in the proto-orthodox church. In essence, Irenaeus believed that Peter and the other disciples received authority that was passed on to them by Jesus (Matthew 28:18–20); thus, leadership in the church in perpetuity is bestowed from one chosen leader to another. Every bishop in the church can trace a heritage back to Peter. In this way, the church leadership "receive[s] simultaneously with the episcopal succession the sure gift of truth."[40]

Elaine Pagels notes the political implications of the struggle between the experientially authenticated membership of the gnostic communities, which welcomed women into leadership roles, and the lineage-authenticated membership, which selected its leaders based on their confirmation by previous bishops.[41] Although numerous aspects of the gnostic church ecclesiology were proclaimed as heretical by proto-orthodox churches, the role of women in leadership roles was the most readily observable violation and, therefore, became the litmus test for determining an "outlaw" church. The introduction of household codes into letters bearing Paul's name (Colossians, Ephesians) and the straightforward relegation of women to the roles of wife and child-bearer (1 Timothy 2:8–15; Titus 2:3–5) became the image of female perfection in the proto-orthodox church. This vision left no room either for the virgin in Corinth whom Paul encouraged to "remain as she is" (1 Corinthians 7:8) or for the heroic Thecla, who battled her mother, fiancée, civic leaders, and numerous wild beasts that sought to make her conform to the role of wife and mother. The perspectives of honorable women of the first and second centuries who sought to suppress the body was subsumed by the vision of the honorable woman who loves her husband and children and is self-controlled, chaste, a good manager of the household, kind, and submissive to her husband (Titus 2:4–5).

KEY POINTS OF CORPOREAL CONTROVERSY
IN THE SECOND CENTURY

This journey through early church conflicts reveals a number of controversies, all involving the place of the body. The proto-orthodox view, I will argue, consistently confirms the necessity of the body, whereas the gnostic view challenges the centrality (and necessity) of the body. The proto-orthodox view eventually won the battle over the body, and the church's conviction of the necessity of the body shaped the way Christians still think about Jesus, the world, and the church. A look at second-century Christian struggles reveals several salient points of commonality with contemporary questions raised by transhumanism: the central role of the body in defining humanity, the central role of the body in theology and Christology, the procreative process as a means of defining social and cultural roles for women, and the role of the body in establishing an authoritative structure in society.

Centrality of the Human Body

Paul's letters, written in the 50s, reveal his struggle to respond to his congregants' questions about how they should think about their bodies now that they are "new creatures" in Christ. He refused to side entirely with the strong in Corinth, who claimed that "it is well for a man not to touch a woman" (1 Corinthians 7:1). Paul admitted that this was his view, but also saw that marriage featuring sexual relations within that marriage was an acceptable choice for many in the church. In what is hardly a resounding endorsement, he stated that if engaged couples go ahead and marry, "it is no sin" (1 Corinthians 7:36). He went on to make a rather tortured argument for a bodily resurrection in 1 Corinthians 15. Using analogies from agriculture, zoology, and astronomy, he insisted that resurrection includes a new, if changed, body (v. 35–49). Paul is also fond of using the body as an analogy for the church. In 1 Corinthians 12:12–27, he describes the many parts of the body in the midst of his argument about how the members of the Corinthian community were to relate to one another. Although there is an order of importance, Paul argued for interdependence and necessity of all the members of the body. He replicated this argument in Romans 12:3–8. In short, Paul affirmed the centrality of the body in the life of the church, although he imagined that the role of the body at the advent of the *parousia* (Jesus's second coming) would be dramatically different.

In the second-century canonical (i.e., Pastoral Epistles) view of the body, the lines were more clearly drawn than in Paul's day. These writings should be read as a counterpoint to the gnostic writings that repudiate the body. First Timothy and Titus both have the same impetus for writing—they seek to define the church leadership through males who procreate and control the use of their own bodies as well as their families' bodies. The proto-orthodox view of the body is one of necessity. Whereas gnostics imagined that their congregants were experiencing resurrection in a mystical sense, the proto-orthodox argued for a bodily resurrection to come. In other words, human life cannot be separated from the corporeal existence, including life after death.

Centrality of the Body in Christology

The prologue of John's gospel is a common starting point for the discussion of Christology and was one of the writings that was adopted by both gnostic and proto-orthodox communities. The proto-orthodox church pointed to John 1:14, "the word (*logos*) *became* flesh," as a foundational text to support the notion of the incarnation of God. The gnostics, for their part, focused on the connection of *logos* to eternal *Sophia* (wisdom). Mark's gospel stresses Jesus's humanity though his emotions (3:5), his inability to know the future (13:32), his stress before his arrest (14:33–36), and his cry of anguish at his death (15:34).[42] Both Paul and the gospels affirm Jesus's resurrection, with Luke and John providing evidence that Jesus inhabited the same physical body after his resurrection. Thomas is encouraged to put his fingers in Jesus's pierced side (John 20:27), and the disciples touch him and eat with him at the end of Luke (24:36–43).

In the second century, the proto-orthodox church declared docetism heretical, naming those who claimed that Jesus did not become human, suffer, die, and rise from the dead in a bodily sense as enemies of the truth. Both Ignatius and Justin connect Jesus's suffering and death with the persecutions that some second-century Christians were undergoing. Without Jesus's purposeful suffering, their current hardships were rendered meaningless. Justin Martyr attacks the gnostics as heretics, suggesting that their lack of persecution signals their false beliefs.[43] Pagels summarizes the historical advantage that the proto-orthodox adherence to somatic Christology reaped:

> Orthodox tradition implicitly affirms bodily experience as the central fact of human life. What one does physically—one eats and drinks, engages in sexual life or avoids it, saves one's life or gives it up—all are vital elements in one's *religious* development. But those gnostics who regarded the essential part of every person as the "inner spirit" dismissed such physical experience, pleasurable or painful, as a distraction from spiritual reality—indeed, as an illusion. No wonder, then, that far more people identified with the orthodox portrait than with the "bodiless spirit" of gnostic tradition. Not only the martyrs, but all Christians who have suffered for 2,000 years, who have feared and faced death, have found their experience validated in the story of the *human* Jesus.[44]

The Body and Women

The participation of women in leadership roles in the church diminished from a robust involvement in the Pauline churches to extremely limited leadership roles in the second and third centuries CE. In part because Paul advocated for an ascetic life for both men and women, we see that women were itinerant preachers of the gospel (e.g., Priscilla, Romans 16:3–4), carried the title of "apostle" (Junia, Romans 16:7), and acted as patrons for Paul's mission (Phoebe, Romans 16:1–2). Paul mentions numerous women who appear without a male counterpart, indicating they were involved in the spread of the gospel as unattached females.[45] These women stand in stark contrast to the ideal women as presented in the Pastoral Epistles, who are commanded to be in subjection to their husbands, bearing children to overcome their condemnation through their ancestor Eve.[46] As reviewed earlier, ascetic practices, particularly for women, became associated with gnostic heresies, and those who did not marry or attempted to assume the typical male role of apostle met with strong social and ecclesial opposition. Procreation became a foundational value for women—indeed, a means of salvation.

The Body and Politics and Power

By the end of the second century, theology of the body became a determining factor in the battle to establish an orthodox church. Pagels notes how the spontaneous, charismatic, open leadership model of gnostic churches challenged the male-dominated leadership of the proto-orthodox church that defined authority through "apostolic succession."[47] The notion that any spiritually inspired person—even a woman—might stand with the same authority as one of the male apostles in Jesus' inner circle posed a true threat to the organized church in the second century. Proto-orthodoxy claimed that one needed to stand in a genealogical line back to the physical body of Jesus to be instated as a bishop in the church. In contrast, any person who encountered the Lord in visions could claim authority among the gnostics. The link to the body for the proto-orthodox was their claim to authority in the church.

THE SECOND-CENTURY BATTLE FOR THE BODY MEETS THE TRANSHUMANIST DEBATE

Under entirely different circumstances, the church in the 21st century finds itself in a battle over the meaning of the body. Tissue and organ replacement, nanotechnology, and robotics have become commonplace in current society. However, with the advent of mind/computer interface and cybernetic immortality, the church will face another crisis of identity. In the second century, the battle lines for the church's identity were drawn over the interpretation of the body; more specifically, belief in the *bodily* resurrection was equated with orthodoxy, whereas rejection of the bodily resurrection defined one as a heretic.[48] However, it is clear that the ramifications of one's decision about this seemingly narrow issue extended into such disparate arenas as Christology, ecclesial authority, and the procreative value of women. At the same time that the church was embracing the body, it was rejecting several concepts through a chain of connectivity to this single question.

What was left behind in the second century is readily apparent in the Christological emphasis of the Nicene and Apostles' Creeds, common confessions of faith for Christians that were composed in the first three centuries of the church.[49] In these foundational statements for the Christian faith, Jesus's import is reduced to his incarnation, death, and resurrection. Despite the wealth of information about Jesus's earthly life and mission, these creeds omit everything between the birth and the arrest. Following are the sections from each creed that address the person of Jesus:

The Nicene Creed
We believe in one Lord, Jesus Christ,
the only Son of God,
eternally begotten of the Father,
God from God, Light from Light,
true God from true God,
begotten, not made,
of one Being with the Father.
Through him all things were made.
For us and for our salvation
he came down from heaven:
by the power of the Holy Spirit
he became incarnate from the Virgin Mary,
and was made man.
For our sake he was crucified under Pontius Pilate;
he suffered death and was buried.
On the third day he rose again
in accordance with the Scriptures;
he ascended into heaven
and is seated at the right hand of the Father.
He will come again in glory to judge the living and the dead,
and his kingdom will have no end.

Apostles Creed
I believe in Jesus Christ, God's only Son, our Lord,
who was conceived by the Holy Spirit,
born of the Virgin Mary,
suffered under Pontius Pilate,
was crucified, died, and was buried;
he descended to the dead.
On the third day he rose again; he ascended into heaven,
he is seated at the right hand of the Father,
and he will come again to judge the living and the dead.

Orthodox belief about Jesus was defined by acceptance of his incarnate birth, his corporeal suffering and death, and his bodily resurrection. Christology related to Jesus's earthly activities, mission, and life are largely lost in this Christological construct. The present-day implications of these creedal emphases are readily apparent. Numerous Christian churches today define Jesus's worth largely on the basis of his suffering, death, and resurrection. In this Christology, Jesus's birth is significant because it allows him to die a sacrificial death approximately 30 years later.

The early church also left behind the contribution of women as another consequence of its focus on the body. Women's value became located primarily in their procreative potential. As a result, the voices of the Pastoral Epistles—women should be subordinate to their husbands, will be redeemed through bearing children, and do not have authority to teach—drowned out the women in Paul's communities who were named as apostles, patrons, co-workers, and leaders. Paul's suggestion that the best way for both men and women to serve the Lord was to remain single was largely ignored. Thecla, the heroine of the *Acts of Paul and Thecla*, who battled both family and beasts to preserve her chastity and follow Paul in single-minded devotion to Christ, was rejected by the early church, and along with her, other Christian women who sought to preach, prophesy, and teach the gospel. Jeanine Thweatt-Bates's work on "postgenderism and theology" addresses the argument made by proponents of transhumanism that certain injustices, such as patriarchy and heterosexism, can be eliminated by transhumanism.[50] They argue that if gender is "a bodily reality that negatively limits the full potential of the human person," then transhumanism should allow people to select the biological traits that they value, thereby allowing equality of access to any human traits to both men and women. However, Thweatt-Bates calls attention to the fact that previously ingrained societal preferences would prove prejudicial toward self-selection of traditional male attributes.

The proto-orthodox church also left behind much of the egalitarian ethos of the Pauline churches in the first century. By establishing authority through apostolic succession, carried out in the physical act of laying on of hands, it discredited the spirit-driven authority of the gnostic communities. The proto-orthodox authority ensured that its authority would rest with men and would be hereafter guarded and directed by a hierarchy of men as well.

With the rise of transhumanism, the church faces a corporeal challenge once again. The lines between "mainstream" and "radical" theology will be drawn based up the centrality of the body in defining what it means to be human. This chapter does not advocate for a particular position for the church with respect to the body and transhumanism. Rather, I urge the church to revisit its own history. The proto-orthodox church's emphasis upon somatic theology sacrificed, whether with clear intention or not, some of the vision of the Jesus of the gospels and of the Pauline letters. The church of the 21st century should soberly survey the landscape of the theology that either embraces or rejects transhumanism. Ecclesial history teaches us that decisions about the body have far-reaching and lasting effects for the life of the church.

NOTES

1. Ronald Cole-Turner, "Transhumanism and Christianity," in *Transhumanism and Transcendence: Christian Hope in an Age of Technological Enhancement*, edited by Ronald Cole-Turner (Washington, DC: Georgetown University Press, 2011), 198.

2. Calvin Mercer, "Sorting out *Soma* in the Debate about Transhumanism: One Protestant's Perspective," in *Transhumanism and the Body: The World Religions Speak*, edited by Calvin Mercer and Derek Maher (New York, NY: Palgrave Macmillan, forthcoming 2014).

3. Francis Fukuyama, "The World's Most Dangerous Ideas: Transhumanism," *Foreign Policy* 144 (2004): 42.

4. Ted Peters, "Progress and Provolution: Will Transhumanism Leave Sin Behind?," in *Transhumanism and Transcendence: Christian Hope in an Age of Technological Enhancement*, edited by Ronald Cole-Turner (Washington, DC: Georgetown University Press, 2011), 72.

5. Ronald Cole-Turner, "Extreme Longevity Research: A Progressive Protestant Perspective," in *Religion and the Implications of Radical Life Extension*, edited by Derek Maher and Calvin Mercer (New York, NY: Palgrave Macmillan, 2009), 53.

6. Pete Estep, "The Evidence-Based Pursuit of Radical Life Extension," in *Religion and the Implications of Radical Life Extension*, edited by Derek Maher and Calvin Mercer (New York, NY: Palgrave Macmillan, 2009), 32.

7. "Proto-orthodox" is a term used to describe the belief system that eventually became accepted as the orthodox view of the church in the era when that determination of correctness had not yet occurred.

8. Brent Waters, "Whose Salvation? Which Eschatology? Transhumanism and Christianity as Contending Salvific Religions," in *Transhumanism and Transcendence: Christian Hope in an Age of Technological Enhancement*, edited by Ronald Cole-Turner (Washington, DC: Georgetown University Press, 2011), 171.

9. Elaine Pagels has written two key works that describe the struggle for orthodoxy in the early church vis-à-vis the gnostic writings and the New Testament texts: *The Gnostic Gospels* (New York, NY: Random House, 1979) and *The Gnostic Paul: Gnostic Exegesis of the Pauline Letters* (Harrisburg, PA: Trinity Press International, 1975).

10. Pagels, *The Gnostic Gospels*, xxxviii.

11. Pagels, *The Gnostic Gospels*, xv–xvi.

12. Irenaeus (c. 180) wrote five volumes entitled *The Destruction and Overthrow of Falsely So-Called Knowledge*; Hippolytus (c. 230) wrote the *Refutation of All Heresies*.

13. Pagels, *The Gnostic Gospels*, xv.

14. Gnosticism as a movement is notoriously difficult to define. A survey of gnostic texts will show a range of beliefs about Jesus, God, and the world. For the purposes of this chapter, some basic tenets of gnostic thought will be highlighted that are emblematic of the conflict that the gnostic followers had with the proto-orthodox movement. I write with the caveat that none of these statements represents the entirety of gnosticism in the early church.

15. Plato's *Timaeus* describes the body as a means of conveyance that carries and supports the head (44D). See Dale E. Martin, *The Corinthian Body* (New Haven, CT: Yale University Press, 1995), 30.

16. Pagels, *The Gnostic Gospels*, 13–14.

17. All citations are from the New Revised Standard Version of the Bible.

18. *Treatise on Resurrection* 48: 34–38 (cited in Pagels, *The Gnostic Gospels*, 14).

19. *De Carne Christi* 5 (cited in Pagels, *The Gnostic Gospels*, 5).

20. Martin, *The Corinthian Body*, 114–127.

21. Martin argues that a bodily resurrection would be seen by upper-class, educated persons in Paul's day as something akin to superstitious belief that would be held by ignorant, lower-class persons. Therefore, the "strong" in Corinth would reject this assumption (*The Corinthian Body*, 107–108).

22. Docetism is considered a subset of gnosticism. There were Christians in the second and third centuries who did not accept the fact that Jesus as a divine being would suffer. Gnostics would have adhered to this belief but may not have focused as much on this particular aspect of Christology.

23. Pagels, *The Gnostic Gospels*, 86–87.

24. Pagels, *The Gnostic Gospels*, 87.

25. A clear example of this perspective is found in the Nag Hammadi text *Zostrianos*, named after a spiritual master who describes his path to enlightenment as starting with removing his physical desires (Pagels, *The Gnostic Gospels*, 163).

26. Richard A. Horsley, "Spiritual Marriage with Sophia," *Vigiliae Christianae* 33 (1979): 30–54.

27. The majority of biblical scholars do not accept Pauline authorship of Colossians and Ephesians and date these letters to the late first century CE.

28. Colossians 3:18–4:1; Ephesians 5:21–6:9. See Margaret Y. MacDonald, "Citizens of Heaven and Earth: Asceticism and Social Integration in Colossians and Ephesians," in *Asceticism and the New Testament*, edited by Leif E. Vaage and Vincent L. Wimbush (New York, NY: Routledge, 1999), 269–298.

29. There are six letters in the New Testament that are claimed to be written by Paul, but whose authorship is in dispute—2 Thessalonians, Colossians, Ephesians, 1 and 2 Timothy, and Titus. These letters are believed to be composed between 80 and 120 CE. First and Second Timothy and Titus constitute a subset of disputed letters called the Pastoral Epistles. These three letters are dated as the latest of the disputed Paul letters—between 100 and 20 CE—and Pauline authorship of these three is largely rejected by biblical scholars.

30. David L. Balch, *Let Wives Be Submissive: The Domestic Code in 1 Peter*, SBLMS 26 (Chico, CA: Scholars Press, 1981).

31. Translation and notes by M. R. James, *The Apocryphal New Testament* (Oxford, UK: Clarendon Press, 1924).

32. Dennis Ronald MacDonald argues that the directives toward women in the Pastoral Epistles are written to counter the wide popularity that the *Acts of Paul and Thecla* held in the second century CE. See The Legend and the Apostle: The Battle for Paul in Story and Canon (Louisville, KY: Westminster John Knox Press, 1983).

33. Margaret Y. MacDonald, "Was Celsus Right? The Role of Women in the Expansion of Early Christianity," in *Early Christian Families in Context: An Interdisciplinary Dialogue*, edited by David L. Balch and Carolyn Osiek (Grand Rapids, MI: William B. Eerdmans, 2003), 183.

34. Scholars Version translation of the Gospel of Thomas by Stephen Patterson and Marvin Meyer in *The Complete Gospels: Annotated Scholars Version* (Salem, OR: Polebridge Press, 1992).

35. Translation from Peter Kirby, "Gospel of Mary," *Early Christian Writings*, March 29, 2014, http://www.earlychristianwritings.com/text/gospelmary.html.

36. Peter Brown, *The Body and Society: Men, Women, and Sexual Renunciation in Early Christianity* (New York, NY: Columbia University Press, 1988), 111.

37. 79.22–30, cited in Pagels, *The Gnostic Gospels*, 48.

38. From the *Tripartite Tractate* 69.7–10, cited in Pagels, *The Gnostic Gospels*, 48.

39. *De Praescriptione Haereticorum* 42, cited in Pagels, *The Gnostic Gospels*, 50.

40. Irenaeus, *Libros Quinque Adversus Haereses* 4.26.3, cited in Pagels, *The Gnostic Gospels*, 54.

41. Pagels, *The Gnostic Gospels*, 14–16.

42. Other gospel writers do not show Jesus's humanity to this extent: see the parallel passages in Matthew and Luke to Mark 3:1–6, where Jesus's anger is redacted, and the parallel passages in Matthew and Luke to Mark 13:32, where Luke omits this verse altogether and Matthew has textual variants that remove the phrase that says that the son does not know. John's portrait of Jesus is devoid of emotion and passion, save for his reaction to the people who mourn Lazarus's death (11:35).

43. Justin, *Apology* II.15, cited in Pagels, *The Gnostic Gospels*, 101.

44. Pagels, *The Gnostic Gospels*, 122.

45. The examples are many—Chloe (1 Corinthians 1:11), Euodia and Syntyche (Philippians 4:2–3), and Mary (Romans 16:6), as representatives from Paul's communities, and Mary Magdalene, Mary the mother of James the younger and of Joses, and Salome from the gospels (see Mark 15:40).

46. The one exception to Paul's support of women in leadership roles (in the undisputed letters) appears in 1 Corinthians 14:33b–35: "women should be silent in the churches. For they are not permitted to speak, but should be subordinate, as the law also says. If there is anything they desire to know, let them ask their husbands at home. For it is shameful for a woman to speak in church." I have argued elsewhere that this passage is a non-Pauline interpolation, based both on the manuscript evidence and on the internal conflict with Paul's expectation for women to pray and prophesy in the church (1 Corinthians 11:4). See Lee A. Johnson, "In Search of the Voice of Women in the Churches: Revisiting the Command to Silence Women in 1 Cor 14:34–35," in *Women in the Biblical World: A Survey of Old and New Testament Perspectives*, edited by Elizabeth McCabe (Lanham, MD: University Press of America, 2009), 135–154.

47. Pagels, *The Gnostic Gospels*, 54.

48. Pagels, *The Gnostic Gospels*, 7.

49. The Apostles' Creed is believed to have origins as far back as 180 CE, but appears for the first time in written form in 390. The Nicene Creed in its earliest form was composed in 325. F. L. Cross and E. A. Livingstone, eds., *The Oxford Dictionary of the Christian Church*, 3rd ed. (Oxford, UK: Oxford University Press, 1997).

50. J. Jeanine Thweatt-Bates, "Artificial Wombs and Cyborg Births: Postgenderism and Theology," in *Transhumanism and Transcendence: Christian Hope in an Age of Technological Enhancement*, edited by Ronald Cole-Turner (Washington, DC: Georgetown University Press, 2011), 103.

19

Flesh Made Data: The Posthuman Project
in Light of the Incarnation[1]

Brent Waters

The posthuman project may be characterized as a movement to use various technologies for the purpose of extending longevity and enhancing physical and cognitive performance. To become posthuman represents the maximization—even perfection—of latent qualities that are frustrated by the limitations imposed by the body. The goal, in short, is to overcome these perceived, unfortunate limitations, thereby making individual human beings better than merely being human. Proponents of this ambitious project include such authors as Nick Bostrom, Max Moore, Aubrey de Grey, James Hughes, Hans Moravec, and Ray Kurzweil, as well as the work of such organizations as Humanity+, Singularity University, Foresight Institute, and Future of Humanity Institute.[2]

What posthumanists of varying stripes hold in common is the belief that it is tragic that our lives come to an end. In the words of Max Moore, "Aging and death victimizes all humans," thereby placing an unacceptable "imposition on the human race."[3] Consequently, technologies should be developed that extend longevity not by a few years but by centuries, perhaps millennia, or even better by achieving immortality. Death should become a matter of choice or misfortune rather than necessity. Currently three, often overlapping strategies are suggested to achieve this goal.

The first may be characterized as *biological immortality*. With anticipated developments in genetics and biotechnologies, the average lifespan can be increased dramatically, perhaps indefinitely. The twofold challenge is to prevent the shortening of the telomeres and to ensure that degenerative mutations do not occur in cellular replication and rejuvenation. In addition, the immune system will be genetically enhanced and deleterious genetic defects removed or corrected to protect individuals from life-threatening and chronic diseases or disabilities. Aubrey de Grey, for instance, contends that living for 150 or 200 years will soon become routine. With further technological innovation, much more dramatic increases will be forthcoming, and immortality is not out of the question because infinite cellar rejuvenation cannot be ruled out in principle. For de Grey, winning the war against aging, and therefore death, is a matter of efficient engineering. The DNA that natural selection haphazardly concocted simply needs to be redesigned in line with human values and purposes. Moreover, a moral imperative drives de Grey's quest for biological immortality, as he insists that mortality is not simply an unfortunate aspect of being human, but rather an unmitigated tragedy that can and should be overcome through appropriate research and technological development.[4]

If human biology proves less pliable than hoped, all is not lost, because the second approach of *bionic immortality* might be employed. With anticipated advances in nanotechnology and robotics, as various body parts wear out they will be replaced with artificial substitutes. Synthetic blood vessels and skin will replace their less durable natural counterparts, and as muscles deteriorate, arms and legs will be assisted or replaced with sophisticated prosthetics. Nanobots will be injected to surgically repair or replace diseased organs, and neuroenhancers inserted into the brain to prevent the deterioration of memory and other cognitive functions. Admittedly, these artificial substitutes will wear out over time, but they will be replaced with new and improved versions. Presumably, such maintenance could be undertaken indefinitely; in principle, a bionic being could live forever so long as the artificial parts are properly maintained, repaired, and replaced as needed. Additionally, physical and cognitive functions will not merely be preserved but actually enhanced. Individuals will enjoy the benefits of improved cardiovascular systems, greater strength and agility, and enhanced intelligence and memory.

There are, unfortunately, some liabilities accompanying this approach. The electronic and mechanical systems can malfunction, and a hybrid or cyborg remains vulnerable to accidents or malicious acts resulting in death. Although a predominantly artificial body is an improvement, it is still not an ideal solution in overcoming the limits of embodiment. This leads to the third, and most speculative, approach: *virtual immortality*. According to such visionary leaders in the fields of artificial intelligence and robotics as Ray Kurzweil and Hans Moravec, the information contained in the brain that constitutes a person's memories, experience, and personality might be digitized. In the near future, they contend, highly sophisticated imaging devices will scan the brain to collect this information and, in turn, upload it into a computer. Once this information has been organized and stored, it can then be downloaded into a robotic or virtual reality host. With frequently updated and multiple backups, the uploading and downloading process can be repeated indefinitely. Consequently, one's virtual self is virtually immortal.

An objection may be raised that a person cannot be reduced to a series of zeroes and ones that can be shuffled about between robotic bodies and virtual reality programs. Kurzweil and Moravec, however, are quick to reply that because the mind is not a material object, and the mind is ultimately what a person is, then it cannot be anything other than information. A personality consists of a pattern of organized data that are created and stored over time. A biological body is merely a natural prosthetic preserving this pattern. Unfortunately, nature has not produced a very reliable or enduring prosthetic, so technology must be used to produce a better model. In liberating the mind from the biological body, nothing essential is lost. That is, if the information pattern of a person's identity is preserved, then, in Moravec's words, "I am preserved. The rest is mere jelly."[5] In short, technology can and should be developed to save individuals from the poor jelly-like conditions of being human.

Critical reactions to the posthuman project usually fall into one of three categories. First, it may be dismissed as idle speculation or fantasy. The posthuman creature envisioned by these daydreamers will never really come into being, it is claimed, so people should quit wasting their time worrying about a so-called posthuman future. Second, the technological feasibility may be challenged. The anticipated developments in biotechnology, nanotechnology, bionics, and information technology are not forthcoming and may not be possible, critics protest, so why waste time arguing about a future that is far from being imminent? Third, posthumanism may be seen as a sinister movement that is creating untold moral and political mischief. Francis Fukuyama, for example, identifies transhumanism as the world's most dangerous idea, and states that it should be vigorously opposed, if not suppressed.[6]

Admittedly, each of these reactions is to a certain extent valid. The posthuman project could very well prove to be vacuous, unachievable, or ominous. What each of these reactions misses, however, is the extent to which posthuman ideas and rhetoric are already shaping the expectations and imaginations of late moderns. Individuals increasingly regard themselves as self-constructed projects, projections, and artifacts of their own will, and they are turning to technology to overcome the bodily limitations that impede them from satisfying their desires. In the stark words of Katherine Hayles, "People become posthuman because they think they are posthuman."[7] Whether the envisioned technological transformations prove feasible or not, a posthuman self-perception is already shaping the late moderns' desires and expectations, as well as the actions they take to fulfill them.

In this respect, posthuman discourse is not so much predictive and futuristic, but rather is more akin to hyperbolic description and commentary on late modernity. A so-called posthuman future amplifies to an intense level the desires, hopes, and dreams that late moderns already hold and which they believe can be increasingly fulfilled through technological development.[8] In brief, they believe that nature and human nature can be reduced to their underlying information and, using appropriate technologies, reshaped in more desirable ways. There is no given order other than what is imposed by those with the power to manipulate the pertinent information. Even the human body is perceived as a biological information network, one that medicine can increasingly redesign, at last giving humans something better than the "mere jelly" bequeathed to them by evolution. Common parlance discloses the extent to which late moderns presume they are progressively asserting greater mastery over nature and human nature, as it is taken for granted that societies, corporations, communities, and individuals can and should routinely remake, reinvent, or recreate themselves. The world and its inhabitants are, at least in principle, infinitely malleable; when sufficient technological power is wielded, they can be, at least potentially, shaped into whatever is willed.

It may be objected that such mastery and malleability are illusory. Even with our best technology, contingency steadfastly refuses to be domesticated. Nonetheless, illusions form perceptions and desires, and the best illusions contain enough elements of truth to command attention and shape desires. Asserting a growing mastery over nature and human nature is an attractive message with an impressive track record that can be referenced. Few would deny that technology has already improved our health and made our lives more comfortable.

Consequently, it is not a fanciful step to claim that posthuman discourse denotes an early stage of creating a myth. A myth is *not* merely a sophisticated illusion. Rather, a myth narrates origin and destiny, and explores how evil is overcome by good in between those two states. A myth, then, is not a fairy tale or a fable, but rather a narrative interpretation of the human condition—a literary device that encapsulates where hope and trust are placed, in turn aligning desires accordingly. Humans cannot live without their myths, because, as Jonathan Gottschall contends, humans are storytelling animals.[9] Some myths are more compelling than others, because they offer what is believed to be a more truthful interpretive narration about the human condition. C. S. Lewis's conversion to Christianity, for example, was prompted in large part by the attraction of its mythology.

The rough storyline of the emerging posthuman myth[10] (and it is a salvific myth) goes something like this: the essence of a human being is the information constituting the mind or will. Unfortunately, this information is confined to a body that imposes unacceptable constraints upon the will and that deteriorates over a relatively short period of time. Embodiment is therefore a curse to be overcome by constructing a better host for the will, preferably one that can be sustained indefinitely. In short, humans must save themselves from their finite and mortal bodies by building a superior prosthetic of the will.

The principal problem with this myth is that it is predicated on an insufficient and potentially perilous anthropology, for a human being cannot be reduced to a will trapped in a body. I will demonstrate this insufficiency by contrasting the posthuman myth with the Christian myth or doctrine of the incarnation. Stated in more prosaic terms, I will compare the differing assessments of finitude, mortality, and natality that are made from the stances of turning flesh into data as opposed to the Word made flesh.

In brief, the incarnation encapsulates the astonishing—some say scandalous—claim that in Jesus Christ God became a particular human being. In more poetic terms, the Word was made flesh; the creator became a creature. This incarnate presence sets in place a redemptive process, culminating in the death, resurrection, and exaltation of Jesus Christ. But it needs to be stressed that in this scheme humans are not rescued from their bodies, but rather, following Paul Ramsey, are saved as "embodied souls" and "ensouled bodies."[11] There is no informational essence that can be separated from the body and placed in a different host. The incarnation, then, affirms the creaturely status of humans, for it was with such inherently limited creatures that the Word was pleased to dwell.[12]

How do these respective posthuman and incarnational visions differ in assessing human finitude, mortality, and natality? For the posthuman, finitude is inimical to human flourishing. To be limited is to be in bondage, because freedom consists of the absence of external constraints upon the will. To be truly free is to live in a world where no options need be foreclosed but are always potentially open. Unfortunately, human bodies impose a multitude of constraints upon the will, preventing humans from doing what they want to do. We often lack the strength or dexterity to perform certain acts, and our brains have a limited ability to store and access memory. When I was young, for example, I wanted to be an athlete—but I do not have an athletic body, so I was not free to satisfy my heart's desire. Instead, I became an academic —but alas, I cannot remember everything that I read, and what I do recall is often a muddle.

The posthuman solution is to free the will from the bondage of finitude by constructing a better prosthetic of the will. This is accomplished either by reengineering and enhancing the body, by exchanging selected parts with superior artificial substitutes, or by (eventually) uploading and downloading the information constituting the will. In each of these options or stages, freedom is enhanced through the creation of an expanding range of options. With some biological and bionic enhancements I can at last become a stellar athlete or in virtual reality enjoy the pleasure of total and accurate recall. The will, then, can become genuinely free only by diminishing the finite limits or constraints of embodiment.

In contrast, the incarnation affirms finite embodiment as a good. To be a human creature means that one is necessarily embodied and therefore finite.

Theologically, this characteristic differentiates humans from their infinite creator, and the difference should serve to remind humans that they are in peril when they ignore or attempt to surmount their creaturely constraints. The problem is amplified given the fallen state of the human condition. As sinners, humans often desire good things badly. It is due to this disordered desire that late moderns in particular are disabled from acknowledging finitude as a good of their creaturely status, instead perceiving it principally as an unfortunate and unwanted constraint that should be overcome, or at least mitigated, to the greatest possible extent.

Freedom, for example, is a good to be affirmed, but it becomes distorted with the belief that it is maximized by having endless options at one's disposal. Rather, freedom is found in limitation. Every affirmation requires a prior negation; one must be free to say "no" to this so as to say "yes" to that. Marriage, for example, requires one to first say "no" to being single so that one is free to be married. Similarly, to say "yes" to what the incarnation affirms requires a corresponding acknowledgment and consent to the finitude entailed in being a creature, and therefore resisting those efforts that attempt to eliminate all finite limits. To perceive all limits as unfortunate constraints against freedom is not so much the predicament of finitude per se as it is the problem of the disordered desires of finite creatures.

For the posthuman, mortality is simply an affront to human dignity. Death is an outrageous tragedy that should be rectified. This outrage accounts, in part, for the moral urgency prompting a technological and medical war against aging and death, against nature itself. This urgency is captured in an excerpt from Max More's "Letter to Mother Nature" "Mother Nature, truly we are grateful for what you made us. No doubt you did the best you could. However, with all due respect, we must say that you have in many ways done a poor job with the human constitution. You have made us vulnerable to disease and damage. You compel us to age and die—just as we are beginning attain wisdom ... What you have made is glorious, yet deeply flawed ... We have decided that it is time to amend the human constitution."[13]

Despite the flamboyant rhetoric, More captures a fundamental complaint about the human condition: most people, particularly if they could maintain their physical and mental health, do not want to die. As Saint Augustine recognized, it is not surprising that almost anyone would greedily grasp an offer of immortality.[14] To the posthumanists' credit, rather than ignoring or glossing over death, they confront it as a brute fact that brings to an end one's hopes and aspirations, and obliterates all that is held near and dear. As Saint Paul insisted, death is the final enemy that should not be warmly embraced. So it is understandable that posthumanists, like most other people, do not want to die. An understandable desire, however, is not necessarily a good desire. The desire to live does not automatically render aging and death an evil flaw of nature that should be relentlessly fought.

In contrast, the incarnation affirms the good of mortality. To be an embodied and finite human creature requires both a beginning and an end. This again differentiates the eternal creator from temporal creatures, and it serves as a reminder that all humans are mortal. Death per se is not a universal tragedy inimical to human flourishing. For Christians, mortality has a twofold meaning: death is the end of life, but it also enables the end or *telos* of eternal fellowship with the triune God. To consent to the necessity of mortality is to simultaneously affirm the good of this fellowship. This affirmation, however, does not authorize us to neglect bodily health or hasten its demise to obtain this greater good. As the ideal of martyrdom teaches, Christians should not fear death, but neither should they seek it.

Unlike the posthuman project, salvation does not consist of liberating the will, mind, or soul from the body. Using Ramsey's words again, the human creature is an "embodied soul" and "ensouled body" that cannot be separated in either life or death. Consequently, it is a psychosomatic unity that humans are born, are redeemed, die, and are raised to eternal fellowship with God. Since the end of eternal fellowship with God does not consist of rescuing immaterial data from a material body, then embodiment should inform both the ordering of desire toward this end of eternal fellowship and temporal fellowship with others.[15] There is nothing wrong with wanting to live, but a finite and mortal creature wanting to live forever is a disordered desire.

The desire and necessity of fellowship lead to the final contrast with regard to natality. It is telling that in posthuman literature virtually nothing is said about offspring, other than a cursory assumption that if individuals, for whatever reasons, want to have children they should have the right to use various technologies to procure desirable ones. This casual disregard for descendants is explicable if one's ultimate goal is personal immortality. If one is endeavoring to live for as long as possible, and perhaps for forever, then future generations are not only unnecessary, but may prove to be another external constraint imposed on the will or, even worse, unwanted competition.

This disdain for generational interdependency discloses both the lynchpin of the posthuman project and the reason why it is a perilous enterprise. The fear of death and subsequent quest for immortality is not an unprecedented phenomenon. Every generation has faced death as, in Hannah Arendt's words, the "only reliable law of life" that inevitably consigns "everything human to ruin and destruction."[16] Surmounting this law has prompted various strategies for achieving immortality. For the ancients, this could have meant participating in an immortal lineage or empire. For moderns, it might mean making contributions to immortal art and literature, or more broadly to an immortal history.

Arendt recognized that what these ancient and modern strategies share in common is a consuming fear of death, resulting in illusory and futile attempts to overcome this only reliable law of life. Lineages die out and empires crumble; works of art and literature are lost and forgotten and history shall come to an end. The fear of death, then, provides an ineffectual, if not deadly, basis for ordering intergenerational fellowship among mortal human beings. Arendt wondered if a more promising conceptual scheme might be found, one oriented toward the transmission or generation of life and away from the fear of death.

Arendt coined the word "natality" as a way of conceiving this reorientation. Birth and death are the two definitive conditions demarcating the human condition. It is pursuing the former rather than avoiding the latter, however, that should provide the principal metaphor for ordering human life and lives. Natality ensures a generational continuity over time, while also encapsulating the possibility for change and improvement. Each new birth embodies simultaneously a continuous line of memory and anticipation—a self-giving that creates a recipient who is both like and yet unlike the giver. The gift of every parent is also the unique possibility of each child. Although death is not something to be embraced lovingly, mortality is not humankind's great curse. When death is perceived as nothing more than a cruel fate, natality is robbed of its power to renew and regenerate. To be fixated on mortality is to promote a social and political order that attempts to cheat that fate. Survival becomes *the* consuming desire, which in turn corrupts all other values and considerations. The birth of a child holds no hope or promise, but serves only as a reminder of a mortal fate to be despised and despaired. Consequently, replication—as opposed to reproduction or procreation—becomes the tyrannous rationale of personal survival, pervading all resulting relationships and associations.

In this respect, what differentiates the posthuman project from both ancient and modern projects for achieving immortality is that it is predicated entirely upon *personal* survival. Although the ancient and modern strategies were illusory and futile, they nevertheless entailed participation in projects that were larger and outlived individual participants. Lineages, empires, art, literature, and history are inherently intergenerationally dependent—the very condition that posthumanists despise and wish to be rid of. Admittedly, the posthuman project is equally futile and illusory, but as mentioned earlier, illusions nonetheless help to form the expectations and imaginations of individuals, and more broadly the expectations and imaginations of a culture. This leads us back to posthuman discourse as hyperbolic description and commentary upon our present circumstances. Through its futuristic rhetoric, posthuman discourse amplifies, exemplifies, and justifies one of the most pervasive late modern illusions—namely, that of an impervious individual autonomy and its resulting narcissism.

Late moderns tend to place a high value on mobility and self-sufficiency as ways of asserting and protecting their autonomy, and increasingly technologies are playing a central role in achieving this goal. Late moderns can travel relatively easily and quickly to almost anywhere they please, they can instantly access remote locales, and they can create alternative, virtual worlds. The late modern world is increasingly nomadic. Moreover, these nomadic inhabitants are coming to believe that they ultimately do not need each other to accomplish whatever they might will, and that whatever need they might have of others is usually temporary, entailing quick, expedient, and anonymous exchanges. The perceived ability to do what one wills has become so engrained and taken for granted that the extent to which so-called autonomy is utterly dependent upon others is simply not perceived.[17]

Imagine, for example, that I need a new computer so I can continue to write books and articles that are read by very few people. I order the computer online. In the few minutes that it takes to complete this task, I initiate a series of global transactions. Although the lead office of the company from which I purchased the computer is located in California, the server hosting the Web site is in Vancouver. An office worker in Dublin reviews and processes my order. The hardware and software are manufactured in such places as Bucharest, Seoul, and Taipei. My customized computer is assembled in Shanghai, then air-freighted and delivered to my door by a corporation headquartered in Memphis. My prized computer is user friendly, so I turn it on, answer a few questions, and in a matter of minutes am up and running. I sit back with a sense of smug satisfaction that I did this all by myself. My smugness is, of course, conceited nonsense: the process of obtaining my computer involves dozens, if not hundreds, of people. The technology that I use to obtain my new computer does not so much enhance my autonomy as it hides my dependency upon others in satisfying my desire to write unread books and articles.

It would not be so troubling if such deceptive autonomy was confined to exchanges in global markets, but the illusion is more pervasive and formative. For nearly three decades Sherry Turkle has been studying the influence of technology on contemporary culture, particularly among teenagers and young adults. In her latest book, *Alone Together*, she identifies a growing preference for virtual or robotic companions, because they are more dependable in meeting one's needs and wants.[18] Friends and family members often disappoint, whereas robots and avatars rarely let their users down, and if they do they can be reprogrammed or easily replaced. Turkle notes that this preference is also on the rise among seniors, especially those confined to institutional care. In Turkle's words, "Technology proposes itself as the architect of our intimacies."[19] She goes on to add, "Sociable robots and online life both suggest the possibility of relationships the way we want them."[20] These so-called relationships, then, are not with an other, but with projections of oneself, akin to gazing at a flattering mirror. The self is truly the center of these relationships, and in every relationship.

It is in such mundane activities as online shopping and keeping company with artificial companions that the hyperbole of posthuman rhetoric best captures and discloses the underlying illusion of autonomy and its accompanying narcissism. The envisioned posthuman is genuinely autonomous, for when finite and mortal limits have been eclipsed, at least imaginatively, the resulting immortal really does not have any need for anyone else. This explains the total lack of interest in natality, because there is no need to be regenerative or self-giving if one is already the center and purpose of the future. In the posthuman vision, a future to which one contributes but will not be in a position to receive directly is not worth pursuing; a future in which the self is not the center is not even worth contemplating or imagining. As Arendt recognized, when the prospect of death becomes a consuming fear, natality is effectively negated and stripped of its meaning. Ironically, the more late moderns come to be believe that finitude and mortality can and should be overcome, the less attentive they become to the needs and welfare of others, thereby effectively diminishing human life and lives over time.

If such posthuman rhetoric could be sequestered to the realm of fantasy, then we (or least I) could rest easier. In reality, it is already subtly influencing certain crucial social practices. It should give us pause when we consider how the contemporary practice of medicine is adopting, largely unwittingly, posthuman premises on how to relieve the human condition. Traditionally, medicine has been properly dedicated to providing curative therapies, maintaining and restoring bodily functions, and relieving pain and suffering. In doing so, it recognized that patients were embodied, finite, and mortal creatures. Consequently, there comes a point when medicine can only care and cannot cure.

Increasingly, this has proved a difficult point for late moderns, both health care professionals and patients, to accept. Instead, there is the growing expectation that with an expanding array of preventive, therapeutic, and enhancement technologies at their disposal, doctors should be able to repair and maintain the body indefinitely. In medical and bioethics literature, aging is now routinely regarded as a disease to be treated and eventually, in principle, be cured. This is tantamount to waging a war against finitude and mortality, and the cost is transforming human creatures into isolated beings they were never created to be—a goal warmly endorsed by posthumanists. This shift away from cure and care to transformation corrupts medicine, because its purpose is not to overcome the constraints of embodiment, but rather to help patients come to terms with and consent to their finitude and mortality. When medicine forsakes this purpose, it grows tone deaf to what Jeremy Taylor described as the voice of suffering.[21]

In light of the incarnation, what might be said in response? The Word made flesh dispels all notions that creatures bearing the *imago Dei* are radically autonomous. Humans are free persons, but that personhood is necessarily shaped and lived out in fellowship with others who share the bonds of imperfection that connect embodied, finite, and mortal people. In short, humans are mutually dependent creatures. This dependency must be stressed, because late moderns tend to believe that all human relations are predicated upon exchange and mutuality. If I have nothing to give, I am of little or no value to anyone. In suffering and dying, such reciprocity grows steadily asymmetrical, but this decline should not be construed as failure. As finite and mortal creatures, we are always dependent upon others; this dependency is total at the end of life as well as the beginning. At these points it is proper—indeed, more blessed—to receive than to give. In consenting to such dependency, we receive care as an affirmation of the goods of fellowship, finitude, and mortality.

In using a baby as her symbol of natality, Hannah Arendt also insisted that it be received as a gift—unto us a child is born. It is only as a gift received that a child embodies a hope in genuinely new and renewing possibilities. Otherwise, it is merely one more artifact created in response to a stultifying fear of death. Ironically, in attempting to become the masters of their own fate by waging a war against finitude and mortality, posthumanists effectively foreclose the possibility of genuinely new and renewing possibilities: they are dedicated to asserting all-encompassing control rather than being receptive to the unanticipated. Despite their futuristic rhetoric, posthumanists are merely attempting to impose a tyranny of the present over the future.

NOTES

1. This chapter is adapted from a lecture I delivered at the Faraday Institute, University of Cambridge, Cambridge, UK, November 12, 2013.

2. For a representative collection of posthuman literature, see Max More and Natasha Vita-More, eds., *The Transhumanist Reader* (Malden, MA: Wiley-Blackwell, 2013); for a critical overview of the posthuman project, see Brent Waters, *From Human to Posthuman: Christian Theology and Technology in a Postmodern World* (Aldershot, UK: Ashgate, 2006).

3. Max More, "On Becoming Posthuman," *Free Inquiry* (Fall 1994): 38–40.

4. See Aubrey de Grey, ed., "Strategies for Engineered Negligible Senescence: Why Genuine Control of Aging May Be Foreseeable,"*Annals of the New York Academy of Science*, 1019 (June 2004), and "The War on Aging," in Immortality Institute, *The Scientific Conquest of Death* (Buenos Aires, Argentina: LibrosEnRed, 2004), 29–45.

5. Hans Moravec, *Mind Children: The Future of Robot and Human Intelligence* (Cambridge, MA: Harvard University Press, 1990); Hans Moravec, *Robot: Mere Machines to Transcendent Mind* (Oxford, UK: Oxford University Press, 1999), 117.

6. Francis Fukuyama, "Transhumanism," *Foreign Policy* (September/October 2004), 42–43.

7. N. Katherine Hayles, *How We Became Posthuman: Virtual Bodies in Cybernetics, Literature, and Informatics* (Chicago, IL: University of Chicago Press, 1999), 6.

8. See Brent Waters, *Christian Moral Theology in the Emerging Technoculture: From Posthuman Back to Human* (Farnham, UK: Ashgate, 2014).

9. Jonathan Gottschall, *The Storytelling Animal: How Stories Make Us Human* (New York, NY: Houghton Mifflin Harcourt, 2012).

10. Ted Chu uses a number of overtly religious in attempting to construct what I am characterizing as a myth; see *Human Purpose and Transhuman Potential: A Cosmic Vision for Our Future Evolution* (San Rafael, CA: Origin Press, 2014).

11. See Paul Ramsey, *The Patient as Person: Explorations in Medical Ethics* (New Haven, CT: Yale University Press, 1970), xiii.

12. For a more detailed account of the incarnation and its implications for Christian ethics, see Brent Waters, *This Mortal Flesh: Incarnation and Bioethics* (Grand Rapids, MI: Brazos, 2009).

13. As quoted in Christina Bieber Lake, *Prophets of the Posthuman: American Fiction, Biotechnology, and the Ethics of Personhood* (Notre Dame IN: University of Notre Dame Press, 2013), 95.

14. See St. Augustine, *Concerning the City of God against the Pagans,* translated by Henry Bettenson (London, UK: Penguin Books, 1984), 461 (VI/27).

15. See Beth Felker Jones, *Marks of His Wounds: Gender Politics and Bodily Resurrection* (Oxford, UK: Oxford University Press, 2007).

16. Hannah Arendt, *The Human Condition* (Chicago, IL: University of Chicago Press, 1998), 246.

17. For a more detailed description and assessment of the nomadic characteristics of late modernity, see Waters, *Christian Moral Theology in the Emerging Technoculture*, eps. part III.

18. Sherry Turkle, *Alone Together: Why We Expect More from Technology and Less from Each Other* (New York, NY: Basic Books, 2011).

19. Turkle, *Alone Together*, 1.

20. Turkle, *Alone Together*, 13.

21. See Jeremy Taylor, *On the Rule and Exercises of Holy Dying* (London, UK: Longmans, 1918).

20

. . . .

Morphological Freedom and the Rebellion against Human Bodiliness: Notes from the Roman Catholic Tradition

Cory Andrew Labrecque

Transhumanists, who lament the many limitations and shortcomings of human corporality, value "morphological freedom" as the right to modify the body if (and as) one wishes and as the right not to be prevented from doing so. There is nothing special, transhumanists say, about the human corpus that beseeches us to preserve it. In the Roman Catholic tradition, as is the case for a number of the world's religions, limitation and finitude are not simply part and parcel of humanhood,[1] but are important dimensions of our anthropology and teleology. Moreover, the Church contends that the body ultimately belongs to God. Like the soul, it serves as a locus of communication that connects (embodied) humankind to the Creator and to Creation. In this chapter, I engage these conflicting perspectives, making particular use of the aging body as a focal point.

LAMENTATIONS: TRANSHUMANISM AND FREEDOM FROM THE NATURE OF HUMANHOOD

Transhumanist philosophers make no secret that there is little to celebrate about human nature, which—as Nick Bostrom contends—is nothing but "a work-in-progress, a half-baked beginning that we can learn to remold in desirable ways."[2] The time has come, they say, to wrest the reins of our evolution away from the mediocrity of Nature. Over the course of a few million years, its best efforts have resulted in a human body fraught with several disappointing inadequacies that "thinking man" (*Homo sapiens*) should no longer have to tolerate. A "paltry seven or eight decade" lifespan,[3] a "three pound, cheese-like thinking machine that we lug around in our skulls"[4] containing—in more than one sense—our cognitive capacities, a vulnerable body, our scantily developed sensory modalities,[5] and a "genetically determined setpoint for our levels of well-being"[6] are among the many shortcomings that—even more regrettably—we have, in our passivity, come to accept as inevitable dimensions of who we are or, even worse, *characteristic* of what it means to be human. In this vein, Bostrom makes plain that:

> Transhumanists promote the view that human enhancement technologies should be made widely available, and that individuals should have broad discretion over which of these technologies to apply to themselves (morphological freedom), and that parents should normally get to decide which reproductive technologies to use when having children (reproductive freedom). Transhumanists believe that, while there are hazards that need to be identified and avoided, human enhancement technologies will offer enormous potential for deeply valuable and humanly beneficial uses. Ultimately, it is possible that such enhancements may make us, or our descendants, "posthuman."[7]

Although embodiment—of some kind—could possibly continue to be an important conduit for transhumanism, the *human* corpus is particularly dispensable (disposable, even), as is the ecosystem that has been an integral part of the human condition since the dawn of our time. As such, a number of transhumanists do not hesitate to champion cryonics and the vitrification of the body[8] or mind uploading, whereby "one neuron could be replaced by an implant or by a simulation in a computer outside of the body. Then another neuron, and so on, until eventually the whole cortex has been replaced and the person's thinking is implemented on entirely artificial hardware."[9] Here, transhumanists clarify that uploading of this kind does not necessitate a disembodiment that would merit the charge of escapism:

> [A]n upload could have a virtual (simulated) body giving the same sensations and the same possibilities for interaction as a non-simulated body. With advanced virtual reality, uploads could enjoy food and drink, and upload sex could be as gloriously messy as one could wish. And uploads wouldn't have to be confined to virtual reality: they could interact with people on the outside and even rent robot bodies in order to work in or explore physical reality.[10]

Both means point to a want for an existence that is bereft of biological senescence, which raises concerns about overpopulation and the correlative exhaustion of the planet's limited resources. One option that transhumanists encourage us to consider is extensive space colonization.[11]

This laissez-faire attitude toward the body and its environmental context means that the "posthumans" of the transhumanist imagination could be completely synthetic artificial intelligences, or they could be enhanced uploads, or they could be the result of making many smaller but cumulatively profound augmentations to a biological human. The latter alternative would probably require either the redesign of the human organism using advanced nanotechnology or its radical enhancement using some combination of technologies such as genetic engineering, psychopharmacology, anti-aging therapies, neural interfaces, advanced information management tools, memory enhancing drugs, wearable computers, and cognitive techniques.[12]

The defense of morphological freedom—which Anders Sandberg understands, at least in part, as an extension of self-ownership—consists of the right to modify one's body if (and as) one wishes to, the right not to be prevented from doing so, and the right not to be required to do so.[13] In transhumanist thought, this freedom is not simply about changing hair color or getting implants. The preceding excerpt notes that transformation—especially of the human to the posthuman—will demand a "redesign" or "radical enhancement" to break the constraints of humanhood, to transcend aging, and to ultimately make even death a voluntary decision.[14]

I turn now to the context of aging, which will help elucidate important distinctions between transhumanist and religious conceptualizations of the human body. Although I am particularly attentive to the theological anthropology of Roman Catholicism, I will bring to the fore here a number of comparable dimensions from other faith traditions—especially the Abrahamic traditions—to broaden the conversation.

THE CULT OF PERFECTION AND THE FUNCTIONAL PERSON: TRANSHUMANIST CONTEMPT FOR THE AGING BODY

In a popular passage from *As You Like It*, Shakespeare describes the seventh age as "second childishness and mere oblivion, / Sans teeth, sans eyes, sans taste, sans everything."[15] The stage is set for ageism: a systematic form of discrimination against the elderly as a homogeneous group of physical and mental incompetents.[16] This sweeping generalization and negative cultural interpretation of advanced age as a time of decline, regression, pathology, and immaturity inevitably leads to stigma, social isolation, infantilization, and dehumanization.[17] Some philosophers argue that an organism's moral claim to life is fundamentally dependent on the individual's capacity for higher mental function. To be a person of full moral status, that is, one must possess self-consciousness, rationality, a sense of the future, a sense of continuity over time, and the ability to suffer. Functional perceptions of personhood—which transhumanists espouse—operate on an "all-or-none" or hierarchical (to the extent that one's degree of function, utility, and performance determines human worth) principle, imposing a conditionality on human dignity that is directly proportional to the proper functioning of the optimal body. The conversation shifts, of course, when the "optimal" is achievable only through redesign or radical enhancement.

Nancy Harding and Colin Palfrey argue that the biomedicalization of dementia, for instance, is nothing more than a pursuit to repel aging and, ultimately, death.[18] Indeed, the Latin *dementia* has come to be translated as "madness," "craziness," or "folly," and the verbal form, *dementire*, means "to rave." Although relatively little research has been conducted on the sociology of the aging body, Harding and Palfrey argue that the major premise of this discipline is that the body is inextricably intertwined with identity.[19] Here, though, we must discard the simplistic notion of the body as a biological machine and instead appreciate it as "an unfinished biological and social phenomenon which is transformed, within certain limits, as a result of its entry into, and participation in, society."[20] If we are to argue that self-identity is bound up with the body, which in itself is amenable to change through social relations, then societal attitudes toward the aging body play an important role in the preservation of personhood. The ethical implications of transhumanism—a philosophy that considers aging to be a deficit model of existence—need not be made plain here.

Accordingly, the social isolation of the aged person, who fails to conform to societal standards of rationality and whose body contests the ideal of a "quintessentially modern individual [who] is young and never dies," poses as much a threat to personhood as the neurological deterioration that causes impairment.[21] "The ageing body is feared, for it shows that all humankind's investment in the body is ultimately useless; deterioration and death cannot be avoided ... dementia, in which the body becomes an empty, mind-free tomb and thus symbolic of death, has, through its medicalisation, come to serve as a proxy for death" and, as such, prompts the separation of the aged from the rest of society.[22] Indeed, social derision of the aged is not simply a ban from the community of persons; it is more a disqualification from the community of the *living*. As the mask of old age exposes the elderly to stigma and arouses in society fear and anxiety about inevitable death, the body becomes "alien territory" from which one must retreat; "with this retreat comes a loss of sense of self."[23] Transhumanists, as such, look to the abolition of aging altogether.

It comes as no surprise that the dominant materialistic worldview of our time views the human body as ultimately significant (personhood is oft bestowed only on those with optimally functioning bodies); it is all that we have, and it is what it all happens to. Paul, in his first letter to the Church at Corinth, delivers his oft-quoted verdict on this matter, calling the body "a temple of the Holy Spirit"[24] that shares in the dignity of the *imago Dei*.[25] Although the spiritual soul is immortal, the perishable body is destined for glorification at the resurrection, when it will be reunited with its animating principle.[26] In the context of a material worldview obsessed with corporeal image, certain bodies—such as those marginalized by functional definitions of personhood—are looked upon with contempt. The aged and the disabled body, for instance, are the antithesis of the image of bodily perfection, which exalts youth and optimal functionality. This mechanistic vision of the body, characteristic of transhumanism, is certainly not novel; indeed, it has been very much a part of the biomedical model of conceptualizing health and illness that many—such as George Engel, who champions a *biopsychosocial* approach[27]—have sought to correct.

For centuries, religions have understood the human person as at once both corporeal and spiritual. In Christianity, it is the whole—the body-soul composite—that is "intended to become, in the body of Christ, a temple of the Spirit."[28] In Advaitin philosophy, *Brahman*, the eternal essence that underlies reality, is present in every human as the *atman*, the true self. In Judaism[29] and Islam,[30] God creates humans from the earth and then breathes life into them, carefully fashioning the person as body and soul. As such, the body is never revered as an absolute value, as it is in the materialist worldview. Likewise, the idolization of physical perfection is either blasphemous or futile, as in the Buddhist concept of *anatman*, where bodily form, as one of the five temporary aggregates, is considered impermanent and empty, or in Hinduism, where the bodily self, as opposed to the true self, is subject to change and decay.[31] In this vein, the Catholic Church warns against the trend "to promote the *cult of the body*" and "to sacrifice everything for its sake," as this corporeal idolization may very well lead to a "selective preference of the strong over the weak" and "a perversion of human relationships,"[32] especially between the generations. Interdependence is an important dimension of how Christianity understands human nature, moral agency, and the Covenant; for transhumanists, in contrast, it is a sign of human weakness.

Although the aging body may arouse fear and anxiety about human finitude, thereby instigating the scientific pursuit of physical immortality, religions are far less troubled by the inevitability of death. In this vein, the psalmist petitions God to "teach us to count our days that we may gain a wise heart"[33]; discernment comes to pass in the recognition of human frailty and mortality. The Abrahamic faith traditions, in this regard, teach that death is a significant part of the life narrative in which the human person only momentarily ceases to exist in the separation of body and soul. God resurrects the dead by granting incorruptibility to human life with the restoration of composite existence.[34]

The religions do not see in the aged an excruciating reminder of human finitude that must be excluded from the community of persons. For example, the Abrahamic faith traditions compel the finest expression of imitating the holiness of God by more fully attending to and accompanying the human person to the very moment of his or her transition from this life into the next —without the need to extend mortal life *ad infinitum*. That the human *body* is both fleeting and corruptible is a truism accepted by religions; it is the integrative human *person*, however, who continues to exist in some fashion after death. In this regard, the resurrection accounts of Jesus in the New Testament, as an example, strongly allude to the biographical continuity of personhood in eternity.[35] That is, while human mortal life ceases at death, the human person survives the passage to immortality with the bonds forged in life remaining unbroken. This natural continuity between life, death, and life eternal is shared by the Abrahamic traditions and has obvious ramifications for their perceptions of personhood.[36] It would seem, then, that transhumanists adopt an exclusively biological/bodily definition of human person that risks subordinating the unenhanced (even though people are assured respect for their autonomy in choosing whether to take up enhancements) or those of questionable performance.

The Abrahamic religions' adamant defense of human life is not a clinging to that which is fleeting or the fear of that which is inevitable; instead, it is gratitude and reverence for that which is considered a special gift from God. Indeed, most strains of Christianity, Islam, and Judaism discourage the aversion of imminent death (this, I must clarify, is not the same as purposely hastening death) by use of extraordinary medical means, which may be burdensome, dangerous, or disproportionate to the expected outcome.[37] At the same time, Christians are called to model Christ's preferential love for the poor and to carry out his healing ministry to the sick and social outcast, thereby according special attention to all those who suffer. Similarly, Jews (who are permitted to violate the commandments if preservation of life and health requires it) and Muslims emphasize the mandate and duty to heal, which is different from prolonging life indefinitely. There is no justification for the interruption of ordinary care for the incurably ill or dying. This solidarity with the suffering of others indicates that the religions remain alert to threats to the human dignity of the vulnerable, who are assured certain consolation and protection within the community of faith. Paul, in his first letter to the Church at Corinth, writes, "If one part suffers, every part suffers with it."[38]

And yet, the common Christian mandate to "[b]e perfect, therefore, as your heavenly Father is perfect,"[39] hints at a possible convergence of sacred and secular understandings of perfectibility in the context of personhood. This perspective, however, is far from imaging the ideal form of an anthropomorphized deity. To be sure, the New Testament is silent about the physical attributes of God made flesh in the person of Jesus. Perfectibility in this tradition is countercultural and is synopsized in Paul's ecstatic experience in which the Lord responds to his appeals from torment: "My grace is sufficient for you, for [my] power is made perfect in weakness."[40] Such is a perfection that is to be sought in voluntary poverty, in humility, in the emulation of divine generosity and holiness; it is the perfection of charity grounded in the denial of the self as opposed to an exaltation of the self (where the self is defined by the body).[41] This vision cannot be further from the ideal of perfection that is pursued by transhumanists, whose disdain for the nonfunctional, nonoptimal, imperfect body paves the way for a particular system of ethics that invites a new classist distinction between the enhanced and unenhanced; for transhumanists, perfection is intentionally escapist and, fortunately, accessible in the here and now.

A ROMAN CATHOLIC THEOLOGY
OF THE (LIMITED) BODY

John Paul II's *Theology of the Body* continues to gain prominence in Catholic bioethical discourse. This should be expected as the Incarnation—the mystery of a God who chooses to assume life in the flesh and, hence, the full spectrum of human vulnerability—lies at the very heart of the Christian tradition. In his preface to the former pontiff's extensive catechesis, Christopher West asks, "How could our bodies—so carnal, so earthy, so mortal—be a 'study of God'?"[42] John Paul II responds accordingly: the human body "has been created to transfer into the visible reality of the world the mystery hidden from eternity in God, and thus be a sign of it."[43] Contrary to certain strands of popular belief, Roman Catholicism does not harbor contempt for the body; images of self-flagellation and of the soul being imprisoned in a vessel that is constantly led into temptation and is subject to decay hardly offer a comprehensive description, to be sure. In fact, not only does the tradition teach—as do Judaism and Islam—that the body ultimately belongs to God (which restrains the transhumanist idea of "self-ownership"), but there is heightened attention to "sins against the body."[44]

The ministry of Jesus, in particular, is bodily in its orientation: the bread and the wine of Passover become his body and blood,[45] touch is central to the healing narratives[46] and is the means by which Thomas comes to recognize the risen Christ as God,[47] and the community of the faithful is called "the body of Christ."[48] The Church holds fast to Tertullian's contention that "the flesh is the hinge of salvation"[49] and the Catechism makes a point to outline this in creedal form: "We believe in God who is creator of the flesh; we believe in the Word made flesh in order to redeem the flesh; we believe in the resurrection of the flesh [that we now possess], the fulfillment of both the creation and the redemption of the flesh."[50]

The corporeal dimension of personhood—while not an absolute value,[51] as we have seen—is neither expendable nor ever truly lost. The Church's rendering of the resurrection adheres to a belief in a *restoration*—not a *replacement*—of our current body:

> Christ is raised with his own body: "See my hands and my feet, that it is
> I myself"; but he did not return to an earthly life. So, in him, "all of them will

rise again with their own bodies which they now bear," but Christ "will change our lowly body to be like his glorious body," into a "spiritual body."[52]

Interestingly, the Church recognizes that the lowly, dependent, defenseless, limited body (whose nature was changed by hereditary sinfulness) is also the one that bears the divine image and is the one that will be glorified—"spiritualized," as it were—in the resurrection. To be clear, reference to the "glorified body" here is not compatible, as some might think, with the redesigned or radically enhanced posthuman of transhumanist imagination. In the resurrection, human beings recover their bodiliness "in the fullness of the perfection proper to the image and likeness of God"[53]; this "spiritualization" is a perfect integration of the body and soul in the composite nature of the risen human.[54] There is continuity between the body that we possess in the here and now and the body that we will possess in the world to come. Even though the referent term "posthuman" suggests some lingering tie between the human and the posthuman, talk of redesign and radical enhancement focuses less on a vision of the perfection of humanhood (and certainly less on a vision of perfection as it is discussed here) and more on salvation from it.

What is considered "lowly" about the body, according to the Catholic tradition, is not the boundary it sets on a person's intellect, mood control, or lifespan. It is out of a deep and abiding aloneness in the visible world, traced to the original solitude of Adam and experienced even now through the reality of the body,[55] that humans yearn to be made complete, a goal that can be fulfilled only in communion with others and with the Other.[56] Enhancements of the kind supported by transhumanism not only would be incapable of quenching this longing, but would actually exacerbate this sense of aloneness. This, the Church would say, is what is truly lamentable.

RETURNING OR RECEIVING THE GIFT FROM NOWHERE

The Catholic understanding of human bodiliness is expectedly theocentric, in stark contrast to the meta-anthropocentric (my rendering of "posthuman-centered") orientation of transhumanism. Students of Hannah Arendt—a political theorist who did not speak out of the Catholic tradition—will recognize an insightful parallel between her words that open *The Human Condition* and the Church's teaching to this end:

> The earth is the very quintessence of the human condition, and earthly nature, for all we know, may be unique in the universe in providing human beings with a habitat in which they can move and breathe without effort and without artifice. The human artifice of the world separates human existence from all mere animal environment, but life itself is outside this artificial world, and through

life man remains related to all other living organisms. For some time now, a great many scientific endeavors have been directed toward making life also "artificial," toward cutting the last tie through which even man belongs among the children of nature. It is the same desire to escape from imprisonment to the earth that is manifest in the attempt to create life in the test tube, in the desire to mix "frozen germ plasma from people of demonstrated ability under the microscope to produce superior human beings" and "to alter [their] size, shape and function"; and the wish to escape the human condition, I suspect, also underlies the hope to extend man's life-span far beyond the hundred-year limit.

This future man, whom scientists tell us they will produce in no more than a hundred years, seems to be possessed by a rebellion against human existence as it has been given, a free gift from nowhere (secularly speaking), which he wishes to exchange, as it were, for something he has made himself. There is no reason to doubt our abilities to accomplish such an exchange, just as there is no reason to doubt our present ability to destroy all organic life on earth. The question is only whether we wish to use our new scientific and technical knowledge in this direction, and this question cannot be decided by scientific means.[57]

Some transhumanists might acknowledge that the earth is "the very quintessence" of the human condition, but this truth should not translate to our being bound to—or identified by—this place. As mentioned previously, for transhumanists, there is no particular need for humankind to stay put. On the contrary, the Catholic Church—like all other traditions that ground their anthropology in the book of Genesis—would not only agree with Arendt here, but would extend the conversation in its understanding of humankind being made from the earth[58] (like the rest of the animal world[59]) to tend the earth.[60] The relationship is neither tenuous nor superfluous, but covenantal: "Man," Arendt contends, "*belongs* among the children of nature."

A reader unfamiliar with the writing of Hannah Arendt might easily detect a certain theocentrism in her prophecy of future humans being "possessed by a rebellion against human existence *as it has been given, a free gift.*" The actual source of this gift is only hinted at. Nevertheless, her concerns about making life "artificial," turning away from humanhood "as it has been given," and divorcing it from the natural world, as well as her references to escapism, possession, and rebellion, point to a repudiation of the very essence of being human that could only ever amount to our own extinction.

NOTES

1. By "humanhood," I am referring collectively to the (changing or unchanging) nature *and* condition of being human. Joseph Fletcher identifies (rightly, I think) the "murky semantic swamp" that words like "humane," "humanistic," and "humanhood" will be until medicine, anthropology, religion, and the other relevant disciplines are

better able to elucidate who and what human beings are. See Joseph Fletcher, *Humanhood: Essays in Biomedical Ethics* (Buffalo, NY: Prometheus, 1979), 8.

2. Nick Bostrom, "Transhumanist Values," 2003, http://www. nickbostrom.com/ethics/values.pdf, accessed March 20, 2014, 4.

3. Bostrom, "Transhumanist Values," 5.

4. Bostrom, "Transhumanist Values," 6.

5. Bostrom, "Transhumanist Values," 7.

6. Bostrom, "Transhumanist Values," 7.

7. Nick Bostrom, "In Defense of Posthuman Dignity," *Bioethics* 19, no. 3 (2005): 203.

8. Nick Bostrom et al., "Transhumanist FAQ," version 3.0, http://humanityplus.org/philosophy/transhumanist-faq/, accessed March 20, 2014.

9. Bostrom et al., "Transhumanist FAQ."

10. Bostrom et al., "Transhumanist FAQ."

11. Bostrom et al., "Transhumanist FAQ."

12. Bostrom et al., "Transhumanist FAQ."

13. Anders Sandberg, "Morphological Freedom: Why We Not Just Want It, but *Need* It," 2001, http://www.aleph.se/Nada/Texts/MorphologicalFreedom.htm, accessed March 20, 2014.

14. Nick Bostrom et al., "Transhumanist FAQ."

15. William Shakespeare, *As You Like It*, edited by George Lyman Kittredge (Boston, MA: Ginn, 1939), 2.7.165–166.

16. Rory H. Fisher, "The Health Care System and the Elderly," *Bioethics Update* 3, no. 1 (2003): 1.

17. Karen A. Lyman, "Living with Alzheimer's Disease: The Creation of Meaning among Persons with Dementia," *Journal of Clinical Ethics* 9, no. 1 (1998): 51.

18. Nancy Harding and Colin Palfrey, *The Social Construction of Dementia: Confused Professionals?* (London, UK: Jessica Kingsley, 1997), 126.

19. Harding and Palfrey, *The Social Construction of Dementia*, 127.

20. C. Shilling, *The Body and Social Theory* (London, UK: Sage, 1993), 12.

21. Shilling, *The Body and Social Theory*, 196.

22. Harding and Palfrey, *The Social Construction of Dementia*, 138–139.

23. Harding and Palfrey, *The Social Construction of Dementia*, 140.

24. 1 Corinthians 6.19.

25. *Catechism of the Catholic Church* (Ottawa, ON: Canadian Conference of Catholic Bishops, 1994), §364.

26. *Catechism of the Catholic Church*, §366.

27. George L. Engel, "The Need for a New Medical Model: A Challenge for Biomedicine," *Science*, New Series 196.4286 (1977): 129–136.

28. *Catechism of the Catholic Church*, §362; §364.

29. Genesis 2.7.

30. *Qur'an*, 15.28–29.

31. *Catechism of the Catholic Church*, §2289.

32. *Catechism of the Catholic Church*.

33. Psalms 90.12.

34. *Catechism of the Catholic Church*, §997; Louis Jacobs, *The Book of Jewish Belief* (West Orange, NJ: Behrman, 1984), 231; Fazlur Rahman, *Health and Medicine in the Islamic Tradition: Change and Identity* (New York, NY: Crossroad, 1989), 126;

Jonathan E. Brockopp, ed., *Islamic Ethics of Life: Abortion, War, and Euthanasia* (Columbia, SC: University of South Carolina Press, 2003), 181.

35. Luke 24.13–35; John 20.12–18.

36. *Order of Christian Funerals* (Ottawa, ON: Canadian Conference of Catholic Bishops, 1990), §4; §272; Rahman, *Health and Medicine*, 126. Elliot N. Dorff, *Matters of Life and Death: A Jewish Approach to Modern Medical Ethics*, 1st ed. (Philadelphia: Jewish Publication Society, 1998), 339.

37. *Catechism*, §2278. Rahman, *Health and Medicine*, 109; Dorff, *Matters of Life and Death*, 185–186, 209.

38. 1 Corinthians 12.26.

39. Matthew 5.48.

40. 2 Corinthians 12.9.

41. Matthew 19.21; Leviticus 19.2; *Catechism of the Catholic Church*, §1968.

42. John Paul II, *Man and Woman He Created Them: A Theology of the Body*, translated by Michael Waldstein (Boston, MA: Pauline, 2006), xxvii.

43. John Paul II, *Man and Woman*, §19.4.

44. 1 Corinthians 6.18.

45. Matthew 26.26–28; Mark 14.22–24; Luke 22.15–20.

46. Matthew 8.1–3; Matthew 8.14–15; Matthew 20.29–34; Mark 5.21–43; Luke 6.19.

47. John 20.24–29.

48. *Catechism of the Catholic Church*, §789; Romans 12.4–5; 1 Corinthians 12. 12–27.

49. *Catechism of the Catholic Church*, §1015.

50. *Catechism of the Catholic Church*, §1015, §1017.

51. *Catechism of the Catholic Church*, §2289.

52. *Catechism of the Catholic Church*, §999.

53. John Paul II, *Man and Woman*, §66.1.

54. John Paul II, *Man and Woman*, §66.5–67.2.

55. John Paul II, *Man and Woman*, §6.3.

56. John Paul II, *Man and Woman*, §5.1–10.5; Nicanor Pier Giorgio Austriaco, *Biomedicine and Beatitude: An Introduction to Catholic Bioethics* (Washington, DC: Catholic University of America Press, 2011), 75.

57. Hannah Arendt, *The Human Condition* (Chicago, IL: University of Chicago Press, 1958), 2–3.

58. Genesis 2.7.

59. Genesis 2.19.

60. Genesis 2.15.

The Fleshless Future: A Phenomenological Perspective on Mind Uploading

Hannah Scheidt

UPLOADED MINDS: ALTERNATIVE VERSIONS

In *The Age of Spiritual Machines*, Ray Kurzweil tells the story of "Jack," a hypothetical futuristic man who, experiencing difficulty with his hearing, receives a simple cochlear implant. This routine surgical procedure improves Jack's life so much that he opts for retinal image-processing implants to improve his vision as well. Intoxicated by his improved cyborgian condition, Jack receives memory implants. Jack then decides to have his entire brain and neural system replaced with electronic circuits that provide "far greater capacity, speed, and reliability" than his previous biological wiring. At this point, Kurzweil suggests, Jack might just as well go in for a complete brain scan and have the data from his electronic circuitry (as Kurzweil understands it, his consciousness) installed in a remote electronic neural computer that would presumably outlast his biological body.

So Jack abandons his organic body—which seems to have done nothing but disappoint him—altogether. For his new body, he could choose a nanotechnology-enhanced one capable of repairing its own immune system and growing replacement organs. Or perhaps he might opt for a virtual body suit that allows for interaction in a virtual tactile environment. In this high-tech haptic interface, he could decide to be a "more attractive" version of himself and would have plenty of virtual companions from which to choose. In these scenarios, Jack has not been destroyed, Kurzweil explains, but has simply been transferred to a more suitable embodiment. Jack is himself, Jack is happy, and Jack's friends are impressed.[1]

Consider, now, an alternative account of the process and the results of mind uploading from the cyberpunk novel *Neuromancer*, by William Gibson. In *Neuromancer*, characters with the proper equipment (an elaborate "deck" with dermatrodes that attach to the forehead) can jack into cyberspace, a Matrix-like graphical representation of abstracted data. Case, a hacker and the novel's main character, has a unique guide for his most challenging hacking assignment in the Matrix grid: a ROM (read-only memory) construct. A ROM construct is Gibson's version of an uploaded mind—someone who "flatlines" (dies) while jacked into cyberspace and has his or her memories and "personality data" copied into the ROM. This particular construct is Dixie Flatline, a former legendary cowboy (read: hacker) who flatlined during a particularly harrowing hacking job. It becomes clear from Case's first interaction with the construct that his existence is miserable—that he is not joyfully exploring the infinite net of the Matrix, unencumbered by his organic body:

"How you doing, Dixie?"
"I'm dead, Case. Got enough time in . . . to figure that one."
"How's it feel?"
"It doesn't."
"Bother you?"
"What bothers me is, nothin' does."
. . .
When the construct laughed, it came through as something else, not laughter, but a stab of cold down Case's spine. "Do me a favor, boy."
"What's that, Dix?"
"This scam of yours, when it's over, you erase this goddamn thing."[2]
Dixie agrees to help Case only if Case agrees to erase him—to erase the data, that is, that constitutes his existence as an uploaded mind.

For now, let these two explorations of mind uploading serve as introductions to the topic. Both include accounts of uploading the data of the mind to a nonbiological substrate; Kurzweil's story also includes a version of the gradual-augmentation model. These are two commonly cited hypothetical mind transfer techniques through which to achieve immortality. Recent decades have brought increasing public awareness of the methods and goals of mind uploading, due in part to popular scientific books like Kurzweil's volume, but also due to a surge in popular cultural products such as novels, movies, and television series. The concept is relatively old, however; indeed, some fictional accounts date back to the mid-20th century and the earliest years of electronic digital computers.[3] Today, hopeful mind uploaders want to achieve synapse-by-synapse mapping of the human brain and build computers that can match the brain in speed and capacity.

Not all posthumanists or transhumanists are committed to mind uploading. In *Cyborg Selves: A Theological Anthropology of the Posthuman*, Jeanine

Thweatt-Bates distinguishes between two divergent constructions of the post-human. On the one hand, we have the cyborg, a "feminist posthuman construction" that serves "as a symbol for the ontological kinship of the human with the nonhuman." Thweatt-Bates credits Donna Haraway with this construction of the cyborg; Haraway's seminal feminist essay "A Cyborg Manifesto" suggested using the cyborg as a site to oppose entrenched boundaries and binaries and to rework social realities. On the other hand, we have an uploaded consciousness, a "transhuman construction" replacing the "problematic biological body" with a more durable and immortal virtual or artificial one.[4] In this chapter, I am avoiding the more general "posthumanist" or "transhumanist" vision and addressing, instead, "hopeful mind uploaders" or "mind transfer advocates."

The two reports of mind uploading involving Jack and Dixie Flatland are obviously vastly different, and I juxtapose them to introduce two related critiques. First, these accounts—Kurzweil's Jack and Gibson's Dixie Flatland—stem from two vastly different assessments of the nature of consciousness, the self, and the relationship between the individual and the phenomenal world. Kurzweil's vision is based on a firm and implicit rejection of the importance of embodiment and embeddedness in human consciousness and experience. To expose and challenge these assumptions, I draw on philosophers and critics of computer consciousness specifically. I also relate their reactionary ideologies to Maurice Merleau-Ponty's philosophy of embodied phenomenology. I borrow emblems from Merleau-Ponty—the notion of the flesh and the famous case of the pathological patient Schneider—to challenge the seamless accounts of mind transfer that appear in popular transfer discourse.

Second, in exposing the ideological, anthropological, and ontological foundations of mainstream mind uploading discourse, I suggest that mind uploading does not, as Kurzweil insists, "start with science."[5] Kurzweil is not alone in his resolve.

Roboticist and mind transfer advocate Hans Moravec conveys a similar sentiment: "It is easy to imagine human thought freed from bondage to a mortal body ... But it is not necessary to adopt a mystical or religious stance to accept the possibility. Computers provide a model for even the most ardent mechanist."[6] Moravec clearly distinguishes between "religious" visions for immortality and his own project, which he portrays as entirely naturalistic and scientific. Prominent transhumanist Nick Bostrom, whose "Transhumanist FAQ" includes descriptions of hypothetical uploading scenarios, identifies transhumanism as being firmly rooted in "rational humanism, which emphasizes science and critical reason rather than revelation and religious authority."[7] These assertions are not truthful, and I critique their anthropological and ontological assumptions, thereby exposing the ideological foundations of the project and the way they "prime" the science that follows. Overall, my aim is not to offer a theological critique of the project or to deny its feasibility entirely, but instead to suggest that the enterprise of mind uploading would be more convincing, honest, and compelling if it acknowledged these foundations and adapted its self-understanding accordingly.

MINDS AND BRAINS: THE ANTHROPOLOGY OF UPLOADING

Kurzweil concludes the story of Jack by writing: "As our understanding of the mechanisms of the brain improves and our ability to accurately and non-invasively scan these features improves, reinstating (reinstalling) a person's brain *should alter a person's mind no more than it changes day to day* [italics added]."[8] He is confident that an uploaded mind will survive in near-seamless continuation with previous mental experience. To upload a mind, Kurzweil explains, we need to reverse-engineer a brain, synapse by synapse. This could be accomplished by analyzing a frozen brain, layer by painstaking layer, or by taking advantage of rapidly improving brain scanning technology. Kurzweil likens this mapping to the Human Genome Project, which seemed to be taking an insurmountable goal when it was launched in 1991 but was completed in 2003. According to this author, gradually (but with increasing speed), we will expose the "complete set of unifying formulas that underlies intelligence."[9] Indeed, in his most recent book on the subject, *How to Build a Mind*, Kurzweil expands on some of these formulas, focusing on the hierarchical pattern recognition of the neocortex, whose structure and functions Kurzweil deems imitable.[10] Finally, we need a suitably powerful computational substrate to act as the transfer destination—that is, a computer that can match the human brain in terms of speed and capacity. Thus a complete scan or a detailed dissection of the human brain will tell us exactly what and how humans think and a nonbiological machine will satisfactorily "run" the software of the human mind.

Other notable artificial intelligence advocates describe similar transfer methods and conceal similar assumptions. For example, Marvin Minsky's explanation of consciousness in *The Society of Mind* likens the workings of human intelligence to the interaction of simple processes. Mindless, semi-autonomous, discrete processes, or "agents," interact in the formation of a more complex process that we recognize as the mind. It does not matter what these agents *are*, only what they *do*. For Minsky, "minds are what brains do" (for now), but the physical parts of the brain could be replaced with suitable alternative parts, provided they support the same *processes* or successions of states.[11] In *Mind Children*, Hans Moravec expresses confidence that, in adequate time, no human function will lack an artificial counterpart.[12] This includes, most importantly, human intelligence. Moravec argues that a human mind transferred into a new body will maintain its original identity if we accept the position of "pattern-identity," which "defines the essence of a person ... as the *pattern* and *process* going on in [the] head and body, not the machinery supporting that process."[13] For both of these thinkers, whose major works are part of the futurist canon, the mind is essentially a substrate-independent pattern.[14]

One of the most widely popularized means of understanding and relating this philosophy of mind is the computer analogy, wherein human thought is functionally akin to computer information processing. The brain is the computer "hardware" and the mind is the "software." Daniel Dennett, although not a self-described transhumanist, directly develops this central analogy in his work: "Conscious human minds are more or less serial virtual machines implemented—*inefficiently*—on the parallel hardware that evolution has provided for us."[15] For Dennett, consciousness itself is a complex of meme effects operating as a virtual machine on organic hardware. The self is a blip of self-representation created by the brain—that is, an informational structure programmed to run on the brain's computer. Dennett's view is consistent with the goals of mind uploading. These "blips" are theoretically transferable, and it does not matter on which media they are played.

Importantly, Dennett (as do most advocates of machine consciousness) locates his theory within a legacy that traces back to mid-20th-century computer scientists Alan Turing and John von Neumann. Turing famously designed a machine according to an introspective analysis of how he, as a mathematician, went about solving problems. He then tried to theoretically replicate his thought process in the operations of a machine. The Turing machine would operate according to a set of relatively simple processes that would result in a hyper-rational phenomenon. This idealization of the thought process became the blueprint for the first actual digital computer, engineered by John von Neumann. A von Neumann machine consists of a random access memory and a central processing unit that copies and registers instructions. Because a single workspace contains *both* instructions and executed results, the machine is characterized by the notorious "von Neumann bottleneck."[16] Despite this apparent flaw, all digital computers to this day are descendants of this design, which Dennett describes as a giant electronic mind.

Although recent futurists frequently trace the origin of their ideas about consciousness to Turing, I question the accuracy of their understanding of Turing's machine "consciousness." His famous Turing Test, an adaptation of a Victorian parlor game in which "questioners" guess the genders of two hidden "responders," became the first standard for judging machine intelligence. The Turing Test replaces one of the responders with a well-programmed machine (a digital computer). If the questioner guesses incorrectly which responder is a computer and which is a human, then we conclude that the machine can think, according to this test.[17] Functionally, if the machine acts like a human consciousness and "fools" a human consciousness, we might as well call it a consciousness. Turing is upfront about the limits of what his test proves and is careful about not overstepping these limits. He reminds readers that the Turing Test shows us a way to consider consciousness as a *perceived* or *endowed* quality: "I do not wish to give the impression that I think there is no mystery about consciousness. . . . But I do not think these mysteries necessarily need to be solved before we can answer the question with which we are concerned in this paper."[18] In other words, Turing invites us to consider how we might identify and know intelligence and consciousness in a relative sense—that is, in the eyes of the beholder. A sense of subjectivity and relationality remains at the heart of Turing's definition.

I do not see these same sentiments in the works of contemporary futurists who are committed to dispelling the "mystery of consciousness." Thinkers like Kurzweil, Dennett, Minsky, and Moravec believe that all mind operations are reducible to symbol-manipulating calculations and that humans "process information" in discrete steps that can be imitated in a machine. Claiming that their intellectual legacy lies with these foundational computer scientists belies the extent to which they have superseded their claims. Somewhere along the way, acknowledgment of the "mystery" of consciousness that Turing identified became a liability. Modern mind uploading advocates harken back to Turing's seminal work on machine intelligence, but their work no longer contains any sense of the relational, subjective nature of the project. Such an acknowledgment would likely complicate their neat models of mental processes that aim to expose, extract, and replicate of the data of the mind. This irresponsible simplification makes the goal of the contemporary project—transfer through immortality—more feasible as a "scientific" venture.

BODIES: LOST AND FOUND

The futurist perspective dismisses the human body and rejects its relevance to and necessity for consciousness, thought, and experience. Material hosts, or bodies, are of secondary importance (if that). In *How We Became Posthuman*, N. Katherine Hayles critiques this contemporary perspective of "virtuality," which imagines information and materiality as distinct and privileges information as essential. People forget, Hayles writes, that information is always instantiated in a medium. This is precisely true in popular mind uploading discourse. When Kurzweil writes about Jack's "virtual body" in its "virtual environment," he does not adequately acknowledge that even a virtual self needs a material host, even if it is just a hard drive. And would not this host proffer its own limitations and its own vulnerability? Kurzweil's writing elsewhere exemplifies an attitude of "bodily arbitrariness." He devotes a section in *The Age of Spiritual Machines* to describing the engineered bodies of the future— necessary, he explains, only because "a disembodied mind will quickly get depressed."[19] Moreover, Kurzweil suggests that by the fourth decade of the

20th century, a man has become able to *know what it feels like to be a woman*, simply through a virtual experience enabled by a neural implant. Bodiliness is secondary, transferable, and arbitrary.

Other authors, such as Moravec, convey an even more radical rejection of the body: "The coming revolution may liberate human minds. ... In the present condition we are uncomfortable half-breeds, part biology, part culture, with many of our biological traits out of step with the inventions of our minds." Moravec speaks of his hopes of rescuing his mind from the "limitations of a mortal body," making it clear that he does not identify at all with his body and, furthermore, does not see its role in the constitution of human thought as anything but restrictive.[20]

To challenge these assumptions and encourage more honest recognition of the ideologies at play, I turn to philosophies that refuse to separate bodies from minds and that reject the ontology that plants subjects in a premade world. The specific specter toward which these philosophers direct their challenges—a future populated by conscious, self-replicating machines—is new. The debate, however, is a reprise of an age-old conversation between those who dismiss the body as peripheral and those who argue for its centrality.

Top-Down versus Global Intelligence: Schneider

The computer/mind analogy adheres to a "top-down" schema of consciousness that places mental activity at the beginning of all experience—and it is here that we encounter a formidable objection from the opposing camp. Although Kurzweil and Dennett are eager to explain consciousness in terms of purely physical phenomena, they largely imagine the brain as the master control center and ignore interactive physicality. John Searle, known mainly for the Chinese Room Argument against strong artificial intelligence, calls for an outlook that integrates the specific human body into an understanding of mental activity and experience. Searle writes that mind and body interact because the brain is part of the body and essentially the "last stop" that consciousness takes: "the mind and body interact, but they are not two different things, since mental phenomena just are features of the brain."[21] Searle argues that using and understanding language is less of a matter of following rules (a function that could be programmed in any machine) and more about a neurophysiological predisposition *particular to* human bodies and brains. He writes, "the way to master the mystery of intentionality is to describe in as much detail as we can how phenomena are caused by biological processes while being at the same time realized in biological systems."[22] Although Searle does not mention him, this argument positively reeks of Spinoza, who scandalously posited centuries ago that the human mind is essentially nothing but the idea of the human body.[23] This view can be read as a reversal of the simple top-down understanding of experience, and as one that refuses to award minds independence from materiality. As Searle understands it, the physical human body is the necessary precondition for human processes like language, perception, and intelligence.

Hubert Dreyfus also challenges the top-down understanding of consciousness. He suggests that higher, determinate forms of intelligence—the pure mental activities that so preoccupy cybernetic futurists—are necessarily derived from global, involved, and embodied "lower" forms of intelligence. These embodied "lower" forms of intelligence (e.g., pattern recognition and categorization of perception stimuli) have been most intractable to artificial intelligence engineers, while tasks demanding "higher" intelligence (e.g., solving math or logic problems) have met with great success. For Dreyfus, nonformal ("lower") information processing such as pattern recognition requires indeterminate, global anticipation enabled by a body that is both a "machine" (object) and the object of experience (subject). Perception, intelligence, and consciousness are products of a holistic process in which parts receive meaning only in terms of the whole. The overall meaning of a sentence, for example, determines the meanings of the individual words. Notes in a melody, similarly, have value only as part of the whole composition, rather than the melody being recognized in terms of independent identified notes. Perception, understood this way, is accessible only to a subject who can anticipate an experience holistically rather than approach it through step-by-step formal analysis. This kind of information processing, Dreyfus argues, cannot be reproduced in a heuristically programmed computer, because computers take in information necessarily in parts and build the whole secondarily. It is the intentionality and materiality of the *body* that anticipates, discovers, and confers meanings.

In making this argument, Dreyfus echoes the phenomenology proposed by Maurice Merleau-Ponty. Indeed, Merleau-Ponty provides us with an icon through which to understand the embodied foundation of every thought: the brain-damaged patient, Schneider. Schneider is able to perform only concrete or habitual movements—he cannot move abstractly or even describe his own passive movements. Schneider can grasp and touch, but not point. When asked to perform a concrete movement, Schneider repeats the order, reorients his entire body in preparation, and finally performs the task, never using less than his entire body or minimizing movement, as a typical patient might: "The patient is conscious of his bodily space as the matrix of his habitual action, but not as an objective setting; his body is at his disposal as a means of ingress into a familiar surrounding, but not as the means of expression of a gratuitous and free spatial thought."[24] Schneider must serially create the world, taking extra steps to understand the position of his body. Schneider knows that he is lying down only because, upon reflection, he feels the pressure of a mattress upon his back. In place of tactile recognition and perception (functions of, in Merleau-Ponty's terms, the phenomenal body), Schneider substitutes a laborious decoding of stimuli and deduction. In Schneider, we have an example of what serial information processing—top-down rather than global—looks like in a human specimen.

Schneider, Merleau-Ponty explains, does not arrive at political or religious convictions, and moreover, he is not motivated to try. He cannot even carry on a conversation that was not in some way planned in advance. All of these scenarios require an abstract level of functioning of which Schneider is incapable. Schneider's relative deficiencies—like the problems inherent in machine intelligence—are beneath the level of abstract intelligence. As Merleau-Ponty writes:

> Consciousness—cognitive life, the life of desire or perceptual life—is subtended by an "intentional arc" which projects round about us our past, our future, our human setting, our physical, ideological and moral situation, or rather which results in our being situated in all these respects.[25]

Schneider lacks a perceiving body and the essential intentional arc that situates the self in the world. A necessary preconsciousness grounds the phenomenal body and not only allows for automatic motor functionality, but also supports higher-level ideological and moral situatedness.

Ontological Challenge: The Flesh

Popular mind uploading scenarios posit that the physical world impinges on our mind, which then organizes the received data. This constitutes the ontological assumption of the project: that reality itself can be analyzed as a set of situation-free determinate elements. Dreyfus, again echoing Merleau-Ponty, argues instead that humans create their own fields of experience in terms of preconscious intentions. Relevance is built into the human field of experience. By being situated—that is, by being in the world—we "know" in a way that is coextensive with the world. Thus what we call the world is constituted (and is always in the process of *being* constituted).

Digital computers as yet have no such process, because the information in a machine's memory is not contextually regulated like that of a human's; computers require formal regulation to bring data into their workspaces. Because they exist in a ready-made world, it is unclear whether a machine can be, like a human, a "subject destined for the world." Contemporary research in computer intelligence has shown how challenging it can be to perform even simple tasks of visual recognition. For example, it took a network of 16,000 computers at Google's labs to recognize a cat in 2012.[26] This difficulty is largely explained by the fact that computers do not have the same intentional relationship to the environment that humans do. This is not to say that a computer cannot derive a means of "gearing in" to the world, but I doubt that it will be a world that resembles our own.

The challenges outlined previously—the argument for the centrality of the body, the preference for global processing rather than a top-down schema of consciousness, and the suggestion that reality is ambiguous rather than ready-made—are formulated in Merleau-Ponty's notion of the flesh. The flesh is the mechanism through which Merleau-Ponty imagines the intertwining and reversibility of the sensate and the sensible. There must exist a relationship that is "the initiation to and the opening upon a tactile world ... this [opening] can only happen if my hand, while it is felt from within, is also accessible from without, itself tangible."[27] The seer, therefore, is not a transcendental ego—immaterial and transferable—but rather a being who is himself or herself of the sensible. It is the body—the surface of the hand, the organ of the eye—that perceives and experiences, because it is the body that is located in the fold of the "flesh."

The ontology of the flesh explains our perception of and interaction with objects, but, Merleau-Ponty argues, it also has a relationship with ideas (remember Schneider and the true extent of his problems). There is a bond between the flesh and the idea, and it is not arbitrary but foundational. Merleau-Ponty writes explicitly about the indebtedness of mind to body:

> The ideas we are speaking of would not be better known to us if we had no body and no sensibility; it is then that they would be inaccessible to us. The "little phrase," the notion of the light ... could not be given to us *as ideas* except in a carnal experience. It is not only that we would find in that carnal experience the occasion to think them; it is that they owe their authority, their fascinating, indestructible power, precisely to the fact that they are in transparency behind the sensible, or in its heart.[28]

The invisible (the idea) is not contrary to the visible world; it is rather the invisible *of* this world and what inhabits it. Here, then, we have a foundational critique—namely, that information is inseparable from materiality. Information inhabits its material substrate. This is something mind uploaders simply cannot accept, because this connection challenges the anthropology that grounds their hopes for immortality.

Any notion of consciousness must account for the primordial property of the flesh, the synergy within and among organisms, and the circle of the touched and the touching. What does this suggest about the enterprise of mind uploading? Is a machine body sensate and sensible (object and subject) in the way that a human body is? A computer is certainly sensate, albeit not in the same way that a human is. The whole point, after all, is to create a "more suitable" embodiment. However, I maintain (along with Dreyfus) that machines are not sensible or intentional in the same way that humans are.

The rejection of philosophical (and, increasingly, scientific) conclusions that challenge uploading scenarios of immortality is unconsciously based on a specific theological anthropology, a doctrine of the human. The way that this attitude toward the body and understanding of the self speak directly to a vision of immortality is symptomatic of the religious nature of the enterprise. Religious thinkers throughout history have engaged in similar negotiations. Early Christian authors Irenaeus and Tertulliam, for example, could not imagine the self without the original organic body, so they argued that the resurrected body is made of exactly the same flesh—the same particles—that are digested in the belly of a lion or buried in the grave. For Origen, in contrast, the earthly body was not as essential in defining one's identity. He argued that we will have bodies in heaven, but that they will be spiritual and luminous: just as bodies change in life, so they will change after death.[29] The approach to the body expressed in mind uploading discourse constitutes a religious ethos, as it is conditioned by prior ideologies that are not always recognized as such.

CONCLUSION

Merleau-Ponty works against the Cartesian rubric and predicts a major shift in cognitive science away from a traditional approach that treats mental life as formal, disembodied, and confined to the brain and toward embodied cognition.[30] His phenomenological project aims at getting as close to direct experience—direct and primitive contact with the world—as possible. Merleau-Ponty argues that returning to things-in-themselves demands a return to the world that precedes knowledge, a world in which scientific schematizations are merely "abstract and derivative sign-language."[31] In other words, science as a discipline and an epistemology will always fail in the phenomenal project because its claims to represent an ideal reality do not take the thinking subject into account.

What, then, do we make of the "scientific" enterprise of mind uploading? Mind uploading looks for and rests upon the absolutes of anthropological dualism and strict reductionist materialism. This approach is actually more reminiscent of the practice of theology, as Merleau-Ponty describes it in his essay, "In Praise of Philosophy." Philosophers, he writes, do not make claims about final transcendence and do not place hopes in any destiny, remaining instead committed to an understanding of the unfixed nature of our relations with nature and the contingency of history. To deny this contingency constitutes a nonphilosophical position—that is, a theology or an inverted theology (Merleau-Ponty's term for fixed antitheism or atheism). The "wide-ranging flexibility" of true philosophy "takes the wind from the sails of theology":

> For theology recognizes the contingency of human existence only to derive it from a necessary being, that is, to remove it. Theology makes use of philosophical wonder only for the purpose of motivating an affirmation which ends it. Philosophy, on the other hand, arouses us to what is problematic in our own

existence and in that of the world, to such a point that we shall never be cured of searching for a solution.[32]

We can think of mind uploading as operating, in light of these distinctions, as a theology, in that it seeks to define absolutes and to bring an end to "wonder." The goals, operation, and posture of transhumanists, with regard to mainstream mind uploading, are actually characteristic of theology.

The claim that mind uploading "starts with science" ultimately does a disservice to the project. Acknowledging the theological scaffolding that serves as the necessary support of the mind uploaders' chosen paradigm of immortality will lead to promises and claims that are more difficult and nuanced. Even so, hopeful mind uploaders should be upfront about their values, clearing the way for productive ethical debate. In my introduction, I included the Dixie Flatland scenario to suggest that more thorough and honest explorations of this vision of immortality are happening elsewhere (in this case, cyberpunk literature). In relaxing disciplinary boundaries, Jack may end up looking a little more like Schneider. Lacking horizons and intentional arcs, there may be no conscious continuity between organic life and reincarnation in a "fleshless" reality. In this case, even Dixie Flatline's frustrating existence in the Matrix is too optimistic. Ultimately, however, claims that acknowledge the underlying ideology rather than insisting that mind uploading "starts with science" will be stronger, more substantial, captivating, and potentially revolutionary.

NOTES

1. Ray Kurzweil, *The Age of Spiritual Machines* (New York, NY: Viking, 1999), 54, 140–144.

2. William Gibson, *Neuromancer* (New York, NY: Ace Books, 1984), 105–106.

3. Early fictional accounts include Arthur C. Clarke, *The City and the Stars* (London, UK: Gollancz, Orion Publishing Group, 1956); and Isaac Asimov, "The Last Question" in *Robot Dreams* (New York, NY: Ace Books, 1956). More recent works include William Gibson, *Neuromancer* (New York, NY: Ace Books, 1984); and Greg Egan, *Permutation City* (London, UK: Gollancz, Orion Publishing Group, 1994). The author suggests using cryobiological procedures to freeze the brain until we arrive at the "ultimate solution" and can read out brain data into computers.

4. Jeanine Thweatt-Bates, *Cyborg Selves: A Theological Anthropology of the Posthuman* (Fardham, UK: Ashgate, 2012), 5–6.

5. This is opposed to religion, which emerged in "prescientific" times. In an interview at a Singularity Summit, Kurzweil insists that the project of mind uploading does *not* start with religion. "Ray Kurzweil: The Singularity Is Not a Religion," FutureBlogger, http://futureblogger.net/futureblogger/show/1231-ray-kurzweil-the -singularity-is-not-a-religion, accessed March 16, 2014. The same sentiment is expressed in an interview on the World Future Society website: "The Futurist

Interviews Ray Kurzweil," World Future Society, http://www.wfs.org/content/futurist
-interviews-ray-kurzweil, accessed March 16, 2014.

6. Hans Moravec, *Mind Children: The Future of Robot and Human Intelligence* (Cambridge, MA: Harvard University Press, 1988), 4.

7. Nick Bostrom, "The Transhumanist FAQ," World Transhumanist Association, http://humanityplus.org/leanr/transhumanist-faq/.

8. Kurzweil, *The Age of Spiritual Machines*, 125.

9. Kurzweil, *The Age of Spiritual Machines*, 73.

10. Ray Kurzweil, *How to Create a Mind* (New York, NY: Viking, 2012).

11. Marvin Minsky, *The Society of Mind* (New York, NY: Simon and Schuster, 1986), 287–289.

12. Moravec, *Mind Children,* 2.

13. Moravec, *Mind Children,* 117.

14. This means that the mind, as a pattern or process, is the same regardless of what material it is "running" on—organic, biological neurons or an electric supercomputer.

15. Daniel Dennett, *Consciousness Explained* (Boston, MA: Little, Brown, 1991), 218.

16. This is a central limitation of von Neumann architecture. The data transfer rate, or "throughput," is limited because program memory and data memory share a single workspace: the central processing unit. This is where the bottleneck occurs. As memory increases, the CPU spends an increasing amount of time waiting for data from memory.

17. Alan Turing, "Computing Machinery and Intelligence," *Mind: A Quarterly Review of Psychology and Philosophy* 59, no. 236 (1950): 433–460.

18. Turing, "Computing Machinery and Intelligence," 447.

19. Kurzweil, *The Age of Spiritual Machines*, 134.

20. Moravec, *Mind Children,* 4–5.

21. John Searle, *Minds, Brains and Science* (Cambridge, MA: Harvard University Press, 1984), 26.

22. Searle, *Minds, Brains and Science,* 53.

23. Baruch Spinoza, *Ethics*, translated by Samuel Shirley (Indianapolis, IN: Hackett Publishing, 1992), IIP11, IIP13.

24. Maurice Merleau-Ponty, *Phenomenology of Perception*, translated by Colin Smith (New York, NY: Routledge, 1958), 118–119, 130.

25. Merleau-Ponty, *Phenomenology of Perception,* 157.

26. John Markoff, "How Many Computers to Identify a Cat? 16,000," *New York Times,* June 25, 2012, http://www.nytimes.com/2012/06/26/technology/in-a-big
-network-of-computers-evidence-of-machine-learning.html?pagewanted=all&_r=0, accessed March 20, 2014.

27. Maurice Merleau-Ponty, *Sense and Non-Sense*, translated by Patricia Allen Dreyfus (Evanston, IL: Northwestern University Press, 1964), 133.

28. Merleau-Ponty, *Sense and Non-Sense,* 150.

29. For a full discussion of the role of the body in imagining selfhood among Christians, see Carolyn Walker Bynum, *The Resurrection of the Body* (New York, NY: Columbia University Press, 1995).

30. See, for example, Hubert Dreyfus, "Merleau-Ponty and Recent Cognitive Science," in *The Cambridge Companion to Merleau-Ponty*, edited by Taylor Carman and Mark B. N. Hansen (New York, NY: Cambridge University Press, 2005), 129–150. Or see Raymond W. Gibbs, Jr., *Embodiment and Cognitive Science* (New York, NY: Cambridge University Press, 2006).

31. Merleau-Ponty, *Phenomenology of Perception*, ix–x.

32. Maurice Merleau-Ponty, *In Praise of Philosophy and Other Essays*, translated by John Wild and James Edie (Evanston, IL: Northwestern University Press, 1970), 43–44.

Section 6

Corporeal Diversity and Religious Experience

22

. . . .

Does Transhumanism Face an Uncanny Valley among the Religious?

Donald M. Braxton

INTRODUCTION

Disgust and fear are deep-seated and rapid emotional responses initially designed to guard bodily integrity against predation and disease. In social species, these emotions are recruited to establish and maintain group boundaries. Among one particular social species, *Homo sapiens*, fear and disgust have been further appropriated for the demarcation of tribal groups, contributing to a robust, species-wide xenophobia. While such xenophobic reactions are not unique to religious groups, they are especially pronounced in religious beliefs and behaviors. Among religious populations, disgust and fear are elicited for the establishment of taboos, the demonization of difference, and moral-aesthetic judgments about the acceptability of body differences. If transhumanism does not wish to generate the political fallout that comes from activating these powerful and primitive emotional systems, it may need to forego certain forms of self-modification, even if those trait modifications are in and of themselves quite desirable. Likewise, it may need to embrace certain forms of self-modification, even if the trait change is a relatively low priority with minimal gain for a larger transhumanist agenda. In this chapter, I discuss the anthropological background to the employment of fear and disgust for religious membership policing, offer a map of its most likely trigger mechanisms, outline an empirical research agenda to test these hypotheses, and deduce some suggestions for how transhumanists might have to adjust their agenda if they wish to engage in a productive dialogue with religious groups.

RELIGION AND THE BODY: A BRIEF
BACKGROUND HISTORY

Anthropological research into the body, religious anxiety, and disgust reaches deeply into the academic study of religion and weaves a fairly consistent thread through more than a century and a half of scholarly work. E. B. Tylor, one of the founders of modern scientific study of religious behavior, advanced the theory that religion is made up of various "survivor" cultural artifacts.[1] He posited that many religious beliefs are prescientific explanations for everyday natural occurrences that have not been weeded out by rational analysis. Tylor's analysis of religion suggests that many religious beliefs surrounding the body, for example, are misplaced causal explanations for health, body integrity, and contagion in a premedical context. While his neat and naïve distinction between scientific and religious (animistic) beliefs has not withstood the test of time, his basic impulse to create a rational ethnography to explain the processes governing religious ideation anticipated the modern cognitive science of religion, with its attention to how basic emotional systems make various propositions more or less salient to human minds and social systems.[2]

By the time of Freud (*Totem and Taboo*, 1913), scholars had begun speculating widely about linkages between basic emotional states such as fear, shame, disgust, and anger and contemporary religious-moral constructs. In Freud's mature reflection on religion, the feeling of the "oceanic" assumes center stage in his psychology (*The Future of an Illusion*, 1927; *Civilization and Its Discontents*, 1930), as he posits a struggle between nature's threat to a fragile human body and modern civilization's body prescriptions. For Freud and his peers, civilization was a precarious accomplishment barely able to restrain very old emotional systems and channel them into socially acceptable, or at least less destructive, behaviors. Freud sees in humans "creatures among whose instinctual endowments is to be reckoned a powerful share of aggressiveness."[3] As was the case for Tylor before him, many of Freud's specific suggestions about the mechanics of religion have fallen by the wayside, yet his push to explain current religious behavior in terms of how psychological mechanisms evolved in response to a deeper, prehistoric past remains a core line of investigation for the cognitive science of religion and evolutionary psychology.[4]

Moving forward 30 years, Mary Douglas offered a highly influential Durkheimian explanation of religious behaviors rooted in anxiety and disgust. In her 1966 book, *Purity and Danger*, Douglas advances the analysis of the mobilization of fear and disgust by placing their activation in more fully fleshed out social and political contexts:

> The body is a model which can stand for any bounded system. Its boundaries can represent any boundaries which are threatened or precarious. The body is a complex structure. The functions of its different parts and their relation afford a source of symbols for other complex structures. We cannot possibly interpret

rituals concerning excreta, breast milk, saliva and the rest unless we are prepared to see in the body a symbol of society, and to see the powers and dangers credited to social structure reproduced in small on the human body.[5]

For Douglas, although the complex systems of taboo and ritual pollution, hygiene, group cleanliness, nonstandard sexual behaviors, and the supposed "dirtiness" of inanimate objects violate the rational expectations of modern medicine, they become rational if we understand that various emotion systems are being recruited for the policing of group identity. The body is a natural template on which social groups etch and dramatize arcane systems of prescriptions and prohibitions for social organizational purposes. Douglas is equivocal on the matter of just how fixed these systems may be—that is, how innate they are to human nature and how open they are to social learning—but presumably they must work with some combination of evolved brain mechanisms and social manipulation if they are to generate predictable, and therefore fungible, social outputs. Such systems cannot occur in an evolutionary vacuum that each society invents from scratch. In the parlance of the cognitive science of religion, Douglas's theory may be "mind-blind" (a shorthand expression meaning oblivious to the mechanisms that the human mind routinely employs) but her views can be reformatted for the modern cognitive study of religion.

Marvin Harris continued Douglas's social argument in his classic essay, "Pig Lovers and Pig Haters." He asks, "Why should gods so exalted as Jahweh and Allah have bothered to condemn a harmless and even laughable beast whose flesh is relished by the greater part of mankind?"[6] In contrast to Douglas, Harris rightly prefers more material, ecological explanations for why some animals make their ways onto taboo lists whereas others are deemed acceptable food sources. He contends that religious systems must pay for themselves in terms of some survival advantages for any given social group—a welcome corrective to the freestanding functionalism of Douglas. Like Douglas, however, Harris recognizes that an emotional system is being enlisted to achieve culturally mediated taxonomies of acceptance and disgust.

Also in the 1970s, but in the very different French tradition of poststructuralism, historian and philosopher Michel Foucault argued that state-sponsored ideological work is accomplished by the various ways in which the body has been categorized, tortured, disciplined, and segregated.[7] His attention is not religion as such, but any cultural system directed at policing human behavior and the state's need to inscribe its power and control on the human body. Foucault's investigation of Western sexuality[8] performs a similar task. He traces the use of the body as a weapon in the ideological warfare of the modern state against unruly "pleasure" impulses. He argues that the modern medicalization of the body is "marked by an increased apprehension, a broader and more detailed definition of the correlations between the sexual act and the body, a closer attention to the ambivalence of its effects and its disturbing consequences . . . fearing it because of its many connections with disease and with evil."[9] In both cases—criminality and sexuality—Foucault contends the body is a malleable palette readily available to be inscribed with political boundary markers, just as Douglas suggests. These markers of familiar and odd, stable and subversive, in-group and out-group, uncanny and comforting, harness the mechanisms of primitive emotions to render social constructions cognitively salient. Group members are subjected to the emotional training necessary to give the taxonomies their ideological bite.

Current cognitive science theories of religion ground religious behaviors surrounding the body in evolved mental systems and their routinized outputs. At the center of this scholarly work is how the mind attends to, biases, and records a wide array of data into memory systems. The answer to these questions of memory in turn shape arguments about which religious ideas have competitive advantages over others and achieve cultural transmission across generations. Factors such as built-in constraints on perception; limits on short-term memory; the means by which the mind consolidates long-term memory; specific modules for environmentally recurrent events such as social intelligence, folk physics, and biology; and the emotive systems that tag various life-world events for relevance are all subjects of intense empirical investigation. Religious behaviors relevant to the human body are, therefore, likely to be complex products of all of these factors. My interest in this chapter is in how the systems governing fear and disgust are activated by perceived violations of presumed body security and integrity among religious believers.

The emerging consensus among cognitive scientists is that religion is not really an object of meaningful investigation. As a category, it is simply too vague. This Western cultural construct lacks any precise boundaries, being more like a soup with many ingredients than a domain of investigation in and of itself. Thus, religion has no coherent essence, no *sui generis* feature that can be explicated only on its own terms as, say, an Eliadian scholar of religion might contend. To deal with this fact, the modern cognitive science of religion tends to study all cultural systems in which adherents report hypothesized counterintuitive agents and, as a result, engage in various behaviors that derive from that supposition. In other words, the term "religion" is a pragmatically employed, shorthand term for a range of mental representations and resultant behaviors that most people can agree are what they mean by the term "religious." In what follows, I base my statements about religious beliefs and behaviors on this open-ended definition.

TRANSHUMANISM, THE BODY, AND RELIGIOUS RESISTANCE

The human body, with all of its marvelous systems that enable sentience, self-consciousness, bipedal locomotion, and wondrous tool usage, still comes with many design flaws and weaknesses from an engineering point of view.

Evolution has fashioned the human form through opportunistic tinkering and the building of novel systems on top of more rudimentary subsystems. These transformations were driven by the need to adapt to rapidly changing climatic conditions in our formative past and the resultant changing selection pressures. Many, if not most, of the abilities our species now enjoys were hacks to existing systems otherwise known as "exaptations."[10] Most of these on-the-fly evolutionary experiments failed and were stamped out through extinction. For example, the facial musculature displayed by the hyper-robust *Australopithecines* points to a commitment to a dietary strategy dominated by the consumption of grasses/grains. A grazing specialization, in turn, does not provide the fruitful foundation for the emergence of an advanced, and initially exapted, social intelligence like the *Australopithecines'* scavenging brethren to the north. Some much smaller number of exaptations produced marginally useful behavioral changes that enabled some success, or at least imposed no real costs in terms of differential survival. Finally, a vanishing few of these innovations proved to be beneficial and served as the basis for preferential survival and reproduction. We who live now and who enjoy the consequences of these few "lucky innovators" are the rare success stories of the blind groping of life toward survival. This is the scientific explanation for the current form our species displays, and this evolutionary background narrative is understood and embraced by most, if not all, transhumanists.

This scientific account is lacking in something that most religions prize very highly in their explanations of our species' origin—something that we might call "the gratuity factor." What I am calling the gratuity factor is, in essence, an emotive response to the fact that there is something rather than nothing. For the religiously minded, our design and the affordances it allows our species are the product of a long nurturance of life governed by wise and benevolent supernatural agencies. This factor is of sacred value. Antagonism by religiously minded individuals toward the transhumanist willingness to experiment with the human form is driven at least in part by a perceived deaf ear to the gratuity of human life. While it is not quite accurate to characterize transhumanists as necessarily lacking in a sense of blessing, the anti-religious flavor of some forms of transhumanist rhetoric can easily give this impression.[11]

In reality, such antagonism seems unnecessary and is, indeed, a serious distraction. What is informative about these competing narratives, however, is what drives the rhetoric. On the one hand, many, if not most, transhumanists construct the value of their worldview as an emancipatory narrative in which escaping a slavish submissiveness to nature's limits is the key feature. To the extent that nature's limits are endowed with an arbitrary sacred value, commitment to transhumanism requires that the exponent throw off the blinders of a false ideology. On the other hand, the most salient feature of sacredness is its binary nature; that is, something either is or is not sacred. Sacred status is derived from some immediate connection to a supernatural agency, and attentiveness to sacredness is structured by social expectations of loyalty to this hypothesized agency. As a result, compromise in regard to "sacred things" becomes quite problematic, tantamount to a betrayal of sacred trust.

Because these competing commitments cut so deeply to the core narratives of transhumanists and the religious, it is difficult to fathom how to bridge the gap.[12] Perhaps the most promising avenue is to seek a minimalist level of agreement on the basis of the "gratuity experience." For transhumanists, the accident of human life can still be valued as a product of great luck and value. We are, after all, quite improbable products of the world. For the religious, we are not accidental beings but the products of loving-kindness. Like Richard Dawkins the atheist, and Ursula Goodenough, the religious naturalist, we can find common ground at least on this simple acknowledgment.[13]

But now back to the transhumanist account of the body and its limits: as marvelous as the abilities of the human base model are, they are nevertheless blind evolutionary hacks. Simple, foresighted design principles of today's well-trained engineers can be applied to how the human body accomplishes its metabolic chores, psychological behaviors, and mobility needs. Those same scientists can imagine superior alternatives. Numerous classic compromise solutions to basic organismal functions have been identified: the shared plumbing of our ingestion and respiratory systems; the chronic back problems of a quadrupedal spinal column transformed into a bipedal support structure; distributed and poorly insulated memory systems with files linked in a hodge-podge of associations resulting in shoddy retrieval results. Regardless of how well or how poorly these hacks get us by, there are often ways to accomplish the same functions more efficiently and reliably. Much of modern medicine is dedicated to correcting for the design flaws of previous evolutionary iterations of our species. Transhumanists simply want to open the gates of experimentation to move beyond maintaining blindly designed, imperfect systems. Transhumanists ask, Why not seek to augment or replace human form and function with more optimal designs?

Among the religious of the world for whom the gratuity of life signals divine intervention, a sacralization of the wonders of the world is an indispensable aspect of the cultural package transmitted extra-genetically through social learning. The world cannot be blind and indifferent, they say, but is rather sacred at some level, usually underwritten by an imagined supernatural wisdom. Religious traditions all claim access to information and insight about the nature of reality and its underlying moral structures. The distribution of life-enhancing or life-debilitating opportunities is mapped by this moral order, best known, and therefore most strategically accessed, by religious specialists and guilds of professional mediators (e.g., priests, prophets, shamans). Consultations with religious elites ensure detection of optimal sources of religious power and avoidance of defiling zones and behaviors. How the believer behaves has the power to accrue merit, personal purity, insight, and righteousness. Likewise, the world is full of debasing temptations that can cause the religious to veer from the path of personal discipline. Sacred and profane, holy and defiled—nothing in the world is merely neutral. Webs of supernatural significance underwrite all reality.

The human body is subject to the same culturally generated valuation. Indeed, it carries a special load of projected values because it houses a sacralized mental life. Bodies have a socially determined normal range of shapes and functionalities. While a normal range of variance is expected and socially acceptable in all cultures, outliers to that prescribed range are often subjected to aesthetic-moral ascriptions that lead to wonder, awe, fear, or rejection. What modern scientific medicine calls mutations, disease states, or disabilities, the religious must fit into an additional cultural schema that maps onto whatever aesthetic-politico-moral narrative they endorse. Normal distributions of variance are regarded as relatively clean (i.e., divinely sanctioned), whereas outliers trigger reactions of cultural contamination. Often modern scientific medicine and religious reactions may overlap and generate little social tension. Sometimes, however, religion prompts treatments regarded as unnecessary or even inhumane under secular regimes of modern human rights, and vice versa.

Transhumanism is likely to run afoul of religious interpretations of human bodies because of its willingness to modify experimentally the baseline form in ways that contradict ambient cultural mores. The severity of the reaction will be determined by how many degrees of deviance any particular modification represents. External attachments to the human form may not trigger much, if any, reaction if the resulting transformation is not especially visible. For example, whereas Google Glass was provoking fears of surveillance as this chapter was being written, far more dangers are posed by contact lenses with the same functionality—but the contact lenses are likely to provoke less resistance. Manipulations that visibly alter normal human form and behavior are far more likely to precipitate the need to run a moral and aesthetic calculus against the interpretive templates of any given religious system. Moreover, revolutionary mergers of flesh and machine creating openings in the skin envelope not "naturally" possible are very likely—and perhaps almost always guaranteed—to aggravate religious sensibilities, producing behaviors and functional shifts that violate religious taboos. For example, we are likely to see a multiplication of sexual forms as the genetics is better understood. It may become possible to choose both male and female sex organs on the same person. As a consequence, people will predictably partake in a widening range of sexual experiences, many of which are very likely to violate the sacred boundaries of normative sexuality of some religions. Borrowing a term from human-robot interaction studies, I will call this moral censure domain "the uncanny valley."

To see how this might be the case, I need to say a few things about how religion appropriates and deploys fear and disgust responses for its own purposes.

HOW RELIGION RECRUITS FEAR AND DISGUST CIRCUITS

The emotions of fear and disgust are among the most primitive affective states that hominids experience. Our evolutionary history is rooted in the need of the organism to protect itself from predation, on the one hand, and from noxious foods and potential parasites, on the other hand. Paleoanthropological evidence now suggests that our species lineage made its living for much of its history by scavenging.[14] This insight represents a movement away from a dated and more heroic narrative where the emphasis was placed on aggressive hunting schemes.[15] The scavenging ecological niche dictates a set of emotions designed to react to constant predatory threats and dependency of marginal food sources. While not altering the picture of human emotional settings much, a recent compromise position has suggested a form of "power scavenging" as our unique behavioral strategy, whereby armed groups of hominids confronted large predators after kills to steal meat and then retreat with their prizes.[16] Whatever the outcome, the debate is an important one because our current baseline emotional systems evolved to cope with our environment and the primary modes of subsistence it afforded us.

Most scholars agree that the addition of a regular meat supply to the human diet would have been a crucial component that could fuel expensive investments in brain size.[17] Growth in brain size enables more sophisticated forms of eye-hand coordination (throwing skills), tool use, more complex forms of social life, growing memory banks full of natural history knowledge, and behavioral flexibility in response to accelerating climatic changes. In other words, the shift to an omnivorous diet played a critical role in hominid survival innovations.

As we have come to appreciate the role of meat scavenging in our species' development, we have also become aware of how fundamental the emotion of disgust, and not just fear, is to human behavior.[18] Disgust is the affective state we feel when we entertain the possibility of questionable protein sources. It is designed to be activated by the presence of certain smells and textures. It generates an instinctual repertoire of facial cues often referred to as the gape face. This facial permutation is amazingly robust independent of social learning.[19] Likewise, disgust triggers modifications in our digestive tract performance to stop the eating process if it is already under way, or to eject potentially dangerous foodstuffs if they have already been ingested. The discovery of larval insects in valuable protein through mere visual inspection, for example, can precipitate very violent reactions in humans, even in the absence of any real threat. This bodily system is rigged to become activated with minimal amounts of evidence as a precautionary bet; such a "better safe than sorry" strategy is a classic evolutionary wager when it comes to risk management.

As with many features in the normal human repertoire of behaviors, the disgust response is open for exaptation—that is, it can be recruited into novel applications for which it was not originally designed. Strong evidence suggests that without obviating its original usage, the disgust mechanism was appropriated by social learning subroutines to attach aversion to various forms of social interaction.[20] In the tribal life of foraging societies, disgust as well as fear served to maintain distance between unrelated social groups and hence to isolate potential or actual disease vectors for which many members would not have had resistance. Contagious diseases breed and spread via social interaction. In the absence of any way to understand communicable disease transmission within social groups, magico-superstitious interpretations may have been the best strategy for isolating the sick from the well. Disgust at the symptoms of the diseased clan member would have protected the rest of the population by attaching a social stigma to that person. Similarly, when encounters between unrelated foraging units occurred, disgust at the out-group's body odor, foodstuffs, hygiene routines, or mere appearance would have safeguarded the in-group against contamination by outsiders. Even if no real threat was present, evolution would have rewarded a "better safe than sorry" xenophobic attitude because false positives in system activation carry minimal costs, whereas false negatives could spell extinction for a particular hominid unit.

The earliest records of historical religions demonstrate a preoccupation with highly advanced codes of clean and unclean foods, disgusting or acceptable social interactions, regulation of body fluids and excreta, and culturally sanctioned or disapproved sexual activities. Modern investigations of these systems tend to focus on how these systems would have served health concerns even when modern medical knowledge was not available to religious bodies.[21]

Less well explained are inclusions of social regulations governing bodily adornment and modifications. These codes seem to have less biological justification than their food-related counterparts, but they are easily understood on the basis of policing social group integrity.[22] If they are interpreted as cultural codes designed to advance group cohesion and solidarity, then they can be best appreciated as more or less arbitrary markers of group identity, membership, and breeding opportunities. In other words, in our hypersocial species, disgust was recruited to build and maintain social group cohesion so as to facilitate that group's competitive advantage over rival groups. In one sense, this recruitment is a powerful tool in generating the willingness of individuals to subsume individual interests to group norms (altruism). In another, more sinister sense, it is the gateway through which xenophobia becomes a default setting in our species.

With this brief overview of hominid foraging life and its resultant moral emotions, the stage is now set to explain the persistent tendency of religiously committed people to demonize out-groups—in this case, transhumanists—in the absence of justified medical knowledge. I propose that the fear of cultural contamination and defilement by transhumans is best explained as a cultural modification of biologically inherited fear and disgust triggers serving a tribally sanctioned normative body form.

My hypothesis is that transhumanists will encounter a rapid, unreflective psychological reaction to any and all deviation from the normal configuration of the human form and its behavioral outputs when it violates cultural (especially religious) norms. Transhumanism will be thrown into an uncanny valley of human discomfort especially by those persons most deeply invested in religious ideation. If the body is sacralized by some teleological-religious interpretation, then biological or cultural modifications to normal human physiology and behavior will be taken as potential signs of underlying pathology that is best avoided by the world's religious populations.

THE UNCANNY VALLEY: LESSONS LEARNED FROM 40 YEARS OF ROBOTICS RESEARCH

The uncanny valley is a psychological phenomenon first identified by the Japanese roboticist Masahiro Mori in 1970.[23] It describes a decrease in comfort levels reported by human observers as robotic apparatuses more closely approximate the human form. Mori's suggested schematic of human reactions looks like this:

Mori's hypothesis states that humans undergo a normative shift in evaluation criteria as the robotic artifacts approach near-human form and behavior. The experience is a form of cognitive confusion because the robot more closely resembles normative expectations of human appearance and behavior, yet betrays subtle cues that activate suspicion. These contradictory impulses generate anxiousness in the perceiver, such that perceptual systems are ramped into intensely alert status. Hypervigilance is the resulting state of mind. Humans experience this state subjectively as uncanniness. Mori further hypothesizes that movement intensifies this effect because movement activates agency templates in the viewer. Agency detection stimulates various instinctual programs for withdrawal and self-preservation in the presence of uncertainty regarding an agency's intentions.

Since 1970, the uncanny valley hypothesis has been subjected to intermittent scientific scrutiny. Most scholars who have investigated it have concluded that this phenomenon is real, but indicate that it is likely more complicated than Mori's original proposal suggests. Although many of these findings employ divergent methodologies that may account for some

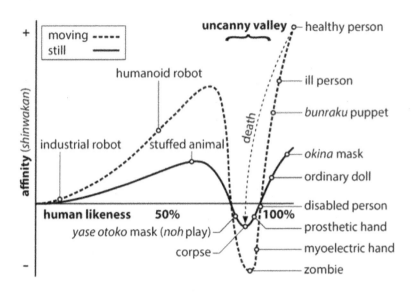

Mori's original diagram of expected reactions to various degrees of anthropomorphism. The name "uncanny valley" is designed to highlight an unexpected dip in a general trend toward greater degrees of emotional comfort as human-like qualities emerge in our perceptions of animate objects in our surroundings. (Excerpted from MacDorman, 2005.)

of the variation in the findings, it also seems clear that more is at play in human reactions.

When we start with exposure to clearly non-anthropomorphic robots such as vacuum cleaners or industrial assembly robots as stimuli, Mori reports that few sensations of uncanniness are detected. The robots are perceived as curiosities but are not sources of anxiety so long as they are diminutive or remain at a safe distance from the perceiver. As the devices begin to approximate animate life forms such as robotic comfort animals for the elderly, perceptions of acceptance actually increase. This sense of ease increases as the robotic entities approximate the human form. At some point, however, the robotic apparatuses so closely approximate human likeness that a phase shift in emotions occurs. Where very subtle cues of nonhumanness in the midst of clearly anthropomorphic intuitions are invoked, powerful and deep-seated anxieties surface. For example, when subjects are exposed to robots with facial expressions mediated through pliable materials designed to replicate human skin, the perception of the plastic texture of the skin causes a sudden downgrading of the subjective comfort ratings. Likewise, when motion designed to simulate human-form movements is scrutinized casually, comfort-levels remain constant. If the subject detects minute nonconforming elements in the motion such as gear-driven granulations in digit manipulation, however, a sense of uncanniness is provoked as evidenced by a sudden phase shift in emotional assessment reports.

As part of efforts to refine Mori's model, scientists have been investigating which emotions are at play and which elements of robotic systems trigger uncanny valley results. Working in the Department of Adaptive Machine Systems at Osaka University, Karl MacDorman reports on the use of androids to elicit the fear of death. The body of research he depends upon comes from so-called terror management theory (TMT); it suggests that exposure to stimuli that induce mortality salience results in ideological entrenchment.[24] MacDorman's findings indicate that encounters with androids can generate ideological entrenchment, but that the eerie sensations evoked are complex combinations not readily identified as simple primal fear or disgust. MacDorman concludes, "[On] average the group exposed to an image of an uncanny robot consistently preferred information sources that supported their worldview relative to the control group."[25]

In a 2006 study, MacDorman further complicated his own version of the uncanny valley by testing the movement component of the effect. Now at the School of Informatics at Indiana University, he reported on the use of video clips of robotic movements as his stimuli. Fourteen video clips were displayed to 56 Indonesian subjects; the video clips contained a wide variety of robotic arrays. Test subjects ranked the images on a mechanical-to-humanlike scale and in terms of strangeness and eeriness. MacDorman's findings resulted in no single uncanny valley phenomenon for a particular threshold approaching human-likeness. He concluded that movement in and of itself does not generate an uncanny valley response when other conditions are controlled.

MacDorman further compounded the complexity by suggesting in a later paper that the vocabulary of the standard questionnaires for testing the uncanny valley may be obscuring the research.[26] According to MacDorman, more nuanced meta-analysis of responses to the uncanny valley points to the need to disentangle the attributional terminology employed in the research and the range of affective states entailed in complex reports of uncanniness. For example, the words "eerie" and "creepy" are closer to the visceral reactions of test subjects than the much more vague descriptor of "strangeness." Likewise, uncanniness seems to be an admixture of emotional responses better understood as aggregations of fear, shock, disgust, and general nervousness.

More recent work has attempted to clarify the confusion surrounding the cognitive components and emotional responses. Taking advantage of more advanced technologies than any of the earlier studies reported so far, Burleigh, Schoenherr, and Lacroix employed human actors to create digitally generated human replicas that have in other studies been shown to evoke reports of unnervingness or the perception of deceptive simulacrums described as wax-museum-like.[27] In the studies conducted by Burleigh et al., still shots were used, so movement was not a factor. These researchers varied the images by introducing atypical features to the human base-form that violated various ontological categories. For example, a continuum of images was generated that slowly morphed a typical human head into more goat-like features. Similarly, a continuum was generated that varied skin texture and facial symmetry in atypical ways. The investigators found that, contrary to Mori's findings, simply approximating human-likeness does not elicit a sensation of eeriness, but the introduction of a category violation for classifying the organism in question does. This was especially the case when the blended images reached the mid-range of continuum, but the effect dissipated at the extremes. At least on the cognitive side of the equation, the findings of Burleigh et al. are more consistent with findings in the study of the religious ideation surrounding supernatural agent concepts in laboratory experiments.[28]

Finally, a 2013 study by Piwek, McKay, and Pollick reported that the researchers failed to confirm that movement was the crucial determinant in the uncanny phenomenon, further reinforcing MacDorman's 2006 results. Recall that Mori suggested two predictors of elicitation: near-human form approximation and motility. Recall also that Burleigh et al. suggested that merely approximating the human form in and of itself does not generate simple excitation of uncanny valley experiences. When Piwek et al. tested the movement component of the hypothesis, they found, once again, that no increase in negative affect was produced by near approximation of normal human movements when all other factors were controlled. On the contrary, the more closely movement approximated human-normal motion, the more comfortable test subjects were. In other words, the relationship is linear without the characteristic uncanny valley dip first hypothesized by Mori.

What is the take-home message of this complex track record of research for transhumanists? First, none of these studies suggest that the uncanny valley response is not real and repeatable. Indeed, too much evidence of its elicitation in some form exists to abandon this concept. Second, no single component of the original hypothesis seems to determine the reaction. Rather, it seems that an admixture of stimuli is really necessary—a gestalt, as it were. Third, methodology in this research matters a great deal. How the stimuli are presented, how the questions are framed, and how the emotional inventories are scored seem to be very important in finding consistent statistical significance. At this point, prudence suggests that not enough consistency exists in the field to make any definitive pronouncements. Fourth, work with robots and androids may not map well onto work with organic life forms, especially when it comes to the disgust reaction. Disgust is an emotion of biological self-preservation. The phase shift in normative judgments (the genesis of an uncanny valley) in robotics may not provoke disgust reactions because they are simulations of biological processes, not biological processes themselves.

In what follows, I will suggest a research agenda that is designed to address these four conclusions.

TRANSHUMANISM EXPERIMENTS

At this point in time, transhumanism is mostly a movement caught in speculation and philosophy derived from ruminations over evolution, advances in medicine, the digital revolution, and advances in technology, especially complexity and miniaturization. Nevertheless, as a movement, it has a sizable investment in its own social and political success. The ability to pursue basic research in biomedical science, computer science, engineering, chemistry, and physics depends on generating a political climate that opens the doors to funding. Thus, in the absence of such basic research in the field, it is difficult to see how transhumanism can become more than a fountain of endless speculation about potential future developments without much consequence.

For this reason, transhumanists have rightly been promoting various political and social discussions surrounding issues of liberal democracy and its ability to tolerate divergent forms of human life.[29] Unfortunately, one consequence of these political discussions is that transhumanism all too often adopts a fairly strident stance toward religion. Perhaps this stridency is the simple product of the current culture wars in the United States over evolution. Whatever its etiology, stridency distorts the reasoning of transhumanists in many ways and cuts short the curiosity of otherwise reasonable people who might be open to understanding the driving forces behind religious apprehension. For example, I know of no program that has given serious attention to the psychology of religious responses to transhumanism. This is what I seek to correct with my suggestions here.

I contend that what has been missing from transhumanism's interactions with religiously inclined people is a willingness to investigate, understand, and transform its discourse in light of what it discovers. Such a research agenda need not be "transhumanist" as such. Even in the absence of a Humanity+ political program, cognitive scientists are already conducting such research. Transhumanism would do well to heed their example, learn from their findings, emulate their methodologies, and ultimately modulate their social and political program accordingly.

Where to begin? First, to be clear, it is reasonable to assume that modifications to the expected normal range of the human form and its behavioral repertoire will fall into an uncanny valley, triggering fear and disgust responses. This emotive response will be especially acute when the modifications are overt and visible on the biological level and when the reactions in question are grounded in religious ideation. The research into the evolution of religion in our species, the cognitive underpinnings of moral reasoning, the history of tribal and xenophobic behaviors, and contemporary research into human-robot interaction clearly point in this direction. To deny this is simply foolish. To dismiss it as mere knee-jerk reactions of close-minded people who have not come to terms with the modern world is blind. To not investigate it on an empirical level so that it can be dealt with more effectively, like any other human behavior, is unscientific. Here is where I argue there is great opportunity.

Second, the good news is that transhumanists may be able to bypass this cultural conflict if they are clear-sighted. On the one hand, while fear and disgust are routinely employed by our species, the social use of disgust at least is a relatively late exaptation and may be quite open to reprogramming through social learning. It may be that we can educate our way beyond the impasse. On the other hand, these trip-wired reactions can be spoofed by some simple and practical cognitive tricks. Fear and disgust elicitations depend on sensory inputs. Shut down or elude these sensory systems, and it is likely that the emotions will stay quiescent. This simple observation implies that as modifications become transparently integral parts of human function and blend more seamlessly into the normal form, it is possible that fear and disgust reactions will decline or even disappear. Perhaps the social confusion that transhumanists now face is simply a temporary function of the crudity of currently available technology. If this is the case, then some augmentations to the human form might prove acceptable almost immediately, whereas other forms of modification may be so striking that no amount of technology will overcome the reactions to them.

The pragmatic conclusion is that social learning may be able to inculcate acceptance as a new normal, but doing so will take time. After all, while evolutionary settings are crucial to understanding how humans behave, these settings are also not entirely fixed—they are not destiny.

HOW TO TEST THE HYPOTHESIS: TRANSHUMANISTS IN THE LAB

Four conclusions were suggested when the uncanny valley research was briefly surveyed earlier:

1. The uncanny valley is real but still poorly understood.
2. The uncanny valley is a product of multiple affective states working in conjunction.
3. The methods employed to investigate the uncanny valley have been too diverse.
4. Hybrids of organic and inorganic devices are likely to add to disgust vectors.

For the empirically minded transhumanist, this list represents a goldmine of research opportunities. Since augmentations to human form and function will necessitate machine mergers with biological tissues, we know that disgust reactions will be waiting in the wings. Thus, I suggest that research should begin there.

Luckily, a fairly extensive body of research already exists with regard to disgust. These experiments entail the casual introduction of hypothesized disgust-elicitors under conditions of deception. For example, participants are told to complete some distractor task required by the experimental cover story. While this task is being completed, one subset of participants is exposed to disgust-elicitors and the other subset serves as a control. In experiments on disgust elicitation among religious test subjects, I have employed heart rate and electrodermal activity monitors to track autonomic nervous responses rather than relying on subjective reports.[30] I have embraced this technique because it does not depend on the wording of a questionnaire or interviewing technique. Nevertheless, I also conduct post-event interviews to collect subjective responses. These responses can be scored and quantified as well.

For transhumanists, I would suggest that a conspirator wear some cosmetic recreation of a body augmentation. At the most basic level, it might be some innocuous device such as a hearing aid. A second condition might add a component of interaction with bodily fluids of a preexisting orifice or opening, perhaps contact lenses or braces for the teeth with highly visible circuitry. A third condition could intensify the violation by opening a novel orifice in the skin envelop, say an IV-like tube in the back of the hand. I would suggest at least two variations for the mock IV tube. In one condition, the entry point to the skin is dry and clean. In the second condition, the opening should appear wet and slightly irritated. A second round of experiments might entail some form of movement violation, such as mechanical ratcheting pantomimed by a conspirator during the distractor task. A similar range of escalating category violations (violations of expected baseline normal conditions) should be explored.

Since we are particularly interested in religious responses to transhuman augmentations, all of these experiments could be run a second time with participants screened for religious backgrounds and orientations. If it is the case that the sacralization of the body results in resistance to its modifications, the reactions of the religious subjects should exceed the reactions of the secular subjects in important ways. It would be very suggestive to find empirical evidence that this is indeed the case.

A third round of experiments might explore xenophobia in the wake of encounters with violations of baseline human appearance and behavior. This question was at the root of MacDorman's 2005 study. When anxiety and disgust are made salient, humans display a tendency to increase their xenophobic behaviors. Typically, xenophobic ideation is handled with a questionnaire designed to map such responses after exposure to a priming condition, as any of the previously described scenarios would be. Regressions could be run to seek correlations between religious background and orientation, on the one hand, and tendency toward xenophobia before and after priming, on the other hand. Again, a great deal of empirical research already makes this outcome seem likely, but nothing like this study design has ever been tried with transhumanist displays.

A fourth round of experiments might be undertaken where the priming conditions are not introduced covertly, but rather are an overt part of the experiment itself. Under these conditions, the conspirator wearing the cosmetic simulation might seek to explain the augmentation as the mock task is being completed. In this scenario, we could begin to test the impact of social learning on calming anxiety and disgust reactions. Perhaps higher executive functions might prove able to tamp down these primitive and very rapid emotional states. That would be a very hopeful result for transhumanists and might result in new insights regarding how to introduce novel augmentations in conflicted political and social climates.

CONCLUSION

In this chapter, I surveyed the role of specific evolved emotional systems in the history of the study of religion. Religion is deeply invested in the sacralization of the body and has recruited various primitive emotions that will likely militate against acceptance of transhumanist agendas. Next, I introduced uncanny valley research to generate a framework for empirical investigation of emotional reactions potential body and behavior modifications. Finally, I suggested a set of four clusters of experiments designed to elucidate hypothesized reactions to anticipated implementations of body alterations. I suggest that transhumanists need to move beyond philosophical discussions of the politics and policies surrounding their agenda and begin to engage in empirical studies of the psychology of social change if they want that agenda to succeed.

NOTES

1. E. B. Tylor, *Primitive Religion: Researches into the Development of Mythology, Philosophy, Art, and Custom* (Cambridge, UK: Cambridge University Press, 2012 [1871]), 16–20.

2. Ilkka Pyysiainen, *Magic, Miracles, and Religion: A Scientist's Perspective* (Walnut Creek, CA: AltaMira, 2004), 101.

3. Sigmund Freud, *Civilization and Its Discontents: The Standard Edition* (New York, NY: W. W. Norton, 2010 [1930]), 59.

4. Jesper Sorenson, *A Cognitive Theory of Magic* (Walnut Creek, CA: AltaMira, 2007), 27–28.

5. Mary Douglas, *Purity and Danger: An Analysis of Concepts of Pollution and Taboo* (London, UK/Headley, UK: Routledge and Kegan Paul, 1976 [1966]), 115.

6. Melvin Harris, *Cows, Pigs, Wars and Witches: The Riddle of Culture* (New York, NY: Random House, 1974), 29.

7. Michel Foucault, *Discipline and Punish: The Birth of the Prison* (New York, NY: Vintage, 1995 [1975]).

8. Michel Foucault, *The History of Sexuality*, 3 vols. (New York, NY: Vintage Books, 1975–1986).

9. Foucault, *The History of Sexuality*, Vol. 3, 238.

10. An exaptation is any evolved device that is co-opted for a novel use because environmental conditions demand it. It always entails a functional shift in how the device is used. For example, human thumbs did not evolve for tool usage. The opposable thumb is a result of an arboreal past. Once our ancestors had thumbs, however, they found thumbs could also be used for complex manual manipulations. The environmental trigger that initiated this transition was climatic. It resulted in various changes, including bipedal locomotion, which in turn freed up the hands for other applications.

An example of a mental tool so exapted is the Theory of Mind. Theory of Mind is the mental device that allows us to represent mental states in others. It enables more complex social interactions. When our species evolved religious behaviors roughly 50,000 years ago, the Theory of Mind was given a new purpose—the ability to represent minds unattached to bodies. This cognitive novelty was the crucial driver that led to the earliest mortuary behaviors and the eventual hypothesis of abiding dead ancestors. Some of these ancestors graduated to the level of supernatural agencies.

For a study of the inability of children on the autism spectrum to generate religious concepts, see Simon Baron-Cohen, *Mindblindness: An Essay on Autism and Theory of Mind* (Cambridge, MA: Bradford Books, 1996).

11. For an example of a religious rejection of transhumanism on these grounds, see Leslie Fain, "The Surprising Spread and Cultural Impact of Transhumanism," *Catholic World Reporter* (October 3, 2013), http://www.catholicworldreport.com/Zone/31/Science.aspx#.UzV4xa1dWQe, accessed January 26, 2014. For an example of a certain degree of callousness to religious emotive responses, see Michael Anissimov, " 'Futurisms': Anti-Transhumanist Intellectuals," *Accelerating Future* (November 25, 2009), http://www.acceleratingfuture.com/michael/blog/2009/11/futurisms-anti-transhumanist-intellectuals/, accessed January 29, 2014.

12. Joshua Green, *Moral Tribes: Emotion, Reason, and the Gap between Us and Them* (New York, NY: Penguin Press, 2013), 289–291.

13. Richard Dawkins, *The God Delusion* (New York, NY: Mariner Press, 2008), 34; Ursula Goodenough, *The Sacred Depths of Nature* (Oxford, UK: Oxford University Press, 1998).

14. Ian Tattersal, *Masters of the Planet* (New York, NY: Palgrave Macmillan, 2012).

15. Richard B. Lee and Irvin Devor, eds., *Man the Hunter* (Piscataway, NJ: Transaction,1973).

16. Henry T. Bunn and Joseph A. Ezzo, "Hunting and Scavenging by Plio-Pleistocene Hominids," *Journal of Archeological Science* 20, no. 4 (1993): 365–398.

17. Craig Stanford, *The Hunting Apes: Meat Eating and the Origins of Human Behavior* (Princeton, NJ: Princeton University Press, 2001).

18. Marc Hauser, *Moral Minds: How Nature Designed Our Universal Sense of Right and Wrong* (New York, NY: Ecco Press, 2006); Daniel Kelly, *Yuck! The Nature and Moral Significance of Disgust* (Cambridge, MA: MIT Press, 2011); Colin McGinn, *The Meaning of Disgust* (Oxford, UK: Oxford University Press, 2011); Jonathan Haidt, *The Righteous Mind: Why Good People Are Divided by Politics and Religion* (New York, NY: Vintage Press, 2012).

19. Kelly, *Yuck!*, 64–69.

20. Hauser, *Moral Minds*; Kelly, *Yuck!*; Haidt, *The Righteous Mind*.

21. Harris, *Cows, Pigs, Wars, and Witches*.

22. Valerie Curtis, *Don't Look, Don't Eat, Don't Touch: The Science behind Revulsion* (Chicago, IL: University of Chicago Press, 2013).

23. Masahiro Mori, "The Uncanny Valley," *Energy* 7, no. 4 (1970): 33–35.

24. Karl F. MacDorman, "Androids as an Experimental Apparatus: Why Is There an Uncanny Valley and Can We Exploit It?", *Toward Social Mechanisms of Android Science: A Cogsci Workshop*, 2005, https://www.lri.fr/~sebag/Slides/uncanny.pdf, accessed January 13, 2014.

25. MacDorman, "Androids as an Experimental Apparatus."

26. Karl F. MacDorman and Z. A. D. Dwi Pramono, "Human Emotion and the Uncanny Valley: A GLM, MDS, and Isomap Analysis of Robot Video Ratings," in *HRI '08 Proceedings of the 3rd ACM/IEEE International Conference on Human Robot Interaction* (New York: ACM, 2008), 169–176.

27. Tyler J. Burleigh, Jordan R. Schoenherr, and Guy L. Lacroix, "Does the Uncanny Valley Exist? An Empirical Test of the Relationship between Eeriness and the Human Likeness of Digitally Created Faces," *Computers in Human Behavior* 29 (2013), 759–771.

28. Pascal Boyer, *Religion Explained* (New York, NY: Basic Books, 2002); Justin Barrett, *Why Would Anyone Believe in God?* (Walnut Creek, CA: AltaMira Press, 2004).

29. Ronald Bailey, "For Enhancing People: Do the Technologies That Enable Human Physical and Intellectual Enhancement Undermine Virtue?", in *The Transhumanist Reader*, edited by Max More and Natasha Vita-More (New York, NY: Wiley-Blackwell, 2013), 327–344.

30. My lab has been testing the use of a mobile sensor assembly for deployment in the field. Test one occurred in the spring of 2012. Thirty subjects were subjected to four anxiogenic conditions, one anxiolytic condition, and one control condition. We succeeded in eliciting a mean 7.8 percent decrease in heart rate variability (HRV) relative to baseline measurements for all anxiogenic stimuli. Our second study ran from the fall of 2013 to the spring of 2014. Forty test subjects were subjected to a contrived biohazard testing site and to control conditions. As before, HRV dipped at a mean of 8.2 percent, as predicted by other studies on precautionary psychology. Our third study will run during May and June 2014 (after the completion of this chapter). Twenty participants will be exposed to a Washington, D.C., neighborhood rich in ethnic Latino signaling and to a control condition (park scene). We anticipate that the social deployment of disgust will register at the same magnitude as seen in the biohazard conditions in tests 1 and 2. The full data set will be published upon completion. This experimental regimen will be implemented for the study of interreligious signaling in the Old City of Jerusalem beginning the fall of 2015.

The Trans-Athlete and the Religion of Sport: Implications of Transhumanism for Elite Sport's Spiritual Dimension

Tracy J. Trothen

Elite sport, and particularly the Olympic Games, is an important context for the development and implementation of cutting-edge technoscience enhancements. The religious-like dimensions of both transhumanism and sport add potency to the meeting of enhancements and elite sport, given that aspects of both can be regarded as sacred by followers. This chapter focuses on three implications of enhancement technologies for elite sport's spiritual dimension.

Significant economic and scientific resources are invested in sport, making it possible to develop such technologies as the much-anticipated Athletic Biological Passport, which will not only detect the use of banned performance-enhancing substances but also establish an athlete's phenotypic profile, thereby providing information helpful to the design of training and nutrition regimens.[1] Transhumanism is being actualized in sport through the application of cybernetics, genetic modification technologies, cognitive science, nanotechnology, sports science, and other means. Sport enhancement options are more plentiful than ever, ranging from vitamins, power drinks, caffeine, meditation, prostheses, anabolic steroids, and recombinant forms of erythropoietin (EPO), to blood doping, tailor-made training programs, and equipment such as Speedo's 2008 Fastskin LZR swim suits, to rumored and anticipated genetic modification technologies (e.g., the genetic modification technology "Repoxygen") and data chip implants.

How will increased technoscience enhancement usage affect what some consider sacred aspects of sport, such as flow experiences, physical effort, physical aliveness of both pain and pleasure, heart, perfection, and hope?

Several scholars have argued that sport is a type of religion or functions in some ways similar to a religion.[2] While academic debates continue regarding whether or how the sacred is "truly" experienced in a sport, many sports participants describe their experiences as "sacred, spiritual, or religious."[3] While subjective religious feeling may or may not be a sufficient ingredient in making a scholarly case for divine presence, it is—as Friedrich Schleiermacher and other theologians have contended—sufficient from the perspective of the sports participant.[4]

Transhumanism, too, may be considered a way of being religious or even a new religious movement[5] that sees humanity moving through a transition point on the way to a much more desirable posthuman state by "improving the human condition through applied reason, especially by developing and making widely available technologies to eliminate aging and to greatly enhance human intellectual, physical, and psychological capacities."[6] Many believe that these enhancement technologies will become available for every human being to choose. Such capacities are held sacred in transhumanism. Insofar as religion concerns that which is perceived as sacred or spiritual, then transhumanism can be considered to function similarly to a religion. According to Nick Bostrom's Humanity+ Web site, "While not a religion, transhumanism might serve a few of the same functions that people have traditionally sought in religion. It offers a sense of direction and purpose and suggests a vision that humans can achieve something greater than our present condition."[7]

Even as some organized religions have seen their numbers decrease, people have been finding alternative ways and places in which to practice spirituality. Studies have suggested that an increased interest in spirituality has accompanied the decrease in mainstream church attendance in North America and the United Kingdom.[8] This mainstream decrease in attendance has been accompanied by the growth, beginning in the 1960s, of the New Age movement. Parts of this movement have been very inner self oriented, with little attention paid to a greater source beyond the self. This way of understanding spirituality is more in line with a postmodernist trend that rejects grand narratives and instead concerns itself with the integrity, power, and particularity of each individual. The strengths of this understanding include individual empowerment and appreciation of difference. Unfortunately, what can be sacrificed is the awareness of the limitations of the individual and accountability to a divine power beyond oneself. A growing North American emphasis on liberal individualism is related to the growth of more individualistic spiritualties.

Both the transhumanist movement and sport, as alternative spiritual loci, espouse an implicit or explicit value set. Values held in both elite sport and transhumanism reflect what their respective followers regard as sacred. Further, it is reasonable to expect an increasing technological impact on sport;

the emphases in sport on utility and efficiency assuredly will continue to grow as sport enhancement technoscience grows.[9] The well-established technological values of utility and efficiency shape the transhumanist understandings of what it means to improve or enhance "intellectual, physical, and psychological capacities"[10] through individual choice to self-improve. As Heidi Campbell notes, transhumanist proponents see it as "perfectly acceptable to sacrifice certain aspects of personhood (embodiment, gender, personality) for the sake of enhancing other aspects of one's existence (capabilities, memory, strength, endurance)."[11] Sacred aspects of personhood are those that are determined to contribute to the goal of immortality through the preservation of those capacities deemed to constitute personhood or the essence of the self. For example, expendable aspects of personhood would include such athletic moments as the joy of completing a marathon, the beauty of a well-executed passing play, or the ability of a team to work together seamlessly. On one level, as philosopher Randolph Feezell demonstrates, these moments in sport are trivial. But their triviality does not render them meaningless; in fact, some of the more meaningful moments in life may occur in sport. As Feezell argues, "A meaningful life is not dependent on the notion that there is an overall meaning of life or that a particular life must have some end."[12] This analysis of meaning as centering on process and moments is contrary to a utility- or ends-driven approach to life such as that embraced by transhumanists in their overriding quest for immortality.

The shift in elite sport to professionalization and commercialization has occurred hand-in-hand with greater use of technoscience to enhance athletic performance. Sociologist Rob Beamish identifies runner Roger Bannister and his 1954 "miracle mile" as "the gateway to modernity and the pursuit of sports through applied science, research, and professionalized training regimes."[13] A medical student, Bannister drew on his knowledge of physiology to develop an effective training regimen. After witnessing Bannister's success at accomplishing what many thought at the time to be impossible (i.e., the sub-four-minute mile), it became clear that if one wanted to compete successfully, much more rigorous and scientifically tailored training was the answer. Such intensive training meant it would become increasingly difficult to compete unless one did so as a professional. Moreover, to get the funding that would allow this single-minded focus on training, an athlete had to win. Research included in the 1969 and 1970 reports from the International Olympic Committee/National Olympic Committee joint commission showed that "from 1950 to 1970, the time track athletes spent training had doubled and in some cases tripled."[14] As technoscience enhancement options increase in the context of a technology-driven global culture, elite sport's emphasis on utility, efficiency, and winning at all costs has intensified, and it will continue to do so.[15] The increase in enhancement technologies is related to the rise of professionalization and commercialization, which in turn are utility driven to

the ends of winning, financial gain, and status. A parallel decrease in the valuing of what Feezell terms sports' "splendid triviality"[16] reflects this shift
toward utility and normative social values in elite sport.

I approach this topic from my perspective as a feminist Protestant Christian
ethicist. I am interested in causal dynamics that undergird values and epistemological claims. One might expect that the intersection of two ways of being
religious or spiritual—transhumanism and sport—will have a doubling[17] effect
on sport-related experiences of the sacred. It is not clear whether such
doubling will enhance, negate, or otherwise affect spiritual experiences in elite
sport.

In this chapter, I begin to explore three of the many potential issues raised
by the intersection of transhumanism and elite sport: individualism and
choice; embodiment; and hope located in perfection. These issues suggest that
growing enhancement use has important implications for the spiritual dimension of sport. I introduce Christian theological reflection at points to help illu-
minate spiritual and social convictions associated with these issues. Scholars
have shown that sport and Christianity reflect and influence North American
cultural norms.[18] Feminist Christian theologies are drawn on as a foil, suggesting
the appearance of an approach informed by marginalized values in contrast to a
transhumanist approach. This chapter is meant only to introduce these three
issues and begin to consider the implications of this intersection of two ways of
being religious for the spiritual dimension of sport.[19]

INDIVIDUALISM AND CHOICE

Spirituality includes a sense of the sacred, and what is sacred is connected to
notions of hope. In Christianity, spirituality is oriented to the Divine Other, of
whom glimpses are available through encounters with the Other created in
God's image; hope concerns justice and relational flourishing in life and
life beyond death as promised in the saving ministry of Jesus Christ.
Transhumanism and much of secular North American society locate hope in
individual choice and notions of human progress toward the extension of life.[20]

Proponents of enhancement availability and use in elite sport do not necessarily subscribe to transhumanism, but they do tend to share many transhumanist values—in particular, the emphasis on individual freedom to choose.
Ethicists Andy Miah and Claudio Tamburrini[21] are representative of those
who argue that athletes should have the freedom to choose whichever
enhancements they desire so long as the intent is not to gain a *covert* competitive advantage. Miah adds the proviso that a desire to "approach a way of
being human that is more reflective of [athletes'] authentic selves" should
inform the choice to use an enhancement.[22] Tamburrini and Tännsjö add
that there is no reason to question the authenticity of an athlete's desire to
use an enhancement—to do so would be paternalistic and disrespectful of

the individual's autonomy, necessarily leading to the conclusion that no one can have authentic desires and make truly free choices.[23]

Critics argue that elite athletes cannot give full authentic consent because they face undue pressure to win. The choice to use enhancements can be a choice between using enhancements and staying competitive in their sport.[24] At least one qualitative study suggests that the desire to stay in the game seems to be the single strongest motivator to use banned substances.[25] Individual choice proponents acknowledge that these decisions can be difficult, but they ultimately reject this as a persuasive reason, citing paternalism.

A second protest is that some enhancements pose significant health risks. This argument is similarly dismissed on the basis that the very nature of elite sport poses serious risks and there is no perceived need to prevent athletes from choosing particularly violent sports. Some of the higher-risk or more-extreme sports include 300-foot ski jumps, skiing arials, and snowboarding. Whitewater kayakers can come close to drowning, yet claim that this very risk enhances the sport—even in a spiritual sense—and draws them to it.[26] Lugers travel down the track at harrowing speeds of up to 90 miles per hour. In ice hockey, protective equipment helps, but there is always significant risk of serious injury owing to the sport's speed, large bodies, hard surfaces, and blades. Given these well-established risks, how might one justify prohibiting these same athletes from choosing enhancements because they may have harmful consequences?

My criticism of the individual choice approach to enhancements is two-fold: it oversimplifies the issue by ignoring powerful underlying dynamics and, by ignoring these dynamics and failing to critically examine normative values, it undermines the value of spirituality in sport. To elaborate on these points, first, I will undertake a brief examination of liberal individualism in contrast to a relational autonomy. Second, I will suggest, through the example of embodied violence, how unexamined sociocultural notions of the good do not always serve individual well-being. Marginalized values may foster well-being, but unless a deliberate critical analysis of values is engaged, there is little possibility for anything other than the deepening of normative values. In other words, without such critical analysis and conversation, elite sport is likely to become more utility driven toward the end of winning and the creation of individual winners rather than fostering a broader appreciation of athletic excellence that includes aesthetics, diversity, teamwork, human vulnerability, and spirituality.

Liberal individualism fails to account for the problematic aspects of choice in a global context of constructed values and systemic power imbalances. Feminist and relational theorists have demonstrated that people do not

> typically discover their own values by introspection and [instead] support the view that persons *determine* their values through dialogue with others and action. Since values are *formed through* social engagement (rather than prior to

it), we should not focus on the question "what does a person want to do now?" but rather on "what are the processes by which he/she has come to hold his current preferences?" . . . Feminist theory has helped to reveal how social conditions can distort an individual's ability to pursue options that support her interests. Specifically, feminists have shown how oppression produces social conditions that make compliance with oppressive norms the most reasonable option available to individuals.[27]

Unlike a liberal individualism, a relational autonomy such as that described here assumes these complexities and does not accept that desires are necessarily authentic and in the best interests of the individual making choices.

Perhaps the best-known example of widespread use of a banned enhancement within a sport is the 1998 Tour de France or, as known popularly, the Tour du Dopage (Tour of Doping). During this event, it was discovered that more than 50 of the riders had used recombinant EPO. A relational autonomy approach suggests that the motivation of these riders likely was informed by a number of factors that warrant careful examination prior to drawing the conclusion that individual choice is an adequate reason to make enhancements available. The question of which processes contributed to the choice by so many riders to use a banned substance would enrich the greater conversation regarding which goods would be promoted by a decision to let each athlete decide which enhancements to use as means to realize their self-identities.

A number of contextual factors influence elite athletes and their decisions about enhancement use. Among the more notable factors are liberal individualism, technology, capitalism, and conservative evangelical Christian theologies. These factors and others inform cultural contexts and can make certain choices seem self-evident when, in fact, these choices are driven by contextually derived values.

The example of accepted violence in sport illustrates this dynamic. This is a place where particular interpretations and values of Christianity and sport could dovetail with a transhumanist vision in a particularly dangerous way. Several theologians writing from marginalized perspectives, particularly women, have shown that traditional Christianity has glorified unnecessary suffering and self-sacrifice, thereby contributing to repeated victimization. Traditional atonement theologies that present Jesus's suffering on the cross as the source of salvation, rather than his ministry, reinforce the message that suffering is good and even salvific. Briefly, there is a significant difference between interpretations that glorify the suffering of the crucifixion and those that understand the crucifixion as a terrible consequence of Jesus's ministry of love and justice. In the latter, God's grace and outrageous love were issued in Jesus's resurrection, *in spite of* the great suffering inflicted by humans.[28]

Additionally, feminist theologians have argued that Jesus carried out his ministry knowing that crucifixion was a possible—albeit not desirable—consequence. According to this view, Jesus was not a passive, innocent self-sacrificing victim commanded by God to suffer, but rather Christ incarnate who proclaimed the good news knowing that entailed risks. Regardless of such critiques and theological reconstructions written from the perspective of marginalized communities, much of Christianity continues to reinforce the notion that suffering and self-sacrifice are noble and desirable in themselves.

This notion, probably not accidentally, is congruent with the conviction in sport that an athlete's injuries are badges of honor. The serious athlete is expected to push his or her body to extremes, training to and past the point of injury. Self-inflicted violence in elite sport includes not only serious risks in the actual performance of the sport, but also rigorous training regimens, unhealthy weight loss to meet weight class parameters and optimal performance criteria,[29] and sometimes possible side effects from permitted and banned performance enhancements. Obviously, these sports examples are not the same as Jesus's ministry of salvation and crucifixion. The point is that traditional interpretations of Christian narrative that—rightly or wrongly— are understood as glorifying suffering have been absorbed into culture and become manifest in various aspects of life, including sport.

The nexus created by transhumanism, conservative Christian theologies of bodily suffering and self-sacrifice, technological values, and an extreme liberal individualism likely will amplify the willingness of athletes, coaches, and fans to accept what might be risky enhancement technologies and science to improve the winning-ness utility of an athletic performance. Individual choice is an important moral principle. Regard for contextual factors need not mitigate regard for autonomy. Rather, it should prompt the examination of *approaches* to individualism and autonomy. The starting point of a normative ethic for sport enhancement ought not be the individual per se, but rather the individual in community.[30] The question of authenticity is complex and not a blithe caveat. Authentic desire cannot be understood within an individual choice paradigm. Without critical attention to normative values and contextual systems, it is not possible to engage alternative values and desires, including those associated with sport's spiritual dimension.

EMBODIMENT

For those who understand sport as a way of being religious or as providing religious-like functions, embodiment is the locus of spirituality. The body is regarded in both similar and very different ways by elite sport and transhumanism. Transhumanists see the body as limiting and in need of strengthening, improvement, or overcoming. Similarly, elite sport is focused on overcoming physical limits through a number of strategies such as strength and endurance training. A goal in elite sport is the optimizing and mastering of the intertwined relationship between the body, mind, heart, and soul. For transhumanists, however, the body is dispensable, necessary to neither personhood nor immortality and only of use insofar as it can be mastered. Transhumanism understands these dimensions to be of relative value and discrete, with only the mind (which is reduced to the brain in this compartmentalized view) seen as sufficiently sacred to be necessary to personhood. The body and emotions, if they are retained, are subsidiary and helpful only insofar as they contribute to overall cognitive improvement and longevity.

As elite athletes physically interface with technoscience enhancements, it is important to consider how this intersection will affect embodiment and spiritual experiences in sport. For many athletes, their spiritual experiences are very embodied. The clearest example of this is what has been called peak experiences,[31] ecstasy, transcendence, Zen states, the zone, or flow.[32] Flow experiences in sport are characterized by intense absorption, a sense of effort-lessness, egoless-ness and connectedness, inner peace and harmony, a change in the sense of time, a loss of fears and anxieties, a sense of mystery and awe, and a sense of control or mastery.[33] The flow experience of a sense of indwelling sacredness and an awareness of something sacred larger than oneself is an analogy for what Lawrence W. Fagg proposes as the "seamless continuum" between experiences of transcendence and immanence.[34] By locating the sacred in the physical—or so-called profane—athletes' flow experiences transgress the normative Western Christian presumption that the sacred is restricted to the spirit as distinct from the body. Epistemological constructs of spirit/body, immanent/transcendent, and the sacred/profane as distinct categories are rendered meaningless by flow experiences.

With this powerful sense of interconnection, the athlete can experience unexpected and awe-inspiring performances and wins. A distance runner, in a study conducted by Jackson and Csikszentmihalyi, said, "You are going faster, and yet it seems easier. . . . It is hard to describe in words unless you experience it. . . . you're going as fast as you can go, and yet you're doing it quite easily."[35] The unexpected surge that can happen with flow makes competitions less predictable, contributing to the hope that anything is possible and helping mitigate complacency in athletic competition.

As bodies change with the addition of more enhancements, flow experiences will be affected. It is possible that focus and attention could be enhanced through physiological or genetic intervention. Presumably, this would contribute to optimal conditions for flow states.[36] At least for now, one cannot simply decide to enter a flow state; it comes when it comes. This unpredictability has been part of the power of flow; it is unanticipated and even with optimal conditions flow may or may not occur. It is more likely that flow will become less valued as enhancements increase. Given that flow is contingent on a number of human factors, including emotional centeredness or deep attention, and appropriate perceived level of skill as compared to the level of challenge,[37] trans-athletes may risk losing flow or may develop a lack of interest in creating the conditions for flow if flow is no longer regarded as necessary to excellence (if excellence is reduced more and more to winning alone). Perhaps an enhancement might consist of the dampening or elimination of emotions, making it more possible for the elite athlete to focus more completely on the mechanics of a winning performance. Flow seems to rely on emotional centeredness, rather than the elimination of emotions. The absence or even decreased prevalence of flow experiences could reinforce perceptions that the body, mind, and spirit are discrete pieces of the increasingly reducible human. The absence of flow would likely make athletic performances more measureable and predictable, diminishing the human capacity to be surprised and awed by sport. Hope generated in sport has been related to unexpected wins and losses amidst the order of the games; the rules and structure of a sport contribute to a known order and rhythm within which the unexpected happens occasionally to the fallible human athlete.

Another way in which the advancement of sport technoscience enhancements might affect embodiment regards visibly nonconforming bodies. Perhaps two of the best-known examples of elite athletes who have not fit normative embodiment categories are South African runners Caster Semenya and Oscar Pistorius. Semenya won the women's 800-meter race at the 2009 International Association of Athletics Federations (IAAF) World Championship by a wide margin of 2.45 seconds. Because of this pronounced superiority to her competitors and speculation that she appeared too masculine, Semenya was suspended from competition while she underwent gender testing.[38] The results remain confidential, but it is rumored that she "failed" the gender tests and had to undergo hormone therapy to "correct" her physiology before resuming competitions. Pistorius riveted the world with his Cheetah legs—carbon-fiber prosthetics—that enabled him to run after being born without fibulae in his lower legs. After the IAAF, in 2008, banned Pistorius from competition because of his prosthetics, the Court of Arbitration for Sport overturned the decision, making it possible for Pistorius to compete in the 2012 Olympics. Instead of raising much discussion about the problems of these embodiment categories (gender, sex, and abled/disabled), the issue was framed mostly as one of competing rights and fairness.

In both cases, detractors claimed that these athletes had unfair advantages.[39] Yet, when other invisible or less visible embodiment differences advantage an athlete, there is not much discussion. Finnish athlete Eero Mäntyranta had a genetic mutation that gave him an estimated 25 to 50 percent greater oxygen-carrying capacity than persons without the mutation. His superior endurance undoubtedly played a role in his winning of seven Olympic medals in the 1960s in cross-country skiing.[40] Swimmer Michael Phelps has several genetic advantages, including larger feet and hands, a greater lung capacity, and a body that produces about half the amount of lactic acid compared to other athletes.[41] Elite athletes are an exceptional group; likely most, if not all, possess at least some genetic advantages. Science has developed to the point where we can test to determine what many of these advantages are and then decide which ones are acceptable.

Those options that are assessed as enhancing and permissible likely will not be judged as conflicting with notions of the essential pure and natural athlete (as God created them); so long as athletes appear "normal," enhancements or advantages tend to be accepted or ignored by the general public. Although the meaning of pure and natural is often connected with God created-ness, those who are born not meeting the human-constructed image of normality often are evaluated as unnatural and in need of fixing. This is another example of the hold on the Western popular imagination of a version of Christian theology. Human-imposed valuations of who counts as a normal, God-created person reinforce judgments that suggest all are not created equally in the image of God. From another Christian theological perspective, if each individual is created in God's image, then, as theologian Mayra Rivera (building on Levinas) posits, it is only through encountering the irreducible and singular other that we can "touch" God; each person can provide a particular glimpse of the Divine Other. Non-normative theologies, such as Rivera's, that are informed by marginalized values derived from the biblical source challenge normative epistemological embodiment categories. However, these theologies have not yet secured a hold on the popular imagination.

Feminist philosopher Donna Haraway has theorized that the creation of technologically enhanced humans has the *potential* to destabilize embodiment categories (and notions of normality) that exclude non-normative bodies by blurring the boundaries between human and machine.[42] Humans, such as Pistorius, interfaced with machine technologies (cybernetic organisms or cyborgs for short) are visibly nonconforming. Haraway sees cyborgs as possible sites of hope only if the relational (including kinship) dimension of humanity is valued in what she imagines as an increasingly visibly diverse society.[43] As Jeanine Thweate-Bates points out, Haraway's cyborg vision diverges markedly from transhumanism and Western liberal individualism. Others are less optimistic, citing research that shows embodiment categories "are more likely to be reaffirmed than challenged by the majority of cultural depictions of the post/human."[44]

Another point of convergence between transhumanism and elite sport is in the suggestion by some theorists that such enhancement technologies as genetic modification could make competitions fairer by "level[ing] out differences in performance capacity established by birth."[45] This approach assumes that fairness requires sameness. Sameness, in turn, implies the selection of one normal and desirable type of body that becomes the benchmark against which all other bodies are measured. This notion fits with the much-critiqued transhumanist assumption that there is one version of the good. Such a benchmark body would be congruent with this one version reinforcing the human tendency, as Parens puts it, to "fear and hate the different."[46] The interface of transhumanism with sport would eventually mean a particular construction of the athletic body.

Sameness would remove much of what has made athletic competition meaningful. The elimination of the mystery of diverse human bodies makes a sport much easier to control and direct toward one goal. For example, a great hockey game would be defined in one particular way, and players constructed to fulfill that idea of greatness. Right now there are a range of ways, culturally influenced, to play the game—a focus on passing plays and finesse, or attention to strength and body contact, or an offensive defense with a focus on shooting. These differences are part of what makes Olympic hockey so exciting—there are clear differences among the players and the teams. By making effort the only defining point and so rendering competition fair, the naturalness of human diversity is undermined, removing the excitement generated by a conflation of factors, known and unknown. Athletic competition is a celebration of exceptionally different embodied persons, which is precisely why so many of us are followers.

PERFECTION AND HOPE

The last issue that I have chosen to consider is perfection as a dimension of hope. Hope is central to, but very differently understood in, transhumanism and sport.[47] Ray Kurzweil argues that an age he calls the "Singularity" is near; it "will represent the culmination of our biological thinking and existence with our technology, resulting in a world that is still human but that transcends our biological roots. There will be no distinction, post-Singularity, between human and machine or between physical and virtual reality. . . . Although the Singularity has many faces, its most important implication is this: our technology will match and then vastly exceed the refinement and suppleness of what we regard as the best of human traits."[48] Kurzweil recognizes that values are not universal, whereas the effects of technological enhancements will be universal. Nevertheless, he does not see this contradiction as a problem, because eventually everyone will be on the same page as they realize the promise of optimal living, or perfection, to be offered by enhancement technologies.[49]

Much has been written about the contrast between transhumanism's eschatology and Christian hope. I will not revisit these arguments but will offer an example of a very different notion of singularity. Rivera's theology of relational transcendence sees each person as irreducibly singular and relational, a complicated mix of good and evil, created in the image of God: "a multiple relational model of transcendence-within acknowledges and grapples with the multiplicity within the radical singularity of each person as well as the multiplicity of relations between subjects" and "God is . . . that multiple singularity that joins together all creatures—creatures that are themselves irreducible in the infinite multiplicity of their own singularity."[50] In Rivera's theology, individuality enhances relationality and relationality enhances individuality, since the Divine can be "touched" (but not grasped) through the awe of truly encountering the other.

Extending Rivera's theology to elite sport, the trans-athlete could be a visible symbol of hope if relational autonomy and mystery outweigh a utility-driven individualism. Conversely, a Kurzweilian elite sport would mean athletes becoming enhanced objects designed to win—performers in a spectacle but not people with whom we identify, experiencing their successes and failures as ours. Sports ethicist Simon raised concerns a number of years ago regarding the impact of doping on sport, wondering if sport would become a contest of "competing bodies" dependent upon how well each body responds to enhancing substances, rather than a "contest between persons" that includes the mix of effort, genetics, phenotype, spirit and all that makes up a person.[51] Even if effort continues to be an element in sports competition, if elite sport is perceived as an exhibition rather than a contest between persons, it will not hold the same meaning or spark the same hope for the impossible. Part of the hope is the identification that the fan experiences with the athlete or team. If this identification is disrupted by elite athletes becoming less vulnerable or invulnerable enhanced transhumans, the fan experience of hope will be disrupted as well.

Both transhumanism and sport quest for perfection and the transcendence of human limits.[52] In transhumanism, perfection is related to a homogenous notion of progress toward enhanced human intellectual, physical, and psychological capacities. In sport, perfection includes winning but is not limited to winning. And it is not enough to just win: perfection is about the sublime, the unforgettable and awe-inspiring unexpected transcendent moments that insist on the possibility of what we think is impossible. These are the " 'perfect moment[s]' accomplished by the 'imperfect performer' " revealing the lie that there is an unbridgeable gap between the transcendent and immanent.[53] It is these moments of realized eschatology—no matter how trivial, and even perhaps because of their triviality—that provide a sense of hope, meaning, and fulfillment to followers.

All too often, the concept of perfection is reduced to normative qualities, squeezing out mystery and evaluating people as either perfect (conforming to normative ideals of beauty, sexuality, gender, age, race, and able-bodiedness) or not. Moreover, as Brent Waters observes, the "quest for perfection cannot ultimately tolerate the imperfect."[54] The notion that God is perfect problematizes the concept of perfection. As humans, we have limited abilities to comprehend divine mystery and tend to impose our own often distorted and at least limited conceptions of perfection on God. These ideas, no matter how much they are projections of our culturally conditioned selves, help to inform our desires. God's perfection does not fit with popular definitions of perfection because the values underlying God's perfection cannot be reduced to utility. God's perfection may well include much of what currently is considered imperfect. Marginalized values and the sense of meaning experienced in the "splendid triviality" of sport[55] are not less important to human flourishing than winning at any costs.

In the end, our rational understanding of perfection is perhaps more limited than our embodied experiential understanding of perfect moments. As Ted Peters writes, "God may be able to deliver perfection. Science cannot."[56] Somewhere in the midst of living as God's created, illusive uncontrolled moments of perfection provide hope that divine awe, wonder, and possibility exist. Sport can be a human locus for such redemptive moments.

The hope of sports followers is that their team will win even when there is no rational reason to believe this outcome will happen. (One has only to consider the dedication of Chicago Cubs fans to know this.) Flow experiences contribute to this kind of hope for athletes. Even though the conviction that sport is a meritocracy and so anything is possible flies in the face of scientific evidence that some athletes have inborn advantages, it persists. What would it take to irrevocably damage such relentless hope? The removal of human frailty and human possibility might achieve this end. The tipping point will be different for each sports follower, but this may be the most significant spiritual risk posed by enhancement technoscience to sport.

CONCLUSION

This chapter began with the establishment of a relationship between religion, and both transhumanism and sport. Building on the understanding that sport and transhumanism function for many in religious-like ways, I identified three of the potential issues raised by the intersection of transhumanism and elite sport: individualism and choice; embodiment; and hope located in perfection. Through the examination of these issues, I showed that growing enhancement use by athletes has important implications for the spiritual dimension of sport.

I suggest that the use of enhancements will affect sport's spiritual dimension —and likely not in an enhancing manner. An emphasis on individualism and utility in elite sport will be amplified unless alternative, marginalized values, including a relational autonomy, are considered deliberately. This amplification probably will mean an increased focus on winning as not only the favored value in elite sport, but possibly the only value. Connected to this trend are implications for embodiment: probably greater control over the body will be emphasized and embodiment diversity minimized as elite trans-athletes are brought to the same or similar standards. With greater mastery of the body, the body will become tailored in ways that reflect normative technological and other cultural values. It may be used increasingly as a tool that, when in optimal condition, can withstand pain and achieve winning performances. As we regard ourselves increasingly as tools for the meeting of ends that seem desirable right now, the mystery of spiritual experiences, such as flow states, likely will become less valued. Yet, the hunger for that which we cannot fully reduce or master persists. It is that hunger that may be the most significant spiritual hope for alternative visions of what it means to be human.

NOTES

1. Pierre-Edouard Sottas, Neil Robinson, Oliver Rabin and Martial Saugy, "The Athlete Biological Passport," *Clinical Chemistry* 57, no. 7 (2011): 969–976.

2. Scholars have called sport a civil religion [Robert N. Bellah, "Civil Religion in America," in *Religion in America*, edited by W. G. McLoughlin and R. N. Bellah (Boston, MA: Houghton Mifflin, 1967), 3–23], a religion [Charles S. Prebish, ed., *Religion and Sport: The Meeting of Sacred and Profane* (Westport, CT: Greenwood Press, 1993), 16], a popular religion [Joseph L. Price, "From Sabbath Proscriptions to Super Sunday Celebrations: Sports and Religion in America," in *From Season to Season: Sport as American Religion*, edited by Joseph L. Price (Macon, GA: Mercer University Press, 2001), 15–38], a folk religion [James Mathisen, "From Civil Religion to Folk Religion: The Case of American Sport," in *Sport and Religion*, edited by Shirl J. Hoffman (Champaign, IL: Human Kinetics Books, 1992), 20], a natural religion [Michael Novak, "The Joy of Sports," in *Religion and Sport: The Meeting of Sacred and Profane*, edited by Charles S. Prebish (Westport, CT: Greenwood Press, 1993), 162], a way of being religious [Tom Sinclair-Faulkner, "A Puckish Reflection on Religion in Canada," in *Religion and Culture in Canada/Religion et Culture au Canada*, edited by Peter Slater (Ottawa, ON: Corporation Canadienne des Sciences Religieuses/ Canadian Corporation for Studies in Religion, 1977), 384], and other characterizations.

3. A. Whitney Sanford, "Pinned on Karma Rock: Whitewater Kayaking as Religious Experience," *Journal of the American Academy of Religion* 75, no. 4 (2007): 888.

4. Eric Baine-Selbo, "Ecstasy, Joy, and Sorrow: The Religious Experience of Southern College Football," *Journal of Religion and Popular Culture* XX (2008): 9.

5. Amarnath Amarasingam, "Transcending Technology: Looking at Futurology as a New Religious Movement," *Journal of Contemporary Religion* 23, no. 1 (2008): 1–16.

6. Humanity+, "Transhumanist FAQ Version 3.0," http://humanityplus.org/ philosophy/transhumanist-faq/#top, accessed February 25, 2014.

7. Humanity+, "Transhumanist FAQ Version 3.0."

8. See, for example, Kevin O'Gorman, *Saving Sport: Sport, Society and Spirituality* (Dublin, Ireland: Columba Press, 2010), 61.

9. Herbert Marcuse, *One Dimensional Man: Studies in the Ideology of Advanced Industrial Society* (Boston, MA: Beacon Press,1964); Jürgen Habermas, *Knowledge and*

Human Interest (Boston, MA: Beacon Press, 1968); Michel Foucault, *Technologies of the Self* (Boston, MA: University of Massachusetts Press, 1988).

10. Humanity+, "Transhumanist FAQ Version 3.0," http://humanityplus.org/philosophy/transhumanist-faq/#top, accessed February 25, 2014.

11. Heidi Campbell, "On Posthumans, Transhumans and Cyborgs: Towards a Transhumanist-Christian Conversation," *Modern Believing* 47, no. 2 (2006): 68–69.

12. Randolph Feezell, *Sport, Philosophy, and Good Lives* (Lincoln, NE: University of Nebraska Press, 2013), 208.

13. Robert Beamish, *Steroids: A New Look at Performance-Enhancing Drugs* (Santa Barbara, CA: Praeger, 2011), 60.

14. Beamish, *Steroids*, 68.

15. Some studies on recreational sport have found that it is possible to cultivate other, more marginalized values, such as diversity and the pleasure of playing the game, or competing intensely regardless of outcome. See, for example, Barbara Ravel and Genevieve Rail, "From Straight to Gaie? Quebec Sportswomen's Discursive Constructions of Sexuality and Destabilizations of the Linear Coming out Process," *Journal of Sport & Social Issues* 32, no. 1 (2008): 4–23.

16. Randolph Feezell, *Sport, Philosophy, and Good Lives*, 70.

17. I am indebted to Ronald Cole-Turner for suggesting the phrase "doubling effect" regarding this intersection.

18. Steven J. Overman, *The Influence of the Protestant Ethic on Sport and Recreation* (Aldershot, UK: Avebury Ashgate, 1997).

19. There are several other issues not dealt with, or only alluded to, in this chapter, such as athletes as role models (will elite trans-athletes become amplified secular religious symbols or even moral exemplars?), the role of emotion in spirituality, human fragility, the celebration of the so-called "natural" body, and the location of ultimate wisdom, among others.

20. Mike McNamee, "Whose Prometheus? Transhumanism, Biotechnology and the Moral Topography of Sports Medicine," *Sport, Ethics and Philosophy* 1, no. 2 (2007): 187.

21. Claudio M. Tamburrini, "What's Wrong with Genetic Inequality? The Impact of Genetic Technology on Elite Sports and Society," *Sport, Ethics and Philosophy* 1, no. 2 (2007): 229–238.

22. Andy Miah, "From Anti-Doping to a 'Performance Policy' Sport Technology, Being Human, and Doing Ethics," *European Journal of Sport Science* 5, no. 1 (2005): 55.

23. Claudio Tamburruni and Torbjörn Tännsjö, "Enhanced Bodies," in *Enhancing Human Capacities*, edited by Julian Savulescu, Ruud ter Meulen, and Guy Kahane (Oxford, UK: Wiley-Blackwell, 2011), 247–290.

24. Robert L. Simon, *Fair Play: The Ethics of Sport*, 2nd ed. (Boulder, CO: Westview Press, 2004), 76–77.

25. Kate Kirby, A. Moran, and S. Guerin, "A Qualitative Analysis of the Experiences of Elite Athlete Who Have Admitted to Doping for Performance Enhancement," *International Journal of Sport Policy and Politics* 3, no. 2 (2011): 205–224.

26. Sanford, "Pinned on Karma Rock."

27. Susan Sherwin, "Genetic Enhancement, Sports and Relational Autonomy," *Sport, Ethics and Philosophy* 1, no. 2 (2007): 177–178.

28. Tracy J. Trothen, "Holy Acceptable Violence? Violence in Hockey and Christian Atonement Theories," *Journal of Religion and Popular Culture*, 21 (2009), doi:10.3138/jrpc.21.suppl_1.003.

29. Michelle M. Lelwica, "Losing Their Way to Salvation: Women, Weight Loss, and the Salvation Myth of Culture Lite," in *Religion and Popular Culture in America*, edited by Bruce David Forbes and Jeffrey H. Mahan (Berkeley, CA: University of California Press, 2000), 180–200.

30. Michael Sandel's concern regarding "hyperagency" leads him to question the integrity of human desire in the enhancement debate. Michael Sandel, "The Case against Perfection: What's Wrong with Designer Children, Bionic Athletes, and Genetic Engineering," in *Human Enhancement*, edited by Julian Salvescu and Nick Bostrom (Oxford, UK: Oxford University Press, 2009), 78.

31. Abraham H. Maslow, *Toward a Psychology of Being* (New York, NY: John Wiley and Sons, 1968).

32. Mihaly Csikszentmihalyi, *Beyond Boredom and Anxiety* (San Francisco, CA: Jossey-Bass, 1975).

33. See, for example, Susan A. Jackson and Mihaly Csikszentmihalyi, *Flow in Sports: The Keys to Optimal Experiences and Performances* (Champaign, IL: Human Kinetics, 1999); Richard Pengelley, "Sport and Spirituality: An Ancient Connection for Our Modern Times." *Dialogue Australasia* 20 (2008): 1–9.

34. Lawrence W. Fagg, "Are There Intimations of Divine Transcendence in the Physical World?", *Zygon* 38, no. 3 (2003): 560.

35. This is taken from an interview in a study by Jackson and Csikszentmihalyi, *Flow in Sports*, 75.

36. Elkington found that there is a "pre-flow" stage with three moments: initial investment of attention, activation and energization, and the trust-flow imperative. Sam Elkington, "Articulating a Systematic Phenomenology of Flow: An Experience-Process Perspective," *Leisure/Loisir* 34, no. 3 (2010): 327–360.

37. Mihaly Csikszentmihalyi and Giovanni B. Moneta, "Models of Concentration in Natural Environments: A Comparative Approach Based on Streams of Experiential Data," *Social Behavior and Personality* 27, no. 6 (1999): 630.

38. Kopano Ratele, "Looks: Subjectivity as Commodity," *Agenda* 90/25, no. 4 (2011): 92–103; April Vannini and Barbara Fornssler, "Girl, Interrupted: Interpreting Semenya's Body, Gender Verification Testing, and Public Discourse," *Cultural Studies Critical Methodologies* 11, no. 3 (2010): 243–257.

39. See, for example, Brendan Burkett, Mike McNamee, and Wolfgang Potthast, "Shifting Boundaries in Sports Technology and Disability: Equal Rights or Unfair Advantage in the Case of Oscar Pistorius?", *Disability & Society* 26, no. 5 (2011): 643–654; Ratele, "Looks."

40. Angela J. Schneider, Matthew N. Fedoruk, and Jim L. Rupert, "Human Genetic Variation: New Challenges and Opportunities for Doping Control," *Journal of Sports Sciences* 30, no. 11 (2012): 1121.

41. George Dvorsky, "Michael Phelps: 'Naturally' Transhuman," Institute for Ethics and Emerging Technologies, 2008, http://ieet.org/index.php/IEET/more/2575, accessed February 25, 2014.

42. Elaine L. Graham, "Post/Human Conditions," *Theology & Sexuality* 10, no. 2 (2004): 13.

43. Thweate-Bates provides an insightful critique of overly simplified approaches to Haraway's hope for the boundary-blurring potential of cyborgs. J. Jeanne Thweate-Bates, "Artificial Wombs and Cyborg Births: Postgenderism and Theology," in *Transhumanism and Transcendence: Christian Hope in an Age of Technological Enhancement*, edited by Ronald Cole-Turner (Washington, DC: Georgetown University Press, 2011), 107.

44. Heather Walton, "The Gender of the Cyborg," Theology & Sexuality 10, no. 2 (2004): 35.

45. Tamburrini, "What's Wrong with Genetic Inequality?," 234.

46. Erik Parens, "The Goodness of Fragility: On the Prospect of Genetic Technologies Aimed at the Enhancement of Human Capacities," in *Contemporary Issues in Bioethics*, 5th ed., edited by Tom L. Beachamp and LeRoy Walters (Belmont, CA: Wadsworth, 1999), 598.

47. As others have ably described, Christian hope for salvation and the eschaton is very different from the transhumanist hope for immortality and enhanced cognitive functioning or the athlete's hope of winning a competition (see this volume or Cole-Turner, ed., *Transhumanism and Transcendence*).

48. Raymond Kurzweil, *The Singularity Is Near: When Humans Transcend Biology* (New York, NY: Viking Press, 2005), 9.

49. Kurzweil, *The Singularity Is Near*, 424.

50. Mayra Rivera, *The Touch of Transcendence* (London, UK: Westminster John Knox Press, 2007), 100, 137.

51. Robert L. Simon "Good Competition and Drug-Enhanced Performance," in *Ethics in Sport*, edited by William J. Morgan, Klaus V. Meier, and Angela J. Schneider (Champaign, IL: Human Kinetics, 2001), 119–129.

52. Nick Bostrom, "Human Genetic Enhancements: A Transhumanist Perspective," *Journal of Value Inquiry* 37 (2003): 497.

53. I am indebted to Michael Grimshaw for his articulation of this insight ["I Can't Believe My Eyes: The Religious Ascetics of Sport as Post-Modern Salvific Moments," *Implicit Religion* 3, no. 2 (2000): 87].

54. Brent Waters, "Whose Salvation? Which Eschatology? Transhumanism and Christianity as Contending Salvific Religions," in *Transhumanism and Transcendence: Christian Hope in an Age of Technological Enhancement*, edited by Ronald Cole-Turner (Washington, DC: Georgetown University Press, 2011), 171.

55. Feezell, *Sport, Philosophy, and Good Lives*, 70.

56. Ted Peters, "Perfect Humans or Trans-Humans?," in *Future Perfect? God, Medicine and Human Identity*, edited by Celia Deane-Drummond and Peter M. Scott, (London, UK: T & T Clark International, 2006),16.

24

. . . .

Spiritual Enhancement

Ron Cole-Turner

Who are the most fervent opponents of transhumanism, if not religious people? We hear this again and again from transhumanists, anti-transhumanists, and just about anyone else who feels a need to comment on technologies of human enhancement. Whether it is really true is debatable.

Given the strength of this assumption, it is ironic that the most readily enhanceable human trait is our capacity for spiritual experience. Compared to cosmetic surgery, spiritual enhancement is inexpensive and painless. Compared to cognitive enhancement, spiritual enhancement is highly effective and enduring. Compared to lifespan extension, compelling evidence indicates that spiritual enhancement actually works in a highly positive and predictable way. The very thing that many see as standing in the way of enhancement technology is the thing most easily enhanced.

Technologies of spiritual enhancement are not new. For millennia, we have known that certain disciplines and techniques can enhance our spiritual awareness. We have also known that certain substances can alter our consciousness in interesting ways. It is even interesting to wonder about moments in the past when people inadvertently consumed some of these substances, experienced mystical or spiritual states of awareness, and became venerated religious leaders, all without any obvious explanation.

In the 20th century, some of these ancient substances were identified and analyzed chemically. Similar substances were synthesized. The most widely known of all these substances, old or new, is lysergic acid diethylamide (LSD), synthesized by the Swiss chemist Albert Hoffman in 1938. Another important substance (or mix of substances, to be more precise) is ayahuasca, a name given to various blends of plant infusions often consumed as a kind of brew.[1] Yet another substance, mescaline, is derived from peyote, a type of cactus. Both ayahuasca and peyote are used today in religious ceremonies as sacramental substances. Limited use of these two substances in religious observance is legally permissible in the United States under the First Amendment's "free exercise" clause. In light of the most recent research, however, the most important of these consciousness-altering substances is psilocybin, derived from various species of "sacred mushrooms."

Substances like psilocybin seem to open the mind to an awareness of a spiritual dimension; for this reason, they are sometimes called "entheogens." More commonly, they are referred to as psychedelics or hallucinogens. In the 1950s and 1960s, these drugs became widely known—perhaps too widely known—and words like "psychedelic" and "hallucinogenic" became associated with drug use in general and with an emerging counterculture seen by many as a threat to social order. At the same time, serious experiments using psychedelics were conducted in psychology and spirituality. Some of these studies yielded intriguing hints about the therapeutic value of entheogens, but failures of experimental rigor and limited research tools meant that the findings were largely inconclusive in terms of supporting claims for any medical or psychological benefit.[2]

Perhaps the best known of these early experiments is the "Marsh Chapel" session, which took place at Boston University's chapel on Good Friday in 1962. A group of seminary students received psilocybin or a placebo. According to various reports published by researchers and participants, those who received psilocybin experienced various levels of mystical or spiritual states of consciousness. Despite its design flaws, the Marsh Chapel experiment offered clear evidence that psilocybin is reliably associated with mystical experience.

Real proof, however, was still decades away. The delay was due mainly to legal restrictions on this line of research.[3] Based on the questionable claim that these substances have no medical value and are highly addictive, they were classified as Schedule I drugs under treaties and laws adopted around 1970. The laws were intended to stop "recreational use" of these compounds, but what they really stopped was scientific research. For decades—roughly the early 1970s until well into the 1990s—almost no biomedical studies used entheogens.

Beginning in the 1990s and building gradually over the past 20 years, research using psychedelics was gradually relaunched in the United States and Europe. After securing a research exemption, research teams are now permitted to engage in limited experimentation in a controlled medical setting.

One of the first questions explored by research teams was whether these drugs offer help in addressing psychological problems. Within a decade, however, a team based at Johns Hopkins University School of Medicine had expanded the scope of the research. In 2006, this research group published the results of a highly significant study, presenting evidence that psilocybin safely and reliably occasions mystical experience in healthy volunteers in a way that is profoundly meaningful.[4]

In terms of technologies of human enhancement, what we are beginning to learn from this latest wave of studies is that these drugs offer a safe and reliable way to enhance the spiritual experience of healthy people. Anyone familiar with the standard bioethics debate about therapy versus enhancement will immediately recognize that if any valid distinction is to be made between the two, the Johns Hopkins research lands squarely on the side of enhancement. At least some of this research involves healthy volunteers, and its purpose is unrelated to any disease but rather solely focused on "occasioning" mystical experience.

Building on some of the findings of the Johns Hopkins research team, neuroscientists based in London have administered psilocybin to volunteers and conducted brain imaging studies while the substance is active in the brain. The London work advances our understanding of how psilocybin acts in the brain, contributing to basic neuroscience and offering intriguing hints about how these drugs might affect brain activity in ways that are associated with mystical experience.

This chapter briefly summarizes some of this research, starting with work done at Johns Hopkins and then moving on to the imaging studies conducted in London. Putting these findings together offers new and intriguing clues to the neuroscience of consciousness and mystical experience. We are only just beginning to understand the complex connections between the ways these substances affect the brain and the subjective, mystical experience that seems reliably to be associated with these neurological correlates. Nevertheless, these findings already invite various interpretations about brains, minds, consciousness, and spiritual experience. Our purpose in the opening sections of the chapter is to report on these findings and then to summarize the hints they offer about the relationship between psilocybin, brain activity, and mystical experience.

This discussion is followed in later sections with questions about what seems to be the newly emerging landscape for technologically mediated spiritual enhancement. Several questions are explored: What does this new research suggest about the possibility of enhancing human spirituality? Is spiritual enhancement really possible, and is it the highest goal or most hostile opponent of transhumanism? How might the possibility of human spiritual enhancement fit within the wider technological project of improving humanity?

PSILOCYBIN AND "COMPLETE" MYSTICAL EXPERIENCE: THE EVIDENCE

Beginning in 2006 and continuing at least through 2014, researchers at Johns Hopkins School of Medicine have been exploring the relationship between psilocybin and mystical experiences. Based on the studies published so far, it can now be said that administering psilocybin in a controlled setting is safe and is reliably correlated with the experience of mystical states. Noting carefully the difference between correlation and causation—a distinction that is especially profound and critically significant when we are talking about the relationship between a chemical substance and a mystical experience—the reports claim only that psilocybin "occasions" mystical experience, not that it "causes" the experience.

In the Johns Hopkins studies, psilocybin is administered orally. Psilocybin occurs naturally in several species of mushrooms. In clinical settings, however, psilocybin is administered in oral form at a dosage of 20 to 30 mg per 70 kg of body weight, and sometimes at a lower dose. The studies at Johns Hopkins involve research volunteers who are carefully prepared and accompanied by two people through the psilocybin session itself. The studies are double-blind, meaning that the researchers involved in a session and the volunteers themselves do not know when a placebo is administered instead of the drug.

Both before and after psilocybin and placebo sessions, volunteer research subjects are put through a battery of questionnaires, including personality inventories (the NEO-PI) and two questionnaires related to spiritual or mystical experience. One of these questionnaires, the "Mysticism Scale" or the Hood scale, has been widely used in mysticism research in recent decades. The other questionnaire was developed in part by William Richards, a member of the Johns Hopkins team. For decades, Richards has encouraged research into the value of entheogens like psilocybin. Working originally with Walter Pahnke, a key leader in an earlier period of research and director of the "Good Friday" study, Richards has developed a questionnaire to measure mystical experience. The Pahnke-Richards questionnaire, also called the "States of Consciousness Questionnaire," includes 43 questions that ask for subjective assessment of types and intensity of spiritual or mystical experience.

Key terms and concepts used in the 43 questions are derived from classic texts on religious and mystical experience, such as William James's *The Varieties of Religious Experience* and W. T. Stace's *Mysticism and Philosophy*. Based on Stace's work in particular, Pahnke and Richards identify seven domains of mystical experience. First is internal unity or a sense of pure awareness, a merging with ultimate reality. The second domain is referred to as external unity, the sense of the unity or oneness of all things or the feeling that all things are alive. This is followed by a sense of sacredness (third domain), and then a sense of a noetic quality that is part of the experience (fourth domain), meaning that somehow the experience is more real than ordinary experience, carrying a sense of intuitive knowledge of ultimate reality. The fifth domain is a sense of transcendence of space and time, followed by the deep feeling of a positive mood of joy, peace, or love (sixth domain). The seventh domain is a sense of paradoxicality and ineffability, the claim that it is hard to put the experience into words.[5]

The questionnaire includes items related to each of these domains, and subjects are asked to respond using a six-point rating, ranging from 0 (not at all or none) to 5 (extreme). The first two domains—internal unity and external unity—are grouped together, resulting in six areas (unity, sacredness, noetic quality, transcendence, positive mood, and ineffability). An individual who identifies strong or intense feelings is judged to have had a complete mystical experience. Specifically, an individual who rates the intensity of experience in each of the six areas at 60 percent or more of the maximum possible is counted as having met the threshold for a complete experience.[6]

The first Johns Hopkins study on psilocybin and mystical experience was published in 2006. It reported that 22 of 36 original volunteers had a "complete" mystical experience. In addition, researchers noted that "[i]t is remarkable that 67 percent of the volunteers rated the experience with psilocybin to be either the single most meaningful experience of his or her life or among the top five most meaningful ... Thirty-three percent of the volunteers rated the psilocybin experience as being the single most spiritually significant experience of his or her life, with an additional 38 percent rating it to be among the top five."[7] When we combine the top two tiers of respondents, we find that a whopping seven out of 10 rated the experience as among the top five most spiritually significant experiences of their lifetime.

LASTING EFFECTS AND ENDURING CHANGES

But does it last? Surely the memories of the entheogen-occasioned mystical experiences fade in time and their importance wears off. To find out whether this is true, the Johns Hopkins team brought back the 2006 study volunteers after 14 months and resurveyed them. Based on what they learned, the researchers had this to say: "When administered under supportive conditions, psilocybin occasioned experiences similar to spontaneously occurring mystical experiences that, over a year later, were considered by volunteers to be among the most personally meaningful and spiritually significant experiences of their lives and to have produced positive changes in attitudes, mood, altruism, behaviour and life satisfaction."[8]

More revealing, perhaps, are the verbatim statements of volunteers presented in the published report of the 14-month follow-up study. For example, one volunteer described the feeling of being "a non-self self held/suspended in an almost tactile field of light." Another spoke of "the utter joy and freedom of letting go—without anxiety—without direction—beyond ego self." Still others described their experiences with these statements: "The sense that all is One, that I experienced the essence of the Universe and the knowing that God asks nothing of us except to receive love." "The experience of death, which initially was very uncomfortable, followed by absolute peace and being in the presence of God. It was so awesome to be with God that words can't describe the experience." "The complete and utter loss of self . . . The sense of unity was awesome . . . I now truly do believe in God as an ultimate reality."[9]

A second major study at Johns Hopkins asked whether there is a relationship between the amount of psilocybin administered and the intensity of the experience. Researchers found that a dose at either 20 or 30 mg per 70 kg of body weight was consistently associated with a personally meaningful spiritual experience. Below that level, the experiences were significant but generally fell short of a "complete" experience. By comparison, at the higher levels, 72 percent of the volunteers met the criteria for a complete mystical experience in one or both of the higher-dose sessions. When they were surveyed 14 months later, "retrospective ratings of mystical experience and spiritual significance did not diminish over time. One month after either or both the two highest dose sessions, 83 percent of participants rated the experience as the single most or among the five most spiritually significant experiences of their life. At the 14-month follow-up, this number was even higher (94 percent)."[10]

One unexpected finding from the Johns Hopkins research is that psilocybin seems to change the personality in lasting ways. Personality traits are known to be relatively stable, especially after age 30. But in a 2011 study, the Johns Hopkins team presented evidence that a psilocybin session is associated with a significant increase in the personality trait of "openness" and that this increase lasts over time. The team uses the "NEO Personality Inventory" to assess personality traits. For the 2011 study, the team reviewed data collected from volunteers at the initial screening, 1 to 2 months after the psilocybin session, and about 14 months afterward. They found that mystical experience "correlated significantly with increases in Openness" and that this increase persisted over time.[11] How great was the increase? According to the study, the increases in Openness "were larger in magnitude than changes in personality typically observed in healthy adults over decades of life experience."[12] As the study notes, "Openness includes a relatively broad range of intercorrelated traits covering aesthetic appreciation and sensitivity, fantasy and imagination, awareness of feelings of self and others, and intellectual engagement. . . . [It] is strongly associated with creativity."[13]

What may be even more significant for our purposes in this chapter are two new insights that arise from this study. First, the changes in Openness are correlated with a "complete mystical experience." According to the study, "Importantly, participants who had a complete mystical experience during their high-dose session, but not others, showed enduring increases in Openness, suggesting that other mystical experiences could occasion similar change."[14] In other words, it is not that psilocybin changes the personality or increases Openness. What is found, instead, is that psilocybin occasions a mystical experience that correlates with Openness.

The second new insight strongly suggested here is that psilocybin is associated not just with an experience, but with a personality trait. A key question about the mystical significance of entheogens was stated half a century ago by Huston Smith: "Drugs appear able to induce religious experiences; it is less evident that they can produce religious lives."[15] How exactly do we define and measure "religious lives" or changes toward them? What is the relationship between "religious traits" and "personality traits"? There are no easy or accepted answers to those questions. If some relationship does truly exist between the personality trait of Openness and the sort of "religious lives" envisioned by Smith, then we can point to the Johns Hopkins study as providing at least a hint of an answer to Smith's question. Psilocybin occasions mystical experience, which in turn occasions an increase in Openness. If we do not yet have evidence of a relationship between entheogens and religious lives— if indeed that evidence always eludes us—at least we now have evidence of a connection between psilocybin, mystical states, and personality traits.

In summary, the research team at Johns Hopkins has shown that while there are risks associated with the use of psilocybin, there is also a strong and reliable association between this entheogen and mystical or spiritual experiences. The risks of a "bad trip," usually consisting of paranoid-like feelings or disorientation, have generally been exaggerated, along with the ideas that these drugs are addictive and that people start to crave them or take them often. Any feelings of fear or paranoia were readily managed by team members, who provided a reassuring presence for volunteers throughout the session. Thus, while it is important to note the need for carefully planning and managing any use of psilocybin, it is also clear that this particularly substance is reliably associated with mystical states of awareness.

This particular point is emphasized at the very end of the 2006 report: "The ability to prospectively occasion mystical experiences should permit rigorous scientific investigations about their causes and consequences, providing insights into underlying pharmacological and brain mechanisms."[16] In terms of scientific research into mystical experience and altered states of consciousness, this "ability" changes everything.

YOUR BRAIN ON DRUGS

When psilocybin enters the human body, it is metabolized as psilocin, a fairly simple chemical that excites serotonin receptor sites in the brain. For several decades, it has been known that psilocin is an agonist that specifically seeks out and affects the serotonin $5\text{-}HT_{2A}$ sites. What happens next was basically unknown territory until 2012, when it was elucidated thanks in large part to a research team led by David Nutt and Robin Carhart-Harris and based at the Imperial College London. The fact that psilocybin reliably and safely "occasions" mystical experience makes it possible to study this experience using sophisticated neuroimaging technology, which is exactly what neuro-scientists in London are doing. First by using functional magnetic resonance imaging (fMRI) and then by using magnetoencephalography (MEG), Imperial College researchers are exploring in detail the activity of the brain when psilocybin is present, and what they are finding has surprised the researchers themselves.

If psilocybin excites serotonin receptor sites, it is reasonable to think that this substance makes the brain more active, possibly even in a way that might generate or create the neural correlate of the mystical experiences so carefully documented by the Johns Hopkins researchers. The London research shows that this commonly held assumption is wrong. Psilocybin and other psyche-delics do not stimulate the brain to become more active. In fact, what researchers found is just the opposite—something that the research report calls "unexpected" and requiring "some explanation." Published in 2012, the report of the first experiment makes this claim: "It has been commonly assumed that psychedelics work by increasing neural activity; however, our results put this into question."[17]

Rather than increasing brain activity, psilocybin seems to decrease it, par-ticularly in a key brain network. In a 2014 article suggesting a theoretical interpretation of their fMRI and MEG imaging data, the London-based researchers call attention to the default mode network (DMN). Ordinarily, the DMN is the most intensely active component of the brain, orchestrating other networks and domains. The DMN is seen as serving "as the highest level of functional hierarchy ... [and] as a central *orchestrator* or *conductor* of global brain activity."[18] When psilocybin is present, however, the activity of the DMN is decreased and its connectivity with other brain regions is diminished.

The article continues with an observation that suggests a relationship between psilocybin, brain function, and subjective spiritual or mystical experi-ence. For millennia, mystics have reported an experience of loss of ego or self-awareness and a sense of union or oneness with surrounding reality. According to the report, "it was remarkable that we recently found a highly significant positive correlation between the magnitude of alpha power *decreases* in the PCC [a region of the DMN] after psilocybin and ratings of the item 'I experi-ence a disintegration of my "self" or "ego." ' ... It is a central hypothesis of this paper that psychedelics induce a primitive state of consciousness ... by relin-quishing the ego's usual hold on reality."[19] In other words, psilocybin dimin-ishes the activity of the very region of the brain that most closely corresponds with the neurologic center of consciousness, and the amount of this decrease correlates with subjective reports of loss of self—a classic hall-mark of mystical experience.[20]

The London researchers expand their interpretation by referring to W. T. Stace's classic book, *Mysticism and Philosophy*. They suggest that their fMRI and MEG findings may correspond or point in the direction of the

neural correlate of mystical experience as Stace defines it. "If we consider contemporary accounts of the mystical consciousness, we can see that the individuality, the 'I,' disappears and is in a sense 'annihilated.' "[21] Carhart-Harris
and his colleagues then add this comment: "Stace's work is particularly useful
because his ideas resonate with the findings of recent neuroimaging studies
relevant to the neurobiology of spiritual experience."[22]

Here again, it is worth reminding ourselves that the language of causality
is tempting but dangerous. Findings and conclusions must be stated carefully.
At most these researchers and their Johns Hopkins colleagues suggest association, correlation, and resonance, claiming reliability but not causality, and
saying that the drugs "occasion" but not do "cause" the experiences.
Knowing *that* something happens is not the same as knowing *why* it happens.
Even knowing that it happens in association with something else merely suggests that some sort of pathway exists. There is a connection that links one
thing (psilocybin) to specific brain states (decreases in the DMN) and to subjective experience that can be described as mystical. Mystical experience is
linked to changes in personality that can be described as increases in
Openness. We know this now on the basis of this research. To claim that we
know that these things are connected is not to claim we have identified the
links in the causal pathway from drug to altered experience, much less to
mystical experience or altered traits of personality.

RELIGION AND SPIRITUAL ENHANCEMENT

Where is this research taking us? All signs point to a future in which entheogens and perhaps other technologies are used to enhance spiritual experience. Compared to the more traditional means of meditation and spiritual
discipline, the reliability and the relative ease with which entheogens occasion mystical experience are bound to be deeply attractive to those who seek
such experience. Some people might embrace these aids while turning away
from more established forms of organized religion. If their goal is to find meaning in their lives through spiritually or personally meaningful experiences,
they may come to see that no organized religion can offer what entheogens
offer. Will today's religious institutions modify themselves to begin to offer
access to psilocybin? Given the generally conservative nature of religious
institutions, this outcome seems unlikely.[23]

As one who teaches in a religious institution and prepares future religious
leaders, I often hear my colleagues suggest that we are in the "meaning" business. If so, we face an impossible competitive challenge. No religious institution in history has ever been able to create or provide religious on-time
ceremonies that more than 70 percent of participants would judge to be in
the top five most meaningful experiences of their personal and spiritual lives.
No religious event has ever occasioned a 61 percent rate of "complete mystical

experience." And yet that is exactly what the Johns Hopkins team reports. If I am in the meaning business, I cannot compete.

Perhaps this is one reason why entheogens are likely to remain illegal for the foreseeable future. Apart from a limited "research exemption," access to drugs like psilocybin involves criminal behavior. The one pathway to legally protected use is in religious ceremonies. In the United States, at least three recognized religious bodies have fought for and won permission to use entheogens in their religious ceremonies under the First Amendment's protection of the free exercise of religion. One of these is the Native American Church, which uses peyote. The other two—*Santo Daime* and *Uniao do Vegetal*—use a brew called ayahuasca.[24] It is not too far-fetched to imagine that other religious institutions might be modified or created to claim this protection. It is generally believed that across the United States, informal groups have already formed for the purpose of providing support for those using entheogens. In time, perhaps, one of these will organize as a religious community and seek legal status and protection. It might potentially create religiously affiliated and legally protected retreat centers, where skilled staff can provide the support and care that is needed for the safe use of entheogens.

Many religious people, however, might find the prospect of entheogen-occasioned mystical states to be troubling. Some might see it as a threat to their institutional survival, while others might see it as a form of spiritual cheating, too cheap to be real and too fast to be authentically religious. Still other religious people might fear entheogen-occasioned mystical experience because they fear mystics and mysticism in general. Mystics tend not to be dogmatic or literalistic in their thinking. They tend not to see the world in binary terms or to create categories that define who is in and who is not. To the extent that some religions, at least, think that they need these things, their defenders might fear all mystics, but perhaps especially entheogen-using mystics, as disloyal followers, interested in spirituality but unwilling to defend the dogmas and the moral markers that define religious boundaries. Not all religions or religious leaders exemplify or encourage the trait of Openness.

Thus we might predict that religiously minded people will react in various ways to the new research on the relationship between entheogens and mystical experience. Some will object, perhaps even to the point of arguing in court for limits on the free exercise of religion. Others will see this new research as just one more sign that a new era of spirituality is dawning, almost like a new phase of human cultural evolution. The familiar phrase, "spiritual but not religious," may point not just to shrinking support for institutional religion and expanding interest in a spiritual dimension of experience, but also to acceptance of the use of entheogens as a new and especially promising path to mystical experience.

TRANSHUMANISM AND SPIRITUAL ENHANCEMENT

Regardless of what religious people might think of entheogens, the value of psilocybin in treating other mental or psychological conditions or its usefulness in mind and brain studies is enough to keep research moving forward. It may turn out, however, that the effectiveness of psilocybin in treating anxiety, depression, or addictions hinges in large part on whether it occasions mystical states of experience. Recall for a moment the association between psilocybin and increases in the personality trait of Openness: the pathway from psilocybin to Openness passes through mystical experience. It may turn out that the same is true of other potential benefits of psilocybin.

Another potential benefit of entheogens might be increased creativity and mental productivity. If so, transhumanists will surely take notice of this potential. If cognitive enhancement through technology is desirable but still largely illusive, why not enhancement of creativity and productivity? Growing anecdotal evidence suggests that entheogens open the mind to a greater range of options and to new solutions to stubborn problems. For example, in *What the Dormouse Said*, John Markoff comments at length on the widespread use of LSD and its impact on the creativity of the early generation of computer scientists and entrepreneurs.

One of the most famous of these is Steve Jobs, co-founder of Apple, Inc. Before his death in 2011, Jobs told biographer Walter Isaacson that "Taking LSD was a profound experience, one of the most important things in my life. LSD shows you that there's another side to the coin, and you can't remember it when it wears off, but you know it. It reinforced my sense of what was important—creating great things instead of making money, putting things back into the stream of history and of human consciousness as much as I could."[25] Others have made similar claims that entheogens unleashed a vital stream of creativity that made them successful in unexpected ways. Also recall what the Johns Hopkins team points out about the association between psilocybin and Openness: it "is strongly associated with creativity."[26]

One transhumanist argument for the limited legalization of entheogens and their carefully supported use might be that they increase Openness and creativity. It might even become clear that these substances increase creativity best when they occasion mystical experience. One can then imagine transhumanists, some of whom already seek cognitive enhancement through technology, embracing entheogens and even enhanced spiritual and mystical experience as a pathway to greater creativity.

Others might embrace entheogens—perhaps more theoretically now and more for others than for themselves—as a path to moral enhancement. Do these substances boost compassion and social engagement? Some of the findings from the Johns Hopkins research team suggest that in the view of acquaintances, the volunteers who experienced mystical states also demonstrated "small but significant positive changes in ... behavior and attitudes."[27] Some transhumanists have argued that moral enhancement is not merely a legitimate option for individuals, but a necessity if humanity is to survive. For example, Ingmar Persson and Julian Savulescu write that "a moral improvement of humankind is requisite to solve the problems" we face precisely because of advanced technology.[28] So far the evidence that entheogens enhance moral·predispositions is limited to a few hints. If it is ultimately shown that they engender not just Openness but also compassion, some transhumanists might have another reason to support their use. In that case, some might find spiritual enhancement tolerable as a means to an end, more perhaps like an unwanted side effect than something sought for its own sake.

In this chapter, however, spiritual enhancement is being considered precisely *as an enhancement per se*. To be fair, our title begs the question of whether spiritual enhancement really is an enhancement. Not everyone will agree that it is. Some might see it as unappealing, if not demeaning, lessening rather than improving humanity. Of course, some anti-transhumanists claim that lifespan extension would not be a real enhancement. But the reasons for objecting are quite different in the case of mystical or spiritual experience, which tends to have the effect of diminishing the sense of self, even to the point of annihilation. If transhumanism is a yearning for maximal self-fulfillment, enhancing the sense of loss of self and union with absolute being is most unappealing, except to the most mystical of transhumanists.

For now it seems fairly obvious that the growing possibility of the use of entheogens for spiritual enhancement will provoke a range of reactions. Some religious people will object because they are not much drawn to mysticism, preferring instead a religion of clarity and objectivity. Other religious people might be drawn to mysticism and want to enrich their mystical experience but think that entheogens are not the right means to this end, while others might judge otherwise. Among those who are more secular or even antireligious in outlook, opposition to all things religious might be enough to make them apprehensive about anything that might boost spiritual experience. They might see entheogens as having other benefits, such as boosted creativity and openness, but perceive that these benefits come at too high a cost. What might they say if the day comes when more than a little evidence shows that entheogen-occasioned mystical experience enhances creativity, Openness, and compassion? Are creativity and Openness really worth the risk of having a mystical experience, particularly a *complete* mystical experience?

These concerns are reminiscent of the worries of Michael Sandel, one of transhumanism's more thoughtful critics. Drawing on a sometimes-religious, sometimes-secular line of argument, Sandel warns us about the dangers of transhumanists and the unexamined risks that come with technologies they love. Enhancement technology, he suggests, exposes us to the risk of developing a misguided mindset, an attitude that life is not so much to be accepted as managed, as if all its unwanted and unpleasant aspects can and should be prevented. Sandel describes this dangerous attitude by drawing on a phrase from the theologian William F. May, saying that too much technology can cost us our "openness to the unbidden."

Having a little fun at Sandel's expense, Nick Bostrom and Julian Savulescu comment, "Perhaps one solution would be for the FDA to require appropriate labeling of enhancement products." Memory-boosting pills, they suggest, might be approved as long as they come with this warning: "May cause constipation, dry mouth, skin rashes, and loss of openness to the unbidden."[29]

The ultimate irony of entheogens in that we now have evidence that a one-time 20 to 30 mg dose of psilocybin—a single dose of a little pill—leads to just the opposite of what Sandel fears. Sandel worries about our losing what little "openness to the unbidden" we still seem to have. Here, quite possibly, is a technology to enhance what seems most absent in the lives of rational, realistic, technologically savvy adults. It occasions an openness to the unbidden. Will Sandel want it? Or Bostrom or Savulescu?

NOTES

1. Cf. G. William Barnard, "Entheogens in a Religious Context: The Case of the Santo Daime Religious Tradition," *Zygon* 49, no. 3 (2014): in press; Marc G. Blainey, "Forbidden Therapies: Santo Daime, Ayahuasca, and the Prohibition of Entheogens in Western Society," *Journal of Religion and Health* 10, doi: 10.1007/s10943-014-9826-2.

2. Walter N. Pahnke and William A. Richards, "Implications of LSD and Experimental Mysticism," *Journal of Religion and Health* 5, no. 3 (1966): 175–208.

3. David J. Nutt, Leslie A. King, and David E. Nichols, "Effects of Schedule I Drug Laws on Neuroscience Research and Treatment Innovation," *Nature Reviews Neuroscience* 14, no. 8 (2013): 577–585.

4. Roland R. Griffiths, William Richards, Una D. McCann, and Robert Jesse, "Psilocybin Can Occasion Mystical-Type Experiences Having Substantial and Sustained Personal Meaning and Spiritual Significance," *Psychopharmacology* 187, no. 3 (2006): 276–277.

5. Roland R. Griffiths, Matthew W. Johnson, William A. Richards, Brian D. Richards, Una McCann, and Robert Jesse, "Psilocybin Occasioned Mystical-Type Experiences: Immediate and Persisting Dose-Related Effects," *Psychopharmacology* 218, no. 4 (2011): 652–653.

6. Griffiths et al., "Psilocybin Occasioned Mystical-Type Experiences," 653.

7. Griffiths et al., "Psilocybin Can Occasion Mystical-Type Experiences Having Substantial and Sustained Personal Meaning," 276–277.

8. Roland R. Griffiths, William. A. Richards, Matthew. W. Johnson, Una. D. McCann, and Robert Jesse, "Mystical-Type Experiences Occasioned by Psilocybin Mediate the Attribution of Personal Meaning and Spiritual Significance 14 Months Later," *Journal of Psychopharmacology* 22, no. 6 (2008): 631.

9. Griffiths et al., "Mystical-Type Experiences Occasioned by Psilocybin Mediate the Attribution of Personal Meaning and Spiritual Significance 14 Months Later," 629.

10. Griffiths et al., "Psilocybin Occasioned Mystical-Type Experiences," 661–662.

11. Katherine A. MacLean, Matthew W. Johnson, and Roland R. Griffiths, "Mystical Experiences Occasioned by the Hallucinogen Psilocybin Lead to Increases in the Personality Domain of Openness," *Journal of Psychopharmacology* 25 (2011): 1456–1457.

12. MacLean et al., "Mystical Experiences Occasioned by the Hallucinogen Psilocybin," 1457.

13. MacLean et al., "Mystical Experiences Occasioned by the Hallucinogen Psilocybin," 1459.

14. MacLean et al., "Mystical Experiences Occasioned by the Hallucinogen Psilocybin," 1460.

15. Huston Smith, "Do Drugs Have Religious Import?" *Journal of Philosophy* 61 (1964): 528–529.

16. Griffiths et al., "Psilocybin Can Occasion Mystical-Type Experiences Having Substantial and Sustained Personal Meaning," 276–277.

17. Robin L. Carhart-Harris, David Erritzoe, Tim Williams, James M. Stone, Laurence J. Reed, Alessandro Colasanti, Robin J. Tyacke, Robert Leech, Andre L. Malizia, Keven Murphy, Peter Hobden, John Evans, Amanda Feilding, Richard G. Wise, and David J. Nutt, "Neural Correlates of the Psychedelic State as Determined by fMRI Studies with Psilocybin," *Proceedings of the National Academy of Sciences* 109, no. 6 (2012): 2141.

18. Robin L. Carhart-Harris, Robert Leech, Peter J. Hellyer, Murray Shanahan, Amanda Feilding, Enzo Tagliazucchi, Dante R. Chialvo, and David Nutt, "The Entropic Brain: A Theory of Conscious States Informed by Neuroimaging Research with Psychedelic Drugs," *Frontiers in Human Neuroscience* 8, article 20 (2014), doi: 10.3389/fnhum.2014.00020.

19. Carhart-Harris et al., "The Entropic Brain."

20. Carhart-Harris et al., "The Entropic Brain."

21. Carhart-Harris et al., "The Entropic Brain."

22. Carhart-Harris et al., "The Entropic Brain." For more on this research, see Ronald Cole-Turner, "Entheogens, Mysticism, and Neuroscience," *Zygon* 49, no. 3 (2014): in press.

23. Leonard Hummel, "By Its Fruits? Mystical and Visionary States of Consciousness Occasioned by Entheogens," *Zygon* 49, no. 3 (2014): in press.

24. For information on legal uses of entheogens, see Martin W. Ball, "Four Legal Entheogens for the Spiritual Explorer," *Spirituality & Health* (November-December 2009), http://spiritualityhealth.com/articles/four-legal-entheogens-spiritual-explorer.

25. Walter Isaacson, *Steve Jobs* (New York, NY: Simon & Schuster, 2011), p. 41.

26. MacLean et al., "Mystical Experiences Occasioned by the Hallucinogen Psilocybin," 1459.

27. Griffiths et al., "Psilocybin Can Occasion Mystical-Type Experiences Having Substantial and Sustained Personal Meaning," 278.

28. Ingmar Persson and Julian Savulescu, "Moral Transhumanism," *Journal of Medicine and Philosophy* 0 (2011):11, doi: 10.1093/jmp/jhq052.

29. Nick Bostrom and Julian Savulescu, "Introduction: Human Enhancement Ethics: The State of the Debate," quoting Michael J. Sandel, "The Case against Perfection: What's Wrong with Designer Children, Bionic Athletes, and Genetic Engineering," in *Human Enhancement*, edited by Nick Bostrom and Julian Savulescu (Oxford, UK: Oxford University Press, 2006), 6. In the original, the warning is in all capital letters.

Conclusion

. . . .

Transhumanism and Religion: Glimpsing the Future of Human Enhancement

Tracy J. Trothen

Implanted computer chips that tell us what we should eat, how much exercise to get, and what our overall health status is may not be far away. GPS tracking capabilities may see us all on "the grid." Life expectancy will be lengthened. Replacement organs may become generated through our stem cells. Emotions may become more controllable. Pain sensations may become alterable. Robots will become more android in appearance. War drones will become more common. Artificial intelligence technologies will grow and mind uploading may become more than the stuff of movies. Even spiritual experiences and openness, as Ron Cole-Turner discusses in his groundbreaking chapter, have potential for enhancement. The possibilities for human enhancement are greater than most people might imagine. While there is no agreement among the authors in this collection regarding how far we should go in the transhumanist quest, all agree that questions of meaning and ethics are pressing. Most are cautious in their approaches, seeing potential for both harms and benefits. Some are more critical either toward transhumanism or, in the case of Don Braxton's chapter, toward religious responses to transhumanism.

This book, as emphasized at the outset, is meant to be a representative slice of the state of the academic discussion of the relationship between transhumanism and religion. Reflective of the discussion so far, we see in this volume a greater focus on the Roman Catholic and Protestant streams of Christianity. While this collection pays some attention to Judaism, Buddhism, Daoism, Confucianism, and secular ways of being religious or spiritual, the number of chapters devoted to these traditions is limited. We surmise that with time the religious traditions (and other ways of being spiritual or religious) will become more evenly represented in this conversation.

Although there is no agreement on how to assess transhumanist thinking, some common themes thread their way through most of these chapters. The most salient are transcendence, sin or moral fallibility, questions of theological anthropology or what it means to be human, relationality, autonomy, embodiment, and perfection and hope. These themes have several coterminous points—notably, the topics of justice and values. In what follows I will chart some of what is said about these themes and add my own brief commentary.

TRANSCENDENCE

As an ethicist, I found myself pondering mandatory and aspirational ethics as I read these valuable chapters. The minimal ethical requirements that bind us in society, largely through law and codes of ethics, are mandatory. Aspirational ethics are more associated with virtue and the duty to do good, with regard to those ideals to which we aspire. We never fully achieve our aspirations but rather continue to work toward their realization.

A faith tradition is one possible source of both mandatory and aspirational ethics. Other worldviews and movements such as capitalism, humanism, and transhumanism also provide value bases for mandatory and aspirational ethics. One important feature that can differentiate these sources concerns accountability: to whom do we look for guidance and virtue? As several of our authors suggest, human action and being are strongly influenced by the answer to this question. Those following a theistic faith tradition look to their transcendent God for ultimacy. Those who follow transhumanism look most to the human ability to reason and create enhancing technologies that allow for the transcending of limits. How one understands the ultimate source of hope for well-being influences human strivings and actions.

As Michael Burdett makes clear, transhumanists locate hope for betterment in the self and other humans. Typically, religious traditions look beyond the self for betterment but they also pay heed to the self. The Judeo-Christian tradition, for example, underscores the divine commandment to love God, self, and others. The point about self-love often gets lost or undervalued. Through the psychological sciences and some faith practices, we are realizing increasingly the importance of attention to the self in the form of self-awareness. Yet we are loath—in the Western world, at least—to exhort self-love and knowledge without immediately adding the caveat to be careful lest you think too much of yourself. At best, this sends a mixed message to more vulnerable people who do not tend to think much of themselves to begin with. It also shifts the focus toward excessive and narcissistic self-love and away from self-knowledge and healthy self-love.

When we plumb the meaning of love, it becomes clear that one cannot authentically love without knowing. As theologian Sallie McFague argued in her book *Super, Natural Christians*, you cannot love what you do not know.[1] This includes love of the self, the Other, and creation. It seems to me that self-knowledge is necessary—and little acknowledged as such—to constructive engagement with issues related to what it means to be human, such as those surfaced by transhumanism. Without healthy self-knowledge and love, it is difficult or impossible to engage in a constructive self-critique or to assume appropriate responsibility. This, in turn, makes it more difficult to discern what is of the transcendent divine and what has deviated from that transcendent source.

MORAL FALLIBILITY

Responsibility, according to the authors who address this topic, is important in minimizing potential harms as we move forward with technological enhancements. Imbued in most chapters are understandings of moral virtue and fallibility (or sin). For example, Todd T. W. Daly discusses original sin and its relationship to death. Drawing on the work of theologian Reinhold Niebuhr, Stephen Garner points to the sins of pride and will-to-power, and other authors, such as Amy Michelle DeBaets and Joseph Wolyniak, provide excellent discussions of the human tendency to supersede limits. While the caution regarding hubris is very important, particularly for the more socially privileged, I wonder if we are ignoring an equally important dimension of sin in the human enhancement discussion.

The feminist, womanist, and mujerista insight that sin for women and marginalized groups is about the denial of self-worth and a giving up of power and responsibility is significant to the transhumanism-religion conversation and to technoscience deliberations more generally. If I see myself as voiceless, powerless, or unworthy, I am apt to accept what I am told. The challenge of finding one's authentic desires (as Patrick Hopkins writes about) and engaging communally in discussions about how best to pursue those desires is fraught with systemic difficulties—in particular, the challenge faced by the marginalized to trust, hear, and claim their voices. It may well be that out of concern for what the privileged are creating technologically, not only have we over-emphasized the precautionary principle (see Daniel McFee's chapter), but we have also misconstrued the scope of the possible harms. In other words, in our concern for the choices being made by the privileged, we have forgotten the dangers of disempowerment.

This multifaceted understanding of sin is a very important point that is relevant to the other themes in this collection. Sin, whether understood from a privileged position or a marginalized position, is about distorted perspective; from a religious viewpoint, sin is a failure to follow paths that bring one closer to God. In the case of the privileged, sin is about greed and arrogance, perhaps fed by fear of not being in control. It could be about greed for money, status, or power. Alternatively, it could simply belie a perverse self-assurance that only I know what is best. As such, it is a denial of human fallibility.

In the case of the underprivileged, sin also takes the shape of self-focus, albeit for very different reasons. When one experiences a lack of power, it might seem that the only recourse is to focus on survival of the self and those for whom one is immediately responsible. The ability to survive is no mean feat for those living in poverty or violence. Yet, the belief that I am alone can eventually lead to unnecessary fragmentation and the perpetuation of the status quo. Finding ways to claim/reclaim power is not easy. Community is necessary. Likewise, it is necessary that the more privileged regularly ask whose voices are missing and why.

For the marginalized, the use of the term "sin" can be experienced as another level of blaming the victim. The concept of sin has been reimagined by theologians writing from the underside as the neglect of self-worth and the relinquishing of power. Even though the type of sin engaged in by the less powerful is usually (not always) self-deprecating, it is nonetheless harmful to the wider community as well as the self. In the case of human enhancements, we should be particularly concerned with the experiences and perspectives of the least powerful. When we accord the marginalized an epistemological privilege in this discussion, a very different version of what is valuable about being human may emerge.

THEOLOGICAL ANTHROPOLOGY

That each person is valuable is intrinsic to a religious perspective. In the Abrahamic faiths, it is claimed that humans are made in the image of God, although fallen. Created as embodied humans, designed for covenantal relationship and the flourishing of all that is living, human beings are believed to have been good creations made in the image of their Creator. Much debate revolves around how we ought to understand this claim. Some, such as Joshua Moritz and Celia Deane-Drummond,[2] have queried elsewhere whether only humans are created in God's image or whether animals also fit this description. Although not a widely held view, if God's image or even likeness is possibly revealed in animals, then it is not a huge leap to imagine that human-created (co-created) forms of life may also be in God's image and thus of God. In this volume, Matthew Zaro Fisher ponders whether an uploaded mind would be a person made in the image of God. Similarly, Jeanine Thweatt-Bates asks whether a form of "friendly AI" might be understood as a relational person created in the image of God. Their conclusions differ, with Fisher answering in the affirmative and Thweatt-Bates responding in the negative. Both ask whether human flesh and conscious awareness of oneself as a person are necessary to being in the image of God. Fisher reasons that there is no clear distinction between the cyborg and the uploaded mind, in this regard, since both have materiality (a pseudo-body). Building on Rahner's concept of the *Vorgriff* (the self-luminosity of being), there is no separation of the material and the spirit; therefore, Fisher argues, we have no reason to assume that the uploaded mind would not be a person in the image of God.

Thweatt-Bates builds on her arguments elsewhere that while the cyborg may be considered potentially liberating (in Donna Haraway's tradition) and a self-conscious person, the uploaded mind is an entirely different matter. In her critique and celebration of Ted Peters's work, Deane-Drummond argues similarly regarding the significance of embodiment to personhood. Further, at what point, if any, do we become created in our own image rather than in God's image?

Some authors, such as Anders Sandberg, may ask why creating ourselves in our own image is problematic. Why not re-create ourselves in such a way that we might live longer, healthier lives? Why not do everything possible to avoid death and allow further flourishing? Sandberg emphasizes that the question of the meaning of life lies at the heart of the various transhumanist strands. If the transhumanist purpose is to transcend human biological limitations and improve the overall state of humanity and the cosmos, he suggests, how can this not fit with any value system that upholds life?

Hava Tirosh-Samuelson would certainly agree, as would most of the writers in this volume, that we should avoid death and seek life. From a Jewish perspective, in particular, life is a gift from God that we are meant to pursue vigorously. This does not mean that Tirosh-Samuelson agrees with the strong pro-enhancement stance held by Sandberg. She explains this qualification: "But to the extent that trans/posthumanism denigrates the biological human body, denies the wisdom of mortality, and celebrates the elimination of human species, Judaism offers a critique." Although the religions offer critiques of some extreme enhancement goals, many of the ideas behind radical life extension are consistent with Judaism, Christianity, and, as Geoffrey Redmond points out, Confucianism, Buddhism, and Daoism. Further, part of the human purpose is to co-create (drawing on Philip Hefner's oft-used concept of the created co-creator). But, as Garner asks, at what point does this co-creating take us away from, rather than closer to, the Divine purpose?

RELATIONALITY

As we edge more deeply into ethical questions of values and principles, the topic of what it means to be a human person reemerges with a focus on relationality. Several of the authors identify the importance of human encounters with the "Other" (see the chapters by Steven Benko and Amelia Hruby, Corey Andrew Labrecque, Jeanine Thweatt-Bates, and Tracy J. Trothen). These authors are concerned with diversity from a religious perspective. In short, given the Abrahamic theological claim that all are created in God's image, then as theologian Mayra Rivera describes, genuine encounters with the irreducible Other can begin bringing one closer to God as the Divine Other. When one truly encounters the Other as "not me" and made in the image of God, then one sees more clearly the effects and wrongness of systemic injustice and devaluing.

The recognition of the Other involves the insight that all life is interconnected and interdependent. Dependence, in normative Western culture, is thought of as undesirable—something to be overcome in much the same way as our bodily limitations are to be conquered. The ideal is independence, freedom, and individual choice. Daly and Labrecque underscore the importance of interdependence as a Christian ideal but note that it is a sign of human weakness or limitation in transhumanism. The perception that I do not need anyone is, as Brent Waters argues, is a false social construction. The emphasis on extreme individualism belies the ways in which we relate to and depend on others. Christian theologians Richard Rohr and Andrea Ebert surmise that, increasingly, the inability of Westerners to encounter and take difference seriously limits our relational and spiritual capacities.[3] The preoccupation with individual rights and wants has cultivated a type of self-centeredness (or narcissism, Waters suggests) that leads to relational fragmentation. The lie, in this case, is that if I can look after me, then my happiness (and likely good things on a global level) will follow (McFee and DeBaets). On the flip side, the alienation from self that is experienced by so many of the less privileged also contributes to an inability to see others. The lie, in this case, is that if I can survive, that is all I deserve.

To encounter the Other, I must see into and then beyond myself. I must also be willing to risk my vulnerability and acknowledge that I am not in control of a mutual relationship, although I can participate in it, confessing and even celebrating my interdependence. Perhaps, as Thweatt-Bates points out, the interfacing of technology with humans creates more visible diversity and therefore more potential for the blurring of discriminatory boundaries, thereby enhancing the possibility of relationship. But the recognition of the Other as not me, and as—at least potentially—in the image of the Divine, must be recognized as necessary to relationship. As Benko and Hruby conclude, "The effort to become transhuman is itself an ethical undertaking that can only remain ethical if one remains predisposed to the otherness of the Other."

So far we humans have not been well disposed toward this fostering of relationship; we remain vulnerable to sin. The assumption that human values and judgment are unassailable is a trap that religions (and societies) have encountered throughout history. Christian groups, even after being persecuted themselves, have demonized and persecuted out-groups, killing and torturing those who are in some way different (e.g., Albigensians and Cathars, witches, Jews, those not conforming to heteronormativity). Don Braxton elucidates this dynamic in his examination of religious disgust reactions to transhumanism.

Will religious humanity discriminate against the more visibly diverse transhumans?

AUTONOMY: FREEDOM OF CHOICE

Another dimension of potential human fallibility involves decisions regarding what constitutes an enhancement and choices about which enhancements ought to be implemented. The risks of implementing our desires through irreversible human enhancement measures are significant. For this reason, even some transhumanists are very cautious regarding enhancement choices that will affect future generations (e.g., germ-line modifications). At the very least, we will make some choices that these future generations would not, choices that we may come to reevaluate later, and choices that cause harm or reinforce existing harms. The desires to look more attractive, reduce physical suffering, live much longer, think faster, run faster, be stronger, and have the freedom to choose such enhancements are understandable. However, as Waters insightfully points out, "An understandable desire . . . is not necessarily a good desire." What we want and why we believe we want these things are constructed based on contextual messages. Also socially constructed is the belief that it is possible to satisfy these desires if only we acquire these things. Hopkins suggests that humans are by their nature unsatisfied, always desiring something more. If this is so, he posits, then we are doomed to never quench this desire (and never achieve contentment), regardless of whatever technological enhancements we may create.

Choice may sound easy—and it is, at one level. I can easily choose what I want for breakfast. Such a choice is easy, that is, until I stop to consider the sociological, political, economic, ethical, family of origin, and other issues behind my choice to eat meat, milk, yogurt, or oatmeal and the kind or brand of each. Most of the time it is easier to ignore these issues. When I do pause to reflect on them, however, my assumption that I am freely choosing these foods comes into question. It can seem as though what I eat for breakfast is my free choice, but I soon realize that my capacity to choose and my thinking that influences what I choose are shaped by external factors and processes. Also, my choices may not be entirely consistent with the faith perspective or worldview that I embrace.

Autonomy, as several authors point out, is a central transhumanist tenet. The freedom for people to choose as they please and the capacity to create technology that can satisfy those choices are very important in transhumanist thought. This freedom and capacity are parts of autonomy. As Sandberg makes clear, transhumanists are convinced that such technological innovations are not merely possible but also probable. Yet, as several of our authors argue, the concept of free choice is linked with several problems. Currently, the normative Western concept of autonomy is conflated with individual rights and choice. This is the version of autonomy that underlies most transhumanist faith claims. A reduction of autonomy to individual choice ignores the uneven global power distribution, as pointed out by Heup Young Kim. The systemic marginalization of women and minorities is seen as largely inconsequential to the process of moving ahead with more enhancements. Truly informed choice, however, requires a critical awareness of the possible harms and benefits. For this reason, it is necessary to have some critical understanding of socially normative values and consequent power distribution.

This power distribution is central to chapters by DeBaets, Kim, Labrecque, and McFee. These authors are not convinced by transhumanist arguments that enhancement technologies will gradually become available and accessible to everyone. Some transhumanists suggest that over time, as with all technologies, the cost will drop, affording everyone the opportunity to choose whichever enhancements they desire.[4] As the boundaries between machine and human become increasingly blurred, it is theorized that humans will learn that embodiment categories can be transcended, bridging much, if not all, of the divisions between groups. In short, proponents claim that transhumanism has the likely potential to solve systemic injustices, albeit over time.

EMBODIMENT: CHOICE AND RELATIONALITY

Writing from a feminist theological perspective, DeBaets shows that when people are reduced to information in their brains, the body becomes invisible and the costs of this invisibility are typically borne by marginalized groups, such as women and minorities. By this, she means that the body and its significance are camouflaged by the transhumanist assumption that all we are is found in our brains. This assumption makes it even more difficult to name the discrimination that happens below the surface. As a result, the discrimination is glossed over and goes unaddressed.

Kim's much-needed Eastern religious perspective adds an important dimension to this critique. For him, transhumanism is not simply a white male-centered movement but a Western imperialist one. Again, Kim makes clear the relevance and the perspectival nature of values to transhumanist aspirations. McFee and Labrecque round out this critique, respectively, by emphasizing the seriousness of global wealth disparity and the negative implications for the aging body. With regard to the latter, transhumanist proponents see aging as a deficit. Labrecque points out, however, that attitudes pose as much a threat to personhood as does the deterioration of the body. Additionally, these authors identify the potential for discrimination against the unenhanced. As Thweatt-Bates queries, which kind of body counts?

Individual choice or extreme autonomy, as Waters charges, manifests and cloaks prejudices. Choice is not unfettered, but rather mirrors socially embedded values. In this way, choice, unfortunately, is more about individualism than about individuality. By this, I mean that "free thinking" is not free of context and commitments. Feminists have long known that humans are perspectival; none of us is value free. This need not be a bad thing, but problems arise when we neglect or refuse to be critically aware of the values and context that drive our choices. Individuality, as I propose it, requires that I be sufficiently aware of cultural, relational, and other influences so that I am able to pose critical questions about my beliefs and opinions. We are formed by many sources, including our families of origin, the media, and politics. In nurturing a sense of individuality, I have to ask myself from where my beliefs come and whether they are consonant with what I really believe. Accessing this authenticity is no easy task. If I deny these questions, however, I make choices that only seem to be mine alone.

According to Sandberg, most transhumanist proponents claim that their vision is not about espousing one particular set of values, aside from individual choice and the technological options for overcoming unnecessary human limitations. But if all worldviews are value laden, then, as the authors in this collection find, values inform even the most basic of transhumanist tenets, such as what is judged to be an enhancement. In other words, how do we know what makes us better? Perhaps these values are not always articulated, but that omission does not mean they are not operative. As Labrecque wonders regarding the aged, will transhumanist thinking simply reinforce and amplify existing prejudice? Will seemingly freely made choices result in greater conformity to contemporary Western norms about beauty, value, and happiness?

Systemic marginalization and devaluing of those who do not visibly fit the norm are concerns raised throughout this collection. One might ask, if our bodies are at the root of so much discrimination, then why would we not want to change our beings to the extent that materiality does not matter? Would this not put an end to most injustices? Perhaps it would—but that outcome is unlikely. It would not necessarily heal the discriminatory values and attitudinal roots. It would also obviate diversity.[5]

Relationality and embodiment are key topics for several authors, including Benko and Hruby, Deane-Drummond, DeBaets, Daly, Labrecque, Thweatt-Bates, Trothen, Lee Johnson, and Hannah Scheidt. Questions about the significance of the body to personhood and being human are prominent when considering enhancement. The most extreme case is mind uploading: who are we if we have no fleshy body? Waters sums up many of the concerns raised by this prospect in his charge that "a human being cannot be reduced to a will trapped in a body." Likewise, Scheidt finds that arguments in favor of mind uploading neglect the embodied and relational dimensions of consciousness. The issue is muddied by Philip A. Douglas's insightful suggestion that a future possibility is the creation of "one mind"—a concept that may be in keeping with Teilard de Chardin's hope for greater spiritual connectedness. Even if mind uploading does not become an option, bodily enhancement options will certainly increase. Whatever is normatively valued will become marketed as "enhancing." As difficult as it is to see the values currently informing our desires, it will surely become more difficult with more lasting consequences as technology "advances."

These concerns are connected to additional religious issues about embodiment. Some authors in this volume see transhumanist ideas and the Christian theological bodily-affirming doctrines of creation, incarnation, and bodily resurrection as incompatible. Yet, Christianity's relationship with the body has been at the least ambivalent; Christianity has a longstanding love-hate relationship with the body. Johnson's chapter provides an evocative discussion illustrating this ambivalent relationship. Drawing clear connections between gnostic discomfort with the body and particularly women's bodies, Johnson suggests that this dynamic has not been resolved. Now a new embodiment identity crisis looms as the church is forced to confront the technological enhancement question.

Talk of the body usually stirs thinking about sexuality. Sexuality is a preoccupation, fascination, and often taboo topic for many people. Thweatt-Bates touches on sexuality in her timely analysis of "friendly" AI, and particularly film portrayals of AI. Many religions have struggled with human sexuality, unsure of sexual desire and its fit with religious convictions. How will sexual desire be affected in the transhuman? Which values and faith convictions (both religious and secular) will inform choices regarding both the erotic and reproductive possibilities? This emotionally charged topic will generate more scholarly attention as corporeal enhancements emerge more visibly in the market.

Braxton cautions theologians, religious studies scholars, and transhumanists alike: taboos and disgust reactions pervade religions as built-in survival mechanisms. They function to maintain the social order. Of course, the social order is neither fully functional nor good (desirable) for everyone. Those who do not fit with the current norms are cast out or otherwise discriminated against. Given the strong reactions generated by embodiment and sexuality generally, it is easy to see that differently appearing bodies would generate particularly strong reactions. Disgust at people who are significantly altered physically, Braxton suggests, functions to maintain the status quo and keep a cap on the use of human enhancements, including enhancements that might otherwise win the support of the religiously minded.

Cole-Turner's chapter is very important because he dares to go where angels fear to tread. The use of pharmaceuticals to induce altered states has long been viewed with disgust. Indeed, these "drugs" have been lumped together as anathema. Yet, as Cole-Turner points out, well-regarded evidence-based research suggests that some entheogens such as psilocybin may safely enhance embodied spiritual openness. If this is so, then why do most faith communities refrain from even talking about this possibility? Braxton's analysis of disgust reactions can shed some light on this paradox:

the use of pharmaceutical drugs to enhance any aspect of humanity (unless it has become viewed as normal) transgresses notions of purity and social norms prohibiting certain "drug" use.

The Christian confession that humans are naturally created in God's image usually serves as a base for maintaining the perceived purity of the body. But, as many scholars have argued persuasively, we have equated socially constructed notions of the "normal" body with the natural, God-inspired body. Some enhancing agents such as vitamins, many surgical procedures, and vaccinations have become so "normal" that they are no longer seen as enhancing but rather are considered natural in some sense. Brian Green's exploration of natural law theory and its relevance in a transhuman world, helps the reader to consider the theological meaning of natural. Cole-Turner's reflections generate more questions about what makes us, as embodied people, "naturally" spiritually open.

HOPE AND PERFECTION

We can extend the reflection on disgust reactions and the question of what is normal and natural. At some level at least, much of Western society sees aging bodies as unnatural, and I strongly suspect that this perception crosses religious and secular lines. Labrecque's examination of this prejudice—if not outright revulsion—demonstrated toward those whose bodies have visibly aged is revealing. Aging and/or disease-ridden bodies are the social location of both disgust and fear of dying and death. These reactions are associated with the hope of transcending aging and death—a hope that is shared by followers of religions and transhumanism.

Not surprisingly, several of the authors in this volume address eschatology; they see it as intersecting with transhumanism. Religions generally understand that there is more than what is realized in human life. Although they may conceptualize the afterlife in very different ways, they believe that humans will continue in some form after death. From a religious outlook, the source of hope lies beyond the self or other humans. For transhumanists, future hope lies in human-created technology that has the potential (or promise) to enhance humanity to the point of virtual immortality. (It is understood that even technology may not be able to save us from all accidents or catastrophic events.) In the transhumanist outlook, the source of hope is humanity. As Daly reflects, "Christians and transhumanists both long for a better kind of existence where death, sickness, and disease will be truly vanquished. There is a shared a sense of disgust over the phenomenon of death. Beyond this shared moral outrage, however, lie divergent understandings of death and its defeat." There are also divergent understandings of life and what it means to live fully.

The notion of perfection is part of these understandings of a full life and future hope. But the concept of perfection is very different as seen through a religious lens compared to a transhumanist one. Burdett refers to transhumanist future hope as "the myth of progress," for which technology serves as its driving force. As with all myths, Burdett points out, the myth of progress carries embedded values, and in particular the value of transcending the limits of human finitude through the "perfecting" of the self. Perfection, then, is a constructed notion formed by ideals emerging out of whatever we think is most desirable at a given point in time.

From a religious perspective, perfection is also striven for but is understood differently. Tirosh-Samuelson describes perfection on earth, from a Jewish perspective, as attained through good works to others. Similarly, in some sense Labrecque and Wolyniak see Christian notions of perfection as partial restoration to the prelapsarian state, the Garden of Eden before the introduction of sin. This is perhaps akin to the concept of the eschatological proviso: through God's grace and human justice work, it is possible and important to edge toward the realization of God's harmonious and Edenic promise, but humanity cannot fully realize that state in this world. The existence of limits is not perceived as a bad thing in Christianity; these limits signal the fallenness of humanity (a caution), the divine imperative to strive toward justice and love, and the promise of more.

Bodily perfection, in Judeo-Christian tradition, is understood as God given. Further, humanity's original state as made in the image of God was as close to perfection as willed by God. Thus, as Labrecque, Wolyniak, and Thweatt-Bates suggest, from a Christian perspective it is restoration of the body that is sought, not replacement of the body. Further, it is not full restoration but, as Wolyniak, reflecting on Bacon's thought, puts it, partial recovery of the Garden of Eden state of humanity. Again, there is the understanding that humanity is limited and must rely on a transcendent Divinity for full recovery from the Fall.

This discussion suggests that Christianity may be amenable to a third option in the therapy/enhancement debate—that of restoration.[6] Traditionally, the most common approach to the enhancement ethics debate has been to evaluate technological interventions on the basis of whether they are therapeutic (good) or enhancing (not good). As Cole-Turner suggests elsewhere regarding the relation of this debate to Christian theology, "The distinction in theology is between redemption and glorification, between God redeeming humanity by restoring us to an original state from which we have fallen and glorifying or transforming us far above any original status."[7]

This third option of restoration or nontherapy lies between interventions clearly defined as therapeutic or enhancing. The question is this: restoration to what state? If humans develop the capacity to move humanity to—what we think is—an almost prelapsarian state, should this be done? From a Jewish perspective, Tirosh-Samuelson appeals to the concept of an open-ended future. In short, humanity must resist actions that close or limit future divine possibilities. At the same time, humanity is to participate fully in good works in accordance with God's will. This concept of discerning and following a moral path that is in accord with something greater than the self is common to most of the religions. Arguably, it both limits human choice and requires efforts to improve humanity that go beyond therapy and acceptance of our current state.

Values, ideals, and human limitation lie at the heart of all these themes. Humans have not demonstrated a good and consistent capacity to make decisions that enhance their overall notion of life. What makes us think we can begin to do so now? What is most concerning about transhumanism is not the possibility of morphing humanity into something different, but rather the lack of critical analysis and awareness of operative values. What is it that we are/will be choosing and why? Does transhumanism espouse a value set or, as Sandberg contends, does it offer an opportunity to realize our diverse interpretations of the meaning of life? At the close of his chapter, Cole-Turner asks whether "spiritual enhancement is really an enhancement." This needs to be asked of all "enhancements." What is it that will make us better?

NOTES

1. Sallie McFague, *Super, Natural Christians: How We Should Love Nature* (Minneapolis, MN: Augsburg Fortress Press, 1997).

2. Joshua M. Moritz, "Evolution, the End of Human Uniqueness, and the Election of the *Imago Dei*," *Theology and Science* 9, no. 3 (2011): 307–339; Celia Deane-Drummond, "God's Image and Likeness in Humans and Other Animals: Performative Soul-Making and Graced Nature," *Zygon* 47/4 (December 2012): 934–948.

3. Richard Rohr and Andreas Ebert, *The Enneagram: A Christian Perspective* (New York, NY: Crossroad Publishing, 2001), 21.

4. See, for example, Claudio M. Tamburrini, "What's Wrong with Genetic Inequality? The Impact of Genetic Technology on Elite Sports and Society," *Sport, Ethics and Philosophy* 1, no. 2 (2007): 233.

5. Diversity may be related to human happiness and capacity for awe and wonder (McFee and Scheidt). See, for example, Hubert Dreyfuss and Sean Dorrance Kelly, *All Things Shining: Reading the Western Classics to Find Meaning in a Secular Age* (New York, NY: Free Press, 2011); Susan A. Jackson and Mihaly Csikszentmihalyi, *Flow in Sports: The Keys to Optimal Experiences and Performances* (Champaign, IL: Human Kinetics, 1999). And certainly diversity is central to the concept of an open-ended future, encountering the Other and, from a theistic perspective, glimpsing the divine; see Mayra Rivera, *The Touch of Transcendence* (London, UK: Westminster John Knox Press, 2007).

6. Andy Miah, "Towards the Transhuman Athlete: Therapy, Non-therapy and Enhancement," *Sport in Society* 13, no. 2 (2010): 221–233.

7. Ronald Cole-Turner, "Introduction: The Transhumanist Challenge," in *Transhumanism and Transcendence: Christian Hope in an Age of Technological Enhancement*, edited by Ronald Cole-Turner (Washington, DC: Georgetown University Press, 2011), 4–5.

Bibliography

PRIMARY SOURCES

"Acts of Paul and Thecla." In *The Apocryphal New Testament*, translation and notes by M. R. James. Oxford, UK: Clarendon Press, 1924.

"Apocalypse of Paul." In *The New International Edition: The Nag Hammadi Scriptures*, edited by James M. Robinson and Marvin Meyer. San Francisco, CA: HarperCollins, 2008.

"Apocalypse of Peter." In *The New International Edition: The Nag Hammadi Scriptures*, edited by James M. Robinson and Marvin Meyer. San Francisco, CA: HarperCollins, 2008.

"Gospel of Mary." In *The New International Edition: The Nag Hammadi Scriptures*, edited by James M. Robinson and Marvin Meyer. San Francisco, CA: HarperCollins, 2008.

"Gospel of Thomas." In *The Complete Gospels: Annotated Scholars Version*, edited by Stephen Patterson and Marvin Meyer. Salem, OR: Polebridge Press, 1992.

"Gospel of Truth." In *The New International Edition: The Nag Hammadi Scriptures*, edited by James M. Robinson and Marvin Meyer. San Francisco, CA: HarperCollins, 2008.

"Gospel to the Egyptians." In *The New International Edition: The Nag Hammadi Scriptures*, edited by James M. Robinson and Marvin Meyer. San Francisco, CA: HarperCollins, 2008.

Hippolytus. "Refutation of All Heresies." In *The Ante-Nicene Fathers*, Vol. 5, edited by J. H. MacMahon. Grand Rapids, MI: Eerdmans, 1981.

Irenaeus. "Against the Heresies." In *The Ante-Nicene Library: The Writings of Irenaeus*, Vol. 2, edited by A. Roberts and W. H. Rambaut. Edinburgh, Scotland: T. & T. Clark, 1869.

Justin Martyr. "Apology." In *St. Justin Martyr: The First and Second Apologies*, translated and edited by Leslie William Barnard. Mahwah, NJ: Paulist Press, 1997.

Plato. "Republic." In *The Collected Dialogues of Plato*, edited by Edith Hamilton and Huntington Cairns, translated by Paul Shorey. Princeton, NJ: Princeton University Press, 1961.

Plato. "Timaeus." In *Timaeus. Critias. Cleitophon. Menexenus. Epistles*. Loeb Classical Library, Vol. IX, translated by R. G. Bury. Cambridge, MA: Harvard University Press, 1929.

"Secret Book of James." In *The New International Edition: The Nag Hammadi Scriptures*, edited by James M. Robinson and Marvin Meyer. San Francisco, CA: HarperCollins, 2008.

Tertullian. "De Carne Christi." In *Tertulliani Opera. Corpus Christianorum, series latina 1*, edited by E. Dekkers. Turnhout, Belgium: Brepolis, 1954.

Tertullian. "De Praescriptione Haereticorum." In *Tertulliani Opera. Corpus Christianorum, series latina 2*, edited by E. Kroymann. Turnhout, Belgium: Brepols, 1954.

"Testimony of Truth." In *The New International Edition: The Nag Hammadi Scriptures*, edited by James M. Robinson and Marvin Meyer. San Francisco, CA: HarperCollins, 2008.

"Tripartite Tractate." In *The New International Edition: The Nag Hammadi Scriptures*, edited by James M. Robinson and Marvin Meyer. San Francisco, CA: HarperCollins, 2008.

Watson, Burton, trans. *The Analects of Confucius*. New York, NY: Columbia University Press, 2007.

"Zostrianos." In *The New International Edition: The Nag Hammadi Scriptures*, edited by James M. Robinson and Marvin Meyer. San Francisco, CA: HarperCollins, 2008.

SECONDARY SOURCES

Abbey, Edward. *The Journey Home: Some Words in Defense of the American West*. New York, NY: Penguin, 1991.

Agar, Nicholas. "Kurzweil and Uploading: Just Say No!" *Journal of Evolution and Technology* 22 (2011): 23–36. http://jetpress.org/v22/agar.htm. Accessed March 28, 2014.

Agar, Nicholas. *Humanity's End: Why We Should Reject Radical Enhancement*. Cambridge, MA: MIT Press, 2011.

Akin, William E. *Technocracy and the American Dream: The Technocrat Movement, 1900–1941*. Berkeley, CA: University of California, 1977.

Allenby, Braden, and Daniel Sarewitz. *The Techno-Human Condition*. Cambridge, MA: MIT Press, 2011.

Allinson, Robert E. "The Ethics of Confucianism and Christianity: the Delicate Balance." *Ching Feng* 33, no. 3 (1990): 158–175.

Amarasingam, Amarnath. "Transcending Technology: Looking at Futurology as a New Religious Movement." *Journal of Contemporary Religion* 23, no. 1 (2008): 1–16.

Anissimov, Michael. " 'Futurisms': Anti-Transhumanist Intellectuals." *Accelerating Future* (November 25, 2009): np. http://www.acceleratingfuture.com/michael/

blog/2009/11/futurisms-anti-transhumanist-intellectuals/. Accessed January 29, 2014.

Arendt, Hannah. *The Human Condition*. Chicago, IL: University of Chicago Press, 1958.

Armstrong, Stuart, and Anders Sandberg. "Eternity in Six Hours: Intergalactic Spreading of Intelligent Life and Sharpening the Fermi Paradox." *Acta Astronautica* 89 (2013): 1–13. doi: 10.1016/j.actaastro.2013.04.002.

Arnhart, Larry. *Darwinian Natural Right: The Biological Ethics of Human Nature*. Albany, NY: State University of New York Press, 1998.

Asimov, Isaac. "The Last Question." In *Robot Dreams*. New York, NY: Ace Books, 1956.

Augustine. *Concerning the City of God against the Pagans*. Translated by Henry Bettenson. London, UK: Penguin Books, 1984.

Augustine. "Confessions." In *The Works of Saint Augustine: A Translation for the 21st Century*, edited by John E. Rotelle et al., Part I, Vol. 1; translated by Maria Boulding. Hyde Park, NY: New City Press, 1997.

Augustine. "The Punishment and Forgiveness of Sins and the Baptism of Little Ones." In *The Works of St. Augustine: A Translation for the 21st Century*, edited by John E. Rotelle et al., Part I, Vol. 23; translated by Roland J. Teske. Hyde Park, NY: New City Press, 1997.

Austriaco, Nicanor Pier Giorgio. *Biomedicine and Beatitude: An Introduction to Catholic Bioethics*. Washington, DC: Catholic University of America Press, 2011.

Badmington, Neil. "Theorizing Posthumanism." *Cultural Critique* 53 (Winter 2003): 10–27.

Bacon, Francis. *The Advancement of Learning*. Edited by G. W. Kitchin. London, UK: 1915.

Bacon, Francis. *The Advancement of Learning (The Oxford Francis Bacon IV)*. Edited by Michael Kiernan. Oxford, UK: Clarendon Press, 2000.

Bacon, Francis. *Francis Bacon: A Critical Edition of the Major Works (The Oxford Authors)*. Edited by Brian Vickers. Oxford, UK: Oxford University Press, 1996.

Bacon, Francis. *The Instauratio Magna Part II: Novum Organum and Associated Texts (The Oxford Francis Bacon IV)*. Edited by Graham Reese and Maria Wakley. Oxford, UK: Clarendon Press, 2004.

Bacon, Francis. *The New Organon*. Edited by Lisa Jardine and Michael Silverthorne. Cambridge, UK: Cambridge University Press, 2000.

Bailey, Ronald. "For Enhancing People: Do the Technologies that Enable Human Physical and Intellectual Enhancement Undermine Virtue?" In *The Transhumanist Reader*, edited by Max More and Natasha Vita-More, 327–344. New York, NY: Wiley-Blackwell, 2013.

Bainbridge, William Sims. "Religion for the Galactic Civilization." In *Science Fiction and Space Futures*. Edited by Eugene M. Emme, 187–201. San Diego, CA: American Astronautical Society, 1982.

Bainbridge, William Sims. "The Transhumanist Heresy." *Journal of Evolution and Technology* 14, no. 2 (2005): 1–10.

Baine-Selbo, Eric. "Ecstasy, Joy, and Sorrow: The Religious Experience of Southern College Football." *Journal of Religion and Popular Culture* 20 (2008): 1–12.

Balch, David L. *Let Wives Be Submissive: The Domestic Code in 1 Peter*, SBLMS 26. Chico, CA: Scholars Press, 1981.

Barbour, Ian G. *Ethics in an Age of Technology: The Gifford Lectures 1989–1991*. Vol. 2. San Francisco, CA: HarperSanFrancisco, 1993.

Barnard, G. William. "Entheogens in a Religious Context: The Case of the Santo Daime Religious Tradition." *Zygon* 49, no. 3 (2014): in press.

Baron-Cohen, Simon. *Mindblindness: An Essay on Autism and Theory of Mind*. Cambridge, MA: Bradford Books, 1996.

Barrett, Justin. *Why Would Anyone Believe in God?* Walnut Creek, CA: AltaMira Press, 2004.

Barrow, John D., and Frank J. Tipler. *The Anthropic Cosmological Principle*. Oxford, UK: Oxford University Press, 1988.

Beamish, Robert. *Steroids: A New Look at Performance-Enhancing Drugs*. Santa Barbara, CA: Praeger, 2011.

Beauchamp, Tom L., and James F. Childress. *Principles of Biomedical Ethics*. 5th ed. New York, NY: Oxford University Press, 2001.

Bellah, Robert N. "Civil Religion in America." In *Religion in America*, edited by W. G. McLoughlin and R. N. Bellah, 3–23. Boston, MA: Houghton Mifflin, 1967.

Benso, Silvia. *The Face of Things: A Different Side of Ethics*. Albany, NY: State University of New York Press, 2000.

Berger, Peter, and Thomas Luckmann. *The Social Construction of Reality: A Treatise in the Sociology of Knowledge*. New York, NY: Anchor Books, 1966.

Best, Stephen, and Douglas Kellner. *The Postmodern Adventure: Science, Technology and Cultural Studies at the Third Millennium*. New York, NY: Guilford Press, 2001.

Best, Stephen, and Douglas Kellner. *Postmodern Theory*. New York, NY: Guilford Press, 1991.

Bilsky, Emily. *Golem! Danger, Deliverance and Art*. New York, NY: Jewish Museum, 1988.

Bimson, John J. "Doctrines of the Fall and Sin after Darwin." In *Theology after Darwin*, edited by Michael S. Northcott and R. J. Berry, 106–122. Milton Keynes, UK: Paternoster, 2009.

Blackford, Russell. "Transhumanism at the Crossroads." Institute for Ethics and Emerging Technologies. http://ieet.org/index.php/IEET/more/119/.

Blainey, Marc G. "Forbidden Therapies: Santo Daime, Ayahuasca, and the Prohibition of Entheogens in Western Society." *Journal of Religion and Health* 10 (2014). doi: 10.1007/s10943-014-9826-2.

Blake, Charlie, Claire Malloy, and Steven Shakespeare, eds. *Beyond Human: From Animality to Transhumanism*. London, UK: Continuum, 2012.

Bleich, David J. *Judaism and Healing*. Jersey City, NJ: Ktav Publishing House, 2002.

Bloch, Ernst. *The Principle of Hope*, 3 vols. Translated by Neville Plaice, Stephen Plaice, and Paul Knight. Cambridge, MA: MIT Press 1995 (1986).

Bloch, Ernst. *The Spirit of Utopia*. Translated by Anthony A. Nassar. Palo Alto, CA: Stanford University Press, 2000.

Blocher, Henri. *Original Sin: Illuminating the Riddle*. Downers Grove, IL: Intervarsity Press, 1997.

Boer, Theo, and Richard Fischer, eds. *Human Enhancement: Scientific, Ethical and Theological Aspects from a European Perspective*. Geneva, Switzerland: Conference of European Churches, 2013.

Bohr, David. *Catholic Moral Tradition*. rev. ed. Huntington, IN: Our Sunday Visitor, 1999.

Bonhoeffer, Dietrich. *Creation and Fall: A Theological Exposition of Genesis 1-3*. Edited by John W. DeGruchy. Translated by Douglas Stephen Bax. Minneapolis, MN: Fortress Press, 1997.

Bonhoeffer, Dietrich. *Sanctorum Communio: A Theological Study of the Sociology of the Church*. Edited by Clifford J. Green. Translated by Reinhard Krauss and Nancy Lukens. Minneapolis, MN: Fortress Press, 1998.

Bostrom, Nick. "Are You Living in a Computer Simulation?" *Philosophical Quarterly* 53, no. 211 (2003): 243-255.

Bostrom, Nick. "Astronomical Waste: The Opportunity Cost of Delayed Technological Development." *Utilitas* 15, no. 3 (2003): 308-314.

Bostrom, Nick. "In Defense of Posthuman Dignity." In *H±: Transhumanism and Its Critics*, edited by Gregory R. Hansell and William Grassie, 55-66. Philadelphia, PA: Metanexus Institute, 2011. Also, *Bioethics* 19, no. 3 (2005): 202-214.

Bostrom, Nick. "Dignity and Enhancement." Chapter 8 in *Human Dignity and Bioethics: Essays Commissioned by the President's Council on Bioethics*. Washington, DC: President's Council on Bioethics, March 2008.

Bostrom, Nick. "Existential Risk Prevention as Global Priority." *Global Policy* 4, no. 1 (2013), np. http://www.jetpress.org/volume9/risks.html. Accessed July 19, 2014.

Bostrom, Nick. "Existential Risks: Analyzing Human Extinction Scenarios and Related Hazards." *Journal of Evolution and Technology* 9 (2002). http://www.nickbostrom.com/existential/risks.html. Accessed July 28, 2014.

Bostrom, Nick. "The Fable of the Dragon Tyrant." *Journal of Medical Ethics* 31 (2005): 273-277.

Bostrom, Nick. "A History of Transhumanist Thought." *Journal of Evolution and Technology* 14, no. 1 (2005): 1-25. http://jetpress.org/volume14/bostrom.html. Accessed March 28, 2014.

Bostrom, Nick. "Human Genetic Enhancements: A Transhumanist Perspective." *Journal of Value Enquiry* 37, no. 4 (December 2003): 493-509.

Bostrom, Nick. "Letter from Utopia." *Studies in Ethics, Law, and Technology* 2, no. 1 (2008): 1-7.

Bostrom, Nick. "The Superintelligent Will: Motivation and Instrumental Rationality in Advanced Artificial Agents." *Minds and Machines* 22, no. 2 (2012): 71-85.

Bostrom, Nick. "The Transhumanist FAQ: A General Introduction 2.1." World Transhumanist Organization, 2003. http://www.transhumanism.org/resources/FAQv21.pdf. Accessed May 11, 2014.

Bostrom, Nick. "The Transhumanist FAQ. Version 3.0." World Transhumanist Association. http://humanityplus.org/leanr/transhumanist-faq/.

Bostrom, Nick. "Transhumanist Values." In *Ethical Issues for the 21st Century*, edited by Frederick Adams. Philosophical Documentation Center Press, 2003; reprinted in Review of Contemporary Philosophy 4 (May 2005). http://www.nickbostrom.com/tra/values.html. Accessed March 4, 2014.

Bostrom, Nick. "Why I Want to Be a Posthuman When I Grow up." In *Medical Enhancement and Posthumanity*, edited by Bert Gordijn and Ruth Chadwick, 107-137. New York, NY: Springer. 2008.

Bostrom, Nick, and Anders Sandberg. "The Wisdom of Nature: An Evolutionary Heuristic for Human Enhancement." In *Human Enhancement*, 375–416. Oxford, UK: Oxford University Press, 2008.

Boyer, Pascal. *Religion Explained.* New York, NY: Basic Books, 2002.

Bradshaw, Heather G., and Ruud Ter Meulen. "A Transhumanist Fault Line around Disability: Morphological Freedom and the Obligation to Enhance." *Journal of Medicine and Philosophy* 35 (2010): 670–684.

British Neuroscience Association. "Effects of Schedule I Drug Laws on Neuroscience Research and Treatment Innovation." 2013. http://www.bna.org.uk/news/view.php?permalink=FX7RLTOWXC. Accessed March 12, 2014.

Brockopp, Jonathan E., ed. *Islamic Ethics of Life: Abortion, War, and Euthanasia.* Columbia, SC: University of South Carolina Press, 2003.

Brooke, John Hedley. "Visions of Perfectibility." *Journal of Evolution & Technology* 14, no. 2 (August 2005): 1–12.

Brown, Peter. *The Body and Society: Men, Women, and Sexual Renunciation in Early Christianity.* New York, NY: Columbia University Press, 1988.

Broyde, Michael J. "Modern Reproductive Technologies and Jewish Law." In *Marriage, Sex and Family in Judaism*, edited by Michael J. Broyde and Michael Augubel, 295–327. Lanham, MD: Rowman and Littlefield, 2005.

Buber, Martin. *Paths in Utopia.* Syracuse, NY: Syracuse University Press, 1996.

Buchanan, Allen, Dan W. Brock, Norman Daniel, and Daniel Wilker. *From Chance to Choice.* Cambridge, UK: Cambridge University Press, 2002.

Budziszewski, J. "The Natural, the Connatural, and the Unnatural." Paper presented at St. Thomas Aquinas and the Natural Law, Jacques Maritain Center, University of Notre Dame, South Bend, IN, July 6–11, 2004. http://www3.nd.edu/Departments/Maritain/ti04/budz.htm. Accessed March 28, 2014.

Bunn, Henry T. and Josephy A. Ezzo. "Hunting and Scavenging by Plio-Pleistocene Hominids." *Journal of Archeological Science* 20, no. 4 (1993): 365–398.

Burdett, Michael S. "Contextualizing a Christian Perspective on Transcendence and Human Enhancement: Francis Bacon, N. F. Fedorov, and Pierre Teilhard de Chardin." In *Transhumanism and Transcendence: Christian Hope in an Age of Technological Enhancement*, edited by Ronald Cole-Turner, 19–36. Washington, DC: Georgetown University Press, 2011.

Burkett, Brendan, Mike McNamee, and Wolfgang Potthast. "Shifting Boundaries in Sports Technology and Disability: Equal Rights or Unfair Advantage in the Case of Oscar Pistorius?" *Disability & Society* 26, no. 5 (2011): 643–654.

Burleigh, Tyler J., Jordan R. Schoenherr, and Guy L. Lacroix. "Does the Uncanny Valley Exist? An Empirical Test of the Relationship Between Eeriness and the Human Likeness of Digitally Created Faces." *Computers in Human Behavior* 29 (2013): 759–771.

Bury, J. B. *The Idea of Progress: An Inquiry into Its Origin and Growth.* London, UK: Macmillan, 1920.

Bynum, Caroline Walker. *The Resurrection of the Body.* New York, NY: Columbia University Press, 1995.

Campa, Riccardo. "Pure Science and the Posthuman Future." *Journal of Evolution & Technology* 19, no. 1 (September 2008): 28–34.

Campany, Robert Ford. *Making Transcendents: Ascetics and Social Memory in Early Medieval China*. Honolulu, HI: University of Hawai'i Press, 2009.

Campbell, Heidi. "On Posthumans, Transhumans and Cyborgs: Towards a Tranhumanist-Christian Conversation." *Modern Believing* 47, no. 2 (2006): 61–73.

Carhart-Harris, Robin L., David Erritzoe, Tim Williams, James M. Stone, Laurence J. Reed, Alessandro Colasanti, Robin J. Tyacke, Robert Leech, Andre L. Malizia, Keven Murphy, Peter Hobden, John Evans, Amanda Feilding, Richard G. Wise, and David J. Nutt. "Neural Correlates of the Psychedelic State as Determined by fMRI Studies with Psilocybin." *Proceedings of the National Academy of Sciences* 109, no. 6 (2012): 2138–2143.

Carhart-Harris, Robin L., Robert Leech, Peter J. Hellyer, Murray Shanahan, Amanda Feilding, Enzo Tagliazucchi, Dante R. Chialvo, and David Nutt. "The Entropic Brain: A Theory of Conscious States Informed by Neuroimaging Research with Psychedelic Drugs." *Frontiers in Human Neuroscience* 8, article 20 (2014). doi: 10.3389/fnhum.2014.00020.

Casebeer, William D. *Natural Ethical Facts: Evolution, Connectionism, and Moral Cognition*. Cambridge, MA: MIT Press, 2003.

Castree, Noel, and Catherine Nash. "Posthuman Geographies." *Social and Cultural Geography* 7, no. 4 (August 2006): 501–504.

Catechism of the Catholic Church. Ottawa, ON: Canadian Conference of Catholic Bishops, 1994.

Chan Wing-tsit, trans. *Instructions for Practical Living and Other Neo-Confucian Writings*. New York, NY: Columbia University Press, 1963.

Chan Wing-tsit, trans. *Source Book in Chinese Philosophy*. Princeton, NJ: Princeton University Press, 1963.

Cheng Chung-ying. "The Trinity of Cosmology, Ecology, and Ethics in the Confucian Personhood." In *Confucianism and Ecology: The Interrelation of Heaven, Earth, and Humans*, edited by Mary Evelyn Tucker and John Berthrong, 211–235. Cambridge, MA: Harvard University Press, 1998.

Childress, Kelly Dahlgren. "Genetics, Disability, and Ethics: Could Applied Technologies Lead to a New Eugenics?" *Journal of Women and Religion* 19, no. 20 (2003): 157–178.

Chu, Ted. *Human Purpose and Transhuman Potential: A Cosmic Vision for Our Future Evolution*. San Raphael, CA: Origins Press, 2014.

Churchland, Patricia, and Terrence Sejnowski. *The Computational Brain*. Cambridge, MA: MIT Press, 1993.

Ćirković, Milan M. "A Resource Letter on Physical Eschatology." *American Journal of Physics* 71 (2003), 122–133. doi: 10.1119/1.1528470.

Clarke, W. Norris. "Technology and Man: A Christian Vision." *Technology and Culture* 3, no. 4 (Autumn 1962): 422–442.

Clarke, Arthur C. *The City and the Stars*. London, UK: Gollancz, Orion Publishing Group, 1956.

Clayton, Philip. *In Quest of Freedom: The Emergence of Spirit in the Natural World*. Goettingen, Germany: Vandenhoeck and Ruprecht, 2009.

Crnkovic, Gordana Dodig. "Information and Energy/Matter." *Information* 3 (2012): 751–755.

Cohen, G. A. *Karl Marx's Theory of History: A Defence*. Princeton, NJ: Princeton University Press, 2001.

Cole-Turner, Ronald. "Entheogens, Mysticism, and Neuroscience." *Zygon* 49, no. 3 (2014): in press.

Cole-Turner, Ronald. "Extreme Longevity Research: A Progressive Protestant Perspective." In *Religion and the Implications of Radical Life Extension*, edited by Derek Maher and Calvin Mercer, 51–61. New York, NY: Palgrave Macmillan, 2009.

Cole-Turner, Ronald. *The New Genesis: Theology and the Genetic Revolution*. Louisville, KY: Westminster John Knox Press, 1993.

Cole-Turner, Ronald. "Science, Technology and Mission." In *The Local Church in a Global Era: Reflections for a New Century*, edited by Max L. Stackhouse, Tim Dearborn, and Scott Paeth, 100–112. Grand Rapids, MI: Eerdmans, 2000.

Cole-Turner, Ronald. "Transhumanism and Christianity." In *Transhumanism and Transcendence: Christian Hope in an Age of Technological Enhancement*, edited by Ronald Cole-Turner, 193–203. Washington, DC: Georgetown University Press, 2011.

Cole-Turner, Ronald, ed. *Transhumanism and Transcendence: Christian Hope in an Age of Technological Enhancement*. Washington, DC: Georgetown University Press, 2011.

Collins, Harry, and Trevor Pinch. *The Golem at Large: What You Should Know about Technology*. Cambridge, UK: Cambridge University Press, 1998.

Collins, John J. "Apocalyptic Eschatology in the Ancient World." In *The Oxford Handbook of Eschatology*, edited by Jerry L. Walls, 40–55. Oxford, UK: Oxford University Press, 2008.

Collins, John J. *The Apocalyptic Imagination: An Introduction to Jewish Apocalyptic Literature*. Grand Rapids, MI: William B. Eerdmans.

Cowen, Tyler. *Average Is over: Powering America beyond the Age of the Great Stagnation*. Ebook: Penguin, 2013.

Creegan, Nicola Hoggard. *Animal Suffering and the Problem of Evil*. Oxford, UK: Oxford University Press, 2013.

Critchley, Simon. *The Ethics of Deconstruction*. Edinburgh, UK: Edinburgh University Press, 1999.

Critchley, Simon. "Prolegomena to Any Post-Deconstructive Subjectivity." In *Deconstructive Subjectivities*, edited by Simon Critchley and Peter Dews, 13–46. Albany, NY: State University of New York Press, 1996.

Critichley, Simon, and Robert Bernasconi. *The Cambridge Companion to Levinas*. Cambridge, UK: Cambridge University Press, 2002.

Critchley, Simon, Robert Bernasconi, and Adriaan Peperzak. *Emmanuel Levinas: Basic Philosophical Writings*. Bloomington, IN: Indiana University Press, 1996.

Critchley, Simon, and Peter Dews. "Introduction." In *Deconstructive Subjectivities*, edited by Simon Critchley and Peter Dews, 1–12. Albany, NY: State University of New York Press, 1996.

Csikszentmihalyi, Mihaly. *Beyond Boredom and Anxiety*. San Francisco, CA: Jossey-Bass, 1975.

Csikszentmihalyi, Mihaly, and Giovanni B. Moneta. "Models of Concentration in Natural Environments: A Comparative Approach Based on Streams of Experiential Data." *Social Behavior and Personality* 27, no. 6 (1999): 603–638.

Curtis, Valerie. *Don't Look, Don't Eat, Don't Touch: The Science Behind Revulsion.* Chicago, IL: University of Chicago Press, 2003.

Daly, Todd T. W. "Chasing Methuselah: Transhumanism and *Theosis* in Critical Perspective." In *Transhumanism and Transcendence: Christian Hope in an Age of Technological Enhancement,* edited by Ronald Cole-Turner, 131–144. Washington, DC: Georgetown University Press, 2011.

Daly, Todd T. W. "Life-Extension in Transhumanist and Christian Perspectives: Consonance and Conflict." *Journal of Evolution & Technology* 14, no. 2 (2005): 57–75.

Darwin, Charles. *The Autobiography of Charles Darwin.* Edited by Nora Barlow. New York, NY: W. W. Norton, 2005.

Davis, Colin. *After Poststructuralism: Reading, Stories and Theory.* New York, NY: Routledge, 2004.

Davis, Colin. *Levinas: An Introduction.* Oxford, UK: Blackwell, 1996.

Davis, Dena S. *Genetic Dilemmas: Reproductive Technology, Parental Choices, and Children's Futures.* Reflective Bioethics. New York, NY: Routledge, 2001.

Dawkins, Richard. *The God Delusion.* New York, NY: Mariner Press, 2008.

Deacon, Terence W. *Incomplete Nature: How Mind Emerged from Matter.* New York, NY: W. W. Norton, 2012.

Deacon, Terence W. "A Role for Relaxed Selection in the Evolution of the Language Capacity." *Proceedings of the National Academy of Sciences* 107 (May 2010): 9000–9006.

Deane-Drummond, Celia. *Biology and Theology Today: Exploring the Boundaries.* London, UK: SCM Press, 2001.

Deane-Drummond, Celia. *The Ethics of Nature.* New York, NY: John Wiley & Sons, 2008.

Deane-Drummond, Celia. "Future Perfect? God, the Transhuman Future and the Quest for Immortality." In *Future Perfect? God, Medicine and Human Identity,* edited by Celia Deane-Drummond and Peter Manley Scott, 168–182. London, UK: T&T Clark, 2006.

Deane-Drummond, Celia. "Taking Leave of the Animal? The Theological and Ethical Implications of Transhuman Projects." In *Transhumanism and Transcendence: Christian Hope in an Age of Technological Enhancement,* edited by Ron Cole-Turner, 115–130. Washington, DC: Georgetown University Press, 2012.

Deane-Drummond, Celia.*The Wisdom of the Liminal: Human Nature, Evolution and Other Animals.* Grand Rapids, MI: Eerdmans, 2014.

Deane-Drummond, Celia, and Agustín Fuentes. "Blurring Boundaries in Human Being and Becoming: Situating Theological Anthropology in Interspecies Relationships." *Philosophy, Theology and the Sciences* 1, no. 1 (2014): 251–275, in press.

Deane-Drummond, Celia, Robin Grove-White, and Bronislaw Szerszynski. "Genetically Modified Theology: The Religious Dimensions of Public Concerns about Agricultural Biotechnology." *Studies in Christian Ethics* 14, no. 2 (2001): 23–41.

De Chardin, Teilhard. *The Phenomenon of Man.* New York, NY: Harper, 1959.

DeGrazia, David. "Enhancement Technologies and Human Identity." *Journal of Medicine and Philosophy* 30 (2005): 261–283.

De Grey, Aubrey, ed. *Strategies for Engineered Negligible Senescence: Why Genuine Control of Aging May Be Foreseeable. Annals of the New York Academy of Science* 1019. New York: New York Academy of Science, June 2004.

De Grey, Aubrey. "The War on Aging." In Immortality Institute, *The Scientific Conquest of Death*, 29–45. Buenos Aires, Argentina: LibrosEnRed, 2004.

Dennett, Daniel. *Consciousness Explained*. Boston, MA: Little, Brown, 1991.

Dennett, Daniel. *Darwin's Dangerous Idea: Evolution and the Meanings of Life*. New York, NY: Touchstone, 1995.

De Rosa, Paul J. "Karl Rahner's Concept of 'Vorgriff': An Examination of Its Philosophical Background and Development." PhD dissertation, Oxford University, Oxford, UK, 1988.

Descartes, Rene. "Principles of Philosophy." In *The Philosophical Works of Descartes*. Translated by E. S. Haldane and G. R. T. Gross, 177–292. Cambridge, UK: Cambridge University Press, 1970.

Devereux, Anne Rogers. "*Der Vorgriff* (The Pre-Apprehension of Being) and the Religious Act in Karl Rahner." PhD dissertation, Georgetown University, Washington, DC, 1973.

Dorff, Elliot N. "Becoming Yet More Like God: A Jewish Perspective on Radical Life Extension." In *Religion and the Implications of Radical Life Extension*, edited by Derek Maher and Calvin Mercer, 63–74. New York, NY: Palgrave Macmillan, 2009. Republished in paperback, forthcoming 2014.

Dorff, Elliot N. "The Body Belongs to God: Judaism and Transhumanism." In *Transhumanism and the Body: The World Religions Speak*, edited by Calvin Mercer and Derek Maher. New York, NY: Palgrave, Macmillan, forthcoming.

Dorff, Elliot N. "Jewish Bioethics: The Beginning of Life." In *The Oxford Handbook of Jewish Ethics and Morality*, edited by Elliot N. Dorff and Jonathan K. Crane, 313–329. Oxford, UK: Oxford University Press, 2013.

Dorff, Elliot N. *Matters of Life and Death: A Jewish Approach to Modern Medical Ethics*. Philadelphia, PA: Jewish Publication Society, 2005 (1998).

Dostoyevsky, Fyodor. *Notes from Underground and the Double*. Translated by Jessie Coulson. Harmondsworth, UK: Penguin Classics, 1972.

Douglas, Mary. *Purity and Danger: An Analysis of Concepts of Pollution and Taboo*. London, UK and Headley, UK: Routledge and Kegan Paul, 1976.

Dreyfus, Hubert. "Merleau-Ponty and Recent Cognitive Science." In *The Cambridge Companion to Merleau-Ponty*, edited by Taylor Carman and Mark B. N. Hansen, 129–150. New York, NY: Cambridge University Press, 2005.

Dupré, John. "On Human Nature." *Human Affairs* 2 (2003): 109–122.

Dupré, John. *Humans and Other Animals*. Oxford, UK: Oxford University Press, 2002.

Dusek, Val. *Philosophy of Technology: An Introduction*. Oxford, UK: Blackwell, 2006.

Dvorsky, George. "Michael Phelps: 'Naturally' Transhuman." Institute for Ethics and Emerging Technologies. 2008. http://ieet.org/index.php/IEET/more/2575. Accessed February 25, 2014.

Dyson, Freeman J. "Time without End: Physics and Biology in an Open Universe." *Reviews of Modern Physics* 51, no. 3 (July 1979): 447–460.

Edelstein, Ludwig. *The Idea of Progress in Classical Antiquity*. Baltimore, MD: Johns Hopkins Press, 1967.

Editors, *Scientific American*. "End the Ban on Psychoactive Drug Research." 2014. http://www.scientificamerican.com/article/end-the-ban-on-psychoactive-drug-research/. Accessed March 9, 2014.

Egan, Greg. *Permutation City*. London, UK: Gollancz, Orion Publishing Group, 1994.

Elkington, Sam. "Articulating a Systematic Phenomenology of Flow: An Experience-Process Perspective." *Leisure/Loisir* 34, no. 3 (2010): 327–360.

Ellul, Jacques. *The Technological Bluff*. Translated by G. W. Bromiley. Grand Rapids, MI: Eerdmans, 1990.

Engel, George L. "The Need for a New Medical Model: A Challenge for Biomedicine." *Science*, New Series 196 (1977): 129–136.

Estep, Pete. "The Evidence-Based Pursuit of Radical Life Extension." In *Religion and the Implications of Radical Life Extension*, edited by Derek Maher and Calvin Mercer, 25–37. New York, NY: Palgrave Macmillan, 2009. Republished in paperback, forthcoming 2014.

Ettinger, Robert C. W. *Man into Superman: The Startling Potential of Human Evolution—and How to Be Part of It*. New York, NY: St. Martin's Press, 1972.

Extropians. "Extropians FAQ List." http://www.ultim8team.com/modules/future/extropy_faq.php. Accessed March 31, 2014.

Fagg, Lawrence W. Are There Intimations of Divine Transcendence in the Physical World? *Zygon* 38, no. 3 (2003): 559–572.

Farias, Miguel, Anna-Kaisa Newheiser, Guy Kahane, and Zoe de Toledo. "Scientific Faith: Belief in Science Increases in the Face of Stress and Existential Anxiety." *Journal of Experimental Social Psychology* 49, no. 6 (2013): 1210–1213.

Fain, Leslie. "The Surprising Spread and Cultural Impact of Transhumanism." *Catholic World Reporter* (October 3, 2–13): np. http:www.catholicworldreport.com/Zone/31/Science.aspx#.UzV4xa1dWQe. accessed January 26, 2014.

Farquhar, Judith, and Qicheng Zhang. *Ten Thousand Things: Nurturing Life in Contemporary Beijing*. New York, NY: Zone Books, 2012.

Fedorov, N. F. *What Was Man Created for? The Philosophy of the Common Task: Selected Works*. Edited by E. Koutiassov and M. Minto. Lausanne, Switzerland: Honeyglen/L'Age d'Homme, 1990.

Feezell, Randolph. *Sport, Philosophy, and Good Lives*. Lincoln: University of Nebraska Press, 2013.

Feinberg, Joel. *Freedom and Fulfilment: Philosophical Essays*. Princeton, NJ: Princeton University Press, 1992.

Fisher, Rory H. "The Health Care System and the Elderly." *Bioethics Update* 3, no. 1 (2003): 1–3.

Fletcher, Joseph. *The Ethics of Genetic Control: Ending Reproductive Roulette*. Garden City, NY: Anchor Press, 1974.

Foerst, Anne. *God in the Machine: What Robots Can Tell Us about God and Humanity*. New York, NY: Plume Books, 2005 (2004).

Foot, Philippa. *Natural Goodness*. Oxford, UK: Oxford University Press, 2001.

Forrester, Duncan B. "Politics and Vision." *The Bible in Transmission* (Autumn 1999): 1–4.

Foucault, Michael. *Discipline and Punish: The Birth of the Prison*. New York, NY: Vintage, 1995 [1975].

Foucault, Michael. *The History of Sexuality*, 3 vols. New York, NY: Vintage Books, 1975–1986.

Foucault, Michael. *Technologies of the Self*. Boston, MA: University of Massachusetts Press, 1988.

Freud, Sigmund. *Civilization and Its Discontents: The Standard Edition*. New York, NY: W. W. Norton, 2010 [1930].

Fukuyama, Francis. *Our Posthuman Future: Consequences of the Biotechnology Revolution*. New York, NY: Picador, 2002.

Fukuyama, Francis. "Transhumanism." *Foreign Policy* (September/October 2004): 42–43. http://www.foreignpolicy.com/articles/2004/09/01/transhumanism. Accessed April 2, 2013.

Fukuyama, Francis. "The World's Most Dangerous Ideas: Transhumanism." *Foreign Policy* 144 (2004): 42–43.

Fuller, R. Buckminster. *Utopia or Oblivion: The Prospects for Humanity*. Harmondsworth, UK: Penguin, 1972.

FutureBlogger. "Ray Kurzweil: The Singularity Is Not a Religion." http://futureblogger .net/futureblogger/show/1231-ray-kurzweil-the-singularity-is-not-a-religion. Accessed March 16, 2014.

Gardner, John. *Biocosm*. Maui, HI: Inner Ocean, 2003.

Gardner, John. *The Intelligent Universe*. Franklin Lakes, NJ: New Page, 2007.

Garner, Stephen. "The Hopeful Cyborg." In *Transhumanism and Transcendence: Christian Hope in an Age of Technological Enhancement*, edited by Ronald Cole-Turner, 87–100. Washington, DC: Georgetown University Press, 2011.

Garreau, Joel. *Radical Evolution: The Promise and Peril of Enhancing Our Minds, Our Bodies and What It Means to Be Human*. New York, NY: Doubleday, 2004.

Geertz, Clifford. *The Interpretation of Cultures*. New York, NY: Basic Books, 1973.

Geraci, Robert M. "Apocalyptic AI: Religion and the Promise of Artificial Intelligence." *Journal of American Academy of Religion* 76, no. 1 (2008): 138–166.

Geraci, Robert M. *Apocalyptic AI: Visions of Heaven in Robotics, Artificial Intelligence, and Virtual Reality*. New York, NY: Oxford University Press, 2010.

Geraci, Robert M. "Cultural Prestige: Popular Science Robotics as Religion-Science Hybrid." In *Reconfigurations: Interdisciplinary Perspectives on Religion in Post-Secular Society*, edited by Alexander D. Ornella and Stefanie Knauss, 43–58. Wien, Austria: Lit Press, 2007.

Geraci, Robert M. Video Games and Transhumanist Inclination. *Zygon: Journal of Religion and Science* 47, no. 4 (2012): 735–756.

Gibbs, Raymond W. Jr. *Embodiment and Cognitive Science*. New York, NY: Cambridge University Press, 2006.

Gibson, William. *Neuromancer*. New York, NY: Ace Books, 1984.

Goggin, Gerard, and Christopher Newell. "Uniting the Nation? Disability, Stem Cells, and the Australian Media." *Disability & Society* 19, no. 1 (January 2004): 47–60.

Good, Irving J. "Speculations Concerning the First Ultraintelligent Machine." *Advances in Computers* 6 (1965): 31–88.

Goodenough, Ursula. *The Sacred Depths of Nature*. Oxford, UK: Oxford University Press, 1998.

Goodman, Lenn E. *Creation and Evolution*. London, UK: Routledge, 2010.

Gottschall, Jonathan. *The Storytelling Animal: How Stories Make Us Human.* New York, NY: Houghton Mifflin Harcourt, 2012.

Goyal, Philip. "Information Physics: Towards a New Conception of Physical Reality." *Information* 3 (2012): 567–594.

Graham, Elaine. "Bioethics after Posthumanism: Natural Law, Communicative Action and the Problem of Self-Design." *Ecotheology* 9, no. 2 (2004): 178–198.

Graham, Elaine. "Post/Human Conditions." *Theology & Sexuality* 10, no. 2 (2004): 13.

Gray, John. *The Immortalization Commission: Science and the Strange Quest to Cheat Death.* New York, NY: Farrar, Straus and Giroux, 205.

Green, Joshua. *Moral Tribes: Emotion, Reason, and the Gap Between Us and Them.* New York, NY: Penguin Press, 2013.

Green, Ronald. *Babies by Design: The Ethics of Genetic Choice.* New Haven, CT: Yale University Press, 2007.

Griffiths, Bede. *Universal Wisdom: A Journey through the Sacred Wisdom of the World.* San Francisco, CA: HarperSanFrancisco, 1994.

Griffiths, Roland R., Matthew W. Johnson, William A. Richards, Brian D. Richards, Una D. McCann, and Robert Jesse. "Psilocybin Occasioned Mystical-Type Experiences: Immediate and Persisting Dose-Related Effects." *Psychopharmacology* 218, no. 4 (2011): 649–665.

Griffiths, Roland R.,William A. Richards, Matthew. W. Johnson, Una D. McCann, and Robert Jesse. "Mystical-Type Experiences Occasioned by Psilocybin Mediate the Attribution of Personal Meaning and Spiritual Significance 14 Months Later." *Journal of Psychopharmacology* 22, no. 6 (2008): 621–632.

Griffiths, Roland R., William A. Richards, Una D. McCann, and Robert Jesse. "Psilocybin Can Occasion Mystical-Type Experiences Having Substantial and Sustained Personal Meaning and Spiritual Significance." *Psychopharmacology* 187, no. 3 (2006): 268–283.

Grimshaw, Michael. "I Can't Believe My Eyes: The Religious Ascetics of Sport as Post-Modern Salvific Moments." *Implicit Religion* 3, no. 2 (2000): 87–99.

Grumett, David. "Transformation and the End of Enhancement: Insights from Pierre Teilhard de Chardin." In *Transhumanism and Transcendence*, edited by Ronald Cole-Turner, 37–49. Washington, DC: Georgetown University Press, 2011.

Habermas, Jürgen. *Knowledge and Human Interest.* Boston, MA: Beacon Press, 1968.

Haidt, Jonathan. *The Righteous Mind: Why Good People Are Divided by Politics and Religion.* New York, NY: Vintage Press, 2012.

Hansell, Gregory R., and William J. Grassie, eds. *H±: Transhumanism and Its Critics.* Philadelphia, PA: Metanexus, 2011.

Hanson, Robin. "Burning the Cosmic Commons: Evolutionary Strategies for Interstellar Colonization" 2010. http://hanson.gmu.edu/filluniv.pdf. Accessed March 31, 2014.

Hanson, Robin. "How to Live in a Simulation." *Journal of Evolution and Technology* 7 (September 2001). http://www.jetpress.org/volume7/simulation.htm. Accessed July 28, 2014.

Harding, Nancy, and Colin Palfrey. *The Social Construction of Dementia: Confused Professionals?* London, UK: Jessica Kingsley, 1997.

Hare, R. M. "Universalisability." *Proceedings of the Aristotelian Society* 55 (1954–1955): 295–312.

Harris, John. *Enhancing Evolution: The Ethical Case for Making Better People*. Princeton, NJ: Princeton University Press, 2007.

Harris, Melvin. *Cows, Pigs, Wars and Witches: The Riddle of Culture*. New York, NY: Random House, 1974.

Harris, Sam. *The Moral Landscape: How Science Can Determine Human Values*. New York, NY: Free Press, 2010.

Harrison, Peter. *The Bible, Protestantism, and the Rise of Modern Science*. Cambridge, UK: Cambridge University Press, 1998.

Harrison, Peter. *The Cambridge Companion to Science and Religion*. Cambridge, UK: Cambridge University Press, 2010.

Harrison, Peter. *The Fall of Man and the Foundation of Science*. Cambridge, UK: Cambridge University Press, 2007.

Harrison, Peter. " 'Science' and 'Religion': Constructing the Boundaries." *Journal of Religion* 86, no. 1 (2006): 81–106.

Hauerwas, Stanley. *In Good Company: The Church as Polis*. Notre Dame, IN: University of Notre Dame Press, 1995.

Hauser, Marc. *Moral Minds: How Nature Designed Our Universal Sense of Right and Wrong*. New York, NY: Ecco Press, 2006.

Hayles, N. Katherine. *How We Became Posthuman: Virtual Bodies in Cybernetics, Literature, and Informatics*. Chicago, IL: University of Chicago Press, 1999.

Hayles, N. Katherine. "The Human in Posthuman." *Cultural Critique* 53 (Winter 2003): 134–137.

Head, Marilyn. "Thanks, But I'd Rather Be Disabled." *New Zealand Listener* 21–27 (January 2006): 48–49.

Hefner, Philip. *The Human Factor: Evolution, Culture and Religion. Theology and the Sciences*. Minneapolis, MN: Fortress Press, 1993.

Heilbroner, Robert L. "Do Machines Make History?" *Technology and Culture* 8, no. 3 (1967): 335–345.

Heilbroner, Robert L. "Technological Determinism Revisited." In *Does Technology Drive History? The Dilemma of Technological Determinism*, edited by Merritt Roe Smith and Leo Marx, 67–98. London, UK: MIT Press, 1994.

Hellsten, Sirkku K. " 'The Meaning of Life' during a Transition from Modernity to Transhumanism and Posthumanity." *Journal of Anthropology* (2012). doi: doi:10.1155/2012/210684.

Hodgson, Peter. *Winds of Spirit: A Constructive Christian Theology*. Louisville, KY: Westminster John Knox, 1994.

Hopkins, Patrick D. "Transcending the Animal: How Transhumanism and Religion Are and Are Not Alike." *Journal of Evolution and Technology* (2005): 11–26. http://www.jetpress.org/volume14/hopkins.html. Accessed March 28, 2014.

Horsley, Richard A. "Spiritual Marriage with Sophia." *Vigiliae Christianae* 33 (1979): 30–54.

Hughes, James. *Citizen Cyborg: Why Democratic Societies Must Respond to the Redesigned Human of the Future*. Cambridge, MA: Westview Press, 2004.

Hughes, James. "The Compatibility of Religious and Transhumanist Views of Metaphysics, Suffering, Virtue and Transcendence in an Enhanced Future." *Global Spiral* 8, no. 2 (May 2007). http://www.metanexus.net/essay/

compatibility-religious-and-transhumanist-views-metaphysics-suffering-virtue
-and-transcendence. Accessed July 19, 2014.

Hughes, James. "The Politics of Transhumanism and the Techno-Millennial Imagination, 1626–2030." *Zygon* 47, no. 4 (2012): 757–776.

Hughes, James. "Report on the 2007 Interests and Beliefs Survey of the Members of the World Transhumanist Association." 2008. http://transhumanism.org/resources/WTASurvey2007.pdf. Accessed March 31, 2014.

Humanity+. "Transhumanist FAQ." http://humanityplus.org/philosophy/transhumanist-faq/#answer_29. Accessed March 30, 2014.

Humanity+. "Transhumanist FAQ Version 3.0." http://humanityplus.org/philosophy/transhumanist-faq/#top. Accessed February 25, 2014.

Hume, David. *Treatise on Human Nature*. Edited by L. A. Selby-Riggs. Oxford, UK: Oxford, 1949.

Hummel, Leonard. "By Its Fruits?: Mystical and Visionary States of Consciousness Occasioned by Entheogens." *Zygon* 49, no. 3 (2014): in press.

Huxley, Julian. *New Bottles for New Wine*. New York, NY: Harper, 1957.

Huxley, Julian. *Religion without Revelation*. New York, NY: Harper, 1927.

Idel, Moshe. *Golem: Jewish Magical and Mystical Tradition on the Artificial Anthropoid*. Albany, NY: State University of New York Press, 1990.

Ihde, Don, and Evan Selinger, eds. *Chasing Technoscience: Matrix for Materiality*. Bloomington, IN: Indiana University Press, 2003.

Immortality Institute. *The Scientific Conquest of Death: Essays on Infinite Lifespans*. Buenos Aries, Argentina: Libros En Red, 2004.

Isaacson, Walter. *Steve Jobs*. New York, NY: Simon & Schuster, 2011.

Jackson, Susan A., and Mihaly Csikszentmihalyi. *Flow in Sports: The Keys to Optimal Experiences and Performances*. Champaign, IL: Human Kinetics, 1999.

Jacoby, Russell. *Picture Imperfect: Utopian Thought for an Anti-Utopian Age*. New York, NY: Columbia University Press, 2005.

James, M. R. *The Apocryphal New Testament*. Oxford, UK: Clarendon Press, 1924.

James, William. *The Varieties of Religious Experience*. New York, NY: Modern Library, 1902.

Jardine, Lisa. *Francis Bacon: Discovery and the Art of Discourse*. Cambridge, UK: Cambridge University Press, 1974.

Jenkins, Peter. "Historical Simulations: Motivational, Ethical and Legal Issues." *Journal of Futures Studies* 11, no. 1 (August 2006): 23–42.

Jenkins, Philip. *The Next Christendom: The Coming of Global Christianity*. Oxford, UK: Oxford University Press, 2011.

Jenson, Robert W. *Systematic Theology. Vol. 2: The Works of God*. Oxford, UK: Oxford University Press, 1999.

John Paul II. *Laborem Exercens*. Rome, Italy: Vatican, 1981.

John Paul II. *Man and Woman He Created Them: A Theology of the Body*. Translated by Michael Waldstein. Boston, MA: Pauline, 2006.

Johnson, Lee A. "In Search of the Voice of Women in the Churches: Revisiting the Command to Silence Women in 1 Cor 14:34–35." In *Women in the Biblical World: A Survey of Old and New Testament Perspectives*, edited by Elizabeth McCabe, 135–154. Lanham, MD: University Press of America, 2009.

Johnson, Monte Ransome. *Aristotle on Teleology*. Oxford, UK: Oxford University Press, 2005.

Jonas, Hans. *The Gnostic Religion: The Message of the Alien God and the Beginning Christianity*, 2nd ed. Boston, MA: Beacon Press, 1963 (1958).

Jonas, Hans. *The Imperative of Responsibility: In Search of an Ethics for the Technological Age*. Chicago, IL: University of Chicago Press, 1984.

Jonas, Hans. *Philosophical Essays: From Ancient Creed to Technological Man*. Englewood Cliffs, NJ: Prentice Hall, 1974.

Jones, Beth Felker. *Marks of His Wounds: Gender Politics and Bodily Resurrection*. Oxford, UK: Oxford University Press, 2007.

Kahane, Guy. "Our Cosmic Insignificance." *Noûs*, forthcoming 2014. http://philpapers.org/archive/KAHOCI.1.pdf.

Kalton, Michael C., trans. *To Become a Sage: The Ten Diagrams on Sage Learning by Yi T'oegye*. New York, NY: Columbia University Press, 1988.

Kass, Leon. "L'Chaim and Its Limits: Why Not Immortality?" *First Things* 113 (2001): 17–24.

Kass, Leon. *Life, Liberty and the Pursuit of Dignity*. San Francisco, CA: Encounter Books, 2002.

Kaufman, Gordon D. *The Theological Imagination: Constructing the Concept of God*. Philadelphia, PA: Westminster Press, 1981.

Kearney, Richard. *The God Who May Be: A Hermeneutics of Religion*. Bloomington, IN: Indiana University Press, 2001.

Kelly, Daniel. *Yuck! The Nature and Moral Significance of Disgust*. Cambridge, MA: MIT Press, 2011.

Kelly, Kevin. "The Third Culture." *Science* 279 (February 13, 1998): 992–993.

Kelly, Kevin. "The *Vorgriff auf esse*: A Study in The Relation of Philosophy to Theology in the Thought of Karl Rahner." PhD dissertation, Yale University, New Haven, CT, 1994.

Kim Heup Young. *Christ and the Tao*. Hong Kong: Christian Conference of Asia, 2003.

Kim Heup Young. "Sanctity of Life: A Reflection on Human Embryonic Stem Cell Debates from an East Asian Perspective." In *Global Perspectives on Science and Spirituality*, edited by Pranab Das, 107–124. West Conshohocken, PA: Templeton Press, 2009.

Kim Heup Young. *Wang Yang-ming and Karl Barth: A Confucian-Christian Dialogue*. Lanham, MD: University of America Press, 1996.

King, Stephanie, and Vincent M. Janik. "Bottlenose Dolphins Can Use Learned Vocal Labels to Address Each Other." *Proceedings from the National Academy of the Sciences of the United States of America* (2013). doi: 10.1073/pnas.130 44591104. Accessed March 30, 2014.

Kirby, Kate, Aidan Moran, and Suzanne Guerin. "A Qualitative Analysis of the Experiences of Elite Athlete Who Have Admitted to Doping for Performance Enhancement." *International Journal of Sport Policy and Politics* 3, no. 2 (2011): 205–224.

Kirby, Peter, trans. "Gospel of Mary." *Early Christian Writings*. March 29, 2014. http://www.earlychristianwritings.com/text/gospelmary.html.

Kirkham, Richard L. *Theories of Truth: A Critical Introduction.* Cambridge, MA: MIT Press, 1992.

Kirkwood, Tom. *Time of Our Lives: The Science of Human Aging.* Oxford, UK: Oxford University Press, 1999.

Klein, Terrence W. "Karl Rahner on the Soul." *Saint Anselm Journal* 6 (2008): 1–10.

Kohn, Livia. "Told You So: Extreme Longevity and Daoist Realization." In *Religion and the Implications of Radical Life Extension*, edited by Derek Maher and Calvin Mercer, 85–96. New York, NY: Palgrave Macmillan, 2009. Republished in paperback, forthcoming 2014.

Kosky, Jeffrey L. "After the Death of God: Emmanuel Levinas and the Ethical Possibility of God." *Journal of Religious Ethics* 24, no. 2 (Fall 1996): 235–259.

Krebs, Teri S., and Pål-Ørjan Johansen. "Over 30 Million Psychedelic Users in the United States." *F1000Research* 2, no. 98 (2013). doi: 10.12688/f1000research.2-98.v1.

Kuhn, Thomas S. "Objectivity, Value Judgement, and Theory Choice." In *Philosophy of Science: Contemporary Readings*, edited by Yuri Balashov and Alexander Rosenberg, 74–86. London, UK: Routledge, 2002.

Kuhn, Thomas S. *The Structure of Scientific Revolutions.* 2nd ed. Chicago, IL: University of Chicago Press, 1970.

Kumar, Krishan. *Utopianism.* Minneapolis, MN: University of Minnesota Press, 1991.

Kurtz, Paul. *Eupraxophy: Living without Religion.* Amherst, NY: Prometheus Books, 1989, 45–62.

Kurzweil, Ray. *The Age of the Spiritual Machines.* London, UK: Orion, 1999.

Kurzweil, Ray. *How to Create a Mind: The Secret of Human Thought Revealed.* New York, NY: Viking, 2012.

Kurzweil, Ray. *How to Create a Mind: The Secret of Human Thought Revealed.* New York: Penguin, 2013.

Kurzweil, Ray. *The Singularity is Near: When Humans Transcend Biology.* New York, NY: Viking Penguin, 2005.

Lake, Christina Bieber. *Prophets of the Posthuman: American Fiction, Biotechnology, and the Ethics of Personhood.* Notre Dame, IN: University of Notre Dame Press, 2013.

Lansing, J. Stephen. *Priests and Programmers: Technologies of Power in the Engineered Landscape of Bali.* Princeton, NJ: Princeton University Press, 1991.

Lassen, Jesper, and Andrew Jamison. "Genetic Technologies Meet the Public: The Discourses of Concern." *Science, Technology, & Human Values* 31, no. 1 (January 2006): 8–28.

Lebacqz, Karen. "Dignity and Enhancement in the Holy City." In *Transhumanism and Transcendence: Christian Hope in an Age of Technological Enhancement*, edited by Ronald Cole-Turner, 51–62. Washington, DC: Georgetown University Press, 2011.

Lee, Richard B. and Irvin Devor, eds. *Man the Hunter.* Piscataway, NJ: Transaction, 1973.

Leibowitz, Yeshayahu. *Judaism, the Jewish People, and the State of Israel* (in Hebrew). Tel Aviv, Israel: Schocken, 1976.

Lelwica, Michelle M. "Losing Their Way to Salvation: Women, Weight Loss, and the Salvation Myth of Culture Lite." In *Religion and Popular Culture in America*, edited by Bruce David Forbes and Jeffrey H. Mahan, 180–200. Berkeley, CA: University of California Press, 2000.

Levinas, Emmanuel. *God, Death, and Time*. Translated by Bettina Bergo. Stanford, CA: Stanford University Press, 2000.

Levinas, Emmanuel. *Nine Talmudic Readings by Emmanuel Levinas*. Translated by Annette Aronowicz. Bloomington, IN: Indiana University Press, 1990.

Levitas, Ruth. *The Concept of Utopia*. Oxford, UK: Peter Lang, 2011.

Lewin, David. *Technology and the Philosophy of Religion*. Newcastle, UK: Cambridge Scholars Press, 2011.

"Lifetime Vaccine against All Types of Flu Could Be Available in 2018." http://www .dailymail.co.uk/health/article-2468561/Super-vaccine-eliminate-need-annual -flu-jabs-years-successful-trials.html. Accessed January 14, 2014.

Liu, Shu-hsien, and Robert E. Allinson, eds. *Harmony and Strife: Contemporary Perspectives, East and West*. Hong Kong: Chinese University Press, 1988.

Loeb, Paul S. "Nietzsche's Transhumanism." *The Agonist* 4, no. 2 (2011). http://www .nietzschecircle.com/AGONIST/2011_08/Loeb_Nietzsche_Transhumanism. pdf. Accessed July 28, 2014.

Lossky, Vladimir. *Orthodox Theology: An Introduction*. Translated by Ian and Ihita Kesarcodi-Watson. Crestwood, NY: St. Vladimir's Seminary Press, 2001.

Lyman, Karen A. "Living with Alzheimer's Disease: The Creation of Meaning among Persons with Dementia." *Journal of Clinical Ethics* 9, no. 1 (1998): 49–57.

Lyotard, Jean-François. *The Postmodern Condition: A Report on Knowledge*. Translated by Geoff Bennington and Brian Massumi. Minneapolis, MN: University of Minnesota Press, 1984.

MacDonald, Dennis Ronald. The Legend and the Apostle: The Battle for Paul in Story and Canon. Louisville, KY: Westminster John Knox Press, 1983.

MacDonald, Margaret Y. "Citizens of Heaven and Earth: Asceticism and Social Integration in Colossians and Ephesians." In *Asceticism and the New Testament*, edited by Leif E. Vaage and Vincent L. Wimbush, 269–298. New York, NY: Routledge, 1999.

MacDonald, Margaret Y. "Was Celsus Right? The Role of Women in the Expansion of Early Christianity." In *Early Christian Families in Context: An Interdisciplinary Dialogue*, edited by David L. Balch and Carolyn Osiek, 157–184. Grand Rapids, MI: William B. Eerdmans, 2003.

MacDorman, Karl. F. "Androids as an Experimental Apparatus: Why Is There an Uncanny Valley and Can We Exploit It?" *Toward Social Mechanisms of Android Science: A Cogsci Workshop, Proceedings of the 27th Annual Meeting of the Cognitive Science Society* (July 21–23, 2005). Stresa, Italy, 2005. https:// www.lri.fr/~sebag/Slides/uncanny.pdf. Accessed January 13, 2014.

MacDorman, Karl F. and Z. A. D. Dwi Pramono. "Human Emotion and the Uncanny Valley: A GLM, MDS, and Isomap Analysis of Robot Video Ratings." In *HRI '08 Proceedings of the 3rd ACM/IEEE International Conference on Human Robot Interaction*, 169–176. New York, NY: ACM, 2008.

MacIntyre, Alasdair. *After Virtue*, 3rd ed. Notre Dame, IN: University of Notre Dame Press, 2007.

MacIntyre, Alasdair. *Dependent Rational Animals: Why Human Beings Need the Virtues*. Chicago, IL: Open Court, 1999.

MacLean, Katherine A., Matthew W. Johnson, and Roland R. Griffiths. "Mystical Experiences Occasioned by the Hallucinogen Psilocybin Lead to Increases in the Personality Domain of Openness." *Journal of Psychopharmacology* 25 (2011): 1453–1461.

Maher, Derek F. "Two Wings of a Bird: Radical Life Extension from a Buddhist Perspective." In *Religion and the Implications of Radical Life Extension*, edited by Derek F. Maher and Calvin Mercer, 111–121. New York, NY: Palgrave Macmillan, 2009. Republished in paperback, forthcoming 2014.

Maher, Derek F., and Calvin Mercer, eds. *Religion and the Implications of Radical Life Extension*. New York, NY: Palgrave Macmillan, 2009. Republished in paperback, forthcoming 2014.

Mahootian, Farzad. "Ideals of Human Perfection: A Comparison of Sufism and Transhumanism." In *Building Better Humans? Refocusing the Debate on Transhumanism*, edited by Hava Tirosh-Samuelson and Kenneth L. Mossman, 133–156. Frankfurt am Main, Germany: Peter Lang, 2011.

Marcuse, Herbert. *One Dimensional Man: Studies in the Ideology of Advanced Industrial Society*. Boston, MA: Beacon Press, 1964.

Markoff, John. "How Many Computers to Identify a Cat? 16,000." *New York Times* (June 25, 2012). http://www.nytimes.com/2012/06/26/technology/in-a-big -network-of-computers-evidence-of-machine-learning.html?pagewanted=all&_r=0. Accessed March 20, 2014.

Markoff, John. *What the Dormouse Said: How the Sixties Counterculture Shaped the Personal Computer Industry*. New York, NY: Viking, 2005.

Martin, Dale E. *The Corinthian Body*. New Haven, CT: Yale University Press, 1995.

Martin, George. "Brief Proposal on Immortality: An Interim Solution." *Perspective in Biology and Medicine* (1971): 339–340.

Marx, Karl. *Capital: A Critique of Political Economy*. Translated by Samuel Moore and Edward Aveling. New York, NY: Random House, 1906.

Marx, Karl. *A Contribution to the Critique of Political Economy*. Translated by N. I. Stone. Chicago, IL: Charles H. Kerr, 1904.

Marx, Leo. "Does Improved Technology Mean Progress?" *Technology Review* 90, no. 1 (1987): 33–41.

Marx, Leo. "The Idea of 'Technology' and Postmodern Pessimism." In *Does Technology Drive History? The Dilemma of Technological Determinism*, edited by Merritt Roe Smith and Leo Marx, 237–257. London, UK: MIT Press, 1994.

Marx, Leo. *The Machine in the Garden: Technology and the Pastoral Ideal in America*. Oxford, UK: Oxford University Press, 2000.

Marx, Leo, and Bruce Mazlish, eds. *Progress: Fact or Illusion?* Ann Arbor, MI: University of Michigan Press, 1996.

Maslow, Abraham H. *Toward a Psychology of Being*. New York, NY: John Wiley and Sons, 1968.

Masson, Robert. "Language, Thinking and God in Karl Rahner's Theology of the Word: A Critical Evaluation of Rahner's Perspective on the Problem of Religious Language." PhD dissertation, Fordham University, New York, NY, 1978.

Mathisen, James. "From Civil Religion to Folk Religion: The Case of American Sport." In *Sport and Religion*, edited by Shirl J. Hoffman, 17–34. Champaign, IL: Human Kinetics Books, 1992.

Matthews, Steven. *Theology and Science in the Thought of Francis Bacon*. Aldershot, UK: Ashgate, 2008.

May, William E. *Catholic Bioethics and the Gift of Human Life*, 3rd ed. Huntington, IN: Our Sunday Visitor, 2013.

Mayr, Ernst. *What Evolution Is*. New York, NY: Basic Books, 2001.

McFayden, Alistair. *Bound to Sin: Abuse, Holocaust, and the Christian Doctrine of Sin*. Cambridge, UK: Cambridge University Press, 2000.

McGinn, Colin. *The Meaning of Disgust*. Oxford, UK: Oxford University Press, 2011.

McKenny, Gerald. "Transcendence, Technological Enhancement, and Christian Theology." In *Transhumanism and Transcendence: Christian Hope in an Age of Technological Enhancement*, edited by Ronald Cole-Turner, 177–192. Washington, DC: Georgetown University Press, 2011.

McKibben, Bill. *Enough Staying Human in an Engineered Age*. New York, NY: Times Books, 2003.

McKnight, Stephen A. *The Religious Foundations of Francis Bacon's Thought*. Columbia, MO: University of Missouri Press, 2006.

McNamee, Mike. "Whose Prometheus? Transhumanism, Biotechnology and the Moral Topography of Sports Medicine." *Sport, Ethics and Philosophy* 1, no. 2 (2007): 181–194.

Mead, Aroha Te Pareake, and Steven Ratuva. *Pacific Genes and Life Patents: Pacific Indigenous Experiences and Analysis of the Commodification and Ownership of Life*. Wellington, NZ: Call of the Earth Llamado de la Tierra and the United Nations University of Advanced Studies, 2007.

Mehlman, Maxwell J. *Transhumanist Dreams and Dystopian Nightmares: The Promise and Peril of Genetic Engineering*. Baltimore, MD: Johns Hopkins University, 2012

Meilaender, Gilbert. *Should We Live Forever? The Ethical Ambiguities of Aging*. Grand Rapids, MI: W. B. Eerdmans, 2013.

Mellars, Paul. "Why Did Modern Human Populations Disperse from Africa *ca*. 60,000 Years Ago? A New Model." *Proceedings from the National Academy of the Sciences of the United States of America* 103 (2006): 9381–9386. doi: 10.1073/pnas.o 510792103. Accessed March 29, 2014.

MemeBox. "Ray Kurzweil: The Singularity Is Not a Religion." October 27, 2008. http://www.youtube.com/watch?v=CLy0tTfw8i0. Accessed May 17, 2012.

Mercer, Calvin. *Slaves to Faith: A Therapist Looks inside the Fundamentalist Mind*. Westport, CT: Praeger, 2009.

Mercer, Calvin. "Sorting out *Soma* in the Debate about Transhumanism: One Protestant's Perspective." In *Transhumanism and the Body: The World Religions Speak*, edited by Calvin Mercer and Derek Maher. New York, NY: Palgrave Macmillan, forthcoming 2014.

Mercer, Calvin, and Derek Maher, eds. *Transhumanism and the Body: The World Religions Speak*. New York, NY: Palgrave Macmillan, forthcoming 2014.

Merleau-Ponty, Maurice. *In Praise of Philosophy and Other Essays*. Translated by John Wild and James Edie. Evanston, IL: Northwestern University Press, 1970.

Merleau-Ponty, Maurice. *Phenomenology of Perception*. Translated by Colin Smith. New York, NY: Routledge, 1958.

Merleau-Ponty, Maurice. *Sense and Non-Sense*. Translated by Patricia Allen Dreyfus. Evanston, IL: Northwestern University Press, 1964.

Metz, Thaddeus. "The Immortality Requirement for Life's Meaning." *Ratio* 16, no. 2 (2003): 161–177. doi: 10.1111/1467-9329.00213.

Miah, Andy. "From Anti-Doping to a 'Performance Policy': Sport Technology, Being Human, and Doing Ethics." *European Journal of Sport Science* 5, no. 1 (2005): 51–57.

Midgley, Mary. *Beast and Man: The Roots of Human Nature*, 2nd ed. London, UK: Routledge, 1995 (1978).

Midgley, Mary. *The Essential Mary Midgley*. Edited by David Midgley. London, UK: Routledge, 2005.

Midgley, Mary. *The Myths We Live by*. London, UK: Routledge, 2003.

Midgley, Mary. *Science as Salvation: A Modern Myth and Its Meaning*. London, UK: Routledge, 1992.

Minsky, Marvin. *The Society of Mind*. New York, NY: Simon and Schuster, 1986.

Moravec, Hans. *Mind Children: The Future of Robot and Human Intelligence*. Cambridge, MA: Harvard University Press, 1988.

Moravec, Hans. *Robot: Mere Machine to Transcendent Mind*. New York, NY: Oxford University Press, 1999.

More, Max. "The Extropian Principles 2.5." *Extropy* 11, 2nd Half (1993).

More, Max. "Extropian Principles 3.0." http://wwwmaxmore.com/extprnn3.htm.

More, Max. "The Extropian Principles 3.0: A Transhumanist Declaration." 1999. http://www.buildfreedom.com/extropian_principles.html.

More, Max. "A Letter to Human Nature." In *The Transhumanist Reader: Classical and Contemporary Essays on the Science, Technology, and Philosophy of the Human Future*, edited by Max More and Natasha Vita-More, 449–450. Oxford, UK: Wiley-Blackwell, 2013.

More, Max. "On Becoming Posthuman." *Free Inquiry* 14, no. 4 (Fall 1994): 38–40. http://eserver.org/courses/spring98/76101R/readings/becoming.html.

More, Max. "The Overhuman in the Transhuman." *Journal of Evolution and Technology*, 21, no. 1 (January 2010): 1–4.

More, Max. "The Philosophy of Transhumanism." In *The Transhumanist Reader: Classical and Contemporary Essays on the Science, Technology, and Philosophy of the Human Future*, edited by Max More and Natasha Vita-More, 3–17. Chichester, UK: John Wiley & Sons, 2013.

More, Max. "The Proactionary Principle." http://www.maxmore.com/proactionary .html. Accessed October 5, 2008.

More, Max. "Transhumanism: Towards a Futurist Philosophy." *Extropy* 6 (Summer 1990): 6–12.

More, Max. "True Transhumanism: A Reply to Don Ihde." In *H±: Transhumanism and Its Critics*, edited by Gregory R. Hansell and William Grassie, 136–146. Philadelphia, PA: Metanexus Institute, 2011.

More, Max, and Natasha Vita-More. *The Transhumanist Reader: Classical and Contemporary Essays on the Science, Technology, and Philosophy of the Human Future*. Ebook: John Wiley-Blackwell, 2013.

Mori, Massahiro. "The Uncanny Valley." *Energy* 7, no. 4 (1970): 33–35.

Muehlhauser, Luke, and Louie Helm. "Intelligence Explosion and Machine Ethics." In *Singularity Hypotheses: A Scientific and Philosophical Assessment*, edited by Amnon Eden, Johnny Søraker, James H. Moor, and Eric Steinhart, 101–126. Berlin, Germany: Springer, 2012.

Muehlhauser, Luke, and Anna Salamon. "Intelligence Explosion: Evidence and Import." In *Singularity Hypotheses: A Scientific and Philosophical Assessment*, edited by Amnon Eden, Johnny Søraker, James H. Moor, and Eric Steinhar, 15–40t. Berlin, Germany: Springer, 2012.

Murphy, Nancey, and George Ellis. *On the Moral Nature of the Universe: Theology, Cosmology & Ethics*. Minneapolis, MN: Augsburg Fortress, 1996.

Muthukumaraswamy, Suresh D., Robin L. Carhart-Harris, Rosalyn J. Moran, Matthew J. Brookes, Tim M. Williams, David Errtizoe, Ben Sessa, Andreas Papadopoulos, Mark Bolstridge, Krish D. Singh, Amanda Feilding, Karl J. Friston, and David J. Nutt. "Broadband Cortical Desynchronization Underlies the Human Psychedelic State." *Journal of Neuroscience* 33, no. 38 (2013): 15171–15183.

Naam, Ramez. *More Than Human: Embracing the Promise of Biological Enhancement*. New York: Broadway Press, 2005.

National Council of the Churches of Christ in the USA. "Fearfully and Wonderfully Made: A Policy on Human Biotechnologies." http://www.ncccusa.org/pdfs/BioTechPolicy.pdf.

Near, Henry. *Where Community Happens: The Kibbutz and the Philosophy of Communism*. Oxford, UK: Peter Lang, 2011.

Newell, Christopher. "Disabled Theologies and the Journeys of Liberation to Where Our Names Appear." *Feminist Theology* 15, no. 3 (2007): 322–345.

Nichols, David E., and Benjamin R. Chemel. "The Neuropharmacology of Religious Experience: Hallucinogens and the Experience of the Divine." In *Where God and Science Meet. Vol. 3: The Psychology of Religious Experience*, edited by Patrick McNamara, 1–33. Westport, CT: Praeger, 2006.

Niebuhr, Reinhold. *The Nature and Destiny of Man: A Christian Interpretation. Vol. 1: Human Nature*. London, UK: Nesbit, 1941.

Niebuhr, Reinhold. *The Nature and Destiny of Man: A Christian Interpretation*. 2 vols. New York, NY: Charles Scribner's Sons, 1964.

Nisbet, Robert A. *History of the Idea of Progress*. London, UK: Heinemann, 1980.

Nisbet, Robert A. "The Idea of Progress: A Bibliographical Essay." *Literature of Liberty* 2, no. 1 (1979): 7–37.

Noble, David F. *The Religion of Technology: The Divinity of Man and the Spirit of Invention*. London, UK: Penguin, 1999.

Nordmann, Alfred. "Science in the Context of Technology." In *Science in the Context of Application*, edited by Martin Carrier and Alfred Nordmann, 467–82. London, UK: Springer, 2011.

Novak, Michael. "The Joy of Sports." In *Religion and Sport: The Meeting of Sacred and Profane*, edited by Charles S. Prebish, 151–173. Westport, CT: Greenwood Press, 1993.

Novak, David. "On Human Dignity." In *David Novak: Natural Law and Revealed Torah*, edited by Hava Tirosh Samuelson and Aaron W. Hughes, 71–88. Boston, MA: Brill, 2013.

Novak, David. "Jewish Eschatology." In *The Oxford Handbook of Eschatology*, edited by Jerry L. Walls, 113–131. New York, NY: Oxford University Press, 2008.

Nussbaum, Martha C. *Women and Human Development: The Capabilities Approach*. Cambridge, UK: Cambridge University Press, 2000.

Nutt, David J., Leslie A. King, and David E. Nichols. "Effects of Schedule I Drug Laws on Neuroscience Research and Treatment Innovation." *Nature Reviews Neuroscience* 14, no. 8 (2013): 577–585.

Nye, David E. *America as Second Creation: Technology and Narratives of New Beginnings.* London, UK: MIT Press, 2003.

O'Gorman, Kevin. *Saving Sport: Sport, Society and Spirituality.* Dublin, Ireland: Columba Press, 2010.

Overman, Steven J. *The Influence of the Protestant Ethic on Sport and Recreation.* Aldershot, UK: Avebury Ashgate, 1997.

Pagels, Elaine. *The Gnostic Gospels.* New York, NY: Random House, 1979.

Pagels, Elaine. *The Gnostic Paul: Gnostic Exegesis of the Pauline Letters.* Harrisburg, PA: Trinity Press International, 1975.

Panikkar, Raymond. *The Cosmotheandric Experience: Emerging Religion Consciousness.* Maryknoll, NY: Orbis, 1993.

Parens, Erik. "The Goodness of Fragility: On the Prospect of Genetic Technologies Aimed at the Enhancement of Human Capacities." In *Contemporary Issues in Bioethics,* 5th ed., edited by Tom L. Beachamp and LeRoy Walters, 596–602. Belmont, CA: Wadsworth, 1999.

Passig, David. *The Future Code: Israel's Future Test* (in Hebrew). Tel Aviv, Israel: Yediot Aharonot and Hemed Library, 2008.

Passig, David. *2048.* Translated by Baruch Gefen. Tel Aviv, Israel: Yedioth Aharonoth Books. Hemed Books, 2013.

Patterson, Stephen, and Marvin Meyer, trans. *The Complete Gospels: Annotated Scholars Version.* Salem, OR: Polebridge Press, 1992.

Pattison, George. *God and Being: An Enquiry.* Oxford, UK: Oxford University Press, 2013.

Peacocke, Arthur R. *Creation and the World of Science: The Bampton Lectures, 1978.* Oxford, UK: Clarendon Press, 1979.

Pearce, David. "The Abolitionist Project." 2007. http://www.abolitionist.com/. Accessed March 31, 2014.

Pearce, David. "Happiness, Hypermotivation and the Meaning of Life." http://wireheading.com/hypermotivation.html. Accessed March 31, 2014.

Pengelley, Richard. "Sport and Spirituality: An Ancient Connection for Our Modern Times." *Dialogue Australasia* 20 (2008): 1–9.

Peperzak, Adriaan. *To the Other: An Introduction to the Philosophy of Emmanuel Levinas.* West Lafayette, IN: Purdue University Press, 1993.

Pepperell, Robert. *The Posthuman Condition: Consciousness beyond the Brain.* Bristol, UK: Intellect, 2003 (1995).

Perry, Mike. *Forever for All: Moral Philosophy, Cryonics, and the Scientific Prospects for Immortality.* Boca Raton, FL: Universal Publishers, 2000.

Pesic, Peter. "Wrestling with Proteus: Francis Bacon and the 'Torture' of Nature." *Isis* 90, no. 1 (1999): 81–94.

Peters, Ted. *Anticipating Omega: Science, Faith and Our Ultimate Future.* Göttingen, Germany: Vandenhoeck & Ruprecht, 2006.

Peters, Ted. "Are We Playing God with Nanoenhancement?" In *Nanoethics: The Ethical and Social Implications of Nanotechnology,* edited by Fritz Allhoff, Patrick

Lin, James Moor, and John Weckert, 173–183. Hoboken, NJ: Wiley-Interscience, 2007.

Peters, Ted. "Perfect Humans or Transhumans." In *Future Perfect: God, Medicine and Human Identity*, edited by Celia Deane-Drummond and Peter Scott, 15–32. London, UK: T & T Clark/Continuum, 2006.

Peters, Ted. *Playing God: Genetic Determinism and Human Freedom*, 2nd ed. London, UK: Routledge, 2003.

Peters, Ted. "Progress and Provolution: Will Transhumanism Leave Sin behind?" In *Transhumanism and Transcendence: Christian Hope in an Age of Technological Enhancement*, edited by Ronald Cole-Turner, 63–86. Washington, DC: Georgetown University Press, 2011.

Peters, Ted. *Science, Theology and Ethics*. Farnham, UK: Ashgate, 2003.

Peters, Ted. *The Stem Cell Debate*. Minneapolis, MN: Fortress Press, 2007.

Peters, Ted. "A Theological Argument for Chimeras." *Nature Reports Stem Cells*. http://www.nature.com/stemcells/2007/0706/070614/full/stemcells.2007.31.html#B4. Accessed February 14, 2011.

Peters, Ted. "Transhumanism and the Posthuman Future: Will Technological Progress Get Us There?" In *H±: Transhumanism and its Critics*, edited by Gregory R. Hansell and William Grassie, 147–175. Philadelphia, MN: Metanexus Institute, 2011.

Peters, Ted, and Gaymon Bennett, Jr. "Stem Cell Research and the Claim of the Other in the Human Subject." *Dialog* 43, no. 3 (Fall 2004): 184–204.

Peters, Ted, and Martinez Hewlett. *Can You Believe in God and Evolution? A Guide for the Perplexed*. Darwin 200th Anniversary Edition. Nashville, TN: Abingdon Press, 2008 (2006).

Peterson, Gregory R. "The Created Co-creator: What It Is and Is Not." *Zygon* 39, no. 4 (December 2004): 827–840.

Plantinga, Alvin. *Where the Conflict Really Lies: Science, Religion, and Naturalism*. Oxford, UK: Oxford University Press, 2011.

Plantinga, Cornelius, Jr. *Not the Way It's Supposed to Be: A Breviary of Sin*. Grand Rapids, MI: W. B. Eerdmans, 1995.

Porter, Jean. *Nature as Reason: A Thomistic Theory of the Natural Law*. Grand Rapids, MI: William B. Eerdmans, 2005.

Post, Stephen G. "Decelerated Aging: Should I Drink from the Fountain of Youth?" In *The Fountain of Youth: Cultural, Scientific, and Ethical Perspectives on a Biomedical Goal*, edited by Stephen G. Post and Robert H. Binstock, 72–93. New York, NY: Oxford University Press, 2004.

Post, Stephen G. "Humanism, Posthumanism, and Compassionate Love." *Technology in Society* 32 (2010): 35–39.

Prainsak, Barbara, and Ofer Fierstein. Science for Survival: Biotechnology Regulation in Israel. *Science and Public Policy* 33, no. 1 (2006): 33–46.

Prebish, Charles S., ed. *Religion and Sport: The Meeting of Sacred and Profane*. Westport, CT: Greenwood Press, 1993.

President's Council on Bioethics and Leon R. Kass. *Beyond Therapy: Biotechnology and the Pursuit of Happiness: A Report of the President's Council of Bioethics*. New York, NY: HarperCollins, 2003.

Price, Joseph L. "From Sabbath Proscriptions to Super Sunday Celebrations: Sports and Religion in America." In *From Season to Season: Sport as American Religion*, edited by Joseph L. Price, 15–38. Macon, GA: Mercer University Press, 2001.

Pyysiainen, Ilkka. *Magic, Miracles, and Religion: A Scientist's Perspective.* Walnut Creek, CA: AltaMira, 2004.

Rahman, Fazlur. *Health and Medicine in the Islamic Tradition: Change and Identity.* New York, NY: Crossroad, 1989.

Ramsey, Paul. *The Patient as Person: Explorations in Medical Ethics.* New Haven, CT: Yale University Press, 1970.

Raner, Karl. "Christology within an Evolutionary View of the World." *Theological Investigations* 5, no. 8 (2004): 1033–1054. Limerick, Ireland: Mary Immaculate College Centre for Culture, Technology and Values. http://www.theway.org. uk/Theological%20Investigations/Theological_Investigations.pdf. Accessed March 30, 2014.

Raner, Karl. *Hearer of the Word.* Translated by Joseph Donceel. New York, NY: Continuum, 1994.

Raner, Karl. "Natural Science and Reasonable Faith." *Theological Investigations* 21, no. 2 (2004): 4055–4078. Limerick, Ireland: Mary Immaculate College Centre for Culture, Technology and Values. http://www.theway.org.uk/ Theological%20Investigations/Theological_Investigations.pdf. Accessed March 30, 2014.

Raner, Karl. "The Unity of Spirit and Matter in the Christian Understanding of Faith." *Theological Investigations* 6, no. 12 (2004): 1345–1360. Limerick, Ireland: Mary Immaculate College Centre for Culture, Technology and Values. http://www.theway.org.uk/Theological%20Investigations/Theological _Investigations.pdf. Accessed March 30, 2014.

Rappaport, Roy A. *Ecology, Meaning, and Religion.* Berkeley, CA: North Atlantic Books, 1979.

Ratele, Kopano. "Looks: Subjectivity as Commodity." *Agenda* 90/25, no. 4 (2011): 92–103.

Ravel, Barbara, and Genevieve Rail. "From Straight to Gaie? Quebec Sportswomen's Discursive Constructions of Sexuality and Destabilizations of the Linear Coming out Process." *Journal of Sport & Social Issues* 32, no. 1 (2008): 4–23.

Ravitzky, Aviezer. *Messianism, Zionism and Jewish Religious Radicalism.* Translated by Michael Swirsky and Jonathan Chipman. Chicago, IL: University of Chicago Press, 1996.

Redding, Micah. "Christianity Is Transhumanism." 2012. http://micahredding.com/ blog/2012/04/25/christianity-transhumanism. Accessed March 31, 2014.

Rees, Martin. *Our Final Hour: A Scientist's Warning: How Terror, Error, and Environmental Disaster Threaten Humankind's Future in This Century—on Earth and Beyond.* New York, NY: Basic Books, 2003.

Richards, William A. "Entheogens in the Study of Religious Experiences: Current Status." *Journal of Religion and Health* 44, no. 4 (2005): 377–389.

Richards, William A. "Here and How: Discovering the Sacred with Entheogens." *Zygon* 49, no. 3 (2014): in press.

Richards, William A. The Rebirth of Research with Entheogens: Lessons from the Past and Hypotheses for the Future. *Journal of Transpersonal Psychology* 41, no. 2 (2009): 139.

Ricoeur, Paul. *History and Truth*. Translated by Charles A. Kelbley. Evanston, IL: Northwestern University Press, 1977.

Rivera, Mayra. *The Touch of Transcendence*. London, UK: Westminster John Knox Press, 2007.

Robbins, Jill, ed. *Is It Righteous to Be? Interviews with Emmanuel Levinas*. Stanford, CA: Stanford University Press, 2002.

Roco, Mihail C., and William Sims Bainbridge, eds. *Converging Technologies for Improved Human Performance: Nanotechnology, Biotechnology, Information Technology and Cognitive Science*. Arlington, VA: National Science Foundation/Department of Commerce, 2002.

Rolnick, Philip A. *Person, Grace, and God*. Grand Rapids, MI: Eerdmans, 2007.

Rosenberg, Alexander. *Philosophy of Science: A Contemporary Introduction*, 2nd ed. London, UK: Routledge, 2005.

Rosenthal, Gideon. "Tikkun ha-Olam: The Metamorphosis of a Concept." *Journal of Religion* 85 (2005): 214–220.

Roughgarden, Joan. *Evolution's Rainbow: Diversity, Gender, and Sexuality in Nature and People*. Berkeley, CA: University of California Press, 2004.

Russell, Robert J. "Five Attitudes toward Nature and Technology from a Christian Perspective." *Theology and Science* 1, no. 2 (October 2003): 149–159.

Rutjens, B. T., J. Van Der Pligt, and F. Van Harreveld. "Things Will Get Better: The Anxiety-Buffering Qualities of Progressive Hope." *Personality and Social Psychology Bulletin* 35, no. 5 (2009): 535–543.

Rutjens, B. T., F. van Harreveld, and J. van der Pligt. "Yes We Can: Belief in Progress as Compensatory Control." *Social Psychological and Personality Science* 1, no. 3 (2010): 246–252.

Sachedina, Abdulaziz. *Islamic Biomedical Ethics: Principles and Application*. Oxford, UK: Oxford University Press, 2009.

Samuelson, Norbert, and Hava Tirosh-Samuelson. "Jewish Perspectives on Transhumanism." In *Building Better Humans? Refocusing the Debate on Transhumanism*, edited by Hava Tirosh-Samuelson and Kenneth L. Mossman, 105–132. Frankfurt, Germany: Peter Lang, 2012.

Sandberg, Anders. "Morphological Freedom: Why We Not Just Want It, But Need It." 2001. http://www.aleph.se/Nada/Texts/Morphological Freedom.htm. Accessed March 20, 2014.

Sandel, Michael. "The Case against Perfection: What's Wrong with Designer Children, Bionic Athletes, and Genetic Engineering." In *Human Enhancement*, edited by Julian Salvescu and Nick Bostrom, 71–90. Oxford, UK: Oxford University Press, 2009.

Sandel, Michael. *The Case against Perfection: Ethics in the Age of Genetic Engineering*. Cambridge, UK: Belknap Press, 2007.

Sandin, Per. "The Precautionary Principle and the Concept of Precaution." *Environmental Values* 13, no. 4 (2004): 461–475.

Sanford, A. Whitney. "Pinned on Karma Rock: Whitewater Kayaking as Religious Experience." *Journal of the American Academy of Religion* 75, no. 4 (2007): 875–895.

Sarewitz, Daniel. "The Idea of Progress." In *A Companion to the Philosophy of Technology*, edited by Jan-Kyrre Berg Olsen, Stig Andur Pedersen, and Vincent F. Hendricks, 303–307. Oxford, UK Wiley-Blackwell, 2009.

Sargent, Lynn Tower. *Utopianism: A Very Short Introduction*. Oxford, UK: Oxford University Press, 2010.

Savage, Marshall T. *The Millennial Project: Colonizing the Galaxy in Eight Easy Steps*, 2nd ed. New York, NY: Little, Brown,1994.

Schneider, Angela J., Matthew N. Fedoruk, and Jim L. Rupert. "Human Genetic Variation: New Challenges and Opportunities for Doping Control." *Journal of Sports Sciences* 30, no. 11 (2012): 1117–1129.

Schwartz, Richard. "Tikkun Olam: Jewish Imperative." *Encyclopedia of Religion and Nature*, Vol. 2, edited by Bron Talyor, 1638–1639. London, UK: Continuum, 2005.

Scott, Peter. "The Technological Factor: Redemption, Nature, and the Image of God." *Zygon* 35, no. 2 (June 2000): 371–384.

Searle, John. *Minds, Brains and Science*. Cambridge, MA: Harvard University Press, 1984.

Seung, Sebastian. *Connectome: How the Brain's Wiring Makes Us Who We Are*. New York, NY: Mariner Books, 2013.

Shakespeare, William. *As You Like It*. Edited by George Lyman Kittredge. Boston, MA: Ginn, 1939.

Shapin, Steven, and Christopher Martyn. "How to Live Forever: Lessons of History." *BMJ* 321 (2000): 1580–1582.

Sheehan, Thomas. "Rahner's Transcendental Project." In *The Cambridge Companion to Karl Rahner*, edited by Declan Marmion and Mary E. Hines, 29–42. Cambridge, UK: Cambridge University Press, 2005.

Sherwin, Byron L. *The Golem Legend: Origins and Implications*. Lanham, MD: University Press of America, 1985.

Sherwin, Byron L. *Golems among Us: How a Jewish Legend Can Help Us Navigate the Biotech Century*. Chicago, IL: Ivan R. Dee, 2004.

Sherwin, Susan. "Genetic Enhancement, Sports and Relational Autonomy." *Sport, Ethics and Philosophy* 1, no. 2 (2007): 171–180.

Shilling, C. *The Body and Social Theory*. London, UK: Sage, 1993.

Simon, Robert L. *Fair Play: The Ethics of Sport*, 2nd ed. Boulder, CO: Westview Press, 2004.

Simon, Robert L. "Good Competition and Drug-Enhanced Performance." In *Ethics in Sport*, edited by William J. Morgan, Klaus V. Meier, and Angela J. Schneider, 119–129. Champaign, IL: Human Kinetics, 2001.

Sinclair-Faulkner, Tom. "A Puckish Reflection on Religion in Canada." In *Religion and Culture in Canada/Religion et Culture au Canada*, edited by Peter Slater, 384–401. Ottawa, ON: Corporation Canadienne des Sciences Religieuses/ Canadian Corporation for Studies in Religion, 1977.

Smith, Huston. "Do Drugs Have Religious Import?" *Journal of Philosophy* 61 (1964): 517–530.

Smith, Merritt Roe. "Technological Determinism in American Culture." In *Does Technology Drive History? The Dilemma of Technological Determinism*, edited by Merritt Roe Smith and Leo Marx, 1–35. London, UK: MIT Press, 1994.

Smith, Merritt Roe, and Leo Marx, eds. *Does Technology Drive History? The Dilemma of Technological Determinism*. London, UK: MIT Press, 1994.

Sorenson, Jesper. *A Cognitive Theory of Magic*. Walnut Creek, CA: AltaMira, 2007.

Sorgner, Stefan L. "Nietzsche, the Overhuman, and Transhumanism." *Journal of Evolution and Technology* 20, no. 1 (March 2009): 29–42. http://jetpress.org/v20/sorgner.htm Accessed July 28, 2014.

Sottas, Pierre-Edouard, Neil Robinson, Oliver Rabin, and Martial Saugy. "The Athlete Biological Passport." *Clinical Chemistry* 57, no. 7 (2011): 969–976.

Spezio, Michael L. "Brain and Machine: Minding the Transhuman Future." *Dialog* 44, no. 4 (Winter 2005): 375–380.

Spinoza, Baruch. *Ethics*. Translated by Samuel Shirley. Indianapolis, IN: Hackett, 1992.

Spinoza, Benedict. *Ethics*. Translated by W. H. White and A. H. Stirling and introduction by Don Garrett. Hertfordshire, UK: Wordsworth Classics, 2001.

Sponheim, Paul. "The Human Factor: Evolution, Culture and Religion: Review of Philip Hefner's 'The Human Factor: Evolution, Culture and Religion.'" *CTNS Bulletin* 14, no. 2 (Spring 1994): 23–26.

Sprat, Thomas. *The History of the Royal Society of London*. London, UK: 1667.

Stace, W. T., and Huston Smith. *Mysticism and Philosophy*. Los Angeles, CA: J. P. Tarcher, 1960, 1987.

Stanford, Craig. *The Hunting Apes: Meat Eating and the Origins of Human Behavior*. Princeton, NJ: Princeton University Press, 2001.

Steinhart, Eric. "Theological Implications of the Simulation Argument." *Ars Disputandi* 10 (2010): 23–37.

Stenmark, Mikael. "Is There a Human Nature?" *Zygon* 47, no. 4 (2012): 890–902.

Stoeger, William. "Entropy, Emergence, and the Physical Roots of Natural Evil." In *Physics and Cosmology: Scientific Perspectives on the Problem of Natural Evil*, Vol. 1., edited by Nancey Murphy, Robert Russell, and William Stoeger, 93–108. Vatican City: Vatican Observatory, 2007.

Tamburruni, Claudio. "What's Wrong with Genetic Inequality? The Impact of Genetic Technology on Elite Sports and Society." *Sport, Ethics and Philosophy* 1, no. 2 (2007): 229–238.

Tamburruni, Claudio, and Torbjörn Tännsjö. "Enhanced Bodies." In *Enhancing Human Capacities*, edited by Julian Savulescu, Ruud ter Meulen, and Guy Kahane, 247–290. Oxford, UK: Wiley-Blackwell, 2011.

Tassone, Giuseppe. *A Study on the Idea of Progress in Nietzsche, Heidegger, and Critical Theory*. Lewiston, NY: Mellen, 2002.

Tattersal, Ian. *Masters of the Planet*. New York, NY: Palgrave Macmillan, 2012.

Taylor, Jeremy. *On the Rule and Exercises of Holy Dying*. London, UK: Longmans, 1918.

Teilhard de Chardin, Pierre. *The Future of Man*. Translated by Norman Denny. New York, NY: Image Books/Doubleday, 2004.

Teilhard de Chardin, Pierre. *The Phenomenon of Man*. New York, NY: Harper and Row, 1965.

Temkin, Larry. "Is Living Longer Living Better?" In *Enhancing Human Capabilities*, edited by Julian Savulescu, Ruud ter Meulen, and Guy Kahane, 350–385. Chichester, UK: Blackwell, 2011.

Terasem. "The Truths of Terasem." 2002. http://terasemfaith.net/beliefs Accessed at 2014-03-27. Accessed March 31, 2014.

Thielicke, Helmut. *Death and Life*. Translated by Edward H. Schoreder. Philadelphia, PA: Fortress Press, 1970.

Thomas Aquinas. *Summa Theologiae*, 1st American ed., 3 vols. Translated by the Fathers of the English Dominican Province. New York, NY: Benziger Bros., 1948.

Thweatt-Bates, Jeanne J. "Artificial Wombs and Cyborg Births: Postgenderism and Theology." In *Transhumanism and Transcendence: Christian Hope in an Age of Technological Enhancement*, edited by Ronald Cole-Turner, 101–114. Washington, DC: Georgetown University Press, 2011.

Thweatt-Bates, Jeanne J. *Cyborg Selves: A Theological Anthropology of the Posthuman*. Edited by Roger Trigg and J. Wentzel van Huyssteen. Burlington, VT: Ashgate, 2012.

Tillich, Paul. *Ultimate Concern: Tillich in Dialogue*. London, UK: SCM Press, 1965.

Tillich, Paul. *What Is Religion?* New York, NY: Harper & Row, 1969.

Tipler, Frank J. *The Physics of Immortality*. New York, NY: Anchor, 1994.

Tirosh-Samuelson, Hava. "Engaging Transhumanism." In *H±: Transhumanism and Its Critics*, edited by Gregory R. Hansell and William Grassie, 19–52. Philadelphia, PA: Metanexus Institute, 2011.

Tirosh-Samuelson, Hava. *Happiness in Premodern Judaism: Virtue, Knowledge and Well-Being*. Cincinnati, OH: Hebrew Union College, 2003.

Tirosh-Samuelson, Hava. "Science and the Betterment of Humanity: Three British Prophets of Transhumanism." In *Building Better Humans? Refocusing the Debate on Transhumanism*, edited by Hava Tirosh-Samuelson and Kenneth L. Mossman, 55–82. Frankfurt, Germany: Peter Lang, 2012.

Tirosh-Samuelson, Hava. "Transhumanism: A Secular Faith for the Post-Secular Age." *Zygon: Journal of Religion and Science* 47, no. 2 (2012): 710–733.

Tirosh-Samuelson, Hava. "Understanding Jonas: An Interdisciplinary Project." In *The Legacy of Hans Jonas: Judaism and the Phenomenon of Life*, edited by HavaTirosh-Samuelson and Christian Wiese, xxi–xlii. Boston, MA: Brill, 2008.

Tirosh-Samuelson, Hava, and Kenneth L. Mossman, eds. Building Better Humans? Refocusing the Debate on Transhumanism. Frankfurt, Germany: Peter Lang, 2012.

Tirosh-Samuelson, Hava, and Christian Wiese, eds. *The Legacy of Hans Jonas: Judaism and the Phenomenon of Life*. Boston, MA: Brill, 2008.

Tolstoy, Leo. *A Confession and Other Religious Writings* (London: Penguin Classics, 1988 [1884]).

Trothen, Tracy J. "Holy Acceptable Violence? Violence in Hockey and Christian Atonement Theories." *Journal of Religion and Popular Culture* 21 (2009). doi: 10.3138/jrpc.21.suppl_1.003.

Tu Wei-ming. "Beyond the Enlightenment Mentality." In *Confucianism and Ecology: The Interrelation of Heaven, Earth, and Humans*, edited by Mary Everlyn Tucker and John Berthrong, 3–22. Cambridge, MA: Harvard University Press, 1998.

Tu Wei-ming. *Centrality and Commonality: An Essay on Confucian Religiousness*. Albany, NY: State University of New York Press, 1989.

Turing, Alan. "Computing Machinery and Intelligence." *Mind: A Quarterly Review of Psychology and Philosophy* 59, no. 236 (October 1950): 433–460.

Turkle, Sherry. *Alone Together: Why We Expect More from Technology and Less from Each Other.* New York, NY: Basic Books, 2011.

Turner, Daniel, et al. "Cognitive Enhancing Effects of Modafinil in Healthy Volunteers." *Psychopharmacology* 165 (2003): 260–269.

Tylor, E. B. *Primitive Religion: Researches into the Development of Mythology, Philosophy, Art, and Custom.* Cambridge, UK: Cambridge University Press, 2012.

United States Central Intelligence Agency. "World Fact Book." https://www.cia.gov/library/publications/the-world-factbook/. Accessed March 25, 2014.

Vannini, April, and Barbara Fornssler. "Girl, Interrupted: Interpreting Semenya's Body, Gender Verification Testing, and Public Discourse." *Cultural Studies Critical Methodologies* 11, no. 3 (2010): 243–257.

Vardy, Peter. *Being Human: Fulfilling Genetic and Spiritual Potential.* London, UK: Darton, Longman and Todd, 2003.

Vedral, Vlatko. "Information and Physics." *Information* 3 (2012): 219–223.

Verdoux, Philippe. "Transhumanism, Progress and the Future." *Journal of Evolution and Technology* 20, no. 2 (2009): 49–69.

Vidal, Fernando. "Human Persons and Human Brains: A Historical Perspective within the Christian Tradition." In *Rethinking Human Nature: A Multidisciplinary Approach,* edited by Malcolm Jeeves, 30–60. Grand Rapids, MI: Eerdmans, 2011.

Viera, Fatima. "The Concept of Utopia." In *The Cambridge Companion to Utopian Literature,* edited by Gregory Claeys, 3–27. Cambridge, UK: Cambridge University Press, 2010.

Vita-More, Natasha. "Bringing Arts/Design into the Discussion of Transhumanism." In *H±: Transhumanism and Its Critics,* edited by Gregory Hansell and William Grassie, 70–83. Philadelphia, PA: Metanexus, 2011.

Vogel, Lawrence. "Natural Law Judaism? The Genesis of Bioethics in Hans Jonas, Leo Strauss, and Leon Kass." In *The Legacy of Hans Jonas: Judaism and the Phenomenon of Life,* edited by Hava Tirosh-Samuelson and Christian Wiese, 287–314. Boston, MA: Brill, 2008.

Volk, Brian. "Mr. Berry Goes to Medical School." In *Wendell Berry and Religion: Heaven's Earthly Life,* edited by Joel James Schuman and L. Roger Owens, 33–49. Lexington, KY: University Press of Kentucky, 2009.

Wahrman, Miriam. *Brave New Judaism: When Science and Scripture Collide.* Hanover, NH: Brandeis University Press, 2004.

Walker, Mark, and Heidi Campbell. "Religion and Transhumanism: Introducing a Conversation." *Journal of Evolution and Technology* 14, no. 2 (2005): i–xiv.

Walton, Heather. "The Gender of the Cyborg." *Theology & Sexuality* 10, no. 2 (2004): 33–44.

Ware, Kallistos. *Act out of Stillness: The Influence of Fourteenth-Century Hesychasm on Byzantine and Slav Civilization,* edited by Daniel J. Sahas. Toronto, ON: Hellenic Canadian Association of Constantinople and Thessalonikean Society of Metro Toronto, 1995.

Waters, Brent. *Christian Moral Theology in the Emerging Technoculture: From Posthuman Back to Human.* Farnham, UK: Ashgate, 2014.

Waters, Brent. *From Human to Posthuman: Christian Theology and Technology in a Postmodern World*. Aldershot, UK: Ashgate, 2006.

Waters, Brent. *This Mortal Flesh: Incarnation and Bioethics*. Grand Rapids, MI: Brazos, 2009.

Waters, Brent. "Whose Salvation? Which Eschatology? Transhumanism and Christianity as Contending Salvific Religions." In *Transhumanism and Transcendence: Christian Hope in an Age of Technological Enhancement*, edited by Ronald Cole-Turner, 163–175. Washington, DC: Georgetown University Press, 2011.

Weijers, Dan. "Optimistic Naturalism: Scientific Advancement and the Meaning of Life." *Sophia* (2013). doi: 10.1007/s11841-013-0369-x.

Wells, Matthew V. *To Die and Not Decay*. Ann Arbor, MI: Association for Asian Studies, 2009.

Weng, Ng Kam. "Co-creator or Priestly Steward: Theological Perspectives on Biotechnology." In *Beyond Determinism and Reductionism: Genetic Science and the Person*, edited by Mark L. Y. Chan and Roland Chia, 74–94. Adelaide, Australia: ATF Press, 2003.

White, Lynn, Jr. "The Historical Roots of Our Ecologic Crisis." *Science* 155, no. 3767 (March 10, 1967): 1203–1207.

White, Susan. *Christian Worship and Technological Change*. Nashville, TN: Abingdon Press, 1994.

Whitehead, Alfred North. *Science and the Modern World*. New York, NY: Pelican Mentor, 1948.

Whitney, Charles. "Francis Bacon's *Instauratio*: Dominion of and over Humanity." *Journal of the History of Ideas* 50, no. 3 (1989): 371–390.

Whitney, Charles. *Francis Bacon and Modernity*. New Haven, CT: Yale University Press, 1986.

Wiese, Christian. *The Life and Thought of Hans Jonas: Jewish Dimensions*. Translated by Jeffrey Grossman and Christian Wiese. Waltham, MA: Brandeis University Press and University Press of New England, 2007.

William of Ockham. *Quodlibetal Questions*, Vols. 1 and 2, Quodlibets 1–7. Translated by A. J. Freddoso and F. E. Kelley. New Haven, CT: Yale University Press, 1991.

Williams, Bernard. "The Makropulos Case: Reflections on the Tedium of Immortality." In *Problems of the Self*, 82–100. Cambridge, UK: Cambridge University Press, 1973.

Wilson, David Sloan. *Darwin's Cathedral: Evolution, Religion, and the Nature of Society*. Chicago, IL: University of Chicago Press, 2002.

Wilson, E. O. *Consilience: The Unity of Knowledge*. New York, NY: Vintage, 1999.

Winner, Langdon. "Technology Today: Utopia or Dystopia?" *Social Research* 64, no. 3 (1997): 989–1017.

Wolf, Susan. "Happiness and Meaning: Two Aspects of the Good Life." *Social Philosophy and Policy* 14, no. 1 (1997): 207–225.

World Future Society. "The Futurist Interviews Ray Kurzweil." http://www.wfs.org/content/futurist-interviews-ray-kurzweil. Accessed March 16, 2014.

World Transhumanist Association. "People of Faith." 2004. http://www.trans humanism.org/index.php/WTA/communities/religious/. Accessed March 31, 2014.

Young, George M. *The Russian Cosmists: The Esoteric Futurism of Nikolai Fedorov and His Followers*. Oxford, UK: Oxford University Press, 2012.

Young, Simon. *Designer Evolution: A Transhumanist Manifesto*. Amherst, NY: Prometheus Books, 2006.

Yudkowsky, Eliezer. "Frequently Asked Questions about the Meaning of Life." 1999. http://yudkowsky.net/obsolete/tmol-faq.html. Accessed March 31, 2014.

Yudkowsky, Eliezer. "The Fun Theory Sequence." *Less Wrong* (2009). http://lesswrong.com/lw/xy/the_fun_theory_sequence/. Accessed March 31, 2014.

Yudkowsky, Eliezer. "Staring into the Singularity 1.2.5." 1996. http://yudkowsky.net/obsolete/singularity.html. Accessed March 31, 2014.

Zahavi, Dan. *Subjectivity and Selfhood: Investigating the First-Person Perspective*. Cambridge, MA: MIT Press, 2008.

Zimmerli, Walther Cristoph. "Human Responsibility for Extra Human Nature." *Nature, Technology and Religion: Transdisciplinary Perspectives* (May 23, 2013). European Forum for the Study of Religion and Environment, Sigtuna Foundation, Sweden, May 22–25, 2013.

Zimmerli, Walther Cristoph. "Human Responsibility for Extra-Human Nature: An Ethical Approach to Technofutures." In *Technofutures: God, Society and Earth Ethics*, edited by C. Deane-Drummond, S. Bergmann, and B. Szerszynski. Basingstoke, UK: Ashgate, 2015, in preparation.

Zimmerman, Michael E. "The Singularity: A Crucial Phase in Divine Self-Actualization?" *Cosmos and History: Journal of Natural and Social Philosophy* 4, nos. 1–2 (2008): 347–380.

Index

Central Conference of American
    Rabbis, 167
Cheng Chung-ying, 106–7
Chinese Room Argument, 321
Choice(s): death as matter of, 85, 291;
    ethics of genetic, 224; and
    individualism, 354–57;
    regarding human enhancement,
    391–92; regarding humanoid
    artificial intelligence, 181;
    regarding technology, 193–94;
    and relationality, 392–95. *See
    also* Freedom of choice
Christianity: death in, 85, 87–92; and
    Enlightenment, 101–3; and
    glorification of suffering, 357;
    versus gnosticism beliefs,
    277–78; and human body, 394;
    identification of human beings,
    235; and incarnation belief, 234;
    messianism of, 166; and
    nonmaleficence principle, 237;
    and permanent satisfaction, 71;
    and personhood, 192; self-
    sacrifice in, 356–57; and
    spirituality, 354; and techno-
    logical enhancement, 251; and
    transhumanism, 6, 231
Christology: centrality of the body in,
    283; and Christ's earthly
    activities, 285; versus proto-
    orthodoxy, 275
The City of the Sun (Campanella), 135
Civilization and Its Discontents
    (Freud), 332
Cloning, 174
Co-evolution, 125
Cog (humanoid robot), 43
Cold War, 100
"College of the Six Days
    Works," 62
Combinatorial optimization
    process, 125
Communism, and transhumanism,
    99–100
The Communist Manifesto (Marx), 136
Comte, Auguste, 136

Conference of European Churches,
    Church and Society
    Commission, 221
Conflict myth, 53
Confucianism: versus Daoism, 151; on
    humanity, 108; on
    transformation, 108
Confucius: on aging, 150–51; on
    innovations, 159–60
Consciousness: anticipatory, 175; and
    artificial intelligence programs,
    219; Dennett on, 319; health,
    155; machine, 319–20; Merleau-
    Ponty on, 323; nature of, 317;
    phenomenal, 78; postmortem,
    158; top-down schema of,
    321–23; transfer of, to
    computers, 26, 158
Conservative Judaism, 168. *See also*
    Judaism
Consilience: The Unity of Knowledge
    (Wilson), 117
Constantine, Emperor, 274–75
"Contextualizing a Christian
    Perspective on Transcendence
    and Human Enhancement," 118
*A Contribution to the Critique of Political
    Economy* (Marx), 136
Corporeal challenge: and bodily
    resurrection, 284–86;
    gnosticism, 274–81; human
    body centrality, 282–83; and
    proto-orthodox church, 284;
    and women, 283–84
Cosmist transhumanism, 14–18; omega
    points, 17–18; universal
    immortalism, 16–17
Cosmos: creation of, 121; described,
    106; gnostic understanding of,
    275; moral, and Buddhism, 157;
    replication of, 124; Valentinus's
    teachings of, 280
Cowen, Tyler, 220
Created co-creators metaphor, 232–33
Creation and Fall (Bonhoeffer), 89
Creatureliness. *See* Human
    creaturehood

About the Editors and Contributors

CALVIN MERCER's 4 books and 25 articles focus on biblical studies and religion and culture. He is co-editor, with Steve Fuller, of the new series, *Palgrave Studies in the Future of Humanity and Its Successors*. He was the founding chair of the American Academy of Religion's "Transhumanism and Religion" group at the annual meeting. He is also trained in clinical psychology, practiced professionally part-time for nearly a decade, and has utilized insights from this discipline in his published work on religion. Representative recent publications include *Slaves to Faith: A Therapist Looks inside the Fundamentalist Mind* (Praeger, 2008) and *Religion and the Implications of Radical Life Extension* (co-editor, Palgrave-Macmillan, 2009). *The Body in Transhumanism: The World Religions Speak*, co-edited, is forthcoming from Palgrave Macmillan. At East Carolina University, Mercer directs the Religious Studies Program. He frequently gives public lectures on religion and human enhancement, as well as his psychological interpretation of fundamentalism.

TRACY J. TROTHEN is Associate Professor of Ethics and Theology in the School of Religion at Queen's University, in Kingston, Ontario. She is a certified Clinical Pastoral Education Specialist and Supervisor. Trothen is the author of two books, the most recent entitled *Shattering the Illusion: Child Sexual Abuse Policies and Canadian Religious Institutions* (Wilfrid Laurier Press, 2012), and more than 25 articles and book chapters. She has a co-edited anthology in press, *Religion and Sexuality: Diversity and the Limits of Tolerance* (University of British Columbia Press), and is completing a book manuscript on sport, enhancements, and religion (Mercer University Press). Her research interests include sexuality, embodiment, sport, and human enhancement. Currently, Trothen co-chairs, with Ronald Cole-Turner, the American Academy of Religion's "Transhumanism and Religion" group.

STEVEN A. BENKO's research and publications have been in the area of ethical subjectivity as it relates to transhuman technology, critical thinking pedagogy, and comedy and ethics. He has presented on these topics at national and regional meetings of the American Academy of Religion, the Pop Culture Association/American Culture Association, and the International Society for Exploring Teaching and Learning. Representative publications include "Ethics, Technology and Posthuman Communities" (2005) and "Ironic Faith in *Monty Python's Life of Brian*" (2012). He is a member of the Religious and Ethical Studies program at Meredith College and director of the college Ethics Bowl team. He frequently gives lectures on critical thinking pedagogy, ethical theory, and religion and popular culture.

DONALD M. BRAXTON is the J. Omar Good Professor of Religious Studies and Chair of the Department of Religious Studies at Juniata College. His current research is the area of interreligious conflict, computational simulation of religious behavior, the evolution of religion, transhumanism, and the use of wearable technology to study the manipulation of emotion for religious purposes. Braxton has published articles in *Method and Theory in the Study of Religion*, *Zygon*, and *Journal of Cognition and Culture*. He has contributed chapters to *The Routledge Companion to Religion and Science* (2011) and *A Christian Naturalistic Faith* (2007).

MICHAEL S. BURDETT is Postdoctoral Fellow in Religion, Science and Technology at Wycliffe Hall, University of Oxford, and is a Visiting Fellow at the University of St. Andrews. He worked in the aerospace and robotics industries with a firm that had contracts with NASA and JPL before becoming a theologian. He holds degrees in engineering, physics, and theology and has been given academic and professional awards in each field. His academic interests lie at the intersection of science and technology, theology, and philosophy. He has published and presented internationally on continental philosophy, transhumanism, the technological society, and Christian theology. He is an editor for the online journal, *The Marginalia Review*, in the area of science, technology, and religion and is author of the forthcoming book *Eschatology and the Technological Future* (Routledge). Currently, he is working on two science and religion grants funded by the Templeton Religion Trust and the BioLogos Foundation.

RON COLE-TURNER teaches theology and ethics at Pittsburgh Theological Seminary, where he has held the H. Parker Sharp Chair since 1996. He is the author and editor of several books focusing on religious and ethical dimensions of new and emerging technologies, including *Transhumanism and Transcendence: Christian Hope in an Age of Technological Enhancement* (edited, Georgetown University Press, 2011) and

Design and Destiny: Jewish and Christian Perspectives on Human Germline Modification (MIT University Press, 2008). Cole-Turner is a member of the Executive Committee of the International Society for Science and Religion, an honorary society, and currently a co-chair of the "Transhumanism and Religion" group of the American Academy of Religion.

TODD T. W. DALY currently serves as Associate Professor of Theology and Ethics at Urbana Theological Seminary in Illinois; he writes regularly about transhumanism, particularly as it relates to life extension. His contributions have appeared in publications, including *Ethics & Medicine*, *Journal of Evolution and Technology*, and *Christianity Today*; he has also published his work in the edited volume, *Transhumanism and Transcendence* (2011). Daly is a scholar at the Paul Ramsey Institute and serves on the ethics committee of Carle Foundation Hospital in Champaign-Urbana. He also a member of the Steering Committee of the American Academy of Religion's "Transhumanism and Religion" group. He is currently writing a book on theological ethics dealing with radical life extension, entitled *Chasing Methuselah*.

CELIA DEANE-DRUMMOND is Professor in Theology at the University of Notre Dame. She holds degrees and doctorates in the natural sciences as well as theology. Her research interests are in the engagement of theology and natural science, including specifically ecology, evolution, animal behavior, and anthropology. Her research has consistently sought to explore theological and ethical aspects of that relationship. She is joint editor of a new journal to be launched in 2014 with Mohr Siebeck (Germany) entitled *Philosophy, Theology and the Sciences*. Relevant recent books include *Wonder and Wisdom* (DLT, 2006); *Genetics and Christian Ethics* (Cambridge University Press, 2006); *Future Perfect*, edited with Peter Scott (Continuum, 2006, 2nd ed. 2010); *Christ and Evolution* (Fortress, 2009); *Creaturely Theology*, edited with David Clough (SCM Press, 2009); and *The Wisdom of the Liminal* (Eerdmans, 2014).

AMY MICHELLE DEBAETS is an assistant professor in the department of bioethics at Kansas City University of Medicine and Biosciences and a faculty scholar with the University of Chicago Program on Medicine and Religion. She received her PhD from Emory University in religion with a concentration in ethics as well as a certificate in women's, gender, and sexuality studies. DeBaets also holds MDiv and ThM degrees from Princeton Theological Seminary and an MA in bioethics. She previously served as an adjunct faculty member at Weill Medical College of Cornell University. She has published on ethical issues in life extension technologies, genomic patents, and inheritable genetic modifications. Her current research project addresses spirituality in osteopathic medicine.

PHILIP A. DOUGLAS currently teaches at the Florida Institute of Technology. He was formerly a Visiting Assistant Professor of Writing, Rhetoric and American Cultures at Michigan State University. His writing interests include a spectrum of topics from biographical writing to transhumanism and its intersections with religion and, specifically, religious conceptions of eschatology. He has previously written and presented on virtual worlds in literature and film and the novels and autobiography of Richard Wright. He is also active in animal welfare issues and has written articles and blog posts for People for the Ethical Treatment of Animals and the Humane Society of the United States.

MATTHEW ZARO FISHER is a PhD candidate in the philosophy of religion and theology program at Claremont Graduate University in Claremont, California. With an MA in systematic theology from Marquette University, his research interests revolve around the epistemological relationship between theological and scientific inquiry and the ways in which science and philosophy can help better inform contemporary theology, particularly concerning issues surrounding human identity. He is also engaged in interreligious dialogue and research through involvement with the Center for Jain Studies at Claremont Lincoln University, an affiliate of the Claremont School of Theology.

STEPHEN GARNER was recently appointed Head of the School of Theology, Mission and Ministry at Laidlaw College, Auckland, New Zealand, after six years teaching theology at the University of Auckland. He holds an MSc in computer science and a PhD in theology and teaches in the areas of ethics, public and contextual theology, science and religion, and spirituality. His PhD dissertation was titled "Transhumanism and the *Imago Dei*: Narratives of Apprehension and Hope," and his recent research has focused on religion and cyborgs, theology and new media, and popular culture and public theology. He served for four years on the New Zealand Interchurch Bioethics Council representing the Presbyterian Church of Aotearoa, New Zealand (PCANZ), and currently co-convenes the PCANZ Leadership Subcommittee.

BRIAN PATRICK GREEN is Assistant Director of Campus Ethics Programs at the Markkula Center for Applied Ethics and Adjunct Lecturer in the School of Engineering at Santa Clara University. His bachelor's degree is in genetics from the University of California, Davis, and his master's and doctoral degrees are in ethics and social theory from the Graduate Theological Union in Berkeley, California. His research centers on investigating the relationship of human nature and technology, particularly the role of technology in human life and flourishing, utilizing a Catholic Thomistic natural law perspective. His associated research interests are in theology and science, bioethics, engineering ethics, ethics of emerging technologies, ethics of space exploration, and transhumanism.

PATRICK D. HOPKINS is a philosopher who specializes in ethics, moral psychology, and philosophical problems of science, medicine, and technology. He has a BA from the University of Mississippi in psychology, worked in neuroscience research for a few years at a major medical school and a primate research center, received his PhD in philosophy from Washington University in St. Louis, and is currently Professor of Philosophy at Millsaps College and Affiliated Faculty of the Center for Bioethics and Medical Humanities at the University of Mississippi Medical Center, both in Jackson, Mississippi. He has published numerous articles on biomedical ethics, science and technology studies, gender studies, and religious studies. He is editor of *Sex/Machine: Readings in Culture, Gender, and Technology* (Indiana University Press, 1999). Currently he is working on a book on the history and criticism of natural law theory.

AMELIA HRUBY is a graduate student pursuing a PhD in philosophy at DePaul University. Her areas of study include 20th-century French philosophy, hermeneutics, phenomenology, and feminist philosophy and predominantly feature thinkers such as Emmanuel Levinas, Jacque Derrida, Michel Foucault, and Martin Heidegger. She has presented on critical thinking and pedagogy and the potential for authentic intersubjectivity in Heidegger's thought. Her research concerns the constitution of subjectivity as it intersects with ethics, literary studies, feminism, and technology.

LEE A. JOHNSON is an Assistant Professor of Religious Studies at East Carolina University. She specializes in Pauline studies and, through her work with the "Performance Criticism of the Bible and Other Ancient Texts" group in the Society of Biblical Literature, explores how written letters would have been presented, performed, and preserved in the New Testament era. She has published numerous articles in *Catholic Biblical Quarterly*, *Biblical Interpretation*, and *Biblical Theology Bulletin*, as well as contributing to volumes in the *Religious Rivalries* series and *Women in the Biblical World*. She is currently completing a manuscript on *Reading Paul: Letter-Writing in a Non-literate Culture*.

HEUP YOUNG KIM's 6 books, 25 book chapters, and numerous articles are in Asian constructive theology, interreligious dialogue, and religion and science. Representative recent publications in English include *Asian and Oceanic Christianities in Conversation: Exploring Theological Identities at Home and in Diaspora* (co-editor, Rodopi, 2011); "The Tao in Confucianism and

Taoism: The Trinity in East Asian Perspective," in *Cambridge Companion to the Trinity* (Cambridge University Press, 2011); and "Sanctity of Life: A Reflection on Human Embryonic Stem Cell Debates from an East Asian Perspective," in *Global Perspectives on Science & Spirituality* (Templeton, 2009). He was a founding member of the International Society for Science and Religion (ISSR), a co-moderator of the Congress of Asian Theologians (CATS), and a president of the Korean Society for Systematic Theology. Kim is Professor Emeritus of Theology at Kangnam University and Visiting Professor of Religion and Science at Hanshin University, South Korea.

CORY ANDREW LABRECQUE is the Raymond F. Schinazi Junior Scholar in Bioethics and Religious Thought at the Center for Ethics and Co-director of Catholic Studies at Emory University in Atlanta, Georgia. His research lies at the intersection of religion, medicine, biotechnology, environment, and ethics; he is interested in the impact of emerging/transformative technologies (especially those related to regenerative and anti-aging medicine) on philosophical and theological perspectives on human nature and the human/nature relationship. Labrecque is author of the forthcoming book, *For Ever and Ever, Amen: Roman Catholicism, Transhumanism, and the Ethics of Radically Extending Human Life in an Ageist Society* (McGill-Queen's Press).

DANIEL McFEE is Associate Professor and Chair of the Religious Studies Department at Mercyhurst University. He is also co-founder and co-director of the Evelyn Lincoln Institute for Ethics and Society at Mercyhurst University. McFee has published and lectured widely on issues of transhumanism, environmental ethics, and politics and religion. He is currently working on a book on religious ethics and transhumanism.

GEOFFREY REDMOND is a medical doctor and Sinologist. He began postgraduate studies at the University of Virginia, emphasizing textual criticism of English Renaissance texts under Professor Fredson Bowers, a leading English language philologist of his era. He then entered medical training at Columbia University College of Physicians and Surgeons. He later returned to his interest in the humanities, now in the religion and philosophy of traditional China. In addition to several medical texts, he has published *Science and Asian Religious Traditions* (Greenwood Press, 2008); *Teaching the Book of Changes (I Ching)* (Oxford University Press, 2014); and *The I Ching (Book of Changes): A Critical Translation of the Ancient Text* (London: Bloomsbury Academic, forthcoming). His perspectives on transhumanism are based on his experience in medical practice as well as his study of Chinese thought. He believes the latter, in which longevity is an explicit goal, can provide a fresh perspective on the cultural effects of extended human lifespan.

ANDERS SANDBERG is James Martin Research Fellow at the Future of Humanity Institute at the Oxford Martin School, Oxford University. He has written a number of papers and chapters on human enhancement ethics, emerging technology, and global catastrophic risk. He has a background in computational neuroscience and has written a number of reports and papers on neuroscience as well as the feasibility and ethics of whole-brain emulation. He is also a research associate to the Oxford Uehiro Centre for Practical Ethics and the Oxford Centre for Neuroethics. He founded the Swedish Transhumanist Association in 1996, and has been an active public lecturer on transhumanist topics over the past 20 years.

HANNAH SCHEIDT is a doctoral student in the Religious Studies Program at Northwestern University. Her work focuses on religion, irreligion, culture, and technology in the contemporary world. She is interested in secular and atheist identity and community formations, and particularly in their use of digital media technologies. In addition, she is interested in the ways digital technologies affect notions of the self. Past and upcoming conference presentations address such topics as transhumanism and religion, religious formations in Internet culture, celebrity and contemporary atheism, and moral contestation in the mediasphere. She graduated from Bowdoin College with a BA in Religious Studies and English Literature.

JEANINE THWEATT-BATES is the author of *Cyborg Selves: A Theological Anthropology of the Posthuman* and has contributed to several volumes on the intersection of transhumanism and religion. She holds a PhD in theology and science from Princeton Theological Seminary. She is a member of the Steering Committee of the "Transhumanism and Religion" group of the American Academy of Religion and an activist for gender justice within religion through gal328.org. She currently teaches philosophy at the College of New Jersey.

HAVA TIROSH-SAMUELSON is Irving and Miriam Lowe Professor of Modern Judaism and Director of the Center for Jewish Studies at Arizona State University. She writes on Jewish intellectual history, Judaism and science, Judaism and ecology, and transhumanism. She is the author of the award-winning *Between Worlds: The Life and Work of Rabbi David ben Judah Messer Leon* (1991) and of *Happiness in Premodern Judaism: Virtue, Knowledge and Well-Being in Premodern Judaism* (2003). She is the editor of *Judaism and Ecology: Created World and Revealed World* (2002); *Women and Gender in Jewish Philosophy* (2004); *Judaism and the Phenomenon of Life: The Legacy of Hans Jonas* (2008); and *Building Better Humans? Refocusing the Debate on Transhumanism* (2011). She is the Editor in-Chief of the Library of Contemporary Jewish Philosophers (2013–). She has received numerous grants to research transhumanism, which have funded symposia, public lectures, faculty seminars, and international conferences. Her essays on transhumanism have appeared in *Zygon: Journal of Religion and Science* and in anthologies devoted to transhumanism.

BRENT WATERS is the Jerre and Mary Joy Professor of Christian Social Ethics and Director of the Jerre L. and Mary Joy Stead Center for Ethics and Values at Garrett-Evangelical Theological Seminary, Evanston, Illinois. He is the author of *Economic Globalization and Christian Ethics* (forthcoming); *Christian Moral Theology in an Emerging Technoculture*; *This Mortal Flesh: Incarnation and Bioethics*; *The Family in Christian Social and Political Thought*; *From Human to Posthuman: Christian Theology and Technology in a Postmodern World*; *Reproductive Technology: Towards a Theology of Procreative Stewardship*; *Dying and Death: A Resource for Christian Reflection*; and *Pastoral Genetics: Theology and Care at the Beginning of Life* (with co-author Ronald Cole-Turner). He is editor of *Christology and Ethics* (with co-editor F. LeRon Shults) and *God and the Embryo: Religious Voices on Stem Cells and Cloning* (with co-editor Ronald Cole-Turner). Waters has also written numerous articles and lectured extensively on the relationship among theology, ethics, and technology. He has served previously as the Director of the Center for Business, Religion and Public Life, Pittsburgh Theological Seminary. He is a graduate of the University of Redlands (BA), the School of Theology at Claremont (MDiv, DMin), and the University of Oxford (DPhil).

JOSEPH WOLYNIAK is a DPhil candidate at the University of Oxford (Harris Manchester College) and visiting scholar at the University of Denver, where he is completing a dissertation on "The Baconian Project" under Professor Peter Harrison (Centre for the History of European Discourses, University of Queensland). He was previously appointed as a Graduate Research Fellow at the Ian Ramsey Centre for Science and Religion (Oxford University) and was a visiting scholar at the Yale Interdisciplinary Center for Bioethics/Yale-Hastings Program in Ethics and Health Policy. An Episcopal Church Foundation Fellow (2012), he currently serves as the vice chair of the Episcopal Church's Executive Council Committee on Science, Technology and Faith.